ANTHOLOGY

OF

PUBLIC SPEECHES

ANTHOLOGY
OF
PUBLIC SPEECHES

∾

Compiled by

MABEL PLATZ, Ph.D.

Radio Division, United States Office of
Education, Washington, D. C.

THE H. W. WILSON COMPANY

New York   1940

TO MY FOREFATHERS *who believed so firmly in the principles of freedom and justice that they left their ancestral homes in the Old World and faced the hardships of pioneer life in the New World in order that they and their children's children might enjoy the benefits of these principles.*

FOREWORD

In modern times oratory, as an art, has undergone changes, because the mode of public speaking has changed. Today a speaker may address millions by the use of the radio, whereas previously a speaker's audience was limited to the range of his own voice. Today a speaker also has the benefit of the public address system and the open forum. Though the technique of public speaking has changed, the spoken word, important through history in time of crisis, is of even greater importance considered from the standpoint of human rights. The history of free speech is indeed the history of man's right to say what he believes in an effort to persuade others to accept his point of view.

A collection of speeches in which freedom of speech is stressed is important at this time as we in the United States are celebrating the 150th anniversary of our Constitution which guarantees the right of free speech. Such a collection is important because history has taught us that we need ever be aware of the ageless struggle to maintain, in a democracy, the right of the individual to speak for himself.

With world events warning us that fundamental human liberties are being imperiled, it is important to bring before the public a collection of speeches which have been influential in shaping the course of history. Such a collection clarifies the nature of the long struggle for free speech.

In commending this volume which has been prepared by one associated with the work of this office I am not thinking of the personal opinions or political views which may be expressed in the individual speeches but rather of the totality of the anthology and its significance to man's struggle for freedom through the ages. Of course, I cannot accept responsibility for the personal opinions and interpretations of the author.

J. W. STUDEBAKER
United States Commissioner of Education
Washington, D. C.

CONTENTS

THE BRITISH PERIOD

THE AMERICAN PERIOD

THE WORLD WAR PERIOD

PREFACE

The Occasion, the Speaker, and the Speech—these are the three essential elements in public speaking. A synchronous effectiveness in these three factors results in successful public speaking.

It is the purpose of this volume to present speeches of representative orators who have figured in the history of public speaking—orators who, as in ancient Greece and Rome, contributed to the art of public speaking as well as those orators who have been able through the spoken word to influence the course of history.

The history of public speaking reveals that freedom of speech has ever been the privilege of democracies. The right of the individual to express his thoughts to others has been the foundation of the republics of the world. It is ever the purpose of autocracies to curb freedom of speech. When one voice rules a nation, the voice of the people is silenced and their freedom limited; when one voice represents the people, the people echo their leader and their freedom is dictated; when the voices of the people are heard, then there is progress toward economic, political, and religious freedom.

This collection of speeches is intended to be used as a companion volume to the author's *History of Public Speaking*, published in 1936 by Noble and Noble of New York City, which presents a comparative study and history of public speaking from a motivated point of view. The speeches in the present volume may be studied in connection with assignments from the history and will clarify the significance of the cycle.

Each selection is introduced by a brief statement of the speaker's life and his contribution to oratory as well as a statement of the occasion on which the speech was made, thus fusing the three essentials: the Occasion, the Speaker, and the Speech.

Grateful acknowledgments are due to the following members of the United States Department of the Interior, Office of Education, Washington, D.C.: Dr. John W. Studebaker, United States Commissioner of Education; Dr. Cyril F. Klinefelter, Administrative Assistant to the Commissioner of Education; Mr. William D. Boutwell, chief of the Division of Radio, Publications, and Exhibits; Miss Olga Jones, chief of the Editorial Division; Mr. John Gordon Studebaker, director of the Educational Radio Script Exchange; Mr. Richard P. Herget, Business Manager of the Educational Radio Division and Forum; Mrs. Edith Wood, Secretary to the chief of the Radio Division; Mr. Delbert L. Eagle, Senior Supervising Clerk of the Radio Division, typist of the manuscript; Miss Jane Ellen Mankin of Vanderbilt University in charge of bibliography; Mr. Jay Clark Waldron of the Radio Division; and to Mr. Wendell S. Gibbs for assistance on translations; and to Emerson Lee Bassett, Chairman Emeritus, Speech Department, Stanford University who was responsible for the original idea of the book.

Sincerest appreciation is also extended to his Excellency, Mehmet Münir Ertegün, Turkish Ambassador to the United States, Washington, D.C., for the use of the speech of Kemal Ataturk; to Dr. Ricardo J. Alfaro, President of Panama, for assistance with the speech of Simon Bolívar; to Monsieur André Liotard of the Modern Language faculty at the University of Maryland for French translations; to Mr. Harry Newton Price of the Washington Post for criticism on the selection of orators; to Mrs. George Price, formerly of the Library of Congress, Washington, D.C., and the staff of the Library of Congress at Washington, D.C.

For the courtesy of re-printing speeches and translations of speeches the author extends thanks to The Macmillan Company; G. P. Putnam's Sons for the use of Carleton Lee's *The World Orators*; to the John C. Winston Company for selections from Charles Morris' *The World's Great Orators and Their Orations*; to Funk and Wagnalls Company for selections from William

Jennings Bryan's compilation of *The World's Famous Orations*;
to the Colonial Press for the use of speeches from Chauncey
Depew's *The Library of Oratory*; to the late Ashley Thorndike
for the use of *Modern Eloquence*; to Charles Scribner's Sons,
D. Appleton-Century Company, Christian Literature Company,
Macmillan Company; and to the Copyright Division of the Library of Congress for its valuable assistance.

THE GREEK PERIOD

INTRODUCTION

The national epics of the leading races of primitive Europe and Asia show that there was an eloquence of a high degree amongst these people, but it was with the Greeks that ancient oratory first found expression as one of the fine arts.

Strength and courage were the property of all ancient Greeks, yet the real leaders were the counsellors who could through their eloquence assume leadership. The words of these early leaders of Greece have been preserved in the works of such historians as Herodotus and Thucydides. It was with the birth of democracy under Pericles in the fifth century B.C. that Greece was launched on her Golden Age of Oratory.

The political institutions which were created in the Greek city-states were most conducive to the development of eloquence. Every citizen was permitted to attend, speak, and vote in the *Popular Assembly.* The *General Assembly*, which consisted of the whole body of male citizens over eighteen years of age, met forty times each year, and on these occasions the orators of Greece addressed the people. There was also the *Athenian Council of 500*, which was selected to debate and administer the affairs of state, and here as well as in the *Athenian Courts* the democratic principles of free speech prevailed. In addition to these institutions there were the *Areopagus*, the most dignified assembly of Athens, and the *Dionysia*, the popular festival of Greece, which offered opportunities for the display of eloquence.

The glory of Attic oratory thus was that its appeal was always to the Athenian democracy—a people taught by life to reason and to judge; but this people also considered oratory as a fine art whose beauty was analogous to the beauty of the body. The Greek public was accustomed to poetical recitation from its oral traditions of poetry and music, and so in addition to valuing public speaking as a safeguard of property and person the Greek orators strove for beauty and perfection in its form and style.

At the time of Demosthenes, when the pinnacle of Greek oratory was reached, there existed three schools of eloquence: that of Lysias, mild and persuasive combining artistic prose with the speech idiom of daily life, quietly engaging the attention and winning the assent of the audience; that of Thucydides, bold and animated, awakening the feelings and powerfully forcing conviction on the mind; and that of Isocrates which was a combination of the two preceding forms. Demosthenes culled what was valuable from the various styles and blended them into a harmonious whole. The chiseled perfection of Greek oratory as an art was thus accomplished by this supreme orator, but more significant than the beauty of his work was the motive prompting it. Demosthenes led the patriotic orators of Greece in their efforts to save the people from the encroachment of monarchy. Greek liberty was ever the theme and purpose of their message, and when their warnings were unheeded the decline of Greek oratory followed with the loss of liberty.

The orations presented here have been chosen as representative of the various forms of Greek oratory.

ACHILLES TO THE ENVOYS

Homer

(9th Century B.C.)

The reply of Achilles to Odysseus, which appears in the
Iliad, is perhaps the noblest example of Homeric oratory.

Achilles had been offended by Agamemnon, who sent an embassy to him pleading that he set aside his grievance and save the
Achaians from defeat. The speeches of the three representatives,
Phoinix, Ajax, and Odysseus, are recorded in the ninth book of
the Iliad. The reply of Achilles to Odysseus is the speech
presented here.

Heaven-sprung son of Laertes, Odysseus of many wiles, in openness
must I now declare unto you my saying, even as I am minded and as
the fulfilment thereof shall be, that ye may not sit before me and coax
this way and that. For hateful to me even as the gates of hell is he that
hideth one thing in his heart and uttereth another; but I will speak
what meseemeth best. Not me, I ween, shall Agamemnon, son of
Atreus, persuade, nor the other Danaäns, seeing we were to have no
thanks for battling with the foeman ever without respite. He that
abideth at home hath equal share with him that fighteth his best, and in
like honor are held both the coward and the brave; death cometh alike
to the untoiling and to him that hath toiled long. Neither have I any
profit for that I endured tribulation of soul, ever staking my life in fight.
Even as a hen bringeth her unfledged chickens each morsel as she
winneth it, and with herself it goeth hard, even so I was wont to watch
out many a sleepless night and pass through many bloody days of battle,
warring with folk for their women's sake. Twelve cities of men have
I laid waste from shipboard, and from land eleven, I do you to wit,
throughout deep-soiled Troy-land; out of all these took I many goodly
treasures, and would bring and give them all to Agamemnon, son of
Atreus, and he staying behind amid the fleet ships would take them and
portion out some few but keep the most. Now, some he gave to be
meeds of honor to the princes and the kings, and theirs are left untouched; only from me of all the Achaians took he my darling lady and
keepeth her—let him sleep beside her and take his joy. But why must
the Argives make war on the Trojans? why hath Atreides gathered his
host and led them hither? is it not for lovely-haired Helen's sake? Do
then the sons of Atreus alone of mortal men love their wives? Surely,

whatsoever man is good and sound of mind loveth his own and cherisheth her, even as I too loved mine with all my heart, though but the captive of my spear. But now that he hath taken my meed of honor from mine arms and hath deceived me, let him not tempt me that know him full well; he shall not prevail. Nay, Odysseus, let him take counsel with thee and all the princes to ward from the ships the consuming fire. Verily without mine aid he hath wrought many things, and built a wall and dug a foss about it wide and deep, and set a palisade therein; yet even so can he not stay murderous Hector's might. But so long as I was fighting amid the Achaians, Hector had no mind to array his battle far from the wall, but scarce came unto the Skaian gates and to the oak tree; there once he awaited me alone and scarce escaped my onset. But now, seeing I have no mind to fight with noble Hector, I will to-morrow do sacrifice to Zeus and all the gods, and store well my ships when I have launched them on the salt seas—then shalt thou see, if thou wilt and hast any care therefor, my ships sailing at break of day over Helles-pont, the fishes' home, and my men right eager at the oar; and if the great Shaker of the earth grant me good journey, on the third day should I reach deep-soiled Phthia. There are my great possessions that I left when I came hither to my hurt; and yet more gold and ruddy bronze shall I bring from hence, and fair-girdled women and gay iron, all at least that were mine by lot; only my meed of honor hath he that gave it me taken back in his despitefulness, even Lord Agamemnon, son of Atreus. To him declare ye everything even as I charge you, openly, that all the Achaians likewise may have indignation, if haply he hopeth to beguile yet some other Danaän, for that he is ever clothed in shame-lessness. Verily not in my face would he dare to look, though he have the front of a dog. Neither will I devise counsel with him nor any enterprise, for utterly he hath deceived me and done wickedly; but never again shall he beguile me with fair speech—let this suffice him. Let him begone in peace; Zeus the lord of counsel hath taken away his wits. Hateful to me are his gifts, and I hold him at a straw's worth. Not even if he gave me ten times, yea twenty, all that now is his, and all that may come to him otherwhence, even all the revenue of Orchomenos or Egyptian Thebes where the treasure-houses are stored fullest—Thebes of the hundred gates, whence sally forth two hundred warriors through each with horses and chariots—nay, nor gifts in number as sand or dust; not even so shall Agamemnon persuade my soul till he have paid me back all the bitter despite. And the daughter of Agamemnon, son of Atreus, will I not wed, not were she rival of golden Aphrodite for fair-ness and for handiwork matched bright-eyed Athene—not even then will I wed her; let him choose him of the Achaians another that is his peer and is more royal than I. For if the gods indeed preserve me and I come unto my home, then will Peleus himself seek me a wife. Many Achaian maidens are there throughout Hellas and Phthia, daughters of princes that ward their cities; whomsoever of these I wish will I make my dear lady. Very often was my high soul moved to take me there a wedded wife, a help meet for me, and have joy of the possessions that the old man Peleus possesseth. For not of like worth with life hold I even all the wealth that men say was possessed of the well-peopled city of Ilios in days of peace gone by, before the sons of the Achaians came; neither all the treasure that the stone threshold of the archer Phoebus Apollo encompasseth in rocky Pytho. For kine and goodly flocks are to be had for the harrying, and tripods and chestnut horses for the purchasing; but to bring back man's life neither harrying nor earning availeth when once it hath passed the barrier of his lips. For thus my goddess mother telleth me, Thetis the silver-footed, that twain fates are bearing me to the issue of death. If I abide here and besiege the Trojans' city, then my returning home is taken from me, but my fame shall be imperishable; but if I go home to my dear native land, my high fame is taken from me, but my life shall endure long while, neither shall the issue of death soon reach me. Moreover, I would counsel you all to set sail homeward, seeing ye shall never reach your goal of steep Ilios; of a surety, far-seeing Zeus holdeth his hand over her and her folk are of good courage. So you go your way and tell my answer to the princess of the Achaians, even as is the office of elders, that they may devise in their hearts some better counsel, such as shall save them their ships and the host of the Achaians amid the hollow ships; since this counsel availeth them naught that they have now devised by reason of my fierce wrath. But let Phoinix now abide with us and lay him to rest, that he may follow with me on my ships to our dear native land to-morrow, if he will; for I will not take him perforce.

Translated by Walter Leaf, Litt. D., for "The Iliad of Homer."
Published by The Macmillan Company.
Reprinted by permission.

THE FUNERAL ORATION RECORDED BY THUCYDIDES

Pericles

(490 B.C.—429 B.C.)

The Funeral Oration attributed by Thucydides to Pericles was delivered in honor of the Athenian citizens who had fallen on the field of battle in the first summer of the Peloponnesian War.

Pericles may be regarded as the first orator of Greece and, perhaps, of the world. Aristophanes refers to him as "the Olympian who thundered and lightninged and shook all Greece." He had a stately, yet vehement, manner of speaking. His bursts of eloquence were interspersed by tranquil passages followed by more rapid movements.

The Funeral Oration is preserved for us by the historian, Thucydides, who was a constant, eager auditor of Pericles. The distinctive manner of the speech compared to other speeches recorded by Thucydides would show that the historian had followed the style and sentiments of Pericles with fidelity. The oration is one of the renowned monuments of ancient eloquence.

Most of those who have spoken here before me have commended the lawgiver who added this oration to our other funeral customs; it seemed to them a worthy thing that such an honor should be given at their burial to the dead who had fallen on the field of battle. But I should have preferred that, when men's deeds have been brave, they should be honored in deed only, and with such an honor as this public funeral, which you are now witnessing. Then the reputation of many would not have been imperilled on the eloquence or want of eloquence of one, and their virtues believed or not, as he spoke well or ill. For it is difficult to say neither too little or too much; and even moderation is apt not to give the impression of truthfulness. The friend of the dead who knows the facts is likely to think that the words of the speaker fall short of his knowledge and of his wishes; another who is not so well informed, when he hears of anything which surpasses his own powers, will be envious and will suspect exaggeration. Mankind are tolerant of the praises of others so long as each hearer thinks that he can do as well or nearly as well himself; but, when the speaker rises above him, jealousy is aroused, and he begins to be incredulous. However, since our ancestors have set the seal of their approval upon the practice, I must obey, and to the utmost of my power shall endeavor to satisfy the wishes and beliefs of all who hear me.

I will speak first of our ancestors, for it is right and becoming that now, when we are lamenting the dead, a tribute should be paid to their memory. There has never been a time when they did not inhabit this land, which by their valor they have handed down from generation to generation, and we have received from them a free State. But if they were worthy of praise, still more were our fathers, who added to their inheritance, and after many a struggle transmitted to us, their sons, this great empire. And we ourselves assembled here to-day, who are still most of us in the vigor of life, have chiefly done the work of improvement, and have richly endowed our city with all things, so that she is sufficient for herself both in peace and war. Of the military exploits by which our various possessions were acquired, or of the energy with which we or our fathers drove back the tide of war, Hellenic or Barbarian, I will not speak; for the tale would be long and is familiar to you. But before I praise the dead, I should like to point out by what principles of action we rose to power, and under what institutions and through what manner of life our empire became great. For I conceive that such thoughts are not unsuited to the occasion, and that this numerous assembly of citizens and strangers may profitably listen to them.

Our form of government does not enter into rivalry with the institutions of others. We do not copy our neighbors, but are an example to them. It is true that we are called a democracy, for the administration is in the hands of the many and not of the few. But while the law secures equal justice to all alike in their private disputes, the claim of excellence is also recognized; and when a citizen is in any way distinguished he is preferred to the public service, not as a matter of privilege, but as the reward of merit. Neither is poverty a bar, but a man may benefit his country whatever be the obscurity of his condition. There is no exclusiveness in our public life, and in our private intercourse we are not suspicious of one another, nor angry with our neighbor if he does what he likes; we do not put on sour looks at him, which, though harmless, are not pleasant. While we are thus unconstrained in our private intercourse, a spirit of reverence pervades our public acts; we are prevented from doing wrong by respect for authority and for the laws, having an especial regard to those which are ordained for the protection of the injured, as well as to those unwritten laws which bring upon the transgressor of them the reprobation of the general sentiment.

And we have not forgotten to provide for our weary spirits many relaxations from toil; we have regular games and sacrifices throughout the year; at home the style of our life is refined; and the delight which we daily feel in all these things helps to banish melancholy. Because of the greatness of our city the fruits of the whole earth flow in upon us, so that we enjoy the goods of other countries as freely as of our own.

Then, again, our military training is in many respects superior to that of our adversaries. Our city is thrown open to the world, and we never expel a foreigner or prevent him from seeing or learning anything of which the secret, if revealed to an enemy, might profit him. We rely not upon management or trickery, but upon our own hearts and hands. And in the matter of education, whereas they from early youth are always undergoing laborious exercises which are to make them brave, we live at ease, and yet are equally ready to face the perils which they face. And here is the proof: The Lacedaemonians came into Attica, not by themselves, but with their whole confederacy following; we go alone into a neighbor's country; and although our opponents are fighting for their homes and we on a foreign soil, we have seldom any difficulty in overcoming them. Our enemies have never yet felt our united strength; the care of a navy divides our attention, and on land we are obliged to send our own citizens everywhere. But they, if they meet and defeat a part of our army, are as proud as if they had routed us all, and when defeated they pretend to have been vanquished by us all.

If, then, we prefer to meet danger with a light heart but without laborious training, and with a courage which is gained by habit and not enforced by law, are we not greatly the gainers? Since we do not antic-ipate the pain, although, when the hour comes we can be as brave as those who never allow themselves to rest; and thus, too, our city is equally admirable in peace and in war. For we are lovers of the beautiful, yet simple in our tastes, and we cultivate the mind without loss of manli-ness. Wealth we employ, not for talk and ostentation, but when there is a real use for it. To avow poverty with us is no disgrace; the true dis-grace is in doing nothing to avoid it. An Athenian citizen does not neglect the State because he takes care of his own household; and even those of us who are engaged in business have a very fair idea of politics. We alone regard a man who takes no interest in public affairs, not as a harmless, but as a useless character; and if few of us are originators, we are all sound judges of a policy. The great impediment to action is, in our opinion, not discussion, but the want of that knowledge which is gained by discussion preparatory to action. For we have a peculiar power of thinking before we act and of acting, too, whereas other men are courageous from ignorance, but hesitate upon reflection. And they are surely to be esteemed the bravest spirits who, having the clearest sense both of the pains and pleasures of life, do not on that account shrink from danger. In doing good, again, we are unlike others; we make our friends by conferring, not by receiving, favors. Now, he who confers a favor is the firmer friend, because he would fain by kindness keep alive the memory of an obligation; but the recipient is colder in his feelings because he knows that in requiting another's generosity he will not be winning gratitude, but only paying a debt. We alone do good to our neighbors, not upon a calculation of interest, but in the confidence of freedom and in a frank and fearless spirit. To sum up: I say that Athens is the school of Hellas, and that the individual Athenian in his own person seems to have the power of adapting himself to the most varied forms of action with the utmost versatility and grace. This is no passing and idle word, but truth and fact; and the assertion is verified by the position to which these qualities have raised the State. For in the hour of trial Athens alone among her contemporaries is superior to the report of her. No enemy who comes against her is indignant at the reverses which he sustains at the hands of such a city; no subject complains that his masters are unworthy of him. And we shall assuredly not be without witnesses; there are mighty monuments of our power which will make us the wonder of this and of succeeding ages; we shall not need the praises of Homer or of any other panegyrist whose poetry may please for the moment, although his representation of the facts will not bear the light of day. For we have compelled every land and every sea to open a path for our valor, and have everywhere planted eternal memorials of our friendship and of our enmity. Such is the city for whose sake these men nobly fought and died; they could not bear the thought that she might be taken from them; and every one of us who survive should gladly toil on her behalf.

I have dwelt upon the greatness of Athens because I want to show you that we are contending for a higher prize than those who enjoy none of these privileges, and to establish by manifest proof the merit of these men whom I am now commemorating. Their loftiest praise has been already spoken. For in magnifying the city I have magnified them, and men like them whose virtues made her glorious. And of how few Hellenes can it be said, as of them, that their deeds when weighed in the balance have been found equal to their fame! Methinks that a death such as theirs has been gives the true measure of a man's worth; it may be the first revelation of his virtues, but is at any rate their final seal. For even those who come short in other ways may justly plead the valor with which they have fought for their country; they have blotted out the evil with the good, and have benefited the State more by their public services than they have injured her by their private actions. None of these men were enervated by wealth or hesitated to resign the pleasures of life; none of them put off the evil day in the hope, natural to poverty, that a man, though poor, may one day become rich. But, deeming that the punishment of their enemies was sweeter than any of these things, and that they could fall in no nobler cause, they determined at the hazard of their lives to be honorably avenged, and to leave the rest. They resigned to hope their unknown chance of happiness; but in the face of death they resolved to rely upon themselves alone. And when the moment came they were minded to resist and suffer, rather than to fly and save their lives; they ran away from the word of dishonor, but on the battle-field their feet stood fast, and in an instant, at the height of their fortune, they passed away from the scene, not of their fear, but of their glory.

Such was the end of these men; they were worthy of Athens, and the living need not desire to have a more heroic spirit, although they may pray for a less fatal issue. The value of such a spirit is not to be expressed in words. Any one can discourse to you forever about the advantages of a brave defence which you know already. But instead of listening to him I would have you day by day fix your eyes upon the greatness of Athens, until you become filled with the love of her; and when you are impressed by the spectacle of her glory, reflect that this empire has been acquired by men who knew their duty and had the courage to do it, who in the hour of conflict had the fear of dishonor always present to them, and who, if ever they failed in an enterprise, would not allow their virtues to be lost to their country, but freely gave their lives to her as the fairest offering which they could present at her feast. The sacrifice which they collectively made was individually repaid to them; for they received again each one for himself a praise which grows not old, and the noblest of all sepulchres—I speak not of that in which their remains are laid, but of that in which their glory survives and is proclaimed always and on every fitting occasion both in word and deed. For the whole earth is the sepulchre of famous men; not only are they commemorated by columns and inscriptions in their own country, but in foreign lands there dwells also an unwritten memorial of them, graven, not on stone, but in the hearts of men. Make them your examples, and, esteeming courage to be freedom and freedom to be happiness, do not weigh too nicely the perils of war. The unfortunate who has no hope of a change for the better has less reason to throw away his life than the prosperous who, if he survives, is always liable to a change for the worse, and to whom any accidental fall makes the most serious difference. To a man of spirit, cowardice and disaster coming together are far more bitter than death striking him unperceived at a time when he is full of courage and animated by the general hope.

Wherefore I do not now commiserate the parents of the dead who stand here; I would rather comfort them. You know that your life has been passed amid manifold vicissitudes; and that they may be deemed fortunate who have gained most honor, whether an honorable death like theirs, or an honorable sorrow like yours, and whose days have been so ordered that the term of their happiness is likewise the term of their life. I know how hard it is to make you feel this, when the good fortune of others will too often remind you of the gladness which once lightened your hearts. And sorrow is felt at the want of those blessings, not which a man never knew, but which were a part of his life before they were taken from him. Some [of you] are of an age at which they may hope to have other children, and they ought to bear their sorrow better; not only will the children who may hereafter be born make them forget their own lost ones, but the city will be doubly a gainer. She will not be left desolate, and she will be safer. For a man's counsel cannot have equal weight or worth, when he alone has no children to risk in the general danger. To those of you who have passed their prime, I say: Congratulate yourselves that you have been happy during the greater part of your days; remember that your life of sorrow will not last long, and be comforted by the glory of those who are gone. For the love of honor alone is ever young, and not riches, as some say, but honor is the delight of men when they are old and useless.

To you who are the sons and brothers of the departed, I see that the struggle to emulate them will be an arduous one. For all men praise the dead, and, however preeminent your virtue may be, hardly will you be thought, I do not say to equal, but even to approach them. The living have their rivals and detractors, but when a man is out of the way, the honor and good-will which he receives is unalloyed. And, if I am to speak of womanly virtues to those of you who will henceforth be widows, let me sum them up in one short admonition: To a woman not to show more weakness than is natural to her sex is a great glory, and not to be talked about for good or for evil among men.

I have paid the required tribute, in obedience to the law, making use of such fitting words as I had. The tribute of deeds has been paid in part; for the dead have been honorably interred, and it remains only that their children should be maintained at the public charge until they are grown up: this is the solid prize with which, as with a garland, Athens crowns her sons living and dead, after a struggle like theirs. For where the rewards of virtue are greatest, there the noblest citizens are enlisted in the service of the State. And now, when you have duly lamented, every one his own dead, you may depart.

Translated by B. Jowett for "Thucydides."
Reprinted by permission of the Macmillan
Company, publishers.

THE ENCOMIUM OF HELEN

Gorgias

(483? B.C.—375 B.C.)

The Sophists were the forerunners of oratorical art in Greece. They devoted attention to grammar, literary criticism, and dialectic. Of this group of Sophists Gorgias was undoubtedly the most influential, for he transplanted rhetoric to Greece from Sicily, where Corax had laid the foundations of the art, and set up a school of rhetoric in Athens in which he sought to teach the power of eloquence by a formula of artificial rhetorical devices.

Gorgias also advocated extemporaneous speech by the memorization of commonplaces on as many subjects as he deemed might be needed by his pupils. Although he is esteemed the creator of the artistic prose of Attic oratory, Gorgias' own style was often very artificial and florid.

Included here is his *Encomium of Helen,* which will give the student some conception of his style and manner.

A city is adorned by good citizenship, the body by beauty, the soul by wisdom, acts by virtue, and speech by truthfulness. But the opposites of these virtues are a disgrace. Man and woman, word and deed, city and government, we ought to praise if praiseworthy, and blame if blameworthy. For it is equally wrong and stupid to censure what is commendable, and to commend what is censurable. Now I conceive it to be my duty in the interest of justice to confute the slanders of Helen, the memory of whose misfortunes has been kept alive by the writings of the poets and the fame of her name. I propose, therefore, by argument to exonerate her from the charge of infamy, to convince her accusers of their error, and remove their ignorance by a revelation of the truth.

There are few indeed who do not know that by birth Helen ranked among the first men and women of her time. Her mother was the celebrated Leda, her father the god Zeus, though Tyndareus was reputed to be her father. The former is the mightiest of gods, the latter the noblest of men.

Born of such parents, she possessed divine beauty, which she made no attempt to conceal. Nearly all who met her were inspired with love for her, and by her personal charms she attracted many great and haughty suitors. Some of them had abundance of wealth; others were renowned for their ancient nobility. Some were distinguished for their physical superiority and prowess in war; others for their mental acquirements. But all in common were filled with contentious love and an irrepressible spirit of rivalry. Now which of them won Helen and how he satisfied his love for her, I shall not pretend to say. For to tell people what they already know is a good enough way to gain credence, but not to give pleasure. Passing over, then, that period in my discourse, I shall now address myself to what I have to say, and set forth, the probable causes of Helen's voyage to Troy.

Now Helen acted as she did either by command of the gods and a decree of fate, or she was carried off by force, or yielded to persuasion, or was led captive by love. If, then, her act was the effect of the first cause, she certainly ought not to be blamed. For human forethought and prudence can never thwart the will of the gods. In fact it is a universal law, not that the stronger should yield to the weaker, but the weaker to the stronger; that the stronger should lead, and the weaker follow. Now the gods are mightier than men in strength and wisdom and all things else. Accordingly we must attribute the fault to fate and the gods, or clear Helen of infamy.

But if she was unlawfully carried off by force and shamefully insulted, evidently it was the perpetrator of this outrage who did wrong; she, on the other hand, is to be pitied for the indignity and misfortune she was compelled to suffer. He alone, then, who attempted this barbarous deed, deserves to pay the penalty of dishonor and reproach, while she ought rather to be pitied than abused for being violently torn from her friends and her native land. Helen was not a sinner, but a sufferer, and our feeling for her should not be one of hatred, but of compassion.

But if it was the power of speech that moved and beguiled her soul, it will not be difficult to free her of all blame on this score. For the power of speech is mighty. Insignificant in themselves, words accomplish the most remarkable ends. They have power to remove fear and assuage pain. Moreover they can produce joy and increase pity. That this is so there can be no doubt, as I shall undertake to show.

All poetry I call, in accordance with my conception of it, measured speech. Now the readers of poetry are affected in various ways. At times they experience a shivering fear; then again they feel a tender pity and mournful longing. In short, every condition of happiness or unhappiness touches a responsive chord in the soul of the reader. Song, then, inspired by the gods, produces pleasure and removes pain. For the spirit of song, harmonizing with the sentiment of the soul, soothes, and persuades, and enchants it. Enchantment differs from magic in that it beguiles the soul, while magic deceives the mind. In this lies the power of song.

How many, then, have been persuaded and are still persuaded by the captivating power of speech! Whereas, if we had perfect memory of the past, full knowledge of the present, and clear foresight of the future, the same language could not so easily present to us the same pictures of the present, past, and future as is now the case. The result would be that in nearly all cases people would not take counsel of their opinions. For opinions are slippery and insecure, and lead those who follow them into slippery and insecure positions.

Since so many have yielded to persuasion, why should we refuse assent to the belief that Helen too was overcome by its irresistible power? And if submission to necessity be a complete defence, why not also submission to persuasion, which is no less powerful than necessity, since it compels assent to what is said and approval of what is done? Paris, I admit, did wrong in exercising upon Helen the compulsory power of persuasion, but in submitting to that power Helen did nothing to merit condemnation.

That persuasion joined with argument can bend the soul to its will, we find illustrated in the discourses of the astronomers, who by overthrowing one theory and setting up another make the unknown and incredible appear clear to the mind's eye. Again we see evidence of this fact in oratorical contests, in which a speech delights and persuades a great multitude, owing its effectiveness rather to the force of rhetorical art than to the power of truth. Finally the discussions of the philosophers show us how easily the mind may be changed by argument and persuasion.

To conclude this part of my argument, then, words have the same effect on the soul that drugs have on the body. For just as different drugs expel different diseases from the body, and some cure sickness and others end life, so words produce various effects on the soul. Some cause pain, and others pleasure. Some terrify, and others encourage, while still others drug and enchant the soul with evil persuasion. In yielding to persuasion, then, Helen did no wrong, but suffered great misfortune.

Let us now consider the case from a fourth point of view; and if we find that Helen acted as she did through love, we must acquit her of all fault. For all things in the visible world are constituted, not as we would have them, but as nature has ordained. And through the sight this visible world affects the soul in various ways. When, for example, the eye catches sight of hostile bodies in conflict, of assault, and of defence, it is troubled and in turn troubles the soul, so that not infrequently people flee in terror when there is no impending danger. Many a man in the past has lost his presence of mind at some terrible sight; to such an extent does fear paralyze the mind. Many, too, through fear, become dreadfully sick or incurably mad; so powerful an impression does the eye make on the mind of the things it has seen. To enumerate instances of sights that inspire terror is unnecessary, since in all cases the effect on the soul is the same as in the example I have given. When, however, from many colors and many forms, a painter produces one perfect form and figure, he delights our eyes. The sight of beautiful images and statues affords us unspeakable pleasure. So, too, the sight of many things and many persons inspires us with love and longing.

Since this is so, what wonder if Helen's eye was captivated by the charms of Paris, and transmitted the sensation of love to her soul? And how, if he was a god and possessed of divine power, could she in her weakness repel his advances? But if this be human frailty we ought not to condemn it as a fault, but regard it as a misfortune. For it comes to us through captivation of the soul, and not by design of the intellect. It results from the necessity of love, and not the premeditation of art.

How, then, can we justly censure Helen? For whether she acted through love, persuasion, force, or divine necessity, her conduct is equally defensible.

I have now, by argument, removed all stain from Helen's reputation, and accomplished the task I set myself at the beginning, by discrediting unjust censure and ignorant opinion. My purpose has been to make this discourse an encomium of Helen and a pastime for myself.

Translated by Francis P. Garland.
Reprinted by courtesy of the Colonial Press.

ON THE MURDER OF HERODES

Antiphon

(*480 B.C.—411 B.C.*)

Antiphon, who has been called the "father of Attic oratory," represents the austere style of Greek oratory.

The art of speech writing had started with Corax in Sicily, who had divided the speech into Proem, Narrative, Argument, Subsidiary remarks, and Peroration. Gorgias had added beauty of diction to this formula together with prose rhythm and antithesis. Antiphon marks the transition from this school of rhetoric to the forensic pleading of the law courts. His strong point was argument in which he emphasized the topic of general probability, basing his plea on what was most natural and probable under the circumstances.

His Tetralogies, delivered at homicide trials, are like modern debates with the affirmative and negative sides presented by one speaker. In them he combines the forensic rhetoric of Sicily with the popular dialectic of the Sophists.

The speech recorded here was written by Antiphon for Helus, a Mitylenaean, accused of the murder of an Athenian citizen, Herodes, who had mysteriously disappeared from the boat in which the two had embarked for Thrace.

I could have wished, gentlemen, that I possessed the gift of eloquence and legal experience proportionate to my adversity. Adversity I have experienced in an unusual degree, but in eloquence and legal experience I am sadly deficient. The result is that, in circumstances where I was compelled to suffer personal ill-usage on a false charge, legal experience did not come to my rescue; and here, when my salvation depends on a true statement of the facts, I feel embarrassed by my incapacity for speaking. Many an innocent man has been condemned because of his inability to present clearly the truth and justice of his cause. Many a guilty man, on the other hand, has escaped punishment through skilful pleading. It follows, then, that if the accused lacks experience in these matters, his fate depends rather on the representations of his prosecutors than on the actual facts and true version of the case.

I shall not ask you, gentlemen, to give me an impartial hearing. And yet I am aware that such is the practice of most men on trial, who have no faith in their own cause or confidence in your justice. No, I make no such request, because I know full well that, like all good men and true, you will grant me the same hearing that you grant the prosecution. I do ask you, however, to be indulgent if I commit any indiscretion of speech, and to attribute it rather to my inexperience than to the justice of my cause. But if my argument has any weight I pray you will ascribe it rather to the force of truth than to rhetorical art.

I have always felt that it is not just either that one who has done wrong should be saved through eloquence, or that one who has done no wrong should be condemned through lack of eloquence. Unskilful speaking is but a sin of the tongue; but wrongful acts are sins of the soul. Now it is only natural that a man whose life is in danger should commit some indiscretion of speech; for he must be intent not only on what he says, but on the outcome of the trial, since all that is still uncertain is controlled rather by chance than by providence. This fact inspires great fear in a man whose life is at stake. In fact, I have often observed that the most experienced orators speak with embarrassment when their lives are in danger. But whenever they seek to accomplish some purpose without danger they are more successful. My request for indulgence, then, gentlemen, is both natural and lawful; and it is no less your duty to grant it than my right to make it.

I shall now consider the case for the prosecution in detail. And first I shall show you that I have been brought to trial here in violation of law and justice, not on the chance of eluding your judgment—for I would commit my life to your decision, even if you were bound by no oath to pronounce judgment according to law, since I am conscious that I have done no wrong and feel assured that you will do me justice; no, my purpose in showing you this is rather that the lawlessness and violence of my accusers may bear witness to you of their bitter feeling towards me.

First, then, though they imprisoned me as a malefactor, they have indicted me for homicide—an outrage that no one has ever before suffered in this land. For I am not a malefactor, or amenable to the law of malefactors, which has to do only with thieves and highwaymen. So far, then, as they have dealt with me by summary processes, they have made it possible for you to make my acquittal lawful and righteous.

But they argue that homicide is a species of malefaction. I admit that it is a great crime, as great as sacrilege or treason. But these crimes are dealt with each according to its own peculiar laws. Moreover, they compel me to undergo trial in this place of public assemblage, when all men charged with murder are usually forbidden to appear; and furthermore they would commute to a fine in my case the sentence of death imposed by law on all murderers, not for my benefit, but for their own private gain, thereby defrauding the dead of lawful satisfaction. Their reason for so doing you will perceive as my argument advances.

In the second place, you all know that the courts decide murder cases in the open air, for no other reason than that the judges may not assemble in the same place with those whose hands have been defiled with blood, and that the prosecutor may not be sheltered beneath the same roof with the murderer. This custom my accusers have utterly disregarded. Nay, they have even failed to take the customary solemn oath that, whatever other crimes I may have committed, they will prosecute me for murder alone, and will allow no meritorious act of mine to stand in the way of my condemnation. Thus do they prosecute me unsworn; and even their witnesses testify against me without having taken the oath. And then they expect you, gentlemen, to believe these unsworn witnesses and condemn me to death, when they have made it impossible for you to accept such testimony by their violation and contempt of the law.

But they contend if I had been set free I would have fled. What motive could I have had? For, if I did not mind exile, I might have refused to come home when summoned, and have incurred judgment by default, or having come, might have left voluntarily after my first trial. For such a course is open to all. And yet my accusers in their lawlessness seek to deprive me alone of the common right of all Greeks.

This leads me, gentlemen, to say a word about the laws that govern my case. And I think you will admit that they are good and righteous, since, though very ancient, they still remain unchanged—an unmistakable proof of excellence in laws. For time and experience teach men what is good and what is not good. You ought not, therefore, to judge by the arguments of my accusers whether the laws are good or bad, but rather judge by the laws whether their claims are just or unjust. So perfect, indeed, are the laws that relate to homicide, that no one has ever dared to disturb them. But these men have dared to constitute themselves lawmakers in order to effect their wicked purposes, and disregarding these ordinances they seek unjustly to compass my ruin.

Their lawlessness, however, will not help them, for they well know that they have no sworn witness to testify against me. Moreover they did not make a single decisive trial of the matter, as they would have done if they had confidence in their cause. No, they left room for controversy and argument, as if, in fact, they meant to dispute the previous verdict. The result is that I gain nothing by an acquittal, since it will be open to them to say that I was acquitted as a malefactor, not as a murderer, and catching me again they will ask to have me sentenced to death on a charge of homicide. Wicked schemers! Would ye have the judges set aside a verdict obtained by fair means, and put me a second time in jeopardy of my life for the same offence? But this is not all.

They would not even allow me to offer bail according to law, and thus escape imprisonment, though they have never before denied this privilege even to an alien. And yet the officers in charge of malefactors conform to the same custom. I, alone, then, have failed to derive advantage from this common right conferred by law. This wrong they have done me for two reasons: First, that they might render me helpless to prepare for my defence; and second, that they might influence my friends, through anxiety for my safety, to bear false witness against me. Thus, would they bring disgrace upon me and mine for life.

In this trial, then, I am at a disadvantage in respect to many points of your law and of justice. Nevertheless, I shall try to prove my innocence. And yet I realize that it will be difficult immediately to dissipate the false impression which these men have long conspired to create. For it is impossible for any man to guard against the unexpected.

Now, the facts in the case, gentlemen, are briefly these: I sailed from Mitylene in the same boat with Herodes, whom I am accused of having murdered. Our destination was the same—Ænus—but our objects were different. I went to visit my father, who happened to be at Ænus at that time; Herodes went to sell some slaves to certain Thracian merchants. Both the slaves and the merchants sailed with us.

To confirm these statements I shall now offer the testimony of competent witnesses.

To continue, then, we were compelled by a violent storm to put in at a port on the Methymnian coast, and there we found the boat on which they allege I killed Herodes.

Now I would have you bear in mind that this whole affair took place not through design on my part, but through chance. For it was by chance that Herodes undertook the voyage with me. It was by chance that we encountered the storm, which compelled us to put in at the Methymnian port. And it was by chance that we found the cabined boat in which we sought shelter against the violence of the storm.

After we had boarded the other boat and had taken some wine, Herodes left us, never to return. But I did not leave the boat at all that night. On the day after Herodes disappeared, however, I sought him as diligently as any of our company, and felt his loss as keenly. It was I who proposed sending a messenger to Mitylene, and when no one else was willing to go I offered to send my own attendant. Of course, I would not have done this if I had murdered Herodes, for I would be sending an informant against myself. Finally, it was only after I was satisfied by diligent search that Herodes was nowhere to be found, that I sailed away with the first favorable wind. Such are the facts.

What inference can you draw from these facts other than that I am an innocent man? Even these men did not accuse me on the spot, while I was still in the country, although they knew of the affair. No, the truth was too apparent at that time. Only after I had departed, and they had had an opportunity to conspire against me, did they bring this indictment.

Now the prosecution have two theories of the death of Herodes. One is that he was killed on shore, the other that he was cast into the sea. First, then, they say that I killed Herodes on shore, by striking him on the head with a stone. This is impossible, since, as I have proved, I did not leave the boat that night. Strange that they should pretend to have accurate knowledge of the manner of his death, and yet not be able satisfactorily to account for the disappearance of his body. Evidently this must have happened near the shore, for, since it was night, and Herodes was drunk, his murderer could have had no reason to take him far from the shore. However that may be, two days' search failed to produce any trace of him. This drives them to their second hypothesis—that I drowned Herodes. If that were so, there would be some sign in the boat that the man was murdered and cast into the sea. No such sign, however, appears. But they say they have found signs in the boat in which he drank the wine. And yet they admit he was not killed in that boat. The utter absurdity of this second view is shown by the fact that they cannot find the boat they say I used for the purpose of drowning Herodes, or any trace of it.

It was not till after I had sailed away to Ænus, and the boat in which Herodes and I made the voyage had returned to Mitylene, that these men made the examination that led to the discovery of blood. At once they concluded that I killed Herodes on that very boat. But when they found that this theory was inadmissible, since the blood was proved to be that of sheep, they changed their course and sought to obtain information by torturing the crew. The poor wretch whom they first subjected to torture said nothing compromising about me. But the other, whom they did not torture till several days later, keeping him near them in the meantime, is the one who has borne false witness against me. . . .

All that it is possible for you to learn, gentlemen, from the testimony of human witnesses, you have now heard. It remains to consider the testimony of the gods, expressed by signs. For by reliance on these heaven-sent signs you will best secure the safety of the state both in adversity and in prosperity. In private matters, too, you ought to attach great weight to these signs. You all know, of course, that, when a wicked man embarks in the same boat with a righteous man, the gods not infrequently cause the shipwreck and destruction of both because of the sinfulness of one alone. Again, the righteous, by associating with the wicked, have been brought, if not to destruction, at least into the greatest dangers that divine wrath can send. Finally, the presence of guilty men at a sacrifice has often caused the omens to be unfavorable Thus do the gods testify to the guilt and wickedness of man.

In the light of divine testimony, then, my innocence is established. For no mariner with whom I sailed has ever suffered shipwreck. Nor has my presence at a sacrifice ever caused the omens to be unfavorable.

Now, I feel sure, gentlemen, that if the prosecution could find evidence that my presence on shipboard or at a sacrifice had ever caused any mishap, they would insist upon this as the clearest proof of my guilt. Since, however, this divine testimony is adverse to their claims, they ask you to reject it, and to have faith in their representations. Thus do they run counter to the practice of all reasonable men. For, instead of testing words by facts, they seek to overthrow facts by words.

Having now concluded my defence, gentlemen, against all that I can recall of the charge against me, I look to you for acquittal. On that depends my salvation and the fulfilment of your oath. For you have sworn to pronounce judgment according to law. Now, I am not liable to the laws under which I was arrested, while as to the acts with which I am charged I can still be brought to trial in the legal form. And if two trials have been made out of one, the fault is not mine, but that of my accusers. When, however, my worst enemies give me the chance of a second trial, surely you, the impartial awarders of justice, will never pronounce on the present issue a premature verdict of murder. Be not so unjust; rather leave something for that other witness, Time, who aids the zealous seekers of eternal truth. I should certainly desire that in cases of homicide the sentence be in accordance with law, but that the investigation, in every possible instance, be regulated by justice. In this way the interests of truth and right would best be secured. For in homicide cases an unjust sentence banishes truth and justice beyond recall. If, then, you condemn me, you are bound to abide by the sentence, however guiltless I may be. No one would dare, through confidence in his innocence, to contravene the sentence passed upon him, nor, if conscious of guilt, would he rebel against the law. We must yield not only to the truth, but to a verdict against the truth, especially if there be no one to support our cause. It is for these reasons that the laws, the oaths, and the solemnities in murder cases differ from those in all other cases. In this class of cases it is of the utmost importance that the issue be clear and the decision correct. For, otherwise, either the murdered will be deprived of vengeance, or an innocent man will suffer death unjustly. It is less serious, however, that the prosecution should accuse unjustly, than that you, the judges, should decide unjustly. For their accusation is not decisive, the result depends on you. Decide, then, justly; for your decision, if wrong, admits of no remedy.

But how, you may ask, will you decide justly? By compelling my accusers to take the customary solemn oath before they put me upon my defence against an indictment for murder. And how are you to accomplish this? By acquitting me now. And remember, even though you acquit me now, I shall not escape your judgment, since in the other trial, too, you will be my judges. By an acquittal now you make it possible to deal with me hereafter as you will, but, if you condemn me now, my case will not be open to reconsideration. If, then, you must make any mistake, an undeserved acquittal is less serious than an unjust condemnation. For the former is a mistake only; the latter an eternal disgrace. Take care, then, that you do no irreparable wrong. Some of you in the past have actually repented of condemning innocent men, but not one of you has ever repented of making an undeserved acquittal. Moreover, involuntary mistakes are pardonable, voluntary unpardonable. The former we attribute to chance, the latter to design. Of two risks, then run the lesser; commit the involuntary mistake; acquit me.

Now, gentlemen, if my conscience were guilty, I should never have come into this city. But I did come—with an abiding faith in the justice of my cause, and strong in conscious innocence. For not once alone has a clear conscience raised up and supported a failing body in the hour of trial and tribulation. A guilty conscience, on the other hand, is a source of weakness to the strongest body. The confidence, therefore, with which I appear before you, is the confidence of innocence.

To conclude, gentlemen, I have only to say that I am not surprised that my accusers slander me. That is their part; yours is not to credit their slander. If, on the one hand, you listen to me, you can afterwards repent, if you like, and punish me by way of remedy, but, if you listen to my accusers, and do what they wish, no remedy will then be admissible. Moreover, no long time will intervene before you can decide lawfully what the prosecution now asks you to decide unlawfully. Matters like these require not haste, but deliberation. On the present occasion, then, take a survey of the case; on the next, sit in judgment on the witnesses; form, now, an opinion; later, decide the facts.

It is very easy, indeed, to testify falsely against a man charged with murder. For, if he be immediately condemned to death, his false accusers have nothing to fear, since all danger of retribution is removed on the day of execution. And, even if the friends of the condemned man cared to exact satisfaction for malicious prosecution, of what advantage would it be to him after his death?

Acquit me, then, on this issue, and compel my accusers to indict me according to law. Your judgment will then be strictly legal, and, if condemned, I cannot complain that it was contrary to law. This request I make of you with due regard to your conscience as well as to my own right. For upon your oath depends my safety. By whichever of these considerations you are influenced, you must acquit me.

AGAINST ERATOSTHENES

Lysias

(*459 B.C.?—380 B.C.?*)

Lysias, who belongs to the canon of Greek orators,[1] had an almost studied plainness of diction. He used the language of daily life—simple, concise, clear, and vivid in style. Dionysius wrote of him, "It is the gift of Lysias to write winningly, gracefully, and with loveliness."

There is pathos in his forceful tirade against Eratosthenes which is presented here. The Thirty Tyrants among their crimes had put to death Polemarchus, brother of Lysias. Eratosthenes was the one of the Thirty who had arrested and imprisoned him. Lysias in his speech directly accuses Eratosthenes of the murder. There are two parts to the speech. The first is a direct charge against Eratosthenes; the second against the crimes of the Thirty Tyrants. The first part is reproduced here.

It is an easy matter to begin this accusation, but to end it will be attended with no small difficulty; for the crimes of Eratosthenes are so great in magnitude and so many in number, that by speaking falsehood I could not make the accusation worse than the facts, nor, however much I wished, would I be able to tell all the truth; but it is necessary either for the accuser to give out from weariness, or for the allotted time to fail.

And I believe that our experience, as accuser of Eratosthenes, will be contrary to all precedent. Heretofore, it was necessary for the accusers to show what enmity existed between themselves and the accused; but now we must inquire from the defendants what enmity they had against the Commonwealth, that led them to sin so enormously against it. I do not speak thus, Athenians, as if I had no personal resentments nor grievances against the Thirty: I only mean that every one has abundant causes for indignation against them, either on private or on public grounds.

[1] See Platz, Mabel. *The history of public speaking.* Noble and Noble. New York. 1935. p. 23.

By the crimes that have been committed, jurors, I, who never before pleaded in my own nor in any other cause, am now compelled to undertake this accusation against Eratosthenes; and so I have frequently been disheartened, for fear that on account of inexperience I should make the accusation for my brother and myself unworthily or unskilfully. Nevertheless, I shall endeavor, in as few words as possible, to establish the truth of these charges.

My father, Cephalus, was persuaded by Pericles to settle in this country, and lived here thirty years; and neither we nor he ever went to law against any one nor were accused ourselves; but we so lived under the democracy that we neither wronged others nor were wronged by others. But when the Thirty, being corrupt men and mercenary accusers, came into power, they affirmed that it was necessary to rid the city of wrong-doers and that the rest of the citizens should turn to virtue and justice. Though they made such pretences, they did not conform their actions to them, as I, first speaking of my own affairs and afterwards of yours, shall endeavor to remind you.

Theognis and Piso said among the Thirty, in regard to the foreign residents, that they were dissatisfied with the constitution. It seemed, therefore, an excellent pretext to bring them to punishment, but in fact to get their money; at any rate, the city was poor, and the government was in need of funds. And without difficulty they persuaded their hearers; for they deemed it of no consequence to put men to death, but the amassing of wealth they regarded of prime importance. They decided, therefore, to arrest ten resident aliens, including among them two poor men, in order that they might have the plea in regard to the remaining eight that these measures had not been taken from mercenary motives, but in the interests of the government, just as they might defend any other measure adopted for satisfactory reasons. Accordingly, distributing the houses, they began their visits.

They found me entertaining a party of friends. Having driven them off, they left me in charge of Piso, while the rest went to the shield-manufactory to take an inventory of the slaves. Left alone with Piso, I asked him if he would take a sum of money to save me. He said he would, if it were considerable. I said that I was ready to give him a talent of silver; and he agreed to do it. I knew, Athenians, that he regarded neither gods nor men, nevertheless, in my present straits, it seemed to me absolutely necessary to take an oath from him. And when he swore, imprecating destruction upon himself and his children, that in return for the talent he would get me off safe, I went into my chamber and opened my money-box. Piso, observing this, came in, and seeing what was in the box, called up two attendants and ordered them to take its whole contents. And when he had, not what I agreed to give him, gentlemen of the Court, but three talents of silver, four hundred cyziceni, a hundred darics, and four silver cups, I begged him to leave me travel-

ling expenses.   He said that I might consider myself lucky if I got off
with my life.

As Piso and I were coming out of the house, Melobius and Mnesi-
theides met us, who had returned from the manufactory.   Overtaking
us at the door, they inquired where we were going.   Piso said to my
brother's, in order to examine his house.   They ordered him then to go
on, but bade me accompany them to Damnippus's.

And Piso, approaching me, bade me keep silence and be of good
cheer, that he also was going to come there.   They found Theognis there
with other prisoners, to whom they gave me, and went off again.   Being
in such a strait, it seemed to me best to neglect no means of escape, as
if death were already facing me.

So having called Damnippus, I spoke to him as follows: "You happen to be a friend of mine; I have come to your house; I have done no
wrong; because I have property I perish; will you then in sympathy for
my wretched plight do all that lies in your power for my safety?"   And
he promised that he would.   But he thought it would be best to mention
it to Theognis, who, he was sure, would do anything for money.   While
he was talking with Theognis (as I happened to be acquainted with the
house, and knew there were two doors), I decided to try to save myself
in this way, deeming that if I escaped I should get off safe; but if I
were caught I thought that, if Theognis should be persuaded by Damnippus to receive a bribe, I should none the less escape, but if not I should
die all the same.   Having thought this out, I began my flight, while they
were stationing a guard at the hall-door.   Though there were three doors
it was necessary for me to go through, all happened to be opened.   Having reached the house of Archeneus, the shipmaster, I sent him to the
city to inquire about my brother; and he returned and said that Eratosthenes had seized him in the street and led him off to prison.

And I, having ascertained this, sailed the following night for Megara.
The Thirty gave the command to Polemarchus—the usual one with
them—to drink the hemlock, before telling the accusation on account
of which he was about to die; so far was he from being tried and
allowed to make a defence.

And when he was brought out of the prison, dead, although we had
three houses, from no one of them did they allow the funeral to take
place, but hired a mean tenement, and there laid out the corpse.   And
though we had clothing, they gave none to us, asking it for his burial,
but of his friends one gave a cloak, another a pillow, and others, what
each chanced to have he presented for his burial.   And although there
were seven hundred shields belonging to us, together with silver and gold
and bronze and finery and furniture and female apparel, to an amount
beyond what they ever imagined they would possess, and, in addition,
a hundred and twenty slaves (of which they kept the best, and the rest
they handed over for the benefit of the treasury), they reached such a
pitch of covetousness and greed, that they made an exhibition of their

character. For from the ears of Polemarchus's wife, Melobius, as soon as he entered the house, took the golden earrings which she happened to be wearing.

And not in the least portion of our property did we obtain compassion from them. But they so wronged us because of our money as others would not have done who were incensed because of great injuries, although we did not deserve such treatment from the city, but paid all the expenses of the choruses, and many special taxes, and acquitted ourselves as orderly citizens, and performed all the legal obligations of resident aliens, and had no private enemies, but ransomed many of the Athenians from their enemies. Of such treatment did they deem us worthy, who showed more attachment to the city as resident aliens than they did as citizens.

For they drove many of the citizens to take refuge with the enemy, and putting many to death unjustly, left them without burial; and many who were in possession of civic rights they deprived of their citizenship; and the daughters of many about to receive marriage portions they prevented from being married. And now they have reached such a state of insolence, that they have come here to defend themselves, declaring that they have done nothing bad or shameless; and I wish that they spoke the truth, for were it so, no small part of this advantage would come to me.

For, as I said before, Eratosthenes put my brother to death, although he had suffered no personal wrongs at his hands, nor had seen him doing any injury to the city, but merely gratifying to the full his own lawlessness.

I wish to put him on the witness-stand and to question him, jurors; for this is my opinion: for this fellow's benefit, I deem it impious to hold conversation even with another, concerning him; but to his injury, I conceive it consistent with self-respect and piety to speak even to himself. Rise up, then, and answer me what I ask you.

Did you arrest Polemarchus or not? "Fearing, what was commanded by the Thirty, I did." Were you in the Council Chamber when speeches were made about us? "I was." Did you support those advocating to kill, or oppose? "I opposed." That we might not be put to death? "That you might not be put to death." Thinking we should be suffering unjustly or justly? "Unjustly."

So then, O basest of all men, did you oppose that you might save us, but arrest that you might kill? And when the majority of you were masters of our safety, do you say you opposed those wishing to kill us, but when it depended on you alone to save Polemarchus or not, you led him off to prison? Then because, as you say, by opposing you availed nothing, do you claim to be considered an honest man; but, because you arrested and put to death, do you not think that you ought to pay the penalty to me and these present?

Nay, moreover, it is not reasonable to believe him in this (admitting that he tells the truth in affirming that he protested), that he was ordered to kill. He will not say, I presume, that, in the case of the resident aliens, they took a pledge from him. To whom, pray, was it less likely to be commanded than to one who happened to oppose them and expressed his opinion? For who was less likely to carry out their instructions than he who protested against what they wished to be done? Furthermore, it seems to me that there is sufficient excuse for the other Athenians to throw the blame of what has occurred upon the Thirty. But how is it reasonable for you to accept the excuses of the Thirty themselves, if they throw the blame upon themselves?

If indeed there had been in the city some authority stronger than that by which he was commanded to put men to death unjustly, perhaps you would reasonably have pardon for him. But now, from whom in the world are you ever to exact punishment, if it shall be possible for the Thirty to say that they did the things commanded by the Thirty?

And, moreover, it was not in his house, but in the street, where he might have let him escape without breaking the decree of the Thirty, that he arrested him and took him to prison; but you are all angry even with those who entered your house, making a search for you or for anything of yours.

But if it is necessary to make allowances for those who put others to death for their own safety, you would more justly pardon them; for they incurred peril if they failed to go when sent, or if when they had found the person at home they denied it. But Eratosthenes might have said that he did not meet Polemarchus, or, at all events, that he did not see him; for these statements could not be disproved or tested, so that they could not have been investigated even by those enemies who wished it.

But you ought, Eratosthenes, if, as you say, you were an honest man, far rather to have become an informer to those who were going to be put to death unjustly, than to arrest those who were going to suffer death unjustly; but now your deeds have become manifest, not as of one vexed, but as of one pleased, at what took place.

And so ought these jurors from your deeds rather than from your words to cast their votes, taking what they know to have actually happened as sure proofs of what was then said, since it is not possible to punish witnesses about these things. Since, so far from being allowed to assist at their councils, it was impossible for us even to remain in our own homes. Hence it is in the power of those who worked all possible evils to the State, to say everything good about themselves. I do not shrink, however, from meeting you on this point, but I acknowledge, if you wish, that you opposed them; but I wonder what, in heaven's name, you would have done if you had been in harmony with the Thirty, seeing that, when claiming you protested, you killed Polemarchus.

Come, now, what would you do if you chanced to be brothers or even sons of his? Would you have acquitted him? For Eratosthenes, gentlemen, must prove one of two things,—either that he did not arrest Polemarchus, or that he did this justly. But he has acknowledged that he arrested him unjustly, so that he has made your decision about him easy.

And, further, many, both citizens and strangers, have come to ascertain what opinion you will hold concerning these men. Some of whom, being your own citizens, will go away having learned either that they will suffer punishment for what wrongs they have committed, or that, having succeeded in what they were aiming at, they will become tyrants of the city; but, if they fail, they will be no worse off than the rest of you. The foreigners in the city will know whether they banished justly the Thirty from their cities, or unjustly, for if they who suffered ill shall acquit the Thirty after having arrested them, surely these strangers will think that they have been overzealous in chastising them in your behalf.

Is it not then a hard thing if you punished with death the generals who conquered in a naval battle, because they said that on account of the storm they were not able to rescue their comrades from the stormy sea, deeming that you ought to exact punishment from them because of the valor of the dead; but these men, who as private citizens did all that lay in their power to bring disaster on your fleet, and who, when they were established in power, acknowledge of their own free will that they put to death many of the citizens without trial,—now ought they not to be punished, both themselves and their children, with the direst punishments?

PERORATION

I wish to conclude, after recalling a few things to the recollection of both parties,—the City Party and the Piraeus Party,—in order that, having before you as warnings the disasters which have come upon you through these men, you may pass sentence.

And first, you of the Town, reflect that by these men you were so severely governed that you were compelled to wage such a war upon brothers, and sons, and citizens, that having been vanquished, you are the equals of the conquerors, but conquering, you would have been slaves of the tyrants.

These men, on the one hand, from their administration, would have acquired wealth for their own houses; you, through the war with each other, have impoverished yours. For they did not deign to have you thrive along with them, though they forced you to become odious in their company; having reached such a pitch of arrogance that, instead of seeking to win your loyalty by sharing with you their prizes, they fancied themselves friendly if they shared with you their dishonors.

Wherefore do you, now that you are in security, to the utmost of your power take vengeance on them, both for yourselves and for the men of the Piraeus, reflecting that these men, villains though they are, were once your masters, but that now you are citizens with the best of men, fighting against the enemy and taking counsel in the interest of the State; and remembering the foreign troops, whom these men posted on the Acropolis, as sentinels of their despotism and your servitude. And to you, though much more might be said, I say only this much.

But you of the Piraeus, remember, in the first place, your army—how, after fighting many a battle on foreign soil, you were deprived of your arms, not by the enemy, but by these men in time of peace; how you were proclaimed exiles from the city bequeathed to you by your fathers; and how, when in exile, they demanded your surrender of the cities.

In return for these things, show resentment, as you resented them when you went into exile; and be mindful also of the other evils which you have suffered at their hands—how some from the market-place, some from the temples they cruelly seized and put to a violent death; how others were torn from children, and parents, and wives, and were compelled to become their own murderers; and they did not even allow them to receive the common decencies of burial, deeming their own empire to be surer than the vengeance from on high.

And those of you who escaped death, after having experienced perils in many places, and wanderings to many cities, and expulsion from all, beggared of the necessaries of life, with children left in that fatherland which had become hostile soil, or in the land of strangers, through many opposing influences, have come to the Piraeus. And though dangers many and great confronted you, being honorable men, you freed some and others you restored to their fatherland.

Had you been unfortunate and failed in those aims, you yourselves would now be exiles in fear of suffering what you suffered before. And neither temples nor altars would have availed you against wrong on account of the character of these men, which things are a source of safety even to evil-doers. And your children, as many as were here, would have been outraged by these men, and those in a foreign land, for the smallest debt, would have been enslaved from the lack of those to assist them.

I do not wish to speak, however, of what might have been, seeing that what these men have done is beyond my power to tell; for it is the work, not of one accuser, nor of two, but of many. Nevertheless, there is in me no lack of indignation—for the temples which these men have bartered away or defiled by entering them; for the city which they impoverished; for the arsenals which they dismantled; for the dead whom you must vindicate by their death, since you could not succor them when alive.

And I fancy they are listening to us, and will know that you are voting, feeling that those who acquit these men have pronounced sentence upon them, but as many as exact retribution from these men have taken vengeance in their names.

I shall cease accusing—you have heard—seen—suffered; you have them—judge.

Translated by Mitchell Carroll, Ph.D.
Published by G. P. Putnam's Sons.
Reprinted by permission.

FOR EUPHILETOS

Isaeus

(*420 B.C.—348 B.C.*)

Isaeus was the teacher of Demosthenes. He was the most perfect master of forensic argument and expressed the transition from the studied plainness of Lysias to the elaboration of style which was climaxed in the orations of Demosthenes. His diction was pure and clear; his composition easy and varied; his arrangement versatile; his logic keen.

The speech which is included here is an appeal composed by Isaeus for Euphiletos whose right to citizenship had been attacked.

You have now heard, judges, not only our evidence, but the testimony of all the kinsfolk, that Euphiletos the plaintiff is our brother. Consider, first, what motive our father could have had for telling an untruth, or for adopting this man if he had not been his son. You will find that all who act thus are constrained either by the want of true-born sons or by poverty, hoping for benefits from the persons who by their means have become Athenians. Neither condition applies to our father. He has, in us, two legitimate sons, so that childlessness could not have prompted the adoption. Nor, again, did he look to Euphiletos for maintenance or wealth; he has substance enough; further, it has been deposed before you that he maintained the plaintiff from infancy, educated him, enrolled him in his clan—and these are no light expenses. Our father, then, was not likely, judges, to attempt anything so unjust when it could do him no good. Nor, again, will I be suspected of such madness as bearing false witness for the plaintiff in order to have my patrimony divided among a larger number. Hereafter, of course, I could not for a moment dispute the relationship; no one of you would endure the sound of my voice, if I, who now, standing in peril of the law, testify that he is our brother, should be found contradicting that statement. The probability is, judges, that true testimony has been borne, not only by us, but by the other kinsmen too. Reflect, in the first place, that the husbands of our sisters would never have perjured themselves in the cause of the plaintiff; his mother was the stepmother of our sisters, and somehow stepmothers and the daughters of a former marriage are wont to disagree: so that, if the plaintiff had been our stepmother's son by another than our father, our sisters, judges, would never have allowed their husbands to be witnesses. Again, our maternal uncle, being, of course, no relation of the plaintiff, would not have gratified the plaintiff's mother by making a false deposition fraught with the manifest injury to us involved in our adoption of a stranger as our brother. Further, judges, how could any of you impute perjury to Demaratos, who stands there, or to Hegesippos, or Nikostratos—men whose whole lives will show a stainless record, and who, being our intimate friends and knowing us all, have severally testified their kinship with Euphiletos?

I should be glad, then, to learn from the most respected of our adversaries whether he could establish his Athenian citizenship by any other proof than those which we have brought for Euphiletos. For my part, I do not think he could do more than show that both his parents are Athenians, and adduce the testimony of his relatives to the truth of that assertion. Then again, judges, supposing our adversaries were in peril, they would expect you to believe their friends rather than their accusers; as it is, though we have all that testimony on our side, shall they require you to put faith in their own story rather than in Euphiletos, in me and my brother, in our clansmen, in our entire family? Moreover, the adversaries are acting from private enmity, without personal risk to one of their number; we, who give our evidence, stand, one and all, within the peril of the law.

In addition to these testimonies, judges, the mother of Euphiletos, whom the adversaries allow to be an Athenian, was willing to take an oath before the arbitrator at the Delphinion that she and our father are the parents of Euphiletos; and who should know better? Then our father, judges, who ought to be the next best authority, was and is willing to swear that Euphiletos is his son by his wedded Athenian wife. If this is not enough, judges, I was thirteen years old, as I said before, when Euphiletos was born, and I am ready to swear that Euphiletos is the son of my father. Justly, then, judges, might you deem our oaths more trustworthy than the adversaries' assertions; we are willing to make oath on a matter of which we have accurate knowledge, while they retail hearsay from the plaintiff's ill-wishers, or inventions of their own. We, moreover, bring our kinsmen as witnesses before you as before the arbitrators,—witnesses who have a claim to be believed; while, since Euphiletos brought his first suit against the corporation and its demarch now deceased, the adversaries have failed to find any evidence that he is not my father's son, though the case was before the arbitrator for two years. To the conductors of the arbitration these facts afforded the strongest presumption of falsehood, and both of them decided against the adversaries. (Read the evidence of the former award.) You have heard that the former arbitration went against them. I claim, judges, that just as the adversaries would have urged an award favorable to themselves in evidence of Euphiletos not being the son of Hegesippos, so the opposite result should now be testimony to the truth of our story, since they were adjudged guilty of having erased the name of Euphiletos, an Athenian citizen, after it had been duly registered. That, then, Euphiletos is our brother and your citizen, and that he has been subjected by the conspirators in his deme to injurious and outrageous treatment, sufficient proof, judges, has, I think, been laid before you.

Translated by R. C. Jebb.
Published by Macmillan Company.
Reprinted by permission.

ENCOMIUM ON EVAGORAS

Isocrates

(436 B.C.—338 B.C.)

Isocrates was master of a literary, rhetorical prose style. Features of his art were purity of diction, a rhythmical prose beauty, the use of the periodic sentence, the avoidance of the hiatus, and a skillful use of figures of speech. His speeches became the models upon which Cicero based his work, for Isocrates, more than any one else influenced the Roman orator.

The works of Isocrates may be roughly classified into four divisions: The Scholastic, including his *Antidosis,* which is a discussion of his theory of culture; the Forensic, best represented by the *Æginiticus*; the Letters, including those to Philip and Alexander; and the Political of which the *Panegyric* on which Isocrates worked for ten years is considered his masterpiece.

Isocrates was disqualified from active participation in public life because of a weak voice. Consequently he opened a school of oratory and directed his skill to the preparation of speeches to be spoken by leaders in political assemblies and in the public courts.

The *Encomium on Evagoras* is an example of the literary style and manner of Isocrates. Milton imitated this work in his noble plea, *Areopagitica,* wherein he advocated the liberty of unlicensed printing.

Evagoras, king of Salamis in Cyprus, had been friendly with the Athenians and sought to establish Hellenic customs and civilization in the Isle of Cyprus. Isocrates presented the eulogy after the assassination of Evagoras.

When I saw, O Nicocles, that you were honoring the tomb of your father, not only with numerous and magnificent offerings, according to custom, but also with dances, musical exhibitions, and athletic contests, as well as with horse-races and trireme-races, on a scale that left no possibility of their being surpassed, I thought that Evagoras, if the dead have any feeling of what happens on earth, while accepting this offering favorably, and beholding with joy your filial regard for him and your magnificence, would feel far greater gratitude to any one who could show himself capable of worthily describing his mode of life and the dangers he had undergone than to any one else; for we shall find that ambitious and high-souled men not only prefer praise to such honors, but choose a glorious death in preference to life, and are more jealous of their reputation than of their existence, shrinking from nothing in order to leave behind a remembrance of themselves that shall never die.

Now, expensive displays produce none of these results, but are merely an indication of wealth; those who are engaged in liberal pursuits and other branches of rivalry, by displaying, some their strength, and others their skill, increase their reputation; but a discourse that could worthily describe the acts of Evagoras would cause his noble qualities to be ever remembered amongst all mankind.

Other writers ought accordingly to have praised those who showed themselves distinguished in their own days, in order that both those who are able to embellish the deeds of others by their eloquence, speaking in the presence of those who were acquainted with the facts, might have adhered to the truth concerning them, and that the younger generation might be more eagerly disposed to virtue, feeling convinced that they will be more highly praised than those to whom they show themselves superior.

At the present time, who could help being disheartened at seeing those who lived in the times of the Trojan wars, and even earlier, celebrated in songs and tragedies, when he knows beforehand that he himself, even if he surpass their noble deeds, will never be deemed worthy of such eulogies? The cause of this is jealousy, the only good of which is that it is the greatest curse to those who are actuated by it. For some men are naturally so peevish that they would rather hear men praised, as to whom they do not feel sure that they ever existed, than those at whose hands they themselves have received benefits.

Men of sense ought not to be the slaves of the folly of such men, but, while despising them, they ought at the same time to accustom others to listen to matters which ought to be spoken of, especially since we know that the arts and everything else are advanced, not by those who abide by established customs, but by those who correct and, from time to time, venture to alter anything that is unsatisfactory.

I know that the task I am proposing to myself is a difficult one—to eulogize the good qualities of a man in prose. A most convincing proof of this is that, while those who are engaged in the study of philosophy are ever ready to speak about many other subjects of various kinds, none of them has ever yet attempted to compose a treatise on a subject like this. . .

When a boy, he was distinguished for beauty, strength, and modesty, the most becoming qualities at such an age. In proof of which witnesses could be produced: of his modesty, those of the citizens who were brought up with him; of his beauty, all who saw him; of his strength, the contests in which he surpassed his compeers.

When he grew to man's estate, all these qualities were proportionately enhanced, and in addition to them he acquired courage, wisdom, and uprightness, and these in no small measure, as is the case with some others, but each of them in the highest degree.

For he was so distinguished for his bodily and mental excellences, that, whenever any of the reigning princes of the time saw him, they were amazed and became alarmed for their rule, thinking it impossible that a man of such talents would continue to live in the position of a private individual, and whenever they considered his character they felt such confidence in him that they were convinced that he would assist them even if any one ventured to attack them.

In spite of such changes of opinion concerning him, they were in neither case mistaken; for he neither remained a private individual, nor, on the other hand, did them injury, but the Deity watched over him so carefully in order that he might gain the kingdom honorably, that everything which could not be done without involving impiety was carried out by another's hands, while all the means by which it was possible to acquire the kingdom without impiety or injustice he reserved for Evagoras. For one of the nobles plotted against and slew the tyrant, and afterwards attempted to seize Evagoras, feeling convinced that he would not be able to secure his authority unless he got him also out of the way.

Evagoras, however, escaped this peril and, having got safe to Soli in Cilicia, did not show the same feelings as those who are overtaken by like misfortunes. Others, even those who have been driven from sovereign power, have their spirits broken by the weight of their misfortunes; but Evagoras rose to such greatness of soul, that, although he had all along lived as a private individual, at the moment when he was compelled to flee, he felt that he was destined to rule.

Despising vagabond exiles, unwilling to attempt to secure his return by means of strangers, and to be under the necessity of courting those inferior to himself, he seized this opportunity, as befits all who desire to act in a spirit of piety and to act in self-defence rather than to be the first to inflict an injury, and made up his mind either to succeed in acquiring the kingdom or to die in the attempt if he failed. Accordingly, having got together fifty men (on the highest estimate), he made preparations to return to his country in company with them.

From this it would be easy to recognize his natural force of character and the reputation he enjoyed amongst others; for, when he was on the point of setting sail with so small a force on so vast an undertaking, and when all kinds of perils stared him in the face, he did not lose heart himself, nor did any of those whom he had invited to assist him think fit to shrink from dangers, but, as if they were following a god, all stood by their promises, while he showed himself as confident as if he had a stronger force at his command than his adversaries, or knew the result beforehand.

This is evident from what he did; for, after he had landed on the island, he did not think it necessary to occupy any strong position, and, after providing for the safety of his person, to wait and see whether any of the citizens would come to his assistance; but, without delay, just as he was, on that eventful night he broke open a gate in the wall, and, leading his companions through the gap, attacked the royal residence.

There is no need to waste time in telling of the confusion that ensues at such moments, the terror of the assaulted, and his exhortations to his comrades; but, when the supporters of the tyrant resisted him, while the rest of the citizens looked on and kept quiet, fearing, on the one hand, the authority of their ruler, and, on the other, the valor of Evagoras; he did not abandon the conflict, engaging either in single combat against numbers, or with few supporters against the whole of the enemy's forces, until he had captured the palace, punished his enemies, succored his friends, and finally recovered for his family its ancestral honors, and made himself ruler of the city.

I think that, even if I were to mention nothing else, but were to break off my discourse at this point, it would be easy to appreciate the valor of Evagoras and the greatness of his achievements; however, I hope that I shall be able to present both even more clearly in what I am going to say.

For while, in all ages, so many have acquired sovereign power, no one will be shown to have gained this high position more honorably than Evagoras. If we were to compare the deeds of Evagoras with those of each of his predecessors individually, such details would perhaps be unsuitable to the occasion, while time would be insufficient for their recital; but if, selecting the most famous of these men, we examine them in the light of his actions, we shall be able to investigate the matter equally well, and at the same time to discuss it more briefly.

Who would not prefer the perils of Evagoras to the lot of those who inherited kingdoms from their fathers? For no one is so indifferent to fame that he would choose to receive such power from his ancestors rather than to acquire it, as he did, and to bequeath it to his children. Further, amongst the returns of princes to their thrones that took place in old times, those are most famous which we hear of from the poets; for they not only inform us of the most renowned of all that have taken place, but add new ones out of their own imaginations. None of them, however, has invented the story of a prince who, after having undergone such fearful and terrible dangers, has returned to his own country; but most of them are represented as having regained possession of their kingdoms by chance, others as having overcome their enemies by perfidy and intrigue.

Amongst those who lived afterwards (and perhaps more than all) Cyrus, who deprived the Medes of their rule and acquired it for the Persians, is the object of most general admiration. But, whereas Cyrus conquered the army of the Medes with that of the Persians, an achievement which many (whether Hellenes or barbarians) could easily accomplish, Evagoras undoubtedly carried out the greater part of what has been mentioned by his own unaided energy and valor.

In the next place, it is not yet certain, from the expedition of Cyrus, that he would have faced the perils of Evagoras, while it is obvious, from the achievements of the latter, that he would readily have attempted the same undertakings as Cyrus. Further, while Evagoras acted in everything in accordance with rectitude and justice, several of the acts of Cyrus were not in accordance with religion; for the former merely destroyed his enemies, the latter slew his mother's father. Wherefore, if any were content to judge, not the greatness of events, but the good qualities of each, they would rightly praise Evagoras more than Cyrus.

But—if I am to speak briefly and without reserve, without fear of jealousy, and with the utmost frankness—no one, whether mortal, demigod, or immortal, will be found to have acquired his kingdom more honorably, more gloriously, or more piously than he did. One would feel still more confident of this if, disbelieving what I have said, he were to attempt to investigate how each obtained supreme power. For it will be manifest that I am not in any way desirous of exaggerating, but that I have spoken with such assurance concerning him because the facts which I state are true.

Even if he had gained distinction only for unimportant enterprises, it were fitting that he should be considered worthy of praise in proportion; but, as it is, all would allow that supreme power is the greatest, the most august, and most coveted of all blessings, human and divine. Who then, whether poet, orator, or inventor of words, could extol in a manner worthy of his achievements one who has gained the most glorious prize that exists by most glorious deeds?

However, while superior in these respects, he will not be found to have been inferior in others, but, in the first place, although naturally gifted with most admirable judgment, and able to carry out his undertakings most successfully, he did not think it right to act carelessly or on the spur of the moment in the conduct of affairs, but occupied most of his time in acquiring information, in reflection, and deliberation, thinking that, if he thoroughly developed his intellect, his rule would be in like manner glorious, and looking with surprise upon those who, while exercising care in everything else for the sake of the mind, take no thought for the intelligence itself.

In the next place, his opinion of events was consistent; for, since he saw that those who look best after realities suffer the least annoyance, and that true recreation consists, not in idleness, but in success that is due to continuous toil, he left nothing unexamined, but had such thorough acquaintance with the condition of affairs, and the character of each of the citizens, that neither did those who plotted against him take him unawares, nor were the respectable citizens unknown to him, but all were treated as they deserved; for he neither punished nor rewarded them in accordance with what he heard from others, but formed his judgment of them from his own personal knowledge.

But, while he busied himself in the care of such matters, he never made a single mistake in regard to any of the events of everyday life, but carried on the administration of the city in such a spirit of piety and humanity that those who visited the island envied the power of Evagoras less than those who were subject to his rule; for he consistently avoided treating any one with injustice, but honored the virtuous, and, while ruling all vigorously, punished the wrong-doers in strict accordance with justice; having no need of counsellors, but, nevertheless, consulting his friends; often making concessions to his intimates, but in everything showing himself superior to his enemies; preserving his dignity, not by knitting brows, but by his manner of life; not behaving irregularly or capriciously in anything, but preserving consistency in word as well as in deed; priding himself, not on the successes that were due to chance, but on those due to his own efforts; bringing his friends under his influence by kindness, and subduing the rest by his greatness of soul; terrible, not by the number of his punishments, but by the superiority of his intellect over that of the rest; controlling his pleasures, but not led by them; gaining much leisure by little labor, but never neglecting important business for the sake of short-lived ease; and, in general, omitting none of the fitting attributes of kings, he selected the best from each form of political activity; a popular champion by reason of his care for the interests of the people, an able administrator in his management of the state generally, a thorough general in his resourcefulness in the face of danger, and a thorough monarch from his pre-eminence in all these qualities. That such were his attributes, and even more than these, it is easy to learn from his acts themselves.

THE FIRST ORATION ON THE CROWN

Æschines

(389 B.C.—314 B.C.)

Æschines was an advocate of the Macedonian party and as such came into frequent open conflict with Demosthenes. He had unusual physical and intellectual abilities. His magnificent voice, graceful manner and gift of expression, made him a powerful speaker, but he lacked nobility of character. This lack of what the Greeks called "ethos," or moral force, was his downfall.

The First Oration on the Crown is presented here because to it Demosthenes replied in his oration *On the Crown*. It opened a word-contest which was a death struggle between not only two champion orators of the day but between two political parties.

Notice the three indictments which Æschines makes:

1. It is illegal for an official who has not passed his audit as treasurer, as is the case with Demosthenes, to be crowned.

2. The proclamation of a crown in the theatre is illegal.

3. Demosthenes has not been a public benefactor and to enter such a statement in the public records is illegal.

You see, Athenians! what forces are prepared, what numbers formed and arrayed, what soliciting made through the assembly, by a certain party;—and all this to oppose the fair and ordinary course of justice in the State. As to me, I stand here in firm reliance, first on the immortal gods, next on the laws and you, convinced that faction never can have greater weight with you than law and justice.

It were to be wished, indeed, that the presidents of our senate and of our popular assembly would attend with due care to the order of their debates; that the laws ordained by Solon to secure the decency of public speaking might still preserve their force; that so our elder citizens might first arise in due and decent form (as these laws direct), without tumult or confusion, and each declare in order the salutary counsels of his sage experience; that after these, our other citizens who chose to speak might severally, and in order, according to their ages, propose their sentiments on every subject. Thus, in my opinion, would the course of government be more exactly regulated, and thus would our assemblies be less frequently engaged in trials. But now, when these institutions, so confessedly excellent, have lost their force; when men propose illegal resolutions without reserve or scruple; when others are found to put them to the vote, not regularly chosen to preside in our assemblies, but men who have raised themselves to this dignity by intrigue; when, if any of the other senators on whom the lot of presidency has fairly fallen, should discharge his office faithfully, and report your voices truly, there are men who threaten to impeach him, men who invade our rights, and regard the administration as their private property; who have secured their vassals, and raised themselves to sovereignty; who have suppressed such judicial procedures as are founded on established laws, and, in the decision of those appointed by temporary decrees, consult their passions; now, I say, that most sage and virtuous proclamation is no longer heard, "Who is disposed to speak of those above fifty years old?" and then, "Who of the other citizens in their turns?" Nor is the indecent license of our speakers any longer restrained by our laws, by our magistrates; no, nor by the presiding tribe which contains a full tenth part of the community.

If such be our situation, such the present circumstances of the State, and of this you seem convinced, one part alone of our polity remains (as far as I may presume to judge)—prosecutions of those who violate the laws. Should you suppress these—should you permit them to be suppressed—I freely pronounce your fate; that your government must be gradually and imperceptibly given up to the power of a few. You are not to be informed, Athenians, that there are three different modes of government established in the world: the monarchical, the government of the few, and the free republic. In the two former the administration is directed by the pleasure of the ruling powers; in free States, it is regulated by established laws. It is then a truth, of which none shall be ignorant, which every man should impress deeply on his mind, that when he enters the tribunal, to decide a case of violation of the laws, he that day gives sentence on his own liberties. Wisely therefore has our legislator prescribed this, as the first clause in the oath of every judge: "I will give my voice agreeably to the laws"; well knowing, that when the laws are preserved sacred in every State, the freedom of their constitution is most effectually secured. Let these things be ever kept in memory, that your indignation may be kindled against all those whose decrees have been illegal. Let not any of their offences be deemed of little moment, but all of the greatest importance; nor suffer your rights to be wrested from you by any power; neither by the combinations of your generals, who, by conspiring with our public speakers, have frequently involved the State in danger; nor by the solicitations of foreigners, who have been brought up to screen some men from justice, whose administration has been notoriously illegal. But as each man among you would be ashamed to desert from his post in battle, so think it shameful to abandon the post this day assigned to you by the laws, that of guardians of the constitution.

Let it also be remembered that the whole body of our citizens has now committed their State, their liberties, into your hands. Some of them are present awaiting the event of this trial; others are called away to attend on their private affairs. Show the due reverence to these, remember your oaths and your laws; and if we convict Ctesiphon of having proposed decrees, assert the freedom of your constitution, and punish those who have administered your affairs in opposition to your laws, in contempt of your constitution, and in total disregard of your interests. If, with these sentiments impressed on your minds, you attend to what is now to be proposed, you must, I am convinced, proceed to a decision just and religious, a decision of the utmost advantage to yourselves, and to the State.

To enter into a minute examination of the life of Demosthenes I fear might lead me into a detail too tedious. And why should I insist on such points as the circumstances of the indictment for his wound, brought before the Areopagus, against Demomeles his kinsman, and the gashes he inflicted on his own head? Or why should I speak of the expedition under Cephisodotus, and the sailing of our fleet to the Hellespont, when Demosthenes acted as a Trierarch, entertained the admiral on board his ship, made him partaker of his table, of his sacrifices and religious rites, confessed his just right to all those instances of affection, as an hereditary friend; and yet, when an impeachment had been brought against him which affected his life, appeared as his accuser? Why, again, should I take notice of his affair with Midias; of the blows which he received in his office of director of the entertainments; or how, for the sum of thirty minae, he compounded this insult, as well as the sentence which the people pronounced against Midias in the theatre? These and the like particulars I determine to pass over; not that I would betray the cause of justice; not that I would recommend myself to favor by an affected tenderness; but lest it should be objected that I produce facts true, indeed, but long since acknowledged and notorious. Say, then, Ctesiphon, when the most heinous instances of this man's baseness are so incontestably evident that his accuser exposes himself to the censure not of advancing falsehoods, but of recurring to facts so long acknowledged and notorious, is he to be publicly honored, or to be branded with infamy? And shall you, who have presumed to form decrees equally contrary to truth and to the laws, insolently bid defiance to the tribunal, or feel the weight of public justice?

My objections to his public conduct shall be more explicit. I am informed that Demosthenes, when admitted to his defence, means to enumerate four different periods in which he was engaged in the administration of affairs. One, and the first, of these (as I am assured) he accounts that time in which we were at war with Philip for Amphipolis: and this period he closes with the peace and alliance which we concluded, in consequence of the decree proposed by Philocrates, in which Demosthenes had equal share, as I shall immediately demonstrate. The second period he computes from the time in which we enjoyed this peace down to the day when he put an end to a treaty that had till then subsisted, and himself proposed the decree for war. The third, from the time when hostilities were commenced down to the fatal battle of Chaeronea. The fourth is this present time.

After this particular specification, as I am informed, he means to call on me, and to demand explicitly on which of these four periods I found my prosecution; and at what particular time I object to his administration as inconsistent with the public interest. Should I refuse to answer, should I attempt the least evasion or retreat, he boasts that he will pursue me and tear off my disguise; that he will haul me to the tribunal, and compel me to reply. That I may then at once confound this presumption, and guard you against such artifice, I thus explicitly reply: before these your judges, before the other citizens spectators of this trial, before all the Greeks who have been solicitous to hear the event of this cause (and of these I see no small number, but rather more than ever yet known to attend on any public trial), I thus reply: I say, that on every one of these four periods which you have thus distinguished, is my accusation founded. And if the gods vouchsafe me their assistance, if the judges grant me an impartial hearing, and if my memory shall faithfully recall the several instances of your guilt, I am fully confident that I shall demonstrate to this tribunal that the preservation of the State is to be ascribed to the gods, and to those citizens who have conducted our affairs with a truly patriotic and well-tempered zeal, and that all our calamities are to be imputed to Demosthenes as their real author. And in this charge I shall observe the very same method which, as I am informed, he intends to use. I shall begin with speaking of his first period, then proceed to the second and the third in order, and conclude with observations on present affairs. To that peace, then, I now go back, of which you, Demosthenes and Philocrates, were the first movers.

And did not the gods warn us of our danger? did they not urge the necessity of vigilance, in a language scarcely less explicit than that of man? Surely never was a State more evidently protected by the gods, and more notoriously ruined by its popular leaders. Were we not sufficiently alarmed by that portentous incident in the mysteries, the sudden death of the initiated? Did not Amyniades still further warn us of our danger, and urge us to send deputies to Delphi to consult the god? And did not Demosthenes oppose this design? Did he not, rude and brutal as he is, insolently presuming on that full power to which your favor raised him, say that the Pythian priestess was inspired by Philip? And did he not at last, without one propitious sacrifice, one favorable omen, to assure us of success, send out armies to manifest and inevitable danger?

Yet he lately presumed to say that Philip did not venture to march into our territories, for this very reason, because his sacrifices had not been propitious. What punishment therefore is due to thy offences, thou pest of Greece? If the conqueror was prevented from invading the territories of the vanquished by unpropitious sacrifices, shouldst thou, who, without the least attention to futurity, without one favorable omen, hast sent our armies to the field—shouldst thou be honored with a crown for those calamities in which thou hast involved the State, or driven from our borders with ignominy?

And what can be conceived surprising or extraordinary that we have not experienced? Our lives have not passed in the usual and natural course of human affairs: no, we were born to be an object of astonishment to posterity. Do we not see the King of Persia, he who opened a passage for his navy through Mount Athos, who stretched his bridge across the Hellespont, who demanded earth and water from the Greeks; he who in his letters presumed to style himself sovereign of mankind from the rising to the setting sun; now no longer contending to be lord over others, but to secure his personal safety? Do we not see those crowned with honor, and ennobled with the command of the war against Persia, who rescued the Delphian temple from sacrilegious hands? Hath not Thebes, our neighboring State, been in one day torn from the midst of Greece? And, although this calamity may justly be imputed to her own pernicious counsels, yet we are not to ascribe such infatuation to any natural causes, but to the fatal influence of some evil genius. . . .

Since you were not personal spectators of their calamities, represent them to your imagination; think that you behold their city stormed, their walls levelled with the ground, their houses in flames, their wives and children dragged to slavery, their hoary citizens, their ancient matrons, unlearning liberty in their old age, pouring out their tears and crying to you for pity; expressing their resentment, not against the instruments, but the real authors of their calamities; importuning you by no means to grant a crown to this pest of Greece, but rather to guard against that curse, that fatal genius which evermore pursues him. For never did any State, never did any private persons conduct their affairs to a happy issue, that were guided by the counsels of Demosthenes. And is it not shameful, my countrymen, that in the case of those mariners who transport men over to Salamis, it should be enacted by a law, that whoever shall overset his vessel in this passage, even inadvertently, shall never be again admitted to the same employment (so that no one may be suffered to expose the persons of the Greeks to careless hazard); and yet that this man, who has quite overset all Greece, as well as this State, should be still intrusted with the helm of government? . . .

But all this is granted; yet he is a "zealous friend to our free constitution." If you consider only his fair and plausible discourses, you may be deceived in this as you have been in other instances. But look into his real nature and character, and you cannot be deceived. Hence it is that you are to form your judgment. And here I shall recount the several particulars necessary to form the character of a faithful citizen and a useful friend to liberty. On the other hand, I shall describe the man who is likely to prove a bad member of society and a favorer of the arbitrary power of a few. Do you apply these two descriptions to him, and consider, not what he alleges, but what he really is.

I presume, then, it must be universally acknowledged that these are the characteristics of a friend to our free constitution. First, he must be of a liberal descent both by father and mother, lest the misfortune of his birth should inspire him with a prejudice against the laws which secure our freedom. Secondly, he must be descended from such ancestors as have done service to the people, at least from such as have not lived in enmity with them; this is indispensably necessary, lest he should be promoted to do the State some injury, in order to revenge the quarrel of his ancestors. Thirdly, he must be discreet and temperate in his course of life, lest a luxurious dissipation of his fortune might tempt him to receive a bribe in order to betray his country. Fourthly, he must have integrity united with a powerful elocution; for it is the perfection of a statesman to possess that goodness of mind which may ever direct him to the most salutary measures, together with a skill and power of speaking which may effectually recommend him to his hearers. Yet, of the two, integrity is to be preferred to eloquence. Fifthly, he must have a manly spirit, that in war and danger he may not desert his country. It may be sufficient to say, without further repetition, that a friend to the arbitrary power of a few is distinguished by the characteristics directly opposed to these.

And now consider which of these agrees to Demosthenes. Let us state the account with the most scrupulous regard to justice. This man's father was Demosthenes of the Paeanian tribe, a citizen of repute (for I shall adhere strictly to truth). But how he stands as to family, with respect to his mother and her father, I must now explain. There was once in Athens a man called Gylon, who by betraying Nymphaeum in Pontus to the enemy, a city then possessed by us, was obliged to fly from his country, in order to escape the sentence of death denounced against him, and settled on the Bosphorus, where he obtained from the neighboring princes a tract of land called "the Gardens," and married a woman who indeed brought him a considerable fortune, but was by birth a Scythian. By her he had two daughters, whom he sent hither with a great quantity of wealth; one of them he settled—I shall not mention with whom, that I may not provoke the resentment of too many; the other Demosthenes, the Paeanian, married in defiance of our laws, and from her is the present Demosthenes sprung—our turbulent and malicious informer. So that by his grandfather, in the female line, he is an enemy to the State, for his grandfather was condemned to death by your ancestors; and by his mother he is a Scythian—one who assumes the lan guage of Greece, but whose abandoned principles betray his barbarous descent.

And what has been his course of life? He first assumed the office of a Trierarch, and, having exhausted his paternal fortune by this ridiculous vanity, he descended to the profession of a hired advocate; but having lost all credit in this employment by betraying the secrets of his clients to their antagonists, he forced his way into the gallery, and appeared a popular speaker. When those vast sums of which he had defrauded the public were just dissipated, a sudden tide of Persian gold poured into his exhausted coffers; nor was all this sufficient, for no fund whatever can prove sufficient for the profligate and corrupt. In a word, he supported himself, not by a fortune of his own, but by your perils. But how does he appear with respect to integrity and force of elocution? Powerful in speaking, abandoned in his sensual gratification, that I cannot describe his practices; I cannot offend that delicacy, to which such shocking descriptions are always odious. And how has he served the public? His speeches have been plausible, his actions traitorous.

As to his courage, I need say but little on that head. Did he himself deny that he is a coward? Were you not sensible of it, I should think it necessary to detain you by a formal course of evidence; but as he has publicly confessed it in our assemblies, and as you have been witnesses of it, it remains only that I remind you of the laws enacted against such crimes. It was the determination of Solon, our old legislator, that he who evaded his duty in the field, or left his post in battle, should be subject to the same penalties with the man directly convicted of cowardice; for there are laws enacted against cowardice. It may, perhaps, seem wonderful that the law should take cognizance of a natural infirmity; but such is the fact. And why? That every one of us may dread the punishment denounced by law more than the enemy; and thus prove the better soldier in the cause of his country. The man, then, who declines the service of the field, the coward, and he who leaves his post in battle, are by our lawgiver excluded from all share in public deliberations, rendered incapable of receiving the honor of a crown, and denied admission to the religious rites performed by the public. But you direct us to crown a person whom the laws declare to be incapable of receiving a crown; and by your decree you introduce a man into the theatre who is disqualified from appearing there; you call into a place sacred to Bacchus him who, by his cowardice, has betrayed all our sacred places. But that I may not divert you from the great point, remember this: when Demosthenes tells you that he is the friend of liberty, examine not his speeches, but his actions; and consider not what he professes to be, but what he really is. . . .

And here, in your presence, would I gladly enter into discussion with the author of this decree, as to the nature of those services for which he desires that Demosthenes should be crowned. If you allege, agreeably to the first clause of the decree, that he has surrounded our walls with an excellent intrenchment, I must declare my surprise. Surely the guilt of having rendered such a work necessary far outweighs the merit of execution. It is not he who has strengthened our fortification, who has dug our intrenchments, who has disturbed the tombs of our ancestors, that should demand the honors of a patriot minister, but he who has procured some intrinsic services to the State. If you have recourse to the second clause, where you presume to say that he is a good man, and has ever persevered in speaking and acting in the interest of the people, strip your decree of its vainglorious pomp; adhere to facts; and prove what you have asserted. I shall not press you with the instances of his corruption in the affairs of Amphissa and Euboea. But if you intend to transfer the merit of the Theban alliance to Demosthenes, you but impose on the men who are strangers to affairs, and insult those who are acquainted with them, and see through your falsehood. By suppressing all mention of the urgent juncture, of the illustrious reputation of these our fellow-citizens, the real causes of this alliance, you fancy that you have effectually concealed your fraud in ascribing to Demosthenes a merit which really belongs to the State. And now I shall endeavor to explain the greatness of this arrogance by one striking example. The King of Persia, not long before the descent of Alexander into Asia, despatched a letter to the State, expressed in all the insolence of a barbarian. His shocking and unmannered license appeared in every part; but in the conclusion, particularly, he expressed himself directly thus: "I will not grant you gold; trouble me not with your demands; they shall not be gratified." And yet this man, when he found himself involved in all his present difficulties, without any demand from Athens, but freely, and of himself, sent thirty talents to the State, which were most judiciously rejected. It was the juncture of affairs, and his terrors, and his pressing want of an alliance which brought this sum; the very causes which effected the alliance of Thebes. You are ever sounding in our ears the name of Thebes, you are ever teasing us with the repetition of that unfortunate alliance; but not one word is ever suffered to escape of those seventy talents of Persian gold which you diverted from the public service into your own coffers. Was it not from the want of money, from the want of only five talents, that the foreign troops refused to give up the citadel to the Thebans? Was it not from the want of nine talents of silver, that when the Arcadians were drawn out, and all the leaders prepared to march, the whole expedition was defeated? But you are in the midst of affluence, you have treasures to satisfy your sensuality; and, to crown all, while he enjoys the royal wealth, the dangers all devolve on you.

The absurdity of these men well deserves to be considered. Should Ctesiphon presume to call upon Demosthenes to speak before you, and should he rise and lavish his praises upon himself, to hear him would be still more painful than all you have suffered by his conduct. Men of real merit, men of whose numerous and glorious services we are clearly sensible, are not yet endured when they speak their own praises. But when a man, the scandal of his country, sounds his own encomium, who can hear such arrogance with any temper? No, Ctesiphon, if you have any sense, avoid so shameless a procedure; make your defence in person. You cannot recur to the pretence of any inability for speaking. It would be absurd that you, who suffered yourself to be chosen ambassador to Cleopatra, Philip's daughter, in order to present our condolements on the death of Alexander, king of the Molossi, should now plead such an inability. If you were capable of consoling a woman of another country in the midst of her grief, can you decline the defence of a decree for which you are well paid? Or is he to whom you grant this crown such a man as must be totally unknown, even to those on whom he has conferred his services, unless you have an advocate to assist you? Ask the judges whether they know Chabrias, and Iphicrates, and Timotheus. Ask for what reason they made them presents and raised their statues. With one voice they will instantly reply, that to Chabrias they granted these honors on account of the sea-fight at Naxos; to Iphicrates because he cut off the detachment of Lacedaemonians; to Timotheus on account of his expedition to Corcyra; and to others as the reward of those many and glorious services which each performed in war. Ask them again why they refuse the like honors to Demosthenes; they will answer, because he is a corrupted hireling, a coward, and a deserter. Crown him! would this be to confer an honor on Demosthenes? Would it not rather be to disgrace yourselves and those brave men who fell in battle for their country? Imagine that you see these here roused in indignation at the thoughts of granting him a crown! Hard indeed would be the case, if we remove speechless and senseless beings from our borders, such as blocks and stones, when by accident they have crushed a citizen to death; if in the case of a self-murderer we bury the hand that committed the deed separate from the rest of the body; and yet that we should confer honors on Demosthenes, on him who was the author of the late expedition, the man who betrayed our citizens to destruction. This would be to insult the dead, and to damp the ardor of the living, when they see that the prize of all their virtue is death, and that their memory must perish.

But to urge the point of greatest moment: should any of your sons demand by what examples they are to form their lives, how would you reply? For you well know that it is not only by bodily exercises, by seminaries of learning, or by instructions in music, that our youth is trained, but much more effectually by public examples. Is it proclaimed in the theatre that a man is honored with a crown for his virtue, for his magnanimity, and his patriotism, who yet proves to be abandoned and profligate in his life? The youth who sees this is corrupted. Is public justice inflicted on a man of base and scandalous vices like Ctesiphon? This affords excellent instruction to others. Does the judge who has given a sentence repugnant to honor and to justice, return home and instruct his son? That son is well warranted to reject his instruction. Advice in such a case may well be called impertinence. Not then as judges only, but as guardians of the State, give your voices in such a manner that you may approve your conduct to those absent citizens who may inquire what has been the decision. You are not to be informed, Athenians, that the reputation of our country must be such as theirs who receive its honors. And surely it must be scandalous to stand in the same point of view, not with our ancestors, but with the unmanly baseness of Demosthenes.

How then may such infamy be avoided? By guarding against those who affect the language of patriotism and public spirit, but whose real characters are traitorous. Loyalty and the love of liberty are words that lie ready for every man. And they are the most prompt to seize them whose actions are the most repugnant to such principles. Whenever, therefore, you have found a man solicitous for foreign crowns, and proclamations of honors granted by the Greeks, oblige him to have recourse to that conduct which the law prescribes; to found his pretensions and proclamations on the true basis, the integrity of his life, and the exact regulation of his manners. Should he not produce this evidence of his merit, refuse your sanction to his honors; support the freedom of your constitution, which is now falling from you. Can you reflect without indignation that our senate and our assembly are neglected with contempt, while letters and deputations are sent to private houses, not from inferior personages, but from the highest potentates in Asia and in Europe, and for purposes declared capital by the laws? That there are men who are at no pains to conceal their part in such transactions; who avow it in the presence of the people; who openly compare the letters; some of whom direct you to turn your eyes on them, as the guardians of the constitution; others demand public honors, as the favorites of their country; while the people, reduced by a series of dispiriting events, as it were to a state of dotage, or struck with infatuation, regard only the name of freedom, but resign all real power into the hands of others; so that you retire from the assembly, not as from a public deliberation, but as from an entertainment, where each man has paid his club and received his share?

That this is a serious truth, let me offer something to convince you. There was a man (it grieves me to dwell so often on the misfortunes of the State) of a private station, who, for the bare attempt of making a voyage to Samos, was, as a traitor to his country, put instantly to death by the council of Areopagus. Another private man, whose timid spirit, unable to support the general consternation, had driven him to Rhodes, was not long since impeached, and escaped only by the equality of voices; had but one vote more been given for his condemnation, banishment or death must have been his fate. To these let us oppose the case now before us. A popular orator, the cause of all our calamities, is found guilty of desertion in the field. This man claims a crown, and asserts his right to the honor of a proclamation. And shall not this wretch, the common pest of Greece, be driven from our borders? Or shall we not seize and drag to execution this public plunderer, whose harangues enable him to steer his piratical course through our government? Think on this critical season, in which you are to give your voices. In a few days the Pythian games are to be celebrated, and the convention of Grecian States to be collected. There shall our State be severely censured on account of the late measures of Demosthenes. Should you crown him, you must be deemed accessories to those who violated the general peace. If, on the contrary, you reject the demand, you will clear the State from all imputation. Weigh this clause maturely, as the interest, not of a foreign State, but of your own; and do not lavish your honors inconsiderately; confer them with a scrupulous delicacy; and let them be the distinctions of exalted worth and merit; nor be contented to hear, but look round you, where your own interest is so intimately concerned, and see who are the men who support Demosthenes. Are they his former companions in the chase, his associates in the manly exercises of his youth? No, by the Olympian God! he never was employed in rousing the wild boar, or in any such exercises as render the body vigorous; he was solely engaged in the sordid arts of fraud and circumvention.

And let not his arrogance escape your attention, when he tells you that by his embassy he wrested Byzantium from the hands of Philip; that his eloquence prevailed on the Acarnanians to revolt; his eloquence transported the souls of the Thebans. He thinks that you are sunk to such a degree of weakness that he may prevail on you to believe that you harbor the very genius of persuasion in your city, and not a vile sycophant. And when at the conclusion of his defence he calls upon his accomplices in corruption, as his advocates, then imagine that we see the great benefactors of your country in this place from whence I speak, arrayed against the villainy of those men: Solon, the man who adorned our free constitution with the noblest laws, the philosopher, the renowned legislator, entreating you, with that decent gravity which distinguished his character, by no means to pay a greater regard to the speeches of Demosthenes than to your oaths and laws: Aristides, who was suffered to prescribe to the Greeks their several subsidies, whose daughters received their portions from the people at his decease, roused to indignation at this insult on public justice, and asking whether you are not ashamed, that when your fathers banished Arthmius the Zelian, who brought in gold from Persia; when they were scarcely restrained from killing a man connected with the people in the most sacred ties, and by public proclamation forbade him to appear in Athens, or in any part of the Athenian territory, yet you are going to crown Demosthenes with a golden crown, who did not bring in gold from Persia, but received bribes himself, and still possesses them. And can you imagine but that Themistocles, and those who fell at Marathon, and those who died at

Plataea, and the very sepulchres of our ancestors, must groan if you confer a crown on this man, who confessedly united with the barbarians against the Greeks?

Translated by Thomas Leland, D.D.
Published by G. P. Putnam's Sons.
Reprinted by permission.

THE FIRST PHILIPPIC

Demosthenes

(383 B.C.—322 B.C.)

Demosthenes represents the culmination of Greek oratory. He blended the arts of his predecessors. All that was excellent in them he perfected.

It is impossible to separate Demosthenes, the orator, from Demosthenes, the statesman, for his whole political career was an unceasing contest against Philip of Macedon, and his best oratory was that directed against the aggressions of that tyrant.

It was in connection with Philip of Macedon that Demosthenes exercised his greatest abilities as statesman and orator. He penetrated the sinister designs of that ambitious monarch and depicted to his countrymen the perils of subjection to Macedonian arms.

Demosthenes was unceasing in his contest against Philip and directed his three famous orations, called Philippics, against the enemy of his country. The First Philippic was delivered in 351 B.C., when Philip was advancing into Thrace. Demosthenes, alarmed by the danger, tried to arouse the Athenians.

Had we been convened, Athenians, on some new subject of debate, I had waited until most of the usual persons had declared their opinions. If I had approved of anything proposed by them, I should have continued silent; if not, I had then attempted to speak my sentiments. But since those very points on which these speakers have oftentimes been heard already are, at this time, to be considered, though I have risen first, I presume I may expect your pardon; for if they on former occasions had advised the necessary measures, ye would not have found it needful to consult at present.

First, then, Athenians, these our affairs must not be thought desperate: no, though their situation seems entirely deplorable; for the most shocking circumstance of all our past conduct is really the most favorable to

our future expectations. And what is this? That our own total indolence hath been the cause of all our present difficulties: for were we
thus distressed, in spite of every vigorous effort which the honor of our
State demanded, there were then no hope of a recovery.

In the next place, reflect—you who have been informed by others,
and you who can yourselves remember—how great a power the Lacedaemonians not long since possessed; and with what resolution, with what
dignity you disdained to act unworthy of the State, but maintained the
war against them for the rights of Greece. Why do I mention these
things? That ye may know, that ye may see, Athenians, that if duly
vigilant ye cannot have anything to fear; that if once remiss, not anything can happen agreeably to your desires: witness the then powerful
arms of Lacedaemon, which a just attention to your interests enabled you
to vanquish; and this man's late insolent attempt, which our insensibility
to all our great concerns hath made the cause of this confusion.

If there be a man in this assembly who thinks that we must find a
formidable enemy in Philip, while he views, on one hand, the numerous
armies which attend him, and, on the other, the weakness of the State
thus despoiled of its dominions—he thinks justly. Yet let him reflect
on this: there was a time, Athenians, when we possessed Pydna, and
Potidaea, and Methone, and all that country round; when many of
those States now subjected to him were free and independent, and more
inclined to our alliance than to his. Had then Philip reasoned in the
same manner, "How shall I dare to attack the Athenians, whose garrisons command my territory, while I am destitute of all assistance?" he
would not have engaged in those enterprises which are now crowned with
success; nor could he have raised himself to this pitch of greatness. No,
Athenians, he knew this well, that all these places are but prizes, laid
between the combatants, and ready for the conqueror: that the dominions
of the absent devolve naturally to those who are in the field; the possessions of the supine to the active and intrepid. Animated by these
sentiments, he overturns whole countries; he holds all people in subjection: some, as by the right of conquest; others, under the titles of allies
and confederates; for all are willing to confederate with those whom
they see prepared and resolved to exert themselves as they ought.

And if you, my countrymen, will now at length be persuaded to
entertain the like sentiments; if each of you, renouncing all evasions,
will be ready to approve himself a useful citizen, to the utmost that his
station and abilities demand; if the rich will be ready to contribute, and
the young to take the field; in one word, if you will be yourselves, and
banish those vain hopes which every single person entertains, that while
so many others are engaged in public business, his service will not be
required; you then (if Heaven so pleases) shall regain your dominions,
recall those opportunities your supineness hath neglected, and chastise
the insolence of this man; for you are not to imagine that, like a god,
he is to enjoy his present greatness forever fixed and unchangeable. No,

Athenians, there are (those) who hate him, who fear him, who envy him, even among those seemingly the most attached to his cause. These are passions common to mankind; nor must we think that his friends only are exempted from them. It is true they lie concealed at present, as our indolence deprives them of all resource. But let us shake off this indolence; for you see how we are situated; you see the outrageous arrogance of this man, who does not leave it to your choice whether you shall act or remain quiet; but braves you with his menaces; and talks, as we are informed, in a strain of the highest extravagance; and is not able to rest satisfied with his present acquisitions, but is even in pursuit of further conquests; and while we sit down, inactive and irresolute, encloses us on all sides with his toils.

When, therefore, O my countrymen! when will you exert your vigor? When roused by some event? When forced by some necessity? What then are we to think of our present condition? To freemen, the disgrace attending on misconduct is, in my opinion, the most urgent necessity. Or say, is it your sole ambition to wander through the public places, each inquiring of the other, "What new advices?" Can anything be more new than that a man of Macedon should conquer the Athenians and give law to Greece? "Is Philip dead?" "No, but in great danger." How are you concerned in those rumors? Suppose he should meet some fatal stroke; you would soon raise up another Philip, if your interests are thus regarded; for it is not to his own strength that he so much owes his elevation as to our supineness. And should some accident affect him, should Fortune, who hath ever been more careful of the State than we ourselves, now repeat her favors (and may she thus crown them!); be assured of this, that by being on the spot, ready to take advantage of the confusion, you will everywhere be absolute masters; but in your present disposition, even if a favorable juncture should present you with Amphipolis, you could not take possession of it while this suspense prevails in your designs and in your councils.

And now, as to the necessity of a general vigor and alacrity; of this you must be fully persuaded; this point, therefore, I shall urge no further. But the nature of the armament which, I think, will extricate you from the present difficulties, the numbers to be raised, the subsidies required for their support, and all the other necessaries; how they may (in my opinion) be best and most expeditiously provided; these things I shall endeavor to explain. But here I make this request, Athenians—that you would not be precipitate, but suspend your judgment till you have heard me fully. And if, at first, I seem to propose a new kind of armament, let it not be thought that I am delaying your affairs; for it is not they who cry out, "Instantly!" "This moment!" whose counsels suit the present juncture (as it is not possible to repel violences already committed by any occasional detachment); but he who will show you of what kind that armament must be, how great, and how supported, which may subsist until we yield to peace, or until our enemies sink beneath our arms; for thus only can we be secured from future dangers. These things, I think, I can point out; not that I would prevent any other person from declaring his opinion. Thus far am I engaged; how I can acquit myself will immediately appear; to your judgments I appeal.

Translated by Thomas Leland, D.D.
Published by G. P. Putnam's Sons.
Reprinted by permission.

SECOND ORATION ON THE CROWN

Demosthenes

(383 B.C.—322 B.C.)

In consideration of the many important services which Demosthenes had performed for the state Ctesiphon proposed to decree a crown of gold to him. Æschines who was Demosthenes' rival on the rostrum, opposed the decree and brought a suit against its instigator. The greatest combat of eloquence the world has ever witnessed followed. Æschines was sarcastic and powerful, but Demosthenes was more convincing and scrupulous. After the verbal combat was concluded, Æschines withdrew into voluntary exile as vanquished as if he had lost a military engagement.

The oration *On the Crown,* which was Demosthenes' reply to the attack of Æschines, is accredited as a supreme attainment of eloquence and is presented here as one of the best examples of the work of Demosthenes.

In the first place, ye men of Athens, I make my prayer to all the powers of Heaven, that such affection as I have ever invariably discovered to this State and all its citizens, you now may entertain for me on this present trial: and (what concerns you nearly, what essentially concerns your religion and your honor: that the gods may so dispose your minds as to permit me to proceed in my defence, not as directed by my adversary (that would be severe, indeed!), but by the laws and by your oath; in which, to all the other equitable clauses, we find this expressly added, "Each party shall have equal audience." This imports not merely that you shall not prejudge, not merely that the same impartiality shall be shown to both; but, still farther, that the contending parties shall each be left at full liberty to arrange and to conduct his pleading as his choice or judgment may determine.

In many instances hath Æschines the entire advantage in this cause. Two there are of more especial moment. First, as to our interests in the contest, we are on terms utterly unequal; for they are by no means points of equal import, for me to be deprived of your affections, and for him to be defeated in his prosecution. As to me—but, when I am entering on my defence, let me suppress everything ominous, sensible as I must be of this the advantage of my adversary. In the next place, such is the natural disposition of mankind, that invective and accusation are heard with pleasure, while they who speak their own praises are received with impatience. His, then, is the part which commands a favorable acceptance; that which must prove offensive to every single hearer is reserved for me. If, to guard against this disadvantage, I should decline all mention of my own actions, I know not by what means I could refute the charge or establish my pretensions to this honor. If, on the other hand, I enter into a detail of my whole conduct, private and political, I must be obliged to speak perpetually of myself. Here, then, I shall endeavor to preserve all possible moderation; and what the circumstances of the case necessarily extort from me must, in justice, be imputed to him who first moved a prosecution so extraordinary.

I presume, ye judges, you will all acknowledge that in this cause Ctesiphon and I are equally concerned; that it calls for my attention no less than his; for in every case it is grievous and severe to be deprived of our advantages, and especially when they are wrested from us by an enemy. But to be deprived of your favor and affections is a misfortune the most severe, as these are advantages the most important; and if such be the object of the present contest, I hope, and it is my general request to this tribunal, that while I endeavor to defend myself fairly and equitably against this charge, you will hear me as the laws direct; those laws which their first author, Solon, the man so tender of our interests, so true a friend to liberty, secured; not by enacting only, but by the additional provision of that oath imposed on you, ye judges; not, as I conceive, from any suspicion of your integrity, but from a clear conviction, that as the prosecutor, who is first to speak, hath the advantage of loading his adversary with invectives and calumnies, the defendant could not possibly prevail against them, unless each of you who are to pronounce sentence should, with a reverent attention to that duty which you owe to Heaven, favorably admit the just defence of him who is to answer, vouchsafe an impartial and equal audience to both parties, and thus form your decision on all that hath been urged by both.

As I am on this day to enter into an exact detail of all my conduct, both in private life and in my public administration, here permit me to repeat those supplications to the gods with which I first began, and in your presence to offer up my prayers; first, that I may be received by you on this occasion with the same affection which I have ever felt for this State and all its citizens; and, in the next place, that Heaven may direct your minds to that determination which shall prove most conducive to the general honor of all, and most exactly consonant to the religious engagements of each individual. . . .

Thus successful in confirming the mutual separation of our States, and encouraged by these decrees and these replies, Philip now leads his forces forward and seizes Elatea; assuming, that at all events Athens and Thebes never could unite. You are no strangers to the confusion which this event raised within these walls. Yet permit me to relate some few striking incidents of our own consternation. It was evening. A courier arrived, and, repairing to the presidents of the senate, informed them that Elatea was taken. In a moment some started from supper, ran to the public place, drove the traders from their stations, and set fire to their sheds; some sent round to call the generals; others clamored for the trumpeter. Thus was the city one scene of tumult. The next morning, by dawn of day, the presidents summoned the senate. The people were instantly collected; and before any regular authority could convene their assembly, the whole body of citizens had taken their places above. Then the senate entered: the presidents reported their advices, and produced the courier. He repeated his intelligence. The herald then asked in form, "Who chooses to speak?" All was silence. The invitation was frequently repeated: still no man rose, though the generals, though the ordinary speakers were all present; though the voice of Athens then called on some man to speak and save her: for surely the regular and legal proclamation of the herald may be fairly deemed the voice of Athens.

If an honest solicitude for the preservation of the State had on this occasion been sufficient to call forth a speaker, then, my countrymen, ye must have all risen and crowded to the gallery; for well I know this honest solicitude had full possession of your hearts. If wealth had obliged a man to speak, the Three Hundred must have risen. If patriotic zeal and wealth united were the qualification necessary for the speaker, then should we have heard those generous citizens whose beneficence was afterward displayed so nobly in the service of the State; for their beneficence proceeded from this union of wealth and patriotic zeal. But this occasion, the great day, called, it seems, not only for a well-affected and an affluent citizen, but for the man who had traced these affairs to their very source; who had formed the exactest judgment of Philip's motives, of his secret intentions in this his conduct. He who was not perfectly informed of these; he who had not watched the whole progress of his actions with consummate vigilance, however zealously affected to the State, however blessed with wealth, was in nowise better qualified to conceive or to propose the measures which your interests demanded on an occasion so critical. On that day, then, I was the man who stood forth. And the counsels I then proposed may now merit your attention on a double account: first, to convince you that of all your leaders and ministers, I was the only one who maintained the post of a zealous patriot in your extremity, whose words and actions were devoted to your service in the midst of public consternation: and, secondly, to enable you to judge more clearly of my other actions, by granting a little thought to this. I spoke as follows:

"Those who are thrown into all this confusion, from an opinion that the Thebans are gained over to the interests of Philip, seem to me entirely ignorant of the present state of affairs. Were this the case, I am convinced you would now hear, not that he was at Elatea, but on our very frontier. His intent (as I clearly see) in seizing this post is to facilitate his schemes in Thebes. Attend, and I will now explain the circumstances of that state. Those of its citizens whom his gold could corrupt or his artifice deceive are all at his devotion; those who at first opposed and continue to oppose him he finds incapable of being wrought on. What then is his design? Why hath he seized Elatea? That by drawing up his forces and displaying his powers on the borders of Thebes he may inspire his adherents with confidence and hopefulness, and may strike such terror into his adversaries that fear or force may drive them into those measures they have hitherto opposed. If then we are resolved in this emergency to cherish the remembrance of every unkindness we may have received from the Thebans—if we regard them with suspicion, as men who have ranged themselves on the side of our enemy—we shall, in the first place, act agreeably to Philip's warmest wishes; and then I am apprehensive that the party which now opposes him may be brought over to his interests, the whole city declare unanimously in his favor, and Thebes and Macedon fall with their united force on Attica. Grant due attention to what I shall propose; let it be calmly weighed, without dispute or cavil, and I doubt not but that my counsels may direct you to the best and most salutary measures and dispel the dangers now impending over the State. What then do I propose?

"First shake off that terror which hath possessed your minds, and, instead of fearing for yourselves, fear for the Thebans; they are more immediately exposed and must be the first to feel the danger. In the next place, let all those of the age for military service, both infantry and cavalry, march instantly to Eleusis, that Greece may see that you too are assembled in arms; and your friends in Thebes be emboldened to assert their rights, when they are assured, that as they who have sold their country to the Macedonian have a force at Elatea to support them, you, too, stand prepared to support their antagonists. I recommend in the last place, that you nominate ten ambassadors, who, with the generals, shall have full authority to determine the time and all other circumstances of this march. When these ambassadors shall arrive at Thebes how are they to conduct this great affair? This is a point worthy your most serious attention. Make no demands at all of the Thebans; at this juncture it would be dishonorable. Assure them that your forces are ready, and but wait their orders to march to their support as you are deeply affected by their danger, and have been so happy as to foresee and to guard against it. If they are prevailed on to embrace these overtures, we shall effect our great purpose and act with a dignity worthy of our State; but should it happen that we are not so successful, whatever misfortunes they may suffer, to themselves these shall be imputed; while your own conduct shall appear in no one instance inconsistent with the honor and renown of Athens."

These and other like suggestions did I offer. I came down amid the universal applause of the assembly, without one word of opposition or dissent. Nor did I thus speak without proposing my decree in form; nor did I propose my decree without proceeding on the embassy; nor did I proceed on the embassy without prevailing on the Thebans. From first to last my conduct was uniform, my perseverance invariable, my whole powers entirely devoted to repel the dangers then encompassing the State. Produce the decree made on this occasion. Say, Æschines, what character are we to ascribe to you on that great day? and in what light am I to be considered? As a Batalus, the odious name your scorn and malice have given me? And you, a hero of no ordinary rank, a dramatic hero, a Cresphontes, a Creon, or an Œnomaus, the character in which your vile performance was punished with such heavy stripes? On that day our country had full proof that I, the Batalus, could perform more worthy service than you, the Œnomaus. You performed no services whatever; I discharged the duty of a faithful citizen in the amplest manner.

Here was the foundation laid; here was the first establishment of our interest in Thebes. Hitherto the traitors had been too successful, and all was animosity, aversion, and suspicion between the cities. But by this decree that danger which hung lowering over our State was in an instant dissipated like a vapor. And surely it was the duty of an honest citizen, if he had any better measures to propose, to have declared them publicly, not to have cavilled now. For the counsellor and the sycophant are characters entirely different in every particular; but in this are they more especially distinguished from each other—that the one fairly declares his opinion previous to the event, and makes himself accountable to those whom he hath influenced, to fortune, to the times, to the world; while the other is silent when he ought to speak, but when some melancholy accident hath happened he dwells on this with the most invidious censure. That was the time (I repeat it) for a man sincerely attached to his country and to truth. Yet, such is my confidence in the abundant merits of my cause, that if any man can now point out a better course, nay, if there be any course at all but that which I pursued, I shall confess myself criminal; for if any more expedient conduct hath been now discovered, I allow that it ought not to have escaped me. But if there neither is, nor was, nor can be such a conduct pointed out, no, not at this day, what was the part of your minister? Was it not to choose the best of such measures as occurred, of such as were really in his power? And this I did, Æschines, when the herald asked in due form, "Who chooses to address the people?" not "Who will inveigh against things past?" not "Who will answer for things to come?" In this juncture you kept your seat in the assembly without uttering one word. I rose up and spoke. Well! though you were then silent, yet now explain your sentiments. Say, what expedient was there which I should have devised? What favorable juncture was lost to the State by my means?

What alliance, what scheme of conduct was there to which I should have rather led my fellow-citizens? Not that the time once elapsed is ever made the subject of debate; for that time no man ever suggests expedients. It is the coming of the present juncture which demands the offices of a counsellor. And in that juncture, when some of our misfortunes, it seems, were coming on, some were already present, consider my intention; do not point your malice at the event; the final issue of all human actions depends on God. Do not then impute it as my offence that Philip was victorious in the battle. This is an event determined by God, not by me. Let it be proved that I did not take every precaution which human prudence could suggest; that I did not exert myself with integrity, with assiduity, with toil even greater than my strength; that the conduct I pursued was not noble, was not worthy of the State, was not necessary;—let this be proved, and then accuse me. But if a sudden clap of thunder, if a furious tempest burst at once on us, and laid prostrate, not our State alone, but every State in Greece,— what then? Am I to be accused? With equal justice might the trader, who sends out his vessel equipped and furnished for a voyage, be deemed guilty of her wreck, when she had encountered a storm so violent as to endamage, nay, to tear down her tackle. He might plead thus: "I was not pilot in the voyage." Nor was I commander of your army, nor I master of Fortune: she it is who commands the world. And let this be duly weighed: if when the Thebans engaged on our side we were yet fated to this calamity, what were we to expect if they had not only been detached from us, but united with our enemy, in compliance with all his urgent solicitations? If when the armies fought at a distance of three days' march from Attica such danger and consternation fell on the city, what if the defeat had happened in our own territory? Think you that we could have stood? that we could have assembled here? that we could have breathed? The respite of one day (at least of two or three) is oftentimes of signal moment to the preservation of a people. In the other case—but I cannot bear to mention what we must have suffered if this State had not been protected by the favor of some god, and the interposition of this alliance, the perpetual subject (Æschines) of your clamorous malice.

All this particular discussion is addressed to you, ye judges, and to those auditors who stand round the tribunal. As to this miscreant, he needs but one short and plain reply. If you, Æschines, were the only man among us who foresaw the issue, it was your duty to have foretold it to your countrymen; if you did not foresee it, you are as accountable for such ignorance as any other citizen! What better right, then, have you to urge this as a crime against me than I to accuse you on the same occasion? When at this juncture, not to mention others, I approved myself so far a better citizen than you, as I was entirely devoted to what appeared the true interest of my country, not nicely weighing, not once considering my private danger; while you never proposed any better measures, else we had not adopted these, nor in the prosecution of these were we assisted by any services of yours. No; the event discovered that your conduct had been such as the basest, the most inveterate enemy of this State must have pursued. And observable, indeed, it is, that at the very time when Aristratus at Naxos and Aristolaus at Thassus, equally the avowed foes of Athens, are harassing the Athenian partisans by prosecutions, here Æschines hath brought his accusations against Demosthenes. But the man who derives his consequence from the calamities of Greece should rather meet his own just punishment than stand up to prosecute another; the man whose interests are advanced by the conjunctures most favorable to those of our public enemies can never, surely, be a friend to our country. And that this is your case, your life, your actions, the measures you have pursued, the measures you have declined, all demonstrate. Is there anything effected which promises advantage to the State? Æschines is mute. Are we crossed by an untoward accident? Æschines rises. Just as our old sprains and fractures again become sensible when any malady hath attacked our bodies.

But since he hath insisted so much on the event, I shall hazard a bold assertion: but in the name of Heaven! let it not be deemed extravagant; let it be weighed with candor. I say, then, that had we all known what fortune was to attend our efforts; had we all foreseen the final issue; had you foretold it, Æschines; had you bellowed out your terrible denunciations (you, whose voice was never heard); yet, even in such a case, must this city have pursued the very same conduct if she had retained a thought of glory, of her ancestors, or of future times; for thus she could only have been deemed unfortunate in her attempts; and misfortunes are the lot of all men whenever it may please Heaven to inflict them. But if that State which once claimed the first rank in Greece had resigned this rank in time of danger, she had incurred the censure of betraying the whole nation to the enemy. If we had indeed given up those points without one blow, for which our fathers encountered every peril, who would not have spurned you with scorn?— you the author of such conduct, not the State, or me? In the name of Heaven! say, with what face could we have met those foreigners who sometimes visit us if such scandalous supineness on our part had brought affairs to their present situation? If Philip had been chosen general of the Grecian army, and some other State had drawn the sword against this insidious nomination, and fought the battle unassisted by the Athenians—that people who in ancient times never preferred inglorious security to honorable danger? What part of Greece, what part of the barbarian world has not heard that the Thebans in their period of success, that the Lacedaemonians whose power was older and more extensive, that the King of Persia would have cheerfully and joyfully consented that this State should enjoy her own dominions, together with an accession of territory ample as her wishes, on this condition—that she should receive law, and suffer another State to preside in Greece? But to Athenians this was a condition unbecoming their descent, intolerable to their spirit, repugnant to their nature. Athens never was once known to live in a slavish, though a secure obedience to unjust and arbitrary power. No; our whole history is one series of noble contests for preeminence; the whole period of our existence hath been spent in braving dangers for the sake of glory and renown. And so highly do you esteem such conduct, so consonant to the Athenian character, that those of your ancestors who were most distinguished in the pursuit of it are ever the most favorite objects of your praise. And with reason; for who can reflect without astonishment on the magnanimity of those men who resigned their lands, gave up their city, and embarked in their ships, to avoid the odious state of subjection? Who chose Themistocles, the adviser of this conduct, to command their forces; and when Cyrcilus proposed that they should yield to the terms prescribed, stoned him to death? Nay, the public indignation was not yet allayed. Your very wives inflicted the same vengeance on his wife; for the Athenians of that day looked out for no speaker, no general to procure them a state of prosperous slavery. They had the spirit to reject even life, unless they were allowed to enjoy that life in freedom. For it was a principle fixed deeply in every breast, that man was not born to his parents only, but to his country. And mark the distinction: he who regards himself as born only to his parents waits in passive submission for the hour of his natural dissolution; he who considers that he is the child of his country also is prepared to meet his fate freely rather than behold that country reduced to vassalage, and thinks those insults and disgraces which he must meet in a State enslaved much more terrible than death. Should I then attempt to assert that it was I who inspired you with sentiments worthy of your ancestors, I should meet the just resentment of every hearer. No; it is my point to show that such sentiments are properly your own; that they were the sentiments of my country long before my days. I claim but my share of merit in having acted on such principles in every part of my administration. He, then, who condemns every part of my adminstration; he who directs you to treat me with severity, as one who hath involved the State in terrors and dangers, while he labors to deprive me of present honors, robs you of the applause of all posterity. For if you now pronounce that, as my public conduct hath not been right, Ctesiphon must stand condemned, it must be thought that you yourselves have acted wrong, not that you owe your present state to the caprice of fortune. But it cannot be! No, my countrymen, it cannot be that you have acted wrong in encountering danger bravely for the liberty and safety of all Greece. No! by those generous souls of ancient times who were exposed at Marathon! by those who stood arrayed at Plataea! by those who encountered the Persian fleet at Salamis, who fought at Artemisium! by all those illustrious sons of Athens whose remains lie deposited in the public monuments! all of whom received the same honorable interment from their country—not those only who prevailed, not those only who were victorious: and with reason. What was the part of gallant men they all performed; their success was such as the Supreme Director of the world dispensed to each.

Well, then, thou miscreant! thou abject scrivener! thou, who, to rob me of the honors and the affections of these my countrymen, talkest of battles, of trophies, of brave deeds of old. And what are these, or any of these to the present cause? Say, thou vile player! when I assumed the character of a public counsellor, and on an object so important as the natural preeminence of my country, with what principles should I have arisen to speak? Those of suggesting measures unworthy of my countrymen? Then must I have met that death I merited. And when the interests of the State come before you, your minds, my fellow-citizens, should be possessed with an extraordinary degree of elevation, beyond what is necessary in private causes. When these are to be decided, you have only to consider the ordinary transactions of the world, the tenor of your laws, and the nature of private facts. But, in questions of State, you are to look up to your illustrious ancestors; and every judge is to suppose, that with the symbols of his authority, he is also invested with the high character of his country. Thus, and thus only, shall he determine on such questions in a manner worthy of these his ancestors.

No, Æschines, if you are determined to examine into my fortune, compare it with your own: and if you find mine superior, let it be no longer the subject of your reproach. Let us trace this matter fully. And here, in the name of all the gods! let me not be censured as betraying any indication of a low mind. No man can be more sensible than I that he who insults poverty, and he who, because he hath been bred in affluence, assumes an air of pride and consequence, are equally devoid of understanding. But the virulence and restless malice of an inveterate adversary hath forced me on this topic, where I shall study to confine myself within as strict bounds as the case can possibly admit.

Know, then, Æschines, it was my fortune, when a youth, to be trained up in a liberal course of education, supplied in such a manner as to place me above the base temptations of poverty: when a man, to act suitably to such an education, to contribute in my full proportion to all the exigencies of the State; never to be wanting in any honorable conduct, either in private or in public life, but on all occasions to prove myself useful to my country and to my friends. When I came into the administration of public affairs, I determined on such a course of conduct as frequently gained me the honor of a crown, both from this and other States of Greece. Nor could you, my enemies, attempt to say that I had determined on a dishonorable course. Such hath been the fortune of my life—a subject on which I might enlarge; but I must restrain myself, lest I should give offense by an affectation of importance.

Come, then, thou man of dignity, thou who spurnest at all others with contempt; examine thy own life; say, of what kind hath thy fortune been? She placed thee when a youth in a state of abject poverty, an assistant to thy father in his school, employed in the menial services of preparing his ink, washing down his benches, and sweeping his room, like a slave rather than a child of a citizen. When arrived at manhood, we find thee dictating the forms of initiation to thy mother, assisting in her trade, every night employed with thy fawnskin and lustral bowls, purifying the novitiates, modelling their little figures of clay and bran, then rousing them, and teaching them to pronounce, "I have escaped the bad; I have found the better;" glorying in this noble accomplishment of howling out such jargon louder than the rest, And it is an honor we must allow him; for, as he pleads with so much vehemence, you may conclude that in his howlings he was equally piercing and clamorous. In the daytime he led his noble Bacchanals through the highways crowned with fennel and poplar, grasping his serpents, and waving them above his head, with his yell of "Evoë! Saboë!" then bounding and roaring out "Hyës! Attës! Attës! Hyës!"—"Leader!—Conductor!—Ivybearer!—Van-bearer!" These were his felicitations from the old women: and his wages were tart, biscuit, and new-baked crusts. In such circumstances, surely we must congratulate him on his fortune.

When you had obtained your enrollment among our citizens—by what means I shall not mention—but when you had obtained it, you instantly chose out the most honorable of employments, that of under-scrivener, and assistant to the lowest of our public officers. And when you retired from this station, where you had been guilty of all those practices you charge on others, you were careful not to disgrace any of the past actions of your life. No, by the powers! You hired yourself to Simylus and Socrates, those deep-groaning tragedies, as they were called, and acted third characters. You pillaged the grounds of other men for figs, grapes, and olives, like a fruiterer; which cost you more blows than even your playing—which was in effect playing for your life; for there was an implacable, irreconcilable war declared between you and the spectators, whose stripes you felt so often and so severely, that you may well deride those as cowards who are unexperienced in such perils. But I shall not dwell on such particulars as may be imputed to his poverty. My objections shall be confined to his principles. Such were the measures you adopted in your public conduct (for you at last conceived the bold design of engaging in affairs of State), that while your country prospered you led a life of trepidation and dismay, expecting every moment the stroke due to those iniquities which stung your conscience; when your fellow-citizens were unfortunate, then were you distinguished by a peculiar confidence. And the man who assumes this confidence when thousands of his countrymen have perished—what should he justly suffer from those who are left alive? And here I might produce many other particulars of his character. But I suppress them, for I am not to exhaust the odious subject of his scandalous actions. I am confined to those which it may not be indecent to repeat.

Take, then, the whole course of your life, Æschines, and of mine; compare them without heat or acrimony. You attended on your scholars; I was myself a scholar. You served in the initiations; I was initiated. You were a performer in our public entertainments; I was the director. You took notes of speeches; I was a speaker. You were an under-player; I was a spectator. You failed in your part; I hissed you. Your public conduct was devoted to our enemies; mine to my country. I shall only add that on this day I appear to be approved worthy of a crown; the question is not whether I have been merely blameless; this is a point confessed. You appear as a false accuser; and the question is, whether you are ever to appear again in such a character. You are in danger of being effectually prevented, by feeling the consequences of a malicious prosecution. The fortune of your life, then, hath been truly excellent; you see it. Mine hath been mean; and you have reason to reproach it. Come, then, hear me while I read the several attestations of those public offices which I have discharged; and, in return do you repeat those verses which you spoiled in the delivery:

> Forth from the deep abyss, behold, I come;
> And the dread portal of the dusky gloom.

And,

> Know, then, howe'er reluctant, I must speak
> Those evils—

Oh, may the gods inflict "those evils" on thee! may these thy countrymen inflict them to thy utter destruction!—thou enemy to Athens! thou traitor! thou vile player!—Read the attestations. (The attestations are read.)

Amid all this shamefully avowed corruption, this confederacy, or (shall I call it by its true name?) this traitorous conspiracy against the liberty of Greece, my conduct preserved the reputation of this State unimpeached by the world; while my character, Athenians, stood equally unimpeached by you. Do you ask me, then, on what merits I claim this honor? Hear my answer. When all the popular leaders through Greece had been taught by your example, and accepted the wages of corruption, from Philip first, and now from Alexander, no favorable moment was found to conquer my integrity; no insinuation of address, no magnificence of promises, no hopes, no fears, no favor—nothing could prevail on me to resign the least part of what I deemed the just rights and interests of my country: nor, when my counsels were demanded, was I ever known, like you and your associates, to lean to that side where a bribe had been, as it were, cast into the scale. No; my whole conduct was influenced by a spirit of rectitude, a spirit of justice and integrity; and, engaged as I was in affairs of greater moment than any statesman of my time, I administered them all with a most exact and uncorrupted faith. These are the merits on which I claim this honor.

As to those public works so much the object of your ridicule, they undoubtedly demand a due share of honor and applause; but I rate them far beneath the great merits of my administration. It is not with stones or bricks that I have fortified the city. It is not from works like these that I derive my reputation. Would you know my methods of fortifying? Examine, and you will find them in the arms, the towns, the territories, the harbors I have secured; the navies, the troops, the armies I have raised. These are the works by which I defended Attica, as far as human foresight could defend it; these are the fortifications I drew round our whole territory, and not the circuit of our harbor or of our city only. In these acts of policy, in these provisions for a war I never yielded to Philip. No; it was our generals and our confederate forces who yielded to fortune. Would you know the proofs of this? They are plain and evident. Consider: what was the part of a faithful citizen? of a prudent, an active, and an honest minister? Was he not to secure Euboea, as our defence against all attacks by sea? Was he not to make Boeotia our barrier on the midland side? the cities bordering on Peloponnesus our bulwark on that quarter? Was he not to attend with due precaution to the importation of corn, that this trade might be protected through all its progress up to our own harbor? Was he not to cover those districts which we commanded by seasonable detachments—as the Proconesus, the Chersonesus, and Tenedos? To exert himself in the assembly for this purpose? while with equal zeal he labored to gain others to our interest and alliance—as Byzantium, Abydus, and Euboea? Was he not to cut off the best and most important resources of our enemies, and to supply those in which our country was defective? And all this you gained by my counsels and my administration—such counsels and such an administration as must appear, upon a fair and equitable view, the result of strict integrity; such as left no favorable juncture unimproved through ignorance or treachery; such as ever had their due effect, as far as the judgment and abilities of one man could prove effectual. But if some superior being; if the power of fortune; if the misconduct of generals; if the iniquity of our traitors; or if all these together broke in on us, and at length involved us in one general devastation, how is Demosthenes to be blamed? Had there been a single man in each Grecian State to act the same part which I supported in this city,—nay, had but one such man been found in Thessaly and one in Arcadia, actuated by my principles, not a single Greek, either beyond or on this side of Thermopylae, could have experienced the misfortunes of this day. All had then been free and independent, in perfect tranquillity, security, and happiness, uncontrolled in their several communities by any foreign power, and filled with gratitude to you and to your State, the authors of these blessings so extensive and so precious. And all this by my means. To convince you that I have spoken much less than I could justify by facts, that in this detail I have studiously guarded against envy, take—read the list of our confederates, as they were procured by my decrees.

These, and such as these, Æschines, are the actions which become a noble-minded, honest citizen.

* * *

There are two distinguishing qualities, Athenians, which the virtuous citizen should ever possess—(I speak in general terms, as the least invidious method of doing justice to myself)—a zeal for the honor and preeminence of the State in his official conduct; on all occasions, and in all transactions, an affection for his country. This nature can bestow. Abilities and success depend on another power. And in this affection you find me firm and invariable. Not the solemn demand of my person; not the vengeance of the Amphictyonic Council, which they denounced against me; not the terror of their threatenings; not the flattery of their promises; no, nor the fury of those accursed wretches whom they roused like wild beasts against me could ever tear this affection from my breast. From first to last I have uniformly pursued a just and virtuous course of conduct; assertor of the honors, of the prerogatives, of the glory of my country; studious to support them, zealous to advance them, my whole being is devoted to this glorious cause. I was never known to march through the city with a face of joy and exultation at the success of a foreign power; embracing and announcing the joyful tidings to those who, I supposed, would transmit it to the proper place. I was never known to receive the successes of my own country with tremblings, with sighings, with eyes bending to the earth, like those impious men who are the defamers of the State, as if by such conduct they were not defamers of themselves; who look abroad, and, when a foreign potentate hath established his power on the calamities of Greece, applaud the event, and tell us we should take every means to perpetuate his power.

Hear me, ye immortal gods! and let not these their desires be ratified in heaven! Infuse a better spirit into these men! Inspire even their minds with purer sentiments!—This is my first prayer.—Or, if their natures are not to be reformed, on them, on them only discharge your vengeance! Pursue them both by land and sea! Pursue them even to destruction! But to us display your goodness in a speedy deliverance from impending evils, and all the blessings of protection and tranquillity.

Translated by Thomas Leland, D.D.
Published by G. P. Putnam's Sons.
Reprinted by permission.

BIBLIOGRAPHY OF THE GREEK PERIOD

Aristotle: *Rhetoric*, trans. W. Rhys Roberts, ed. W. D. Ross, The Clarendon Press, London, 1924.

Baldwin, Charles: *Ancient Rhetoric and Poetic*, The Macmillan Company, New York, 1924.

Barker, Ernest: *Library of Greek Thought, Greek Civilization and Character*, E. P. Dutton and Company, Inc., New York, 1924.

Blass, F. W.: *Geschichte der attischen Beredsamkeit*, B. G. Teubner, Leipzig, 1890.

Bosanquet, B.: *Education of the Young in Plato's Republic*, Cambridge University Press, London, 1900.

Brown, Hazel Louise: *Extemporary Speech in Antiquity*, dissertation for Ph.D. degree, Library of Columbia University, New York, 1928.

Cope, E. M.: *An Introduction to Aristotle's Rhetoric*, Cambridge University Press, London, 1867.

Coppens, Charles: *Art of Oratorical Composition*, Schwartz, Kirwin, and Fauss, New York, 1885.

Demosthenes: *Orations*, trans. Chas. Rann Kennedy, D. Appleton and Company, New York, 1912.

Dobson, J. F.: *Ancient Education and its Meaning to Us*, Longmans, Green and Company, New York, 1932.

Hardwicke, Henry: *History of Oratory and Orations*, G. P. Putnam's Sons, New York, 1896.

Holliday, Carl: *The Dawn of Literature*, The Thomas Crowell Y. Company, New York, 1931.

Holy Bible, The: King James Version.

Homer: *The Iliad*, trans. Walter Leaf, The Macmillan Company, New York, 1919.

Jebb, R. C.: *The Attic Orators from Antiphon to Isaeus*, Cambridge University Press, London, 1876.

Jowett, Benjamin: *Thucydides*, The Clarendon Press, London, 1900.

Lee, Carleton, ed.: *The World's Orators*, G. P. Putnam's Sons, New York, 1899.

Longinus, Cassius: *On the Sublime*, trans. W. Rhys Roberts, University Press, Cambridge, 1899.

Morey, William C.: *Outlines of Greek History*, American Book Company, New York, 1903.

Pickard, A. W.: *Heroes of the Nations*, Cambridge University Press, London, 1891.

Platz, Mabel: *The History of Public Speaking*, Noble and Noble, New York, 1935.

Plutarch's Lives: trans. John Dryden, Bigelow, Brown and Company, Inc., New York, 1911.

Ross, W. D.: *Aristotle,* Methuen and Company, Ltd., London, 1923.

Saintsbury, George: *History of Criticism and Literary Taste in Europe from the Earliest Times to the Present Day,* W. Blackwood and Sons, Ltd., London, 1909.

Sears, Lorenzo: *History of Oratory,* S. C. Griggs Company, Chicago, 1896.

Stobart, J. C.: *The Glory That Was Greece,* Sidgwick and Jackson, Ltd., London, 1915.

Thucydides: *The History of the Peloponnesian War,* introduction, Richard Crawley, E. P. Dutton and Company, New York, 1910.

Wells, H. G.: *Outline of History,* The Macmillan Company, New York, 1930.

Wilkins, A. S.: *National Education in Greece,* G. E. Stechert and Company, New York, 1911.

THE ROMAN PERIOD

INTRODUCTION

In the beginning Roman speech was crude and vehement, for Roman leaders were men of action who gained attention by force. Their speech was sturdy, energetic, and practical, expressing the thoughts of an active and progressive people. The conquest of Greece brought Rome for the first time into contact with a people who made her intellectually conscious. Consequently Roman oratory became somewhat imitative of the Greek, but where imagination and artistry predominated in the Greek style force and strength appeared in the Roman.

As in Greece early oratory was recorded by historians, so in Rome the speeches of the early Roman generals were preserved by Rome's great historians, Sallust, Livy, Tacitus, and Plutarch; for it was not until the time of Cato that the orators themselves began to leave written records of their speeches.

It was the Gracchi who really marked the beginning of Latin eloquence, and their successors, studying at Athens, elevated the art of Roman oratory to the eminence attained by the Greek. Cicero, the supreme master of Roman eloquence, acknowledged Demosthenes, the crowning orator of Greece, as his master, but where Demosthenes had plainness of diction and somberness of thought Cicero had wordiness, vivacity, and wit. These two leading orators of the ancient world set up the standards of the Greek and Roman styles which have served as models for subsequent ages of orators.

During the existence of the monarchy there was little opportunity for eloquence in Rome. In the days of the Republic it was the democratic institutions of Rome which fostered the best oratory. Most important of these were the *Roman Forum*, which was the meeting place for the courts of justice; the *Public Assemblies*, where people met to deliberate on the proposals of new laws; and the *Senate*, which furnished the greatest opportunity for eloquence to its members in the discussion of the affairs of state. The Roman educational system also stressed the study of oratory in order to prepare the youth of the country for assuming leadership. Under such democratic institutions leaders like the Gracchi arose and plead for social justice, and the state was saved from the machinations of Catiline by the eloquence of Cicero whose last words rang out against the overthrow of the Republic.

As in Greece, Roman oratory flourished under a democracy and declined with the fall of the Republic. In the selection of orations made for this period both the style of the work and the motive prompting the speech have been considered as criteria of choice.

ON PUNISHING THE CONSPIRATORS

Caius Julius Caesar

(100 B.C.—44 B.C.)

C. Sallustius Crispus, the historian, had talents as an orator and politician. He had risen from the ranks to a position of prominence at Rome and in his public life frequently addressed the Romans in the Law Courts, Forum, and Senate. The speeches which he recorded in his history are therefore a result of his own oratorical training. His style may be defined as classic and cultivated but a trifle archaic.

Notable among the speeches preserved by Sallust are those connected with the Catilinian conspiracy. Catiline, the leader of the conspirators, was generally regarded as a deliberate foe of law and order and morality. Sallust presents Catiline in this light while, as a political partisan of Caesar, he attempts to clear the latter of all complicity, although Caesar was suspected of being privy to the conspiracy because he advocated leniency. The oration which Caesar delivered *On Punishing the Conspirators* is believed to be preserved by Sallust essentially as Caesar delivered it, and is valuable as the only extant speech of Julius Caesar.

It becomes all men, Conscript Fathers, who deliberate on dubious matters, to be influenced neither by hatred, affection, anger, nor pity. The mind, when such feelings obstruct its view, cannot easily see what is right; nor has any human being consulted, at the same moment, his passions and his interest. When the mind is freely exerted, its reasoning is sound; but passion, if it gain possession of it, becomes its tyrant, and reason is powerless.

I could easily mention, Conscript Fathers, numerous examples of kings and nations, who, swayed by resentment or compassion, have adopted injudicious courses of conduct; but I had rather speak of those instances in which our ancestors, in opposition to the impulse of passion, acted with wisdom and sound policy.

In the Macedonian war, which we carried on against King Perses, the great and powerful state of Rhodes, which had risen by the aid of the Roman people, was faithless and hostile to us; yet, when the war was ended, and the conduct of the Rhodians was taken into consideration, our forefathers left them unmolested, lest any should say that war was made upon them for the sake of seizing their wealth, rather than of punishing their faithlessness. Throughout the Punic wars, too, though the Carthaginians, both during peace and in suspension of arms, were guilty of many acts of injustice, yet our ancestors never took occasion to retaliate, but considered rather what was worthy of themselves than what might justly be inflicted on their enemies.

Similar caution, Conscript Fathers, is to be observed by yourselves, that the guilt of Lentulus, and the other conspirators, may not have greater weight with you than your own dignity, and that you may not regard your indignation more than your character. If, indeed, a punishment adequate to their crimes be discovered, I consent to extraordinary measures; but if the enormity of their crime exceeds whatever can be devised, I think that we should inflict only such penalties as the laws have provided.

Most of those who have given their opinions before me have deplored, in studied and impressive language, the sad fate that threatens the republic; they have recounted the barbarities of war, and the afflictions that would fall on the vanquished; they have told us that maidens would be dishonored, and youths abused; that children would be torn from the embraces of their parents; that matrons would be subjected to the pleasure of the conquerors; that temples and dwelling-houses would be plundered; that massacres and fires would follow; and that every place would be filled with arms, corpses, blood, and lamentation. But to what end, in the name of the eternal gods! was such eloquence directed? Was it intended to render you indignant at the conspiracy? A speech, no doubt, will inflame him whom so frightful and monstrous a reality has not provoked! Far from it: for to no man does evil, directed against himself, appear a light matter; many, on the contrary, have felt it more seriously than was right.

But to different persons, Conscript Fathers. different degrees of license are allowed. If those who pass a life sunk in obscurity commit any error, through excessive anger, few become aware of it, for their fame is as limited as their fortune; but of those who live invested with extensive power, and in an exalted station, the whole world knows the proceedings. Thus in the highest position there is the least liberty of action; and it becomes us to indulge neither partiality nor aversion, but least of all animosity; for what in others is called resentment is in the powerful termed violence and cruelty.

I am, indeed, of opinion, Conscript Fathers, that the utmost degree of torture is inadequate to punish their crime; but the generality of mankind dwell on that which happens last, and, in the case of malefactors, forget their guilt, and talk only of their punishment, should that punishment have been inordinately severe. I feel assured, too, that Decimus Silanus, a man of spirit and resolution, made the suggestions which he offered, from zeal for the state, and that he had no view, in so important a matter, to favor or to enmity; such I know to be his character, and such his discretion. Yet his proposal appears to me, I will not say cruel (for what can be cruel that is directed against such characters?), but foreign to our policy. For, assuredly, Silanus, either your fears, or their treason, must have induced you, a consul-elect, to propose this new kind of punishment. Of fear it is unnecessary to speak, when, by the prompt activity of that distinguished man our consul, such numerous forces are under arms; and as to the punishment, we may say, what is, indeed, the truth, that in trouble and distress death is a relief from suffering, and not a torment; that it puts an end to all human woes; and that, beyond it, there is no place either for sorrow or joy.

But why, in the name of the immortal gods, did you not add to your proposal, Silanus, that, before they were put to death, they should be punished with the scourge? Was it because the Porcian law forbids it? But other laws forbid condemned citizens to be deprived of life, and allow them to go into exile. Or was it because scourging is a severer penalty than death? Yet what can be too severe, or too harsh, toward men convicted of such an offence? But if scourging be a milder punishment than death, how is it consistent to observe the law as to the smaller point, when you disregard it as to the greater?

But who, it may be asked, will blame any severity that shall be decreed against these parricides of their country? I answer that time, the course of events, and fortune, whose caprice governs nations, may blame it. Whatever shall fall on the traitors, will fall on them justly; but it is for you, conscript fathers, to consider well what you resolve to inflict on others. All precedents productive of evil effects had had their origin from what was good; but when a government passes into the hands of the ignorant or unprincipled, any new example of severity, inflicted on deserving and suitable objects, is extended to those that are improper and undeserving of it. The Lacedaemonians, when they had conquered the Athenians, appointed thirty men to govern their state. These thirty began their administration by putting to death, even without a trial, all who were notoriously wicked, or publicly detestable; acts at which the people rejoiced, and extolled their justice. But afterward, when their lawless power gradually increased, they proceeded, at their pleasure, to kill the good and bad indiscriminately, and to strike terror into all; and thus the state, overpowered and enslaved, paid a heavy penalty for its imprudent exultation.

Within our own memory, too, when the victorious Sylla ordered Damasippus, and others of similar character, who had risen by distressing their country, to be put to death, who did not commend the proceeding? All exclaimed that wicked and factious men, who had troubled the state with their seditious practices, had justly forfeited their lives. Yet this proceeding was the commencement of great bloodshed. For whenever any one coveted the mansion or villa, or even the plate or apparel of another, he exerted his influence to have him numbered among the proscribed. Thus they, to whom the death of Damasippus had been a subject of joy, were soon after dragged to death themselves; nor was there any cessation of slaughter, until Sylla had glutted all his partisans with riches.

Such excesses, indeed, I do not fear from Marcus Tullius, or in these times. But in a large state there arise many men of various dispositions. At some other period, and under another consul, who, like the present, may have an army at his command, some false accusation may be credited as true; and when, with our example for a precedent, the consul shall have drawn the sword on the authority of the senate, who shall stay its progress, or moderate its fury?

Our ancestors, Conscript Fathers, were never deficient in conduct or courage; nor did pride prevent them from imitating the customs of other nations, if they appeared deserving of regard. Their armor, and weapons of war, they borrowed from the Samnites; their ensigns of authority, for the most part, from the Etrurians; and, in short, whatever appeared eligible to them, whether among allies or among enemies, they adopted at home with the greatest readiness, being more inclined to emulate merit than to be jealous of it. But at the same time, adopting a practice from Greece, they punished their citizens with the scourge, and inflicted capital punishment on such as were condemned. When the republic, however, became powerful, and faction grew strong from the vast number of citizens, men began to involve the innocent in condemnation, and other like abuses were practiced; and it was then that the Porcian and other laws were provided, by which condemned citizens were allowed to go into exile. This lenity of our ancestors, Conscript Fathers, I regard as a very strong reason why we should not adopt any new measures of severity. For assuredly there was greater merit and wisdom in those, who raised so mighty an empire from humble means, than in us, who can scarcely preserve what they so honorably acquired. Am I of opinion, then, you will ask, that the conspirators should be set free, and that the army of Catiline should be set free, and that the army of Catiline should thus be increased? Far from it: my recommendation is, that their property be confiscated, and that they themselves be kept in custody in such of the municipal towns as are best able to bear the expense; that no one hereafter bring their case to the senate, or speak on it to the people, and that the senate now give their opinion that he who shall act contrary to this will act against the republic and the general safety.

AGAINST THE CONSPIRATORS

Marcus Porcius Cato

(234 B.C.—149 B.C.)

Cato, the Censor, opposed the leniency which Caesar urged in his speech for the conspirators. A man of caustic language, pitiless sarcasm, and subtle argument Cato was indeed a Roman of the old school—austere in manner, bitter in condemnation of wrong. The speech included here is recorded by Sallust as a direct reply to Caesar's speech.

My feelings, Conscript Fathers, are extremely different when I contemplate our circumstances and dangers, and when I revolve in my mind the sentiments of some who have spoken before me. Those speakers, as it seems to me, have considered only how to punish the traitors who have raised war against their country, their parents, their altars, and their homes; but the state of affairs warns us rather to secure ourselves against them than to take counsel as to what sentence we should pass upon them. Other crimes you may punish after they have been committed; but with this, unless you prevent its commission, you will, when it has once taken effect, appeal to justice in vain. When the city is taken, no power is left to the vanquished.

But in the name of the immortal gods, I call upon you who have always valued your mansions and villas, your statues and pictures, at a higher price than the welfare of your country, if you wish to preserve those possessions, whatever kind they are, to which you are attached; if you wish to secure quiet for the enjoyment of your pleasures, arouse yourselves, and act in defence of your country. We are not debating on the revenues, or on injuries done to our allies; our liberty and our lives are at stake.

Often, Conscript Fathers, have I spoken at great length in this assembly; often have I complained of the luxury and avarice of our citizens, and, by that very means, have incurred the displeasure of many. I, who never excused to myself, or to my own conscience, the commission of any fault, could not easily pardon the misconduct or condone the licentiousness of others. But though you little regarded my remonstrances, yet the Republic remained secure; its own strength was proof against your remissness. The question, however, at present under discussion, is not whether we live in a good or bad state of morals; not how great or how splendid is the Empire of the Roman people; but whether these things around us, of whatever value they are, are to remain our own or are to fall, with ourselves, into the hands of the enemy.

In such a case, does anyone talk to me of gentleness and compassion? For some time past, it is true, we have forgotten the real names of things; for to lavish the property of others is called generosity, and audacity in wickedness is called heroism; and hence the State is reduced to the brink of ruin. But let those who thus misname things be liberal, since such is the practice, out of the property of our allies; let them be merciful to the robbers of the treasury; but let them not lavish our blood, and, while they spare a few criminals, bring destruction on all the guiltless.

Caius Caesar, a short time ago, spoke in fair and elegant language before this assembly on the subject of Life and Death; considering as false, I suppose, that which is said of the dead: that the bad, going a different way from the good, inhabit places which are gloomy, desolate, dreary, and full of horror. He accordingly proposed that the property of the conspirators should be confiscated, and themselves kept in custody in the municipal towns; fearing, it seems, that if they remain at Rome they may be rescued either by their accomplices in the conspiracy or by a hired mob; as if, forsooth, the mischievous and profligate were to be found only in the city and not throughout the whole of Italy, or as if desperate attempts would not be more likely to succeed where there is less power to resist them. His proposal, therefore, if he fears any danger from them, is absurd; but if, amidst such universal terror, he alone is free from alarm, it the more concerns me to fear for you and for myself.

Be, sure, then, that when you decide on the fate of Lentulus and the other prisoners, you at the same time determine that of the army of Catiline and of all the conspirators. The more spirit you display in your decision, the more will their confidence be diminished; but if they perceive you in the smallest degree irresolute, they will advance upon you with fury.

Do not suppose that our ancestors, from so small a commencement, raised the Republic to greatness merely by force of arms. If such had been the case, we should now enjoy it in a most excellent condition; for of allies and citizens, as well as arms and horses, we have a much greater abundance than they. But there were other things which made them great, but which no longer exist among us: such as industry at home, equitable government abroad, and minds impartial in council, uninfluenced by any immoral or improper feeling. Instead of such virtues, we have luxury and avarice, public distress and private superfluity; we extol wealth, and yield to indolence; no distinction is made between good men and bad; and ambition usurps the honors due to virtue. Nor is this wonderful, since each of you studies his own interest, since at home you are slaves to pleasure, and here to money or to favor; and hence it happens that an attack is made on the defenceless State.

But on these subjects I shall say no more. Certain citizens, of the highest rank, have conspired to ruin their country; they are inciting the Gauls, the bitterest foes of the Roman name, to join in a war against us; the leader of the enemy is ready to make a descent upon us, and do you hesitate, even in such circumstances, how to treat armed incendiaries arrested within your walls? I advise you to have mercy upon them; they are young men who have been led astray by ambition; send them away, even with arms in their hands. But if they turn those arms against you, such mercy and such clemency will end in misery to yourselves. The case, assuredly, is dangerous, but you do not feel it; yes, you fear it greatly, but through weakness and want of spirit you hesitate how to act, waiting one for another, and trusting to the immortal gods, who have so often preserved your country in the greatest dangers. But the protection of the gods is not obtained by vows and womanish supplications; it is by vigilance, activity, and prudent measures that general welfare is secured. When you are once resigned to sloth and indolence, it is in vain that you implore the gods; they are then indignant and threaten vengeance.

In the days of our forefathers, Titus Manlius Torquatus, during a war with the Gauls, ordered his own son to be put to death, because he had fought with an enemy contrary to orders. That noble youth suffered for excess of bravery; and do you hesitate in determining what sentence to pass on the most inhuman of traitors? Perhaps their former life is at variance with their present crime. Spare, then, the dignity of Lentulus, if he has ever spared his own honor or character, or had any regard for gods or for men. Pardon the youth of Cethegus, unless this be the second time that he has made war upon his country. As to Gabinius, Statilius, Coeparius, why should I make any remark upon them? Had they ever possessed the smallest share of discretion, they would not have engaged in such a plot against their country.

In conclusion, Conscript Fathers, if there were time to amend an error, I might easily suffer you, since you disregard words, to be corrected by experience of consequences. But we are beset by dangers on all sides: Catiline, with his army, is ready to devour us, while there are other enemies within the walls and in the heart of the city; and no measures can be taken, no plans arranged, without their knowledge. The more necessary is it, therefore, to act with promptitude. What I advise, then, is this: since the State, by a treasonable combination of abandoned citizens, has been brought into the greatest peril, and since the conspirators have been convicted, on the evidence of Titus Volturcius and of the deputies of the Allobroges, and on their own confession, of having concerted massacres, conflagrations, and other horrible and cruel outrages against their fellow-citizens and their country, that, therefore, punishment

ought to be inflicted, according to the usage of our ancestors, on the prisoners who have confessed their guilt, as on men convicted of capital crimes.

The World's Orations.
Published by G. P. Putnam's Sons.
Reprinted by permission.

TO HIS SOLDIERS

Publius Cornelius Scipio

(?—211 B.C.)

Titus Livius, the Roman historian, was preeminently an orator. He had studied and taught the art of rhetoric. Therefore his *History of Rome* includes many oratorical passages which he attributes to the Roman generals. Livy had a talent for an orderly sequence of arrangement, the ability to move the emotions, nobility of language, and patriotic sincerity. He records the speech of the Roman Consul, P. Cornelius Scipio which was addressed to his soldiers before the first important battle against the Carthaginians under Hannibal, 218 B.C. The speech is one of the most celebrated Roman military orations. Although this particular speech is serious in character, Scipio has been called the wittiest speaker of his day.

If, soldiers, I were leading out to battle that army which I had with me in Gaul, I should have thought it superfluous to address you; for of what use would it be to exhort either those horsemen who so gloriously vanquished the cavalry of the enemy at the river Rhone, or those legions with whom, pursuing this very enemy flying before us, I obtained, in lieu of victory, a confession of superiority, shown by his retreat and refusal to fight? But now because that army, levied for the province of Spain, maintains the war under my auspices and the command of my brother, Cneius Scipio, in the country where the Senate and the people of Rome wished him to serve; and since I have offered myself voluntarily for this contest, that you might have a consul for your leader against Hannibal and the Carthaginians, a few words are required to be addressed from a new commander to soldiers unacquainted with him.

That you may not be ignorant of the nature either of the war or of the enemy, let me remind you, Soldiers, that you have to fight with those whom in the former war you conquered both by land and sea; from whom you have exacted tribute for twenty years; from whom you hold Sicily and Sardinia, taken as the prizes of victory. In the present contest, therefore, you and they will have those feelings which are wont to belong to the victors and the vanquished. They are now about to fight, not because they are daring, but because it is unavoidable; unless you can believe that those who declined the engagement when their forces were entire should have now gained more confidence when two thirds of their infantry and cavalry have been lost in the passage of the Alps, and when almost greater numbers have perished than survive. Yes, they are few, indeed (some may say), but they are vigorous in mind and body; men whose strength and power almost no force may withstand. On the contrary, they are but the semblances, nay, they are rather the shadows of men; for they are worn out with hunger, cold, dirt, and filth, and bruised and enfeebled among stones and rocks. Besides all this, their joints are frost-bitten, their sinews stiffened with the snow, their limbs withered up by the frost, their armor battered and gaping, their horses lame and powerless. With such cavalry, with such infantry, you have to fight; you will not have enemies in reality, but rather their last remains. And I fear nothing more than that when you have fought Hannibal, the Alps may appear to have conquered him. But perhaps it was fitting that the gods themselves should, without any human aid, commence and carry forward a war against a leader and a people who violate the faith of treaties; and that we, who have been injured next to the gods, should finish the contest thus commenced and now nearly completed.

I do not fear lest any one should think that I say this ostentatiously for the sake of encouraging you, while in my own mind I am differently affected. I was at liberty to go with my army into Spain, my own province, whither I had already set out. There I should have had a brother as a sharer of my councils and my dangers, and Hasdrubal for my antagonist, and without question a less laborious war. Nevertheless, as I sailed along the coast of Gaul, I landed on hearing of this enemy, and having sent forward the cavalry, I moved my camp to the Rhone. In a battle of cavalry, for with that part of my forces the opportunity was afforded of engaging, I routed the enemy; and because I could not overtake by land his army of infantry, which was rapidly hurried away as if in flight, having returned to the ships with all the speed I could, after compassing such an extent of sea and land, I have met him at the foot of the Alps. Do I appear to have fallen in unexpectedly with this dreaded foe while declining the contest, or to encounter him in his track, to challenge him and drag him out to decide the contest? I am anxious to try whether the earth has suddenly, in these twenty years, sent forth a new race of Carthaginians, or whether these are the same who fought at the islands of Ægates, and whom you permitted to depart from Eryx, valued at eighteen denarii a head; and whether this Hannibal be, as he himself gives out, the rival of the expeditions of Hercules, or one left by his father the tributary, the subject and the slave of the Roman people; who, if his guilt at Saguntum did not drive him to frenzy, would certainly reflect, if not upon his conquered country, at least on his family, his father, and the treaties written by the hand of Hamilcar; who, at the command of our consul, withdrew the garrison from Eryx; who, indignant and grieving, submitted to the harsh conditions imposed on the conquered Carthaginians; who agreed to depart from Sicily and pay tribute to the Roman people.

I would therefore have you fight, Soldiers, not only with that spirit with which you are wont to encounter other enemies, but with a certain indignation and resentment, as if you saw your slaves suddenly taking up arms against you. We might have killed them, when shut up in Eryx, by hunger, the most dreadful of human tortures; we might have carried our victorious fleet over to Africa, and in a few days have destroyed Carthage without any opposition. We granted pardon to their prayers; we released them from the blockade; we made peace with them when conquered; and we afterwards considered them under our protection when they were oppressed by the African war. In return for these benefits, they come, under the command of a furious youth, to attack our country. And I wish that the contest on your side was for glory, and not for safety. It is not about the possession of Sicily and Sardinia, concerning which the dispute was formerly, but for Italy, that you must fight; nor is there another army behind, which, if we should not conquer, can resist the enemy; nor are there other Alps, during the passage of which fresh forces may be procured. Here, Soldiers, we must make our stand, as if we fought beneath the walls of Rome. Let every one consider that he defends with his weapons not only his own person, but his wife and young children; nor let him only entertain domestic cares and anxieties, but at the same time let him bear in mind that the Senate and people of Rome are now anxiously regarding our efforts; and that, according to what our strength and valor shall be, such henceforward will be the fortune of that city and of the Roman Empire.

Published by G. P. Putnam's Sons.
Reprinted by permission.

THE PEOPLES' RIGHTS ABOVE PRIVILEGE

Caius Gracchus

(153 B.C.—121 B.C.)

The Gracchi brothers, socialists of ancient Rome, became prominent in Roman affairs at a time ripe for oratory. The elder of the two brothers, Tiberius Gracchus, was the greatest orator of his day. He patterned his speeches after Greek models, but it was their moral tone and earnest sincerity which distinguished them. The younger brother, Caius Gracchus, strove to supplant the aristocratic, republican form of government by the rule of a pure democracy. Many critics date the history of Roman oratory from Caius Gracchus. To his brother's virtues Caius added intensity—a reserved force and power which has been acknowledged as the hightest virtue of oratory. Only fragments from the speeches of these eminent orators have been preserved. The lost books of Livy may have contained many of their speeches, but it is from Plutarch that most of the now extant fragments have come. A new style of oratory was set by the Gracchi. They dropped the earlier harshness and introduced a milder, freer tone of speech. Included here is a part of Caius Gracchus' speech, *The People's Rights Above Privilege*, delivered to persuade the Roman people to refuse a measure to increase the taxes.

If you choose, fellow Romans, to be guided by wisdom and to look into the matter, you will find that no one comes forward here without hope of reward. All of us who speak strive for something; we are actuated by a desire to carry off some recompense for our pains. I, myself, in urging you to increase your revenues, that you may the better look after your interests and the public weal, do not come here for nothing. It is not, however, money that I seek from you, but your good opinion and esteem. Those, on the other hand, who come here to dissuade you from accepting this proposed law, care not for your esteem, but Nicomedes'

money.   Those, too, who persuade you to accept the law, ask not your
good opinion, but money enough from Mithridates to buy some property.
Those, moreover, who now sit silent in the same seats, are most eager
in the quest of reward; for they accept rewards from all parties alike,
deceiving them all equally.   In thinking them above this, in thinking
that they keep silent for some reason of their own, you are bestowing
your good opinion upon them undeservedly; for all the while they are
receiving bribes from the ambassadors of foreign kings.   Their case
reminds me of Demades and the tragic actor.   The latter was boasting that
a whole talent had been given him for a single play; whereupon Demades,
the most eloquent orator of Athens, is reported to have said: "Does it
seem wonderful to you that you have received a talent for speaking?   For
not speaking I have received ten talents from a king."   So now yonder
men have been richly rewarded for their silence.

Translated by Francis P. Garland.
Reprinted by courtesy of the Colonial Press.

FIRST ORATION AGAINST VERRES

Marcus Tullius Cicero

(106 B.C.—43 B.C.)

In Cicero the culmination of Roman oratory was reached. He had no equal in his day, and his work remains classic. Cicero was born in perilous times. The old Republic was crumbling; the army was becoming autocratic; the Empire was impending; the freedom of the people was impaired. Cicero was particularly aroused by three enemies of the people: Verres, Catiline, and Antonius.

The first of these, Caius Verres, was held for atrocities which he committed while governor of Sicily and for the confiscation of large sums of money from Rome. His misdeeds were manifold. He was a man heinous and ruthless of purpose. In 70 B.C. Verres was impeached. The trial marked a crisis in the affairs of state, for the oligarchical administration of the provinces and the right of the Senate to act as a jury were involved. Hortensius, the great advocate of Rome, was secured by Verres to take his case. Cicero, then only thirty-six years of age, incensed by the great wrongs of the culprit prepared six speeches for the accusation.

It is unfortunate that none of the works of Hortensius, the opponent of Cicero in the famous trial, are extant. Hortensius was gifted by nature with a splendid voice and bearing but was known to be unscrupulous. Cicero so vividly exposed the crimes of Verres in his first speech for the accusation that Verres fled into voluntary exile and the case was dismissed.

That which was above all things to be desired, O judges, and which above all things was calculated to have the greatest influence toward allaying the unpopularity of your order, and putting an end to the discredit into which your judicial decisions have fallen, appears to have been thrown in your way, and given to you not by any human contrivance, but almost by the interposition of the gods, at a most important crisis of the republic. For an opinion has now become established, pernicious to us, and pernicious to the republic, which has been the common talk of every one, not only at Rome, but among foreign nations also,—that in the courts of law as they exist at present, no wealthy man, however guilty he may be, can possibly be convicted.

Now at this time of peril to your order and to your tribunal, when men are ready to attempt by harangues, and by the proposal of new laws, to increase the existing unpopularity of the senate, Caius Verres is brought to trial as a criminal—a man condemned in the opinion of every one by his life and actions, but acquitted by the enormousness of his wealth according to his own hope and boast. I, O judges, have undertaken this cause as prosecutor with the greatest good wishes and expectation on the part of the Roman people, not in order to increase the unpopularity of the senate, but to relieve it from the discredit which I share with it. For I have brought before you a man, by acting justly in whose case you have an opportunity of retrieving the lost credit of your judicial proceedings, of regaining your credit with the Roman people, and of giving satisfaction to foreign nations; a man, the embezzler of the public funds, the petty tyrant of Asia and Pamphylia, the robber who deprived the city of its rights, the disgrace and ruin of the province of Sicily. And if you come to a decision about this man with severity and a due regard to your oaths, that authority which ought to remain in you will cling to you still; but if that man's vast riches shall break down the sanctity and honesty of the courts of justice, at least I shall achieve this, that it shall be plain that it was rather honest judgment that was wanting to the republic, than a criminal to the judges or an accuser to the criminal.

I, indeed, that I may confess to you the truth about myself, O judges, though many snares were laid for me by Caius Verres, both by land and sea, which I partly avoided by my own vigilance, and partly warded off by the zeal and kindness of my friends, yet I never seemed to be incurring so much danger, and I never was in such a state of great apprehension, as I am now in this very court of law. Nor does the expectation which people have formed of my conduct of this prosecution, nor this concourse of so vast a multitude as is here assembled, influence me (though indeed I am greatly agitated by these circumstances) so much as his nefarious plots which he is endeavoring to lay at one and the same time against me, against you, against Marcus Glabrio, the pretor, and against the allies, against foreign nations, against the senate, and even against the very name of senator; whose favorite saying it is that they have got to fear who have stolen only as much as is enough for themselves, but that he has stolen so much that it may easily be plenty for many; that nothing is so holy that it can not be corrupted, or so strongly fortified that it can not be stormed by money. But if he were as secret in acting as he is audacious in attempting, perhaps in some particular he might some time or other have escaped our notice.

But it happens very fortunately that to his incredible audacity there is joined a most unexampled folly. For as he was unconcealed in committing his robberies of money, so in his hope of corrupting the judges he has made his intentions and endeavors visible to every one. He says that only once in his life has he felt fear, at the time when he was first impeached as a criminal by me; because he was only lately arrived from his province, and was branded with unpopularity and infamy, not modern but ancient and of long standing; and, besides that, the time was unlucky, being very ill-suited for corrupting the judges. Therefore, when I had demanded a very short time to prosecute my inquiries in Sicily, he found a man to ask for two days less to make investigations in Achaia; not with any real intention of doing the same with his diligence and industry, that I have accomplished by my labor, and daily and nightly investigations. For the Achaian inquisitor never even arrived at Brundusium. I in fifty days so traveled over the whole of Sicily that I examined into the records and injuries of all the tribes and of all private individuals, so that it was easily visible to every one, that he had been seeking out a man not really for the purpose of bringing the defendant whom he accused to trial, but merely to occupy the time which ought to belong to me.

Now that most audacious and most senseless man thinks this. He is aware that I am come into court so thoroughly prepared and armed, that I shall fix all his thefts and crimes not only in your ears, but in the very eyes of all men. He sees that many senators are witnesses of his audacity; he sees that many Roman knights are so, too, and many citizens, and many of the allies besides to whom he has done unmistakable injuries. He sees also that very numerous and very important deputations have come here at the same time from most friendly cities, armed with the public authority and evidence collected by their states.

In truth, what genius is there so powerful, what faculty of speaking, what eloquence so mighty, as to be in any particular able to defend the life of that man convicted as it is of so many vices and crimes, and long since condemned by the inclinations and private sentiments of every one? And, to say nothing of the stains and disgraces of his youth, what other remarkable event is there in his questorship, that first step to honor, except that Cnaeus Carbo was robbed by his questor of the public money? that the consul was plundered and betrayed? his army deserted? his province abandoned? the holy nature and obligations imposed on him by lot violated?—whose lieutenancy was the ruin of all Asia and Pamphylia, in which provinces he plundered many houses, very many cities, all the shrines and temples; when he renewed and repeated against Cnaeus Dolabella his ancient wicked tricks when he had been questor, and did not only in his danger desert, but even attack and betray the man to whom he had been lieutenant, and proquestor, and whom he had brought into odium by his crimes; whose city pretorship was the destruction of the sacred temples and the public works, and, as to his legal decisions, was the adjudging and awarding of property contrary to all established rules and precedents. But now he has established great and numerous monuments and proofs of all his vices in the province of Sicily, which he for three years so harassed and ruined that it can by no possibility be restored to its former condition, and appears scarcely able to be at all recovered after a long series of years, and a long succession of virtuous pretors. While this man was pretor the Sicilians enjoyed neither their own laws, nor the decrees of our senate, nor the common rights of every nation. Every one in Sicily has only so much left as either escaped the notice or was disregarded by the satiety of this most avaricious and licentious man.

No legal decision for three years was given on any other ground but his will; no property was so secure to any man, even if it had descended to him from his father and grandfather, but he was deprived of it at his command; enormous sums of money were exacted from the property of the cultivators of the soil by a new and nefarious system. The most faithful of the allies were classed in the number of enemies. Roman citizens were tortured and put to death like slaves; the greatest criminals were acquitted in the courts of justice through bribery; the most upright and honorable men, being prosecuted while absent, were condemned and banished without being heard in their own defense; the most fortified harbors, the greatest and strongest cities, were laid open to pirates and robbers; the sailors and soldiers of the Sicilians, our own allies and friends, died of hunger; the best built fleets on the most important stations were lost and destroyed, to the great disgrace of the Roman people. This same man while pretor plundered and stripped those most ancient monuments, some erected by wealthy monarchs and intended by them as ornaments for their cities; some, too, the work of our own generals, which they either gave or restored as conquerors to the different states in Sicily. And he did this not only in the case of public statues and ornaments, but he also plundered all the temples consecrated in the deepest religious feelings of the people. He did not leave, in short, one god to the Sicilians which appeared to him to be made in a tolerable workmanlike manner, and with any of the skill of the ancients.

I am prevented by actual shame from speaking of his nefarious licentiousness as shown in rapes and other such enormities; and I am unwilling also to increase the distress of those men who have been unable to preserve their children and their wives unpolluted by his wanton lust. But, you will say, these things were done by him in such a manner as not to be notorious to all men. I think there is no man who has heard his name who cannot also relate wicked actions of his; so that I ought rather to be afraid of being thought to omit many of his crimes, than to invent any charges against him. And indeed I do not think that this multitude which has collected to listen to me wishes so much to learn of me what the facts of the case are, as to go over it with me, refreshing its recollection of what it knows already.

And as this is the case, that senseless and profligate man attempts to combat me in another manner. He does not seek to oppose the eloquence of any one else to me; he does not rely on the popularity, or influence, or authority of any one. He pretends that he trusts to these things; but I see what he is really aiming at (and indeed he is not acting with any concealment). He sets before me empty titles of nobility—that is to say, the names of arrogant men, who do not hinder me so much by being noble, as assist me by being notorious; he pretends to rely on their protection, when he has in reality been contriving something else this long time. What hope he now has, and what he is endeavoring to do, I will now briefly explain to you, O judges.

But first of all, remark, I beg you, how the matter has been arranged by him from the beginning. When he first returned from the province, he endeavored to get rid of this prosecution by corrupting the judges at a great expense; and this object he continued to keep in view till the conclusion of the appointment of the judges. After the judges were appointed, because in drawing lots for them the fortune of the Roman people had defeated his hopes, and in the rejecting of some my diligence had defeated his impudence, the whole attempt at bribery was abandoned. The affair was going on admirably; lists of your names and of the whole tribunal were in every one's hands. It did not seem possible to mark the votes of these men with any distinguishing mark or color or spot of dirt; and that fellow, from having been brisk and in high spirits, became on a sudden so downcast and humbled, that he seemed to be condemned not only by the Roman people but even by himself. But lo! all of a sudden, within these few days, since the consular comitia have taken place, he has gone back to his original plan with more money, and the same plots are now laid against your reputation and against the fortunes of every one, by the instrumentality of the same people; which fact at first, O judges, was pointed out by me by a very slight hint and indication; but afterward, when my suspicions were once aroused, I arrived at the knowledge of all the most secret counsels of that party without any mistake.

For as Hortensius, the consul-elect, was being attended home again from the Campus by a great concourse and multitude of people, Caius Curio fell in with that multitude by chance,—a man whom I wish to name by way of honor rather than disparagement. I will tell you what if he had been unwilling to have it mentioned, he would not have spoken of in so large an assembly so openly and undisguisedly; which, however, shall be mentioned by me deliberately and cautiously, that it may be seen that I pay due regard to our friendship and to his dignity. He sees Verres in the crowd by the arch of Fabius; he speaks to the man, and with a loud voice congratulates him on his victory. He does not say a word to Hortensius himself, who had been made consul, or to his friends and relations who were present attending on him; but he stops to speak to this man, embraces him, and bids him cast off all anxiety. "I give you notice," said he, "that you have been acquitted by this day's comitia." And as many most honorable men heard this, it is immediately reported to me the first thing. To some it appeared scandalous, to others, again, ridiculous—ridiculous to those who thought that this cause depended on the credibility of the witnesses, on the importance of the charges, and on the power of the judges, and not on the consular comitia; scandalous to those who looked deeper, and who thought that this congratulation had reference to the corruption of the judge.

In truth, they argued in this manner—the most honorable men spoke to one another and to me in this manner—that there were now manifestly and undeniably no courts of justice at all. The very criminal who the day before thought that he was already condemned, is acquitted now that his defender has been made consul. What are we to think then? Will it avail nothing that all Sicily, all the Sicilians, that all the merchants who have business in that country, that all public and private documents are now at Rome? Nothing, if the consul-elect wills it otherwise. What! will not the judges be influenced by the accusation, by the evidence, by the universal opinion of the Roman people? No. Everything will be governed by the power and authority of one man.

In the meantime my comitia began to be held; of which that fellow thought himself the master, as he had been of all the other comitia this year. He began to run about, that influential man, with his son, a youth of engaging and popular manners, among the tribes. The son began to address and to call on all the friends of his father—that is to say, all his agents—for bribery; and when this was noticed and perceived, the Roman people took care with the most earnest good will that I should not be deprived of my honor through the money of that man, whose riches had not been able to make me violate my good faith. After that I was released from the great anxiety about my canvass, I began, with a mind much more unoccupied and much more at ease, to think of nothing and to do nothing except what related to this trial. I find, O judges, these plans formed and begun to be put in execution by them, to protract the matter, whatever steps it might be necessary to take in order to do so, so that the cause might be pleaded before Marcus Metellus as pretor. That by doing so they would have these advantages: firstly, that Marcus Metellus was most friendly to them; secondly, that not only would Hortensius be consul, but Quintus Metellus also; and listen while I show you how great a friend he is to them. For he gave him a token of his good will of such a sort, that he seemed to be giving it as a return for the suffrages of the tribes which he had secured to him. Did you think that I would say nothing of such serious matters as these? and that, at a crisis of such danger to the republic and my own character, I would consult anything rather than my duty and my dignity? The other consul-elect sent for the Sicilians; some came, because Lucius Metellus was pretor in Sicily. To them he speaks in this manner: that he is the consul; that one of his brothers has Sicily for a province; that the other is to be judge in all prosecutions for extortion; and that care had been taken in many ways that there should be no possibility of Verres being injured.

I ask you, Metellus, what is corrupting the course of justice, if this is not,—to seek to frighten witnesses, and especially Sicilians, timid and oppressed men, not only by your own private influence, but by their fear of the consul, and by the power of two pretors? What could you do for an innocent man or for a relation, when for the sake of a most guilty man, entirely unconnected with you, you depart from your duty and your dignity, and allow what he is constantly saying to appear true to any one who is not acquainted with you? For they said that Verres said, that you had not been made consul by destiny, as the rest of your family had been, but by his assistance. Two consuls, therefore, and the judge are to be such because of his will. We shall not only, says he, avoid having a man too scrupulous in investigating, too subservient to the opinion of the people, Marcus Glabrio, but we shall have this advantage also: Marcus Caesonius is the judge, the colleague of your accuser, a man of tried and proved experience in the decision of actions. It will never do for us to have such a man as that on the bench, which we are endeavoring to corrupt by some means or other; for before, when he was one of the judges on the tribunal of which Junius was president, he was not only very indignant at that shameful transaction, but he even betrayed and denounced it.

But as for what I had begun to say—namely, that the contest is between you and me, this is it—I, when I had undertaken this cause at the request of the Sicilians, and had thought it a very honorable and glorious thing for me that they were willing to make experiment of my integrity and diligence, who already knew by experience my innocence and temperance: then, when I had undertaken this business, I proposed to myself some greater action also by which the Roman people should be able to see my good will toward the republic. For that seemed to me to be by no means worthy of my industry and efforts, for that man to be brought to trial by me who had been already condemned by the judgment of all men, unless that intolerable influence of yours, and that grasping nature which you have displayed for some years in many trials, were interposed also in the case of that desperate man. But now, since all this dominion and sovereignty of yours over the courts of justice delights you so much, and since there are some men who are neither ashamed of their licentiousness and their infamy, nor weary of it, and who, as if on purpose, seem to wish to encounter hatred and unpopularity from the Roman people, I profess that I have undertaken this,—a great burden perhaps, and one dangerous to myself, but still worthy of my applying myself to it with all the vigor of my age, and all diligence.

And since the whole order of the senate is weighed down by the discredit brought on it by the wickedness and audacity of a few, and is overwhelmed by the infamy of the tribunals, I profess myself an enemy to this race of men, an accuser worthy of their hatred, a persevering, a bitter adversary. I arrogate this to myself, I claim this for myself, and I will carry out this enmity in my magistracy, and from that post in which the Roman people has willed that from the next first of January I shall act in concert with it in matters concerning the republic, and concerning wicked men. I promise the Roman people that this shall be the most honorable and the fairest employment of my ædileship. I warn, I fore-warn, I give notice beforehand to those men who are wont either to put money down, to undertake for others, to receive money, or to promise money, or to act as agents in bribery, or as go-betweens in corrupting the seat of judgment, and who have promised their influence or their im-pudence in aid of such a business, in this trial to keep their hands and inclinations from this nefarious wickedness.

And what do you suppose will be my thoughts, if I find in this very trial any violation of the laws committed in any similar manner? espe-cially when I can prove by many witnesses that Caius Verres often said in Sicily, in the hearing of many persons, "that he had a powerful friend, in confidence with whom he was plundering the province; and that he was not seeking money for himself alone, but that he had so distributed the three years of his Sicilian pretorship, that he should say he did ex-ceedingly well, if he appropriated the gains of one year to the augmenta-tion of his own property, those of the second year to his patrons and defenders, and reserved the whole of the third year, the most productive and gainful of all, for the judges."

From which it came into my mind to say that which, when I had said it lately before Marcus Glabrio at the time of striking the list of judges, I perceived the Roman people greatly moved by: that I thought that foreign nations would send ambassadors to the Roman people to procure the abrogation of the law, and of all trials, about extortion; for if there were no trials, they think that each man would only plunder them of as much as he would think sufficient for himself and his children; but now, because there are trials of that sort, every one carries off as much as it will take to satisfy himself, his patrons, his advocates, the pretor, and the judges; and that this is an enormous sum; that they may be able to satisfy the cupidity of one most avaricious man, but are quite unable to incur the expense of his most guilty victory over the laws. O trials worthy of being recorded! O splendid reputation of our order! when the allies of the Roman people are unwilling that trials for extortion should take place, which were instituted by our ancestors for the sake of the allies. Would that man ever have had a favorable hope of his own safety, if he had not conceived in his mind a bad opinion of you? on which account, he ought, if possible, to be still more hated by you than he is by the

Roman people, because he considers you like himself in avarice and wickedness and perjury.

And I beg you, in the name of the immortal gods, O judges, think of and guard against this; I warn you, I give notice to you, of what I am well assured, that this most seasonable opportunity has been given to you by the favor of the gods, for the purpose of delivering your whole order from hatred, from unpopularity, from infamy, and from disgrace. There is no severity believed to exist in the tribunals, nor any scruples with regard to religion; in short, there are not believed to be any tribunals at all. Therefore we are despised and scorned by the Roman people; we are branded with a heavy and now long standing infamy. Nor, in fact, is there any other reason for which the Roman people has with so much earnestness sought the restoration of the tribunician power: but when it was demanding that in words, it seemed to be asking for that, but in reality it was asking for tribunals which it could trust.

But now men are on the watch-towers; they observe how every one of you behaves himself in respecting religion and observing the laws. They see that, ever since the passing of the law for restoring the power of the tribunes, only one senator, and he, too, a very insignificant one, has been condemned. And though they do not blame this, yet they have nothing which they can very much commend. For there is no credit in being upright in a case where there is no one who is either able or who endeavors to corrupt one. This is a trial in which you will be deciding about the defendant, the Roman people about you;—by the example of what happens to this man it will be determined whether, when senators are the judges, a very guilty and a very rich man can be condemned.

On which account, in the first place, I beg this of the immortal gods, which I seem to myself to have hopes of, too—that in this trial no one may be found to be wicked except he who has long since been found to be such; secondly, if there are many wicked men, I promise this to you, O judges, I promise this to the Roman people, that my life shall fail rather than my vigor and perseverance in prosecuting their iniquity. But that iniquity, which, if it should be committed, I promise to prosecute severely, with however much trouble and danger to myself, and whatever enmities I may bring on myself by so doing, you, O Marcus Glabrio, can guard against ever taking place by your wisdom, and authority, and diligence. Do you undertake the cause of the tribunals. Do you undertake the cause of impartiality, of integrity, of good faith and religion. Do you undertake the cause of the senate, that, being proved worthy by its conduct in this trial, it may come into favor and popularity with the Roman people. Think who you are and in what a situation you are placed; what you ought to give to the Roman people and what you ought to repay to your ancestors. Let the recollection of the Acilian Law passed by your father occur to your mind, owing to which law the Roman people has had this advantage of most admirable decisions and very strict judges in cases of extortion.

I am resolved not to permit the pretor or the judges to be changed in this cause. I will not permit the matter to be delayed till the lictors of the consuls can go and summon the Sicilians, whom the servants of the consuls-elect did not influence before, when by an unprecedented course of proceeding they sent for them all; I will not permit those miserable men, formerly the allies and friends of the Roman people, now their slaves and supplicants, to lose not only their rights and fortunes by their tyranny, but to be deprived of even the power of bewailing their condition; I will not, I say, when the cause has been summed up by me, permit them after a delay of forty days has intervened, then at last to reply to me when my accusation has already fallen into oblivion through lapse of time; I will not permit the decision to be given when this crowd collected from all Italy has departed from Rome, which has assembled from all quarters at the same time on account of the comitia, of the games, and of the census.

The reward of the credit gained by your decision, or the danger arising from the unpopularity which will accrue to you if you decide unjustly, I think ought to belong to you; the labor and anxiety to me; the knowledge of what is done and the recollection of what has been said by every one, to all. I will adopt this course, not an unprecedented one, but one that has been adopted before, by those who are now the chief men of our state,—the course, I mean, of at once producing the witnesses.

What you will find novel, O judges, is this, that I will so marshall my witnesses as to unfold the whole of my accusation; that when I have established it by examining my witnesses, by arguments, and by my speech, then I shall show the agreement of the evidence with my accusation: so that there shall be no difference between the established mode of prosecuting, and this new one, except that, according to the established mode, when everything has been said which is to be said, then the witnesses are produced; here they shall be produced as each count is brought forward, so that the other side shall have the same opportunity of examining them, of arguing and making speeches on their evidence. If there be any one who prefers an uninterrupted speech and the old mode of conducting a prosecution without any break, he shall have it in some other trial. But for this time let him understand that what we do is done by us on compulsion (for we only do it with the design of opposing the artifice of the opposite party by our prudence). This will be the first part of the prosecution. We say that Caius Verres has not only done many licentious acts, many cruel ones, toward Roman citizens, and toward some of the allies, many wicked acts against both gods and men; but especially that he has taken away four hundred thousand sesterces out of Sicily contrary to the laws. We will make this so plain to you by witnesses, by private documents, and by public records, that you shall decide that, even if we had abundant space and leisure days for making a long speech without any inconvenience, still there was no need at all of a long speech in this matter.

Translated by Charles Duke Yonge.
Published by Funk and Wagnalls Company.
Reprinted by permission.

FIRST ORATION AGAINST CATILINE

Marcus Tullius Cicero
(106 B.C.—43 B.C.)

While Consul at Rome, Cicero detected and exposed the treasonable designs of Catiline, a conspirator against Rome. Catiline, a man of noble birth, had led a profligate life which had burdened him with debts. Pressed by his debtors he planned a political revolution, so he might become ruler of Rome. His plans included the sacking and burning of Rome and the murdering of all opposed to his conspiracy. On November 7, 63 B.C., Cicero rose in the Senate and delivered his *First Oration against Catiline*. This eloquent speech of condemnation and indignation so aroused the Senate that Catiline was forced to flee. In the series of four speeches against Catiline Cicero exposed the entire scheme of treason and outrage.

How long, O Catiline, will you abuse our patience? How long is that madness of yours still to mock us? When is there to be an end of that unbridled audacity of yours, swaggering about as it does now? Do not the guards placed by night on the Palatine Hill: do not the watches posted throughout the city: does not the alarm of the people, and the union of all good men: does not the precaution taken of assembling the Senate in this most defensible place: do not the looks and countenances of this venerable body here present, have any effect upon you? Do you not feel that your plans are detected? Do you not see that your conspiracy is already arrested and rendered powerless by the knowledge which every one here possesses of it? What is there that you did last night, what the night before: where is it that you were: who was there that you summoned to meet you: what design was there which was adopted by you, with which you think that any one of us is unacquainted?

Shame on the age and on its principles! The Senate is aware of these things; the consul sees them; and yet this man lives. Lives! ay, he comes even into the Senate. He takes a part in the public deliberations; he is watching and marking down and checking off for slaughter every man among us. And we, gallant men that we are, think that we are doing our duty to the Republic if we keep out of the way of his frenzied attacks.

You ought, O Catiline, long ago to have been led to execution by command of the consul. That destruction which you have been long plotting against us ought already to have fallen on your own head.

What! Did not that most illustrious man, Publius Scipio, the Pontifex Maximus, in his capacity of a private citizen, put to death Tiberius Gracchus, though but slightly undermining the Constitution? And shall we, who are the consuls, tolerate Catiline, openly desirous to destroy the whole world with fire and slaughter? For I pass over older instances, such as how Caius Servilius Ahala with his own hand slew Spurius Maelius when plotting a revolution in the State. There was—there was once such virtue in this Republic that brave men would repress mischievous citizens with severer chastisement than the most bitter enemy. For we have a resolution of the Senate, a formidable and authoritative decree against you, O Catiline; the wisdom of the Republic is not at fault, nor the dignity of this senatorial body. We, we alone—I say it openly,—we, the consuls, are wanting in our duty.

The Senate once passed a decree that Lucius Opimius, the consul, should take care that the Republic suffered no injury. Not one night elapsed. There was put to death, on some mere suspicion of disaffection, Caius Gracchus, a man whose family had borne the most unblemished reputation for many generations. There were slain Marcus Fulvius, a man of consular rank, and all his children. By a like decree of the Senate the safety of the Republic was intrusted to Caius Marius and Lucius Valerius, the consuls. Did not the vengeance of the Republic, did not execution overtake Lucius Saturninus, a tribune of the people, and Caius Servilius, the pretor, without the delay of one single day? But we, for these twenty days, have been allowing the edge of the Senate's authority to grow blunt, as it were. For we are in possession of a similar decree of the Senate, but we keep it locked up in its parchment—buried, I may say, in the Sheath; and according to this decree you ought, O Catiline, to be put to death this instant. You live—and you live, not to lay aside, but to persist in your audacity.

I wish, O Conscript Fathers, to be merciful; I wish not to appear negligent amid such danger to the State; but I do now accuse myself of remissness and culpable inactivity. A camp is pitched in Italy, at the entrance of Etruria, hostile to the Republic; the number of the enemy increases every day; and yet the general of that camp, the leader of those enemies, we see within the walls—ay, and even in the Senate—planning every day some internal injury to the Republic. If, O Catiline, I should now order you to be arrested, to be put to death, I should, I suppose, have to fear lest all good men should say that I had acted tardily, rather than that any one should affirm that I acted cruelly. But yet this, which ought to have been done long since, I have good reason for not doing as yet; I will put you to death, then, when there shall be not one person possible to be found so wicked, so abandoned, so like yourself, as not to admit that it has been rightly done. As long as one person exists who can dare to defend you, you shall live; but you shall live as you do now, surrounded by my many and trusty guards, so that you shall not be able to stir one finger against the Republic: many eyes and ears shall still observe and watch you, as they have hitherto done, though you shall not perceive them.

For what is there, O Catiline, that you can still expect, if night is not able to veil your nefarious meetings in darkness, and if private houses can not conceal the voice of your conspiracy within their walls—if everything is seen and displayed? Change that purpose of yours: trust me: forget the slaughter and conflagration you are meditating. You are hemmed in on all sides; all your plans are clearer to us than the day; let me remind you of them. Do you recollect that on the 21st of October I said in the Senate, that on a certain day, which was to be the 27th of October, C. Manlius, the satellite and servant of your audacity, would be in arms? Was I mistaken, Catiline, not only in so important, so atrocious, so incredible a fact, but, what is much more remarkable, in the very day? I said also in the Senate that you had fixed the massacre of the nobles for the 28th of October, when many chief men of the Senate had left Rome, not so much for the sake of saving themselves as of checking your designs. Can you deny that on that very day you were so hemmed in by my guards and my vigilance, that you were unable to stir one finger against the Republic; when you said that you would be content with the flight of the rest, and the slaughter of us who remained? What! When you made sure that you would be able to seize Praeneste on the 1st of November by a nocturnal attack, did you not find that that colony was fortified by my order, by my garrison, by my watchfulness and care? You do nothing, you plan nothing, think of nothing, which I not only do not hear, but which I do not see and every particular of which I do not know.

Listen while I speak of the night before. You shall now see that I watch far more keenly for the safety than you do for the destruction of the Republic. I say that you came the night before (I will say nothing obscurely) into the Scythe-dealers' street, to the house of Marcus Lecca; that many of your accomplices in the same insanity and wickedness came there also. Do you dare to deny it? Why are you so silent? I will prove it if you do deny it; for I see here in the Senate some men who were there with you.

O ye immortal gods, where on earth are we? in what city are we living? what Constitution is ours? There are here—here in our body, O Conscript Fathers, in this the most holy and dignified assembly of the whole world, men who meditate my death, and the death of all of us, and the destruction of this city, and of the whole world. I, the consul, see them; I ask them their opinion about the Republic, and I do not yet attack, even by words, those who ought to be put to death by the sword. You were, then, O Catiline, at Lecca's that night; you divided Italy into sections; you settled where every one was to go; you fixed whom you were to leave at Rome, whom you were to take with you; you portioned out the divisions of the city for conflagration; you undertook that you yourself would at once leave the city, and said that there was then only this to delay you,—that I was still alive. Two Roman knights were found to deliver you from this anxiety, and to promise that very night, before daybreak, to slay me in my bed. All this I knew almost before your meeting had broken up. I strengthened and fortified my house with a stronger guard; I refused admittance, when they came, to those whom you sent in the morning to salute me, and of whom I had foretold to many eminent men that they would come to me at that time.

As, then, this is the case, O Catiline, continue as you have begun. Leave the city at last: the gates are open; depart. That Manlian camp of yours has been waiting too long for you as its general. And lead forth with you all your friends, or at least as many as you can; purge the city of your presence; you will deliver me from a great fear when there is a wall between me and you. Among us you can dwell no longer—I will not bear it, I will not permit it, I will not tolerate it. Great thanks are due to the immortal gods, and to this very Jupiter Stator, in whose temple we are, the most ancient protector of this city, that we have already so often escaped so foul, so horrible, and so deadly an enemy to the Republic. But the safety of the Commonwealth must not be too often allowed to be risked on one man. As long as you, O Catiline, plotted against me while I was the consul elect, I defended myself not with a public guard, but by my own private diligence. When, in the next consular comitia, you wished to slay me when I was actually consul, and your competitors also, in the Campus Martius, I checked your nefarious attempt by the assistance and resources of my friends, without publicly exciting any disturbance. In short, as often as you attacked me, I by myself opposed you, and that, too, though I saw that my ruin was connected with great disaster to the Republic. But now you are openly attacking the entire Republic.

You are summoning to destruction and devastation the temples of the immortal gods, the houses of the city, the lives of all citizens— in short, all Italy. Wherefore, since I do not yet venture to do that which is the best thing, and which belongs to my office and to the discipline of our ancestors, I will do that which is more merciful, if we regard its rigor, and more expedient for the State. For if I order you to be put to death, the rest of the conspirators will still remain in the Republic; if, as I have long been exhorting you, you depart, your companions, these worthless dregs of the Republic, will be drawn off from the city too. What is the matter, Catiline? Do you hesitate to do that when I order you which you were already doing of your own accord? The consul orders an enemy to depart from the city. Do you ask me are you to go into banishment? I do not order it; but, if you consult me, I advise it.

For what is there, O Catiline, that can now afford you any pleasure in this city? for there is no one in it, except that band of profligate conspirators of yours, who does not fear you—no one who does not hate you. What brand of domestic baseness is not stamped upon your life? What disgraceful circumstance is wanting to your infamy in your private affairs? From what licentiousness have your eyes, from what atrocity have your hands, from what iniquity has your whole body ever abstained? Is there one youth, when you have once entangled him in the temptations of your corruption, to whom you have not held out a sword for audacious crime, or a torch for licentious wickedness?

What! When lately, by the death of your former wife, you had made your house empty and ready for a new bridal, did you not even add another incredible wickedness to this wickedness? But I pass that over, and willingly allow it to be buried in silence, that so horrible a crime may not be known to have existed in this city without having been chastised. I pass over the ruin of your fortune, which you know is hanging over you against the Ides of the very next month; I come to those things which relate not to the infamy of your private vices, not to your domestic difficulties and baseness, but to the welfare of the Republic and to the lives and safety of us all.

Can the light of this life, O Catiline, can the breath of this atmosphere be pleasant to you, when you know that there is not one man of those here present who is ignorant that you, on the last day of the year, when Lepidus and Tullus were consuls, stood armed in the assembly; that you had prepared your hand for the slaughter of the consuls and chief men of the State, and that no reason or fear of yours hindered your crime and madness, but the fortune of the Republic? And I say no more of these things, for they are not unknown to every one. How often have you endeavored to slay me, both as consul elect and as actual consul? how many shots of yours, so aimed that they seemed impossible to be escaped, have I avoided by some slight stooping aside, and some dodging, as it were, of my body? You attempt nothing, you execute nothing, you devise nothing that can be kept hid from me at the proper time; and yet you do not cease to attempt and to contrive. How often already has that dagger of yours been wrested from your hands? how often has it slipped through them by some chance, and dropped down? and you can not any longer do without it; and I know not to what sacred mysteries it is consecrated and devoted by you that you think it necessary to plunge it in the body of the consul.

But, now, what is that life of yours that you are leading? For I will speak to you not so as to seem influenced by the hatred I ought to feel, but by pity, nothing of which is due to you. You came a little while ago into the Senate: in so numerous an assembly, who of so many friends and connections of yours saluted you? If this never happened to any one else in the memory of man, are you waiting for insults by word of mouth, when you are overwhelmed by the most irresistible condemnation of silence? Is it nothing that at your arrival all those seats were vacated? that all the men of consular rank, who had often been marked out by you for slaughter, the very moment you sat down left that part of the benches bare and vacant? With what feelings do you think you ought to bear this? On my honor, if my slaves feared me as all your fellow-citizens fear you, I should think I must leave my house. Do you not think you should leave the city? If I saw that I was even undeservedly so suspected and hated by my fellow-citizens, I would rather flee from their sight than be gazed at by the hostile eyes of every one. And do you, who, from the consciousness of your wickedness, know that the hatred of all men is just and has been long due to you, hesitate to avoid the sight and presence of those men whose minds and senses you offend? If your parents feared and hated you, and if you could by no means pacify them, you would, I think, depart somewhere out of their sight. Now, your country, which is the common parent of all of us, hates and fears you, and has no other opinion of you than that you are meditating parricide in her case; and will you feel neither awe of her authority, deference for her judgment, nor fear of her power?

And she, O Catiline, thus pleads with you, and after a manner silently speaks to you: There has now for many years been no crime committed but by you; no atrocity has taken place without you; you alone, unpunished and unquestioned, have murdered the citizens, have harassed and plundered the allies; you alone have had power not only to neglect all laws and investigations, but to overthrow and break through them. Your former actions, though they ought not to have been borne, I did yet bear as well as I could; but now that I should be wholly occupied with fear of you alone, that at every sound I should dread Catiline, that no design should seem possible to be entertained against me which does not proceed from your wickedness,— this is no longer endurable. Depart, then, and deliver me from this fear; that, if it be a just one, I may not be destroyed; if an imaginary one, that at least I may finally cease to fear.

If, as I have said, your country were thus to address you, ought she not to obtain her request, even if she were not able to enforce it? What shall I say of your having said, for the sake of avoiding suspicion, that you were willing to dwell in the house of Marcus Lepidus? And when you were not received by him, you dared even to come to me, and begged me to keep you in my house; and when you had received answer from me that I could not possibly be safe in the same house with you, when I considered myself in great danger as long as we were in the same city, you came to Quintus Metellus, the praetor, and being rejected by him, you passed on to your associate, that most excellent man, Marcus Marcellus, who would be, I suppose you thought, most diligent in guarding you, most sagacious in suspecting you, and most bold in punishing you; but how far can we think that man ought to be from bonds and imprisonment who has already judged himself deserving of being given into custody?

Since, then, this is the case, do you hesitate, O Catiline, if you can remain here with tranquillity, to depart to some distant land, and to trust your life, saved from just and deserved punishment, to flight and solitude? Make a motion, say you to the Senate (for that is what you demand), and if this body votes that you ought to go into banishment, you say that you will obey. I will not make such a motion, it is contrary to my principles, and yet I will let you see what these men think of you. Begone from the city, O Catiline, deliver the Republic from fear; depart into banishment, if that is the word you are waiting for. What now, O Catiline? Do you not perceive, do you not see the silence of these men? They permit it, they say nothing; why wait you for the authority of their words when you see their wishes in their silence?

But had I said the same to this excellent young man, Publius Sextius, or to that brave man, Marcus Marcellus, before this time the Senate would deservedly have laid violent hands on me, consul though I be, in this very temple. But as to you, Catiline, while they are quiet they approve, while they permit me to speak they vote, while they are silent they are loud and eloquent. And not only they, whose authority forsooth is dear to you, though their lives are unimportant, but the Roman knights also, those most honorable and excellent men, and the other virtuous citizens who are now surrounding the Senate, whose numbers you may see, whose desires you may know, and whose voices you a few minutes ago could hear—ay, whose very hands and weapons I have for some time been scarcely able to keep off from you; but those, too, I will easily bring to attend you to the gates if you leave these places you have been long desiring to lay waste.

And yet, why am I speaking? that anything may change your purpose? that you may ever amend your life? that you may meditate flight or think of voluntary banishment? I wish the gods may give you such a mind; though I see, if, alarmed at my words, you bring your mind to go into banishment, what a storm of unpopularity hangs over me; if not at present, while the memory of your wickedness is fresh, at all events hereafter. But it is worth while to incur that, as long as that is but a private misfortune of my own and is unconnected with the dangers of the Republic. But we cannot expect that you should be concerned at your own vices, that you should fear the penalties of the laws, or that you should yield to the necessities of the Republic, for you are not, O Catiline, one whom either shame can recall from infamy, or fear from danger, or reason from madness.

Wherefore, as I have said before, go forth, and if you wish to make me, your enemy as you call me, unpopular, go straight into banishment. I shall scarcely be able to endure all that will be said if you do so; I shall scarcely be able to support my load of unpopularity if you do go into banishment at the command of the consul; but if you wish to serve my credit and reputation, go forth with your ill-omened band of profligates; betake yourself to Manlius, rouse up the abandoned citizens, separate yourself from the good ones, wage war against your country, exult in your impious banditti, so that you may not seem to have been driven out by me and gone to strangers, but to have gone invited to your own friends.

Though why should I invite you, by whom I know men have been already sent to wait in arms for you at the Forum Aurelium; who I know has fixed and agreed with Manlius upon a settled day; by whom I know that that silver eagle, which I trust will be ruinous and fatal to you and to all your friends, and to which there was set up in your house a shrine as it were of your crimes, has already been sent forward. Need I fear that you can long do without that which you used to worship when going out to murder, and from whose altars you have often transferred your impious hand to the slaughter of citizens?

You will go at last whither your unbridled and mad desire has been long hurrying you. And this causes you no grief, but an incredible pleasure. Nature has formed you, desire has trained you, fortune has preserved you for this insanity. Not only did you never desire quiet, but you never even desired any war but a criminal one; you have collected a band of profligates and worthless men, abandoned not only by all fortune but even by hope.

Then what happiness will you enjoy! with what delight will you exult! in what pleasure will you revel! when in so numerous a body of friends, you neither hear nor see one good man. All the toils you have gone through have always pointed to this sort of life: your lying on the ground, not merely to lie in wait to gratify your unclean desires, but even to accomplish crimes; your vigilance, not only when plotting against the sleep of husbands, but also against the goods of your murdered victims, have all been preparations for this. Now you have an opportunity of displaying your splendid endurance of hunger, of cold, of want of every thing; by which in a short time you will find yourself worn out. All this I effected when I procured your rejection from the consulship, that you should be reduced to make attempts on your country as an exile, instead of being able to distress it as consul, and that that which had been wickedly undertaken by you should be called piracy rather than war.

Now that I may remove and avert, O Conscript Fathers, any in the least reasonable complaint from myself, listen, I beseech you, carefully to what I say, and lay it up in your inmost hearts and minds. In truth, if my country, which is far dearer to me than my life—if all Italy—if the whole Republic were to address me, "Marcus Tullius, what are you doing? Will you permit that man to depart whom you have ascertained to be an enemy? whom you see ready to become the general of the war? whom you know to be expected in the camp of the enemy as their chief, the author of all this wickedness, the head of the conspiracy, the instigator of the slaves and abandoned citizens, so that he shall seem not driven out of the city by you, but let loose by you against the city? Will you not order him to be thrown into prison, to be hurried off to execution, to be put to death with the most prompt severity? What hinders you? is it the customs of our ancestors? But even private men have often in this Republic slain mischievous citizens. Is it the laws which have been passed about the punishment of Roman citizens? But in this city those who have rebelled against the Republic have never had the rights of citizens. Do you fear odium with posterity? You are showing fine gratitude to the Roman people which has raised you, a man known only by your own actions, of no ancestral renown, through all the degrees of honor at so early an age to the very highest office, if from fear of unpopularity or of any danger you neglect the safety of your fellow-citizens. But if you have a fear of unpopularity, is that arising from the imputation of vigor and boldness, or that arising from that of inactivity and indecision, more to be feared? When Italy is laid waste by war, when cities are attacked and houses in flames, do you not think that you will be then consumed by a perfect conflagration of hatred?"

To this holy address of the Republic, and to the feelings of those men who entertain the same opinion, I will make this short answer: If, O Conscript Fathers, I thought it best that Catiline should be punished with death, I would not have given the space of one hour to this gladiator to live in. If, forsooth, those excellent men and most illustrious cities not only did not pollute themselves, but even glorified themselves by the blood of Saturninus, and the Gracchi, and Flaccus, and many others of old time, surely I had no cause to fear lest for slaying this parricidal murderer of the citizens any unpopularity should accrue to me with posterity. And if it did threaten me to ever so great a degree, yet I have always been of the disposition to think unpopularity earned by virtue and glory not real unpopularity.

Though there are some men in this body who either do not see what threatens, or dissemble what they do see; who have fed the hope of Catiline by mild sentiments, and have strengthened the rising conspiracy by not believing it; influenced by whose authority many, and they not wicked, but only ignorant, if I punished him would say that I had acted cruelly and tyrannically. But I know that if he arrives at the camp of Manlius to which he is going, there will be no one so stupid as not to see that there has been a conspiracy, no one so hardened as not to confess it. But if this man alone were put to death, I know that this disease of the Republic would be only checked for a while, not eradicated forever. But if he banishes himself, and takes with him all his friends, and collects at one point all the ruined men from every quarter, then not only will be extinguished and eradicated this full-grown plague of the Republic, but also the root and seed of all future evils.

We have now for a long time, O Conscript Fathers, lived among these dangers and machinations of conspiracy; but somehow or other, the ripeness of all wickedness, and of this long-standing madness and audacity, has come to a head at the time of my consulship. But if this man alone is removed from this piratical crew, we may appear, perhaps, for a short time relieved from fear and anxiety, but the danger will settle down and lie hid in the veins and bowels of the Republic. As it often happens that men afflicted with a severe disease, when they are tortured with heat and fever, if they drink cold water seem at first to be relieved, but afterward suffer more and more severely, so this disease which is in the Republic, if relieved by the punishment of this man, will only get worse and worse, as the rest will be still alive.

Wherefore, O Conscript Fathers, let the worthless begone—let them separate themselves from the good—let them collect in one place—let them, as I have often said before, be separated from us by a wall; let them cease to plot against the consul in his own house—to surround the tribunal of the city praetor—to besiege the Senate-house with swords—to prepare brands and torches to burn the city; let it, in short, be written on the brow of every citizen what are his sentiments about the Republic. I promise you this, O Conscript Fathers, that there shall be so much diligence in us the consuls, so much authority in you, so much virtue in the Roman knights, so much unanimity in all good men, that you shall see every thing made plain and manifest by the departure of Catiline—every thing checked and punished.

With these omens, O Catiline, begone to your impious and nefarious war, to the great safety of the Republic, to your own misfortune and injury, and to the destruction of those who have joined themselves to you in every wickedness and atrocity. Then do you, O Jupiter, who were consecrated by Romulus with the same auspices as this city, whom we rightly call the stay of this city and Empire, repel this man and his companions from your altars and from the other temples—from the houses and walls of the city—from the lives and fortunes of all the citizens; and overwhelm all the enemies of good men, the foes of the Republic, the robbers of Italy, men bound together by a treaty and infamous alliance of crimes, dead and alive, with eternal punishments.

Published by G. P. Putnam's Sons.
Reprinted by permission.

FIRST ORATION AGAINST ANTONY or THE FIRST PHILIPPIC [1]

Marcus Tullius Cicero

(106 B.C.—43 B.C.)

Cicero's final oratorical effort was against Mark Antony. After Caesar's death, that wily politician, Mark Antony, had sought to make himself dictator of Rome. He stole Caesar's property and by fraud and violence established a hold on the state. Caius Octavius, nephew and heir of Caesar, came to Rome to claim his heritage and was opposed by Antony. Cicero was entreated by Octavius to combat Antony's designs which were jeopardizing the welfare of Rome. On August 30, Cicero, the grand old statesman of Rome, refused to attend the Senate at Antony's request and was thereupon attacked with bitter invective by Antony. Cicero, aroused by these attacks and threats of his ruin, delivered his *First Oration Against Antony*. There were fourteen of these attacks in all of which the second is often considered his masterpiece. This oration, however, was not delivered by Cicero, who had withdrawn to Naples for safety. He sent the manuscript to Brutus and Cassius who were much pleased with it. The first oration is included here, for Cicero delivered it before the Senate in 44 B.C. The speeches against Antony have been called Philippics because of their resemblance to the speeches of Demosthenes against Philip. Cicero's words swayed Rome, but Roman freedom was under the sword of the enemy, and Cicero was assassinated in 43 B.C. in the 64th year of his life.

Cicero was to Roman oratory what Demosthenes was to the Greek. Cicero added wit and vivacity to the more somber Greek style. Like Demosthenes he also possessed the honesty and sincerity essential to great oratory.

Before, O Conscript Fathers, I say those things concerning the republic which I think myself bound to say at the present time, I will explain to you briefly the cause of my departure from, and of my return to the city. When I hoped that the republic was at last recalled to a proper respect for your wisdom and for your authority, I thought that it became me to remain in a sort of sentinelship, which was imposed upon me by my position as a senator and a man of consular rank. Nor did I depart anywhere, nor did I ever take my eyes off from the republic, from the day on which we were summoned to meet in the temple of Tellus; in which temple I, as far as was in my power, laid the foundations of peace, and renewed the ancient precedent set by the Athenians; I even used the Greek word, which that city employed in those times in allaying discords, and gave my vote that all recollection of the existing dissensions ought to be effaced by everlasting oblivion.

The oration then made by Marcus Antonius was an admirable one; his disposition, too, appeared excellent; and lastly, by his means and by his sons', peace was ratified with the most illustrious of the citizens and everything else was consistent with this beginning. He invited the chief men of the state to those deliberations which he held at his own house concerning the state of the republic; he referred all the most important matters to this order. Nothing was at that time found among the papers of Caius Caesar except what was already well known to everybody; and he gave answers to every question that was asked of him with the greatest consistency. Were any exiles restored? He said that one was, and only one. Were any immunities granted? He answered, None. He wished us even to adopt the proposition of Servius Sulpicius, that most illustrious man, that no tablet purporting to contain any decree or grant of Caesar's should be published after the Ides of March were expired. I pass over many other things, all excellent—for I am hastening to come to a very extraordinary act of virtue of Marcus Antonius. He utterly abolished from the constitution of the republic the dictatorship, which had by this time attained to the authority of regal power. And that measure was not even offered to us for discussion. He brought with him a decree of the senate, ready drawn up, ordering what he chose to have done; and when it had been read, we all submitted to his authority in the matter with the greatest eagerness; and, by another resolution of the senate, we returned him thanks in the most honorable and complimentary language.

A new light, as it were, seemed to be brought over us, now that not only the kingly power which we had endured, but all fear of such power for the future, was taken away from us; and a great pledge appeared to have been given by him to the republic that he did wish the city to be free, when he utterly abolished out of the republic the name of dictator, which had often been a legitimate title, on account of our late recollection of a perpetual dictatorship. A few days afterward the senate was delivered from the danger of bloodshed, and a hook was fixed into that runaway slave who had usurped the name of Caius Marius. And all these things he did in concert with his colleague. Some other things that were done were the acts of Dolabella alone; but, if his colleague had not been absent, would, I believe, have been done by both of them in concert.

I have now explained to you, O Conscript Fathers, my design in leaving the city. Now I will set before you, also, my intention in returning, which may, perhaps, appear more unaccountable. As I had avoided Brundusium, and the ordinary route into Greece, not without good reason, on the first of August I arrived at Syracuse, because the passage from that city into Greece was said to be a good one. And that city, with which I had so intimate a connection, could not, though it was very eager to do so, detain me more than one night. I was afraid that my sudden arrival among my friends might cause some suspicion if I remained there at all. But after the winds had driven me, on my departure from Sicily, to Leucopetra, which is a promontory of the Rhegian district, I went up the gulf from that point, with the view of crossing over. And I had not advanced far before I was driven back by a foul wind to the very place which I had just quitted. And as the night was stormy, and as I had lodged that night in the villa of Publius Valerius, my companion and intimate friend, and as I remained all the next day at his house waiting for a fair wind, many of the citizens of the municipality of Rhegium came to me. And of them there were some who had lately arrived from Rome; from them I first heard of the harangue of Marcus Antonius, with which I was so much pleased that, after I had read it, I began for the first time to think of returning. And not long afterward the edict of Brutus and Cassius was brought to me; which (perhaps because I love those men, even more for the sake of the republic than of my own friendship for them) appeared to me, indeed, to be full of equity. They added besides (for it is a very common thing for those who are desirous of bringing good news to invent something to make the news which they bring seem more joyful) that parties were coming to an agreement; that the senate was to meet on the first of August; that Antonius having discarded all evil counselors, and having given up the provinces of Gaul, was about to return to submission to the authority of the senate.

But on this I was inflamed with such eagerness to return, that no oars or winds could be fast enough for me; not that I thought that I should not arrive in time, but lest I should be later than I wished in congratulating the republic; and I quickly arrived at Velia, where I saw Brutus; how grieved I was, I can not express. For it seemed to be a discreditable thing for me myself, that I should venture to return into that city from which Brutus was departing, and that I should be willing to live safely in a place where he could not. But he himself was not agitated in the same manner that I was; for, being elevated with the consciousness of his great and glorious exploit, he had no complaints to make of what had befallen him, though he lamented your fate exceedingly.   And it was from him that I first heard what had been the language of Lucius Piso, in the senate of August; who, although he was but little assisted (for that I heard from Brutus himself) by those who ought to have seconded him, still according to the testimony of Brutus (and what evidence can be more trustworthy?) and to the avowal of every one whom I saw afterward, appeared to me to have gained great credit.   I hastened hither, therefore, in order that as those who were present had not seconded him, I might do so; not with the hope of doing any good, for I neither hoped for that, nor did I well see how it was possible; but in order that if anything happened to me (and many things appeared to be threatening me out of the regular course of nature, and even of destiny), I might still leave my speech on this day as a witness to the republic of my everlasting attachment to its interests.

What reason had Marcus Antonius for endeavoring, with such bitter hostility, to force me into the senate yesterday? Was I the only person who was absent?   Have you not repeatedly had thinner houses than yesterday?   Or was a matter of such importance under discussion, that it was desirable for even sick men to be brought down?   Hannibal, I suppose, was at the gates, or there was to be a debate about peace with Pyrrhus, on which occasion it is related that even the great Appius, old and blind as he was, was brought down to the senate house.   There was a motion being made about some supplications—a kind of measure when senators are not usually wanting; for they are under the compulsion, not of pledges, but of the influence of those men whose honor is being complimented; and the case is the same when the motion has reference to a triumph.   The consuls are so free from anxiety at these times, that it is almost entirely free for a senator to absent himself if he pleases.   And as the general custom of our body was well known to me, and as I was hardly recovered from the fatigue of my journey, and was vexed with myself, I sent a man to him, out of regard for my friendship with him, to tell him that I should not be there.

But he, in the hearing of you all, declared that he would come with masons to my house; this was said with too much passion and very intemperately.   For what known crime is there such a heavy punishment appointed as that—that any one should venture to say in this assembly that he, with the assistance of a lot of common operatives, would pull down a house which had been built at the public expense in accordance with a vote of the senate?   And who ever employed such compulsion as the threat of such an injury as that to a senator? or what severer punishment has ever been imposed for absence than the forfeiture of a pledge, or a fine?   But if he had known what opinion I should have delivered on the subject, he would have remitted somewhat of the rigor of his compulsion.

Do you think, O Conscript Fathers, that I would have voted for the resolution which you adopted against your own wills, of mingling funeral obsequies with supplications? of introducing inexplicable impiety into the republic? of decreeing supplications in honor of a dead man? I say nothing about who the man was. Even had he been that great Lucius Brutus who himself also delivered the republic from kingly power, and who has produced posterity nearly five hundred years after himself of similar virtue, and equal to similar achievements—even then I could not have been induced to join any dead man in a religious observance paid to the immortal gods; so that a supplication should be addressed by public authority to a man who has nowhere a sepulcher at which funeral obsequies may be celebrated.

I, O Conscript Fathers, should have delivered my opinion, which I could easily have defended against the Roman people, if any heavy misfortune had happened to the republic, such as war, or pestilence, or famine; some of which, indeed, do exist already; and I have my fears lest others are impending. But I pray that the immortal gods may pardon this act, both to the Roman people, which does not approve of it, and to this order, which voted it with great unwillingness. What! may I not speak of the other misfortunes of the republic? At all events it is in my power, and it always will be in my power, to uphold my own dignity and to despise death. Let me have only the power to come into this house, and I will never shrink from the danger of declaring my opinion!

In the first place, then, I declare my opinion that the acts of Caesar ought to be maintained; not that I approve of them (for who indeed can do that?) but because I think that we ought above all things to have regard to peace and tranquillity. I wish that Antonius himself were present, provided he had no advocates with him. But I suppose he may be allowed to feel unwell, a privilege which he refused to allow me yesterday. He would then explain to me, or rather to you, O Conscript Fathers, to what extent he himself defended the acts of Caesar. Are all the acts of Caesar which may exist in the bits of note-books, and memoranda, and loose papers, produced on his single authority, and indeed not even produced, but only recited, to be ratified? And shall the acts which he caused to be engraved on brass, in which he declared that the edicts and laws passed by the people were valid forever, be considered as of no power? I think, indeed, that there is nothing so well entitled to be called the acts of Caesar as Caesar's laws. Suppose he gave any one a promise, is that to be ratified, even if it were a promise that he himself was unable to perform? As, in fact, he has failed to perform many promises made to many people. And a great many more of those promises have been found since his death, than the number of all the services which he conferred on and did to people during all the years that he was alive would amount to.

What law was ever better, more advantageous, more frequently demanded in the best ages of the republic, than the one which forbade the pretorian provinces to be retained more than a year, and the consular provinces more than two? If this law be abrogated, do you think that the acts of Caesar are maintained? What! are not all the laws of Caesar respecting judicial proceedings abrogated by the law which has been proposed concerning the third decury? And are you the defenders of the acts of Caesar who overturn his laws? Unless, indeed, anything which, for the purpose of recollecting it, he entered in a note-book, is to be counted among his acts, and defended, however unjust or useless it may be; and that which he proposed to the people in the comitia centuriata and carried, is not to be accounted one of the acts of Caesar. But what is that third decury? The decury of centurions, says he. What! was not the judicature open to that order by the Julian Law, and even before that by the Pompeian and Aurelian Laws? The income of the men, says he, was exactly defined. Certainly, not only in the case of a centurion, but in the case, too, of a Roman knight. Therefore, men of the highest honor and of the greatest bravery, who have acted as centurions, are and have been judges.

I am not asking about those men, says he. Whoever has acted as centurion let him be a judge. But if you were to propose a law, that whoever had served in the cavalry, which is a higher post, should be a judge, you would not be able to induce any one to approve of that; for a man's fortune and worth ought to be regarded in a judge. I am not asking about those points, says he; I am going to add as judges, common soldiers of the legion of Alaudae, for our friends say, that that is the only measure by which they can be saved. Oh, what an insulting compliment it is to those men whom you summon to act as judges though they never expected it! For the effect of the law is to make those men judges in the third decury who do not dare to judge with freedom. And in that how great, O ye immortal gods! is the error of those men who have desired that law. For the meaner the condition of each judge, is, the greater will be the severity of judgment with which he will seek to efface the idea of his meanness; and he will strive rather to appear worthy of being classed in the honorable decuries, than to have deservedly ranked in a disreputable one.

Men have been recalled from banishment by a dead man; the freedom of the city has been conferred, not only on individuals, but on entire nations and provinces by a dead man; our revenues have been diminished by the granting of countless exemptions by a dead man. Therefore, do we defend these measures which have been brought from his house on the authority of a single, but, I admit, a very excellent individual; and as for the laws which he, in your presence, read, and declared, and passed—in the passing of which he gloried, and on which he believed that the safety of the republic depended, especially those concerning provinces and concerning judicial proceedings—can we, I say, we who defend the acts of Caesar, think that those laws deserve to be upset?

And yet, concerning those laws which were proposed, we have, at all events, the power of complaining; but concerning those which are actually passed we have not even had that privilege. For they, without any proposal of them to the people, were passed before they were framed. Men ask, what is the reason why I, or why any one of you, O Conscript Fathers, should be afraid of bad laws while we have virtuous tribunes of the people? We have men ready to interpose their veto; ready to defend the republic with the sanctions of religion. We ought to be strangers to fear. What do you mean by interposing the veto? says he; what are all these sanctions of religion which you are talking about? Those, forsooth, on which the safety of the republic depends. We are neglecting those things, and thinking them too old-fashioned and foolish.

The forum will be surrounded, every entrance of it will be blocked up; armed men will be placed in garrison, as it were, at many points. What then?—whatever is accomplished by those means will be law. And you will order, I suppose, all those regularly-passed decrees to be engraved on brazen tablets. "The consuls consulted the people in regular form"—(is this the way of consulting the people that we have received from our ancestors?)—"and the people voted it with due regularity." What people? That which was excluded from the forum? Under what law did they do so? Under that which has been wholly abrogated by violence and arms? But I am saying all this with reference to the future, because it is the part of a friend to point out evils which may be avoided; and if they never ensue, that will be the best refutation of my speech. I am speaking of laws which have been proposed, concerning which you have still full power to decide either way. I am denouncing violence and arms; away with them, too!

You and your colleagues, O Dolabella, ought not, indeed, to be angry with me for speaking in defense of the republic. Although I do not think that you yourself will be, I know your willingness to listen to reason. They say that your colleague, in this fortune of his, which he himself thinks so good, but which would seem to me more favorable if (not to use any harsh language) he were to imitate the example set him by the consulship of his grandfathers and of his uncle,—they say that he has been exceedingly offended. And I see what a formidable thing it is to have the same man angry with me and also armed; especially at a time when men can use their swords with such impunity. But I will propose a condition which I myself think reasonable, and which I do not imagine Marcus Antonius will reject. If I have said anything insulting against his way of life or against his morals, I will not object to his being my bitterest enemy. But if I have maintained the same habits that I have already adopted in the republic—that is, if I have spoken my opinions concerning the affairs of the republic with freedom—in the first place, I beg that he will not be angry with me for that; but, in the next place, if I can not obtain my first request, I beg, at least, that he will show his anger only as he legitimately may show it to a fellow citizen.

Let him employ arms, if it is necessary, as he says it is, for his own defense; only let not those arms injure those men who have declared their honest sentiments in the affairs of the republic. Now, what can be more reasonable than this demand? But if, as has been said to me by some of his intimate friends, every speech which is at all contrary to his inclination is violently offensive to him, even if there be no insult in it whatever—then we will bear with the natural disposition of our friend. But those men, at the same time, say to me, "You will not have the same license granted to you who are the adversary of Caesar as might be claimed by Piso his father-in-law." And then they warn me of something which I must guard against; and certainly, the excuse which sickness supplies me with, for not coming to the senate, will not be a more valid one than that which is furnished by death.

But, in the name of the immortal gods! for while I look upon you, O Dolabella, who are most dear to me, it is impossible for me to keep silence respecting the error into which you are both falling; for I believe that you, being both men of high birth, entertaining lofty views, have been eager to acquire, not money, as some too credulous people suspect—a thing which has at all times been scorned by every honorable and illustrious man—nor power procured by violence and authority such as never ought to be endured by the Roman people, but the affection of your fellow citizens, and glory. But glory is praise for deeds which have been done, and the fame earned by great services to the republic; which is approved of by the testimony borne in its favor, not only by every virtuous man, but also by the multitude. I would tell you, O Dolabella, what the fruit of good actions is, if I did not see that you have already learned it by experience beyond all other men.

What day can you recollect in your whole life, as ever having beamed on you with a more joyful light than the one on which, having purified the forum, having routed the throng of wicked men, having inflicted due punishment on the ringleaders of wickedness, and having delivered the city from conflagration and from fear of massacre, you returned to your house? What order of society, what class of people, what rank of nobles even was there who did not then show their zeal in praising and congratulating you? Even I, too, because men thought that you had been acting by my advice in those transactions, received the thanks and congratulations of good men in your name. Remember, I pray you, O Dolabella, the unanimity displayed on that day in the theater, when every one, forgetful of the causes on account of which they had been previously offended with you, showed that in consequence of your recent service they had banished all recollection of their former indignation. Could you, O Dolabella—(it is with great concern that I speak)—could you, I say, forfeit this dignity with equanimity?

And you, O Marcus Antonius—(I address myself to you, though in your absence)—do you not prefer that day on which the senate was assembled in the temple of Tellus, to all those months during which some who differ greatly in opinion from me think that you have been happy? What a noble speech was that of yours about unanimity! From what apprehensions were the veterans, and from what anxiety was the whole state relieved by you on that occasion! when, having laid aside your enmity against him, you on that day first consented that your present colleague should be your colleague, forgetting that the auspices had been announced by yourself as augur of the Roman people; and when your little son was sent by you to the Capitol to be a hostage for peace. On what day was the senate ever more joyful than on that day? or when was the Roman people more delighted? which had never met in greater numbers in any assembly whatever. Then, at last, we did appear to have been really delivered by brave men, because, as they had willed it to be, peace was following liberty. On the next day, on the day after that, on the third day, and on all the following days, you went on without intermission, giving every day, as it were, some fresh present to the republic; but the greatest of all presents was that when you abolished the name of the dictatorship. This was in effect branding the name of the dead Caesar with everlasting ignominy, and it was your doing—yours I say. For as, on account of the wickedness of one Marcus Manlius, by a resolution of the Manlian family it is unlawful that any patrician should be called Manlius, so you, on account of the hatred excited by one dictator, have utterly abolished the name of dictator.

When you had done these mighty exploits for the safety of the republic, did you repent of your fortune, or of the dignity and renown and glory which you had acquired? Whence then is this sudden change? I cannot be induced to suspect that you have been caught by the desire of acquiring money; every one may say what he pleases, but we are not bound to believe such a thing, for I never saw anything sordid or anything mean in you. Although a man's intimate friends do sometimes corrupt his natural disposition, still I know your firmness; and I only wish that, as you avoid that fault, you had been able also to escape all suspicion of it.

What I am more afraid of is lest, being ignorant of the true path to glory, you should think it glorious for you to have more power by yourself than all the rest of the people put together, and lest you should prefer being feared by your fellow citizens to being loved by them. And if you do think so, you are ignorant of the road to glory. For a citizen to be dear to his fellow citizens, to deserve well of the republic, to be praised, to be respected, to be loved, is glorious; but to be feared, and to be an object of hatred, is odious, detestable; and moreover, pregnant with weakness and decay. And we see that, even in the play, the very man who said,

> "What care I tho all men should hate my name,
> So long as fear accompanies their hate?"

found that it was a mischievous principle to act upon.

I wish, O Antonius, that you could recollect your grandfather, of whom, however, you have repeatedly heard me speak. Do you think that he would have been willing to deserve even immortality, at the price of being feared in consequence of his licentious use of arms? What he considered life, what he considered prosperity, was the being equal to the rest of the citizens in freedom, and chief of them all in worth. Therefore, to say no more of the prosperity of your grandfather, I should prefer that most bitter day of his death to the domination of Lucius Cinna, by whom he was most barbarously slain.

But why should I seek to make an impression on you by my speech? For, if the end of Caius Caesar can not influence you to prefer being loved to being feared, no speech of any one will do any good or have any influence with you; and those who think him happy are themselves miserable. No one is happy who lives on such terms that he may be put to death not merely with impunity, but even to the great glory of his slayer. Wherefore, change your mind, I entreat you, and look back upon your ancestors, and govern the republic in such a way that your fellow citizens may rejoice that you were born; without which no one can be happy nor illustrious.

And, indeed, you have both of you had many judgments delivered respecting you by the Roman people, by which I am greatly concerned that you are not sufficiently influenced. For what was the meaning of the shouts of the innumerable crowd of citizens collected at the gladiatorial games? or of the verses made by the people? or of the extraordinary applause at the sight of the statue of Pompeius? and at that sight of the two tribunes of the people who are opposed to you? Are these things a feeble indication of the incredible unanimity of the entire Roman people? What more? Did the applause at the games of Apollo, or, I should rather say, testimony and judgment there given by the Roman people, appear to you of small importance? Oh! happy are those men who, though they themselves were unable to be present on account of the violence of arms, still were present in spirit, and had a place in the breasts and hearts of the Roman people. Unless, perhaps, you think that it was Accius who was applauded on that occasion, and who bore off the palm sixty years after his first appearance, and not Brutus, who was absent from the games which he himself was exhibiting, while at that most splendid spectacle the Roman people showed their zeal in his favor though he was absent, and soothed their own regret for their deliverer by uninterrupted applause and clamor.

I myself, indeed, am a man who have at all times despised that applause which is bestowed by the vulgar crowd; but at the same time, when it is bestowed by those of the highest, and of the middle, and of the lowest rank, and, in short, by all ranks together, and when those men who were previously accustomed to aim at nothing but the favor of the people keep aloof, I then think that, not mere applause, but a deliberate verdict. If this appears to you unimportant, which is in reality most significant, do you also despise the fact of which you have had experience—namely, that the life of Aulus Hirtius [2] is so dear to the Roman people? For it was sufficient for him to be esteemed by the Roman people as he is; to be popular among his friends, in which respect he surpasses everybody; to be beloved by his own kinsmen, who do love him beyond measure; but in whose case before do we ever recollect such anxiety and such fear being manifested? Certainly in no one's.

What, then, are we to do? In the name of the immortal gods, can you interpret these facts, and see what is their purport? What do you think that those men think of your lives, to whom the lives of those men who they hope will consult the welfare of the republic are so dear? I have reaped, O Conscript Fathers, the reward of my return, since I have said enough to bear testimony of my consistency whatever event may befall me, and since I have been kindly and attentively listened to by you. And if I have such opportunities frequently without exposing both myself and you to danger, I shall avail myself of them. If not, as far as I can I shall reserve myself not for myself, but rather for the republic. I have lived long enough for the course of human life, or for my own glory. If any additional life is granted to me, it shall be bestowed not so much on myself as on you and on the republic.

Translated by Charles Duke Yonge.

Published by Funk and Wagnalls Company.

Reprinted by permission.

[1] Close personal and political friend of Caesar.

ON TRAJAN

Caius Plinius Caecilius Secundus
(62?-114? A.D.)

After Cicero, oratory declined with the passing of freedom.
It became dry and sententious, full of labored phrases and panegyrics and servile compliments to tyrants. Quintilian stemmed
the tendency of the age to decry the Ciceronian style and made
Cicero the great model of his *Institutes of Oratory* in which he
used the maxim of Cato "that the orator is a good man who is
skilled in speaking." Among the pupils of Quintilian, Pliny, the
Younger, took the highest place.

Of the panegyrics so popular in his day Pliny's *On Trajan* is
esteemed by critics to be the best. It was delivered before the
Emperor Trajan and the Senate at Rome in the first century A.D.

Pliny began his career as an advocate at the age of 19. He
was more or less of a dilettante, amiable and painstaking, but
self complacent and somewhat lacking in force of character and
originality. He was a contemporary and friend of the historian
and orator, Tacitus, of whose orations unfortunately none remain.
A passage from Pliny's speech *On Trajan* is included here.

It was a good and wise custom of our ancestors to begin no act or
speech without prayer. They believed it only proper and prudent to
reverence the gods and seek their aid and guidance. How much more
ought we now to have recourse to prayer when, by command of the
senate and the will of the people, your consul is about to make an expression of gratitude to a good prince! For what gift of the gods is
better or nobler than a chaste, pious, godlike prince? And I am sure that
even if there were still doubt as to whether rulers are given to the world
by chance or by divine will, we should all feel that our prince was chosen
by divine direction. For he was not found out by the secret power of fate,
but by the open manifestation of Jupiter's will, and was chosen amid

sacred altars in the same temple in which Jupiter dwells in person as clearly as he does in the starry heavens. It is therefore all the more fitting that I should turn in prayer to thee, Jupiter, most mighty and good, and ask that my address may prove worthy of me as consul, worthy of our senate, and worthy of our prince; that my words may bear the stamp of freedom, faith, and truth, and lack as much the semblance, as they do the need. of flattery.

Not only a consul, but every citizen, should strive to say nothing of our prince that might seem proper enough if spoken of some other prince. Let us, therefore, repress the utterances of fear. Let us speak as we feel. Let us emphasize clearly in our discourse the difference between the present and the past. Let our language show unmistakably that it is Trajan we thank and his age that we praise. But let us not address him with the flattering title of a god or divinity; for we speak not of a tyrant. but of a fellow citizen; not of a master, but of a father. He boasts that he is one of us; nor does he forget that he is only a man, though the ruler of men. Let us, then, appreciate our good fortune and prove ourselves worthy of it. Let us, too, consider again and again how unworthy it would be to show greater regard for princes who rejoice in the servitude of their fellow citizens than for those who rejoice in their freedom. The people of Rome, who have retained the right to choose their princes, now praise the courage of Trajan as enthusiastically as they did the beauty of Domitian, and applaud his devotion, self-restraint, and humanity as vociferously as they did the voice and the bearing of Nero. What, then, shall we commend? The divinity of our prince, his culture, his self-control, or his affability? We can do nothing worthier of our citizens and our senate than we have already done in conferring on him the surname of the Good—a title made peculiarly his by the arrogance of former princes. It is only natural and reasonable, then, that we should esteem ourselves happy and our prince happy, and pray that he may ever do deeds deserving of our praise. At all this he is affected even to tears, for he knows and feels that we speak of him as a man, not as a prince.

Let us retain, then, individually, in the hour of calm reflection, the same spirit that we had in the first heat of our devotion; and let us bear in mind that there is no kind of gratitude more sincere or more acceptable than that which, like the acclamations of the populace, is too spontaneous to be feigned. So far as I can, I shall try to adapt my address to the modesty and moderation of our prince, and shall consider not less what his delicacy will permit than what his merits deserve. It is the peculiar glory of our prince that, when I am about to render him an expression of gratitude, I fear not that he will think me niggardly, but lavish in his praise. This is my only anxiety; this my only difficulty. For it is an easy matter to render thanks to one who deserves them. Nor is there any danger that he will mistake the praise of culture for the censure of conceit; the praise of frugality for the censure of luxury; the praise of clemency for the censure of cruelty;

the praise of liberality for the censure of avarice; the praise of benignity for the censure of malice; the praise of continence for the censure of lust; the praise of industry for the censure of laziness; or the praise of courage for the censure of fear. I do not even fear that I shall seem grateful or ungrateful according as I say a great deal or very little. For I have observed that even the gods themselves are pleased not so much by flawless perfection in the form of prayer, as by the uprightness and piety of their votaries. They prefer him who brings to their altars a pure heart, to him who brings a studied prayer.

But I must comply with the will of the senate, which has decreed for the public advantage that the consul, by way of an address of thanks, shall remind good princes of what they have done, and bad princes of what they ought to do. This is all the more necessary now because our prince suppresses all private expressions of gratitude, and would prevent also public ones if he were permitted to forbid what the senate has decreed. In both cases, Caesar Augustus, you show moderation; for, in permitting here the expression of gratitude that you forbid in private, you honor not yourself, but us. Since, then, you have yielded to our wishes, the important thing is not for us to proclaim your merits, but for you to hear them.

I have often reflected how good and great the man should be whose beck and nod control the earth and sea, peace and war. But I should never, even if I had power equal to that of the gods, have conceived of a prince like ours. One man becomes great in war, but sinks into obscurity in peace. Another gains distinction in the arts of peace, but not in the profession of arms. One is feared because he is cruel; another loved because he is humble. One loses in public life the renown he gained in private; another loses in private life his public reputation. In short, there has been no prince in the past whose virtues have not been tarnished by vices. But our prince has obtained unprecedented praise and glory. His seriousness is not lessened by his cheerfulness, his gravity by his simplicity, or his dignity by his humanity. He is steady, tall, and stately in mien and bearing; and though he is in the prime of life his hair is becoming gray—a sign of approaching age. These are the marks that proclaim the prince. . . .

But though you possessed the proper qualifications, Caesar, you were unwilling to become emperor. You had therefore to be forced. Yet you could not have been forced but for the danger that threatened our country; you would not have assumed the imperial power were it not to save the empire. And I feel sure that the praetorians revolted because great force and danger were necessary to overcome your modesty. Just as the sea is calmer and the sky clearer after a storm, so the peace and security we now enjoy under your rule is greater after that uprising. So through all the vicissitudes of life adversity follows prosperity, prosperity adversity. The source of both lies hidden. Indeed the causes of good and evil in general deceive us by false appearances.

The revolt of the praetorians was a great disgrace to our age, a grave injury to the commonwealth. The emperor and father of the human race was besieged, taken, and shut up; the power of saving men was taken from the mildest of old men; our prince was deprived of his most salutary power—freedom of action. If only such calamity could induce you to assume the reins of government I should say that it was worth the price. The discipline of the camp was corrupted, that you might correct it; a bad example was set, that you might set a good one; finally a prince was forced to put men to death against his will, that he might give the world a prince who could not be forced. You were destined to be adopted at some time or other; but we should never have known how much the empire owed you, had you been adopted sooner. Adopted by the emperor and called upon by your countrymen, you responded as did the great generals of old when summoned from abroad to defend their country. Thus father and son made an exchange at one and the same time: he gave you the empire; you restored it to him. Nay you even put the giver under obligation; for in sharing the imperial power with him you assumed the burden of care, while he enjoyed greater security. . . .

During the preceding reigns the barbarians had become insolent, and no longer struggled to gain their liberty, but fought to enslave us. But on your accession they were again inspired with fear and a willingness to obey your commands. For they saw that you were a general of the old stamp—one of those who had earned their title on fields heaped high with slaughter, or on seas resounding with the shouts of victory. The result is that we now accept hostages; we do not buy them. Nor do we now make peace on disadvantageous terms in order to keep up the appearance of success. Our enemies seek and implore peace; we grant or deny it according as the dignity of the empire requires. Those who obtain their request thank us; those to whom it is denied dare not complain, for they know that you have attacked the fiercest nations at that very time of the year which has hitherto been deemed most favorable for them and most unfavorable for us. I mean the season when the Danube is spanned with ice and supports on its hardened back the ponderous engines of war—the season when the savage tribes of the north are armed, not only with weapons, but with the fury of the elements. But the elements have no terrors for you, and on your approach the enemy shut themselves up in their hiding-places while our troops cross the river triumphantly and hurl against the barbarians the fury of their own winter. Such is the awe with which you have inspired the barbarians. . . .

Above all we ought to feel grateful because you allow the men whom you have made consuls to act with consular power. You offer no dangers, no causes of fear, to swerve the consuls from their duty; they listen to nothing against their will, nor do they make decrees under compulsion. The dignity of the office still remains and will remain; and the consuls will not lose their security while they continue in power. If by any chance the consular power is diminished, the fault will be ours, not that of our age; for so far as our prince is concerned men may now be consuls who were formerly princes. Is there any adequate return we can make for the benefits we have received? None, except that we can always remember that we were consuls under you. Let us feel and vote, then, as becomes the dignity of our office, and let our conduct show that we believe the commonwealth still exists. Let us not withdraw our counsel or active service, or feel that we have been severed from the consulate, but rather let us feel that we are inseparably bound up with it. Finally let us cheerfully endure the labors and cares of our office; its honors and dignity we enjoy in full measure.

In conclusion I invoke upon all mankind the blessing of the guardian gods of our empire; and I pray you, especially, Jupiter Capitolinus, to favor us and add to all your other gifts the gift of perpetuity. You have heard us curse a wicked prince; now hear us bless a good one. We shall not weary you with a multitude of prayers; for we ask not peace, or security, or wealth, or honors; our simple and all-embracing prayer is the health of our prince. Nor will you be reluctant to grant it; for you already received him under your protection when you snatched him from the clutches of a rapacious robber. Otherwise, at a time when the high and mighty of the empire were shaken, he who was higher than all could not have stood unmoved. He remained unnoticed by a bad prince, though he could not but attract the attention of a good prince. If, then, he rules the empire well and for the advantage of all, I ask you, Jupiter, to spare him for our grandsons and great-grandsons, and to give him a successor of his own blood whom he shall have instructed and made worthy of adoption; or, if fate deny him this, I ask you to point out to him some one worthy of being adopted in the Capitol.

My indebtedness to you, Conscript Fathers, I need hardly speak of, for it is recorded on public monuments. You have borne witness in a most gratifying manner to the peace and quiet of my tribuneship, to my moderation and discretion as praetor, and to the zeal and constancy with which I looked after the interests of our allies. You have approved, too, of my appointment as consul with such unanimity as to show me that I must make a constant effort to retain and increase your good will, for I know that we cannot tell whether a candidate deserves office until he has obtained it. Although I saw, then, what short roads led to office, I preferred the longer road of honor. I have passed through a period of gloom and fear to an era of security and happiness. I have been hated by a bad prince; I love a good one. I shall always, therefore, show you the respect and deference due you from a man who looks upon himself not as a consul or ex-consul, but as a candidate for the consulship.

Translated by Francis P. Garland.
Reprinted by courtesy of the Colonial Press.

BIBLIOGRAPHY OF THE ROMAN PERIOD

Baldwin, Charles: *Ancient Rhetoric and Poetic*, The Macmillan Company, New York, 1924.

Botta, Charlotte: *Handbook of Universal Literature*, Houghton Mifflin Company, Boston, 1923.

Bryan, William Jennings, ed: *The World's Famous Orations*, Funk and Wagnalls Company, New York, 1906.

The Cambridge Ancient History, The Macmillan Company, New York, 1927.

Cicero: *De Oratore*, 2nd ed., introd., E.N.P. Moor, Methuen and Company, Ltd., London, 1892.

Cicero: *The Verrine Orations*, trans., L. H. G. Greenwood, 2 vols. G. P. Putnam's Sons, New York, 1929.

Cruttwell, Charles Thomas: *History of Roman Literature*, C. Griffin and Company, Ltd., London, 1898.

Cubberley, E. P.: *The History of Education*, Houghton Mifflin Company, Boston, 1920.

Depew, Chauncey, ed: *The Library of Oratory*, Colonial Press, New York, 1902.

Encyclopedia Americana, vol. 6, Americana Corporation, New York.

Gibbon, Edward: *The Decline and Fall of the Roman Empire*, Bigelow, Brown and Company, New York, 1923.

Gudeman, Alfred: *Latin Literature of the Empire*, Harper & Brothers, New York, 1898.

Hardwicke, Henry: *History of Oratory and Orators*, G. P. Putnam's Sons, New York, 1896.

Holmes, Rice: *The Roman Republic*, The Clarendon Press, London, 1923.

Huelsen, Christian, and Tanzar, Helen, H.: *The Forum and the Palatine*, A. Bruderhausen, New York, 1928.

Jebb, R. C.: *Attic Orators From Antiphon to Isaeus*, The Macmillan Company, New York, 1893.

Lee, Carlton, ed.: *The World's Orators*, G. P. Putnam's Sons, New York, 1899.

Livy: *History of Rome*, E. P. Dutton and Company, New York, 1912.

Messala: "On the Decline of Oratory," Alfred Gudeman, *Latin Literature of the Empire*, Harper & Brothers, New York, 1898.

Monroe, Paul: *Educational Encyclopedia*, "Ancient Roman Education," The Macmillan Company, New York, 1913.

Morris, Charles, ed: *The World's Great Orators and Their Orations*, The John C. Winston Company, Philadelphia, 1902.

Niebuhr, B. G.: *Romische Geschichte*, 3 vols., S. Calvary and Company, Berlin, 1873-74.

Platz, Mabel: *The History of Public Speaking,* Noble and Noble, New York, 1935.

Polybius: *Roman Character*, G. P. Putnam's Sons, New York, 1922-27.

Plutarch: *Lives*, trans., John Dryden, Bigelow, Brown and Company, Inc., New York, 1917.

Quintilian: *Institutes of Oratory*, trans., John Watson, H. G. Bohn, London, 1856.

Rostovtzeff, M. I.: *Social and Economic History of the Roman Empire*, The Clarendon Press, London, 1926.

Sears, Lorenzo: *History of Oratory*, S. C. Griggs Company, Chicago, 1896.

Stobart, J. C.: *The Grandeur That Was Rome*, Sidgwick and Jackson, Ltd., London, 1912.

Tacitus: *Works*, "A Dialogue Concerning Oratory," Oxford translation, H. G. Bohn, London, 1854.

Teuffel, Wilhelm Sigismund: *History of Roman Literature*, trans., W. Wagner, G. Bell and Sons, Ltd., London, 1873.

Wells, H. G.: *Outline of History*, The Macmillan Company, New York, 1930.

THE PATRISTIC PERIOD

INTRODUCTION

With the loss of freedom Roman oratory declined. Under the Empire it became servile and drifted into panegyrics, and the speakers of the day, as Tacitus lamented, "became pleaders and advocates and barristers and anything rather than orators."

It was not until the ancient world was shaken by a new philosophy in the teachings of Jesus of Nazareth that men again became eloquent. This great teacher, who had been reared as a carpenter in Galilee, used a simple, sincere, conversational method of speech which contrasted strangely with the labored rhetorical phrases of the Romans. So persuasive was he in his appeal that people from all classes of life flocked to hear him. He drew about him twelve followers whom he instructed in his teachings and who recorded and saved his words for posterity. His followers, likewise, adopted the direct persuasive method of their teacher, and when Christ was crucified because the power of his message was feared by the Roman and Jewish authorities they continued his preaching and teaching. In spite of persecution, the effectiveness of the preaching of the disciples won many converts to the new religion, so that the story of the spread of Christianity colored the pages of history for centuries.

The orators presented in the present chapter are the leaders in the movement and the founders of the early Church which became the official organ of the religion. As the church grew in power and influence the style of its oratory changed in order to meet the new conditions. There developed a style of delivery known as exegesis, a critical and detailed explanation of a text or portion of the scripture with allegorical explanatory notes.

The orations which follow are representative of the different types of speech prevailing during the patristic period. The orators of the Eastern Church—Gregory Thaumaturgus, Gregory Nazianzus, Basil the Great, and John Chrysostom—are considered by critics superior in many respects to those of the Western Church—Saint Ambrose, Saint Augustine, Leo the Great, and Gregory the Great. Works from each group are included here for comparative study.

ADDRESS BEFORE KING AGRIPPA

Saint Paul of Tarsus
(? —67? A.D.)

Paul of Tarsus was an educated Jew who had been trained in oratory and rhetoric in Jerusalem and at Tarsus which was a university town. After his conversion to the Christian faith Paul undertook a missionary journey with Saint Barnabus through Asia Minor. Later he travelled with Silas, Timothy, and Mark on a similar journey through Asia Minor and Greece, everywhere preaching and teaching the new gospel. After a third missionary journey through Galatia and Phrygia he was imprisoned in Jerusalem, but appealed to the Emperor as a Roman citizen and was consequently sent to Rome where he was permitted considerable freedom in his preaching. He was later beheaded under the Emperor Nero between the years 64 and 67 A.D.

The Book of Acts in the Bible covers the missionary journeys of Paul in which he addressed large groups of people. Speeches recorded on these occasions constitute the first oratorical works of the Christian church. Included here is the famous *Address before King Agrippa* which Saint Paul delivered in presenting his case as a Roman citizen upon the occasion of King Agrippa's visit to Rome. The power of his words must have been compelling, for it is recorded that after he had finished King Agrippa said to Paul, "Almost thou persuadest me to be a Christian," and to Festus, "This man might have been set at liberty if he had not appealed to Caesar." The construction of the speech is simple and direct as is characteristic of the Christian teaching of the early patristic period.

I think myself happy, King Agrippa, because I shall answer for myself this day before thee touching all the things whereof I am accused of the Jews: especially because I know thee to be expert in all customs and questions which are among the Jews; wherefore I beseech thee to hear me patiently.

My manner of life from my youth, which was at the first among mine own nation at Jerusalem, know all the Jews; which knew me from the beginning, if they would testify, that after the straitest sect of our religion I lived a Pharisee. And now I stand and am judged for the hope of the promise made of God unto our fathers: unto which promise our twelve tribes, instantly serving God day and night, hope to come. For which hope's sake, King Agrippa, I am accused of the Jews.

Why should it be thought a thing incredible with you that God should raise the dead? I verily thought with myself that I ought to do many things contrary to the name of Jesus of Nazareth. Which things I also did in Jerusalem: and many of the saints did I shut up in prison, having received authority from the chief priests, and when they were put to death, I gave my voice against them. And I punished them oft in every synagogue, and compelled them to blaspheme; and being exceedingly mad against them, I persecuted them even unto strange cities.

Whereupon as I went to Damascus with authority and commission from the chief priests, at midday, O King, I saw in the way a light from heaven, above the brightness of the sun, shining round about me and them which journeyed with me. And when we were all fallen to the earth, I heard a voice speaking unto me, and saying in the Hebrew tongue,

"Saul, Saul, why persecutest thou Me? It is hard for thee to kick against the pricks."

And I said, "Who art Thou, Lord?"

And He said, "I am Jesus whom thou persecutest. But rise and stand upon thy feet: for I have appeared unto thee for this purpose, to make thee a minister and a witness both of these things which thou hast seen, and of those things in the which I will appear unto thee; delivering thee from the people, and from the Gentiles, unto whom now I send thee, to open their eyes, and to turn them from darkness to light, and from the power of Satan unto God, that they may receive forgiveness of sins, and inheritance among them which are sanctified by faith that is in Me."

Whereupon, O King Agrippa, I was not disobedient unto the heavenly vision, but showed first unto them of Damascus, and at Jerusalem, and throughout the coasts of Judea, and then to the Gentiles, that they should repent and turn to God, and do works meet for repentance. For these causes the Jews caught me in the temple, and went about to kill me.

Having, therefore, obtained help of God, I continue unto this day, witnessing both to small and great, saying none other things than those which the prophets and Moses did say should come: that Christ should suffer, and that He should be the first that should rise from the dead, and should show light unto the people and to the Gentiles.

The Holy Bible
King James Version
Acts 26:2-24

PANEGYRIC ON ORIGEN

Gregory Thaumaturgus

(213-270 A.D.)

Gregory Thaumaturgus was known as the "Wonderworker" because of the miracles which he performed. Of noble parentage he had been educated for a legal career, but became a disciple of the Christian religion under the influence of the great teacher, Origen, who was then at the height of his power in Cæsarea in Palestine. Later Gregory became Bishop of his native city. and through his labors was loved by pagans and Christians. Gregory's panegyric on his beloved teacher, Origen, which was Gregory's farewell to his teacher before leaving for Alexandria, is one of the choicest works of antiquity. It is the first great oration of the Church as distinguished from running comment upon a passage of Scripture.

Ingratitude appears to me a grievous offence—grievous, yea, the most grievous of offences. For if one has received some kindness, failure to attempt to make any return, by at least the oral expression of his gratitude where nothing more is possible, brands him as a man insensible to benefits or devoid of memory. Again, though one be sensible of kindness and conscious of the benefits received, yet unless he retain in memory to future days the kindnesses bestowed, and show some feeling of obligation to the source of his blessings, such a person is obtuse, ungrateful, impious. He is guilty of an offence which cannot be overlooked, either in the case of the great or in that of the small: if, for instance, a great and noble man should fail to acknowledge with all gratitude and honor the great benefits which he has received; or if a mean and contemptible man should not with all zeal praise and magnify his benefactor, not simply for great services, but also for small ones.

Upon the great and the learned, therefore, it is incumbent, from their greater resources and larger possessions, to render in proportion to their ability greater and more illustrious praises to their benefactors. But it is becoming to the poor and humble also neither to be neglectful nor indifferent toward those who have done them kindness, nor to despair if they can offer in return nothing worthy or perfect; but though poor indeed, yet, as grateful in heart and as measuring not the resources of him whom they honor, but only their own, they ought to render him gratitude according to their present ability—a tribute which will without doubt be acceptable and pleasing to the benefactor, and no less highly regarded by him than it would have been if it had been some magnificent offering, provided that it be presented with becoming zeal and with an honest heart.

Thus it is related in the Holy Scriptures that a certain poor and humble widow, when the rich and mighty were contributing of their abundance, alone of all cast in a small, yea, the smallest gift, which was, however, all she possessed, and received the commendation of having given more than they all. For, as I judge, the Holy Scriptures measure the value and excellence of the offering, not by the amount given, but rather by the heart and disposition of the giver. Wherefore it does not behoove us in any manner to shirk this responsibility with the vain fear that the tokens of our gratitude may not be adequate to the benefits which we have received; but, on the other hand, we ought to dare and attempt everything; so that, though we do not offer adequate returns, yet we have done so to the extent of our power. And may my discourse in honor of Origen, even though it fall short of what the occasion demands, yet in some degree measure up to the standard, and at least escape all appearance of ingratitude. . . .

From the time of my birth, my training was under the care of my parents; and the manner of life in my father's house was one of error. From this, I fancy, no one anticipated that I should be delivered, nor was there in me any expectation of this, boy and void of understanding that I was, and under the instructions of a superstitious father. Then came the loss of my father and my orphanhood; which was perchance to me the beginning of the knowledge of the truth. For then I was for the first time brought over to the Word of truth and salvation, in what manner I know not, but by compulsion rather than of mine own free will. For what judgment had I, a boy of but fourteen years, at that time? Yet somehow from that very time the Sacred Word began to come to me, as soon as the faculty of reason, common to all men, attained its development in me. . . .

And when I meditate upon this, I am filled at the same time with joy and apprehension: with joy, forsooth, at the leadings of Providence; yet with apprehension, lest after experiencing such blessings, I myself should be a castaway. Yet indeed I know not how my address has delayed so long on this subject, though it was pleasing to me to recount the wonderful dispensations of Providence which led me to this man (Origen). Nevertheless, I am anxious to pass with few words to the subject of my discourse; not indeed with the hope of rendering a worthy tribute of praise, or gratitude, or piety to him (for it would

seem arrogant in me thus to speak, and I could present nothing worthy
of my theme), but merely with a view to present a simple narrative,
or confession, or whatever other humble title it deserves. . . .

From the very first day on which he received us—which was in
truth to me the first day, the most precious of all days, if I may so
express myself, when for the first time the Sun of Truth began to rise
upon me—while at first, like wild beasts, or fishes, or birds caught
in the toils or nets and attempting to slip out and escape, we were
bent on deserting him and making off to Berytus or our native land,
he endeavored in every manner to restrain us and bind us to him.
To that end he directed all kinds of arguments, he set every rope in
motion, he bent all his energies. With that intent, he lauded philosophy
and its votaries with many fitting encomiums. He asserted that they
alone live well and follow a manner of life truly worthy of beings
endowed with reason, who endeavor to lead an upright life and to
first of all know themselves, what manner of men they are. He next
recounted the truly good things which man should seek to attain, and
the really evil things which man ought to avoid. Then he censured
ignorance and all the ignorant, of whom there is a vast throng; who,
like dumb beasts, are darkened in their understanding and have wandered
far astray, as if wholly bereft of reason; they neither themselves know
the nature of good and evil, nor do they care to learn it from others;
they struggle eagerly for wealth and reputation and political honors
and bodily comforts, as if these were the real good; esteeming those
things of value, yea, as surpassing all else, they prize the arts by
which they can be acquired and the different lines of life which lead
to them; namely, the military profession, and the forensic, and the
study and practice of law. These are the things, he adroitly added,
which enervate and keep us ignorant, when we despise the reason
which ought to rule in us.

I cannot tell how many addresses of this kind he made to induce
us to undertake the study of philosophy. Nor was it only for a single
day that he thus discoursed with us, but for many days; in fact, as
often as we went to him at the beginning; and from the very first
we were transfixed with his discourse on our arrival (for he was a
rare combination of sweetness and grace and persuasion and a certain
irresistibleness), though still somehow wavering and debating with
ourselves. We adhered to the pursuit of philosophy, though not
wholly converted to it, while yet somehow unable to entirely withdraw
from it; and thus we were always drawn toward him by his addresses
as by some superior power.

He further declared that no one could be truly devout toward the
common Lord of all, apart from philosophy—a gift with which man
alone of all the creatures of the earth has been honored; and a gift
which every man whatsoever, whether wise or ignorant,—unless he
has lost all his intelligence through some mental obliquity,—reasonably

embraces. He accordingly affirmed that no one who did not devote himself to philosophy could be at all pious; until at length, by instilling into us many such arguments one after another, he overcame us by his arts and indissolubly joined us to himself, as if by some divine power.

Moreover, the stimulus of personal devotion was brought to bear upon us,—an influence not easily resisted, but subtle and most effective,—the argument of kindliness and benignity and affection, which manifested themselves when he mingled with us and conversed with us. For he did not aim merely to get the better of us by his arguments; his endeavor was, through prudence and affection and kindness, to save us and make us partakers of the blessings of philosophy, and especially of those other blessings with which God had endowed him beyond most men, or we may say beyond all other men of our time: I mean the power which inculcates piety, the saving Word which comes indeed to many, and subjugates all upon whom it falls; for there is nothing which can resist it, which both is, and is to be, king of all; although indeed it is hidden and is not recognizable either with ease or with difficulty by the many, so that when questioned they can speak of it with knowledge. Then, like some spark illumining our inmost soul, love was enkindled and grew bright within us, both for the Sacred Word—most lovable of all things, soothing all by its ineffable beauty—and toward this man, His friend and interpreter. I was most violently smitten by this love, and I persuaded myself to despise all those objects and pursuits which seem becoming to us; even the practice of law, of which I had been so proud; yea, even my native land and my friends, both those who were then present with me and those whom I had left behind. And one object only seemed to me lovable and worthy of desire: philosophy, and that master of philosophy, this inspired man.

"And the soul of Jonathan was knit with the soul of David." It was not until afterward that I read this passage in the Holy Scriptures, but I experienced it before that time none the less keenly, as if it had been pronounced by the clearest of all revelations. For it was not simply Jonathan that was knit with David; but their very souls, which are the ruling powers in man; things which, though all the visible parts of man be severed, cannot by any force be separated when they themselves are unwilling. Indeed, the soul is free, and cannot be forced by any means; not even if you confine it and guard it in a prison. For where the intelligence is, there, by its own nature and by the first reason, is the soul; but if it seems to you to be in a prison, it is conceived by you to be there by a sort of second reason. But for all that, it cannot be precluded from being there where it wishes; but rather it can only be, and is reasonably believed to be, wheresoever and in connection with what things soever the actions peculiar to it alone are in operation.

Wherefore, what happened to me has been very clearly set forth in this brief statement that "the soul of Jonathan was knit to the soul of David"; things which, as I have said, cannot be separated in any manner against their will, and which of their own inclination will not easily agree to separation. Nor is it, I imagine, in the power of the inferior, who is capricious and inclined to vary in purpose, to loose the sacred bond of this affection; in whom alone there was not the capacity for union at first; but it is rather in the superior one, who is steadfast and not readily shaken, and through whom the welding of those bonds and the tying of that sacred knot was possible. Consequently it is not the soul of David which is knit by the divine Word to the soul of Jonathan; but, on the contrary, the soul of the inferior is thus affected and is said to be knit with the soul of David. For the superior, since it is self-sufficient, would not desire to be knit with the inferior; but the inferior, which is in need of help of the nobler, ought properly to be knit with the nobler; so that the latter, still retaining its self-sufficiency, might suffer no loss from its union with the inferior; and the former, which is of itself undisciplined, being bound and joined with the stronger, might be subdued to the stronger by the constraint of such bonds. Wherefore the uniting of the bonds is the part of the superior, not the inferior; but to be knit to the other is the part of the inferior; and that so firmly as not to be able to loose itself from the bonds. By a similar tie did this David of ours bind us to himself, and he has held us captive ever since that time; nor, if we wished, could we loose ourselves from his bonds. And not even if we should go away would he release those souls of ours, which, as the Holy Scripture puts it, he holds so firmly knit unto himself. . . .

To speak briefly, he was in very truth a paradise to us, after the similitude of that paradise of God; in which indeed it was not our task to cultivate the soil beneath us, nor to become gross by nourishing the body; but it was granted us to increase the resources of our minds with all gladness and delight, planting, so to speak, in ourselves some beautiful growths, or having them planted in us by the Author of all things.

Here truly is the paradise of enjoyment; here are truly delights and gladness, as we have ever enjoyed them in the period which has just elapsed—no short time indeed in itself, yet too short, if this is really to be its conclusion, when we shall separate and depart hence. For I know not from what misfortune, from what fault of mine it comes, that I should now depart, than I should now be expelled. . . .

It is related that enemies once attacked a great and sacred city, in which God was worshipped, and carried off its inhabitants, both singers and priests, into captivity in their own country, which was Babylon; and that these captives, when they were held in bondage, refused, even when asked by their captors, to sing the songs of Zion or to play in a strange land; but they hung their harps on the willows, and wept by the rivers of Babylon. I seem to myself to be like one of that number, driven by force from this sacred city and fatherland of mine, where by day and by night the holy oracles are proclaimed, and hymns and songs and spiritual discourses are heard; where also the sunlight is perpetual, both by day, as we discourse on the divine mysteries, and by night, when in dreams we are still engaged with what the soul has said and done during the day; and where, in short, the divine afflatus perpetually pervades all. From this city, I say, I am driven out; I am borne away captive to a strange land, where I shall not be able to pipe, for I shall, like those of old, hang my instrument of music on the willows; and I shall pass my time by the river, and I shall have to work in mud, and I shall be unwilling to sing hymns, though I remember them; and it may perhaps be that, through other occupation, I shall forget everything, robbed and bereft of memory itself. Would that, in going away, I only went away against my will, as a captive! but I depart constrained not by another, but by myself, it being possible to remain. And perchance in setting out I shall be taking no safe journey, as sometimes happens when one leaves some secure and peaceful city; and it is indeed probable that in making the journey I shall fall among thieves and be taken prisoner, and be stripped and wounded with many stripes, and be cast aside, to lie half-dead on the roadside.

But why do I indulge in such lamentations? There lives indeed the Savior of all men, even of the half-dead and of those despoiled by thieves; the Guardian and Physician of all, the Sacred Word, the sleepless Keeper of all. There are also the seeds of truth which thou hast taught us to have and hold, and whatever else we have received from thee; those noble admonitions and precepts, with which we set out on our journey; and though we indeed weep, as those who set forth on a journey, yet we bear with us those seeds. Perchance, then, our Keeper who presides over us will guard us; perchance we shall again come to thee, bringing with us the fruits and handfuls yielded by these seeds, far indeed from perfect (for how could they be that?), but still such as it is possible to produce from the acts of civil life, though marred by a faculty either altogether fruitless or prone to bear bad fruits, yet one not destined, I trust, to be further misused, if God grant us His favor.

Translated by Mitchell Carroll, Ph.D
Published by G. P. Putnam's Sons.
Reprinted by permission.

PANEGYRIC ON SAINT BASIL

Gregory Nazianzus

(329-389 A.D.)

The son of a bishop of the church, Gregory Nazianzus had a background conducive toward religious affairs. He had a disposition toward an ascetic life of retirement. The pattern of his life was therefore a constant ebb and flow of the retirement which he loved and the public life into which he was forced through his services for the church. It was Basil the Great who forced him into the bishopric, and the lives of the two men thereafter were closely interwoven, so that at the death of Basil, Gregory was most fitted to deliver the *Panegyric on Saint Basil* which is included here.

Gregory Nazianzus rarely preached from a text, but he was a complete master of an oratorical style of a high order; yet critics have condemned him for an over-indulgence in epithets and exclamations. His own tendencies as a recluse also made him somewhat self-conscious and sensitive.

It has been ordained that the great Basil who used so constantly to furnish me subjects for my discourses, of which he was quite as proud as any man might be of his own, should now furnish me with the grandest subject which has ever fallen to the lot of an orator. For I think that if any one wished, in making trial of his powers of eloquence, to test them by the standard of that one of all his subjects which he preferred (as painters do with epoch-making pictures), he would choose what of all others stood first, but this he would set aside as beyond the powers of human eloquence. So great a task is the praise of such a man, not only to me, who have long ago laid aside all thought of emulation, but even to those who devote their whole life to eloquence, and whose sole object is the gaining of glory by subjects like this. Such is my opinion, and, as I persuade myself, it is entirely just. But I know not what subject I can treat with eloquence, if not this; or what greater favor I can do to myself, than express our admiration for this man. To me it is the discharge of a most sacred debt. And our speech is a debt beyond all others due to those who have been gifted, in particular, with powers of speech. To the admirers of virtue, a discourse is at once a pleasure and an incentive to virtue. For when I have learned the praises of men, I have a distinct idea of their progress: now there is none of us all who does not have it within his power to attain to any point whatsoever in that progress. As for eloquence itself, in either case, all must go well with it. For, if the discourse be almost worthy of its subject, eloquence will give an exhibition of its power; if it fall far short of it, as must be the case when the praises of Basil are set forth, by an actual demonstration of its incapacity it will have declared the superiority of the excellencies of its subject to all expression in words.

Who more than Basil honored virtue or punished vice? Who evinced more toward the upright, or more severity toward offenders? His very smile was often praise; his silence, reproof, in the depths of conscience reaching and rousing the sense of guilt. Grant that he was no light prattler, no jester, no general favorite. Grant that he did not ingratiate himself with the multitude by becoming all things to all men, and courting their favor: what of that? Should he not receive, from all that judge reasonably, praise for this rather than blame? Is it deemed a fault in the lion that he has not the appearance of the ape; that his aspect is terrible and regal; that his movements, even in sport, are majestic, and excite wonder and delight? Do we regard it as proof of courtesy and true benevolence in actors that they gratify the populace, and move them to laughter by blows in the face?

But, should one pursue this inquiry, who was so delightful as Basil in company?—as I know, and my acquaintance with him has been of very long standing. Who was more graceful in narration, more refined in raillery, more tender in reproof? Neither was his censure arrogance, nor his mildness indulgence, but, avoiding excess in both, he made use of both in reason and season, following the rule of Solomon, who assigns to everything its season.

But what is all this, compared with his extraordinary eloquence and that resistless might of his instruction which has made its own the extremities of the globe? We are still lingering about the base of the mountain, to the neglect of its summit. We still push our bark across the strait, leaving the broad and open sea. For assuredly, if there ever was, or ever shall be, a trumpet sounding far out upon the air, or a voice of God encompassing the world, or some unheard-of and wondrous earthquake, such was his voice, such his intellect, as far surpassing and excelling that of his fellows as man excels the nature of the brute. Who more than he purified himself by the Spirit, and thus made himself worthy to unfold the divine oracles? Who was more enlightened with the light of knowledge, and explored more profoundly the deep things of the Spirit, and with the aid of God surveyed the things of God? And who has possessed a diction that was a more perfect interpreter of his thoughts? Not with him, as with most men, was there a failure, either of thought sustaining his diction, or of language keeping pace with thought; but, alike distinguished in both, he showed himself as an orator throughout, self-consistent and complete. It is the office of the Spirit, according to St. Paul, to search all things, yea, the deep things of God, not as ignorant of them, but as delighting in their contemplation. But all the mysteries of the Spirit were profoundly investigated by Basil; and from these sources he trained and disciplined the characters of all; he taught loftiness of thought, and, withdrawing men from things present, he directed them to the things to come.

The sun is praised by David for his beauty and magnitude, for the swiftness of his course and his power, resplendent as a bridegroom, mighty as a giant. Its circuit has such power that it sheds light from one end of heaven to the other, and distance lessens not the power of its beams. But the beauty of Basil was virtue; his greatness, theology; his course, perpetual activity, ever tending upward to God; his power, the sowing and distribution of the Word. So that I need not hesitate to apply to him the language which St. Paul, borrowing from David, applies to the Apostles, that his sound went into all lands, and the power of his words to the ends of the world. What other source of pleasure at the present day in our assemblies? What at our banquets, in the forum, in the churches? What constitutes the delight alike of magistrates and private citizens, of monks and of those who mingle in society, of men of business and of men of leisure, of the votaries of profane and of sacred science? The one all-pervading and highest source of enjoyment is the writings and labors of Basil. Nay, even to writers, he is the sole material of their works. The ancient commentaries on the divine records cease to be heard; the new take their place; and he stands first in sacred eloquence who best knows the writings of Basil, and most frequently utters his words and explains them in our ears. A single man more than suffices as a substitute for all others to the training of the studious.

I mention but this single instance. When I explore the pages or repeat the words of his Hexaemeron, I am brought into the presence of the Creator; I understand the laws of the creation; and employing only the sense of sight as my teacher, more than ever before I admire the Creator. When I read his books against the heretics, I see the fires of Sodom, by which men of impious and lawless tongues are reduced to ashes, or the Tower of Babel, impiously built and righteously overthrown. When I read his writings on the Spirit, I find the God whom I possess reveals Himself, and I declare the truth with boldness, on account of the support of his theology and contemplation. His other treatises, in which for those of dull intellect, he gives explanations in a threefold way, inscribing them on the solid tablets of his heart, persuaded me to stay no longer by the literal or merely symbolical interpretation; but to pass beyond, to go on from depth to depth, one deep calling another, and discovering light after light, till I reach the utmost limit of truth. When I study his panegyrics on the martyrs, combatants for the faith, I despise the body, and joining the company of those he praises, I am incited to the same struggle. When I read his ethical and practical discourses, they purify me, soul and body, and make me a fitting temple of God, an instrument played upon by the Spirit, hymning forth the divine power and glory. Thus am I reduced to harmony and order, and through successive stages transformed with a divine transformation.

Since I have spoken of theology and of his sublime treatises in the science, I wish yet to add the following. For it is eminently desirable that the multitude should not receive harm themselves by having an unjustifiably low opinion of his piety. My remarks are directed specially against those base persons who, by calumniating others, conceal their own depravity. For in defence of the orthodox doctrine and the union and co-equal Godhead of the Holy Trinity—to use terms as clear and exact as possible—he was ready not only to sacrifice his episcopal see, to which he never aspired, but to accept exile, death, and its preliminary tortures, not as evil but as gain. Witness, in proof of this, what he has actually endured. When condemned to banishment for the truth, he merely bade one of his attendants take up his writing tablet and follow him. But, following the counsel of David, he deemed it necessary to guide his words with discretion, and thus, during the time of war and the reign of heresy, to forbear a little until a season of freedom and calm should be restored, admitting freedom of speech. They indeed aimed to assail the bare and naked declaration of "the Spirit of God" (a truth deemed impious by them and by their nefarious leader in impiety), in order that, banishing him and his religious teachings from the city, they might take possession of the Church, and making it the starting-point and stronghold of their wickedness, thence, as from a citadel, they might overrun and devastate with their wicked doctrine the whole world. He meanwhile, by other Scripture terms, and unambiguous testimonies having the same import, as well as by unanswerable reasonings, so over-powered his opponents that they were unable to assail him, and—which is the highest triumph of power and skill in argument—were held fast in the fetters of their own chosen expressions. Take in proof his discourse on the subject in which he used his pen as under the very impulse of the Spirit. The exact term, nevertheless, he forbore for a time to use, begging his fellow-champions of the faith and the Spirit Himself not to be displeased at his proceeding, nor, amid the temporary distractions of the faith, sacrifice the whole cause by tenacious adherence to a word. He assured them that no harm would accrue by a slight change of terms, or by conveying the truth in other language. For our salvation does not depend upon words, but rather upon actions; nor would we reject even the Jewish people, if, substituting the term "Anointed" for that of "Christ," they should be willing to rank themselves among His followers. But to the whole Christian body it would be a source of infinite harm that the Church should be seized by heretics.

That he held with the profoundest conviction that the Spirit is God is clear from his publicly proclaiming the doctrine on every occasion, and unhesitatingly avowing it when questioned in private. And in his communications to me, from whom he concealed nothing, he has spoken yet more clearly, not only affirming it, but in an unwonted manner imprecating upon himself the fearful doom of being abandoned of the Spirit if he failed to worship Him as consubstantial and co-equal with the Father and the Son. And if any one will regard me as a co-worker with him in this matter, I will explain one point not generally known. On account of the difficulties of the times, he was prudent in his expressions for himself, but allowed me entire freedom of speech, for I was not in danger of being dragged from my seclusion to trial or banishment. He did this in order that by our united efforts we might the more securely establish the Gospel. It is not for the sake of defending his reputation that I have made these statements; for he is superior to all accusations. It is rather that none, regarding the terms employed by him as the law and limit of the truth, may have their faith shaken; that none may pervert his mode of discussion, produced by stress of circumstances and with the sanction of the Spirit, to the strengthening of their own error; but rather that, weighing the import and aim of his words, they may be drawn to the truth, and may seal the lips of the impious. To me, and to all who are dear to me, may his doctrines be an inheritance. Such is my conviction of his purity in this matter, that in this, as in other things, I would gladly unite my lot to his, and ask a common judgment alike from God and from all impartial men. None surely would affirm that the Evangelists conflict with each other, because some have dwelt at greater length upon the humanity of Christ, others attempted to show the heights of His divinity; some have commenced their account with what is within our experience, others with what is beyond and above our experience. For by their varying representations they have met the wants of those whom they addressed, being informed and actuated by the Spirit within them.

There have been, both in ancient and recent times, many men distinguished for piety,—law-givers, generals, prophets, teachers, valiant even to the shedding of their blood: let us compare our Basil with them, and thus recognize the merit of his virtues. Adam was deemed worthy of the fashioning hand of God, the delights of Paradise, and the first giving of the law. But, to say nothing irreverent of our great ancestor, he failed to keep the commandment. But Basil both received and kept it, was unharmed by the tree of knowledge, and, passing by the flaming sword, has, I am well assured, inherited Paradise. Enos first ventured to call upon the Lord; Basil both himself invoked Him and, what is yet more honorable, proclaimed Him to others. Enoch was translated as a reward for an imperfect piety (for his faith was yet amid shadows), and thus escaped the perils of after life; Basil's entire life was a translation, and he was proved to the end in a completed life. Noah was intrusted with the ark, and with the seeds of a new world, committed to a small vessel, and preserved amid the waters; Basil escaped a deluge of impiety, rendered his own city an ark of safety that floated lightly above the waves of heresy, and thus reclaimed the entire world. Abraham was illustrious, at once a Patriarch and the Priest of a new sacrifice, offering, to Him who had bestowed it, the child of promise, hastening a ready and cheerful victim to the altar. But not slight was the offering of Basil, who offered himself unto God, and that with no substitute interposed to prevent the sacred rite from being consummated. Isaac was promised before his birth; but Basil voluntarily promised himself; and his bride, the Church, he wooed not from afar, but near at hand; not through the ministry of servants, but confided to him by the immediate hand of God. Nor was he overreached in assigning the precedence to his children; but such rewards as reason and the Spirit dictated he allotted to each according to their deserts. I extol the ladder of Jacob, the pillar which he anointed to God, and that wrestling with him which, in my opinion, was but the confronting of human weakness with the Divine Majesty, and whence he bears the tokens of a vanquished nature. I praise also his skillful devices with respect to the flocks of Laban, and the twelve Patriarchs his offspring, and the sublime prophetic foresight with which he bestowed on them his blessing. But in Basil I praise still more the ladder, not merely seen, but ascended by successive advances in virtue; the pillar which he did not anoint, but reared to God, a monument of the eternal infamy of the impious; his wrestling, not against God but for Him, in overthrowing the doctrines of the heretics; the pastoral skill by which he grew rich, having gained, as spiritual wealth, a number of marked sheep greater than the unmarked; the multitude of his spiritual children divinely begotten; and the blessing with which he established many.

. . . . . .

Gather yourselves around me now, all ye who are from abroad, aid me in celebrating his praises, by each supplying or demanding the account of his virtues. Princes, extol the lawgiver; politicians, the statesman; citizens, the orderly and exemplary citizen; votaries of learning, the instructor; virgins, the leader of the bride; wives, the teacher of chastity. Let the hermits commemorate him who lends them wings for their flight; cenobites, the judge; the simple-minded, the guide; the contemplative, the theologian; those in prosperity, the curber of pride; those in affliction, the consoler; age, its staff; youth, its guardian; poverty, its provider; abundance, its steward and dispenser. Methinks I hear the widows praising their protector; orphans, their father; the poor, their friend;

strangers, the lover of hospitality; brethren, the brotherly minded; the sick, their physician, whatever be their sickness or the healing they need; the well, the preserver and guardian of health; all, in short, praise him who became all things to all that he might, if possible, gain all.

This tribute, O Basil, is offered to thee from a tongue once most delightful to thee, and which shared in thy honor and companionship. If it approaches thy deserts, to thee be thanks, for, confiding in thee, I entered on this discourse. But if it fall far below thy merits and my hopes, it will be pardoned to one who is worn by age, disease, and sorrow for thee. But God accepts according to our ability. But do thou, O divine and sainted one, look upon us from above, and that thorn in our flesh which God has sent for our discipline, do thou remove by thine intercessions, or persuade us to bear with patience, and direct our entire life to that which shall be most for our profit. And when we depart hence, may we be received into thine own abode, that living together, and together surveying more purely and perfectly the Holy and Blessed Trinity, whose image we have but faintly received here, we may have our longings satisfied, and find a recompense for all our conflicts in propagation or defence of the truth. To thee, therefore, this tribute is rendered by us; but who shall render a like service to us, lingering in life after thee, if indeed we achieve anything worthy of commendation in Jesus Christ, our Lord, to whom be glory forever? Amen.

Revised translation by the Editors of The World's Orators.
Published by G. P. Putnam's Sons.
Reprinted by permission.

FIRST HOMILY FROM THE HEXÆMERON

Basil the Great

(330-379 A.D.)

Basil the Great was born into a family famous in the church of Cæsarea; he, himself, became bishop of his native city of Cæsarea. His greatest personal contributions to the church were the propagation of a monastic life which substituted hard labour, works of charity, and the common life for the existing hermitical asceticism and for the improvement of the liturgy which is still used in the Eastern church. Basil is the first preacher of practical rhetorical sermons. His works are dominated by force and clearness rather than elegance and phraseology and are logical as well as eloquent. Generally he delivered his sermons without text and extemporaneously. A homily from the *Hexaemeron,* his most admired work, is presented here. The entire set of nine homilies on Genesis were given as extemporaneous addresses during the Lenten season and judging from the context were delivered to an audience composed largely of artisans and working people.

I desire for you to be so profoundly impressed with the wonders of creation that everywhere, wherever you may be, and whatever kind of plant you may observe, you will remember the Creator. If indeed you see the grass and flower of the field, let the thought of human nature occur to you and recall this comparison of the wise Isaiah: "All flesh is grass, and all the goodliness thereof is as the flower of the field." Truly the shortness of life, the brief and fleeting happiness resulting from human prosperity, most admirably accord with the similitude of the prophet. To-day one is vigorous in body, is surrounded with every luxury, is in the prime of life, is radiant with the glow of health, is strong and powerful and of resistless energy: tomorrow he will be an object of pity, withered by age and emaciated by sickness. Another is endowed with all the gifts of fortune; about him are grouped a multitude of flatterers; a company of pretended friends gather round in quest of his favor; here a crowd of relatives, and these only from pretence; there a multitude of attendants, who swarm about him to provide his food and other wants: and, as he comes and goes, this endless train of followers arouses envy in all the passers-by. Add also to his riches political power, honors bestowed by kings, the government of nations, and the command of armies; a herald, crying with a loud voice, preceding him; lictors to right and left, inspiring awe in his subjects; blows, confiscations, banishments, imprisonments, and all the means of increasing the intolerable terror of his subjects. And what then? One night either fever, or pleurisy, or inflammation of the lungs snatches this man away from the midst of his fellows, strips him in a trice of all his stage trappings, and all this glory of his turns out to be but a dream. Therefore the prophet compared human glory to the feeblest flower.

Published by G. P. Putnam's Sons.
Reprinted by permission.

HOMILY ON THE STATUES

John Chrysostom of Antioch
(347-407 A.D.)

As a youth in Antioch, Syria, Chrysostom studied oratory in order to enter the legal profession, but upon his conversion he became a monk instead and a preacher of such eloquence and sincerity that he has been considered the greatest of the ancient world. Upon his appointment to the Archbishopric of Constantinople he started a reform of the vices of the court which brought down the hatred of the political authorities of the state upon him and ultimately led to his exile and death as a martyr.

Posterity has proclaimed Chrysostom as "the golden mouthed" for the perfection of his eloquence. He used many illustrations to clarify his subject and this practical method distinguished his work as much as did his ability to combine the classical, rhetorical, and biblico-exegetical. His work was based upon a thorough grammatical study and not upon the allegorical interpretation of Origen and the Alexandrine school.

Chrysostom's *Homilies on the Statues* are regarded as his masterpieces. The Emperor Theodosius had levied an exorbitant tax upon the city of Antioch in Syria. There was a rebellious riot amongst the lower class of people which culminated in the act of dragging the statues of Theodosius through the city streets in an abusive and insulting manner. After the riot had subsided, a panicky fear of punishment gripped the people. It was at the Lenten season when Chrysostom delivered his famous sermons on the statues to allay the people's fear and prepare them for retribution. On the first Tuesday in Lent, when the imperial authorities arrived to investigate the sedition, Chrysostom delivered the sermon included here.

Tell me, what is there in death which is terrible? Is it because it transports thee more quickly to the peaceful haven, and to that life which is free from tumult? Although man should not put thee to death, will not the very law of nature, at length stealing upon thee, separate the body from the soul? and if this event which we fear does not happen now, it will happen shortly.

I speak thus, not anticipating any dread or melancholy event: God forbid! but because I am ashamed for those who are afraid of death. Tell me why, whilst expecting such good things as "eye hath not seen, nor ear heard, nor have entered the heart of man," thou dost demur about this enjoyment, and art negligent and slothful; and not only slothful, but fearful and trembling? What is it but shameful? Thou art in pain on account of death, when Paul groaned on account of the present life, and writing to the Romans said, "The creation groaneth together, and ourselves also which have the first fruits of the Spirit do groan." And he spoke thus, not condemning the things present, but longing for the things to come. "I have tasted," saith he, "of the grace, and I cannot contain myself in the delay. I have the first fruits of the Spirit, and I press on towards the whole. I have ascended to the third heaven; I have seen that glory which is unutterable; I have beheld the shining palaces; I have learned what joys I am deprived of, while I linger here, and therefore do I groan." For suppose any one had conducted thee into princely halls, and all the rest of the glorious show? if from thence he had led thee back afterward to a poor man's hut, and promised that in a short time he would bring thee back to those palaces, and would there give thee a perpetual mansion; tell me, wouldest thou not indeed languish with desire, and feel impatient, even at these few days? Thus think then of heaven and of earth, and groan with Paul, not because of death, but because of the present life!

But give me, saith one, to be like Paul, and I shall never be afraid of death. Why, what is it that forbids thee, O man, to become like Paul? Was he not a poor man? Was he not a tent-maker? Was he not a man of mean rank? For if he had been rich and well born, the poor, when called upon to imitate his zeal, would have had their poverty to plead; but now thou canst say nothing of this sort. For this man was one who exercised a manual art, and supported himself too by his daily labors. And thou, indeed, from the first hast inherited true religion from thy fathers, and from thy earliest age hast been nourished in the study of the sacred writings; but he was "a blasphemer, and a persecutor, and injurious," and ravaged the Church! Nevertheless, he so changed all at once, as to surpass all in the vehemence of his zeal, and he cries out, saying, "Be ye followers of me, even as I also am of Christ." He imitated the Lord; and wilt not thou who hast been educated in piety from the first, imitate a fellow-servant; one who by a great change was brought to the faith at a later period of life? Knowest thou not, that they who are in sin are dead whilst they live; and that they who live in righteousness, although they be dead, yet they live? And this is not my word. It is the declaration of Christ speaking to Martha, "He that believeth in Me, though he were dead, yet shall he live." Is our doctrine, indeed, a fable? If thou art a Christian, believe in Christ; if thou believest in Christ, show me thy faith by thy works. But how mayest thou show this? By thy contempt of death: for in this we differ from the unbelievers. They may well fear death, since they have no hope for a resurrection. But thou, who art travelling towards better things, and hast the opportunity of meditating on the hope of the future, what excuse hast thou, if, whilst assured of a resurrection, thou art yet at the same time as fearful of death as those who believe not in the resurrection?

But I have no fear of death, says one, nor of the act of dying, but of dying basely, of being beheaded. Did John then, I ask, die basely? for he was beheaded. Or did Stephen die basely? for he was stoned; and all the martyrs have thus died miserably, according to this objection: since some have ended their lives by fire, and others by the sword; and others cast into the ocean, others down a precipice, and others into the jaws of wild beasts, have so come by their death. This, O man! is not to die basely, to come to one's end of a violent death, but to die in sin! Hear, at least, the prophet uttering wisdom on this very matter, and saying, "Evil is the death of sinners." He does not say that a violent death is evil; but what then? "Evil is the death of sinners." And justly so; for after the departure from this life, there is an intolerable punishment; torments that are immortal, the envenomed worm, the fire unquenchable, the outer darkness, the chains indissoluble, the gnashing of teeth, the tribulation, the anguish, and the eternal vengeance.

Since therefore such evils await sinners, what advantage can it be to them, though they should end their days at home, and in their beds? Even so, on the other hand, it can do no harm to the righteous to lay down the present life through sword, or steel, or fire, when they are to depart to the good things that are immortal. Truly "the death of sinners is evil." Such a death was that of the rich man, who despised Lazarus. He, when he had terminated his life by a natural end, at home and on his bed, and with his relatives about him, experienced on his departure a fiery torment; nor was he able to obtain there even a little comfort, out of all the pleasure he had enjoyed in the present life! But not so was it with Lazarus; lying upon the pavement, while the dogs came and licked his sores, he had suffered a violent death (for what could be more painful than hunger?); but on his departing hence he enjoyed eternal blessings, luxuriating on the bosom of Abraham! In what respect, then, did it injure him that he died a violent death? or what did it profit the rich man, that he died not with violence?

But some one says, "We have no fear of the violence of the death, but of dying unjustly, and of being punished in a similar way with the guilty,— we who have had nothing to do with the crimes of which we are suspected." What sayest thou, tell me? Art thou afraid of dying unjustly, and wouldest thou wish to die justly? But who is there so wretched and miserable, that, when he had the alternative of dying unjustly, would rather depart by an act of justice? For if it be necessary to fear death, it is necessary to fear it when it comes upon us justly; since he indeed who dies unjustly is by this very means made a partaker with all the saints. For many of those who were approved and distinguished by God have submitted to an unjust end; and first of all Abel. For it was not that he had sinned against his brother, or done Cain any harm; but inasmuch as he had honored God, therefore was he slaughtered. But God permitted it. Was it, think you, because He loved him, and wished to make his crown the brighter, by that most unjust murder? Seest thou then, that it becomes us not to be afraid of dying by violence; nor of dying unjustly: but of dying in a state of sin? Abel died unjustly. Cain lived, groaning and trembling! Which then, I would ask, was the more blessed of the two: he who went to rest in righteousness, or he who lived in sin; he who died unjustly, or he who died justly punished? Would you have me declare unto you clearly whence it is that we are afraid of death? The love of the kingdom hath not penetrated us, nor the desire of things to come inflamed us: otherwise we should despise all present things, even as the blessed Paul did. Add to this, on the other hand, that we do not stand in awe of hell; therefore, instead of sin, we fear death; since if the fear of the one held possession of our souls, the fear of the other would not be able to enter.

And this I will endeavor to make manifest, not from anything of a remote nature, but from what is at our own doors, and from the events which have happened among us in these days. For when the Emperor's letter came, ordering to be imposed the tribute which was thought to be so intolerable, all were in a tumult; all quarrelled with it, thought it a sore grievance, resented it, and when they met one another said, "Our life is not worth living; the city is undone; no one will be able to stand under this heavy burden"; and they were distressed as if placed in the extremest danger. After this, when the rebellion was actually perpetrated, certain vile, yea, thoroughly vile persons, trampled under foot the laws, threw down the statues, and placed the utmost peril over the heads of all; and now that we are in fear of our very lives, through the indignation of the Emperor, the loss of money no longer stings us. But instead of such complaints, I hear from all a language of a different kind. "Let the Emperor take our substance; we will gladly be deprived of our fields and possessions, if any one will but ensure us a safe body, with nothing besides." As, therefore, before the fear of death pressed upon us, the loss of our wealth tormented us; and after these lawless outrages had been perpetrated, the fear of death, succeeding, expelled the grief for that loss; so if the fear of hell had held possession of our souls, the fear of death would not have been there. But even as with the body, when two kinds of pain seize upon us, that which is more powerful usually makes that which is inferior unnoticed, so also would it now happen, if the dread of future punishment remained in the soul; that would make all human fear imperceptible. So that if any one endeavors always to have remembrance of hell, he will deride every kind of death; and this will not only deliver him from the present distress, but will even snatch him from that flame. For he who is always afraid of hell, will never fall into the fire of hell; being made sober by this continual fear!

Permit me, that I now say to you at a fitting time, "Brethren, be not children in understanding; howbeit in malice be ye children." For this is a childish terror of ours, if we fear death but are not fearful of sin. Little children too have a fear of masks, but fear not the fire. On the contrary, if they are carried by accident near a lighted candle, they stretch out the hand without any concern towards the candle and the flame; yet a mask, which is so utterly contemptible, terrifies them; whereas they have no dread of fire, which is really a thing to be afraid of. Just so we too have a fear of death, which is a mask that might well be despised; but have no fear of sin, which is truly dreadful, and, even as fire, devours the conscience! So that if we once were to consider what death is, we should at no time be afraid of it. What then, I pray you, is death? Just what it is to put off a garment. For the body is about the soul as a garment; and after laying this aside for a short time by means of death, we shall resume it again with the more splendor. What is death at most? It is a journey for a season; a sleep longer than usual. So that if thou fearest death, thou shouldest also fear sleep. If thou art pained for those who are dying, grieve for those too who are eating and drinking; for as this is natural, so is that! Let not natural things sadden thee; rather let things which arise from an evil choice make thee sorrowful. Sorrow not for the dying man; but sorrow for him who is living in sin!

Would you have me mention another reason on account of which we fear death? We do not live with strictness, nor keep a clear conscience; for if this were the case nothing would alarm us, neither death, nor famine, nor the loss of wealth, nor anything else that is. For he who lives virtuously cannot be injured by any of these things, or be deprived of his inward pleasure. For, being supported by favorable hopes, nothing will be able to throw him into dejection. What is there that any one can possibly effect, by which he can cause the noble-minded man to become sorrowful? Take away his riches? He has yet wealth that is in the heavens! Cast him out of his country? He will take refuge in that city which is above! Load him with fetters? He has still his conscience free, and is insensible to the external chain! Put his body to death? Yet he shall rise again! And as he who fights with a shadow, and beateth the air, will be unable to hit any one, so he who is at war with the just man is but striking at a shadow and wasting his own strength, without being able to inflict any injury upon him. Grant me then to be sure of the kingdom of heaven; and, if thou wishest, slay me this day. I shall be thankful to thee for the killing; forasmuch as thou sendest me quickly to the possession of those good things! "This, however," says some one, "is what we especially lament, that, prevented as we are by the multitude of our sins, we shall not attain to that kingdom." Such being the case, then, have done lamenting death, and lament thy sins, in order that thou mayest be freed from them! Grief, indeed, hath had its existence, not that we should sorrow for the loss of wealth, nor for death, nor for anything else of that kind, but that we may employ it for the taking away of our sins. And I will make the truth of this evident by an example. Healing medicines have been made for those diseases only which they are able to remove; not for those which are in no respect assisted by them. That is to say (for I wish to make the matter still plainer), the medicine which is able to benefit a malady of the eyes only, and no other disease, one might justly say was made only for the sake of the eyes; not for the stomach, nor for the hands, nor any other member. Let us then transfer this observation to the subject of grief; and we shall find, that in none of those things which happen to us is it of any advantage, except to correct sin; whence it is apparent that it hath had its existence only for the destruction of sin. Let us now take a passing view of each of those evils which befall us, and let us place sadness in conjunction with them, and we shall see what sort of advantage results from it.

Some one is mulcted in property; he becomes sad, but this does not make good his loss. Some one hath lost a son; he grieves, but he cannot raise the dead, nor benefit the departed. Some one hath been scourged, beaten, and contemptuously treated; he becomes sorrowful. This does not remove the ignominy. Some one falls into sickness, and a most grievous disease; he is dejected. This does not remove his disease, but only makes it the more grievous. Do you see that in none of these cases does sadness answer any purpose? Suppose that any one hath sinned, and is sad. He blots out the sin; he gets free from the transgression. How is this shown? By the declaration of the Lord; for, speaking of a certain one who had sinned, He said, "Because of his iniquity I made him sad for a while; and I saw that he was grieved, and he went on heavily; and I healed his ways." Therefore also Paul saith, "Godly sorrow worketh repentance unto salvation." Since then what I have said clearly shows that neither the loss of riches, nor ignominy, nor calumny, nor stripes, nor sickness, nor death, nor any other thing of that kind can possibly be relieved by the interference of grief, but sin only can it blot out and do away, it is evident that for this reason only it hath its existence. Let us therefore no more grieve for the loss of wealth, but then alone, when we commit sin. For great in this case is the gain that comes with sadness. Art thou amerced? Be not sad, for thus thou wilt not be at all benefited. Hast thou sinned? Then be sad: for it is profitable; and consider the skill and wisdom of God. Sin hath brought forth for us these two things, grief and death. "For in the day thou eatest (He saith) thou shalt surely die"; and to the woman, "In sorrow thou shalt bring forth children." And by both of these things He took away sin and provided that the mother should be destroyed by her off-spring. For that death as well as grief takes away sin is evident, in the first place, from the case of the martyrs; and it is plain too from what Paul saith to those who had sinned, speaking on this wise: "For this cause many are weak and sickly among you, and many sleep." Inasmuch, he observes, as ye have sinned, ye die, so that ye are freed from sin by death. Therefore he goes on to say: "For if we would judge ourselves, we should not be judged. But when we are judged, we are chastened of the Lord, that we should not be condemned with the world." And even as the worm is brought forth from the wood, and devours the wood; and a moth consumes the wool, from whence it originates; so grief and death were born of sin, and devour sin.

Let us not then fear death, but let us only fear sin, and grieve on account of this. And these things I speak, not anticipating anything fearful, God forbid! but wishing you when alarmed to be always thus affected, and to fulfil the law of Christ in very deed. For Christ saith, "he that taketh not his cross and followeth after Me, is not worthy of Me." This He said, not that we should always have death before our eyes. Even so as Paul, that is, died daily, and laughed at death, and despised the present life. For indeed thou art a soldier, and standest continually to arms; but a soldier who is afraid of death will never perform a noble action. Thus then neither will a Christian man, if fear-ful of dangers, perform anything great or admirable; nay, besides this, he will be apt to be easily vanquished. But not so is it with the man who is bold and lofty-minded. He remains impregnable and unconquerable. As then the Three Children, when they feared not the fire, escaped from the fire, so also we, if we fear not death, shall entirely escape from death. They feared not the fire (for it is no crime to be burned), but they feared sin, for it is a crime to commit impiety. Let us also imitate these and all such, and let us not be afraid of dangers, and then we shall altogether escape dangers.

Translated by C. Marriott.
Published by G. P. Putnam's Sons.
Reprinted by permission.

THE SERMON ON BELIEF IN THE RESURRECTION

Saint Ambrose of Milan

(340-397 A.D.)

Ambrose is the earliest expression of the oratory of the Western church. Educated in law at Rome for the imperial service he established his official residence at Milan. Here his justice and benevolence, nobility of character, and eloquence so won the esteem of both Catholics and Arians that he was unanimously chosen Bishop of Milan. The Empire was rapidly losing hold on men's minds and the Church was on the point of assuming leadership. At this crisis Ambrose became the leading representative of the Church. He distinguished himself by his opposition to paganism, his exposition of the Nicene orthodoxy, and his insistence on penance from the Emperor Theodosius after the horrible massacre of Thessalonica.

St. Ambrose adopted the oratorical style of the period which was marked by allegory and mysticism. His orations were connected treatises and commentaries and cannot rank with the lofty works of the orators of the Eastern Church. The *Funeral Orations* are perhaps his best work. Included here is *The Sermon on Belief in the Resurrection* which was the second discourse delivered by St. Ambrose on the death of his own brother, Satyrus. Upon St. Ambrose's appointment as Bishop of Milan this brother, Satyrus, devoted himself to the management of St. Ambrose's secular affairs so that nothing might distract Ambrose from his episcopal duties. The intense grief of St. Ambrose at the death of this like-minded brother was expressed in two exquisite discourses—one on his brother's decease and the other on the resurrection from the dead.

Who is so patient in suffering as not to pray for death? who has such endurance in weakness as not to wish rather to die than to live in debility? Who is so brave in sorrow as not to desire to escape from it even by death? But if we ourselves are dissatisfied while life lasts, although we know that a limit is fixed for it, how much more weary should we become of this life if we saw that the troubles of the body would be with us without end! For who is there who would wish to be excepted from death? Or what would be more unendurable than a miserable immortality? "If in this life only," he says, "we hope in Christ, we are more miserable than all men"; not because to hope in Christ is miserable, but because Christ has prepared another life for those who hope in Him. For this life is liable to sin; that life is reserved for the reward.

And how much weariness do we find that the short stages of our lives bring us! The boy longs to be a young man; the youth counts the years leading to riper age; the young man, unthankful for the advantage of his vigorous time of life, desires the honour of old age. And so to all there comes naturally the desire of change, because we are dissatisfied with that which we now are. And lastly, even the things we have desired are wearisome to us; and what we have wished to obtain, when we have obtained it, we dislike.

Wherefore holy men have not without reason often lamented their lengthy dwelling here: David lamented it, Jeremiah lamented it, and Elijah lamented it. If we believe wise men, and those in whom the Divine Spirit dwelt, they were hastening to better things; and if we enquire as to the judgment of others, that we may ascertain that all agree in one opinion, what great men have preferred death to sorrow, what great men have preferred it to fear! esteeming forsooth the fear of death to be worse than death itself. So death is not feared on account of evils which belong to it, but is preferred to the miseries of life, since the departure of the dying is desired and the dread of the living is avoided.

So be it, then. Granted that the Resurrection is preferable to this life. What! have philosophers themselves found anything with which we should have a greater delight to continue than to rise again? Even those indeed who say that souls are immortal do not satisfy me, seeing they only allow me a partial redemption. What grace can that be by which I am not wholly benefited? What life is that if the operation of God dies out in me? What righteousness is that which, if death is the end of natural existence, is common to the sinner and the just? What is that truth, that the soul should be considered immortal, because it moves itself and is always in motion? As regards that which in the body is common to us with beasts, it is perhaps uncertain what happens before the body exists, and the truth is not to be gathered from these differences but destroyed.

But is their opinion preferable, who say that our souls, when they have passed out of these bodies, migrate into the bodies of beasts, or of various other living creatures? Philosophers, indeed, themselves are wont to argue that these are ridiculous fancies of poets, such as might be produced by draughts of the drugs of Circe; and they say that not so much they who are represented to have undergone such things, as the senses of those who have invented such tales are changed into the forms of various beasts as it were by Circe's cup. For what is so like a marvel as to believe that men could have been changed into the forms of beasts? How much greater a marvel, however, would it be that the soul which rules man should take on itself the nature of a beast so opposed to that of man, and being capable of reason should be able to pass over to an irrational animal, than that the form of the body should have been changed? You yourselves, who teach these things, destroy what you teach. For you have given up the production of these portentous conversions by means of magic incantations.

Poets say these things in sport, and philosophers blame them, and at the same time they imagine that those very things are true of the dead which they consider fictitious as regards the living. For they who invented such tales did not intend to assert the truth of their own fable, but to deride the errors of philosophers, who think that that same soul which was accustomed to overcome anger by gentle and lowly purpose, can now, inflamed by the raging impulses of a lion, impatient with anger and with unbridled rage, thirst for blood and seek for slaughter. Or again, that that soul, which as it was by royal counsel used to moderate the various storms of the people, and to calm them with the voice of reason, can now endure to howl in pathless and desert places after the fashion of a wolf; or that that soul which, groaning under a heavy burden, used to low in sad complaint over the labours of the plough, now changed into the fashion of a man, seeks for horns on his smooth brow; or that another, which used of old to be borne aloft on rapid wing to the heights of heaven, now thinks of flight no longer in its power, and mourns that it grows sluggish in the weight of a human body.

Perchance you destroyed Icarus through some such teaching, because the youth, led on by your persuasion, imagined, it may be, that he had been a bird. By such means too have many old men been deceived so as to submit to grievous pain, having unhappily believed the fables about swans, and thought that they, whilst soothing their pain with mournful strains, would be able to transmute their gray hair into downy feathers.

How incredible are these things! how odious! How much more fitting is it to believe in accordance with nature, in accordance with what takes place in every kind of fruit; to believe in accordance with the pattern of what has happened, in accordance with the utterances of prophets, and the heavenly promise of Christ! For what is better than to be sure that the work of God does not perish, and that those who are made in the image and likeness of God cannot be transformed into the shapes of beasts; since in truth it is not the form of the body but of the spirit which is made after the likeness of God. For in what manner could man, to whom are subjected the other kinds of living creatures, migrate with the better part of himself into an animal subjected to himself? Nature does not suffer this, and if nature did grace would not.

But I have seen what you, Gentiles, think of each other, and indeed it ought not to seem strange that you who worship beasts should believe that you can be changed into beasts. But I had rather that you judged better concerning what is due to you, that you may believe that you will be not in the company of wild beasts, but in the companionship of angels.

The soul has to depart from the surroundings of this life, and the pollutions of the earthly body, and to press on to those heavenly companies, though it is for the saints alone to attain to them, and to sing praise to God (as in the prophet's words we hear of those who are harping and saying: "For great are Thy marvellous works, O Lord God Almighty, just and true are Thy ways, Thou King of the nations; who shall not fear and magnify Thy Name, for Thou only art holy, for all nations shall come and worship before Thee"), and to see Thy marriage feast, O Lord Jesus, in which the Bride is led from earthly to heavenly things, while all rejoice in harmony, for "to Thee shall all flesh come," now no longer subject to transitory things, but joined to the Spirit, to see the chambers adorned with linen, roses, lilies, and garlands. Of whom else is the marriage so adorned? For it is adorned with the purple stripes of confessors, the blood of martyrs, the lilies of virgins, and the crowns of priests.

Holy David desires beyond all else for himself that he might behold and gaze upon this, for he says: "One thing have I asked of the Lord, that will I seek after; that I may dwell in the house of the Lord all the days of my life, and see the pleasure of the Lord."

It is a pleasure to believe this, a joy to hope for it; and certainly, not to have believed it is a pain, to have lived in this hope a grace. But if I am mistaken in this, that I prefer to be associated after death with angels rather than with beasts, I am gladly mistaken, and so long as I live will never suffer myself to be cheated of this hope.

For what comfort have I left but that I hope to come quickly to thee, my brother, and that thy departure will not cause a long severance between us, and that it may be granted me, through thy intercessions, that thou mayest quickly call me who long for thee. For who is there who ought not to wish for himself beyond all else that "This corruptible should put on incorruption, and this mortal put on immortality"? that we who succumb to death through the frailty of the body, being raised above nature, may no longer have to fear death.

ON THE LORD'S PRAYER

Saint Augustine
(354-430 A.D.)

The experiences of Saint Augustine, who became the famous Bishop of Hippo in Africa, are woven into a pattern of conflict between his natural and spiritual desires. Of Pagan-Christian parentage, he early in life secured the training and education which in succession made him a teacher of rhetoric at Carthage, Rome, and Milan. It was in the latter location that he met Saint Ambrose and through his eloquence became converted to the orthodox faith. A few years later he was ordained Bishop of Hippo in North Africa which bishopric through his influence became the intellectual center of the western world. His pen was really mightier than his eloquence for he, himself, never went beyond Africa, but his writings gave him a distinguished position in philosophy, psychology, and history.

His sermons are marked rather by spiritual insight than by adherence to grammatical and philological exegesis. He excelled in coining phrases and was most fastidious in his choice of words. The selection used here is an excellent example of his analytical oratorical method. It was delivered to the Competentes, or last class of the Catechomens.

The order established for your edification requires that ye learn first what to believe, and afterward that "they who call upon the name of the Lord shall be saved." This testimony blessed Paul cited out of the prophet; for by the prophet were those times foretold when all men should call upon God; "Whosoever shall call upon the name of the Lord shall be saved." And he added, "How then shall they call on him in whom they have not believed? And how shall they believe in him of whom they have not heard? Or how shall they hear without a preacher? Or how shall they preach except they be sent?" Therefore were preachers sent. They preached Christ. As they preached, the people heard; by hearing they believed, and by believing called upon him. Because, then, it was most rightly and most truly said, "How shall they call on him in whom they have not believed?" therefore have ye first learned what to believe: and to-day have learned to call on him in whom ye have believed.

The Son of God, our Lord Jesus Christ, hath taught us a prayer; and though he be the Lord himself, as ye have heard and repeated in the Creed, the only Son of God, yet he would not be alone. He is the only Son, and yet would not be alone; he hath vouchsafed to have brethren. For to whom doth he say, "Our Father which art in heaven"? Whom did he wish us to call our Father save his own Father? Did he grudge us this? Parents sometimes, when they have gotten one, or two, or three children, fear to give birth to any more, lest they reduce the rest to beggary. But because the inheritance which he promised us is such as many may possess and no one be straitened, therefore hath he called into his brotherhood the peoples of the nations; and the only Son hath numberless brethren who say, "Our Father which art in heaven." So said they who have been before us; and so shall say those who will come after us. See how many brethren the only Son hath in his grace, sharing his inheritance with those for whom he suffered death. We had a father and mother on earth, that we might be born to labors and to death: but we have found other parents, God our Father, and the Church our Mother, by whom we are born unto life eternal. Let us then consider, beloved, whose children we have begun to be; and let us live so as becomes those who have such a Father. See how that our Creator has condescended to be our Father!

We have heard whom we ought to call upon, and with what hope of an eternal inheritance we have begun to have a Father in heaven; let us now hear what we must ask of Him. Of such a Father what shall we ask? Do we not ask rain of him to-day, and yesterday, and the day before? This is no great thing to have asked of such a Father, and yet ye see with what sighings and with what great desire we ask for rain when death is feared,—when that is feared which none can escape. For sooner or later every man must die, and we groan, and pray, and travail in pain, and cry to God, that we may die a little later. How much more ought we to cry to him that we may come to that place where we shall never die!

Therefore is it said, "Hallowed be thy name." This we also ask of him that his name may be hallowed in us; for holy is it always. And how is his name hallowed in us, except while it makes us holy? For once we were not holy, and we are made holy by his name; but he is always holy, and his name always holy. It is for ourselves, not for God, that we pray. For we do not wish well to God, to whom no ill can ever happen. But we wish what is good for ourselves, that his holy name may be hallowed, that that which is always holy may be hallowed in us.

"Thy kingdom come." Come it surely will, whether we ask or no. Indeed, God hath an eternal kingdom. For when did he not reign? When did he begin to reign? For his kingdom hath no beginning, neither shall it have any end. But that ye may know that in this prayer also we pray for ourselves, and not for God (for we do not say "Thy kingdom come" as though we were asking that God may reign), we shall be ourselves his kingdom if, believing in him, we make progress in this faith. All the faithful, redeemed by the blood of his only Son, will be his kingdom. And this his kingdom will come when the resurrection of the dead shall have taken place; for then he will come himself. And when the dead are arisen he will divide them, as he himself saith, "and he shall set some on the right hand, and some on the left." To those who shall be on the right hand he will say, "Come, ye blessed of my Father, receive the kingdom." This is what we wish and pray for when we say, "Thy kingdom come,"—that it may come to us. For if we shall be reprobates, that kingdom will come to others, but not to us. But if we shall be of that number who belong to the members of his only-begotten Son, his kingdom will come to us and will not tarry. For are there as many ages yet remaining as have already passed away? The apostle John hath said, "My little children, it is the last hour." But it is a long hour proportioned to this long day; and see how many years this last hour lasteth. But, nevertheless, be ye as those who watch, and so sleep, and rise again, and reign. Let us watch now, let us sleep in death; at the end we shall rise again and shall reign without end.

"Thy will be done as in heaven, so in earth." The third thing we pray for is that his will may be done as in heaven so in earth. And in this too we wish well for ourselves. For the will of God must necessarily be done. It is the will of God that the good should reign and the wicked be damned. Is it possible that this will should not be done? But what good do we wish ourselves when we say, "Thy will be done as in heaven, so in earth?" Give ear. For this petition may be understood in many ways, and many things are to be in our thoughts in this petition when we pray God, "Thy will be done as in heaven, so in earth." As thy angels offend thee not, so may we also not offend thee. Again, how is "Thy will be done as in heaven, so in earth," understood? All the holy patriarchs, all the prophets, all the apostles, all the spiritual are, as it were, God's heaven; and we in comparison with them are earth. "Thy will be done as in heaven, so in earth;" as in them, so in us also. Again, "Thy will be done as in heaven, so in earth"; the Church of God is heaven, his enemies are earth. So we wish well for our enemies, that they too may believe and become Christians, and so the will of God be done as in heaven, so also in earth. Again, "Thy will be done as in heaven, so in earth." Our spirit is heaven, and the flesh earth. As our spirit is renewed by believing, so may our flesh be renewed by rising again, and "the will of God be done as in heaven, so in earth." Again, our mind whereby we see the truth, and delight in this truth, is heaven; as, "I delight in the law of God, after the inward man." What is the earth? "I see another law in my members, warring against the law of my mind." When this strife shall have passed away, and a full concord be brought about of the flesh and spirit, the will of God will be done as in heaven, so also in earth. When we repeat this petition, let us think of all these things, and ask them all of the Father. Now all these things which we have mentioned, these three petitions, beloved, have respect to the life eternal. For if the name of God is sanctified in us, it will be for eternity. If his will be done as in heaven, so in earth, in all ways which I have explained, it will be for eternity.

There remain now the petitions for this life of our pilgrimage; therefore follows, "Give us this day our daily bread." Give us eternal things, give us things temporal. Thou hast promised a kingdom, deny us not the means of subsistence. Thou wilt give everlasting glory with thyself hereafter, give us in this earth temporal support. Therefore is it "day by day," and "today," that is, in this present time. For when this life shall have passed away, shall we ask for daily bread then? For then it will not be called "day by day," but "to-day." Now it is called "day by day" when one day passes away and another day succeeds. Will it be called "day by day" when there will be one eternal day? This petition for daily bread is doubtless to be understood in two ways, both for the necessary supply of our bodily food and for the necessities of our spiritual support. There is a necessary supply of bodily food, for the preservation of our daily life, without which we cannot live. This is food and clothing, but the whole is understood in a part. When we ask for bread, we thereby understand all things. There is a spiritual food also which the faithful know, which ye too will know when ye shall receive it at the altar of God. This also is "daily bread," necessary only for this life. For shall we receive the Eucharist when we shall have come to Christ himself and begun to reign with him forever? So, then, the Eucharist is our daily bread; but let us in such wise receive it that we be not refreshed in our bodies only, but in our souls. For the virtue which is apprehended there is unity, that, gathered together into his body, and made his members, we may be what we receive. Then will it indeed be our daily bread.

Again, what I am handling before you now is "daily bread"; and the daily lessons which ye hear in church are daily bread, and the hymns ye hear and repeat are daily bread. For all these are necessary in our state of pilgrimage. But when we shall have got to heaven, shall we hear the word, we who shall see the Word himself, and hear the Word himself, and eat and drink him as the angels do now? Do the angels need books, and interpreters, and readers? Surely not. They read in seeing, for the Truth itself they see and are abundantly satisfied from that fountain from which we obtain some few drops. Therefore has it been said, touching our daily bread, that this petition is necessary for us in this life.

"Forgive us our debts, as we forgive our debtors." Is this necessary except in this life? For in the other we shall have no debts. For what are debts but sins? See, ye are on the point of being baptized, then all your sins will be blotted out, none whatever will remain. Whatever evil ye have done, in deed, or word, or desire, or thought, all will be blotted out. And yet if, in the life which is after baptism, there were security from sin, we should not learn such a prayer as this, "Forgive us our debts." Only let us by all means do what comes next, "As we forgive our debtors."

Do ye, then, who are about to enter in to receive a plenary and entire remission of your debts, do ye, above all things, see that ye have nothing in your hearts against any other, so as to come forth from baptism secure, as it were free and discharged of all debts, and then begin to purpose to avenge yourselves on your enemies who in time past have done you wrong. Forgive, as ye are forgiven. God can do no one wrong, and yet he forgiveth who oweth nothing. How, then, ought he to forgive who is himself forgiven, when he forgiveth all who oweth nothing that can be forgiven him?

"Lead us not into temptation, but deliver us from evil." Will this, again, be necessary in the life to come? "Lead us not into temptation" will not be said except where there can be temptation. We read in the book of holy Job, "Is not the life of man upon earth a temptation?" What, then, do we pray for? Hear what. The apostle James saith, "Let no man say when he is tempted, I am tempted of God." He spoke of those evil temptations whereby men are deceived and brought under the yoke of the devil. This is the kind of temptation he spoke of. For there is another sort of temptation which is called a proving; of this kind of temptation it is written, "The Lord your God tempteth (proveth) you to know whether ye love Him." What means "to know?" "To make you know," for he knoweth already. With that kind of temptation whereby we are deceived and seduced, God tempteth no man. But undoubtedly in his deep and hidden judgment he abandons some. And when he hath abandoned them the tempter finds his opportunity. For he finds in him no resistance against his power, but forthwith presents himself to him as his possessor, if God abandon him. Therefore, that he may not abandon us, do we say, "Lead us not into temptation." "For every one is tempted," says the same apostle James, "when he is drawn away of his own lust and enticed. Then lust, when it hath conceived, bringeth forth sin; and sin, when it is finished, bringeth forth death."

What, then, has he hereby taught us? To fight against our lusts. For ye are about to put away your sins in holy baptism; but lusts will still remain, wherewith ye must fight after that ye are regenerate. For a conflict with your own selves still remains. Let no enemy from without be feared: conquer thine own self, and the whole world is conquered. What can any tempter from without, whether the devil or the devil's minister, do against thee? Whosoever sets the hope of gain before thee to seduce thee, let him only find no covetousness in thee; and what can he who would tempt thee by gain effect? Whereas, if covetousness be found in thee, thou takest fire at the sight of gain, and art taken by the bait of this corrupt food. But if he find no covetousness in thee, the trap remains spread in vain.

Or should the tempter set before thee some woman of surpassing beauty; if chastity be within, iniquity from without is overcome. Therefore, that he may not take thee with the bait of a strange woman's beauty, fight with thine own lust within; thou hast no sensible perception of thine enemy, but of thine own concupiscence thou hast. Thou dost not see the devil, but the object that engageth thee thou dost see. Get the mastery, then, over that of which thou art sensible within. Fight valiantly, for he who hath regenerated thee is thy Judge; he hath arranged the lists, he is making ready the crown. But because thou wilt without doubt be conquered if thou have not him to aid thee, if he abandon thee: therefore dost thou say in the prayer, "Lead us not into temptation." The Judge's wrath hath given over some to their own lusts; and the Apostle says, "God gave them over to the lusts of their hearts." How did he give them up? Not by forcing, but by forsaking them.

"Deliver us from evil" may belong to the same sentence. Therefore, that thou mayst understand it to be all one sentence, it runs thus, "Lead us not into temptation, but deliver us from evil." Therefore he added "but," to show that all this belongs to one sentence, "Lead us not into temptation, but deliver us from evil." How is this? I will propose them singly. "Lead us not into temptation, but deliver us from evil." By delivering us from evil he leadeth us not into temptation; by not leading us into temptation he delivereth us from evil.

And truly it is a great temptation, dearly beloved, it is a great temptation in this life, when that in us is the subject of temptation whereby we attain pardon if, in any of our temptations, we have fallen. It is a frightful temptation when that is taken from us whereby we may be healed from the wounds of other temptations. I know that ye have not yet understood me. Give me your attention, that ye may understand. Suppose avarice tempts a man, and he is conquered in any single temptation (for sometimes even a good wrestler and fighter may get roughly handled): avarice, then, has got the better of a man, good wrestler though he be, and he has done some avaricious act. Or there has been a passing lust; it has not brought the man to fornication, nor reached unto adultery—for when this does takes place, the man must at all events be kept back from the criminal act. But he "hath seen a woman to lust after her:" he has let his thoughts dwell on her with more pleasure than was right; he has admitted the attack, excellent combatant though he be, he has been wounded, but he has not consented to it; he has beaten back the motion of his lust, has chastised it with the bitterness of grief, he has beaten it back, and has prevailed. Still, in the very fact that he had slipped has he ground for saying "Forgive us our debts." And so of all other temptations, it is a hard matter that in them all there should not be occasion for saying, "Forgive us our debts." What, then, is that frightful temptation which I have mentioned, that grievous, that tremendous temptation which must be avoided with all our strength, with all our resolution: what is it? When we go about to avenge ourselves. Anger is kindled, and the man burns to be avenged. O frightful temptation! Thou art losing that whereby thou hadst to attain pardon for other faults. If thou hadst committed any sin as to other senses and other lusts, hence mightst thou have had thy cure in that thou mightst say "Forgive us our debts, as we also forgive our debtors." But whoso instigateth thee to take vengeance will lose for thee the power thou hadst to say "As we also forgive our debtors." When that power is lost, all sins will be retained; nothing at all is remitted.

Our Lord and Master and Saviour, knowing this dangerous temptation in this life when he taught us six or seven petitions in this prayer, took none of them for himself to treat of and to commend to us with greater earnestness than this one. Have we not said, "Our Father which art in heaven" and the rest which follows? Why, after the conclusion of the prayer, did he not enlarge upon it to us, either as to what he had laid down in the beginning, or concluded with at the end, or placed in the middle? For why said he not, If the name of God be not hallowed in you, or if ye have no part in the kingdom of God, or if the will of God be not done in you, as in heaven, or if God guard you not, that ye enter not into temptation; why none of all these? but what saith he? "Verily I say unto you, that if ye forgive men their trespasses," in reference to that petition, "Forgive us our debts, as we also forgive our debtors." Having passed over all the other petitions which he taught us, this he taught us with an especial force. There was no need of insisting so much upon those sins in which, if a man offend, he may know the means whereby he may be cured: need of it there was with regard to that sin in which, if thou sin, there is no means whereby the rest can be cured. For this thou oughtst to be ever saying, "Forgive us our debts." What debts? There is no lack of them; for we are but men; I have talked somewhat more than I ought, have said something I ought not, have laughed more than I ought, have eaten more than I ought, have listened with pleasure to what I ought not, have drunk more than I ought, have seen with pleasure what I ought not, have thought with pleasure on what I ought not; "Forgive us our debts, as we also forgive our debtors." This if thou hast lost, thou art lost thyself.

Take heed, my brethren, my sons, sons of God, take heed, I beseech you, in that I am saying to you. Fight to the uttermost of your powers with your own hearts. And if ye shall see your anger making a stand against you, pray to God against it, that God may make thee conqueror of thyself, that God may make thee conqueror, I say, not of thine enemy without, but of thine own soul within. For he will give thee his present help and will do it. He would rather that we ask this of him than rain. For ye see, beloved, how many petitions the Lord Christ hath taught us; and there is scarce found among them one which speaks of daily bread, that all our thoughts may be moulded after the life to come. For what can we fear that he will not give us who hath promised and said, "Seek ye first the kingdom of God and his righteousness, and all these things shall be added unto you; for your Father knoweth that ye have need of these things before ye ask him." "Seek ye first the kingdom of God and his righteousness, and all these things shall be added unto you." For many have been tried even with hunger, and have been found cold, and have not been forsaken by God. They would have perished with hunger if the daily inward bread were to leave their heart. After this let us chiefly hunger. For, "Blessed are they who hunger and thirst after righteousness, for they shall be filled." But he can in mercy look upon our infirmity, and see us, as it is said, "Remember that we are dust." He who from the dust made and quickened man, for that his work of clay's sake, gave his only Son to death. Who can explain, who can worthily so much as conceive, how much he loveth us?

SERMON ON THE COMMUNITY OF GOODS

Leo the Great

(390-461 A.D.)

Leo the Great became Bishop of Rome in 400 A.D. He was so commanding and fearless that his embassy to Attila in 450 was successful in delivering Rome from the fierce Huns. It was also his conception of the Petrine prerogative which became dominant in the church. He was equally successful in extirpating heresy and maintaining discipline at a time when disputes raged. Among the Latin fathers Leo ranks rather as a practical preacher than a cultivated orator. His sermons were usually short, pithy, practical discourses. His style was earnest forcible, and full of thought although at times heavy and obscure through ornateness. As the first great preacher in Rome he was unrivalled in the West. Included here are two short sermons representative of his style of oratory.

It is a great and very precious thing, beloved, in the Lord's sight, when Christ's whole people engage together in the same duties, and all ranks and degrees of either sex co-operate with the same intent: when one purpose animates all alike of declining from evil and doing good; when God is glorified in the works of His slaves, and the Author of all godliness is blessed in unstinted giving of thanks, the hungry are nourished, the naked are clothed, the sick are visited, and men seek not their own but "that which is another's," so long as in relieving the misery of others each one makes the most of his own means; and it is easy to find "a cheerful giver," where a man's performances are only limited by the extent of his power. By this grace of God, "which worketh all in all," the benefits and the deserts of the faithful are both enjoyed in common. For they, whose income is not like, can yet think alike, and when one rejoices over another's bounty his feelings put him on the same level with him whose powers of spending are on a different level. In such a community there is no disorder nor diversity,

for all the members of the whole body agree in one strong purpose
of godliness, and he who glories in the wealth of others is not put to
shame at his own poverty. For the excellence of each portion is the
glory of the whole body, and when we are all led by God's Spirit, not
only are the things we do ourselves our own but those of others also
over the doing of which we rejoice.

THE BLESSEDNESS OF PEACE-MAKING

Leo the Great

(390-461 A.D.)

"Blessed are the peace-makers, for they shall be called the sons of God." This blessedness, beloved, belongs not to any and every kind of agreement and harmony, but to that of which the Apostle speaks: "have peace towards God"; and of which the Prophet David speaks: "Much peace have they that love Thy law, and they have no cause of offence." This peace even the closest ties of friendship or the exactest likeness of mind do not really gain, if they do not agree with God's will. Similarity of bad desires, leagues in crimes, associations of vice, cannot merit this peace. The love of the world does not consort with the love of God, nor doth he enter the alliance of the sons of God who will not separate himself from the children of this generation. Whereas they who are in mind always with God, "giving diligence to keep the unity of the Spirit in the bond of peace," never dissent from the eternal law, uttering that prayer of faith, "Thy will be done as in heaven so on earth." These are "the peacemakers," these are thoroughly of one mind, and fully harmonious, and are to be called sons "of God and joint-heirs with Christ," because this shall be the record of the love of God and the love of our neighbour, that we shall suffer no calamities, be in fear of no offence, but all the strife of trial ended, rest in God's most perfect peace, through our Lord, Who, with the Father and the Holy Spirit, liveth and reigneth for ever and ever. Amen.

A SERMON ON JOB

Gregory the Great
(540-604 A.D.)

During the sixth and seventh centuries Gregory was the most prominent oratorical figure of the church. He united in equal measure charity and grace with firmness and energy. He displayed great zeal for the conversion of heretics, the advancement of monachism, the rigid enforcement of celibacy among the clergy, and the cause of missions among the Anglo-Saxons. Gregory's literary taste was somewhat crude; he discredited the study of classical languages and made little effort to avoid barbarisms in his own work. His style is, however, clear. Gregory was a master of the allegorical method of interpretation, and beyond doubt his sermons served to popularize this system of exegesis during the Middle Ages.

The *Sermons on Job* were delivered by Gregory before his fellow monks in the monastery. They planned first to give an allegorical interpretation of the passage of Scripture and then make a moral application of the text. One of these sermons is included here.

In silver the power of speaking, in gold brightness of life or of wisdom, is used to be denoted. And because heretics are so filled with pride for the brilliancy of their speaking that they are not based firmly on any authority of the sacred books (which books are for speaking like a kind of veins of silver to us, because from those identical books we derive the spring and source of our speaking), he recalls them to the pages of sacred authority, that if they have a desire to speak in a true way, they may from that source draw forth what to say. And he saith, "The silver hath the beginnings of its veins, and to the gold there is a place, where they fine it."

As if he said in plain words: "He that is fitting himself for the words of true preaching, the originals of the cases he must of necessity derive from the sacred page, so as to bring round everything that he speaks to a foundation of divine authority, and in that set firm the edifice of his own speaking." For, as we before said, oftentimes heretics, whilst they are eager to prop up what is bad of their own, broach things which assuredly are not maintained in the page of the sacred books. And hence the great Preacher admonishes His disciple, saying, "O Timothy, keep that which is committed to thy trust, avoiding profane novelties of speaking," for whereas heretics long to be extolled as if for excellency of wit, they as it were bring out new things which are not maintained in the old books of the ancient Fathers, and thus it follows, that whilst they desire to appear wise, they scatter seeds of foolishness to their wretched hearers.

And it is well added: "And to the gold there is a place, where they fine it." As if he said in plain terms: "The true wisdom of believers, which has the Church Universal for its place, undergoes tribulation by your persecuting her, but from all the dross of sins by the fire of your persecution she is purified." Whence it is written: "For gold is tried in the fire, and acceptable men in the furnace of adversity." In which passage this too may be appropriately taken for the meaning, that for their foolish suffering heretics might seem to be rebuked. For oftentimes for the name of Jesus Christ, our Lord and Redeemer, they suffer much, and by those same sufferings they look for themselves to become His martyrs. To which persons it is now said by the voice of the holy man: "And to the gold there is a place, where they fine it." For according to that which has been already said even before us, he that suffers out of the unity of the Church, punishments he may suffer, but a martyr he cannot be made; for "to the gold there is a place, where they fine it." What then, ye heretics, say ye to these things? Ye are minded to be "fined" by the afflicting of the flesh, nay even by martyrdom, but the place where ye must be fined, ye know not. Hear ye what is spoken by the voice of the holy preacher: "To the gold there is a place, where they fine it." So then, seek ye this "place for the fining," this furnace, wherein the gold may be fitly purged, find ye out.

There is one Church, in which he that may have attained to be fined may likewise be purified from all the dross of sins. If for the sake of God ye undergo aught of bitterness, if aught of tribulation, being without her pale, ye can only be burnt, ye cannot be purified. Let Jeremiah tell, let him tell in what way the fire of your fining is void of all efficacy. "The finer melteth in vain; for their wickednesses are not done away." See how the fire externally melting at once administers a punishment of hard suffering, and yet does not clear off the sin of misbelief; it both furnishes torments of cruel punishments, and does not cause additions of good merits. Moreover the fire of this fining which is undergone out of the Catholic Church, how utterly it is void of all efficacy the Apostle Paul instructs us, when he says, "And though I give my body to be burned, and have not charity, it profiteth me nothing." For some think wrong things touching God, and others hold what is right about the Creator but do not maintain unity with their brethren; the one are sundered by erroneousness of faith, and the others by the commission of schism. And hence in the very first part of the Decalogue the sins of both sides are checked, seeing that it is said by the voice of God, "And thou shalt love the Lord thy God with all thine heart, and with all thy soul, and with all thy might." And it is immediately added, "And thou shalt love thy neighbor as thyself." For whoso imagines what is wrong about God, surely it is evident that he does not "love God." But he who, while he entertains right notions about God, is divided from the unity of the Holy Church, it is plain that he does not love his neighbor, whom he refuses to have for his fellow.

Whosoever, then, is divided from this unity of the Church our Mother, either through heresy in entertaining wrong notions concerning God, or by the erroneousness of schism in not loving his neighbor, is bereft of the grace of that charity, concerning which Paul saith what we have before given: "And though I give my body to be burned, and have not charity, it profiteth me nothing." As if he expressed himself in plain utterance: "Without the bounds of its place, the fire of fining being applied to me only afflicts me with torment, and does not purify me by its cleansing." This place all that are lovers of holy peace seek with heartiest endeavors, this on seeking they find, this finding they keep, knowing the remission of sin, as to where, or when, or to what sort it is vouchsafed. For where is it, save in the bosom of our Catholic Mother? When, but before the day of coming departure? Because, "Behold, now is the accepted time; behold, now is the day of salvation." And, "Seek ye the Lord while He may be found, call ye upon Him while He is near." To what sort of persons, but to the converted, who after the imitating of little children are fashioned by humility as their mistress? To whom it is said: "Suffer little children to come unto Me, and forbid them not; for of such is the kingdom of heaven." And therefore, because there are no true martyrs made saving in the Catholic Church, it is rightly said, "To the gold there is a place, where they fine it." Because the soul would not be made bright in the radiance of everlasting beauty, except, so to say, it were first burnt here in the workshop of charity.

Moreover, we are to consider that there are some whom Almighty God by His secret counsel preserving in innocency from their very beginnings, promotes to the topmost heights of virtuous attainments, that, as their age increases, both numerousness of years and loftiness of merits should simultaneously advance in them. But others abandoning in their outset, He suffers to go with bad habits fermenting by headlong ways. Yet for the most part even these He has regard to, and for the following after Him He kindles them with the fire of holy love, and the itchings of bad propensities ingrained in their hearts He converts into a fervor of virtue, and they are the more set on fire to the desire of beseeching the mercy of God, in proportion as they are the more ashamed at the recollection of their own wickedness; as it often happens, that in the conflict of the fight the soldier who is placed before the eyes of his leader

basely yields to the enemy's valor, and that while he powerlessly turns his
back he is struck; yet nevertheless being ashamed of this very thing that
he has done disgracefully before his leader's eyes, from the mere sense of
shame he gathers greater force; and afterwards executes deeds of prowess,
to so high degree that he may at once achieve present credit of his valor,
and cover past disgrace of weakness. In a like way, these persons are
sometimes more actively established in the service of God by consequence
of past weakness, and such persons for the keeping of His commandments both the desire of things future draws on, and the remembrance
of things past urges forward, that on the one side affection to that which
is to come should stimulate, and, on the other, shame for that which is
past spur on. Which same however, while the enemies of the Church
see to be endowed with the highest virtues, and in their present life cannot any way find out that whereby they may derogate from their merit,
they set themselves to impeach them of the past, as the Manichaean assails
our Moses, in whom he endeavors to soil with the sin of a past homicide
the grace of subsequent virtuous attainments, in whom he heeds not how
patient he was afterwards to endure, but how precipitate he was before
to strike. Such adversaries as these blessed Job encountering with the
exactest eye of observation, after that he said, "Silver hath the beginnings
of its veins, and to gold there is a place where they fine it," he justly
added, "Iron is taken out of the earth."

Heretics are used to pride themselves against us by the self-priding
of their righteousness, and to boast high their practices with the swelling
of ostentation, and ourselves, as we have said, they impeach either for
being or having been bad persons. Accordingly in a most humble confession, and in a truthful defence against those, the holy man speaks,
saying, Iron is taken out of the earth. As if he said in plain speech:
"Men of strength, who by the sharpest swords of their tongues are
become iron in this pitched battle of the defending of the faith, were
one time but 'earth' in the lowest sphere of actions." "For to man on his
sinning it was spoken: Earth thou art, and unto earth shalt thou return."
But "iron is taken out of the earth" when the hardy champion of the
Church is separated from an earthly course of conduct, which he before
maintained. Accordingly he ought not to be involved in anything whatever
that he was, who has already begun to be that which he was not. Was not
Matthew found in the earth, who, involved in earthly matters, served the
business of the receipt of custom? But having been taken out of the
earth, he was strengthened into the forcibleness of iron, in that by his
tongue, as by the sharpest sword, the Lord in the enforcing of the Gospel
pierced the hearts of unbelievers. And he that before was weak and
contemptible by his earthly occupations, was afterwards made strong for
heavenly preachings.

Revised translation by the Editors of The World's Orators.
Published by G. P. Putnam's Sons.
Reprinted by permission.

THE MEDIAEVAL PERIOD

INTRODUCTION

There are four distinctive features to the oratory of mediae-valism, influenced by the historical events of the period. The influx of the Norsemen and the consequent political confusion within the Empire caused people to withdraw from the existing evils of the world and to occupy their thoughts with the world to come. This withdrawal resulted in the cloistered life of mediaevalism. To this influence was added oriental mysticism which also gave content to the world to come. The growth of the Empire and the Crusades which were an expression of monasticism also threw Christianity into conflict with Islamism and forced the Church to present a systematic body of doctrine and define all that Christianity meant as opposed to Islamism. A direct result of this influence was the scholasticism of the 11th century.

Each of these movements very definitely affected the pattern of oratory, for the spoken word was the agency through which each movement found expression. Therefore, although the mediaeval oratory is hardly definable as a high type of eloquence, it did serve as a link between ancient and modern oratory and as such forms a background for subsequent oratory.

Representative speeches of each type of speech current throughout the period are included here. Bede is indicative of monasticism; Tauler of mysticism; Saint Bernard of the Crusades; and Abélard of scholasticism.

SERMON ON ALL SAINTS

The Venerable Bede

(673-735 A.D.)

The Venerable Bede, the English historian, was not primarily an orator, but one of his sermons is included here as representative of the oratory of the early mediaeval period. Great stress was laid in his day on homiletical art. The selection chosen from Bede is really quite free from the subtleties of this style and is consequently more eloquent. Bede, himself, is chiefly associated with the monastery at Jarrow where he became the leading scholar of his day. In his lectures in the classroom at the monastery Bede had a charm and vivacity of delivery which endeared him to his pupils. His knowledge was largely encyclopedic and naturally was directed toward the service of the church. His method was allegorical to a large extent, and since he was adept in the use of Greek, Hebrew, and Latin, he used all of these languages in his sermons.

The sermon included here is considered Bede's best address. In the middle ages it was often read during the period of the Feast of All Saints.

To-day, beloved, we celebrate in the joy of one solemnity, the festival of All Saints: in whose companionship the heaven exults; in whose guardianship the earth rejoices; by whose triumphs Holy Church is crowned; whose confession, as braver in its passion, is also brighter in its honor,—because while the battle increased, the glory of them that fought in it was also augmented,—and the triumph of martyrdom is adorned with the manifold kind of its torments, because the more severe the pangs, the more illustrious also were the rewards; while our Mother, the Catholic Church, was taught by her Head, Jesus Christ, not to fear contumely, affliction, death; and more and more strengthened,—not by resistance, but by endurance,—inspired all of that illustrious number who suffered imprisonment or torture, with one and equal ardor to fight the battle for triumphal glory.

O truly blessed Mother Church! so illuminated by the honor of divine condescension, so adorned by the glorious blood of triumphant martyrs, so decked with the inviolate confession of snow-white virginity! Among its flowers neither roses nor lilies are wanting. Endeavor now, beloved, each for yourselves, in each kind of honor, to obtain your own dignity—crowns, snow-white for chastity, or purple for passion. In those heavenly camps, both peace and war have their own flowers wherewith the soldiers of Christ are crowned.

For the ineffable and unbounded goodness of God has provided this also, that the time for labor and for agony should not be extended,—not long, not enduring, but short, and, so to speak, momentary; that in this short and little life should be the pain and the labors, that in the life which is eternal should be the crown and the reward of merits; that the labors should quickly come to an end, but the reward of endurance should remain without end; that after the darkness of this world they should behold that most beautiful light, and should receive a blessedness greater than the bitterness of all passions; as the Apostle beareth witness, when he saith, "The sufferings of this present time are not worthy to be compared with the glory that shall be revealed in us."

With how joyous a breast the heavenly city receives those that return from flignt! How happily she meets them that bear the trophies of the conquered enemy! With triumphant men, women also come, who rose superior both to this world, and to their sex, doubling the glory of their welfare; virgins with youths, who surpassed their tender years by their virtues. Yet not they alone, but the rest of the multitude of the faithful shall also enter the palace of that eternal court, who in peaceful union have observed the heavenly commandments, and have maintained the purity of the faith.

Now, therefore, brethren, let us enter the way of life; let us return to the celestial city, in which we are citizens enrolled and inscribed. For we "are no more strangers and foreigners, but fellow-citizens of the saints, and of the household of God," "heirs of God, and joint-heirs with Christ." The gates of this city are opened to us by fortitude; and faith will afford us a broad entrance. Let us consider, therefore, the felicity of that heavenly habitation, in so far as it is possible to consider it—for to speak the truth, no words of man are sufficient to comprehend it.

Of that city it is written in a certain place thus: "that grief, and sorrow, and sighing shall flee away." What can be happier than that life where there is no fear of poverty, no weakness of disease; where none can be hurt, none can be angry; where none can envy, none can be impure; where none can be tormented with the desire of honor or the ambition of power? No fear there of the devil; no snares there of evil spirits; no terror there of hell; no death there, either of soul or body, but a life blessed in the life of immortality. No discord there forever, but all things in harmony, all things in agreement: because there will be one concord of all saints—one peace and one joy. Tranquil are all things there, and quiet. Perpetual is the splendor there; not such as the sunlight which now is, but both more glorious and more happy; because that city, as we read, needeth not the light of the sun, for the Lord God giveth it light, and its brightness is the Lamb. There, "they that be wise shall shine as the brightness of the firmament, and they that turn many to righteousness, as the stars for ever and ever."

Wherefore, there is no night there,—no darkness, no gathering of clouds, no asperity of cold or heat; but such will be the nature of things, as "eye hath not seen, nor ear heard, neither hath it entered into the heart of man," except of those who are counted worthy to inherit it, whose names are written in the Book of Life, who have washed their robes in the Blood of the Lamb, and are before the throne of God, and serve Him night and day. There is no old age there, nor misery of old age; while all "come to a perfect man, to the measure of the stature of the fulness of Christ."

But above all these things is the being associated with the companies of angels and archangels, thrones and dominations, principalities and powers, and the enjoyment of the watches of all the celestial virtues,— to behold the squadron of the saints, adorned with stars; the patriarchs, glittering with faith; the prophets, rejoicing in hope; the Apostles, who in the twelve tribes of Israel, shall judge the whole world! the martyrs, decked with the purple diadems of victory; the virgins, also, with their wreaths of beauty. But of the King, who is in the midst, no words are able to speak. That beauty, that virtue, that glory, that magnificence, that majesty, surpasses every expression, every sense of the human mind. For it is greater than the glory of all saints; but to attain to that ineffable sight, and to be made radiant with the splendor of His countenance, it were worth while to suffer torment every day—it were worth while to endure hell itself for a season, so that we might behold Christ coming in glory, and be joined to the number of the saints. So is it not then well worth while to endure earthly sorrows, that we may be partakers of such good, and of such glory?

What, beloved brethren, will be the glory of the righteous; what that great gladness of the saints, when every face shall shine as the sun; when the Lord shall begin to count over in distinct orders His people, and to receive them into the kingdom of His Father, and to render to each the rewards promised to their merits and to their works,—things heavenly for things earthly, things eternal for things temporal, a great reward for a little labor; to introduce the saints to the vision of His Father's glory; and "to make them sit down in heavenly places," to the end that God may be all in all; and to bestow on them that love Him that eternity which He hath promised to them—that immortality for which He has redeemed them by the quickening of His own blood; lastly, to restore them to Paradise, and to open the kingdom of heaven by the faith and verity of His promise!

Let these things be ingrafted firmly in our senses—be understood by the fulness of our faith—be loved with the whole heart—be acquired by perseverance of unceasing works. The thing itself lies in the power of him that acts,—because "the kingdom of heaven suffereth violence." This thing, O man, that is, the kingdom of heaven, requires no other price than thyself. It is worth what thou art worth; give thyself, and thou shalt have that. Why shouldst thou be troubled about the price? Christ surrendered Himself, that He might win thee as a kingdom to God the Father. In like manner do thou give thyself, that thou mayest become this kingdom, that "sin may not reign in thy mortal body," but the spirit may rule there, to the acquiring of life. Let it be our joy then to stretch forth after the palm of salutary works. Let us one and all willingly and readily strive in this contest of righteousness; let us run with God and Christ for spectators, and if we have already begun to rise superior to this world and this life, let us not allow our course to be retarded by any hankering after it. If the last day shall find us running without hindrance and swiftly in this race, the Lord will never deny remuneration to our merit. For He who will give a purple crown for their passion to them that conquer in persecution, the same will bestow a snow-white diadem, according to the merits of their righteousness, to them that triumph in peace. For neither Abraham, nor Isaac, nor Jacob was slain; and yet, honored by the merits of their faith and righteousness, they were reckoned the first among the patriarchs; and whoever shall be found faithful, and just, and praiseworthy, shall sit down with them at the banquet. These are the footsteps which the saints, as they were returning to their country, left behind, that, treading in their prints, we might also follow them in their joys.

Let us consider that Paradise is our country, as well as theirs; and so we shall begin to reckon the patriarchs as our fathers. Why do we not, then, hasten and run, that we may behold our country and salute our parents? A great multitude of dear ones is there expecting us; a vast and mighty crowd of parents, brothers, and children, secure now of their own safety, anxious yet for our salvation, long that we may come to their right and embrace them, to that joy which will be common to us and to them, to that pleasure expected by our fellow-servants as well as ourselves, to that full and perpetual felicity. . . . If it be a pleasure to go to them, let us eagerly and covetously hasten on our way, that we may soon be with them, and soon be with Christ: that we may have Him as our Guide in this journey, who is the Author of Salvation, the Prince of Life, the Giver of Gladness, and who liveth and reigneth with God the Father Almighty and with the Holy Ghost.

Translated by the Rev. John Mason Neale.
Published by G. P. Putnam's Sons.
Reprinted by permission.

GOD ALONE

John Tauler

(1300-1361 A.D.)

John Tauler, the famous German mystic, renounced in his youth a great fortune to enter the Dominican cloisters. Later in life he became a member of the mystic movement known as "Friends of God" and in this cause he preached with remarkable success in Strasbourg and its environs. His preaching was in the German language and was intermingled with Latin.

Tauler's mysticism was active rather than passive. It accepted silence and suffering as the most perfect work but taught primarily the love of others and accented the amelioration of society rather than asceticism. It opposed the pantheism of the mystic, Eckhart.

Tauler's sermons are some of the finest in the German language and are so simple and direct in their appeal to human nature that they are adaptable to the present day audience.

The more that a loving soul is loved by God, the more restless does it become. It is a trait of love never to be content to be inactive. Love does a great work in a man; and if it does not work it is not love. The noblest part of a man is his heart, and of this, love takes possession. That heart will know no rest until it loves God and honors and thanks and praises Him perfectly. Such is its joy; for loving the Beloved is dearer to it than its own self.

Now it is necessary to distinguish between true love and false love. This is shown by the three traits of a true living and growing love. These are observed in the will, in the intention, and in the desires of the soul. For a man must will and intend, and desire nothing whatsoever, interiorly or exteriorly, except that he love God purely and exclusively. He must refer all that he has, all that he does, to God alone; and for the reason that God is good, and that out of His goodness He made us and redeemed us by His blood. And he must thank God for the many other good things He has done us and daily continues to do us, yea, and will forever continue to do us—which spirit of thanksgiving is a yet better gift. Behold how love can have no rest or respite, but incessantly goes on, watching every chance to thank God and to praise Him, wishing to respond to His love for us, in however feeble a manner.

But this is not all. Our loving servitor will not only always keep God in view and love Him, but all creatures will be dear to him for God's sake. Besides, for God's sake he suffers all kinds of oppression and opposition. He forsakes all irregularities of life and conduct for God's everlasting honor; himself alone he never seeks under any pretext, whether in matters temporal or external. And by temporal things, we mean all desires likely to lead to sinful pleasures; for by nature, a man holds beautiful things dear and those that attract the senses, or in any wise minister joy to us. Mark well, that a loving soul is bounden to overcome all this with an eager zeal. The need of doing so is soon learned, if one will but carefully consider his life in the activity of the bodily senses, and in what things his affections are likely to go beyond his control.

The lover of Christ who aspires to be perfect, must differ from beginners in this holy love. For beginners many spiritual comforts are lawful, such as sweetnesses of devotion, and a smooth course of spiritual experience. Not so the more perfect soul; for he must seek nothing for self, no, not even what comes to him in spiritual guise. Pure love accepts nothing whatsoever for self alone; it will rest in no interior joy, nor cleave to any spiritual comfort. For this would be to put one's trust more in God's gifts than in God Himself, which is straight against upright and clean and perfect love. And it is because some men fail to practise this rightly ordered love, that God often withdraws these same gifts from them. Their souls are presently left dry, they can no longer think of God or spiritual things, and a miserable dullness settles upon them. This happens in order that they shall learn to fly to God in perfect abandonment of all spiritual joy, serve Him alone in faith, hope, and love, putting self to death. They must learn to suffer the loss of all spiritual taste. They must rely upon God's self alone, resting wholly in His goodness, thinking only of His boundless mercy; for out of that comes forth His gift of virtue to us and our power to accept it.

It is also a quality of purified love, that a soul shall have as faithful a love for God in this state of desolation as in the time of sensible grace. If this be not the case, then it is manifest that one sets greater store by the gift of God than by God Himself: this is to commit gluttony with God's grace. It is, to be sure, for our own gain that we are practising self-denial of joy in God's gifts; but nevertheless this must be without consciousness of self-interest. We must seek God's graces, His sweetness, His goodness, for an end beyond themselves, namely, to arrive by their means at the possession of the interior, spiritual good that is God's very self. He dwells in our inmost soul; and once we have gained Him there, we can come forth to the outward life of truest virtue, practising it in a spirit of detachment.   Thus it is that one first gains possession of God.

Yet we must not forget that a good man may lawfully desire devotional sweetness, according to his needs, or for God's honor, or to fit him the better for the salvation of other men's souls; for these gifts make one more zealous for virtue.   That is a motive of reasonable self love; and a reasonable enjoyment of any good thing, spiritual or bodily, is not to be blamed.

You must also know that for a beginner in the way of love it is lawful to seek for devotional sweetness, so that he may the sooner die to all the sweetness of sin.   He thus learns how good and sweet it is to seek God and Him alone, to cleave to Jesus alone, to renounce all the vanity of this earthly life, and all its sinful desires.   Thus does he learn to relish God in his devout practises.   But when God has thus gifted these souls with spiritual joy, after a while He lessens it; and then the time has come to enter on the way we have herein previously treated of. For while men still hanker after the devotional sentiments which are withdrawn from them, treating them as they do, as if they were the truest spiritual good, they can never attain to what is in very deed the truest spiritual good.   Nor can they in that way advance a single step in true virtue.   They are under self-deception; they do not really know themselves nor their sinfulness; they cannot appreciate what is or what is not permitted them; nor can they detect and resist the temptations incident to the spiritual life.   With some of these souls the end is falling helplessly into grave sins.   Now all this concerns those transitory spiritual favors, which pure and watchful love of God must not allow itself to seek after.

Listen to this: pure love must not over eagerly seek after certain eternal good things, such as the glory which shall be the heavenly reward of our good works.   It is unbecoming pure love of God, it is unbecoming perfect virtue, to seek anything for itself but God alone.   It loves and desires everything, all work, all rest, all suffering, with a single mind for God's glory.   God gives heaven, He takes heaven away; He saves, He damns: pure love has nothing to do with all this, only hoping to be saved.   Pure love has God's honor at heart and God's will; He knows best what to will and to do.   Whatsoever He wills, that He loves, and His love is the best love.   Yea, this loving soul, if it stand right in this case, would not cease to love God, to advance His glory, to practice His highest virtues, even if it thought (if such a thing were permitted or possible, which it is not), that He would condemn it to hell, there to punish its vices, never to forgive its sins.   This thought (however practically impossible), would but stimulate it to greater virtue, for it seeks itself in nothing, it thinks only of God's eternal glory in all things: such a one thus rightly observes God's first and greatest commandment.

The contrary is the case with beginners, for their love is that of the hireling, and is mixed with anxious thoughts about the future, saying:

If I could hope for no reward for my labors and penances, I would not do them. To beginners this is allowed, but not to genuine lovers. God's first commandment says that we must love God above all things, even above ourself. Whosoever will acquire this love, let him search his inner soul, let him scrutinize his outward conduct. In whatsoever thought, word or deed he finds himself falling short of this pure love, let him heartily set about his improvement. Let him aspire constantly to attain to love true and pure. In due time thou shalt have good fruit, thou shalt practice many virtues. Act otherwise, and thou shalt remain in thy defective love until God brings thee out of it, and leads thee to watchful and living love, lest thou fallest asleep in guilty ignorance. God guide us to true love. Amen.

THE DELIVERANCE OF THE HOLY LAND

Saint Bernard

(1090-1153 A.D.)

As Abbot of Clairvaux in France Saint Bernard exercised a powerful influence upon the ecclesiastical affairs of Europe. He made Innocent II pope at Rome, inducing the Emperor to take up arms in his support; he healed a schism within the church; stemmed a heresy in Languedoc; and was influential in condemning the writings of Abélard as heretical.

Primarily a mystic Saint Bernard became the embodiment of mediaeval monasticism. Because of the force and earnestness of his writings he has been called "The Last of the Fathers." He had an over-powering persuasiveness which can be only imperfectly judged from his surviving sermons which were delivered in Latin and full of biblical quotations. His adaptability made him appeal to the unlearned as well as to the learned.

At the Pope's request in 1146 Bernard preached a second crusade. Under the inspiration of his preaching King Louis VII of France and Conrad, King of the Romans, took the cross. All through northern France, the Rhine provinces, and Flanders his eloquence filled the ranks of the Crusaders.

Included here is his sermon on *The Deliverance of the Holy Land* which was preached in behalf of the Second Crusade.

You cannot but know what we live in a period of chastisement and ruin; the enemy of mankind has caused the breath of corruption to fly over all regions; we behold nothing but unpunished wickedness. The laws of men or the laws of religion have no longer sufficient power to check depravity of manners and the triumph of the wicked. The demon of heresy has taken possession of the chair of truth, and God has sent forth His malediction upon His sanctuary.

Oh, ye who listen to me, hasten then to appease the anger of Heaven, but no longer implore His goodness by vain complaints; clothe not yourselves in sackcloth, but cover yourselves with your impenetrable bucklers; the din of arms, the dangers, the labors, the fatigues of war are the penances that God now imposes upon you. Hasten then to expiate your sins by victories over the infidels, and let the deliverance of holy places be the reward of your repentance.

If it were announced to you that the enemy had invaded your cities, your castles, your lands; had ravished your wives and your daughters, and profaned your temples—which among you would not fly to arms? Well, then, all these calamities, and calamities still greater, have fallen upon your brethren, upon the family of Jesus Christ, which is yours. Why do you hesitate to repair so many evils—to revenge so many outrages? Will you allow the infidels to contemplate in peace the ravages they have committed on Christian people? Remember that their triumph will be a subject for grief to all ages and an eternal opprobrium upon the generation that has endured it. Yes, the living God has charged me to announce to you that He will punish them who shall not have defended Him against His enemies.

Fly then to arms; let a holy rage animate you in the fight, and let the Christian world resound with these words of the prophet, "Cursed be he who does not stain his sword with blood!" If the Lord calls you to the defense of His heritage think not that His hand has lost its power. Could He not send twelve legions of angels or breathe one word and all His enemies would crumble away into dust? But God has considered the sons of men, to open for them the road to His mercy. His goodness has caused to dawn for you a day of safety by calling on you to avenge His glory and His name.

Christian warriors, He who gave His life for you, to-day demands yours in return. These are combats worthy of you, combats in which it is glorious to conquer and advantageous to die. Illustrious knights, generous defenders of the Cross, remember the example of your fathers who conquered Jerusalem, and whose names are inscribed in Heaven; abandon then the things that perish, to gather unfading palms, and conquer a Kingdom which has no end.

THE DIVINE TRAGEDY

Abélard

(1079-1142 A.D.)

Scholastic philosopher, teacher, and theologian, Abélard was one of the founders of the system of scholastic philosophizing which had as its object a formally rational expression. He created enemies among the teachers who lectured in France by defeating them in debate. He overthrew Platonic realism and stressed the Aristotelian philosophy. His lectures were enlivened by illustrations which he drew from a wide range of reading. In his *Sic et Non* Abélard introduced a fashion of discussing the tenets of Christianity. His premise was that the master key of knowledge is a persistent and frequent questioning. "By doubting we come to examine and by examining we come to know the truth." Abélard was influential in the founding of the University of Paris.

Persecuted both for his doctrines and his love of Héloise, Abélard fled from monastery to monastery and finally died on his way to Rome where he was to be imprisoned by the Church.

Included here is a portion of his sermon on *The Divine Tragedy*, which shows the style of scholastic reasoning.

Whether, therefore, Christ is spoken of as about to be crowned or about to be crucified it is said that He "went forth"; to signify that the Jews, who were guilty of so great wickedness against Him, were given over to reprobation, and that His grace would now pass to the vast extent of the Gentiles, where the salvation of the Cross and his own exaltation by the gain of many peoples, in the place of the one nation of the Jews, has extended itself. Whence, also, to-day we rightly go forth to adore the Cross in the open plain, showing mystically that both glory and salvation had departed from the Jews and had spread themselves among the Gentiles. But in that we afterward returned (in procession) to the place whence we had set forth, we signify that in the end of the world the grace of God will return to the Jews; namely, when, by the preaching of Enoch and Elijah, they shall be converted to Him.

Whence the apostle: "I would not, brethren, that ye should be ignorant of this mystery, that blindness in part has fallen upon Israel, until the fulness of the Gentiles shall be come, and so all Israel shall be saved." Whence the place itself of Calvary, where the Lord was crucified, is now, as we know, contained in the city; whereas formerly it was without the walls. "The crown wherewith His Mother crowned Him in the day of His espousals, and in the day of the gladness of His heart." For thus kings are wont to exhibit their glory when they betroth queens to themselves and celebrate the solemnities of their nuptials. Now the day of the Lord's crucifixion was, as it were, the day of His betrothal; because it was then that He associated the Church to Himself as His bride, and on the same day descended into Hell, and setting free the souls of faithful, accomplished in them that which He had promised to the thief: "Verily I say unto thee, to-day shalt thou be with me in Paradise."

"To-day," He says, of the gladness of His heart, because in His body He suffered the torture of pain; but while the flesh inflicted on Him torments through the outward violence of men His soul was filled with joy on account of our salvation, which He thus brought to pass. Whence, also, when He went forth to His crucifixion He stilled the women that were lamenting Him and said, "Daughters of Jerusalem, weep not for me, but weep for yourselves and your children." As if He said, "Grieve not for me in these my sufferings, as if by their means I should fall into any real destruction; but rather lament for that heavy vengeance which hangs over you and your children because of that which they have committed against me."

So we, also, brethren, which rather weep for ourselves than for Him; and for the faults which we have committed, not for the punishments which He bore. Let us so rejoice with Him and for Him, as to grieve for our own offenses, and for that the guilty servant committed the transgression, while the innocent Lord bore the punishment. He taught us to weep who is never said to have wept for Himself, tho He wept for Lazarus when about to raise him from the dead.

BIBLIOGRAPHY OF THE PATRISTIC AND MEDIAEVAL PERIODS

Bardenhewer, Otto: *Les Pères de l'Église, leurs Vies et leurs Œuvres,* tome 1, Bloud et Barrel, Paris, 1898-99. (English translation, T. J. Shahan, B. Herder, St. Louis, 1908).

Baur, F. C.: *Church History of the First Three Centuries,* Williams and Norgate, Ltd., London, 1878-79.

Boak, Arthur: *A History of Rome to 565 A. D.,* The Macmillan Company, New York, 1929.

Brewer, D. J., ed: *The World's Best Orations,* Kaiser Company, New York, 1908.

Bury, J. B.: *The Cambridge Medieval History,* Vol. 1, "The Christian Roman Empire," The Macmillan Company, New York, 1911.

Clark, T. and T., ed: *Ante-Nicene Fathers,* The Christian Literature Company, New York, 1890.

Clayton, Joseph: *Saint Anselm,* Bruce Publishing Company, Milwaukee, 1933.

Cody, Sherwin, ed: *World's Great Orations,* McClurg and Company, Chicago, 1928.

Cubberley, E. P.: *History of Education,* Houghton, Mifflin Company, Boston, 1920.

Depew, Chauncey, ed: *Library of Oratory,* Colonial Press, New York, 1902.

Dill, Samuel: *Roman Society,* The Macmillan Company, New York, 1899.

Encyclopedia Britannica, 14th ed., Encyclopedia Britannica Company, Ltd., London, 1929.

Farrar, F. W.: *Lives of the Fathers,* The Macmillan Company, New York, 1907.

Giles, J. A., ed: *The Venerable Bede's Ecclesiastical History of England,* Bell and Daldy, London, 1871.

Holy Bible, The: King James Version.

Lee, Carleton, ed: *The World's Orators,* G. P. Putnam's Sons, New York, 1900.

Lightfoot, J. B.: *Apostolic Fathers,* The Macmillan Company, London, 1885.

Menzies, Allen: *The Ante-Nicene Fathers,* The Christian Literature Company, New York, 1886.

Migne, J. P.: *Patrologiae Cursus Completus,* P. Geuthner, Paris, 1928.

Monroe, Paul: *A Cyclopedia of Education,* The Macmillan Company, New York, 1928.

Morris, Charles, ed: *The World's Great Orators and Their Orations,* The John C. Winston Company, Philadelphia, 1917.

Munroe, Sontag: *The Middle Ages,* The Century Company, New York, 1928.

Pfeiffer, F., ed: *Deutsche Mystiker,* vol. 2, trans., C. B. Evans, Leipzig, 1845.

Platz, Mabel: *The History of Public Speaking,* Noble and Noble, New York, 1935.

Roberts, Alexander, and Donaldson, James, eds: *Ante-Nicene Fathers,* The Christian Literature Company, New York, 1885.

Robinson, James H.: *An Introduction to the History of Western Europe,* Ginn and Company, Boston, 1924.

Romestin, H. de, ed: *Nicene and Post-Nicene Fathers,* vol. 10, The Christian Literature Company. New York, 1876.

Rostovtsev, M. I.: *History of the Ancient World,* The Clarendon Press, London, 1926.

Ryssel, Victor: *Gregorius Thaumaturgus, Sein Leben and Seine Schriften,* L. Fernau, Leipzig, 1880.

Salmond, S. F., ed: *Ante-Nicene Library of the Fathers,* T. and T. Clark, Edinburgh, 1871.

Schaff, P., ed: *Nicene and Post-Nicene Fathers,* Charles Scribner's Sons, New York, 1899.

Sears, Lorenzo: *History of Oratory,* S. C. Griggs and Company, Chicago, 1896.

Thompson, James Westfall: *The Middle Ages,* Alfred A. Knopf, Inc., New York, 1931.

Welch, A. C.: *Anselm and His Work,* Charles Scribner's Sons, New York, 1901.

Wells, H. G.: *Outline of History,* The Macmillan Company, New York, 1930.

Winkworth, S.: *History and Life of John Tauler,* Allenson and Company, Ltd., London, 1905.

THE REFORMATION PERIOD

INTRODUCTION

During the fifteenth century, when the Church had attained a position of supreme authority in matters of Church and State, there arose a reaction against the power of the Church which became known as the Reformation.

Primary causes of this reaction were the growth of new nations which rebelled against the international hierarchy of the Pope; the rise of vernacular literature outside of the Church which added to the spirit of national consciousness; the revival of interest in classical antiquity through the Renaissance which encouraged an intellectual criticism of mediaeval standards, and the consequent development of individuality in the expression of art, literature, and eloquence.

This individuality crept into the Church and man emerged from his mediaeval shell into the realization that he could trust his own reason and instinct and that his individual conscience and judgment as to the implication of the Holy Scriptures should be his guide rather than the authority of the Church. Criticism of the clergy resulted and heresies arose.

This criticism attacked also the style of mediaeval preaching. The patristic fathers had used the style of exegesis, a critical detailed explanation of a text or a portion of the Scripture, with explanatory notes. During the mediaeval ages this style was superseded by the syllogistic reasoning of scholasticism, a logical analysis of disputation. The leaders of the Renaissance scoffed at this hair-splitting argument of the schoolmen.

Since the Reformation orators were largely men educated in the leading universities of the day who had imbibed the spirit of the Renaissance, it was they who largely exposed the fallacies of the scholastic doctrine. Martin Luther through his use of the vernacular in his sermons encouraged the growth of a German national popular speech and by thus turning from the Latin threw off the yoke of scholasticism. John Calvin did much the same thing for the French language, and in England where the controversies were carried on in the English rather than in the Latin language the simplicity, terseness, and power of Tyndale's version of the Bible in English set the standard of the vernacular. Since the preaching of the reformers was based on the Scriptures, it is obvious how important was this use of the vernacular in fixing the speech for succeeding generations.

The Reformation orators presented here are representative of the movement in the various countries. John Wycliffe in England, Savonarola in Italy, and John Huss in Bavaria were really forerunners of the movement; while Martin Luther in Germany, Hugh Latimer in England, John Knox in Scotland, and John Calvin and Huldreich Zwingli in Switzerland represent the movement at its crest.

Although the Reformation may be considered as closing with the Peace of Westphalia in 1648, which ended almost a century of bitter and vindictive religious strife, its influence was felt long afterward. Within the Catholic church itself there was a counter-reformation represented by Francis de Sales and a group of orators at the court of Louis XIV—Bossuet, Fléchier, Bourdaloue, and Massillon—who gained much of their prestige as a direct outgrowth of their rivalry with the reformed preachers.

SERMON ON PRAYER

John Wycliffe

(1320—1384 A.D.)

Wycliffe, called the Morning Star of the Reformation, was connected with Oxford University where his influence was powerful. He started an attack on the established order of the Church because he objected to the holding of temporal wealth by the Church and resented the relationship which the Crown of England held to the papacy and the enormous tribute which was exacted by the Church from the realm.

This leader was twice summoned before the Convocation because of his attacks on the clergy but was exonerated. Later he carried his criticism of the established order into the streets by instituting "simple priests" to preach the "plain straight-forward work of God" throughout the country and by translating the Vulgate Bible into English.

Wycliffe was a great preacher because he had the ability to impress the common people with the simplicity of his message. He built his sermons on a theme and divided them logically. This organization of a system of popular preaching was carried by Huss to Prague, and, from Huss, Martin Luther received his impulse.

The selection included here is representative of the simple, practical teaching which Wycliffe sought to foster.

Christ telleth in this Gospel how His disciples should be helped by virtue of their prayer, when He was (ascended) into heaven. And first he saith a general word, and taking both His (natures) to witness that if they ask aught of the Father of Heaven in His name, He shall give it them. But, as Christ saith, unto that time His disciples asked not in His name, and therefore afterward should they ask that their joy were full, and they should take. All the hardness of this matter is to (know) perfectly to ask in Christ's name, for he shall have that

asketh thus.   But since our Lord is truth and health of men that trust
in Him, that man asketh in Christ's name, that asketh in truth his
soul's health.   Christ is most lord of all, and therefore He will have
despite, (unless) men ask Him a great thing; for (otherwise) His lordship and that asking accord not to His name.   And so, if thou wilt ask in
Christ's name, ask the bliss that ever shall last; and since Christ is
truth and reason, look thy asking be reasonable, and then may thou
be sure to have the thing that thou asketh thus.   And therefore Christ
in this Gospel biddeth us to ask our full joy, and then shall we have
it, if that we ask in reason; for no man hath but half joy, (unless) he
be full of bliss.   And this great lord will not be asked but this bliss,
or means thereto; and if man ask thus in reason that he be worthy
to have it, he shall have it without doubt when best time were that
he had it; and he shall have on the best manner the thing that he
asketh thus.

And therefore the seven askings that Christ teacheth in the
Paternoster meaneth this form of asking; and (by all means) to ask
in charity; and therefore men that live in war are unable to have their
asking: but they ask their own (condemnation) in the fifth petition,
for there they ask that God forgive them their debt that they owe to
Him, right as they forgive men that are debtors unto them.   And here
we shall understand that each man is debtor to God, and each man
oweth to each other to do him good in charity.   And so failing to
love God of all thine heart and all thy will, thou runnest in great debt
both against God and man.   And so in this fifth asking these men
that war now-a-days, asking Him as they would mean,—forgive us
for we are even with Thee, or else take vengeance in ire of us, as we
take vengeance of our brethren.   And this is no good prayer, but
more asking of God vengeance; and for this cause many men are unheard in their prayer and are turned into more evil for their unskillful
prayer.   And such men were better to leave than to pray on such manner.
For many men pray for vengeance and for (worldly) prosperity, and in
the ire of God He giveth them that they ask; but it were better to them
to pray not thus, nor to have these things.   And thus men of (foreign)
lands pray God in great processions; and for unworthiness of their prayer
they were better to sit at home.   And, for men (know) not for what
thing they should pray God in such causes, therefore good living profiteth,
and the Holy Ghost asketh then for them.   And whoever stirreth men to
evil life, if they are friars that cry high, God heareth them not to good,
but rather to take vengeance on them.   For Christ saith, that not each
man that saith unto Him Lord, Lord, shall come into the bliss of
heaven, but he that endeth in right life, for he prayeth in the name
of the Trinity.   And thus Zebedee's sons prayed for good, but in evil
manner.   And so (by all means) right life is the best in man's prayer,
for such life prayeth better to God than the voices of hypocrites.

And after saith Christ to His Apostles, that these things He saith to them in proverbs and mistily; but now is come the time when He shall not speak thus unto them in proverbs, but openly of His Father, (and) He shall tell them as best is. In that day shall Christian men ask in Christ's name unto their bliss. And now He saith unto them that He shall pray His Father for them, for they shall be (like) to Christ and make His (kingdom). Wherefore He prayeth, that the Father love these Apostles and other men that (follow) Him, for they loved Jesus Christ and trowed that He came from God; yea, that Christ by His manhood came of God in His Godhead. Christ came from the Father and came into the world, and now when Christ hath done His message, He forsaketh again the world, and goeth by His manhood to His Father. And Christ's disciples said to Him, Lo, now Thou speakest openly, and Thou sayest now no proverb; and therefore we (know) well that Thou knowest all things, and it is to Thee no need that any man ask Thee aught, for Thou (knowest) before the asking, what men should ask and what things leave. In this we trow that Thou come from God as His own Son.

And this belief is ground to men to have of God what (they) needeth, and to (know) what is best for them, (even) if (it) displease the world. But, as men that are in fevers desire not that were best for them, so men here in sin covet not best things for them. For the world said that the Apostles were fools and forsaken of God, and so it would (say) today of men that lived like to them, for world's joy and earthly good pleaseth them, with means thereto, and they savor not heavenly good nor right (seeking) after Christ. And this judgment now in the world is open witness against men, that they be not whole in soul, but turned amiss to worldly things. For as a mouth of a sick man, distempered from good meat, moveth him to covet things contrary to his health, so it is of man's soul that savoreth not God's law. And as wanting of appetite is a sign deadly to man, so wanting of God's wit is sign of his second death. And so judgment that now reigneth of worldly prosperity is token of men that they are fools and savor not God's law. For the world saith commonly that if a man have worldly bliss and the world (laughs) to him in killing of his enemies, then God loveth him and doth miracles for his sake. But, Lord! where is our belief that we should trow in love of God, that it standeth not in this but rather hate of God! And, as Gregory saith, as a bull that shall be killed goeth in corn at his will, and is not pained nor travelled with other beasts, so a (member) of the fiend is left from the grace of God, to figure his damnation, and suffered to do much harm here, to large his pain hereafter. We should leave these sensible signs and take ensample of holy men, as of Christ and of His Apostles; how they had not their bliss here. But here Christ ordained pains and hate of the world and pursuing to men that He most loved, to teach us that come after them. And thus signs of patience and pursuing in this earth should be tokens of God's love and not signs of Anti-Christ.

Arnold's Select English Works of Wyclif.
Published by G. P. Putnam's Sons.
Reprinted by permission.

ON THE DEGENERATION OF
THE CHURCH

Girolamo Savonarola

(1452—1498 A.D.)

Savonarola, the noted Italian preacher and reformer, was the son of a court physician. As a youth he became repulsed by the avarice and greed which he saw in the rules of the Church and a disappointment in love at the age of nineteen aided him in his decision to take monastic vows at Bologna.

It was in 1492 when Savolarola went to Florence, then under the sway of Lorenzo the Magnificent, that his disgust with the luxury and wantonness of his day drove him to open denunciation. In a vision he became persuaded that he was a prophet sent from God. Although his faith in the dogma of the Roman Catholic Church never swerved, his strenuous protests against papal corruption, his reliance on the Bible as the surest guide, and his intense moral earnestness undoubtedly connect Savonarola with the Reformation.

The boldness and fervor of this preacher drew such crowds of people that Saint Mark's Cathedral in Florence could not contain them. Later Savonarola's oratory prevented Italy from falling into the hands of King Charles of France and he became the practical law-giver of all Florence. He used his power in allaying poverty, unemployment, and taxation and above all exhorted men to trust in God. His eloquence flooded the city and ascetic garb was adopted by the once frivolous Florentines; but his denunciations of Alexander's personal wickedness brought about his excommunication, and in 1498 he was burned on a cross at Florence.

Savonarola was one of the greatest preachers that ever lived. He was a religious enthusiast who had the courage to raise his voice in reproach of corruption and evil-doing. His delivery was emphatic, simple, and direct. His thoughts centered about a text around which his imagination pictured vivid scenes. His voice and gestures emphasized truths which had taken complete possession of him.

The speech included here shows the fearlessness and directness of Savonarola's preaching.

Now there is one thing only in which great delight is taken in the temple of religion. The great anxiety is that it should be all painted and gilded; thus, our churches have exterior things, many fine ceremonies in the solemnization of ecclesiastical offices, with magnificent adornments for the altars and hangings for the walls, candelabra of gold and silver, so many costly chalices and ciboriums. You behold there those great prelates with fine mitres, adorned with gold and precious gems, on their heads, with crosiers of silver. You behold them with brocaded vestments at the altar, singing our beautiful vespers and our high masses, adagio, with so many imposing ceremonies, organs, and numerous singers, that your senses are astounded; and they seem to you men of great gravity and sanctimony, and you do not believe they can err, but that which they say and do is to be observed as the precepts of the gospel; behold, to what a pass the modern church is come!

Men nurture themselves on these trivialities and recreate themselves with these ceremonies, and they say the church of Jesus Christ never flourished so much, and that divine worship was never so well performed as at the present time; as a great prelate once said that the church was never held in such honor, nor were their prelates ever in such estimation, and the first prelates of the church were only insignificant priests in comparison with the bishops of our days.

But Asaph of the Psalms, how does he feel at hearing these words? He whispers in my ear and says, "It is true the first prelates were only insignificant priests, because they were humble and poor, and they had not so many fat bishoprics and so many rich glebe possessions as our modern bishops. They had not so many mitres of gold, moreover, nor so many chalices, and even the few which they possessed they disposed of for the necessities of the poor. Our prelates, to possess chalices, take the substance of the poor, without which they cannot live."

But do you comprehend what I wish to say to you?

In the primitive church the chalices were of wood and the prelates were of gold; to-day the prelates are of wood and the chalices are of gold.

It was said once to St. Thomas of Aquinas by a great prelate, and perhaps it might be said of all who entertain similar opinions, that he exhibited a large vessel, and perhaps more than one, full of ducats, and said, "Master Thomas, look here, the church can no longer say, as St. Peter said, 'Silver and gold have I none.'" St. Thomas, in reply, said "Neither can the church say now that which follows immediately, and was said by the Apostle, 'In the name of our Lord Jesus Christ of Nazareth, arise and walk.'"

They who did these things were then only insignificant priests, as far as temporalities go, but they were great prelates, that is to say, of great virtue and sanctity, great authority; they were greatly reverenced by the people; whether on account of their virtues or of the miracles they performed. . . .

If you go to those prelati ceremoniosi of later times, they give you the best mild words you ever heard; if you condole with them on the present state of the church, that it is bad, speedily they say, "Father, you speak the truth, it will be impossible any longer to live if God does not repair the evil the faith is suffering." But internally they are full of malice, and they speak another language, and they say, "Let us remain at rest, all days are feasts of the Lord on earth:" as if they wished to say, "Let us make the feasts and solemnities of God festivals and functions of the devil; let us introduce them," they say, "with our authority, with an example, so that the true feasts and solemnities of God shall cease, and the festivals of Satan shall be honored." And they say one to another, "What think you of this our faith? what opinion have you of it?" Another replies, "You appear to me a fool. That which has been said of calamities in the church is a dream, a thing spoken of by women and of friars, e uno sogno, e cosa da femminucce, e da frati. . . . 'Che fai tu adunque, Signore? perche dormi tu? Quare abdormis, Domine? exurge, et ne repellas in finem.' . . . Lord, do you not see our tribulations? Have you become unmindful of your church? Do you love it no more? Is it no longer dear to you? It is still your spouse! Do you not recognize it? It is the same for which you came down from heaven and took up your abode in the womb of Mary, for which you took human flesh, for which you suffered all manner of opprobrium, for which you were pleased to shed your blood on the cross. Therefore, since it has cost you so much, O Lord, we beseech of you that you come speedily to liberate it."

A CHRISTMAS MEDITATION

John Huss
(1373-1415 A.D.)

John Huss, the Bohemian reformer, was educated at Prague, where he came into contact with the writings of Wycliffe, translating them into Bohemian and lecturing on them at the University and from the pulpit. As rector of Bethlehem Chapel and confessor of the Queen, Huss stood in such a prominent position that his sympathy with Wycliffe, who has been condemned as a heretic, attracted wide attention. Ultimately, because of his denunciation of the corruption of the Church, he with his followers was excommunicated. Later Huss gave out a University debate on the question of the indulgences which widened the breach between him and the clergy and also between him and the University authorities.

In 1414 Huss was summoned to Constance where he was accused as a heretic and denied the privilege of defense in an open debate. He refused to recant his statements and consequently was burned at the stake in his 46th year, and his ashes were thrown into the Rhine. So great had been his favor with the people that the reaction following his martyrdom led to the so-called Hussite War.

Huss was a popular preacher and a scholar of high repute as well as a man of irreproachable character. It has been justly said that it was he who carried the torch of the Reformation from Wycliffe and handed it on to Martin Luther. The following excerpt from his sermons is illustrative of the homiletical method which he used in his popular preaching before his congregation at Bethlehem Chapel.

To-day, as it were, an angel is saying to the shepherds: "I bring you good tidings of great joy that shall be to all people." And suddenly a multitude of the angels exclaim, saying: "Glory to God in the highest and on earth peace to men of good-will." As you commemorate these things, dearest friends, rejoice that to-day God is born a man, that there may be glory to God in the highest and on earth peace to men of good-will. Rejoice that to-day the infinitely Great One is born a child, that there may be glory to God in the highest and on earth peace to men of good-will. Rejoice that to-day a Reconciler is born to reconcile man to God, that there may be glory to God in the highest and on earth peace to men of good-will. Rejoice that to-day He is born to cleanse sinners from their sin, to deliver them from the devil's power, to lead them from eternal perdition, to bring them to eternal joy, that there may be glory to God in the highest and on earth peace to men of good-will. Rejoice with great joy that to-day is born unto us a King, to bestow in its fulness upon us the heavenly kingdom, a Bishop to grant His eternal benediction, a Father of the ages to come, to keep us as His children by His side forever: yea, there is born a Brother beloved, a wise Master, a sure Leader, a just Judge, to the end that there may be glory to God in the highest and on earth peace to men of good-will. Rejoice, ye wicked, that God is born as a Priest, who hath granted to every penitent absolution from all sins, that there may be glory to God in the highest and on earth peace to men of good-will. Rejoice that to-day the Bread of Angels—that is, God, is made the Bread of men, to revive the hungry with His body, that there may be peace among them, and on earth peace to men of good-will. Rejoice that God immortal is born, that mortal man may live forever. Rejoice that the rich Lord of the universe lies in a manger, like a poor man, that He may make us needy ones rich. Rejoice, most dearly beloved, that what the prophets prophesied has been fulfilled, that there may be glory to God in the highest and on earth peace to men of good-will. Rejoice that there is born to us a Child all powerful and that a Son is given to us full of wisdom and grace, that there may be glory to God in the highest and on earth peace to men of good-will. Oh, dearest friends, ought there to be only a moderate rejoicing over these things? Nay, a mighty joy! For indeed the angel saith: "I bring you good tidings of great joy," for that there is born a Redeemer from all misery, a Saviour from sin, a Governor of His faithful ones; there is born a Comforter for those in sorrow, and there is given to us the Son of God that we may have great joy and that there may be glory to God in the highest and on earth peace to men of good-will. May it please God born this day to grant to us His good-will, His peace, and withal, His joy.

Published by Charles Scribner's Sons.
Reprinted by permission.

DEFENSE BEFORE THE DIET
OF WORMS

Martin Luther

(1483-1546 A.D.)

Martin Luther, leader of the Reformation in Germany, was of poor peasant parentage and earned his early education at Magdeburg by the common practice of singing in the streets. After he had taken his A.B. and M.A. degrees at the University of Erfurt, Luther suddenly entered the Augustinian monastery, where he became constantly tormented by religious conflicts until he came under the influence of the mystics. In 1508 he took the degree of Doctor of Theology at the University of Wittenberg and was at once called to lecture there on Biblical Literature. His natural gift of eloquence made these lectures very popular.

On a pilgrimage to Rome in 1510 Luther was deeply impressed with the low moral standard of the Holy City and the frivolity of the papal court which was in the heyday of the artistic and literary splendor of the Renaissance. He returned to Wittenberg deeply agitated and immediately became an ardent reformer.

At this time the purchase of indulgences or papal remissions for the penalties of sin was being greatly abused in order to fill the papal treasuries. John Tetzel and other preachers were doing a brisk business in the sale of these pardons when Martin Luther opened an attack on them because of their nefarious moral and spiritual effects. The most dramatic and significant episode of the conflict was Luther's nailing of his historic 95 theses against the evils of the papacy to the doors of the Church at Wittenberg. This act led to a public controversy between Luther and Eck, the recognized apologist of the established order of the Church.

Luther's sermons became increasingly bitter and controversial and he soon enlisted the German people in his cause. In 1521 he was excommunicated and in 1521 was called to the Diet of Worms to recant his heretical statements. Upon his refusal to do so he was placed under the ban of the Empire but continued the work of his translation of the Bible into German and his reform agitations. By 1530 he had been so successful in his work that the Augsburg Confession, which laid stress on individual conscience as a means of judgment rather than the authority of the Church, was presented as the accepted faith.

Luther's manner of speech was sharp and bitter in reproof but amiable and kindly in private intercourse. He was essentially a popular preacher and sought to make his sermons appeal to even the simplest men. He had a power of observation and the ability to read character and this, coupled with his wide knowledge and gift of language, and his own powerful personality made him most effective in the pulpit.

Included here is his *Defense before the Diet of Worms.* It is recorded that Luther, after delivering the address in German, was required to repeat the entire speech in Latin, which he did in a most worthy manner.

In obedience to your commands given me yesterday, I stand here, beseeching you, as God is merciful, so to deign mercifully to listen to this cause, which is, as I believe, the cause of justice and of truth. And if through inexperience I should fail to apply to any his proper title, or offend in any way against the manners of courts, I entreat you to pardon me as one not conversant with courts, but rather with the cells of monks, and claiming no other merit than that of having spoken and written with that simplicity of mind which regards nothing but the glory of God and the pure instruction of the people of Christ.

Two questions have been proposed to me: Whether I acknowledge the books which are published in my name, and whether I am determined to defend or disposed to recall them. To the first of these I have given a direct answer, in which I shall ever persist that those books are mine and published by me, except so far as they may have been altered or interpolated by the craft or officiousness of rivals. To the other I am now about to reply; and I must first entreat your Majesty and your Highnesses to deign to consider that my books are not all of the same description. For there are some in which I have treated the piety of faith and morals with simplicity so evangelical that my very adversaries confess them to be profitable and harmless and deserving the perusal of a Christian. Even the Pope's bull, fierce and cruel as it is, admits some of my books to be innocent, though even these, with a monstrous perversity of judgment, it includes in the same sentence. If, then, I should think of retracting these, should I not stand alone in my condemnation of that truth which is acknowledged by the unanimous confession of all, whether friends or foes?

The second species of my publications is that in which I have inveighed against the papacy and the doctrine of the papists, as of men who by their iniquitous tenets and examples have desolated the Christian world, both with spiritual and temporal calamities. No man can deny or dissemble this. The sufferings and complaints of all mankind are my witnesses, that, through the laws of the Pope and the doctrines of men, the consciences of the faithful have been insnared, tortured, and torn in pieces, while, at the same time, their property and substance have been devoured by an incredible tyranny, and are still devoured without end and by degrading means, and that too, most of all, in this noble nation of Germany. Yet it is with them a perpetual statute, that the laws and doctrines of the Pope be held erroneous and reprobate when they are contrary to the Gospel and the opinions of the Fathers.

If, then, I shall retract these books, I shall do no other than add strength to tyranny and throw open doors to this great impiety, which will then stride forth more widely and licentiously than it has dared hitherto; so that the reign of iniquity will proceed with entire impunity, and, notwithstanding its intolerable oppression upon the suffering vulgar, be still further fortified and established; especially when it shall be proclaimed that I have been driven to this act by the authority of your serene Majesty and the whole Roman Empire. What a cloak, blessed Lord, should I then become for wickedness and despotism!

In a third description of my writings are those which I have published against individuals, against the defenders of the Roman tyranny and the subverters of the piety taught by men. Against these I do freely confess that I have written with more bitterness than was becoming either my religion or my profession; for, indeed, I lay no claim to any especial sanctity, and argue not respecting my own life, but respecting the doctrine of Christ. Yet even these writings it is impossible for me to retract, seeing that through such retraction despotism and impiety would reign under my patronage, and rage with more than their former ferocity against the people of God.

Yet since I am but man and not God, it would not become me to go further in defence of my tracts than my Lord Jesus went in defence of his doctrine; who, when he was interrogated before Annas, and received a blow from one of the officers, answered: "If I have spoken evil, bear witness of the evil; but if well, why smitest thou me?"

If then the Lord himself, who knew his own infallibility, did not disdain to require arguments against his doctrine even from a person of low condition, how much rather ought I, who am the dregs of the earth and the very slave of error, to inquire and search if there be any to bear witness against my doctrines! Wherefore, I entreat you, by the mercies of God, that if there be any one of any condition who has that ability, let him overpower me by the sacred writings, prophetical and evangelical. And for my own part, as soon as I shall be better instructed I will retract my errors and be the first to cast my books into the flames.

It must now, I think, be manifest that I have sufficiently examined and weighed, not only the dangers, but the parties and dissensions excited in the world by means of my doctrine, of which I was yesterday so gravely admonished. But I must avow that to me it is of all others the most delightful spectacle to see parties and dissensions growing up on account of the word of God, for such is the progress of God's word, such its ends and object. "Think not I am come to send peace on earth; I came not to send peace, but a sword. For I am come to set a man at variance against his father, and the daughter against her mother, and the daughter-in-law against her own household."

Moreover we should reflect that our God is wonderful and terrible in his counsels; so that his work, which is now the object of so much solicitude, if we should found it in the condemnation of the word of God, may be turned by his providence into a deluge of intolerable calamity; and the reign of this young and excellent prince (in whom is our hope after God) not only should begin, but should continue and close under the most glowing auspices.

I could show more abundantly by reference to Scriptural examples— to those of Pharaoh, the King of Babylon, the kings of Israel—that they have brought about their own destruction by those very counsels of worldly wisdom which seemed to promise them peace and stability. For it is he who taketh the wise in their craftiness and removeth the mountains, and they know not, and overturneth them in his anger. So that it is the work of God to fear God. Yet I say not these things as if the great personages here present stood at all in need of my admonitions, but only because it was a service which I owed to my native Germany, and it was my duty to discharge it. And thus I commend myself to your serene Majesty and all the princes, humbly beseeching you not to allow the malice of my enemies to render me odious to you without a cause. I have done. . . .

Since your most serene Majesty and the princes require a simple answer, I will give it thus: Unless I shall be convinced by proofs from Scripture or by evident reason—for I believe neither in Popes nor councils, since they have frequently both erred and contradicted themselves—I cannot choose but adhere to the word of God, which has possession of my conscience; nor can I possibly, nor will I ever make any recantation, since it is neither safe nor honest to act contrary to conscience! Here I stand; I cannot do otherwise; so help me God! Amen.

THE SERMON ON THE PLOW

Hugh Latimer

(1490-1555 A.D.)

Hugh Latimer, the English reformer, was a graduate of Cambridge University and was won to the Reformation not so much by its doctrinal views, for he had a natural distaste for theological discussion, but because of a sincere desire to improve the moral condition of the people. Latimer restricted his preaching to the inculcation of practical righteousness and the censure of abuse, and soon wielded a powerful influence on the learned and unlearned alike. He had a ready and formidable wit which frequently disconcerted his opponents.

In 1529 at Cambridge he preached his two *Sermons on the Cards* which started a violent controversy at the University, but Henry VIII, whose marriage to Catherine of Aragon Latimer had defended, protected him and appointed him royal chaplain. In 1535 Latimer was appointed Bishop of Worcester and at the convocation preached two powerful and impressive sermons urging the necessity of reform. Thereafter he was looked upon with jealousy and so closely watched that a sermon which he preached in London furnished opportunity to bring him to trial, and have him excommunicated and imprisoned. He was again released at the King's intervention and later was influential in securing Henry's repudiation of the authority of the Pope. Latimer continued his preaching to which crowds of people thronged in London and its environs. Upon the accession of Mary, however, he was summoned to appear before the council, was tried, and condemned to be burned at the stake.

Latimer's sermons are classics and are valuable historically because they portray the social and political life of the period. His style was vivid, witty, and terse, and yet sagacious in its religious advice on human conduct.   The sermon included here is one of the most favorable examples of Latimer's pulpit style and power.

Preaching of the Gospel is one of God's plow-works, and the preacher is one of God's plowmen.   Ye may not be offended with my similitude, in that I compare preaching to the labor and work of plowing, and the preacher to a plowman.   Ye may not be offended with this my similitude, for I have been slandered of some persons for such things.   But as preachers must be wary and circumspect, that they give not any just occasion to be slandered and ill-spoken of by the hearers, so must not the auditors be offended without cause.   For Heaven is in the Gospel likened to a mustard seed; it is compared also to a piece of leaven; and Christ saith that at the last day he will come like a thief.   And what dishonor is this to God?   Or what derogation is this to Heaven?   Ye may not, then, I say, be offended with my similitude for because I liken preaching to a plowman's labor, and a prelate to a plowman.

But now you will ask me whom I call a prelate.   A prelate is that man, whatever he be, that hath a flock to be taught of him; whosoever hath any spiritual charge in the faithful congregation, and whosoever he be that hath cure of souls.   And well may the preacher and the plowman be likened together: First, for their labor at all seasons of the year; for there is no time of the year in which the plowman hath not some special work to do—as in my country, in Leicestershire, the plowman hath a time to set forth, and to assay his plow, and other times for other necessary works to be done.   And then they also may be likened together for the diversity of works and variety of offices that they have to do.   For as the plowman first setteth forth his plow, and then tilleth his land, and breaketh it in furrows, and sometimes ridgeth it up again; and at another time harroweth it and clotteth it, and sometimes dungeth it and hedgeth it, diggeth it and weedeth it, purgeth it and maketh it clean; so the prelate, the preacher, hath many diverse offices to do.   He hath first a busy work to bring his parishioners to a right faith, as Paul calleth it; and not a swerving faith, but to a faith that embraceth Christ, and trusteth to his merits; a lively faith; a justifying faith; a faith that maketh a man righteous without respect of works; as ye have it very well declared and set forth in the homily. He hath then a busy work, I say, to bring his flock to a right faith, and then to confirm them in the same faith—now casting them down with the law, and with threatenings of God for sin; now ridging them up again with the Gospel, and with the promises of God's favor; now weeding them by telling them their faults, and making them forsake sin; now clotting them, by breaking their stony hearts, and by making soft hearts, and apt for doctrine to enter in; now teaching them to know

God rightly, and to know their duty to God and their neighbors; now exhorting them when they know their duty that they do it, and be diligent in it; so that they have a continual work to do.

Great is their business, and, therefore, great should be their hire. They have great labors, and, therefore, they ought to have good livings, that they may commodiously feed their flock—for the preaching of the Word of God unto the people is called meat. Scripture calleth it meat, not strawberries, that come but once a year, and tarry not long, but are soon gone—but it is meat; it is no dainties. The people must have meat that must be familiar and continual, and daily given unto them to feed upon. Many make a strawberry of it, ministering it but once a year; but such do not the office of good prelates. For Christ saith: "Who think you is a wise and faithful servant? He that giveth meat in due time." So that he must at all times convenient preach diligently; therefore, saith he: "Who trow ye is a faithful servant?" He speaketh it as though it were a rare thing to find such a one, and as though he should say there be but few of them to find in the world. And how few of them there be throughout this world that give meat to their flock as they should do, the visitors can best tell. Too few, too few, the more is the pity, and never so few as now.

By this, then, it appeareth that a prelate, or any that hath cure of souls, must diligently and substantially work and labor. Therefore saith Paul to Timothy: "He that desireth to have the office of a bishop, or a prelate, that man desireth a good work." Then, if it be a good work, it is work; ye can but make a work of it. It is God's work, God's plow, and that plow God would have still going. Such, then, as loiter and live idly are not good prelates or ministers. And of such as do not preach and teach and do their duties, God saith by his prophet Jeremy: "Cursed be the man that doeth the work of God fraudulently, guilefully, or deceitfully;" some books have it "negligenter," "negligently," or "slackly." How many such prelates, how many such bishops, Lord, for thy mercy, are there now in England! And what shall we in this case do? Shall we company with them? O Lord, for thy mercy! Shall we not company with them? O Lord, whither shall we flee from them? But "cursed be he that doeth the work of God negligently or guilefully." A sore word for them that are negligent in discharging their office or have done it fraudulently; for there is the thing that maketh the people ill. . . .

And now I would ask a strange question: Who is the most diligent bishop and prelate in all England that passeth all the rest in doing his office? I can tell, for I know him who he is; I know him well. But now I think I see you listening and hearkening that I should name him. There is one that passeth all the others, and is the most diligent prelate and preacher in all England. And will ye know who it is? I will tell you; it is the devil. He is the most diligent preacher of all others; he is never out of his diocese; he is never from his care; ye shall never find him unoccupied; he is ever in his parish; he keepeth residence at all times; ye shall never find him out of the way; call for him when you will, he is ever at home; the diligentest preacher in all the realm; he is ever at his plow; no lording nor loitering can hinder him; he is ever applying his business; ye shall never find him idle, I warrant you!

From The World's Great Orators and Their
Orations by Charles Morris.
Courtesy of the John Winston Company.

GOD'S POWER OVER THAT OF KINGS

John Knox

(1505-1572 A.D.)

John Knox, representative of the reformation in Scotland, is one of the most picturesque figures in the history of the movement. He was a Roman Catholic until 1542, but after that time became a zealous preacher of the reform doctrines. He attended Glasgow University, where he studied for the Church, but his gifts as a preacher were first fully realized at the parish church of St. Andrews, where his voice rang out in severest denunciation of popery. When the castle of St. Andrews was taken by the French fleet, Knox was made a galley slave for 19 months. At the request of King Edward VI he was released, returned to England, and was appointed a royal chaplain. Here he associated with Cranmer and other reformers. On Queen Mary's accession to the throne Knox was driven to the continent where he became a friend of John Calvin in Geneva. On his return to Scotland in 1559 he became the leader of the Reformation there and did not flinch before royalty and bitterly attacked the idolatries of the Church.

Knox's sermons are attacks on morals and manners of Christian living. At times they are overly logical and at times his strong sense of humor becomes savagely sarcastic, but these qualities are mitigated by a kindly tenderness. He also had indomitable courage and sagacity and one of his auditors remarked that Knox in his preaching put more life in him than could 600 trumpets.

The last important utterance of Knox was his sermon upon securing the news of the massacre of St. Bartholomew's Day, when his last strength was summoned to condemn the cruel and barbarous act. The Earl of Morton in delivering the funeral oration for Knox stated "here lies one who in all his life never feared the face of man."

Included here is a fragment of a sermon preached in Edinburgh on the text Isaiah 26:13-16 which shows his dauntless courage in the face of autocracy.

The first thing then, that God requires of him who is called to the honor of a king, is the knowledge of His will revealed in His Word.

The second is an upright and willing mind, to put in execution such things as God commands in His law, without declining to the right or to the left hand.

Kings, then, have not an absolute power to do in this government what pleases them, but their power is limited by God's Word; so that if they strike where God has not commanded, they are but murderers; and if they spare where God has commanded to strike, they and their thrones are criminal and guilty of the wickedness which abounds upon the face of the earth, for lack of punishment.

Oh that kings and princes would consider what account shall be craved of them, as well for their ignorance and misknowledge of God's will as for the neglecting of their office!

Wouldst thou, O Scotland! have a king to reign over thee in justice, equity, and mercy? Subject thou thyself to the Lord thy God, obey His commandments, and magnify thou the Word that calleth unto thee, "This is the way, walk in it;" and if thou wilt not, flatter not thyself; the same justice remains this day in God to punish thee, Scotland, and thee, Edinburgh, especially, which before punished the land of Judah and the city of Jerusalem. Every realm or nation, saith the prophet Jeremiah, that likewise offendeth shall be likewise punished, but if thou shalt see impiety placed in the seat of justice above thee, so that in the throne of God (as Solomon complains) reigns nothing but fraud and violence, accuse thine own ingratitude and rebellion against God; for that is the only cause why God takes away "the strong man and the man of war, the judge and the prophet, the prudent and the aged, the captain and the honorable, the counselor and the cunning artificer; and I will appoint," saith the Lord, "children to be their princes, and babes shall rule over them. Children are extortioners of my people, and women have rule over them."

If these calamities, I say, apprehend us, so that we see nothing but the oppression of good men and of all godliness, and that wicked men without God reign above us, let us accuse and condemn ourselves, as the only cause of our own miseries. For if we had heard the voice of the Lord our God, and given upright obedience unto the same, God would have multiplied our peace, and would have rewarded our obedience before the eyes of the world. But now let us hear what the prophet saith further: "The dead shall not live," saith he, "neither shall the tyrants, nor the dead arise, because thou hast visited and scattered them, and destroyed all their memory."

From The World's Great Orators and Their Orations by Charles Morris.
Courtesy of the John Winston Company.

ON MERCENARY SOLDIERS

Huldreich Zwingli
(1484-1531 A.D.)

Huldreich Zwingli, the Swiss reformer, was hailed by his friends as the undoubted Cicero of his age because of his profound knowledge of the classics and his pulpit ability. After his education at Bern, Vienna, and Basle he was elected parish priest of Glarus, where he remained for ten years. During this time he also served as chaplain in the War of Lombardy in the cause of the Pope against France. His active work as a reformer began in 1516 at Einsiedeln where he became incensed at the practices associated with the pilgrimages to the miraculous image of the Virgin. At Zurich he preached a series of sermons against the errors and superstitions of the times which laid the foundations of his work as a reformer, and by 1525 the Reformation was practically victorious in that city.

Zwingli engaged in many public debates—one at Bern against the Romanists lasted 19 days; his famous debate with Luther at Marbourg delivered over the significance of the Eucharist resulted in the formation of two camps in the protestant movement and added to the agitation which culminated in a civil war between the Catholics and Reformers in the cantons of Switzerland. It was in this way that Zwingli, who was serving as chaplain for the Evangelical faction, was slain.

Zwingli used the Swiss dialect in his preaching, but showed his knowledge of the classics by frequently quoting Greek and Hebrew in his sermons. He was forceful and energetic in his delivery.

The foreign lords have so wheedled and enticed us, simple confederates, seeking their own profit, that at length they have brought us into such danger and disagreement between ourselves that we, not regarding our fatherland, have more care how to maintain them in their wealth and power than to defend our own houses, wives, and children. And this were less had we not shame and damage out of this pact. We have at Naples, at Navarre, at Milan, suffered greater loss in the service of these masters than since we have been a Confederacy; in our own wars we have been ever conquerors, in foreign wars often vanquished; such evils, it is to be feared, have been brought about by those who seek more their own private gain than the true interests of their country.

Let each one for himself reflect on the evils of war and think how it would be with him if he were treated in the manner in which we use our fellow Christians. Think, now, that a foreign mercenary came into thy land with violence; laid waste thy meads, thy fields, thy vineyards; drove off thy cattle; bound thy house furniture together and carted it away; slew thy son in the attack, who would defend himself and thee; violated the chastity of thy daughters; kicked with his feet the dear wife of thy bosom, who went before thee and fell down at the feet of this foreign soldier, begging mercy for thee and herself; dragged out thyself, pious, worthy, old man, even in thine own house and home, from the place where thou wert crouching in fear, knocked thee down in presence of thy wife, despite her cries, and despite thine own trembling, venerable, pleading gray hairs; and then at last set fire to thy dwelling and burned it to the ground,—wouldst thou not think within thyself, if the Heaven did not open and spit fire on such villainy, if the earth did not yawn and swallow up such monsters, there were no God? And yet thou doest all this to another and callest it, forsooth, "the right of war!"

Those who, for truth, religion, justice, and native country, venture their lives in war, are true men, and their cause is sacred. But as for those bloodthirsty, mercenary soldiers who take the field for gain, of whom the world is now full, and those wars which princes carry on, from day to day, out of lust of power, filling the earth with bloodshed, I, for my part, not only can not approve them, but I believe there is nothing more wicked and criminal, and have the opinion that such men deserve to be branded as highway robbers, and that they are unworthy of the name of Christians.

The second danger that threatens us from the foreign lords and their wars is that justice between man and man is stopped; and an old proverb says, "When arms are up in the hands, laws are under the feet." The term "right of war" means nothing but violence, use it as you will, turn it over as you will. Yet it is objected—force must be employed to reduce the disobedient if they refuse to yield obedience to things lawful and right. Yea, verily, it were good it went no farther, and that the thunderbolt of war struck these alone, and that each forced only the disobedient to obedience in things lawful. But what sayest thou of the man who takes money and helps a foreign master to plunder, lay waste, and rob those who have done him no injury whatever; nay, who carries his sword to such masters whom it does not become to go to war at all, bishops, popes, abbots, and this, too, for vile money? Further, the foreign lords do prejudice to the cause of justice in so far that their gifts blind the eyes of every man, be he as wise as you will, and deprive him of his reason as well as of his piety; as Moses teaches, "A gift doth blind the eyes of the wise and pervert the words of the righteous."

The third danger is that with foreign money and foreign wars our manners will become corrupted and debased. This we see very clearly, for our people have never returned from the foreign wars without bringing something new in clothes for themselves and their wives, or without importing home some new extravagance in eating and drinking, some new oaths; the bad they see and learn with readiness, so that we have reason to fear, if these wars be not desisted from, we shall be inundated with still worse evils.

The morality of the women, too, is corrupted. A woman is a weak creature, and desirous of new, handsome things, ornaments, fine clothes, jewels (as we see in Dinah, who went to Sechem out of curiosity, and was there humbled), and when such like things are made to flash in their eyes, and offered to them, think you that they will not be moved by these things, and that the temptation will not be too strong for them? It is to be feared, too, that in time the number of the males will be diminished, altho as yet this has been less noticeable. But at least they are unmanned by luxury. Now no one will work to obtain a living, the lands are out of cultivation, and lie waste in many places, because laborers are not to be got, altho there be people enough, and a land that could well nourish us all. If it bear not cinnamon, ginger, malmsey, cloves, oranges, silk, and other such dainties for the palate, it bears at least butter, milk, horses, sheep, cattle, lint, wine, and corn, and that to the full, so that we can rear a fine, strong race of men, and as to what we want in our own country we can obtain it elsewhere against our own produce. That we do not hold to this comes from the selfishness that has been introduced among us, and which leads us on from labor to idleness.

And yet to work is noble: it saves from wantonness and vice; it yields good fruit, so that a man can richly nourish his body without care, and without the fear that he sully himself with the blood of the innocent, and live by it. It makes the body, too, hale and strong, dissipates diseases engendered by idleness, and last of all, fruit and increase follow the hand of the worker, as creation itself came from the hand of the all-working God at the beginning, so that, in external things, there is nothing in the universe so like God as the worker.

It is to selfishness we owe it that all our strength and power, which ought to defend our country, are consumed in the service of foreign masters. Behold how unlike we are to our ancestors! These would not suffer foreign masters in their land, but now we lead them in among us by the hand, if they have but money, that some may get hold of the money while many get the stripes. And when a pious man has brought up a well-doing son, then come the captains and steal him away, and he must expose himself to the danger of dying of hunger, disease, murder, shot, or wounds. And if he reckon up his bargained money he will find he could have won more by threshing, without speaking of his being run through the body with a spear ere the account comes to be paid; and last of all, his poor old father that brought him up, and whom he should have maintained in his old age, is reduced to carry the beggar's staff.

But those who get the money want for nothing. They force us into alliances with foreign masters, but only after they themselves have been bought over by heavy bribes. And, when it comes to loss, your neighbor or your neighbor's son must bear it, while they come off scotfree. And altho it stands in the conditions that none is to be forced, yet recruiting parties spread themselves over the whole land, and then it is seen what young blood will do when it is up. And with the remuneration it is to be taken into account that those who get the largest bribes conceal them, but, these living in riot and expense, another, who thinks he can not be less than they, goes to the like expense. And if he can not afford this, then he is at the mercy of the briber, who at last takes his vineyard, fields, and meadows. Then he helps him to a small pension, on which he can not live, and so, having lost his all, he must in the end face war and wounds for a wretched pay. In this manner we lose our best sons, who for vile money are consumed in a foreign land. But few, indeed, become rich, but these so rich that they might buy off the rest.

The fourth danger is that the gifts of the foreign lords breed hatred and distrust among us. The Almighty granted to our ancestors grace and favor in his sight, so that they freed themselves from a tyrannous nobility and lived in concord with one another. They prospered; while right and justice were so well administered in this land that all who were oppressed in foreign countries fled hither as to an asylum of safety. Then fear seized the hearts of the princes, who would not themselves act justly, and who yet stood in awe of our bold and unflinching attitude. But seeing that the Lord was strong on our side, so that they could not overcome us by force, they seduced us by the bait of bribes, and reduced us by enslaving us first to selfishness. They laid their schemes and considered that if one of us were to see a friend or a neighbor suddenly growing rich without any trade or profession, and living at his ease in riches, he, too, would be stirred up, in order that he might dress finely, live in idleness, carousing, and wantonness, like his neighbor; to hunt after riches (for all men incline naturally against work and toward idleness), and that, if the like riches were not vouchsafed to him, he would join himself to the ranks of their opponents; that in this manner disunion would be created, so that father should be against son, brother against brother, friend against friend, neighbor against neighbor, and then that the kingdom, as the Son of God himself says, thus divided against itself, would not stand, and there would be an end of the Confederacy. This was what they calculated upon.

And if any one should inquire, "How are we to deliver ourselves from these evils, and return again to union?"—I answer, "By abstaining from selfishness. For, if this base passion did not reign among us, the Confederacy were more a union of brothers than of confederates. If one rejoins to this, Selfishness is implanted in the human heart, from whence it can not be eradicated, for God alone can know and change the heart, then I answer, "Do earnestly that which lies in your power. Where you find it punishable, punish it, and let it not grow. And that it may be extirpated out of the very hearts of men, give heed that the divine Word be faithfully preached."

For where God is not in the heart there is nothing but the man himself. Where there is nothing but the man himself, he cares for nothing but that which serves to his interests, pleasures, and lusts. But when God possesses the heart, then man has regard to that which pleases God, seeks the honor of God, and the profit of his fellow man. Now, the knowledge of God can come to us in no way clearer than from the Word of God. Will you, then, have the knowledge of God spread among you, so that you may live in peace and in the fear of God? Then see to it that the Word of God is purely preached, according to its natural sense, unadulterated by the glosses and inventions of man.

SERMON ON ENDURING PERSECUTION

John Calvin

(1519-1564 A.D.)

In the 16th century the city of Geneva, Switzerland, was often termed Protestant Rome and here it was that John Calvin, who may well be ranked as second only to Luther among the reformers, did his greatest work. Calvin was educated and designed for the Roman clergy, but at a very early age he dissented from the theology of his church and began to preach the doctrines of protestantism. Forced to leave France he adopted Geneva as his home. Here he met Farel, the Elijah of the French reformation, who likewise had taken refuge in Geneva where he had introduced the reformed faith. By the year 1541 Calvin's rule of Geneva became undisputed. His *Institutes of the Christian Religion* became the basis of Calvinism as the reformed religion in Switzerland; for a protracted dispute between Calvin and Luther had resulted in a break of the reformers into Calvinists and Lutherans.

Calvin is often described as a cold stern man and his sermons seem to reflect a like character. Their style is clear, calm, and logical—unimaginative yet full of intense earnestness and piety. A concept of Calvin's style may be gained from the *Sermon on Enduring Persecution* quoted here.

All the exhortations which can be given us to suffer patiently for the name of Jesus Christ, and in defense of the gospel, will have no effect if we do not feel assured of the cause for which we fight. For when we are called to part with life it is absolutely necessary to know on what grounds. The firmness necessary we cannot possess unless it be founded on certainty of faith.

It is true that persons may be found who will foolishly expose themselves to death in maintaining some absurd opinions and reveries conceived by their own brain, but such impetuosity is more to be regarded as frenzy than as Christian zeal; and, in fact, there is neither firmness nor sound sense in those who thus, at a kind of haphazard, cast themselves away. But, however this may be, it is in a good cause only that God can acknowledge us as his martyrs. Death is common to all, and the children of God are condemned to ignominy and tortures just as criminals are; but God makes the distinction between them, inasmuch as he cannot deny his truth.

On our part, then, it is requisite that we have sure and infallible evidence of the doctrine which we maintain; and hence, as I have said, we cannot be rationally impressed by any exhortations which we receive to suffer persecution for the gospel, if no true certainty of faith has been imprinted in our hearts. For to hazard our life upon a peradventure is not natural, and though we were to do it, it would only be rashness, not Christian courage. In a word, nothing that we do will be approved of God if we are not thoroughly persuaded that it is for him and his cause we suffer persecution and the world is our enemy.

Now, when I speak of such persuasion, I mean not merely that we must know how to distinguish between true religion and the abuses or follies of men, but also that we must be thoroughly persuaded of the heavenly life, and the crown which is promised us above, after we shall have fought here below. Let us understand, then, that both of these requisites are necessary, and cannot be separated from each other. The points, accordingly, with which we must commence, are these: We must know well what our Christianity is, what the faith which we have to hold and follow—what the rule which God has given us; and we must be so well furnished with such instructions as to be able boldly to condemn all the falsehoods, errors, and superstitions which Satan has introduced to corrupt the pure simplicity of the doctrine of God. Hence we ought not to be surprised that, in the present day, we see so few persons disposed to suffer for the gospel, and that the greater part of those who call themselves Christians know not what it is. For all are as it were lukewarm, and, instead of making it their business to hear or read, count it enough to have had some slight taste of Christian faith. This is the reason why there is so little decision, and why those who are assailed immediately fall away. This fact should stimulate us to inquire more diligently into divine truth, in order to be well assured with regard to it.

Still, however, to be well informed and grounded is not the whole that is necessary. For we see some who seem to be thoroughly imbued with sound doctrine, and who, notwithstanding, have no more zeal or affection than if they had never known any more of God than some fleeting fancy. Why is this? Just because they have never comprehended the majesty of the holy Scriptures. And, in fact, did we, such as we are, consider well that it is God who speaks to us, it is certain that we would listen more attentively and with greater reverence. If we would think that in reading Scripture we are in the school of angels, we would be far more careful and desirous to profit by the doctrine which is propounded to us.

We now see the true method of preparing to suffer for the gospel. First, We must have profited so far in the school of God as to be decided in regard to true religion and the doctrine which we are to hold; and we must despise all the wiles and impostures of Satan, and all human inventions, as things not only frivolous but also carnal, inasmuch as they corrupt Christian purity; therein differing, like true martyrs of Christ, from the fantastic persons who suffer for mere absurdities. Second, Feeling assured of the good cause, we must be inflamed, accordingly, to follow God whithersoever he may call us: His word must have such authority with us as it deserves, and, having withdrawn from this world, we must feel as it were enraptured in seeking the heavenly life.

But it is more than strange that, though the light of God is shining more brightly than it ever did before, there is a lamentable want of zeal! If the thought does not fill us with shame, so much the worse. For we must shortly come before the great Judge, where the iniquity which we endeavor to hide will be brought forward with such upbraidings that we shall be utterly confounded. For, if we are obliged to bear testimony to God according to the measure of the knowledge which he has given us, to what is it owing, I would ask, that we are so cold and timorous in entering into battle, seeing that God has so fully manifested himself at this time that he may be said to have opened to us and displayed before us the great treasures of his secrets? May it not be said that we do not think we have to do with God? For had we any regard to his majesty we would not dare to turn the doctrine which proceeds from his mouth into some kind of philosophic speculation. In short, it is impossible to deny that it is to our great shame, not to say fearful condemnation, that we have so well known the truth of God and have so little courage to maintain it!

Above all, when we look to the martyrs of past times, well may we detest our own cowardice! The greater part of those were not persons much versed in holy Scripture, so as to be able to dispute on all subjects. They knew that there was one God, whom they behoved to worship and serve; that they had been redeemed by the blood of Jesus Christ, in order that they might place their confidence of salvation in him and in his grace; and that, all the inventions of men being mere dross and rubbish, they ought to condemn all idolatries and superstitions. In one word, their theology was in substance this: There is one God, who created all the world, and declared his will to us by Moses and the Prophets, and finally by Jesus Christ and his apostles; and we have one sole Redeemer, who purchased us by his blood, and by whose grace we hope to be saved; all the idols of the world are cursed and deserve execration.

With a system embracing no other points than these, they went boldly to the flames or to any other kind of death. They did not go in twos or threes, but in such bands that the number of those who fell by the hands of tyrants is almost infinite. We, on our part, are such learned clerks, that none can be more so (so at least we think), and, in fact, so far as regards the knowledge of Scripture, God has so spread it out before us that no former age was ever so highly favored. Still, after all, there is scarcely a particle of zeal. When men manifest such indifference it looks as if they were bent on provoking the vengeance of God.

What, then, should be done in order to inspire our breasts with true courage? We have, in the first place, to consider how precious the Confession of our Faith is in the sight of God. We little know how much God prizes it, if our life, which is nothing, is valued by us more highly. When it is so, we manifest a marvellous degree of stupidity. We cannot save our life at the expense of our confession without acknowledging that we hold it in higher estimation than the honor of God and the salvation of our souls.

A heathen could say that "it was a miserable thing to save life by giving up the only things which made life desirable!" And yet he and others like him never knew for what end men are placed in the world and why they live in it. It is true they knew enough to say that men ought to follow virtue, to conduct themselves honestly and without reproach; but all their virtues were mere paint and smoke. We know far better what the chief aim of life should be, namely, to glorify God, in order that he may be our glory. When this is not done, woe to us! And we cannot continue to live for a single moment upon the earth without heaping additional curses on our heads. Still we are not ashamed to purchase some few days to languish here below, renouncing the eternal kingdom by separating ourselves from him by whose energy we are sustained in life.

Were we to ask the most ignorant, not to say the most brutish persons in the world, why they live, they would not venture to answer simply that it is to eat and drink and sleep; for all know that they have been created for a higher and holier end. And what end can we find if it be not to honor God, and allow ourselves to be governed by him, like children by a good parent; so that after we have finished the journey of this corruptible life we may be received into his eternal inheritance? Such is the principal, indeed the sole end. When we do not take it into account, and are intent on a brutish life, which is worse than a thousand deaths, what can we allege for our excuse? To live and not know why is unnatural. To reject the causes for which we live, under the influence of a foolish longing for a respite of some few days, during which we are to live in the world while separated from God—I know not how to name such infatuation and madness.

But as persecution is always harsh and bitter, let us consider how and by what means Christians may be able to fortify themselves with patience, so as unflinchingly to expose their life for the truth of God. The text which we have read out, when it is properly understood, is sufficient to induce us to do so. The Apostle says, "Let us go forth from the city after the Lord Jesus, bearing his reproach." In the first place he reminds us, although the swords should not be drawn over us nor the fires kindled to burn us, that we cannot be truly united to the Son of God while we are rooted in this world. Wherefore, a Christian, even in repose, must always have one foot lifted to march to battle, and not only so, but he must have his affections withdrawn from the world, although his body is dwelling in it. Grant that this at first sight seems to us hard, still we must be satisfied with the words of St. Paul, "We are called and appointed to suffer." As if he had said, "Such is our condition as Christians; this is the road by which we must go if we would follow Christ."

Meanwhile, to solace our infirmity and mitigate the vexation and sorrow which persecution might cause us, a good reward is held forth: In suffering for the cause of God we are walking step by step after the Son of God and have him for our guide. Were it simply said that to be Christians we must pass through all the insults of the world boldly, to meet death at all times and in whatever way God may be pleased to appoint, we might apparently have some pretext for replying, "It is a strange road to go at a peradventure." But when we are commanded to follow the Lord Jesus, his guidance is too good and honorable to be refused. Now, in order that we may be more deeply moved, not only is it said that Jesus Christ walks before us as our Captain, but that we are made comformable to his image; as St. Paul speaks in the eighth chapter to the Romans, "God hath ordained all those whom he hath adopted for his children, to be made conformable to him who is the pattern and head of all."

Are we so delicate as to be unwilling to endure anything? Then we must renounce the grace of God by which he has called us to the hope of salvation. For there are two things which cannot be separated, —to be members of Christ and to be tried by many afflictions. We certainly ought to prize such a conformity to the Son of God much more than we do. It is true that in the world's judgment there is disgrace in suffering for the gospel. But since we know that unbelievers are blind, ought we not to have better eyes than they? It is ignominy to suffer from those who occupy the seat of justice, but St. Paul shows us by his example that we have to glory in scourgings for Jesus Christ, as marks by which God recognises us and avows us for his own. And we know what St. Luke narrates of Peter and John, namely, that they rejoiced to have been "counted worthy to suffer infamy and reproach for the name of the Lord Jesus."

Ignominy and dignity are two opposites: so says the world which, being infatuated, judges against all reason, and in this way converts the glory of God into dishonor. But, on our part, let us not refuse to be vilified as concerns the world, in order to be honored before God and his angels. We see what pains the ambitious take to receive the commands of a king, and what a boast they make of it. The Son of God presents his commands to us, and every one stands back! Tell me, pray, whether in so doing are we worthy of having anything in common with him? There is nothing here to attract our sensual nature, but such, notwithstanding, are the true escutcheons of nobility in the heavens. Imprisonment, exile, evil report, imply in men's imagination whatever is to be vituperated; but what hinders us from viewing things as God judges and declares them, save our unbelief? Wherefore let the Name of the Son of God have all the weight with us which it deserves, that we may learn to count it honor when he stamps his marks upon us. If we act otherwise our ingratitude is insupportable.

Were God to deal with us according to our deserts, would he not have just cause to chastise us daily in a thousand ways? Nay, more, a hundred thousand deaths would not suffice for a small portion of our misdeeds! Now, if in his infinite goodness he puts all our faults under his foot and abolishes them, and, instead of punishing us according to our demerit, devises an admirable means to convert our afflictions into honor and a special privilege, inasmuch as through them we are taken into partnership with his Son, must it not be said, when we disdain such a happy state, that we have indeed made little progress in Christian doctrine?

Accordingly St. Peter, after exhorting us to walk so purely in the fear of God as "not to suffer as thieves, adulterers, and murderers," immediately adds, "If we must suffer as Christians, let us glorify God for the blessing which he thus bestows upon us." It is not without cause he speaks thus. For who are we, I pray, to be witnesses of the truth of God, and advocates to maintain his cause? Here we are poor worms of the earth, creatures full of vanity, full of lies, and yet God employs us to defend his truth—an honor which pertains not even to the angels of heaven! May not this consideration alone well inflame us to offer ourselves to God to be employed in any way in such honorable service?

Many persons, however, cannot refrain from pleading against God, or, at least, from complaining against him for not better supporting their weakness. It is marvellously strange, they say, how God, after having chosen us for his children, allows us to be so trampled upon and tormented by the ungodly. I answer: Even were it not apparent why he does so, he might well exercise his authority over us and fix our lot at his pleasure. But when we see that Jesus Christ is our pattern, ought we not, without inquiring further, to esteem it great happiness that we are made like to him? God, however, makes it very apparent what the reasons are for which he is pleased that we should be persecuted. Had we nothing more than the consideration suggested by St. Peter, we were disdainful indeed not to acquiesce in it. He says, "Since gold and silver, which are only corruptible metals, are purified and tested by fire, it is but reasonable that our faith, which surpasses all the riches of the world, should be tried."

It were easy indeed for God to crown us at once without requiring us to sustain any combats; but as it is his pleasure that until the end of the world Christ shall reign in the midst of his enemies, so it is also his pleasure that we, being placed in the midst of them, shall suffer their oppression and violence till he deliver us. I know, indeed, that the flesh kicks when it is to be brought to this point, but still the will of God must have the mastery. If we feel some repugnance in ourselves it need not surprise us; for it is only too natural for us to shun the cross. Still let us not fail to surmount it, knowing that God accepts our obedience, provided we bring all our feelings and wishes into captivity and make them subject to him.

When the prophets and apostles went to death it was not without feeling within some inclination to recoil. "They will lead thee whither thou wouldst not," said our Lord Jesus Christ to Peter. When such fears of death arise within us, let us gain the mastery over them, or rather let God gain it; and meanwhile let us feel assured that we offer him a pleasing sacrifice when we resist and do violence to our inclinations for the purpose of placing ourselves entirely under his command. This is the principal war in which God would have his people to be engaged. He would have them strive to suppress every rebellious thought and feeling which would turn them aside from the path to which he points. And the consolations are so ample that it may well be said we are more than cowards if we give way.

In ancient times vast numbers of people, to obtain a simple crown of leaves, refused no toil, no pain, no trouble; nay, it even cost them nothing to die, and yet every one of them fought for a peradventure, not knowing whether he was to gain or lose the prize. God holds forth to us the immortal crown by which we may become partakers of his glory. He does not mean us to fight at haphazard, but all of us have a promise of the prize for which we strive. Have we any cause, then, to decline the struggle? Do we think it has been said in vain, "If we die with Jesus Christ we shall also live with him?" Our triumph is prepared, and yet we do all we can to shun the combat.

THE PASSION OF CHRIST

Louis Bourdaloue

(1632-1704 A.D.)

The French Jesuit preacher, Bourdaloue, was one of the great pulpiteers of the reign of Louis XIV. Educated in the Society of Jesus he joined the order and acted as professor of theology and philosophy in the Jesuit College of Bourges. In 1669 he was called to Paris to occupy the pulpit of the church of St. Louis, where his eloquence was so marked that he was called to the Court of Louis XIV and preached frequently before the King. After the revocation of the Edict of Nantes, Bourdaloue went to Languedoc to convert the Protestants back to Catholicism.

Particularly outstanding were his Lenten sermons preached at Montpellier in 1686. His frankness and sincerity won him friends among Protestants as well as Catholics. He knew how to adapt his eloquence to his audience and was equally a favorite with the common people and the learned and great; yet he never spared vice whether on the throne or in the gutter. He had the attributes of solidity and close reasoning, zeal, piety, and earnestness. Unlike Bossuet, he did not excel in the funeral sermon, but rather in sermons with appeal to conscience and reason. The latter years of his life, which was one of great saintliness, sweetness, and gentleness, he devoted to service in hospitals, prisons, and charitable societies.

Included here is a portion of one of Bourdaloue's most famous sermons preached before King Louis XIV, which shows his manner of applying his topic.

The Passion of Jesus Christ, however sorrowful and ignominious it may appear to us, must nevertheless have been to Jesus Christ himself an object of delight, since this God-man, by a wonderful secret of his wisdom and love, has willed that the mystery of it shall be continued and solemnly renewed in his Church until the final consummation of the world. For what is the Eucharist but a perpetual repetition of the Saviour's Passion, and what has the Saviour supposed in instituting it, but that whatever passed at Calvary is not only represented but consummated on our altars? That is to say, that he is still performing the functions of the victim anew, and is every moment virtually sacrificed, as though it were not sufficient that he should have suffered once. At least that his love, as powerful as it is free, has given to his adorable sufferings that character of perpetuity which they have in the Sacrament, and which renders them so salutary to us. Behold, Christians, what the love of a God has devised; but behold, also, what has happened through the malice of men! At the same time that Jesus Christ, in the sacrament of his body, repeats his holy Passion in a manner altogether mysterious men, the false imitators, or rather base corrupters of the works of God, have found means to renew this same Passion, not only in a profane, but in a criminal, sacrilegious, and horrible manner!

Do not imagine that I speak figuratively. Would to God, Christians, that what I am going to say to you were only a figure, and that you were justified in vindicating yourselves to-day against the horrible expressions which I am obliged to employ! I speak in the literal sense; and you ought to be more affected with this discourse, if what I advance appears to you to be overcharged; for it is by your excesses that it is so, and not by my words. Yes, my dear hearers, the sinners of the age, by the disorders of their lives, renew the bloody and tragic Passion of the Son of God in the world; I will venture to say that the sinners of the age cause to the Son of God, even in the state of glory, as many new passions as they have committed outrages against him by their actions! Apply yourselves to form an idea of them; and in this picture, which will surprise you, recognize what you are, that you may weep bitterly over yourselves! What do we see in the Passion of Jesus Christ? A divine Saviour betrayed and abandoned by cowardly disciples, persecuted by pontiffs and hypocritical priests, ridiculed and mocked in the palace of Herod by impious courtiers, placed upon a level with Barabbas, and to whom Barabbas is preferred by a blind and inconstant people, exposed to the insults of libertinism, and treated as a mock-king by a troop of soldiers equally barbarous and insolent; in fine, crucified by merciless executioners! Behold, in a few words, what is most humiliating and most cruel in the death of the Saviour of the world! Then tell me if this is not precisely what we now see, of what we are every day called to be witnesses. Let us resume; and follow me.

Betrayed and abandoned by cowardly disciples: such, O divine Saviour, has been thy destiny. But it was not enough that the Apostles, the first men whom thou didst choose for thine own, in violation of the most holy engagement, should have forsaken thee in the last scene of thy life; that one of them should have sold thee, another renounced thee, and all disgraced themselves by a flight which was, perhaps, the most sensible of all the wounds that thou didst feel in dying. This wound must be again opened by a thousand acts of infidelity yet more scandalous. Even in the Christian ages we must see men bearing the character of thy disciples, and not having the resolution to sustain it; Christians, prevaricators, and deserters from their faith; Christians ashamed of declaring themselves for thee, not daring to appear what they are, renouncing at least in the exterior what they have professed, flying when they ought to fight; in a word, Christians in form, ready to follow thee even to the Supper when in prosperity, and while it required no sacrifice, but resolved to abandon thee in the moment of temptation. It is on your account, and my own, my dear hearers, that I speak, and behold what ought to be the subject of our sorrow.

A Saviour mortally persecuted by pontiffs and hypocritical priests. Let us not enter, Christians, into the discussion of this article, at which your piety would, perhaps, be offended, and which would weaken or prejudice the respect which you owe to the ministers of the Lord. It belongs to us, my brethren, to meditate to-day on this fact in the spirit of holy compunction; to us consecrated to the ministry of the altars, to us priests of Jesus Christ, whom God has chosen in his Church to be the dispensers of his sacraments. It does not become me to remonstrate in this place. God forbid that I should undertake to judge those who sustain the sacred office! This is not the duty of humility to which my condition calls me. Above all, speaking as I do, before many ministers, the irreprehensible life of whom contributes so much to the edification of the people, I am not yet so infatuated as to make myself the judge, much less the censor of their conduct. But though it should induce you only to acknowledge the favors with which God prevents you, as a contrast, from the frightful blindness into which he permits others to fall, remember that the priests, and the princes of the priests, are those whom the Evangelist describes as the authors of the conspiracy formed against the Saviour of the world, and of the wickedness committed against him. Remember that this scandal is notoriously public, and renewed still every day in Christianity. Remember, but with fear and horror, that the greatest persecutors of Jesus Christ are not lay libertines, but wicked priests; and that among the wicked priests, those whose corruption and iniquity are covered with the veil of hypocrisy are his most dangerous and most cruel enemies. A hatred, disguised under the name of zeal and covered with the specious pretext of observance of the law, was the first movement of the persecution which the Pharisees and the priests raised against the Son of God. Let us fear lest the same passion should blind us! Wretched passion, exclaims St. Bernard, which spreads the venom of its malignity even over the most lovely of the children of men, and which could not see a God upon earth without hating him! A hatred not only of the prosperity and happiness, but what is yet more strange, of the merit and perfection of others! A cowardly and shameful passion, which, not content with having caused the death of Jesus Christ, continues to persecute him by rending his mystical body, which is the Church; dividing his members, which are believers; and stifling in their hearts that charity which is the spirit of Christianity! Behold, my brethren, the subtle temptation against which we have to defend ourselves, and under which it is but too common for us to fall!

A Redeemer reviled and mocked in the palace of Herod by the impious creatures of his court! This was, without doubt, one of the most sensible insults which Jesus Christ received. But do not suppose, Christians, that this act of impiety ended there. It has passed from the court of Herod, from that prince destitute of religion, into those even of Christian princes. And is not the Saviour still a subject of ridicule to the libertine spirits which compose them? They worship him externally, but internally how do they regard his maxims? What idea have they of his humility, of his poverty, of his sufferings? Is not virtue either unknown or despised? It is not a rash zeal which induces me to speak in this manner; it is what you too often witness, Christians; it is what you perhaps feel in yourselves; and a little reflection upon the manners of the court will convince you that there is nothing that I say which is not confirmed by a thousand examples, and that you yourselves are sometimes unhappy accomplices in these crimes.

Herod had often earnestly wished to see Jesus Christ. The reputation which so many miracles had given him excited the curiosity of this prince, and he did not doubt but that a man who commanded all nature might strike some wonderful blow to escape from the persecution of his enemies. But the Son of God, who had not been sparing of his prodigies for the salvation of others, spared them for himself, and would not say a single word about his own safety. He considered Herod and his people as profane persons, with whom he thought it improper to hold any intercourse, and he preferred rather to pass for a fool than to satisfy the false wisdom of the world. As his kingdom was not of this world, as he said to Pilate, it was not at the court that he designed to establish himself. He knew too well that his doctrine could not be relished in a place where the rules of worldly wisdom only were followed, and where all the miracles which he had performed had not been sufficient to gain men full of love for themselves and intoxicated with their greatness. In this corrupted region they breathe only the air of vanity; they esteem only that which is splendid; they speak only of preferment: and on whatever side we cast our eyes, we see nothing but what either flatters or inflames the ambitious desires of the heart of man.

What probability then was there that Jesus Christ, the most humble of all men, should obtain a hearing where only pageantry and pride prevail? If he had been surrounded with honors and riches, he would have found partisans near Herod and in every other place. But as he preached a renunciation of the world both to his disciples and to himself, let us not be astonished that they treated him with so much disdain. Such is the prediction of the holy man Job, and which after him must be accomplished in the person of all the righteous; "the upright man is laughed to scorn." In fact, my dear hearers, you know that, whatever virtue and merit we may possess, they are not enough to procure us esteem at court. Enter it, and appear only like Jesus Christ clothed with the robe of innocence; only walk with Jesus Christ in the way of simplicity; only speak as Jesus Christ to render testimony to the truth, and you will find that you meet with no better treatment there than Jesus Christ. To be well received there, you must have pomp and splendor. To keep your station there, you must have artifice and intrigue. To be favorably heard there, you must have complaisance and flattery. Then all this is opposed to Jesus Christ; and the court being what it is, that is to say, the kingdom of the prince of this world, it is not surprising that the kingdom of Jesus Christ cannot be established there. But woe to you, princes of the earth! Woe to you, men of the world, who despise this incarnate wisdom, for you shall be despised in your turn, and the contempt which shall fall upon you shall be much more terrible than the contempt which you manifest can be prejudicial.

Published by the Colonial Press.
Reprinted by permission.

FUNERAL ORATION ON MARSHAL TURENNE

Esprit Fléchier

(1632-1710 A.D.)

Esprit Fléchier, the French ecclesiastic who became best known as Bishop of Nîmes, does not rank as high as Bourdaloue or Bossuet, but, like Bossuet, he excelled in the funeral sermon. He was appointed reader to the Dauphin by Louis XIV and made a member of the French Academy. It was through his efforts, leniency, and tact that the Edict of Nantes was greatly softened.

Fléchier's style is ingenious and witty, inclined to the grandness of the French preachers who employed art to enhance the effectiveness of their sermons. He may be accused of affectation and an excessive use of antithesis, but his style nevertheless remains clear in spite of this ornateness, and his own delivery of his sermons made them most effective.

Among Fléchier's funeral orations the most celebrated are those delivered on the death of M. de Montausier, the wife of his patron; the Duchess d'Aiguillon; and the one on Marshal Turenne, which is included here. This sermon is expressive of the ornate rhetorical school of oratory, and the diction is therefore highly polished. Marshal Turenne, who had been a Protestant before he was converted to the Catholic faith, had on three outstanding occasions been most valiant in the service of France.

I cannot, gentlemen, at the outset, give you a higher idea of the mournful subject with which I am about to occupy your attention, than by citing the noble and expressive terms used by Holy Scripture to praise the life and deplore the death of the sage and valiant Maccabaeus, the man who spread the glory of his nation to the ends of the earth; who covered his camp with a buckler, and forced that of the enemy with the sword; who gave mortal grief to the kings leagued against him, and rejoiced Jacob with those virtues and exploits, the memory of which shall endure forever.

This man, who defended the cities of Judah, who subdued the pride of the children of Ammon and Esau, and returned loaded with the spoils of Samaria, after having burned upon their own altars the gods of foreign nations; this man, whom God had thrown around Israel like a wall of iron, against which all the hordes of Asia had so frequently dashed themselves to pieces; who, after he had defeated numerous armies, and disconcerted the proudest and most accomplished generals of the King of Syria, came annually like the least of the Israelites, to repair, with his own triumphant hands, the ruins of the sanctuary, and desired no other recompense for the services he had rendered his country, than the honor of having served it; this valiant man, while driving before him, with invincible courage, the enemies whom he had reduced to a shameful flight, at last received a mortal wound, and remained buried, as it were, in his own triumph. At the first report of this disaster, all the cities of Judah were moved, and floods of tears ran from the eyes of all the inhabitants. For a time they were confounded, dumb, and motionless. At length breaking the long and mournful silence, in a voice interrupted by sobs, they gave utterance to the grief, the pity and fear, which oppressed their hearts, and exclaimed: "Why is that great man dead, who saved the people of Israel?" At this cry, Jerusalem redoubled its weeping; the arches of the temple trembled; Jordan was troubled, and all its banks reechoed the sound of those mournful words: "Why is that great man dead, who saved the people of Israel?"

Christians, whom a mournful ceremony has assembled in this place, do you not call to mind what you saw and felt five months ago? Do you not recognize yourselves in the affliction which I have described, and in your minds substitute for the hero spoken of in Scripture him of whom I purpose to speak? The virtues and the fate of the one resemble those of the other, and to the latter nothing is wanting to-day but a eulogy worthy of him. Oh, if the Spirit divine, Spirit of power and truth, should enrich my discourse with those natural and vivid images which represent virtue, and, at the same time, persuade to its practice, with what lofty conceptions should I fill your minds, and what noble impressions should I communicate to your hearts, by the recital of so many edifying and glorious actions!

What subject was ever better fitted to receive all the ornaments of a grave and solemn eloquence than the life and death of the high and mighty Prince Henry de la Tour d'Auvergne, Viscount Turenne, Marshal-general of the Camps and Armies of the King, and Colonel-general of the Light Cavalry? Where else shine with such lustre the glorious results of military virtue, the conduct of armies, sieges of castles, storming of cities, passages of rivers, bold attacks, honorable retreats, well-ordered encampments, vigorous combats, battles gained, enemies vanquished by force, scattered by address, or worn out and consumed by a sage and lofty prudence? Where else can be found such numerous and striking examples, than in the action of a man wise, modest, liberal, disinterested, devoted to the service of his king and country, great in adversity by his fortitude, in prosperity by his moderation, in difficulties by his prudence, in danger by his valor, in religion by his piety?

What subject can inspire sentiments more just and affecting than a death so sudden and surprising; a death which suspended the course of our victories, and dissipated the fondest hopes of peace? Powerful enemies of France, ye live, and the spirit of Christian charity forbids me to cherish a wish for your death. Only may ye recognize the justice of our arms, accept the peace which, in spite of your losses, ye have so often refused, and in the abundance of your tears extinguish the fires of a war which ye have unfortunately kindled. God forbid that I should extend my wishes further. Inscrutable are the judgments of God! But ye live; and I mourn in this pulpit, a wise and virtuous General, whose intentions were pure, and whose virtue seemed to merit a longer life and a more extended career.

But let us suppress our complaints; it is time to commence his eulogy, and to show how that powerful man triumphed over the enemies of the State by his bravery, over the passions of his soul by his wisdom, over the errors and vanities of the world by his piety. If I interrupt the order of my discourse, pardon a little confusion in a subject which has caused us so much grief. I may sometimes confound the general of the army with the sage and the Christian. I shall praise now his victories, and now the virtues which gained them. If I cannot rehearse all his actions, I shall discover them in their principles; I shall adore the God of armies, I shall invoke the God of peace, I shall bless the God of mercy, and through the whole I shall win your attention, not by the force of eloquence, but by the reality and greatness of the virtues about which I shall speak.

Do not suppose, gentlemen, that I shall follow the custom of orators, and praise M. de Turenne as ordinary men are praised. If his life had less of glory, I shall dwell upon the grandeur and nobility of his house; and if his portrait were less beautiful, would discover those of his ancestors. But the glory of his actions effaces that of his birth, and the smallest praise that can be given him is, that he sprang from the ancient and illustrious house of Tour d'Auvergne, which has mingled its blood with that of kings and emperors, has given rulers to Aquitaine, princes to all the courts of Europe, and queens even to that of France. But what do I say? It is not for me to praise him in this respect; it is for me to mourn him. How glorious was the source from which he took his rise! The heresy of recent times had, however, infected it, and he received with noble blood principles of error and falsehood, and even among the members of his household he found some ignoring and some combating the truth. Let us not make the matter of his

eulogy that which was for him an occasion for penitence; let us see
the paths of glory and honor which the providence of God opened
to him in the world before His mercy recalled him from the ways of
perdition and the mistakes of his fathers.

Before his fourteenth year he began to carry arms. Sieges and
battles were the exercises of his youth, and his first amusements were
victories. Under the discipline of his maternal uncle, the Prince of
Orange, he learned the art of war, in the quality of a simple soldier,
and neither pride nor indolence restrained him from one of the employments which required labor and obedience. He was seen in this
lowest rank of military service, neither refusing any labor, nor dreading
any peril; doing from a sense of honor what others did from necessity,
and distinguishing himself from them only by a greater attachment to
fatigue and a nobler application to all his duties.

Then commenced a life whose career was yet to become so glorious,
like those rivers which deepen and expand the farther they extend from
their source, and which carry wealth and prosperity to all the regions
through which they flow. From that time, he lived only for the glory
and welfare of his country. He performed all the services which could
be expected from a mind firm and active, lodged in a robust and
healthy frame. In his youth he had all the prudence of mature age,
and in his mature age all the vigor of youth. His days were full, to
use the language of Scripture; and as he did not lose his early years
in luxury and pleasure, he was not compelled to spend his last in
weakness and inactivity.

What enemy of France has not felt the effects of his valor, and
what part of our frontier has not served as the theatre of his glory?
He crosses the Alps, and in the famous actions of Casal, of Turin, and
of the rout of Quiers, he signalizes himself by his courage and prudence.
Italy regards him as one of the principal instruments of those great and
prodigious successes which posterity will scarcely credit. He passes
from the Alps to the Pyrenees, to aid in the conquest of two important
places, which puts one of our finest provinces under protection from
all the efforts of Spain. He goes to collect, beyond the Rhine, the
remnants of a defeated army; he takes cities, and assists in gaining
battles. Thus by degrees, and by his own merit, he rises to supreme
command, and shows, during the whole course of his life, what can
be done for the defense of a kingdom by a general who is rendered
worthy to command by obeying, and who joins to courage and genius
application and experience.

Then it was that his mind and heart displayed all their energies.
Whether called to prepare matters, or to decide them; to pursue victory
with ardor, or wait for it with patience; whether to counteract the
designs of the enemy by bravery, or dissipate the fears and jealousies
of his allies by wisdom; whether to control himself amid the successes
or sustain himself amid the reverses, of war;—his soul was always equal

to the occasion. He had only to change virtues when fortune changed her face; elated, but without pride; depressed, but with dignity; almost equally admirable when, with judgment and boldness, he saved the remains of his troops beaten at Mariandel, as when he himself beat the Imperials and the Bavarians; or when, with triumphant troops, he forced all Germany to ask peace from France. . . .

Let us follow this prince in his last campaigns, during which so many difficult enterprises, so many glorious successes, are to be regarded as proofs of his courage, and rewards of his piety. To commence his marches with prayer, to repress impiety and blasphemy, to protect sacred persons and property against the insolence and avarice of the soldiers, to invoke in every danger the God of armies, is the common care and duty of all generals. But he goes far beyond this. Even while commanding the army, he regards himself as a simple soldier of Jesus Christ. He sanctifies wars by the purity of his intentions, by the desire of a happy peace, and by the laws of Christian discipline. He looks upon his soldiers as his brethren, and believes himself under obligation to exercise Christian charity in a cruel profession, wherein general humanity itself is lost. Animated by these lofty motives, he surpasses himself, and proves that courage becomes firmer when sustained by the principles of religion, that there is a pious magnanimity which wins success in spite of perils and obstacles, and that a warrior is invincible when he combats with faith and stretches forth pure hands to the God of armies, who protects him.

As from God he derives all his glory, so to Him he returns it all, and cherishes no other confidence than that which is founded on the divine approbation. Here let us set before you one of those critical occasions, when he attacks with a small number of troops the entire forces of Germany! He marches three days, crosses three rivers, meets the enemy, and gives them battle. With numbers on one side, and valor on the other, fortune is long doubtful. At last courage fires the multitude; the enemy is confused, and begins to yield. "Victory!" shouts a voice. At once the General checks all emotion which gives ardor to battle, and in a severe tone says: "Silence! Our fate is not in our own hands, and we ourselves will be vanquished, if God does not succor us!" With these words, he raises his hands to heaven, whence cometh help, and continuing to give his orders, he waits, with submission between hope and fear, for the execution of heaven's will.

How difficult it is to be at once victorious and humble! Military success leaves in the mind I know not what exquisite pleasure, which fills and absorbs it. In such circumstances one attributes to himself a superiority of force and capacity. He crowns himself with his own hands; he decrees to himself a secret triumph; he regards as his own the laurels which he gathers with infinite toil and frequently moistens with his blood; and even when he renders to God solemn thanks and hangs in His temples the torn and bloodstained trophies which he has taken from the enemy, is not vanity liable to stifle a portion of his gratitude, and mingle with the vows which he pays to God applauses which he thinks due to himself; at least does he not retain some grains of the incense which he burns upon His altars?

It was on such occasions that Marshal Turenne, renouncing all pretensions, returned all the glory to Him to whom it legitimately belongs. If he marches, he acknowledges that it is God who protects and guides him; if he defends fortresses, he knows that he defends them in vain if God does not guard them; if he makes an intrenchment, he feels that it is God who forms a rampart around him to defend him from every attack; if he fights, he knows whence to draw all his force; and if he triumphs, he thinks that he sees an invisible hand crowning him from heaven. Referring thus all the favors he receives to their origin, he thence derives new blessings. No longer does he fear the enemies by whom he is surrounded; without being surprised at their numbers or strength, he exclaims with the prophet: "Some trust in their horses and chariots, but we will trust in the Almighty." In this steadfast and just confidence he redoubles his ardor, forms great designs, executes great things, and begins a campaign which appears as if it must prove fatal to the empire.

He passes the Rhine, and eludes the vigilance of an accomplished and prudent general. He observes the movements of the enemy. He raises the courage of the allies, and controls the suspicions and vacillating faith of neighboring powers. He takes away from the one the will, from the other the means, of injuring him; and profiting by all those important conjunctures which prepare the way for great and glorious events, he leaves to fortune nothing which human skill and counsel can take from it. Already the enemy tremble in their camp, confused and disconcerted. Already has that eagle whose bold approach once alarmed our provinces, taken its flight to the mountains. Those brazen mouths, invented by hell for the destruction of men, thunder on all sides, to favor and precipitate the retreat; and France in suspense awaits the success of an enterprise which, according to all the rules of war, must be infallible.

Alas! we knew all that we might hope, but we knew not all that we might fear. Divine Providence concealed from us a calamity greater than the loss of a battle. It was to cost a life which each of us would have been willing to redeem with his own: and all that we could gain was of less value than what we were to lose. O God! terrible but just in Thy counsels toward the children of men, Thou disposest of victors and victories! To fulfil Thy pleasure, and cause us to fear Thy judgments, Thy power casts down those whom it has lifted up. Thou sacrificest to Thy Sovereign Majesty the noblest victims, and strikest, at Thy pleasure, those illustrious heads which Thou hast so often crowned!

Do not suppose, gentlemen, that I am about to open here a tragic scene: to represent that great man stretched upon his own trophies; to uncover that body, blood-stained and ghastly, over which still lingers the smoke of the thunder which struck it; to cause his blood, like that of Abel's, to cry from the ground, or expose to your eyes the mournful images of your country and religion in tears! In slight losses, we may thus surprise the pity of our auditors, and by studied efforts draw from their eyes a few forced and useless tears. But we describe without art a death which we mourn without deceit. Every one finds in himself the source of his grief, and reopens his own wound; and it is not necessary to excite the imagination in order to affect the heart.

Here I am almost forced to interrupt my discourse. I am troubled, gentlemen! Turenne dies! All is confusion; fortune vacillates; victory leaves us; peace takes its flight; the good intentions desire only to adore! But Thou art just, and Thou hast afflicted us. And in an age so corrupt as ours, we need not seek the causes of our calamities elsewhere than in the evil of our ways.

Let us then, gentlemen, derive from our sorrows motives for penitence, and seek only true and substantial consolation in the piety of that great man. Citizens, strangers, enemies, nations, kings, and emperors, mourn and revere him. Yet what can all this contribute to his real happiness? His King even—and such a King!—honors him with his regrets and tears: a noble and precious mark of affection and esteem for a subject, but useless to a Christian. He shall live, I acknowledge, in the minds and memories of men; but the Scripture teaches me that the thoughts of man, and man himself, are but vanity. A magnificent tomb may enclose his piteous remains; but he shall rise again from that superb monument, not to be praised for his heroic exploits, but to be judged according to his works, whether good or bad. His ashes shall mingle with those of the numerous kings who governed the kingdom which he so generously defended; but, after all, what remains under those precious marbles, any more to those kings than to him, of human applause, the pomp of courts, or the splendor of fortune, except an eternal silence, a frightful solitude, and a terrible expectation of the judgment of God? Let the world, then, honor as it will the glory of man, God only is the recompense of faithful Christians.

O death, too sudden! nevertheless, through the mercy of God, long anticipated: of how many edifying words and holy examples hast thou deprived us! We might have seen him, sublime spectacle! a Christian, dying humbly in the midst of triumphs and victories. With what profound sincerity would he have mourned his past errors, abasing himself before the majesty of God, and imploring the succor of His arm, no longer against visible enemies, but against the enemies of his salvation! His living faith and fervent charity, doubtless, would have deeply affected our hearts; and he might have remained to us a model of confidence without presumption, of fear without feebleness, of penitence without artifice, of constancy without affectation, and of a death precious in the sight both of God and man.

Are not these conjectures just? They were involved in his character. They were his cherished designs. He had resolved to live in a manner so holy that it is presumed he would have died in the same way. Ready to cast all his crowns at the feet of Jesus Christ like the conquerors in the Apocalypse, ready to gather together all his honors and dispossess himself of them by a voluntary renunciation, he was no longer of the world, though Providence retained him in it. In the tumult of armies, he solaced himself with the sweet and secret aspirations of solitude. With one hand he smote the Amalekites, and with the other, stretched out to heaven, he drew down the blessing of God. This Joshua, in battle, already performed the functions of Moses upon the Mount, and under the arms of a warrior bore the heart and will of a penitent.

O God! who piercest the profoundest depths of our conscience, and seest the most secret intentions of our hearts, even before they are formed, receive into the bosom of Thy glory that soul, ever occupied with thoughts of Thine eternity! Honor those desires which Thou Thyself didst inspire. Time failed him, but not the courage to fulfil them. If Thou requirest works with desires, behold the charities which he made or destined for the comfort and salvation of his brethren; behold the misled souls which, by his assistance, his counsel, and by his example, he brought back to Thee; behold the blood of Thy people which he so frequently spared; behold his own blood which he so generously shed on our behalf; and yet more than all, behold the blood shed for him by Jesus Christ.

Ministers of God, complete the holy Sacrifice! Christians, redouble your vows and prayers, that God, as a recompense of his toils, may admit his spirit to the place of everlasting repose, and give him an infinite peace in heaven, who three times procured for us a peace on earth, evanescent it is true, yet ever delightful, ever desirable!

Translated by the Associate Editor of The World's Orators.
Published by G. P. Putnam's Sons.
Reprinted by permission.

FUNERAL ORATION ON THE PRINCE DE CONDÉ

Jacques Bénigne Bossuet
(1627-1704 A.D.)

The great French pulpiteer, Bossuet, became the champion in France of the Roman Church and made it the great aim of his life to convert Protestants back to the Catholic faith. At the College of Jesuits in Dijon and at the College of Navarre in Paris, where he was educated, Bossuet distinguished himself as a classical scholar and as an extraordinary orator. After his schooling he was ordained into the priesthood, undertook a mission to Lorraine and later for three years preached in the Convent of St. Thomas Aquinas in Paris. The fame of his preaching brought him to the attention of King Louis XIV, who in 1669 appointed him instructor to the Dauphin and in 1681 aided his nomination to the bishopric of Meaux. Through his eloquence in a sermon on *The Unity of the Church* delivered to the assembly of the French clergy in 1682 Bossuet was able to secure freedom for the Gallician church and the privileges claimed by the King against the prerogatives of the Pope.

Bossuet is often considered the greatest ecclesiastical orator in history. He was gifted with a rich and pleasing voice, a beautiful and commanding personal appearance, grace and charm of manner, and complete self-control. He had an unusual grasp of his subject matter and remarkable ability in the use of beautiful metaphors. These qualities coupled with his sincere religious enthusiasm made him a most powerful and eloquent speaker.

Among his numerous controversies was one, not altogether irreprehensible, with Fénelon, a former pupil of his, against the movement known as Pietism. Bossuet had a special gift in the composition and delivery of funeral orations. Outstanding

among these are his orations on the deaths of the Queen
Dowager of England, wife of Charles I; and of her daughter,
the Duchess of Orleans; and of the Prince of Condé, one of the
greatest captains of the 17th century. The latter oration is included here, for it is usually considered his masterpiece. It was
delivered in the church of Notre Dame in Paris, March 10, 1687,
and was Bossuet's last.

In beginning this address, in which I purpose to celebrate the immortal glory of Louis de Bourbon, Prince de Condé, I feel myself
overweighted both by the grandeur of the subject and, to be frank, by
the fruitlessness of the effort. What part of the inhabited world has
not heard of the victories of the Prince de Condé and the wonders of
his life? They are recounted everywhere; the Frenchman who boasts
of them in the presence of the foreigner tells him nothing which the
latter does not know; and in no matter how exalted a strain I might
sound his praises, I should still feel that in your hearts you were convinced that I deserved the reproach of falling far short of doing him
justice. An orator, feeble as he is, cannot do anything for the perpetuation of the glory of extraordinary souls. Le Sage was right when
he said that "their deeds alone can praise them"; no other praise is
of any effect where great names are concerned; and it needs but the
simple story of his deeds faithfully recorded to sustain the glory of
the Prince de Condé. But, while awaiting the appearance of the history
which is to tell the story of his life to coming ages, it is necessary to
satisfy as best we may the public recognition of his merit and bow
to the order of the greatest of all sovereigns. What does not the kingdom owe to a prince who has honored the house of France, the French
name, his century, and, so to speak, all mankind? Louis the Great
himself shares these sentiments; after having mourned this great man,
and by his tears, shed in the presence of his entire court, rather than
by words, uttered the most glorious eulogy he could receive, he assembled together in this celebrated temple all that is most august in
his realm, in order that the last rites to the memory of this prince
might there be celebrated; and he wishes that my feeble voice should
animate all this funeral equipage. Let us try, then, to forget our grief.
Here an object greater and worthier of this pulpit presents itself to my
mind: it is God who makes warriors and conquerors. "It is thou,"
said David unto Him, "who hast trained my hand to battle, and my
fingers to hold the sword." If He inspires courage, no less is He the
bestower of other great qualities, both of heart and of mind. His
mighty hand is the source of everything; it is He who sends from
heaven generous sentiments, wise counsels and every worthy thought.
But He wishes us to know how to distinguish between the gifts He

abandons to His enemies and those He reserves for His servants. What distinguishes His friends from all others is piety. Until this gift of Heaven has been received, all others not only are as naught, but even bring ruin on those who are endowed with them; without this inestimable gift of piety what would the Prince de Condé have been, even with his great heart and great genius? No, my brethren, if piety had not, as it were, consecrated his other virtues, these princes would have found no consolation for their grief, nor this pontiff any confidence in his prayers, nor would I myself utter with conviction the praises which I owe so great a man. Let us, by this example, then, set human glory at naught; let us destroy the idol of the ambitious, that it might fall to pieces before this altar. Let us to-day join together (for with a subject so noble we may do it) all the finest qualities of a superior nature; and, for the glory of truth, let us demonstrate, in a prince admired of the universe, that what makes heroes, that what carries to the highest pitch worldly glory, worth, magnanimity, natural goodness— all attributes of the heart; vivacity, penetration, grandeur and sublimity of genius—attributes of the mind; would be but an illusion were piety not a part of them—in a word, that piety is the essence of the man. It is this, gentlemen, which you will see in the forever memorable life of the most high and mighty Prince Louis de Bourbon, Prince de Condé, first prince of the blood.

God has revealed to us that He alone creates conquerors, and that He makes them serve his designs. What other created a Cyrus if it is not God who named him two hundred years before his birth in the Prophecies of Isaiah? "Thou art as yet unborn," He said unto him, "but I see thee, and I name thee by thy name; thou shalt be called Cyrus. I will walk before thee in battle; at thy approach I will put kings to flight; I will break down doors of brass. It is I that stretch out the heavens, that support the earth, that name that which is not as that which is," that is to say, it is I that create everything and I that see, from eternity, all that I create. What other could fashion an Alexander, if it is not this same God who caused the unquenchable ardor of Daniel, his prophet, to see from so great a distance and by means of foreshadowings so vivid. "Do you see him," he says, "this conqueror; with what rapidity he rises from the west by bounds, as it were, and touches not the earth?" In the boldness of his leaps, and the lightness of his tread like unto some powerful and frisking beast, he advances by quick and impetuous bounds, and nor mountain nor precipice arrests his progress. Already has the king of Persia fallen into his hands. "At his sight he was exasperated; efferatus est in eum," says the prophet; "he strikes him down, he tramples him under foot; nor can anyone save him from his blows nor cheat him of his prey." But to hear these words of Daniel, whom would you suppose you perceived, gentlemen, under that figure of speech—Alexander or the Prince de Condé? God gave him that dauntless valor that France might enjoy safety during the minority of a king but four years old. Let him grow up, this king, cherished of Heaven, and all will yield to his exploits; rising above his own followers, as well as his enemies, he will know how sometimes to make use of, and at others to dispense with, his most illustrious captains, and alone, under the hand of God, who will be his constant aid, he will be seen to be the stanch rampart of his dominions. But God chose the Duc d'Enghien to defend him in his infancy. So, toward the first days of his reign, at the age of twenty-two years, the duke conceived a plan in the armor of which the seasoned veterans could find no vulnerable point; but victory justified his course at Rocroi. The opposing force, it is true, is stronger; it is composed of those old Walloon, Italian, and Spanish regiments that, up to that time, could not be broken; but at what valuation should be placed the courage inspired in our troops by the pressing necessities of the state, by past successes, and by a young prince of the blood in whose eyes could be read victory? Don Francisco de Mellos awaits the onset with a firm foot; and, without being able to retreat, the two generals and the two armies seemed to have wished to imprison themselves in the woods and the marshes in order to decide the issue of combat like two champions in the lists. Then what a sight is presented to the eye! The young prince appears another man; touched by an object so worthy, his great soul displays all its sublimity; his courage waxes with the dangers it has to encounter and his penetration becomes keener as his ardor increases. That night, which had to be spent in the presence of the enemy, like the vigilant commander that he was, he was the last to retire. But never were his slumbers more peaceful. On the eve of so momentous a day, when the first battle is to be fought, his mind is entirely tranquil, so thoroughly is he in his element; and it is well known that, on the morrow, at the hour he had indicated, it was necessary to awaken this second Alexander from a deep slumber. Do you see him as he rushes on to victory or death? No sooner had he inspired the ranks with the ardor with which his soul was animated than he was seen almost at the same time to press the right wing of the enemy, support our own shaken by the shock of the charge, rally the disheartened and almost vanquished French forces, put to flight the victorious Spaniards, carrying dismay everywhere, and terrifying by his lightning glances those who escape his blows. There still remained that dreaded infantry of the Spanish army, whose great battalions in close line of battle like so many towers, but towers which knew how to repair their breaches, were unshaken by the onset, and, though the rest of the army was put to rout, maintained a steady fire. Thrice the young conqueror attempted to break the ranks of these intrepid warriors, thrice was he repulsed by the valorous Comte de Fontaines, who was borne to the scene of combat in his invalid's chair, by reason of his bodily infirmities, thus demonstrating that the warrior's soul has the ascendant over the body it animates. But at last was he forced to yield.

In vain does Beck, with a body of fresh cavalry, hasten his march through the woods in order to attack our exhausted soldiers; the prince has forestalled him; the defeated battalions are asking quarter. But victory for the Duc d'Enghien was destined to be more terrible than the combat. While, with an air of confidence, he advances to receive the surrender of these brave fellows, they, on their part, still on their guard, are in dread of being surprised by a fresh attack. The frightful havoc wrought by the discharge of their musketry infuriates our troops. Carnage is now rampant; the blood-shed intoxicates the soldiers to a high degree. But the prince, who could not bear to see these lions slaughtered like so many lambs, calmed their overwrought feelings and enhanced the pleasure of victory by that of pardoning the vanquished. What, then, was the astonishment of these veteran troops and their brave officers when they perceived that their only salvation was to give themselves up to their conqueror! With what wonder did they regard the young prince, whose victory had rendered still more impressive his customary proud bearing, to which, however, his clemency had imparted a new grace. How willingly would he have saved the life of the brave Comte de Fontaines, but unhappily he lay stretched upon the field of battle among the thousands of dead bodies, those whose loss is still wept by Spain. Spain knew not that the prince who caused her the loss of so many of her old regiments on the day of Rocroi was to finish the rest on the plains of Lens. Thus the first victory was the guarantee of many others. The prince bent his knee and on the field of battle rendered to the Lord of Hosts the glory He had sent him. There was celebrated the deliverance of Rocroi, and thanksgivings were uttered that the threats of a once dreaded enemy had resulted in his own shameful defeat; that the regency was strengthened, France calmed, and a reign which was to be so illustrious begun by an augury so auspicious. The army led in thanksgiving; all France followed; the first venture of the Duc d'Enghien was lauded to the skies. Praise sufficient to render others forever illustrious; but for him it was but the first stage in his career!

As a result of this first campaign, and after the capture of Thion-ville, a prize worthy of the victory gained at Rocroi, he was regarded as an adversary equally to be feared at sieges and in battles. But there is one trait in the character of the victorious young prince no less admirable than that which was brought out by victory. The court, which at his arrival was prepared to welcome him with the plaudits he deserved, was surprised at the manner in which he received them. The queen-regent assured him that the king was well pleased with his services. This from the lips of his sovereign was a fitting recompense for his labors. If others dared to praise him, however, he treated their eulogies as insults, and, impatient of flattery, he was in dread even of its semblance. Such was the delicacy, or rather the solidity of character, of this prince. Moreover his maxim was (listen; for it is a maxim which makes great men), that, in the performance of great deeds, one's sole thought should be to perform them well, and leave glory to follow in the train of virtue. It is this which he has endeavored to instil into others, and by this principle has he himself ever been guided. Thus false glory had no temptation for him. It was with truth and greatness alone that he was concerned. Thus it came about that his glory was wrapped up in the service of the king and in the happiness and well being of the state; they were the objects nearest his heart; these were his first and most cherished desires. The court had but little charm for him, or occupation suited to his talents, though he was there regarded as its greatest hero. It was deemed needful to exhibit everywhere in Germany, as in Flanders, the intrepid defender whom God had given us. Remark well what is about to transpire: There is being formed against the prince an enterprise of a more formidable nature than that at Rocroi; and, in order to put his talents to the test, warfare is about to drain all its resources, and call to its aid every known invention. What is it that is presented to my vision? I see not merely men to meet in combat but inaccessible mountains: on one side are ravines and precipices; on the other impenetrable forests in the heart of which are marshes, and in proximity to streams are impregnable intrenchments; everywhere are lofty fortresses and forests of felled trees lying across roads which are frightful; and there arises Merci, with his worthy Bavarians inflated by the large measure of success which has fallen to their arms and by the capture of Fribourg; Merci, whom none has ever seen retreat from the combat; Merci, whom the Prince de Condé and the vigilant Turenne have never surprised in a movement that was not in accord with the rules of warfare, and to whom they have conceded this great mark of admiration—that never has he lost a single favorable opportunity, nor failed to anticipate their designs as though he had taken part in their councils. Here, then, in the course of eight days, and by four separate attacks, is seen how much can be supported and undertaken in war. Our troops seem as much dispirited by the frightful condition of the field of battle as by the resistance of the enemy, and for a time the prince sees himself, so to speak, abandoned. But like a second Maccabee, "his right arm abandons him not, and his courage, inflamed by so many perils, came to his aid." No sooner had he been seen on foot the first to scale those inaccessible heights, than his ardor drew the whole army after him. Merci sees himself lost beyond redemption; his best regiments are defeated; nightfall is the salvation of the remainder of his army. But a severe rainstorm serves to add to our difficulties and discouragements, so that we have at the same time to contend with not only the highest courage and the perfection of art, but the forces of nature as well. In spite of the advantage that an enemy, as able as he is bold, takes of these conditions, and the fact that he intrenches himself anew in his impregnable mountains, hard pressed on every side, he is forced not only to allow his cannon and baggage to fall a prey to the Duc d'Enghien, but also all the country bordering the Rhine. See how everything is shaken to its foundation: Philipsburg is in dire distress in ten days, in spite of the winter now close at hand; Philipsburg, which so long held the Rhine captive under our laws, and whose loss the greatest of kings so gloriously retrieved. Worms, Spire, Mayence, Landau, twenty other places I might name, open their portals: Merci is unable to defend them, and no longer faces his conqueror. It is not enough; he must fall at his feet, a worthy victim of his valor. Nordlingen will witness his overthrow; it will there be admitted that it is no more possible to withstand the French in Germany than in Flanders. And all these benefits we will owe to this selfsame prince. God, the protector of France and of a king whom He has destined to perform His great works, thus ordains.

The orator, continuing the story of the great deeds of the hero, leads us by gradual transition to a eulogy of the qualities of his heart. He pictures him in his family relations, and continues as follows:

It was not merely for a son nor for his family that he had such tender sentiments: I have seen him (and do not think that I here speak in terms of exaggeration), I have seen him deeply moved by the perils of his friends. Simple and natural as he was, I have seen his features betray his emotions at the story of their misfortunes, and he was ever ready to confer with them on the most insignificant details as well as on affairs of the utmost importance. In the adjustment of quarrels, he was ever ready to soothe turbulent spirits with a patience and good nature that one would little have expected from a disposition so excitable, nor from a character so lofty. What a contrast to heroes devoid of human sympathy! Well might the latter command respect and charm the admiration, as do all extraordinary things, but they will not win the heart. When God fashioned the heart of man and endowed him with human affection, He first of all inspired him with the quality of kindness, like unto the essence of the divine nature itself, as a token of the beneficent hand that fashioned us. Kindness, therefore, ought to be the mainspring and guide of our heart, and ought at the same time to be the chief attraction that should, as it were, be a part of our very being, with which to win the hearts of others. Greatness, which is but the result of good fortune, so far from diminishing the quality of kindness, is but given one that he might the more freely spread broadcast its beneficent effects like a public fountain, which is but erected that its waters might be scattered to the sunlight. This is the value of a good heart; and the great who are devoid of the quality of kindness, justly punished for their disdainful insensibility to the misfortunes of their fellows, are forever deprived of the greatest blessing of human life, that is to say, of the pleasures of society. Never did man enjoy these pleasures more keenly than the prince of whom I am speaking; never was man less inspired with the misgiving that familiarity breeds contempt. Is this the man who carried cities by storm and won great battles? Verily, he seems to have forgotten the high rank he so well knew how to sustain. Do you not recognize in him the hero, who, ever equable and consistent, never having to stand on tiptoe to seem taller than he is, nor to stoop to be courteous and obliging, found himself by nature all that a man ought to be toward his fellow, like a majestic and bountiful stream, which peacefully bears into the cities the abundance it has spread in the fields that it has watered, which gives to all and never rises above its normal height, nor becomes swollen except when violent opposition is offered to the gentle slope by which it continues on its tranquil course. Such, indeed, has also been the gentleness and such the might of the Prince de Condé. Have you a secret of importance? Confide it boldly to the safekeeping of this noble heart; he will reward your confidence by making your affair his own. To this prince nothing is more inviolable than the sacred rights of friendship. When a favor is asked of him, he acts as though he himself were under obligation; and never has a joy keener and truer been witnessed than he felt at being able to give pleasure to another.

Here the orator gives a description of the qualities of the prince's mind. He praises the warlike talents of his hero, and takes occasion to compare him with Turenne, another great captain of the same period.

It was a grand spectacle to see during the same period, and in the same campaigns, these two men, who in the common opinion of all Europe could be favorably compared to the greatest captains of past ages, sometimes at the head of different bodies of troops; sometimes united more indeed by the concord of their thoughts than by the orders which the subaltern received from his superior; sometimes at the head of opposing forces, and each redoubling his customary activity and vigilance, as though God, who, according to the Scriptures, often in His wisdom makes a sport of the universe, had desired to show mortals the wonders in all their forms that He could work with men. Behold though more impetuous, yet never acting with undue precipitation; the perils, the resources of these brave men! Has there ever been beheld in two men virtues such as these in characters so different, not to say diametrically opposite? The one appears to be guided by deep reflection, the other by sudden illumination; the latter as a consequence, though more impetuous, yet never acting, with undue precipitation;

the former, colder of manner, though never slow, is bolder of action than of speech, and even while having the outward appearance of embarassment, inwardly determined and resolved. The one, from the moment he appears in the army, conveys an exalted idea of his worth and makes one expect of him something out of the ordinary; nevertheless, he advanced in regular order, and performed, as it were, by degrees, the prodigious deeds which marked the course of his career. The other, like a man inspired from the date of his first battle, showed himself the equal of the most consummate masters of the art of warfare. The one by his prompt and continued efforts commanded the admiration of the human race and silenced the voice of envy; the other shone so resplendently from the very beginning that none dared attack him. The one, in a word, by the depth of his genius and the incredible resources of his courage, rose superior to the greatest perils and even knew how to profit by every kind of fickleness of fortune; the other, by reason of the advantages derived from high birth, by his great conceptions derived from Heaven, and by a kind of admirable instinct, the secret of which is not given to ordinary men, seemed born to mold fortune to conform to his designs and bring destiny to his feet. And that the great though diverse characters of these two men might be clearly discerned, it should be borne in mind that the one, his career cut short by an unexpected blow, died for his country like another Judas Maccabeus, mourned by the army as for a father, while the court and all the people lamented his fate. His piety as well as his courage were universally lauded, and his memory will never fade from the minds of men. The other, raised to the very summit of glory by force of arms like another David, dies like him in his bed sounding the praises of God and leaving his dying behests to his family, while all hearts were impressed as much by the splendor of his life as by the gentleness of his death.

TRUE AND FALSE SIMPLICITY

François de Fénelon

(1651-1715 A.D.)

François de Fénelon, the illustrious French prelate who became Archbishop of Cambrai, was a descendant of a distinguished family. At the close of a brilliant college career he entered the seminary of Saint Sulpice, and at the age of 24 received holy orders. He never realized his desire to be a missionary, but devoted his life instead to educational writings, foremost of which is *De l'Éducation des Filles*; to the education of Louis XIV's grandson, the Duke of Burgundy; and to his duties as Archbishop of Cambrai.

A friendship with Madame Guyon, the leader of the Pietists, drew Fénelon to her support in a controversy with Bossuet and led to his ultimate banishment from the court. Thereafter he devoted his time entirely to the care of his diocese and to deeds of charity.

Fénelon objected to the memorization of sermons because they lacked naturalness; he, himself, always spoke from notes. He ever pleaded for greater simplicity in the pulpit, and in his own work had a pure, simple, and natural delivery. A contemporary because of his eloquence called him "the Swan of Cambrai." His gravity, courtliness, dignified earnestness, and wit were in-bred characteristics which were accentuated by his distinguished appearance of refinement and good-breeding. The sermon included here is most indicative of his style.

There is a simplicity that is a defect, and a simplicity that is a virtue. Simplicity may be a want of discernment. When we speak of a person as simple, we may mean that he is credulous and perhaps vulgar. The simplicity that is a virtue is something sublime; every one loves and admires it; but it is difficult to say exactly what this virtue is.

Simplicity is an uprightness of soul that has no reference to self; it is different from sincerity, and it is a still higher virtue. We see many people who are sincere, without being simple; they only wish to pass for what they are, and they are unwilling to appear what they are not; they are always thinking of themselves, measuring their words, and recalling their fear that they have done too much or too little. These persons are sincere, but they are not simple; they are not at ease with others, and others are not at ease with them; they are not free, ingenuous, natural; we prefer people who are less correct, less perfect, and who are less artificial. This is the decision of man, and it is the judgment of God, who would not have us so occupied with ourselves, and thus, as it were, always arranging our features in a mirror.

To be wholly occupied with others, never to look within, is the state of blindness of those who are entirely engrossed by what is present and addressed to their senses; this is the very reverse of simplicity. To be absorbed in self or whatever engages us, whether we are laboring for our fellow beings or for God—to be wise in our own eyes, reserved, and full of ourselves, troubled at the least thing that disturbs our self-complacency, is the opposite extreme. This is false wisdom, which, with all its glory, is but little less absurd than that folly which pursues only pleasure. The one is intoxicated with all it sees around it; the other with all that it imagines it has within; but it is delirium in both. To be absorbed in the contemplation of our own minds is really worse than to be engrossed by outward things, because it appears like wisdom and yet is not; we do not think of curing it; we pride ourselves upon it; we approve of it; it gives us an unnatural strength; it is a sort of frenzy; we are not conscious of it; we are dying, and we think ourselves in health.

Simplicity consists in a just medium, in which we are neither too much excited, nor too composed. The soul is not carried away by outward things, so that it cannot make all necessary reflections; neither does it make those continual references to self, that a jealous sense of its own excellence multiplies to infinity. That freedom of the soul, which looks straight onward in its path, losing no time to reason upon its steps, to study them, or to contemplate those that it has already taken, is true simplicity.

The first step in the progress of the soul is disengagement from outward things, that it may enter into itself, and contemplate its true interests: this is a wise self-love. The second is to join to this the idea of God whom it fears: this is the feeble beginning of true wisdom; but the soul is still fixed upon itself; it is afraid that it does not fear God enough; it is still thinking of itself. These anxieties about ourselves are far removed from that peace and liberty which a true and simple love inspires; but it is not yet time for this; the soul must pass through this trouble; this operation of the spirit of God in our hearts comes to us gradually; we approach step by step to this simplicity. In the third and last state, we begin to think of God more frequently, we think of ourselves less, and insensibly we lose ourselves in Him.

The more gentle and docile the soul is, the more it advances in this simplicity. It does not become blind to its own defects, and unconscious of its imperfections; it is more than ever sensible of them; it feels a horror of the slightest sin; it sees more clearly its own corruption; but this sensibility does not arise from dwelling upon itself, but by the light from the presence of God we see how far removed we are from infinite purity.

Thus simplicity is free in its course, since it makes no preparation; but it can only belong to the soul that is purified by a true penitence. It must be the fruit of a perfect renunciation of self, and an unreserved love of God. But tho they, who become penitents, and tear themselves from the vanities of the world, make self the object of thought, yet they must avoid an excessive and unquiet occupation with themselves, such as would trouble, and embarrass, and retard them in their progress. Dwelling too much upon self produces in weak minds useless scruples and superstition and in stronger minds a presumptuous wisdom. Both are contrary to true simplicity, which is free and direct, and gives itself up, without reserve and with a generous self-forgetfulness, to the Father of spirits. How free, how intrepid are the motions, how glorious the progress that the soul makes, when delivered from all low. and interested, and unquiet cares!

If we desire that our friends be simple and free with us, disencumbered of self in their intimacy with us, will it not please God, who is our truest friend, that we should surrender our souls to Him without fear or reserve, in that holy and sweet communion with Himself which He allows us? It is this simplicity which is the perfection of the true children of God. This is the end that we must have in view, and to which we must be continually advancing.

This deliverance of the soul from all useless, and selfish, and unquiet cares, brings to it a peace and freedom that are unspeakable; this is true simplicity. It is easy to perceive, at the first glance, how glorious it is; but experience alone can make us comprehend the enlargement of heart that it produces. We are then like a child in the arms of its parent; we wish nothing more; we fear nothing; we yield ourselves up to this pure attachment; we are not anxious about what others think of us; all our motions are free, graceful and happy. We do not judge ourselves, and we do not fear to be judged. Let us strive after this lovely simplicity; let us seek the path that leads to it. The further we are from it, the more we must hasten our steps toward it. Very far from being simple, most Christians are not even sincere. They are not only disingenuous, but they are false, and they dissemble with their neighbor, with God, and with themselves. They practice a thousand little arts that indirectly distort the truth. Alas! every man is a liar;

those even who are naturally upright, sincere, and ingenuous, and who are what is called simple and natural, still have this jealous and sensitive reference to self in everything, which secretly nourishes pride, and prevents that true simplicity, which is the renunciation and perfect oblivion of self.

FUNERAL ORATION ON LOUIS XIV

Jean Baptiste Massillon

(1663-1742 A.D.)

Massillon, the last in order of the great pulpiteers of the Court of Louis XIV, joined the Congregation of the Oratory at the age of 18 and later taught in the colleges of this order. An eloquent funeral sermon which he delivered on the Archbishop of Vienne led to his appointment as head of the Seminary of Saint Magloire, where a course of lectures delivered in the seminary established his reputation. In 1699 he was selected as advent preacher at the Court of Versailles and for four years preached the Lenten sermons before the Court. He preached before Louis XIV and delivered the funeral sermon of the great monarch. In 1715, after being made Bishop of Clermont, Massillon preached before the new king Louis XV, who was but nine years of age, a series of Lenten sermons called *Petit Carême*, the first sermons addressed to a child. Other masterpieces are his sermons on *The Prodigal Son, On Death, For Christmas Day, On the Small Number of the Elect,* and the *Funeral Oration On Louis XIV*. His last great sermon was at the funeral of the Dowager Duchess of Orleans. In 1717 Massillon was consecrated Bishop of Claremont and in 1719 was elected a member of the French Academy.

His diction was simple and unaffected. He was a master of pathos and had a gift of insight into the human emotions. Since he was not vindictive and avoided argument, Massillon's manner was most engaging and pleasing; for he combined grace with genius. Although he used few, if any gestures, Massillon had what a contemporary critic described as an "eloquent eye" which could serve his every purpose. He was also the master of the art of amplification, the development of a thought in one

long composite sentence made of a series of intensifying clauses.
Voltaire so admired Massillon that he used him as a model of
eloquence and called him "the preacher who had best understood
the world."

Included here are the introduction and peroration to the
Funeral Oration on Louis XIV.

I communed with mine own heart, saying, lo, I am come to great
estate, and have gotten more wisdom than all they that have been
before me in Jerusalem; yea, my heart had great experience of wisdom
and knowledge.

And I gave my heart to know wisdom, and to know madness and
folly; I have perceived that this also is vexation of spirit.

Eccles. 1:16-17

God alone is great, my brethren, and, above all, during these last
moments, when He presides at the death of earthly Kings: the more
their glory and their power have flamed, the more in fading they render
homage to His supreme greatness: God reveals all that He is; and man
is no longer all that he believed himself to be.

Happy is the Prince whose heart is not exalted in the midst of
his prosperity and his glory; who, like Solomon, has not waited 'till
all his greatness has expired with him on death's bed, to confess that
glory is only vanity and affliction of spirit; and who has humbled
himself under the hand of God at the very time when adulation seemed
to place him above man!

Yea, my brethren, the greatness and the victories of the King we
mourn have been previously sufficiently proclaimed: the magnificence
of the praise has equalled that of the occasion; men have already said
everything in his praise. What is left to us here if not to speak of it
for our own instruction?

This King, terror of his neighbors, astonishment of the universe,
father of Kings, greater than all his ancestors, more magnificent than
Solomon in all his glory, has recognized, as Solomon, that all is vanity.
The world has been dazzled by the splendor which surrounded him;
his enemies have envied his power; strangers have come from the most
remote islands to lower their eyes before the glory of his Majesty; his
subjects have almost erected altars for him; but the prestige which
surrounded him was unable to beguile him.

Thou hast filled him, Oh my Lord, with the fear of Thy Name;
Thou hast written his name in the Eternal Book, in the succession of
holy Kings who should govern Thy people; Thou hast clothed him
with grandeur and magnificence. But this was not enough; he had
yet to be marked with the proper sign of Thy chosen; Thou hast recompensed his faith with tribulations and disgraces. The Christian use

of prosperity can give us right to the Kingdom of Heaven; but only affliction and violence can make it certain to us.

Do we behold with the same eyes, my brethren, the vicissitudes of human things? Without looking back to the centuries of our fore-fathers, what lessons has not God given to us? We have seen the entire Royal race almost extinguished; [1] The Princes, hope and bulwark of the Throne, harvested in the flower of their age; the august husband and wife, amid their most beautiful days, enclosed in the same tomb, and the ashes of the child following sadly and augmenting the doleful display of their funeral; the King who has passed from a stormy minor-ity to the most glorious reign in our history, falling back from this glory into misfortunes almost greater than his previous successes, raising himself again still higher from all these losses, and surviving so many varied events in order to give glory to God, and confirm himself in the faith of immutable blessing.

These great facts pass before our eyes as fabulous scenes: the heart gives way for a moment at the spectacle; compassion ends with the display; and it seems that God operates so many revolutions here below only to play in the universe and to entertain rather than instruct us.

Let us add, therefore, the words of faith to this sad ceremony, which without them preaches to us in vain; let us recall not the mar-velous deeds of a reign which men have already so exalted, but the marvelous deeds of God to a King who is taken away from us. Let us here remember his virtues rather than his victories: let us show him even higher on his deathbed than he was on his throne during his days of glory. Let us take away the praise of vanity only to give it back to divine grace; and although he has been great, in the wonderful unheard of splendor of his reign, and in the heroic sentiments of his piety, (two reflections on which are based this religious duty which we render to the memory of the High, very powerful and excellent Prince, Louis XIV, by name, King of France and of Navarre) let us speak of the glory and of the greatness of his reign only to show the perils and nothingness he knew; and of his devotion, only to propose and immortalize the examples of it.

. . . .

Return, therefore, to the bosom of God from whence you have come, heroic and Christian soul! Already your heart is where your treasure lies. Break these feeble ties of your mortality which prolong your desires, and which retard your hope: the day of our mourning is the day of your glory and of your triumphs. May the Guardian Angels of France come to welcome you in order to conduct you with pomp

---

[1] In his latter days Louis XIV suffered bereavement for his eldest son, the Dauphin, who died in April, 1711; his grandson and consort, the Duke and Duchess of Burgundy, who died in 1712; and his great-grandson the Duke of Brittany, who died in the same year; then the succession to the throne fell on the frail shoulders of his great-grandchild of four years, who became Louis XV.

to the Throne which is destined for you in Heaven beside holy Kings, your ancestors, Charlemagne and Saint Louis. Go to join Thérèse, [2] Louis, [3] Adélaïde, [4] who are waiting for you, and dry near them, in the sojourn of immortality, the tears you have shed upon their ashes; and if, as we hope, the holiness and the uprightness of your intentions have made up before God for any deficit in the merit of your works and the integrity of your justice during the course of such an extended reign, look down from the Heavenly abode on a Kingdom which you leave in affliction, on a child king [5] who has not had the leisure to grow and mature under your eyes and under your examples; and see the end of the misfortunes which overwhelm us, and the crimes which seem to multiply with our misfortunes.

And Thou, almighty God, cast down from Heaven Thy eyes of mercy upon this desolate Monarchy, where the glory of Thy name is better known than among other nations, where faith is as ancient as the Crown, and where it has always been as pure on the Throne as the blood of our Kings who have occupied it. Defend us from the troubles and dissensions to which Thou usually deliverest the infancy of Kings; leave us at least the consolation of peacefully mourning our misfortunes and our losses. Extend the wings of Thy protection over the precious Child that Thou hast placed at the head of Thy people; this august offspring of so many Kings, this innocent victim alone escaped from the shafts of Thine ire and from the extinction of the entire Royal race.

Give him a submissive heart toward the teachings which are going to be upheld by great examples: may piety, clemency, humanity, and many other virtues, which are going to preside at his education, spread over all the course of his reign. Be his God and his Father; teach him to be the father of his subjects; and lead us all together to a most blessed immortality. Thus be it. (Amen)

Translated by M. André Liotard of the Modern Language Department, the University of Maryland, and Minister to the French Congregation at Washington, D.C.

[2] Thérèse, wife of Louis XIV.
[3] Louis, the Dauphin, who died April, 1711.
[4] Adélaïde of Savoy.
[5] Louis XIV's great-grandchild, who became Louis XV.

DIVINE LOVE IN PRAYER

François de Sales

(1567-1622 A.D.)

François de Sales was of noble descent and received unusual care in his education. After taking his doctorate in law at the University of Padua, he entered the priesthood and was sent to the province of Chablais, which had become Calvinistic, to convert the Protestants back to Catholicism. His preaching was so effective that by 1598 the province was again Catholic. In Paris also his simple, fervid, and direct preaching distinguished him so that he came into the closest relation with the Court of Henry IV. He helped to organize the Order of Visitation for "strong souls with weak bodies" and spent much time in deeds of mercy.

De Sales' charm of diction lay in brevity and clearness, the avoidance of subtle argument, and the turgid ornament and rhetorical affectation common to the sermons of his day. He re-echoed the style of the patristic fathers in the sweetness of his writings. It was ever his aim to inspire his audience to lead a godly life rather than to impress them with a display of his own eloquence. Included here is a selection representative of de Sales' style.

There are two ways of exercising our love for God: one affective, the other effective, and as St. Bernard calls it, active. By the first, we place our affections in God, and all that he loves becomes interesting to us; by the second, we serve God, and accomplish what he ordains. The former unites us to the goodness of God; the latter renders us submissive to his holy will. By the one a kind of correspondence is established between us and God, by the communication of his spirit to our souls, and hence arise sentiments of complacency, of benevolence, transports, ecstasies, desires, sighs, and spiritual ardours; the other imparts solidity to our resolutions, and an inviolable fidelity to our obedience, which enables us to accomplish the will of God—to suffer—to accept and embrace everything that he pleases to order. By the first, our happiness and delight are centred in God, and by the second we please and obey him. Affective love conceives the work, if I may say so, and effective love brings it forth. By the former we put the Almighty as a seal upon our heart, or rather as a banner under which all the affections of the soul are ranged; by the latter we place God upon our arm, as a sword to enable us to perform exploits of spiritual valour, in the practice of virtue. Effective love is principally exercised in prayer, wherein the emotions of the heart are so multiplied and varied that it is impossible to distinguish them all; not only on account of their being very numerous, but also because they are spiritual, and consequently so imperceptible as to escape the penetration of the mind. The best trained dogs are liable to be at a fault, and to lose the track of the stag; for its cunning teaches it a thousand stratagems and subtleties, by which it gives the hounds a wrong scent, and thereby escapes their pursuit. In the same manner, we often lose sight of our own heart, and are totally incapable of understanding its operations; it has so many different movements, and these succeed each other so rapidly, that its ways become indiscernible.

God, whose knowledge is infinite, can alone read clearly into its recesses, and fathom its most secret foldings. He sees our thoughts, even before we have formed them; he discovers our most hidden paths, he views all our stratagems and evasions. This is what occasioned the Royal Prophet to say, "Thy knowledge has become wonderful to me; it is high, and I cannot reach to it." (Psalms, cxxxviii.6.) To reflect on all our ordinary actions by a continual self-examination, would be to entangle ourselves in a labyrinth from which we could never be extricated. Besides this, the continual attention and restraint would be insupportable, if it were necessary by incessant reflection to enter into ourselves, and to remember that we are thinking, to observe that we are considering, to see that we are seeing, to discern that we are discerning, to reflect that we are meditating. In this confusion and variety of thoughts, the mind would engage itself in a labyrinth from whose mazes it would vainly seek to disengage itself. We may infer from this, that only persons endowed with the spirit of prayer can clearly explain this subject. Moreover, by prayer we do not here understand it in the sense of St. Basil, who confounds it with the simple petitions which the faithful offer to God when they implore any grace from his clemency; but according to the definition of St. Bonaventure, who says that prayer, in general, comprehends all the acts of contemplation; or in the sense of St. Gregory of Nyssa, who calls it a conversation between the soul and God; or of St. Chrysostom, who speaks of it as an interview with the Divine Majesty; or, in fine, of St. Augustine and St. John Damascen, who call it an elevation of the soul to God— a transport of the mind in God. But if it be an elevation of the soul, an interview, a conversation, it is certain that by prayer we converse with God, and that in return the Almighty speaks to us: that we tend to

God, and that God descends to us; that we live—that we breathe in God, and that, reciprocally, the Almighty dwells in us, and infuses his spirit into our souls.

But what is the subject of our interview in prayer? It is God. For what can a person inflamed with love speak of, but the object of his affections. On this account, prayer and mystical theology are but one and the same thing. It is called theology, because it has God for its object, as well as the speculative theology taught in schools; but there are three points in which a difference exists. 1st. Scholastic theology treats of the Almighty as God, and considers the Divinity in the Supreme Goodness;—mystical theology treats of the Almighty as a being sovereignly amiable, and considers the supreme goodness in the Divinity. 2nd. Speculative theology speaks of God to man and with man;—mystical theology treats of God to God, and with God himself. 3rd. The end of speculative theology is to teach us to know God;—and the object of mystical theology is to teach us to love him. One produces learned men, doctors, theologians;—whilst the other forms saints, ardent lovers of the Almighty, devoted to his service, and burning with zeal for his interests.

This theology is called mystical, because it is concealed. The conversation which passes in prayer between God and the soul is carried on in the secret recesses of the heart: it is a communication of feelings impenetrable to all but those who speak. The language of friends is of so singular a nature, that it can be understood only by themselves. "I sleep and my heart watcheth," said the sacred Lover, "the voice of my Beloved knocking." Who would have imagined that this holy Spouse conversed with her Beloved even when asleep? Yet it was the case; because where love reigns, the sound of words and the ministry of the senses are unnecessary for the conveyance of sentiments and ideas. Prayer, or mystical theology, is, then, nothing more than an amorous intercourse between the soul and God; the subject of this interview is the sovereign and infinitely amiable goodness, to which the soul longs to be united.

Prayer may be called a manna, on account of the different flavours and divine sweets which love discovers to those who make use of it. But it is a hidden manna which falls in the desert before the dawn of day; that is to say, it is not the fruit of lights and science; its sweets can only be tasted in solitude. When we converse with God alone, then we may say of the soul, "Who is she that goeth up by the desert, as a pillar of smoke of aromatical spices, of myrrh and frankincense, and of all the powders of the perfumer?" It is the Spouse herself, who entreats her Beloved to conduct her into solitude, that they may both converse in secret: "Come, my Beloved, let us go forth into the field: let us abide in the villages." On this account the sacred Lover is compared to the turtle dove, which seeks gloomy and lonely spots, and there warbles her melody to gratify her mate during his life, and to mourn for him when dead.

It is also for this reason that the holy Spouse and her divine Lover represent their reciprocal love, under the idea of a continual interview. If their friends sometimes mingle in the conversation, it is without interrupting or disturbing it, for a short time only, as it were, by stealth. The great attraction which persons of prayer experience is to converse with God in perfect solitude. The blessed mother Teresa of Jesus relates of herself, that in the commencement of her spiritual career she had a singular devotion to those mysteries which represent only the person of our Lord; as during his prayer in the Garden of Olives, or when he waited for the Samaritan woman near the well; she thought, that when her divine master was alone he would attract her more powerfully, and that she would be sooner united to him.

Love seeks not for witnesses of its words; and even when those who love have nothing to communicate which requires secrecy, they take pleasure in conversing in private. The reason of this probably is, that they only speak for each other; and it would seem to them they did not speak for themselves alone, if their interview could be overheard. Besides this, they make the most ordinary observations in a manner so peculiar, as to mark the love from which their words proceed. There is nothing uncommon in the words they use; but the tone, the emphasis, and the manner which accompanies everything they say, renders their language so singular, that they alone can understand it. The title of friend publicly conferred on any individual signifies but little; but when uttered in private it comprehends a great deal, and becomes more expressive in proportion to the secrecy with which it is spoken.

If we compare several theologians who speak eloquently of the Almighty, but who love him little, with those who loved him ardently, as the Ignatiuses, the Cyprians, the Chrysostoms, the Augustines, the Hilaries, the Ephrems, the Gregories, the Bernards, and several other illustrious men of antiquity, oh! what a difference shall we discover in this language! We all use the same expressions; but the words pronounced by those lovers of the Almighty were inflamed and embalmed, if we may say so, with the delicious perfume of divine love; whereas, with us they are only cold expressions, which neither contain the energy nor the sweetness of charity.

Everything speaks in those who love: not only their tongue, but also their eyes; their signs, their countenance, their very silence is eloquent. "My heart hath said to thee: My face hath sought thee: thy face, O Lord will I still seek." (Psalms, xxvi.8.) "My eyes have failed for thy word, saying, When wilt thou comfort me?" (Psalms, cxviii. 82.) "Hear, O Lord, my prayer: give ear to my supplication in thy truth." (Psalms, cxlii. 1.) "Give thyself no rest, and let not the apple of thy eye cease," said the inhabitants of Jerusalem, addressing their desolate city. (Lamentations, ii. 18.) Those who love, need not speak to express their affliction; they can make themselves understood by the motion of their eyes and the abundance of their tears.

As the principal exercise of mystical theology is speaking to God and listening to his voice, which is heard in the hidden recesses of the heart, and as this conversation is carried on in secret, commenced and continued without the help of words, by aspirations on the part of the soul and inspirations on the part of God, may we not justly call it a prayer of silence, in which the eyes speak to the eyes, and the heart to the heart, and in which no one can hear what passes except God and the soul, who converse together?

THE REPENTANCE OF THE UNCHASTE WOMAN

Jacques Saurin

(1667-1730 A.D.)

Probably the best result ensuing from the French school of oratory of the period was in the influence exerted over Jacques Saurin, who studied the French manner and transferred it to the Protestant pulpit when he was driven from France at the Revocation of the Edict of Nantes. He established himself at Prague and there was unconsciously instrumental in fusing the sterner, more logical Calvinistic theology with the sound and effective oratory of the French school.

Jacques Saurin was the son of a distinguished French lawyer who had fled from Nîmes, France, at the Revocation of the Edict of Nantes and taken refuge in Geneva. Here, as a young man, Saurin was educated among some of the most intellectual men of all Europe for whom Geneva had become a mecca. He started his career as a pulpiteer in 1701 in a Walloon congregation in London; but in 1705 went to the Hague to the church of French refugees who assembled in the chapel of the Prince of Orange. Here he dedicated many of his sermons to the king and queen who were among his patrons. His extreme popularity aroused the jealous enmity of his clerical colleagues who charged him with heresy and shortened his life by petty persecutions.

Saurin, born a Frenchman, educated in the logic of Calvinistic Geneva, exposed in London to the style of the English pulpit, so happily combined his native and acquired characteristics that he has been likened to the great Bossuet. He may thus be called one of the greatest of Protestant preachers, for he could appeal to both reason and emotion.

Included here are portions of his sermon on *The Repentance of the Unchaste Woman.*

'Let me fall into the hands of the Lord, for his mercies are great: but let me not fall into the hand of man,' *2 Sam. 24:14.* This was the request that David made in the most unhappy moment of his life.

My brethren, the wish of David under his consternation may direct ours in regard to all the spots that have defiled our lives. True, the eyes of God are infinitely more pure than those of men. He indeed discovers frailties in our lives which have escaped our notice, and 'if our heart condemns us, God is greater than our heart.' It is true, he hath punishments to inflict on us infinitely more dreadful than any mankind can invent, and if men can 'kill the body, God is able to destroy both soul and body in hell.' However, this Almighty God, this terrible, this avenging God, is a merciful God, 'great are his tender mercies:' but men, men are cruel; yea, the very men who allow themselves to live in the most shameful licentiousness, men who have the most need of the patience of others, men who themselves deserve the most rigorous punishments, these very men are usually void of all pity for their fellows. Behold a striking example. The unchaste woman in the text experienced both, and by turns made trial of the judgment of God, and the judgment of men. But she met with a very different treatment. In Jesus Christ she found a very severe legislator, who left her awhile to shed tears, and very bitter tears; a legislator, who left her awhile to her own grief, and sat and saw her hair dishevelled, and her features distorted: but who soon took care to dry up her tears, and to address this comfortable language to her, 'Go in peace.' On the contrary, in the hands of men she found nothing but barbarity and cruelty. She heard a supercilious Pharisee endeavour to arm against her the Redeemer of mankind, try to persuade him to pronounce on her sentence of death, even while she was repenting of her sin, and to do his utmost to cause condemnation to flow from the very fountain of grace and mercy. . . .

We must then suppose that the tears now shed by this woman were not the first, which she had shed at the remembrance of her sins. She had already performed several penitential exercises under a sense of forgiveness, and the repetition of these exercises proceeded both from a sense of gratitude for the sentence pronounced in her favour, and from a desire of receiving a ratification of it. On this account we have not assigned the fear of punishment as a cause of the grief of this penitent, as we ought to have done had we supposed that she had not already obtained forgiveness. Our supposition supported by our comment on the words of the text, in my opinion, throw great light on the whole passage. The Pharisee is offended because Jesus Christ suffered a woman of bad character to give him so many tokens of her esteem. Jesus Christ makes at the same time an apology both for himself and for the penitent. He tells the Pharisee, that the great esteem of this woman proceeds from a sense of the great favours which she had received from him: that the Pharisee thought he had given sufficient proof of his regard for Jesus Christ by receiving him into his house, without any extraordinary demonstrations of zeal, without giving him 'water to wash his feet, oil to anoint his head,' or 'a kiss' in token of friendship; and that what prevented him from giving greater marks of esteem was his considering himself in the condition of the first debtor, of whom only a little gratitude was required, because he had been released from an obligation to pay only a small and inconsiderable sum: but that this woman considered herself in the condition of the other debtor, who had been forgiven 'five hundred pence'; and that therefore she thought herself obliged to give her creditor the highest marks of esteem. 'Seest thou this woman? I entered into thine house, thou gavest me no water for my feet: but she hath washed my feet with tears, and wiped them with the hairs of her head. Thou gavest me no kiss: but she hath not ceased to kiss my feet. My head with oil thou didst not anoint: but she hath anointed my feet with ointment. Wherefore I say unto thee, her sins, which are many are forgiven. On this account she hath loved much,' and has given me all these proofs of affection, which are so far superior to those, which I have received at your table, 'for he, to whom little is forgiven, loveth little.'

At length, Jesus Christ turns himself towards the penitent, and, affected at her weeping afresh, repeats his assurances of forgiveness, and appeases that sorrow, which the remembrance of her crimes excited in her heart, though she no longer dreaded punishment. 'Go,' says he, 'thy sins are forgiven. . . . Go in peace.' . . .

BIBLIOGRAPHY OF THE REFORMATION PERIOD

Beard, Charles: *Reformation of 16th Century*, Charles Scribner's Sons, New York, 1927.

Bourdaloue, Louis: *Œuvres Complètes*, 16 vols., ed. Père Bretonneau, Mequignon-Havard, Paris, 1822.

Bryan, William Jennings, ed.: *The World's Famous Orations*, Funk and Wagnalls Company, New York, 1906.

Calvin, John: *Collected Works*, Calvin Translation Society, Edinburgh, 1843-55.

The Cambridge Modern History, The Macmillan Company, New York, 1907.

Carter, C. S.: *English Church and the Reformation*, Longmans, Green and Company, New York, 1925.

Cobbett, William: *History of the Reformation in England and Ireland*, J. Murphy Company, Dublin, 1830.

Cubberley, E. P.: *History of Education*, Houghton, Mifflin Company, Boston, 1920.

D'Aubigné, Merle J. H.: *History of the Reformation*, trans. H. White, American Tract Society, New York, 1849-53.

Depew, Chauncey, ed.: *The Library of Oratory*, Colonial Press, New York, 1902.

Fénelon, François: *Dialogues on Eloquence,* trans. J. Creighton, printed by J. Moyes for W. Baynes, London, 1808.

Fisher, G. P.: *History of the Christian Church*, Charles Scribner's Sons, New York, 1887.

Fisher, G. P.: *The Reformation*, Charles Scribner's Sons, New York, 1906.

Guizot, François Pierre: *History of Civilization*, trans. William Hazlitt, Colonial Press, New York, 1899.

Haskins, Charles Homer: *Renaissance of the 12th Century*, Harvard University Press, Cambridge, 1927.

Hulme, Edward M.: *The Renaissance and the Reformation*, The Century Company, New York, 1914.

Kelly, C. G.: *French Protestantism*, Johns Hopkins Press, Baltimore, 1918.

Latimer, Hugh: *Sermon on the Ploughers and Seven Sermons Preached before Edward VI*, E. Arber, London, 1869.

Laurin, Jacques: *Sermons*, trans. Robinson, Hunter, and Sutcliffe, S. Burder for R. Baynes, London, 1836.

Lee, Carleton, ed.: *The World's Orators*, G. P. Putnam's Sons, New York, 1900.

Lindsay, Thomas Martin: *History of the Reformation*, Charles Scribner's Sons, New York, 1910.

Luther, Martin: *Works*, 24 vols., Halle M. Niemeyer, St. Louis, 1888.

Macaulay, Thomas: *Essays*, Oxford University Press, New York, 1861.

Massillon, Jean Baptiste: *Works*, ed. Abbé Blampignon, Bar-le-Duc, etc., L. Gúerin, 1865-67.

Murray, R. H.: *Erasmus and Luther*, The Macmillan Company, New York, 1920.

Platz, Mabel: *The History of Public Speaking*, Noble and Noble, New York, 1935.

Pollard, A. F.: *Thomas Cranmer and the English Reformation*, G. P. Putnam's Sons, New York, 1904.

Schapiro, J. S.: *Social Reform and Reformation*, Columbia University Press, New York, 1909.

Sears, Lorenzo: *History of Oratory*, S. C. Griggs Company, Chicago, 1896.

Seebohm, Frederic: *Oxford Reformers of 1489*, E. P. Dutton and Company, New York, 1914.

Smith, Preserved: *The Age of the Reformation*, Henry Holt and Company, Inc., New York, 1909.

Ullman, Carl: *Reformatoren vor der Reformation*, trans. R. Menzies, T. and T. Clark, Edinburgh, 1874-77.

Vedder, Henry Clay: *Reformation in Germany*, The Macmillan Company, New York, 1914.

Zwingli, Huldreich: *Selected Works of Huldreich Zwingli*, ed. S. M. Jackson, Press of the University of Pennsylvania, Philadelphia, 1901.

THE FRENCH REVOLUTIONARY PERIOD

INTRODUCTION

The French Revolution was the French people's expression of a deep and instinctive need for certain changes in the existing structure of their political and social life. The orators who through these days represented the Revolution did not present new ideas but made concise those ideas which were dimly moving through the minds of the people. From this Revolution, consequently, came the most volatile oratory France has ever known, and the cries of "liberty, equality, and fraternity," which sprang from the throat of the French Revolution, were destined to echo through centuries of European history.

During the period of the Revolution the divine and the advocate were eclipsed by the orators of the Legislative Hall, for it was the Convention of the States-General and the National Assembly which were the forums of the Revolution. The deputies of the people in the session of the States-General found themselves in conflict with the throne and aristocracy. The nation had to be saved from famine, distress, and bankruptcy. Eloquent tongues were needed to bind together the Assembly and encourage it to put forth those acts which the welfare of the nation demanded.

The orators of the Revolution, moreover, were not only the men who represented the nation during the critical periods from 1798 to 1871 but those whose voices were heard in shaping the policies of the counter-revolutionary measures following that period, for the French Revolution was continuous.

Included here are Mirabeau, the leading orator of the Revolution; Danton, the leader of the Jacobins who were the ultra-radicals of the revolutionary process; Vergniaud, the leading orator of the conservative revolutionaries who were known as Girondists; Napoleon Bonaparte of the Empire, the greatest of military orators; Benjamin Constant and Royer Collard, the constitutionalists of the Restoration; Thiers and Guizot, the leading voices of the Parliament of 1830; Lamartine, the poet orator who was prominent in the revolutionary movement of 1848; and Gambetta, who was the leading voice in the voting of the Constitution of 1875.

Echoes of the French revolutionary voices were found in other European countries. The processes of thought which had fomented in France and found expression in the Revolution there were at work also in other lands. As soon as the news of the Revolution in Paris arrived in Hungary her great patriot, Louis Kossuth, in a compelling speech demanded parliamentary government for Hungary. In Italy the cry of the Revolution was re-echoed when the Italian patriot, Mazzini, founded the "Young European Association" of men believing in a future of liberty, equality, and fraternity for all mankind, while in Spain Emilio Castelar devoted his entire life to advancing the principles of republicanism fostered first by the Revolution in France. Speeches delivered by these leaders are therefore included under this period.

Latin America also received her first ideas of independence from the French Revolution; and this French influence has been woven through the whole pattern of the Latin American republics. It has been ably said that "the French Revolution still marches on in Latin America" in the present century, for the ideas of Montesquieu, Lamartine, and Rousseau nurtured many of her leaders. Simon Bolivar has therefore been selected as a representative exponent of the struggle for political freedom in South America.

AND YET YOU DELIBERATE

Comte de Mirabeau
(1749-1791)

Born of nobility, educated for the army, forced to take refuge
in England because of his disgraceful escapades, failing in a
diplomatic mission to Prussia, Mirabeau at the crucial moment
of his country's need used the funds of information gleaned from
all these experiences to become the leading voice of the States-
General. A contemporary member of the Tiers-État described
him as a wild beast with a tiger's face who could never speak
without convulsions, yet his terrific voice overcame the fears and
vacillations of the members, and the charm of his oratory subjugated even those who feared and hated him. He was not only
the greatest orator but the greatest statesman of the French Revolution. Had he lived the Revolution might have been spared its
hideous bloodshed, for Mirabeau attempted moderation and
sought to defend the monarchy by remodelling it after the English constitutional monarchy. He was naturally suspected by the
more radical and thwarted by the ignorance and obstinacy of the
Assembly. The tragedy of the Revolution was that Mirabeau died
before he could have his policies accepted. His own vices, also,
as he well knew, lessened his influence.

Audacious, daring, imperious was this master of the French
rostrum. His knowledge of human nature was profound. Impulsive and impetuous, he was yet controlled by a sound and
intelligent judgment. He was a born tribune of the people and
inspired confidence in his followers. In debate he was invincible
and was spurred by opposition. His speeches were not always his
own compositions, for he used his friends to aid him in speech
writing—Dumont, Durival, and Reybaz supplied him with the
material for his speeches, but it was Mirabeau's own genius which

immortalized them. Often he would receive his notes as he ascended the rostrum and weave them dexterously into the texture of his discourse. In his greater speeches, however, he abandoned the extemporaneous. The famous speeches *On the Constitution, The Royal Veto,* and *National Education* were painstakingly premeditated. Imaginative appeal, bitter sarcasm, strength and delicacy of innuendo, and a matchless arrangement of argument were employed in presenting the views of this giant of oratory. His voice helped in the regeneration of France and the establishment of liberty under constitutional forms.

The speech presented here shows the compromise on the King's policy which Mirabeau sought in behalf of the people of France.

Gentlemen, the time presses. I reproach myself for every moment that I steal from your sage deliberations; and I hope that these considerations, rather indicated than presented by me,—but whose evidence appears to me irresistible,—will be sufficient to pass the motion which I have the honor now to propose to you:—

That there be presented to the King a humble address, describing to his Majesty the vivid alarm which has been felt in this National Assembly of his kingdom by reason of the abuse which has been made of the King's name, within a short time, in order to permit the approach to the capital, and to this city of Versailles, of an artillery train, and of enormous bodies of troops, foreign and national; a large number of which troops are already quartered in neighboring villages: and also, through this abuse of the King's name, the announced formation of fixed camps in the neighborhood of these two cities.

That there be represented to the King, not only how much these measures are opposed to the gracious intentions of his Majesty toward relieving his people, in the present unhappy conditions of the dearness and scantiness of grain, but also how much these measures are contrary to the liberty and to the honor of the National Assembly; how adapted they are to alter that mutual confidence between the King and his people which makes the glory and the security of a monarch, and which alone can insure the repose and the tranquillity of his kingdom; and, in fine, procure for the nation the inestimable results which the country awaits from the labors and the zeal of this Assembly.

That his Majesty most respectfully be urged to reassure his faithful subjects, by giving all necessary orders for the immediate cessation of these measures, which are equally useless, dangerous, and alarming; and also for the prompt return of the troops in question, and of the artillery train, to the places from which they have been brought.

And while waiting for this measure to be decided, and in consequence of the disquietude and alarm which such a state of affairs has brought to pass in the heart of the people, and in order provisionally to maintain calm and tranquillity, let his Majesty be begged to issue a command that in the two cities of Paris and Versailles there shall be a levy of the civil guard, which acting under the orders of the King, will entirely suffice for such duty without augmenting around the two cities in question a population that must be supplied with food.

ADDRESS TO THE KING

SIRE—You have invited the National Assembly to bestow on you a mark of its confidence; in such a request you have gone further than the most eager of its fervent hopes.

We have been imparting to your Majesty our most vivid alarms: if we only were the object of them, if we had been so weak as to be fearful only for ourselves, then your goodness would condescend to reassure us; and moreover, in blaming us for having been doubtful of your intentions toward us, you would concentrate all our inquietudes, you would dissipate the cause of them, and you would leave no uncertainty as to the position before you of the National Assembly.

But, Sire, we do not implore your protection, for that would be to accuse your justice: we have indeed felt fears, and we dare to say that our fears are a part of the purest patriotism,—the interest of those who trust in us, of public tranquillity, and of the happiness of that dear monarch, who, in making smooth for our feet the road of happiness, certainly deserves to walk in it himself without obstacles.

The promptings of your own heart, Sire—behold in them the true safety of the French people. As soon as troops pour in from all sides, as soon as camps are formed around us, the very capital invested, we ask ourselves with astonishment, "Does the King distrust the fidelity of his own people? If he had doubted that, would he not have confided to us his paternal chagrin? What are we to understand by this menacing procedure? Where are those enemies of the State and of the King to be overcome? Where are the rebels, the conspirators, that it is necessary to reduce to subjection?" One unanimous voice replies to this in the capital and throughout the kingdom: "Our King is true to us; we bless Heaven for the gift which Heaven has bestowed upon us in his love."

Sire, the religious convictions of your Majesty cannot wave except under the pretext of public benefit.

If those who have given these counsels to our King had had enough confidence in their own principles to unfold them to us, such a moment would bring in the fairest triumph of truth.

The State has nothing to dread from the evil ideas of those who dare to lay siege even to the throne, who do not respect the confidence of the purest and most virtuous of princes. And how do they contrive, Sire, to make you disbelieve in the attachment of the love of your subjects? Have you shed their blood? Are you cruel, implacable? Have you abused justice? Do the people impute to you their own misfortunes? Do they connect your name with their calamities? Can they have said to you that the nation is impatient under your yoke, that it is weary of the sceptre of the Bourbons? No, no, they have not done this. The calumny they employ is at least not absurd; they seek something like probability to give color to their dark treacheries.

Your Majesty has seen recently all your own government can do for your people: subordination is re-established in your perturbed capital; the prisoners set at liberty by the multitude have themselves reassumed their chains; public order, which would perhaps have cost torrents of blood to re-establish had it been done by force, has been re-established by one single word from your mouth. But that word was a word of peace; it was the expression of your heart, and your subjects feel it their glory never to resist that. How grand to exercise such authority! It is that of Louis IX, of Louis XII, of Henri IV; it is the only authority which can be worthy of you.

We should deceive you, Sire, if we did not add, forced by circumstances, that this kind of rule is the only one which to-day it would be possible to exercise in France. France will not tolerate the abuse of the best of kings, or that there should be set aside, through untoward measures, that noble plan which he himself has outlined. You have called us hither to adjust, in concert with you, the Constitution; to take measures for the regeneration of the kingdom: this National Assembly has just declared solemnly to you that your wishes shall be accomplished, that your promises are not vain, and that difficulties and terrors shall not retard the work of the Assembly, nor intimidate in any way its courage.

But our enemies will presume to say, "What now is the harm in the coming together of the troops?"

The danger, Sire, is pressing, is general, beyond all the calculations of human prudence.

The danger affects the people of your provinces. Once alarmed as to our liberty, this alarm cannot be checked. Distance only makes more of the matter, exaggerates everything, doubles, sharpens, and poisons their disquietude.

The danger threatens the capital. With what sort of an eye can a people in poverty, and tormented by most cruel anxieties, see the poor relics of its own daily bread quarreled over by a host of menacing soldiery? The mere presence of the military will kindle excitement, and produce a general fermentation; and the first act of real violence, originating under the pretext of a matter for the police, may be the beginning of a horrible series of calamities.

The danger threatens the troops themselves. French soldiers brought near to the very centre of discussion, sharing in the passions as well as in the interests of the people, can easily forget that enlistment has made them soldiers, in remembering that nature has made them men.

The danger, Sire, menaces our own labors, which are our first duty, and which will not have full success, genuine permanence, except so far as the people regard them as the work absolutely of our own free will. Besides this, there is a contagion in passionate popular movements. We are only men. Our defiance of ourselves, the fear of appearing weak, can make us overshoot our mark; we are besieged by violent and unregulated counsels; calm reason and tranquil wisdom do not utter their oracles in the midst of tumult, disorders, and scenes of faction.

The danger, Sire, is even more terrible; judge of its extent by the alarms which bring us to you. Great revolutions have had causes much less intelligible; more than one enterprise fatal to nations and to kings has announced itself in a way less sinister and less formidable. Do not give credence to those who speak lightly to you of the nation at large; those who do not know how to represent it before you except according to their own views—sometimes as insolent, rebellious, seditious—sometimes as submissive, docile under the yoke, and ready to bend its head to receive it. These two pictures are equally untruthful.

Always ready to obey you, Sire, since you command us in the name of the law, our fidelity is without limits, as it is without stain.

Ready to resist to a man the arbitrary commands of those who are abusing your name—since they are enemies of the law—our devotion to your Majesty itself commands such resistance; and it shall be to our eternal honor to have merited the reproaches that our firmness may bring upon us.

Sire, we conjure you, in the name of our fatherland, in the name of your happiness and your glory, send back your soldiers to the garrison posts whence your counselors have brought them; dismiss that artillery destined to protect our frontiers; and above all, send away the foreign troops—those allies of the nation that we paid to defend and not to disturb our firesides. Your Majesty has no need of them: why should a monarch, adored by twenty-five millions of Frenchmen, at an enormous cost draw together around his throne so many thousands of foreigners?

Sire, surrounded by your children, let our love be your guard! The deputies of the nation are summoned to consecrate with you the supreme rights of royalty, upon the immovable basis of a people's liberty: while they reason on these things will you expose them to the suspicion of having yielded not to their sentiment, but to fear? Ah! the authority that all hearts confer on you is the only authority that is pure, the only authority that cannot be defied; it is the just return for your benefits, and it is the immortal appanage of princes, of whom you are the model.

TO DARE, TO DARE AGAIN;
ALWAYS TO DARE

Georges Jacques Danton
(1759-1794)

Born of a bourgeois family, educated in law at Troyes and Paris, Danton was by 1785 a practitioner of law before the Parlement in Paris. He attached himself to the extremists and was one of the founders of the ultra-Jacobin Cordeliers club. Here his violence in speech and counsel as well as his dominant force of personality soon made him the leader of his party. He led the attack on the Tuileries of August 10, 1792, and voted for the death of Louis XVI. Although he sought to save them from violent harm, he was also responsible for the suppression of the Girondists, whom he considered anti-revolutionists. Danton's aim may have been to conciliate the various revolutionary and republican factions into a stable and peaceful government, but he was deterred by the rise of Robespierre, who advocated violence rather than moderation. Danton and his followers fell under the guillotine during The Terror on April 5, 1794.

Danton, like Mirabeau, placed action first. He extemporized his speeches, searching to produce a grand effect of terror or enthusiasm, to incite his hearers to immediate action. His own appearance contributed to this effect, for he was extremely large of physique, and his ugly face could express almost brutal passion. His actions were over-quick, hot and passionate, and his terrible voice thundered when he spoke.

Included here are portions of two speeches most indicative of Danton's style of delivery as well as his statesmanship. The first, against foreign invaders, was delivered before the Assembly on September 2, 1792, and has become famous for its closing words: "To dare, to dare again, always to dare." The second speech, *Freedom of Worship*, shows the moderation of the man when dealing with his opponents, for Vergniaud whom he supports in this speech was a Girondist, of the political faction opposed to the Jacobins whose president Danton was.

It seems a satisfaction for the ministers of a free people to announce to them that their country will be saved. All are stirred, all are enthused, all burn to enter the combat.

You know that Verdun is not yet in the power of our enemies and that its garrison swears to immolate the first who breathes a proposition of surrender.

One portion of our people will guard our frontiers, another will dig and arm the intrenchments, the third with pikes will defend the interior of our cities. Paris will second these great efforts. The commissioners of the Commune will solemnly proclaim to the citizens the invitation to arm and march to the defence of the country. At such a moment you can proclaim that the capital deserves the esteem of all France. At such a moment this National Assembly becomes a veritable committee of war. We ask that you concur with us in directing this sublime movement of the people, by naming commissioners to second and assist all these great measures. We ask that any one refusing to give personal service or to furnish arms shall meet the punishment of death. We ask that proper instructions be given to the citizens to direct their movements. We ask that carriers be sent to all the departments to notify them of the decrees that you proclaim here. The tocsin we shall sound is not the alarm signal of danger, it orders the charge on the enemies of France. (Applause) To conquer we have need to dare, to dare again, always to dare! And France will be saved!

(Pour les vaincre, il nous faut de l'audace; encore de l'audace; toujours de l'audace; et la France est sauvée.)

FREEDOM OF WORSHIP

Georges Jacques Danton

(1759-1794)

We have appeared divided in counsel, but the instant we seek the good of mankind we are in accord. Vergniaud has told us grand and immortal truths. The Constitutional Assembly, embarrassed by a king, by the prejudices which still enchain the nation, and by deep-rooted intolerance, has not up-rooted accepted principles, but has done much for liberty in consecrating the doctrine of tolerance. To-day the ground of liberty is prepared and we owe to the French people a government founded on bases pure and eternal! Yes! we shall say to them: "Frenchmen, you have the right to adore the divinity you deem entitled to your worship: the liberty of worship, which it is the object of law to establish, means only the right of individuals to assemble to render in their way homage to the Deity." Such a form of liberty is enforcible only by legal regulations and the police, but you do not wish to insert regulating laws in your declaration of rights. The right of freedom of worship, a sacred right, will be protected by laws in harmony with its principles. We will have only to guarantee these rights. Human reason cannot retrograde; we have advanced too far for the people ever to believe they are not absolutely free in religious thought, merely because you have failed to engrave the principle of this liberty on the table of your laws. If superstition still seems to inhere in the movements of the Republic, it is because our political enemies always employ it. But look! everywhere the people, freed from malevolent espionage, recognize that any one assuming to interpose between them and their God is an impostor.

Reprinted by courtesy of the Colonial Press.

ON THE SITUATION IN FRANCE

Pierre Victurnien Vergniaud
(1759-1793)

Vergniaud, the greatest orator of the Girondist section of the Revolutionary Assembly in Paris, was second only to Mirabeau as a great orator of the French Revolution. His parents educated him in the Jesuit College of Limoges, his birthplace. Later he studied law and in 1782 was admitted to the bar. In 1789 he delivered his famous speech on *The State of the French Peasantry.* In 1792, a year after he became a member of the Legislative Assembly, he delivered one of his greatest orations before that assembly on *The Trial of the King,* picturing the fatal prostration of the country should the vengeance which controlled the Parisian mob and the policies of the convention succeed in the murder of the king. Yet in the last analysis Vergniaud's own vote was cast for the death of the monarch.

Vergniaud's speech, *The Call to Arms,* delivered on January 18, resulted in a declaration of war against the King of Bohemia and Austria. His continued opposition to Robespierre and to the Revolutionary Tribunal resulted in an accusation against Vergniaud being laid before the Convention, but he frustrated the attack by a brilliant extemporaneous speech. Later, however, his opposition to the atrocities and the anarchy of the Terrorists resulted in his proscription, imprisonment, and death at the guillotine with his allies. His was the crime of moderation at a time of wild and unreasoning frenzy.

Vergniaud was not the equal of Mirabeau in statesmanship. He used the greatest care in the preparation of his speeches, often burdening them with classical references. His oratorical brilliance came in flashes. The effect of his most compelling orations was often weakened by his inability to sustain his efforts over a period of time; thus his most successful speeches were those purposed to secure immediate action.

Included here is one of his speeches delivered July 3, 1792, *On the Situation in France.*

What, then, is the strange position in which the National Assembly finds itself? What fatality pursues us and signalizes each day with great events, carrying disorder into our works and giving us over to the tumultuous agitation of apprehensions, hopes, and passions? What fates prepare for France this terrible ebullition, in the midst of which, did we understand less well the imperishable love of the people for liberty, we should be tempted to doubt whether the Revolution is retrograding, or whether it will run its proper course?

At the moment when your armies of the north seemed to be making progress in Brabant and flattered our courage with auguries of victory, suddenly they were forced to fall back before the enemy; they abandon advantageous positions which they have conquered; they are led back to our own territory, whence the theater of war is fixed; and nothing of us will remain with the unfortunate Belgians but the memory of the fires which will have lighted our retreat. On another side and on the banks of the Rhine our frontiers are threatened by Prussian troops, whose march the ministerial reports have made us hope would not be so sudden. Such is our political and military situation, and never were so necessary the wise arrangement of plans, the prompt execution of means, the union, the accord of all authorities to whom the Constitution delegates the use of armed force; never might become so disastrous the least misinformation, the slightest suspension, the most trifling missteps.

How does it happen that precisely at the last period of the most violent crisis, on the edge of the abyss into which the nation may plunge, the movement of our armies is suspended; that by a sudden disorganization of the ministry the chain of works has been shattered, the bonds of confidence broken, the safety of the empire given up to the inexperience of hands chosen at random, the difficulties of execution multiplied, and its success jeopardized by mistakes which must happen, even with the most enlightened patriotism, in the apprenticeship of a great administration? If plans are conceived which may expedite the completion of our armies, for increasing our means of conquest, or of making our defeats less disastrous, why are they preceded to the throne by calumny and there stifled by the most perfidious malevolence? Can it be true that our triumphs are dreaded? Is it of the blood of the army of Coblentz or of our own that they are sparing?

And you, gentlemen, what great thing are you going to undertake for the commonwealth? You whose courage the enemies of the Constitution insolently flatter themselves that they have shaken; you whose consciences they try each day to alarm by styling the love of liberty as the spirit of faction—as if you could have forgotten that a despotic court also gave the name of factionists to the representatives of the people who went to take the oath of the Tennis-Court; [1] that the cowardly heroes of the aristocracy have constantly lavished it upon the conquerors of the Bastille, upon all those who made and maintained the Revolution, and which the Constituent Assembly believed it to be its duty to honor by proclaiming in one of its addresses that the nation was composed of twenty-four millions of factionists; you who have been so calumniated because you are almost all foreign to the caste which the Revolution threw down into the dust, and because the intriguers who desired to reestablish it, and the degraded men who regret the infamous pleasure of groveling before it have not hoped to find accomplices in you; you, against whom they let loose with so much fury only because you form a truly popular assembly, and because in you they wished to dishonor the people; you who have been so cowardly accused of tarnishing the glory of the constitutional throne, because several times your avenging hand struck those who wished to make it the throne of a despot; you to whom have been infamously and absurdly attributed intentions contrary to your oaths, as if your well-being was not attached to the Constitution—as if, invested with another power than that of the law, you had a civil list to hire counter-revolutionary satellites; you, whom, by the perfidious use of calumny and the language of a hypocritical moderation, they wished to chill toward the interests of the people, because they know that you hold your mission from the people, that the people is your support, and that if by a guilty desertion of its cause you deserved to be abandoned by it, in turn it would be easy to dissolve you; you whom they wanted and, it must be said with sorrow, whom they have succeeded in weakening by fatal divisions, but who doubtless in the present crisis, when the nation is fixing her anxious gaze on you, will feel the need of gathering together all your forces; who will postpone until after the war our noisy quarrels and our wretched dissensions; who will lay down at the foot of the altar of liberty our pride, our jealousies, and our passions; who will not find this mutual hatred so sweet that you will prefer its infernal enjoyment to the welfare of the country; you whom they wanted to terrify with armed petitions as if you did not know that in the beginning of the Revolution the sanctuary of liberty was surrounded by the satellites of despotism, that Paris was besieged by an army, and that those days of danger were those of veritable glory for the Constituent Assembly; you, to whom I have believed I ought to present these swift reflections because at the moment when it is important to stir deeply public opinion it seemed to me indispensable to do away with all the illusions, all the errors which might lessen the effect of your measures;

[1] June 20, 1789.

you, finally, to whom each day discloses a vast horizon of conspiracies, treacheries, dangers; who are placed on the crater of Ætna to ward off the thunderbolt—what are your resources? What does the necessity command you? What does the Constitution allow you?

First, I will call your attention to interior troubles. They have two causes: aristocratic maneuvers, and priestly maneuvers. Both tend to the same end—counter-revolution. You will prevent the action of the first by means of a wise and vigorous police. We must hasten to discuss the bases of it; but when you have done everything that in you lay to save the people from the terrible influence of the second, the Constitution leaves at your further disposal only a last resort: it is simple; nevertheless, I believe that it is just and efficacious. This is it:

The King has refused his sanction to your resolution upon the religious troubles. [2] I do not know whether the somber spirit of the Medici and the Cardinal de Lorraine still wander beneath the arches of the palace of the Tuileries; if the sanguinary hypocrisy of the Jesuits La Chaise and Le Tellier lives again in the soul of some monster burning to see a revival of Saint Bartholomew and the Dragonades; I do not know whether the King's heart is disturbed by the fantastic ideas suggested to him and his conscience disordered by the religious terrors with which he is environed.

But it is not possible to believe, without wronging him and accusing him of being the most dangerous enemy of the Revolution, that he wishes to encourage, by impunity, the criminal attempts of pontifical ambition, and to give to the proud agents of the tiara the disastrous power with which they have equally oppressed peoples and kings. It is not possible to believe, without wronging him and accusing him of being the enemy of the people, that he approves or even looks with indifference on the underhanded schemes employed to divide the citizens, to cast the leaven of hatred into the bosoms of sensitive souls, and to stifle in the name of the Divinity the sweetest sentiments of which He has composed the felicity of mankind. It is impossible to believe, without wronging him and accusing him of being the enemy of the law, that he withholds his consent to the adoption of repressive measures against fanaticism, in order to drive citizens to excesses which despair inspires and the laws condemn; that he prefers to expose unsworn priests, even when they do not disturb the peace, to arbitrary vengeance, rather than to subject them to a law which, affecting only agitators, would cover the innocent with an inviolable egis. Finally it is not possible to believe, without wronging him and accusing him of being the enemy of the Empire, that he wishes to perpetuate sedition and to eternalize the disorders and all the revolutionary movements which

[2] The King vetoed a measure against priests who refused to swear to the Constitution of 1790.

are urging the empire toward civil war, and which, through civil war, would plunge it into dissolution.

It is in the name of the King that the French princes have tried to enlist all the courts of Europe against the nation; it is to avenge the dignity of the King that the treaty of Pilnitz was concluded and the monstrous alliance between the courts of Vienna and Berlin formed; it is to defend the King that we have seen the old companies of life-guards, under the colors of rebellion, hastening to Germany; it is in order to come to the King's aid that the emigrants are soliciting and obtaining places in the Austrian army and are prepared themselves to rend their country; it is to join those valiant knights of the Royal prerogative that other worthies full of honor and delicacy abandon their post in the face of the enemy, violate their oaths, steal the military chests, strive to corrupt their soldiers and thus plunge their glory in dastardliness, perjury, subordination, theft, and assassination; it is against the nation, or the National Assembly alone, and in order to maintain the splendor of the throne, that the king of Bohemia and Hungary makes war upon us, and the king of Prussia marches upon our frontiers; it is in the name of the King that liberty is attacked, and if they succeeded in its overthrow it would be in his name that they indemnify the allied powers for their expenses; because we understand the generosity of kings; we know with what disinterestedness they dispatch their armies to desolate a foreign land, and up to what point they would exhaust their treasuries to maintain a war which could not be profitable to them. Finally, of all the evils which they are striving to heap upon our heads, and of all those which we have to fear, the name alone of the King is the pretext or the cause.

If the King, charged with watching over the external safety of the State, with notifying the legislative body of imminent hostilities, informed of the movements of the Prussian army and not making it known in any way to the National Assembly; informed, or at least able to presume, that this army would attack us in a month, was slow in making preparations for repulsion; if there was a just anxiety about the progress the enemy might make into the interior of France, and if a reserve camp were evidently necessary to check or stop this progress; if there was a resolution making the formation of this camp an immediate certainty; if the King rejected this resolution and substituted for it a plan whose success was uncertain and which demanded so much time for its execution that the enemy would have time to make it impossible; if the legislative body passed resolutions of general safety; if the imminence of the peril allowed no delay; if nevertheless the royal assent was refused or deferred for two months; if the King should trust the command of an army to an intriguing general, [3] suspected by the nation because of the most serious faults, and the most pronounced

[3] Lafayette

attempts upon the Constitution; if another general, [4] bred far from the corruption of courts, and familiar with victory, should ask, for the glory of our arms, a reinforcement which it would be easy to grant him; if, by refusing, the King should clearly say to him: "I forbid you to conquer"; if, profiting by this baleful temporizing, by so much incoherence in our political course, or rather such constant perseverance in treachery, the league of tyrants should strike fatal blows at liberty— could it be said that the King had made the constitutional resistance, that he had taken, for the defense of the State, the steps contemplated by the Constitution which he had made along the line of the formal act which it prescribes?

Coming to present circumstances, I do not think that if our armies are not yet at their full complement, it is through the malevolence of the King. I hope that he will soon increase our means of resistance by a useful employment of battalions so uselessly scattered in the interior of the kingdom; finally I hope that the march of the Prussians through our national guards will not be as triumphal as they have the proud madness to imagine. I am not tormented by the fear of seeing realized the horrible suppositions that I have made; however, as the dangers with which we are invested impose upon us the obligation to foresee everything; as the facts that I have supposed are not devoid of striking conformity with several of the King's speeches; as it is certain that the false friends surrounding him have sold themselves to the conspirators of Coblentz; [5] as they are burning to ruin him in order that some one of their chiefs may reap the fruit of the conspiracy; as it is important for his personal safety, as well as for the tranquillity of the kingdom, that his conduct be no longer encompassed with suspicions; as only great frankness in his proceedings and in his explanations can prevent extreme measures and the bloody quarrels which the latter would give rise to, I should propose a message in which, after such interpellations as circumstances may make it advisable to address to him, would be presented the truths that I have stated; in which it would be demonstrated that the system of neutrality which they seem to be anxious to have him adopt toward Coblentz and France would be arrant treason in the king of the French; that it would bring him no other glory than profound horror from the nation and signal contempt from the conspirators; that, having already chosen France, he should loudly proclaim his unshakeable resolution to triumph or perish with her and the Constitution.

Will you wait until weary of the hardships of the Revolution or corrupted by the habit of groveling around a castle and the insidious preachings of moderantism [6]—until weak men become accustomed to

[4] Lückner
[5] Coblentz was used as headquarters by the Emigrés.
[6] The term Moderantist was applied to the Moderate party.

speak of liberty without enthusiasm and slavery without horror? How does it happen that the constituted authorities block one another in their course; that armed forces forget that they exist to obey; that soldiers or generals undertake to influence the legislative body, and distempered citizens to direct, by the machinery of violence, the action of the chief of the executive authority? Do they wish to establish a military government? That is perhaps the most imminent, the most terrible of our dangers. Murmurs are arising against the court: who shall dare to say they are unjust? It is suspected of treacherous plans; what facts can be cited to dispel these suspicions?

They speak of popular movements, of martial law; they try to familiarize the imagination with the blood of the people; the palace of the king of the French is suddenly changed to a redoubt; yet where are his enemies? Against whom are these cannons and these bayonets pointed? The defenders of the Constitution have been repulsed by the ministry; the reins of the Empire have been hanging loose at the moment when it needed as much vigor as patriotism to hold them. Everywhere discord is fomenting, fanaticism triumphing. Instead of taking a firm and patriotic attitude to save it from the storm, the government lets itself be driven before the tempest; its instability inspires foreign powers with scorn; the boldness of those who vomit armies and swords against us chills the good will of the peoples who wish in secret for the triumph of liberty.

This means is worthy of the august mission which you fill, of the generous people whom you represent; it might even gain some celebrity for the name of that people and make you worthy to live in the memory of men: it will be to imitate the brave Spartans who sacrificed themselves at Thermopylae; those venerable men who, leaving the Roman senate, went to await, at the thresholds of their homes, the death which marched in the van of the savage conqueror. No, you will not need to offer up prayers that avengers may spring from your ashes. Ah! The day when your blood shall redden the earth, tyranny, its pride, its protectors, its palaces, its satellites, will vanish away forever before the national omnipotence. And if the sorrow of not having made your country happy embitters your last moments you will at least take with you the consolation that your death will hasten the ruin of the people's oppressors and that your devotion will have saved liberty.

AGAINST GIVING THE KING A TRIAL

Maximilien Marie Isadore de Robespierre
(1758-1794)

Robespierre, the bloodhound of the Revolution, was by nature a political and religious fanatic who was steeped in the doctrines of Rousseau. Educated for the bar he was elected a member of the States-General in 1789; joined the Jacobin Club of which he became a leader, and through his force and determination of character won over the Parisian Commune. He became the inspiration of the Reign of Terror, which triumphantly sent the chief men of the Girondists to the scaffold.

After the execution of Danton, when the public tide began to turn against him, Robespierre inaugurated a reign of virtue by instituting the worship of the Supreme Being. He won the assent of the Assembly to a festival in this new cause and on June 8 delivered his speech *On the Festival of the Supreme Being* in the midst of the horrors of The Terror.

Robespierre's *Last Speech* was delivered before the convention two days before his own execution and is considered one of his masterpieces. Of greater importance, however, was his speech on the King's trial in which he opposed the Girondists, who desired to have the King tried in a ceremonious manner. By this speech and his attitude throughout the trial Robespierre was able to force even the Girondists to take what to them was an illogical position and vote for the execution of the king.

Lamartine has described Robespierre as a man destitute of exterior graces and the gift of extemporaneous speech, but a man who painstakingly labored for perfection in his utterances and succeeded in the end in a warmth and suppleness of style and a transformation of his stiff and meagre figure, shrill voice, and abrupt gesticulation into an engine of eloquence, of conviction, and of passion.

The speech included here is the one delivered in the Convention on December 3, 1792, *Against Giving the King a Trial.*

The Assembly has unwittingly been drawn far from the actual question. There is no question of a trial. Louis is not an accused; you are not judges; you are only, you can be only, statesmen, and the representatives of the nation. You have no sentence to render for or against a man; but a measure of public safety to take, an act of national providence to perform. A dethroned king, in a Republic, is good only for two purposes—either to trouble the tranquillity of the State and to unsettle liberty, or to establish both. But I maintain that the character which your deliberation has hitherto taken on tends directly against the goal.

Louis was king and the Republic is founded; the great question which occupies you is decided by these words alone. Louis has been dethroned for his crimes; Louis denounced the French people as rebels; to chastise them he has invoked the arms of his brother tyrants. Victory and the people have decided that he was the rebel: hence Louis cannot be judged; he is judged already. He is condemned, or the Republic is not absolved. To propose a trial for Louis XVI in any way whatever is to retrograde toward royal and constitutional despotism; it is a counter-revolutionary idea, for it is putting the revolution itself on trial.

Indeed, if Louis can still be the object of a trial, Louis can be absolved; he can be innocent. What do I say? He is presumed to be so until he is judged. But if Louis is absolved, if Louis can be presumed to be innocent, what does the Revolution become? If Louis is innocent, all the defenders of liberty become calumniators. All the rebels were friends of truth and the defenders of oppressed innocence; all the manifestoes of foreign courts are but legitimate protestations against a ruling faction. Even the confinement which Louis has suffered until the present time is an unjust persecution; the confederates, the people of Paris, all the patriots of the French dominion are guilty; and this great trial pending in the court of nature, between crime and virtue, between liberty and tyranny, is finally decided in favor of crime and tyranny.

When a nation has been forced to resort to the right of insurrection it returns to a state of nature as regards its tyrant. How can the latter invoke the social compact? He has annihilated it. The nation can preserve it still, if it thinks fit, in whatever concerns the interrelations of its citizens: but the effect of tyranny and insurrection is to break it entirely as regards the tyrant; it is to throw them into mutual war; the tribunals, the judiciary procedures, are made for the members of the city. It is a gross contradiction to suppose that the Constitution can preside over this new state of things; that would be to suppose that it survived itself. What are the laws which replace it? Those of nature, which is the basis of society itself; the safety of the people. The right to punish the tyrant and that to dethrone him are the same thing. The one does not admit of different forms from the other. The tyrant's trial is insurrection; his judgment is the fall of his power; his penalty, whatever the liberty of the people demands.

People do not judge like judiciary courts. They pass no sentences; they hurl the thunderbolt. They do not condemn kings: they thrust them back into oblivion; and this justice is not inferior to that of courts. If they arm themselves against their oppressors for their own safety, why should they be bound to adopt a mode of punishing them which would be a new danger to themselves?

We have allowed ourselves to be misled by foreign examples which have nothing in common with us. Since Cromwell caused Charles I to be judged by a tribunal which he controlled, and Elizabeth had Mary Queen of Scots condemned in the same way, it is natural that tyrants who sacrifice their kind, not to the people, but to their own ambition, should seek to deceive the crowd by illusive forms. It is a question neither of principles, nor of liberty, but of trickery and intrigue. But the people! What other law can they follow but justice and reason supported by their omnipotence?

A trial for Louis XVI! But what is this trial, if it is not the call of insurrection to a tribunal or to some other assembly? When a king has been annihilated by the people, who has the right to resuscitate him in order to make of him a new pretext for trouble and rebellion? And what other effects can this system produce? In opening an arena to the champions of Louis XVI you resuscitate all the strife of despotism against liberty; you consecrate the right to blaspheme against the Republic and against the people, because the right to defend the late despot imports the right to say everything that concerns his cause. You arouse all the factions; you revive, you encourage dying royalism. The people might freely take part for or against it. What more legitimate, what more natural than to repeat everywhere the maxims that his defenders would be free to profess at your bar and from your very tribune? What kind of a Republic is it whose founders raise up adversaries on every side to attack it in its cradle!

It is a great cause, it is said, which must be judged with wise and slow circumspection. It is you who make a great cause of it. What do I say? I say that it is you who make a cause of it. What do you find great in it? Is it its difficulty? No. Is it the person? In the eyes of liberty there is none more vile; in the eyes of humanity there is none more guilty. He can impose again only on those who are more cowardly than himself. Is it the utility of the result? That is one more reason for hastening it. A great cause is a project of popular law; a great cause is that of an unfortunate oppressed by despotism. What is the motive of these everlasting delays which you recommend to us? Are you afraid of wounding popular opinion? As if the people themselves feared anything but the weakness or ambition of their mandatories! As if the people were a vile troop of slaves, stupidly attached to the stupid tyrant whom they have proscribed, desiring at whatever price to wallow in baseness and servitude! You speak of opinion; is it not for you to direct it, to fortify it? If it goes astray, if it becomes depraved, whom must it blame if not you yourselves? Are you afraid of displeasing the foreign kings leagued against us? Oh! without doubt, the way to conquer them is to appear to fear them: the way to confound the criminal conspiracy of the despots of Europe is to respect their accomplice. Are you afraid of foreign peoples? Then you still believe in the inborn love of tyranny.

Why then do you aspire to the glory of emancipating the human race? By what contradiction do you suppose that the nations which have not been astonished by the proclamation of the rights of humanity will be terrified by the chastisement of one of its most cruel oppressors? Finally, you fear, it is said, the verdict of posterity. Yes, posterity will be astonished indeed at your inconsistency and your weakness; and our descendants will laugh both at the presumption and the prejudices of their ancestors. It has been said that genius is necessary to penetrate this question. I maintain that it requires only good faith: it is much less a matter of self-enlightenment than of not wilfully blinding one's self. Why does a thing which seems clear to us at one time seem obscure at another?

I have heard the defenders of inviolability advance a bold principle which I should have almost hesitated to express myself. They said that those who would have slain Louis XVI on the tenth of August would have performed a virtuous action. But the sole basis of this opinion can be the crimes of Louis XVI and the rights of the people. Has an interval of three months changed his crimes or the rights of the people? If then he was snatched away from public indignation it was without doubt solely that his punishment, solemnly ordered by the National Convention in the name of the nation, should be more imposing to the enemies of humanity; but to bring up the question whether he is guilty or whether he can be punished is to betray the trust of the French people.

Of what importance to the people is the contemptible person of the last of the kings? Representatives, what is important to them, what is important to yourselves, is that you fulfil the duties which their confidence has imposed upon you. You have proclaimed the Republic, but have you given it to us? We have not yet made a single law which justifies that name; we have not yet reformed a single abuse of despotism. Away with names; we have still tyranny complete, and in addition, factions more vile and charlatans more immoral, with new ferments of troubles, and of civil war. The Republic! and Louis still lives! and you still place the person of the king between us and liberty! Let us fear to make criminals of ourselves on account of our scruples; let us fear that by showing too much indulgence for the guilty we may place ourselves in his place.

A new difficulty! To what punishment shall we condemn Louis? The punishment of death is too cruel. No, says another, life is more cruel still. I ask that he may live. Advocates of the king, is it through pity or cruelty that you wish to save him from the penalty of his crimes? As for me, I abhor the penalty of death so lavish in your laws, and I have neither love nor hatred for Louis. Crimes only I hate. I have asked the Assembly, which you still call Constituent, for the abolition of the death penalty, and it is not my fault if the first principles of reason seem to it moral and political heresies. But if you never bethought yourselves to invoke them in favor of so many unfortunates whose offenses are less their own than those of the government, by what fatality do you remember them only to plead the cause of the greatest of all criminals? You ask an exception to the death penalty for him alone against whom it can be legitimate! Yes, the penalty of death generally is a crime, and for that reason alone, according to the indestructible principles of nature, it can be justified only in cases when it is necessary for the safety of individuals or the social body. Public safety never demands it against ordinary offenses, because society can always guard against them by other means and make the offender powerless to harm it. But a dethroned king in the bosom of a revolution which is anything but cemented by laws, a king whose name suffices to draw the scourge of war on the agitated nation, neither prison nor exile can render his existence immaterial to the public welfare; and this cruel exception to ordinary laws which justice approves can be imputed only to the nature of his crimes.

It is with regret that I utter this fatal truth. But Louis must die, because the country must live. Among a people at peace, free and respected at home and abroad, the counsels to generosity given you might be entertained. But a people whose liberty is still contested after so many sacrifices and combats; a people among whom the laws are still inexorable only toward the unfortunate; a people among whom the crimes of tyranny are still the subjects of debate, must long for vengeance; and the generosity with which we are flattered would seem too much like that of a band of brigands dividing the spoils.

I move to resolve forthwith upon the fate of Louis XVI. As for his wife, you will send her back to the courts, as well as all other persons accused of the same criminal attempts. His son shall be guarded at the Temple, until such time as peace and public liberty shall have been established. As for him, I ask that the Convention declare him, from this moment, a traitor to the French nation, a criminal toward humanity. I ask that it make a great example before the world on the very spot where died, the tenth of August, a noble martyr of liberty. I ask that this memorable event be commemorated by a monument designed to nourish in the hearts of the people the consciousness of their rights and the horror of tyrants; and in the souls of tyrants a salutary terror of the people's justice.

TO THE SOLDIERS ON ENTERING MILAN

Napoleon Bonaparte

(1769-1821)

Napoleon Bonaparte, the greatest military orator of whom we have record, stood alone as the orator of France in the interim between the Directory and the Restoration. He established the strictest censorship over the press and speech, so that men dared not speak except to echo him. The freedom of speech by which the revolutionary leaders had gained power was forgotten, for the Empire had at Napoleon's touch replaced the Republic. He deified the "Glory of France," and by appealing to that concept became the greatest military leader and orator of the world.

Napoleon spoke with power, for his actions were eloquent; he addressed his troops before and after battle; he also issued bulletins and addresses which are unique in the history of oratory. According to any established standard these speeches are not eloquent—under ordinary circumstances they would have been mere declamations. His sentences were short, his words simple but directed to the hearts of his soldiers. He was profuse in his praise of their valor and ever inspired them to greater achievements. The tremendous energy of these speeches gave them point and weight. He knew the correct thing to say at the correct time, and his authoritative and commanding presence and his rare intuition of human nature made him the most beloved and powerful of military geniuses. Even after Waterloo, Napoleon remained eloquent to the end. His last wish was oratorical:

"I desire that my ashes repose on the banks of the Seine in the midst of the people whom I have loved so much."

Included here are two of his speeches. The first one was addressed to his soldiers, May 15, 1796, on entering Milan while

he was at the height of his power.   The second speech is his farewell to his soldiers at Fontainebleau, April 20, 1814, when he
was about to depart into exile.

SOLDIERS—You have rushed like a torrent from the top of the Apen-
nines; you have overthrown and scattered all that opposed your march.
Piedmont, delivered from Austrian tyranny, indulges her natural senti-
ments of peace and friendship toward France.   Milan is yours, and the
Republican flag waves throughout Lombardy.   The Dukes of Parma and
Modena owe their political existence to your generosity alone.

The army which so proudly threatened you can find no barrier to
protect it against your courage; neither the Po, the Ticino, nor the Adda
could stop you for a single day.   These vaunted bulwarks of Italy opposed
you in vain; you passed them as rapidly as the Apennines.

These great successes have filled the heart of your country with joy.
Your representatives have ordered a festival to commemorate your victories, which has been held in every district of the Republic.   There your
fathers, your mothers, your wives, sisters, and mistresses rejoiced in your
good fortune and proudly boasted of belonging to you.

Yes, soldiers, you have done much—but remains there nothing more
to do?   Shall it be said of us that we knew how to conquer, but not how
to make use of victory?   Shall posterity reproach us with having found
Capua in Lombardy?

But I see you already hasten to arms.   An effeminate repose is tedious
to you; the days which are lost to glory are lost to your happiness.   Well,
then, let us set forth!   We have still forced marches to make, enemies to
subdue, laurels to gather, injuries to revenge.   Let those who have sharpened the daggers of civil war in France, who have basely murdered our
ministers and burnt our ships at Toulon, tremble!

The hour of vengeance has struck; but let the people of all countries
be free from apprehension; we are the friends of the people everywhere,
and those great men whom we have taken for our models.   To restore
the capitol, to replace the statues of the heroes who rendered it illustrious, to rouse the Roman people, stupefied by several ages of slavery—
such will be the fruit of our victories; they will form an era for posterity;
you will have the immortal glory of changing the face of the finest part
of Europe.   The French people, free and respected by the whole world,
will give to Europe a glorious peace, which will indemnify them for the
sacrifices of every kind which for the last six years they have been making.   You will then return to your homes and your country.   Men will
say, as they point you out, "He belonged to the Army of Italy."

FAREWELL TO THE OLD GUARD

Napoleon Bonaparte

(1769-1821)

SOLDIERS OF MY OLD GUARD—I bid you farewell. For twenty years I have constantly accompanied you on the road to honor and glory. In these latter times, as in the days of our prosperity, you have invariably been models of courage and fidelity. With men such as you our cause could not be lost; but the war would have been interminable; it would have been civil war, and that would have entailed deeper misfortunes on France.

I have sacrificed all my interests to those of the country.

I go, but you, my friends, will continue to serve France. Her happiness was my only thought. It will still be the object of my wishes. Do not regret my fate; if I have consented to survive, it is to serve your glory. I intend to write the history of the great achievements we have performed together. Adieu, my friends. Would I could press you all to my heart.

Napoleon then ordered the eagles to be brought, and, having kissed them, he added:

I embrace you all in the person of your general. Adieu, soldiers! Be always gallant and good.

DEMOCRACY IN FRANCE

François Guizot

(1787-1874)

Guizot was born of Protestant parents. His father having perished on the scaffold during the Reign of Terror, Guizot was brought up by his mother in Geneva. In 1812 he was called to France to fill the chair of modern history at the Sorbonne. By 1820 Guizot was one of the leaders of the liberal opposition to the government of Charles X. In 1830 he was elected to the Chamber of Deputies; his first speech to the Chamber being a defense of the celebrated address of the 221. After the second Restoration, Guizot served as director of the Ministry of the Interior. He was one of the leaders of the Doctrinaires who desired a *juste milieu* between absolutism and democracy. In the year 1840 Guizot started an administration which lasted eight years—the last regime under the constitutional monarchy of France. During this period, through his indomitable courage and splendid eloquence, Guizot was able to restore amicable relations with the other powers of Europe and to establish in France a consciousness based on thrift and prudence rather than on ambition and glory.

Guizot was a master of parliamentary tactics, more powerful in defense than in opposition. His style was austere and terse rather than persuasive and humorous, but was always most effectively concise. In *Democracy in France* Guizot shows very ably his political acumen.

Mirabeau, Barnave, Napoleon, and Lafayette, who died at distant and very dissimilar periods, in bed or on the scaffold, in their own country or in exile, all died under the influence of one sentiment—a sentiment of profound melancholy. They thought their hopes deceived, their labors abortive. They were assailed by doubts of the success of their cause, and by misgivings as to the future.

King Louis Philippe reigned above seventeen years, for more than eleven of which I had the honor to be his minister. If to-morrow it pleased God to summon us into His presence, should we quit this earth very confident in the future destiny and the constitutional order of our country?

Is then the French Revolution destined to give birth only to doubt and deception?—to bury all its triumphs under ruins?

Yes: so long as France shall suffer the true and the false, the upright and the perverse, the practicable and the chimerical, the salutary and the pestilent to be constantly mingled and confounded in her opinions, her institutions, and the government of her affairs, such will be the unfailing and inevitable result.

Until a people which has gone through a great revolution has passed on the principles, the passions, and the doctrines which have led to this revolution, a sentence like that which shall be passed on all human things at the Last Day, "severing the wheat from the tares, and the corn from the straw that shall be cast into the fire," it can never surmount the perils, nor reap the advantages, of the struggle in which it has been engaged.

So long as this judgment is deferred, chaos reigns; and chaos, if prolonged in the midst of a people, would be death.

Chaos is now concealed under one word—Democracy.

This is now the sovereign and universal word which all parties invoke, all seek to appropriate as a talisman.

The Monarchists say, "Our Monarchy is a Democratic Monarchy: therefore it differs essentially from the ancient Monarchy, and is adapted to the modern condition of society."

The Republicans say, "The Republic is Democracy governing itself. This is the only form of government in harmony with a democratic society, its principles, its sentiments, and its interests."

Socialists, Communists, and Montagnards require that the republic should be a pure and absolute democracy. This, in their estimation, is the condition of its legitimacy.

Such is the power of the word Democracy, that no government or party dares to raise its head, or believe its own existence possible, if it does not bear that word inscribed on its banner; and those who carry that banner aloft with the greatest ostentation and to the extremest limits, believe themselves to be stronger than all the rest of the world.

Fatal idea, which incessantly excites and foments social war amongst us! This idea must be extirpated; for on its extirpation depends social peace, and, in her train, liberty, security, prosperity, dignity, all the benefits, material or moral, which social peace alone can insure.

The following are the causes to which the word Democracy owes its power.

It is the banner of all the social hopes and ambitions of man—pure or impure, noble or base, rational or irrational, possible or chimerical.

Now it is the glory of man to be ambitious. He alone, of all created beings, does not passively resign himself to evil; he alone incessantly aspires after good; not only for himself, but for his fellow-creatures. He respects and loves the race to which he belongs; he wishes to find a remedy for their miseries, and redress for their wrongs.

But man is no less imperfect than he is ambitious. Amidst his ardent and unceasing struggles to eradicate evil and to achieve good, every one of his virtuous inclinations is accompanied by an evil inclination which treads closely on its heels, or strives with it for precedence. The desire for justice and the desire for vengeance—the spirit of liberty and the spirit of tyranny—the wish to rise and the wish to abase what has risen—the ardent love of truth and the presumptuous temerity of fancied knowledge;—we may fathom all the depths of human nature; we shall find throughout, the same mingled yet conflicting qualities, the same danger from their close and easy approximation.

To all these instincts, at once contrary and parallel—to all indiscriminately, the bad as well as the good—the word Democracy holds out an interminable vista and infinite promises. It fosters every propensity, it speaks to every passion, of the heart of man; to the most generous and the most shameful, the most moral and the most immoral, the gentlest and the harshest, the most beneficent and the most destructive; to the former it loudly offers, to the latter it secretly and dimly promises, satisfaction.

Such is the secret of its power.

I am wrong in saying, the secret. The word Democracy is not new, and in all ages it has signified what it signifies now. But what is new and proper to our times is this: the word Democracy is now pronounced every day, every hour, and in every place; and at every time and place it is heard by all men. This formidable appeal to all that is most potent, for good and for evil, in man and in society, was formerly heard only transiently, locally, and among certain classes, which, though bound to other classes by the ties of a common country, were distinct and profoundly different from them. They lived at a distance from each other; each obscurely known to the other. Now there is but one society; and in this society there are no more lofty barriers, no more great distances, no more mutual obscurities. Whether it be false or true, noxious or salutary, when once a social idea arises, it penetrates everywhere, and its action is universal and constant. It is a torch that is never extinguished; a voice that is never wearied or hushed. Universality and publicity are from henceforth the conditions of all the great provocations addressed to men—of all the great impulses given to society.

This is doubtless one of those absolute and sovereign facts which enter into the designs of God with regard to mankind.

Such being the fact, the empire of the word Democracy is not to be regarded as a transitory or local accident. It is the development—

others would say the explosion—of all the elements of human nature throughout all the ranks and all the depths of society; and consequently the open, general, continuous, inevitable struggle of its good and evil instincts; of its virtues and its vices; of all its powers and faculties, whether to improve or to corrupt, to raise or to abase, to create or to destroy. Such is, from henceforth, the social state, the permanent condition of our nation.

Published by D. Appleton & Company.
Reprinted by permission.

ON THE WASTEFULNESS OF IMPERIAL FRANCE

Adolphe Louis Thiers
(1797-1877)

Thiers was one of the most influential political leaders ever produced by France. Distinguished as a student at the lycée he was encouraged to study law and later enrolled as a contributor to the *Constitutional,* the leading Liberal organ. Under Louis Philippe, Thiers was elected a member of the Chamber of Deputies where he frequently appeared as an eloquent spokesman of the Opposition. In 1863 he entered the Corps Législatif, where he assailed the Imperial policies in a series of masterly speeches. In 1867 he made a speech against Napoleon's foreign policy and in 1870 vigorously opposed the war with Prussia, declaring that Napoleon had committed another blunder. When the Empire collapsed, Thiers undertook diplomatic trips to England, Prussia, Italy, and Austria on behalf of France and won thereby the gratitude of his countrymen. When the French Republic was organized in 1871, Thiers was elected President and in the three years he served in that capacity accomplished much to overcome the evil effects of the war. He used his influence always to defend the Republic against monarchism.

In stature Thiers was small and clumsy, and slovenly in dress. His voice had a nasal twang, and he never lost a provincial singsong dialect. He chatted when he spoke—interspersing his speech with anecdotes and historical allusions. His first attempts at oratory were reported as being ridiculous, but when he adopted the rapid, incisive style suited to his personality, he became a most powerful speaker.

Included here is a portion of the speech *On the Wastefulness of Imperial France* in which Thiers uses sarcasm most effectively.

Since our new institutions diminished the share which our nation took in managing its own affairs, it was feared that the activity of mind with which I am reproached might be dangerous, unless means should be found to occupy the attention of the country. These means, sometimes dangerous, always odious, have been wars abroad, and enormous expenditure and great speculations at home. After great wars come small ones—small, if we consider the number of men engaged, but large if we consider their distance and the serious complications they may cause. The war in Mexico has already cost us more than the Italian war, to say nothing of the complications it may entail. The war expenditure, has, of course, been met by loans, and the public debt has consequently been considerably increased. Next come our great public works, an excellent employment for the country's savings in times of peace, as every sensible man will acknowledge; but we ought to proceed prudently.

It is a mistake to suppose, as some do, that there need be no limit to the application of our savings to public works; agriculture and manufactures ought to have their share, and if only a portion should be employed by the State in improving roads, canals and other means of communication, still less should be devoted to the mere embellishment of towns. It is certainly necessary to widen the streets and improve the salubrity of cities, but there is no necessity for such vast changes as have been operated in Paris, where, I think, all reasonable limits have been exceeded. The contagion of example is to be feared. The proverb says that he who commits one folly is wise. If Paris only were to be rebuilt I should not have much to say against it, but you know what La Fontaine wittily says:

"Every citizen must build like a lord,
Every little prince have his ambassadors,
Every marquis have his pages."

The glory of the Prefect of the Seine has troubled all the prefects. The Prefect of the Seine has rebuilt the Tuileries, and the Prefect of the Bouches-du-Rhone wants to have his Tuileries also.

Last year the Minister of State answered me that only a trifling expenditure was intended, not more than six millions; but it appears from the debates of the Council-General that the expense will be twelve or fourteen millions, and some persons say as much as twenty millions. I know that the Prefect of the Bouches-du-Rhone is a senator; but if it takes twelve millions to build him a residence, that is a large sum. All the other prefects will be eager to follow his example, as the Prefect of Lisle is already. The sub-prefects, also, will want new residences and new furniture. Where would all this lead to? The Minister of Public Works, full of glory, must have more consideration for the cares of the Minister of Finance. But here we have a new Minister of

Public Works, with a new glory to make, and demands for millions multiply.

The Minister of Finance defends himself as well as he can, but appears to be conquered; he might resist by resigning, certainly; but that is a means borrowed from past days. A compromise is at least effected. To spare the Treasury, one hundred millions are to be obtained by selling part of the State forests. For this, however, your consent is necessary; but the matter is settled in principle, and the public domain will supply the funds which the Treasury refuses. By whom is this torrent of expenditure to be arrested? By yourselves, gentlemen! Your wisdom, courage and patriotism can alone achieve the task. Your responsibility is great, especially in financial matters; in politics your powers may be contested to a certain extent, but in questions of finance they are undisputed. In finances you, therefore, are responsible for everything. It is time to halt in this course of expenditure, and not to imitate those sinners who are always talking of reforming and, after all, die in financial impenitence.

We are often told that financial science is obscure, but the assertion is untrue. Sciences are never obscure, except through the dullness of those who expound them, or the charlatanism of those who assume a false air of profundity. I will take my examples from private life. Let us suppose two fathers; one methodical, strict and somewhat morose; the other easy and good natured. The former will regulate his expenditure according to his income, and fix limits which he will not pass; during the year this may cause some deprivation to himself and his family, but when settling day comes he has neither anxiety nor embarrassment. The latter takes no such precautions; he passes quietly thru the year, restricting neither his own expenditures nor that of his family; but when he settles his accounts he finds that he has exceeded his income and is obliged to encroach on his capital to pay his debts; and this goes on from year to year with ever increasing embarrassment until ruin stares him in the face. The stern father, meanwhile, has preserved or even increased his estate, and taught his children that which will be useful to them through life. As in private life, so it is in public affairs. Statesmen have the same passions as other men, and it is only by resisting these passions that they can save the State. . . .

I ask your pardon for speaking so warmly, but it is impossible to treat a graver or more interesting subject. I repeat that you are running toward the double rock, either of failing in your engagements, or of rendering inevitable the imposition of various taxes which may give rise to deplorable divisions. I abjure you to reflect most seriously on this state of affairs. You are on the brink of a financial gulf if you persist in the present course. I ask pardon for distressing you, but it is my duty to tell you the truth, and I tell it, whatever the result may be.

FREE SPEECH NECESSARY FOR GOOD GOVERNMENT

Benjamin Constant

(1767-1830)

Among the orators of the Restoration was Benjamin Constant, who came from Switzerland, the land of his birth, in 1795 as a protégé of Madame de Staël and settled in Paris. Here he took an active part in the politics of the day and wrote and argued in favor of constitutional liberty and freedom of the press. Banished by Napoleon, he returned after the Restoration of the Bourbon monarchy. Following a second exile he was elected to the Chamber of Deputies and continued to hold a seat in that body until 1830. Included here is *Free Speech Necessary for Good Government,* an address delivered in the Chamber of Deputies at Paris, March 23, 1820.

I would ask the minister if he has reflected on the inevitable consequences incident to the suspension, temporary or otherwise, of the free circulation of our newspapers. It may render him ignorant of all that is passing in the cliques of parasites and flatterers at court. All governments, whether liberal or despotic (you see I eschew the words "foreign to the interests or rights of the people"), must rely for security on some means of knowing what is transpiring in the State. Even in Turkey the viziers are sometimes irritated at being deceived by their pashas as to the situation of the provinces, and perhaps much may be attributed to the inexact knowledge a neighbor prince had of the dispositions of his garrisons when he saw them declare against him. Now, gentlemen, I assert it as a fact, that in suspending the free circulation of newspapers, the government condemns itself to know nothing, except from the advices of its salaried servants; that is to say, it will never know more than half the facts, and frequently it will believe the opposite of the true conditions. To prove this truth I shall not resort to reasoning. Reasoning is too near liberty to need to be availed of. I shall invoke only a few facts, because facts are always the same. As we have seen, the chartered rights of the people may be demolished, but the facts remain impregnable.

Well, then, gentlemen, will you remember the occurrence in Lyons in June, 1817? France was then under the exceptional laws under which you had placed her. Individual liberty was then, as it again will be, at the mercy of a ministry, and the censor made of journalism what you will do here in a week, if you adopt this proposed law.

What was the result then, gentlemen? A real or a sham conspiracy resulted. The severest measures were taken. Many men were put to death, and for a long time persecution was a political method. Well! All this was done and the government did not know just what it was agitating for. The government saw its error itself, for after all these executions had taken place, when, as a result, the conditions were irreparable, a marshal of France was sent to the field of these bloody severities to enlighten the Ministry on the true state of things. In the meanwhile, they incarcerated, judged, condemned, executed, and all without knowing wherefore; for had it not been felt necessary to inform them, the tardy mission of M. le Maréchal Marmont would not have been thought necessary. I shall not enter into this lugubrious history, nor judge between those who affirm or deny their authority in the conspiracy. Who is right or wrong—this has no bearing on what I would prove. What is important is that for months the government was in ignorance of the facts, and they had to send a personal messenger to report eye-witness on which they could depend.

But, gentlemen, it might have been otherwise. If in the Department of the Rhone there had been a single liberal journal, this journal—Jacobin, revolutionary, or whatever you would call it—might present things from a different point of view from the local authorities. The government might hear the two sides. It should not commence by striking without reason, afterward to send to find if it had any cause for striking.

I may be mistaken, but I think this side of the question has never been indicated, and that it is worthy examination. In suspending the free circulation of newspapers, the Ministry announce that they desire to hear or learn nothing save by their own agents—that is to say if their agents are by imprudence, by any personal motives or passions, on a false route, they will learn from them only that which they think plausible to place their merit in evidence or to assure their justification. Is this to the interest of government? I ask the Ministry to reflect. If at all times I treat this only from the stand-point of the interest of the Ministry, it is because I would address them words they would hear. If it concerned them alone, I need not speak. All authority brings with it the penalties of its responsibilities, its vexations, and false measures; nothing can be more just, and what the result would be to the ministry is to me indifferent.

But as the example at Lyons has shown us, the people resent this, and I would save the poor people a part of the sufferings toward which this new régime is inevitably conducting us. I call this a new régime, because it is different from what the charter had commenced to introduce in France. But I might as well and more justly call it the old régime, for it is the old régime which we are reconstructing piece by piece; lettres de cachet, censures, oligarchic elections—these are the bases of the edifice! The columns and the capitals will come later! I ask the Ministry if they intend to govern France without knowing her. Will they adopt measures depending on events of which they are informed only by men whose interests are presumably to disguise them; to commit thus without profit to themselves much injustice which they can never repair? If this be their intent, the suspension of the liberty of the press is a sure method of its fulfilment. But if they find that the French people value the right of being heard before being condemned, and that twenty-eight million citizens should not be struck upon uncertain and possibly false reports, then the journals must be left free in their field of labor. Whatever the result, I am happy to have thus put the question. France will know if this be refused how much importance the Ministry attach to her requests by the lightness with which they treat them. I ask if they will do me the honor to reply, that they refute the example cited in the case of Lyons and not lose themselves in vague declamations in reply to the citation of a precise case.

Let us pass to another subject on which two words of explanation will be useful. To suspend the free circulation of the press is to place the newspapers in the hands of a minister, and to authorize the insertion in them of what he pleases.

Have you forgotten, gentlemen, what occurred when a law, similar to the one you would resurrect, gave to a cabinet minister this power? I would not speak of the elections. I should be ashamed to recapitulate facts so well known. It were idle almost to tell the damage caused, for in three successive elections the minister discredited the official articles attacking the candidates. He only contributed to their election. On my part, I owe him gratitude in this respect and I pardon his intentions for their favorable results.

The facts I want you to consider are much more important. You will probably remember that in the summer of the year 1818 several individuals who had filled responsible functions were arrested because they were suspected of conspiracy. I am not called on to explain or to defend these individuals. Their innocence or their guilt has nothing to do with this matter. They were detained; they were ironed; they had yet to be judged; and as they were to be exposed to the rigors of justice, they had a rightful claim on its safeguards. General Canuel was among the number. Well, gentlemen, while General Canuel was incarcerated, what did the minister do? He selected a journal of which the editors were friendly to the inculpated, and in it inserted the most damaging articles, and as they related to a man who was untried and unconvicted, I call them the most infamous. These articles circulated throughout France, and he against whom they had been directed had not the power to respond with a line. Do you find in this ministerial usage of the press anything delicate, loyal, legitimate? It is this slavish use of the press they would solicit you to enact anew.

This condition can never be renewed. The constituency of our present ministry is a guarantee against it.

By a law against universal liberty, you place the rights of all citizens at the discretion of a ministry. By suspending the freedom of the press, you will place at their mercy all reputations. I shall not stop to examine the promises of the Minister of the Interior on this anodyne measure, which is to "stop personalities," to "encourage enlightenment," and to "leave writers free." What opinion have the censors?

Censors are to thought what spies are to innocence; they both find their gains in guilt, and where it does not exist they create it. Censors class themselves as lettered. Producing nothing themselves, they are always in the humor of their sterility. No writer who respects himself would consent to be a censor. The title of royal censor was almost a reproach under the ancient régime. Has it been rehabilitated under the imperial censorship? These men will bring into the monarchy all the traditions of the empire. They will treat the liberty of the press as they do the administration, and we shall be marching under the guidance of the errors of Bonaparte, without the prestige of his imperial glory and the quiet of its unity.

AGAINST PRESS CENSORSHIP

Pierre Paul Royer-Collard

(1763-1845)

Royer-Collard at the outbreak of the Revolution was practicing law in Paris. He took the popular side with the Girondists, but became disgusted with the Reign of Terror, so retired to his lectureship in Philosophy at the University of France where he exercised a powerful influence on the philosophic thought of all France. He was elected to the French Academy in 1827 and in 1828 became President of the Chamber of Deputies. It was in the latter capacity that he presented the famous address of the 221 deputies in March, 1830, refusing to support the government— a speech which the king refused to have read to him.

There is a virility in Royer-Collard's speeches which reminds one of Mirabeau. De Cormenin, a French contemporary, states that Royer-Collard did more than any other man to form the manners of French constitutionalism. Included here is his speech *Against Press Censorship,* delivered before the French Chamber of Deputies at Paris in 1828.

In the ideas of some men, it was imprudent on the great day of creation to allow man, a free and intelligent being, to escape into the midst of the universe! A more lofty wisdom is now about to repair this fault of Providence and to render humanity, sagely mutilated, the service of elevating it at last to the happy innocence of the brute creation! The Author of all things formerly thought otherwise; but he was wrong! Truth is a good, say these men, more provident than nature, but error is an evil. Perish, then, both truth and error! As a prison is the natural remedy for liberty, ignorance will be the natural remedy for intelligence; ignorance is the true science of men and of society! Gentlemen, a law which thus denies the existence of mind is an atheistical law and should not be obeyed! Alas! we have passed through periods when, the authority of the law having been usurped by tyranny, evil was called good, and virtue crime. During this fearful test we did not seek for the rule of our actions in the law, but in our consciences: we obeyed God rather than men. Must we, under the legitimate government, be brought back to these deplorable recollections? We shall still be the same men! Your law, be it well understood, will be vain, for France is better than its government! Counsellors of the crown, what have you done hitherto? Who has raised you above your fellow-citizens that you assume a right to impose a tyranny upon them? Obscure and ordinary men like ourselves, you only surpass us in temerity! Such senseless audacity can only be met with in factions. Your law, therefore, denounces a faction in the government with as much certainty as if this faction had denounced itself. I shall not ask it what it is, whence it comes, or whither it is going, for it would tell me falsehoods! I judge this faction by its works! It now proposes to you to destroy the liberty of the press; last year it exhumed from the Middle Ages the right of primogeniture, and the year before it introduced sacrilege! It is thus retrograding. It matters not to me whether it be called counter-revolution or otherwise; it is going backward in religion and policy! It clings to fanaticism, to privilege, to ignorance, and to barbarism, or to the absurd domination which barbarism favors! The enterprise, however, will not be so easy to accomplish. In future not another line is to be printed in France! With all my heart! A brazen frontier shall preserve us from foreign contagion! Well and good! But for a long time discussion has existed in the world between good and evil, between the true and the false. It fills innumerable volumes, which have been read over and over, day and night, by an inquisitive generation. Whole libraries of books have passed into the minds of men. It is from thence you must banish them: have you a law ready for that purpose? So long as we shall not forget what we know, we shall be ill-disposed to brutishness and slavery. But the action of mind is not solely derived from books; springing from freedom of condition, it exists in labor, in riches, and in leisure; while it is nourished by the assemblages of towns and the facility of communication. To enslave men it is necessary to disperse and to impoverish them, for misery is the safeguard of ignorance. Believe me, reduce the population, discard the men of industry from the soil, burn the manufactories, fill up the canals, plow up the highways. If you do not effect all this, you will have accomplished nothing; if the plow does not pass entirely over civilization, that which remains will be sufficient to baffle your efforts.

I cannot support the amendments of the committee, or indeed any amendments. The law is neither worthy nor susceptible of any. There is no arrangement to be made with the principle of tyranny by which it was dictated. I reject it purely and simply out of respect for humanity which it degrades, and for justice by which it is outraged.

Reprinted by courtesy of the Colonial Press.

REPLY TO THE POLISH DEPUTATION

Alphonse de Lamartine
(1790-1869)

By nature and temperament Lamartine was a poet. The grace and beauty which mark his prose and poetry are also found in his speeches, but when found in the latter they appear rather emotional.

On February, 1848, when a seditious mob crowded the streets of Paris demanding a red flag of anarchy instead of the tri-color of the Republic, Lamartine, a member of the Revolutionary Government, in a passionate burst of eloquence calmed the furor and brought reason out of chaos. It was one of the most remarkable triumphs of oratory in history and placed Lamartine high in the rank of political orators. He subsequently became the moderator of the Revolution, repressing violence through his eloquence, courage, and magnanimity.

Lamartine's speech on the *Question of the East,* embracing proposals for the basis of a new European system, gave him a position in the Chamber of Deputies. When his popularity waned, Lamartine applied himself to his historical writings.

Included here is a speech delivered in 1848, when he was minister of foreign affairs, in reply to a request for assistance in re-establishing Polish nationality.

France owes you not only good wishes and tears, but moral and eventual assistance in return for the Polish blood with which you have bedewed every battlefield in Europe during our great wars. France will pay her debt; rely on that; trust to the hearts of thirty-six millions of Frenchmen. Only leave to France that which exclusively belongs to her—the season, the moment, and the form, of which providence shall determine the choice and suitability, to restore you, without aggression or bloodshed, to that place which is your due in the catalogue of nations.

You may be acquainted with the principles which the provisional government of the Republic has universally adopted in its foreign policy. In case you are not, let me recapitulate them: The Republic is undoubtedly republican, and she openly proclaims it to the world; but the Republic is not at open or secret war with any nation or existing government so long as these nations and governments do not declare themselves at war with her.

She will not, therefore, commit or voluntarily suffer to be committed any act of violence or aggression against the Germanic nations. They, at this moment, are occupied in modifying their internal system of confederation, and in assuring the security and rights of those peoples who can claim a place among them. We should be either mad or traitors to the liberty of the world were we to interrupt this labor by warlike demonstrations, and were we to change into hostility, apprehension, or hatred the tendency to freedom that now makes them lean toward us and toward you.

What moment do you bid us choose for this measure, so utterly opposed to right policy and liberty! Is the treaty of Pilnitz being revived against us? Does a coalition of the despotic monarchs now threaten our frontiers and yours? No. You see, each courier brings us tidings of the victorious acclamation with which people adopt our principles and strengthen our cause, precisely because we have declared that these principles are those of respect for the rights, wishes, forms, government, and territories of nations. Are the results of the external policy of the government so discouraging that we must compel them to change it by force and present ourselves on the frontiers with a sword instead of with freedom and peace?

No; this policy, alike firm and pacific, answers the expectations of the Republic too well for us to change it before the hour when the powers shall change it of themselves. Look at Belgium; look at Switzerland, at Italy, at all the south of Germany; look at Vienna, Berlin. What more do you need? The very possessors of your territories open a path for you to your country and call on you to reconstitute them peacefully. Be not unjust toward God, toward the Republic, or toward us. The nations sympathizing with Germany, the king of Prussia opening the gates of his fortresses to your martyrs, the gates of Poland opened, Cracow freed, the grand duchy of Posen again a Polish province —such are the weapons with which one month of our policy has supplied you.

Ask no others at our hands. The provisional government will not suffer its policy to be changed by a foreign nation, however great the sympathy that may be inspired. Poland is dear to us; Italy is dear to us; all oppressed peoples are dear to us; but France to us is dearer than all, and the responsibility of her destinies, and possibly those of Europe, rests with us. We will surrender this responsibility to the nation alone. Trust to the nation and to the future; trust to those last thirty days which have already gained for the cause of French democracy more ground than thirty pitched battles could have gained, and do not disturb by force of arms, or by an agitation which would only injure our common cause, the work which providence accomplishes without other arms than its ideas for the regeneration of the people and the fraternity of the human race.

As Poles you have spoken admirably.   As for us it is our duty to speak as Frenchmen.   We must both of us fulfil our respective duties. As Poles you are justly impatient to fly to the land of your fathers, and to respond to the appeal which the already liberated portion of Poland has made to her generous sons.   We can only applaud this sentiment and furnish, as you desire, all those pacific means which will aid the Poles in returning to their country, and can only rejoice at the commencement of independence at Posen.

We, as Frenchmen, have not to consider the interests of Poland alone; we have to consider the universality of that European policy which corresponds to all the horizons of France and all those interests of liberty of which the French Republic is the second outbreak, and we trust the most glorious and the last, in Europe.   The importance of these interests, the gravity of these resolutions, render it impossible for the provisional government of the Republic to surrender into the hands of any partial nationality—any party in a nation, however sacred its cause may be—the responsibility and freedom of its resolutions.

If the policy toward Poland, forced upon us under the monarchy, be no longer the line of policy dictated by the Republic, the latter at least has spoken to the world in terms to which we will adhere: the Republic will suffer no power on the face of the earth to say to her: "Your words are different from your actions."   The Republic must and will not act in contradiction to her word; the respect paid to it is purchased at this price, and she will never suffer it to fall into disrepute by falsifying it.

What were her expressions in her manifesto to the powers?   Her thoughts were with you when she said that on the day when it shall seem to us that the moment has arrived for the resurrection of a nation unjustly effaced from the map, we shall hasten to its assistance.   But we have reserved to ourselves that which pertains to France alone— the choice of time, justice, and the reasons which would make it our duty to interfere.

Well, up to this moment we have chosen and resolved that these means shall be pacification.   See yourselves, and let France and Europe see, if these pacific means have deceived us or deceived you.   In thirty-one days the natural and peaceful results of this system of peace and fraternity which we have declared we would adopt have proved of more avail to the cause of France, liberty, and Poland herself than ten battles and torrents of human blood.

Such is the progress of the Republic, thanks to this system of respect for the freedom of the land and the blood of mankind. We shall never retreat into another system. The straight path, rest assured, will lead us to that disinterested object we seek to attain far better than the tortuous paths of diplomacy. Do not seek to induce us to deviate from it, even through the fraternal sentiments we entertain toward you. Our reason restrains and guides our feelings toward Poland.

Suffer us to listen to the promptings of this sentiment in the full freedom of our thoughts, and learn that these thoughts do not separate two people whose blood has so often mingled on the battle-plain. Our care for you, like our hospitality, shall extend to your own frontiers; our eyes shall follow you into your own country. Bear thither with you the hope of that regeneration which begins for you in Prussia, where your banner floats at Berlin. France asks no other return for the asylum she has afforded you than the amelioration of your national destinies and the recollections you will carry home with you of the French name.

Published by the Funk & Wagnalls Company.
Reprinted by permission.

THE REGENERATION OF FRANCE

Léon Gambetta
(1838-1882)

Léon Gambetta first gained recognition as an orator while he was studying for the bar in Paris. Here he exerted his influence over the students in the Quartier Latin in opposition to the imperial government. In 1858 he was called to the Parisian bar and was a deputy of advanced liberal opinions representing the "irreconcilables" of Marseilles and Belleville. His panegyric of republicanism, delivered in May, 1870, gained great notoriety for him.

Gambetta was, at first, opposed to the war with Germany, but when it became inevitable he was whole-hearted in his efforts for national defense. In October, 1871, he made a sensational escape from Paris through the besieging German lines in a balloon. At his call all southern France rose in arms and for five months Gambetta became the virtual dictator of his country.

After the fall of the Empire he was made Minister of the Interior. Orations delivered at Bordeaux and at Grenoble on November 26, 1872, in which he referred to the political power as lying in the hands of *les nouvelles couches sociales*, showed him at the height of his oratorical power. His tact and parliamentary dexterity coupled with his eloquence secured the voting of the constitution in February, 1875. He was instrumental in the downfall of Thiers and the resignation of the conservative MacMahon. In 1877 he was imprisoned for the virulence of his speech, but in 1881 Premier of France. He resigned from this latter post in 1882 and died soon afterward.

Gambetta had statesmanship and eloquence of the highest order. The violence of his invective and the sincerity of his con-

cepts for the good of his country overshadowed a certain careless-
ness in form and diction. Included here is a speech which is
characteristic of the appeals which he so often delivered in an
effort to arouse the people of France.

The peasantry is intellectually several centuries behind the enlightened and educated classes of the country. Yes, the distance is immense
between them and us, who have received a classical or scientific education—even the imperfect one of our day. We have learned to read our
history, to speak our language, while (a cruel thing to say) so many
of our countrymen can only babble! Ah! that peasant, bound to the
tillage of the soil, who bravely carries the burden of his day, with no
other consolation than that of leaving to his children the paternal fields,
perhaps increased an acre in extent! All his passions, joys, fears, are
concentrated on the fate of his patrimony. Of the external world, of
the society in which he lives, he apprehends but legends and rumors;
he is the prey of the cunning and the fraudulent. He strikes, without
knowing it, the bosom of the Revolution, his benefactress; he gives
loyally his taxes and his blood to a society for which he feels fear as
much as respect. But there his role ends, and if you speak to him of
principles, he knows nothing of them.

It is to the peasantry, then, that we must address ourselves. They
are the ones we must raise and instruct. The epithets the parties have
bandied of "rurality" and "rural chamber" must not be the cause of
injustice. It is to be wished that there were a "rural chamber," in the
profound and true sense of the term, for it is not with hobble-de-hoys
a "rural chamber" can be made, but with enlightened and free peasants
able to represent themselves. And instead of being the cause of raillery,
this reproach of a "rural chamber" would be a tribute rendered to the
progress of the civilization of the masses. This new social force could
be utilized for the general welfare. Unfortunately, we have not yet
reached that point, and this progress will be denied us as long as the
French democracy fails to demonstrate that if we would remake our
country, if we would return her to her grandeur, her power, and her
genius, it is the vital interest of her superior classes to elevate, to emancipate this people of workers, who hold in reserve a force still virgin
and able to develop inexhaustible treasures of activity and aptitude. We
must learn and then teach the peasant what he owes to society and what
he has the right to ask of her.

On the day when it will be well understood that we have no grander
or more pressing work; that we should put aside and postpone all
other reforms; that we have but one task, the instruction of the people,
the diffusion of education, the encouragement of science—on that day
a great step will have been taken in your regeneration. But our action

needs to be a double one, that it may bear upon the body as well as the mind. To be exact, each man should be intelligent, trained not only to think, read, reason, but able to act, to fight. Everywhere beside the teacher we should place the gymnast and the soldier, to the end that our children, our soldiers, our fellow-citizens, should be able to hold a sword, to carry a gun on a long march, to sleep under the canopy of the stars, to support valiantly all the hardships demanded of a patriot. We must push to the front these two educations. Otherwise you make a success of letters, but do not create a bulwark of patriots.

Yes, gentlemen, if they have outclassed us, if you had to submit to the supreme agony of seeing the France of Kléber and of Hoche lose her two most patriotic provinces, those best embodying at once the military, commercial, industrial and democratic spirit, we can blame only our inferior physical and moral condition. To-day, the interests of our country command us to speak no imprudent words, to close our lips, to sink to the bottom of our hearts our resentments, to take up the grand work of national regeneration, to devote to it all the time necessary, that it may be a lasting work. If it need ten years, if it need twenty years, then we must devote to it ten or twenty years. But we must commence at once, that each year may see the advancing life of a new generation, strong, intelligent, as much in love with science as with the Fatherland, having in their hearts the double sentiment that he serves his country well only when he serves it with his reason and his arm.

We have been educated in a rough school. We must therefore cure ourselves of the vanity which has caused us so many disasters. We must also realize conscientiously where our responsibility exists, and seeing the remedy, sacrifice all to the object to be attained—to remake and reconstitute France! For that, nothing should be accounted too good, and we shall ask nothing before this; the first demand must be for an education as complete from base to summit as is known to human intelligence. Naturally, merit must be recognized, aptitude awakened and approved, and honest and impartial judges freely chosen by their fellow-citizens, deciding publicly in such a way that merit alone will open the door. Reject as authors of mischief those who have put words in the place of action; all those who have put favoritism in the place of merit; all those who have made the profession of arms not a means for the protection of France but a means of serving the caprices of a master, and sometimes of becoming the accomplices in his crimes.

ON HIS WELCOME TO NEW YORK

Louis Kossuth

(1802-1894)

Never was a more valiant effort made for national independence than in Hungary in the years 1848-49 under the leadership of her great patriot, Louis Kossuth. Kossuth was elected to the Diet in 1847 and was soon famous as a speaker. On March 3, 1848, when the news of the revolution in Paris arrived in Hungary, Kossuth in a compelling speech demanded parliamentary government for Hungary. He immediately became the leader of the European revolution in his own country. His speech was read aloud in the streets of Vienna and incited insurrection there. By April 19, 1849, Kossuth issued his famous Declaration of Independence for Hungary. The intervention of Russia, which came to the aid of Austria, frustrated the Hungarian struggle for freedom, and Kossuth fled to Turkey where he was imprisoned. At the intervention of England and the United States he was released from prison and immediately continued his agitation for home rule for Hungary, traversing England and the United States making speeches in the English language. Twenty years later Hungary did become an equal associate of Austria in the combined kingdom of Austria-Hungary.

Kossuth was a fiery and enthusiastic speaker and most eloquently pictured the wrongs and sufferings of his native land. His visit to the United States in 1851 as a refugee created much excitement, and he was everywhere received with enthusiastic popular demonstrations. There is presented here an excerpt from his first speech in America.

Let me, before I go to work, have some hours of rest upon this soil of freedom, your happy home. Freedom and home; what heavenly music in those two words! Alas! I have no home, and the freedom of my

people is downtrodden. Young Giant of free America, do not tell me
that thy shores are an asylum to the oppressed and a home to the home-
less exile. An asylum it is; but all the blessings of your glorious country, can they drown into oblivion the longing of the heart and the fond
desires for our native land? My beloved native land, thy very sufferings
make thee but dearer to my heart; thy bleeding image dwells with me
when I wake, as it rests with me in the short moments of my restless
sleep. It has accompanied me over the waves. It will accompany me
when I go back to fight over again the battle of thy freedom once more.
I have no idea but thee; I have no feeling but thee.

Even here, with this prodigious view of greatness, freedom, and
happiness which spreads before my astonished eyes, my thoughts are
wandering toward home; and when I look over these thousands of thousands before me, the happy inheritance of yonder freedom for which your
fathers fought and bled—and when I turn to you, citizens, to bow before
the majesty of the United States, and to thank the people of New York
for their generous share in my liberation, and for the unparalleled honor
of this reception—I see, out of the very midst of this great assemblage,
rise the bleeding image of Hungary, looking to you with anxiety, whether
there be in the luster of your eyes a ray of hope for her; whether there
be in the thunder of your huzzas a trumpet-call of resurrection. If there
were no such ray of hope in your eyes, and no such trumpet-call in your
cheers, then woe to Europe's oppressed nations. They will stand alone in
the hour of need. Less fortunate than you were, they will meet no
brother's hand to help them in the approaching giant struggle against the
leagued despots of the world; and woe, also, to me. I will feel no joy
even here; and the days of my stay here will turn out to be lost to my
fatherland—lost at the very time when every moment is teeming in the
decision of Europe's destiny.

Gentlemen, I have to thank the people, Congress, and government of
the United States for my liberation from captivity. Human tongue has
no words to express the bliss which I felt, when I—the downtrodden
Hungary's wandering chief—saw the glorious flag of the Stripes and
Stars fluttering over my head—when I first bowed before it with deep
respect—when I saw around me the gallant officers and the crew of the
Mississippi frigate—the most of them the worthiest representatives of
true American principles, American greatness, American generosity—and
to think that it was not a mere chance which cast the Star-spangled Banner
around me, but that it was your protecting will—to know that the United
States of America, conscious of their glorious calling, as well as of their
power, declared, by this unparalleled act, to be resolved to become the protectors of human rights—to see a powerful vessel of America coming to
far Asia to break the chains by which the mightiest despots of Europe
fettered the activity of an exiled Magyar, whose very name disturbed the
proud security of their sleep—to feel restored by such a protection, and,
in such a way, to freedom, and by freedom to activity; you may be well

aware of what I have felt, and still feel, at the remembrance of this proud moment of my life. Others spoke—you acted; and I was free! You acted; and at this act of yours, tyrants trembled; humanity shouted out with joy; the downtrodden people of Magyars—the downtrodden, but not broken—raised their heads with resolution and with hope, and the brilliancy of your Stars was greeted by Europe's oppressed nations as the morning star of rising liberty. Now, gentlemen, you must be aware how boundless the gratitude must be which I feel for you.

Humble as I am, God, the Almighty, has selected me to represent the cause of humanity before you. My warrant to this capacity is written in the sympathy and confidence of all who are oppressed, and of all who, as your elder brother, the people of Britain, sympathize with the oppressed —my warrant to this capacity is written in the hopes and expectations you have entitled the world to entertain, by liberating me out of my prison, and by restoring me to activity. But it has pleased the Almighty to make out of my humble self yet another opportunity for a thing which may prove a happy turning-point in the destinies of the world. I bring you a brotherly greeting from the people of Great Britain. I speak not in official character, imparted by diplomacy, whose secrecy is the curse of the world, but I am the harbinger of the public spirit of the people, which has the right to impart a direction to its government, and which I witnessed, pronouncing itself in the most decided manner, openly—that the people of England, united to you with enlightened brotherly love, as it is united in blood—conscious of your strength, as it is conscious of its own, has forever abandoned every sentiment of irritation and rivalry, and desires the brotherly alliance of the United States to secure to every nation the sovereign right to dispose of itself, and to protect the sovereign right of nations against the encroaching arrogance of despots; and leagued to you against the league of despots, to stand together, with you, godfather to the approaching baptism of European liberty.

I came not to your glorious shores to enjoy a happy rest—I came not with the intention to gather triumphs of personal distinction, but as humble petitioner, in my country's name, as its freely chosen constitutional chief, humbly to entreat your generous aid; and then it is to this aim that I will devote every moment of my time, with the more assiduity, with the more restlessness, as every moment may bring a report of events which may call me to hasten to my place on the battle-field, where the great, and I hope, the last battle will be fought between liberty and despotism—a moment marked by the finger of God to be so near that every hour of delay of your generous aid may prove fatally disastrous to oppressed humanity. And, thus having stated my position to be that of a humble petitioner in the name of my oppressed country, let me respectfully ask: Do you not regret to have bestowed upon me the high honor of this glorious reception, unparalleled in history?

I say unparalleled in history, though I know that your fathers have welcomed Lafayette in a similar way; but Lafayette had mighty claims to your country's gratitude. He had fought in your ranks for your freedom and independence; and, what was still more, in the hour of your need he was the link of your friendly connection with France—a connection the results of which were two French fleets of more than thirty-eight men-of-war and three thousand gallant men, who fought side by side with you against Cornwallis, before Yorktown; the precious gift of twenty-four thousand muskets; a loan of nineteen millions of dollars; and even the preliminary treaties of your glorious peace negotiated at Paris by your immortal Franklin. I hope the people of the United States, now itself in the happy condition to aid those who are in need of aid, as itself was once in need, will kindly remember these facts; and you, citizens of New York, you will yourselves become the Lafayettes of Hungary. Lafayette had great claims to your love and sympathy, but I have none. I came a humble petitioner, with no other claims than those which the oppressed have to the sympathy of freemen who have the power to help, with the claim which the unfortunate has to the happy, and the downtrodden has to the protection of eternal justice and of human rights. In a word, I have no other claims than those which the oppressed principle of freedom has to the aid of victorious liberty.

TO THE YOUNG MEN OF ITALY

Giuseppe Mazzini

(1805-1872)

In April, 1834, the "Young European Association of men believing in a future of liberty, equality, and fraternity for all mankind" was founded under the influence of the Italian patriot, Giuseppe Mazzini. Mazzini himself was in exile the greater portion of his vari-colored life, but always strongly supported the cause of liberty. For fifty years he worked for a united Italy and lived to see his life's desire when Rome became the capital of that United Italy under the statesmanship of Cavour and the leadership of Garibaldi. Mazzini was a literary orator who used a poetical diction of great charm and beauty. The loftiness of his own spirit pervaded and animated all his public utterances.

The selection included here was delivered by Mazzini at Milan, July 25, 1848, as a eulogy on the death of his fellow patriots, the brothers Bandiera and their accomplices, who were executed by the Neapolitan government at Cosenza for effecting an uprising of patriots.

When I was commissioned by you, young men, to proffer in this temple a few words sacred to the memory of the brothers Bandiera and their fellow-martyrs at Cosenza, I thought that some of those who heard me might exclaim with noble indignation: "Wherefore lament over the dead? The martyrs of liberty are only worthily honored by winning the battle they have begun; Cosenza, the land where they fell, is enslaved; Venice, the city of their birth, is begirt by foreign foes. Let us emancipate them, and until that moment let no words pass our lips save words of war."

But another thought arose: Why have we not conquered? Why is it that, while we are fighting for independence in the north of Italy, liberty is perishing in the South? Why is it that a war which should have sprung to the Alps with the bound of a lion, has dragged itself along for four months, with the slow uncertain motion of the scorpion surrounded by a circle of fire? How has the rapid and powerful intuition of a people newly arisen to life been converted into the weary helpless effort of the sick man turning from side to side? Ah! had we all arisen in the sanctity of the idea for which our martyrs died; had the holy standard of their faith preceded our youth to battle: had we reached that unity of life which was in them so powerful, and made of our every action a thought, and of our every thought an action; had we devoutly gathered up their last words in our hearts, and learned from them that Liberty and Independence are one, that God and the People, the Fatherland and Humanity, are the two inseparable terms of the device of every people striving to become a nation; that Italy can have no true life till she be One, holy in the equality and love of all her children, great in the worship of eternal truth, and consecrated to a lofty mission, a moral priesthood among the peoples of Europe—we should now have had, not war, but victory; Cosenza would not be compelled to venerate the memory of her martyrs in secret, nor Venice be restrained from honoring them with a monument; and we, gathered here together, might gladly invoke their sacred names, without uncertainty as to our future destiny, or a cloud of sadness on our brows, and say to those precursor souls: "Rejoice! for your spirit is incarnate in your brethren, and they are worthy of you."

The idea which they worshipped, young men, does not as yet shine forth in its full purity and integrity upon your banner. The sublime program which they, dying, bequeathed to the rising Italian generation, is yours; but mutilated, broken up into fragments by the false doctrines, which, elsewhere overthrown, have taken refuge among us. I look around, and I see the struggles of desperate populations, an alternation of generous rage and unworthy repose; of shouts for freedom and of formulae of servitude, throughout all parts of our peninsula; but the soul of the country, where is it? What unity is there in this unequal and manifold movement? Where is the Word which should dominate the hundred diverse and opposing counsels which mislead or seduce the multitude? I hear phrases usurping the national omnipotence—"The Italy of the North—the league of the States—Federative compacts between Princes," but Italy, where is it? Where is the common country, the country which the Bandiera hailed as thrice Initiatrix of a new era of European civilization?

Intoxicated with our first victories, improvident for the future, we forgot the idea revealed by God to those who suffered; and God has punished our forgetfulness by deferring our triumph. The Italian movement, my countrymen, is, by decree of Providence, that of Europe. We arise to give a pledge of moral progress to the European world. But neither political fictions, nor dynastic aggrandizements, nor theories of expediency, can transform or renovate the life of the peoples. Humanity lives and moves through faith; great principles are the guiding stars that lead Europe towards the future. Let us turn to the graves of our martyrs, and ask inspiration of those who died for us all, and we shall find the secret of victory in the adoration of a faith. The angel of martyrdom and the angel of victory are brothers; but the one looks up to heaven, and the other looks down to earth; and it is when, from epoch to epoch, their glance meets between earth and heaven, that creation is embellished with a new life, and a people arises from the cradle of the tomb— evangelist or prophet. . . .

Love, young men, love and venerate the ideal. The ideal is the Word of God. High above every country, high above humanity, is the country of the spirit, the city of the soul, in which all are brethren who believe in the inviolability of thought and in the dignity of our immortal soul; and the baptism of this fraternity is martyrdom. From that high sphere spring the principles which alone can redeem the peoples. Arise for the sake of these, and not from impatience or suffering or dread of evil. Anger, pride, ambition, and the desire of material prosperity, are arms common alike to the peoples and their oppressors, and even should you conquer with these to-day, you would fall again to-morrow; but principles belong to the peoples alone, and their oppressors can find no arms to oppose them. Adore enthusiasm, the dreams of the virgin soul, and the visions of early youth, for they are a perfume of paradise which the soul retains in issuing from the hands of its Creator. Respect above all things your conscience; have upon your lips the truth implanted by God in your hearts, and, while laboring in harmony, even with those who differ with you, in all that tends to the emancipation of our soul, yet ever bear your own banner erect and boldly promulgate your own faith.

Such words, young men, would the martyrs of Cosenza have spoken, had they been living amongst you; and here, where it may be that, in- voked by our love, their holy spirits hover near us, I call you to gather them up in your hearts and to make of them a treasure amid the storms that yet threaten you; storms which, with the names of our martyrs on your lips and their faith in your hearts, you will overcome.

God be with you, and bless Italy!

PLEA FOR A REPUBLIC IN SPAIN

Emilio Castelar

(1832-1899)

Emilio Castelar, the Spanish republican, was earlier in his life successfully engaged as a professor of history at the University of Madrid and was a journalist and novelist of consequence. In 1854 he made his entrance into the field of political debate with such success that he became recognized as one of the most brilliant orators of Spain. In 1866 he was condemned to death as a revolutionist but escaped with his life only to return as a participant in the Revolution of 1868. At the downfall of King Amadeus in 1873 Castelar was made the President of the Republic and began a practical dictatorship. At the overthrow of this Republic he fled to Paris but was returned to the Spanish Cortes in 1876 and continued to speak there until his withdrawal from public life.

Castelar was always more of an orator than a man of action and devoted his life completely to the principles of republicanism. His style is naturally tempered to the Spanish public and consequently abounds with enthusiasm and fire. It is said that whenever he spoke the Chamber was crowded and cards of admission were to be secured at a high premium. All parties alike delighted to hear his eloquent rhapsodies.

Included here is his *Plea for a Republic in Spain* delivered in the Spanish Cortes December 18, 1869.

Before replying to Minister Sagasta's speech, I desire to say that my public life forbids me to defend myself against personal attacks such as the gentleman seems to delight in. The minister of government was extremely kind in speaking of my address as brilliant, but extremely severe when he declared it to be wanting in truth. Neither criticism was just. Gentlemen, I should not have to defend my own speeches if they had the splendor and beauty attributed to them by Mr. Sagasta. I should be content to let them shine, confident, with the most eloquent and greatest of ancient philosophers that "Beauty is the splendor of truth."

After all, if there be any grand quality in this Assembly it is eloquence—the expression of grand sentiments and sublime ideas in fervent language. I have heard such speeches come from every side of the Assembly and I should like to hear one, in the language of moderation, from the government. Discussions carried on in that manner, with eloquence and good judgment, give us hope for the future; for the laws of history do not permit a dictatorship to fasten itself upon a people whose faces are lighted by the fires of eloquence.

Mr. Sagasta defended the dictatorship, and in doing so he drew an awful picture of our social condition, talking of crimes and criminals, and telling you that our education in the past had been very bad, and that the corruption of to-day was very great. And what have the republicans to learn from that? For three centuries, yes, more than three centuries, our Church has been an enemy to the human conscience.

For many centuries it has been inimical to the national will. Consequently, if there is anything very bad or vicious here to-day, it is owing to institutions with which we have nothing to do. And more, this evil, this viciousness, owe their existence to a lack of respect among the people for law. This lack of respect for law is born of the systematic abuse of power by our arbitrary government. Judges nominated by a party and appointed to revise the electoral lists; schools, so-called, for filling convents and military barracks; the jury outlawed; public life closed to the democracy; political corruption extending from above down in all directions—this is the product, and these are the products, of a sore and wounded people painted by Mr. Sagasta, people who are the natural offspring of a long heredity of crime and error. It is impossible to cure the people if the system be not changed.

Well, deputies, what form of government has come to Spain since the September revolution? The republican form has come and is still here. It so happens that you have not been able yet to implant monarchical institutions in its place. After being fifteen days in power you declared yourselves monarchists and us outlaws. Did you create the monarchy in the primaries? When the Assembly convened, the monarchy was proposed. There we had great battles. Has the monarchy been established? The Conservatives, although they have not said so, have, I believe, agreed upon a candidate; the Radicals, more loquacious, have named theirs; but have you, separated or united, produced a monarchy?

The Conservatives have a candidate who really represents the latest privilege granted to the middle classes. Why is it that they do not bring him here? Because they know that this is a democratic monarchy, based, as it is nominally, on universal suffrage, and because the candidate has not had, and never will have, the votes, the indorsement, the backing of the people. And you? You want a monarchy to keep up appearances; a monarchy in order that Europe may say: "See how prudent, how God-fearing, how wise, how intelligent are the Spaniards: they have a disguised republic!"

After a provisional government and a provisional regency you want a provisional monarchy also. You do not expect or want to be strong in the right, in liberty, in the will of the people or in national sovereignty. All you want is a king who shall represent the predominance and the egotism of a party. You ought to know that as the candidate of the Conservatives can not come here without the consent of the people, your candidate can not come without the consent of the Conservatives. Do you believe that your candidate will last if all the Conservative forces do not support him? Notwithstanding all that the Conservatives have declared to their representatives here, not one of them has said that he renounces his dynastic faith. Therefore, deputies, you can not establish the monarchy.

On Saturday, I pictured to you, in colors more or less vivid, the prestige which monarchical institutions have enjoyed in our country, and for this the minister of state upbraided me without understanding my arguments. I ask you to concentrate your attention for a moment upon the parallel which I am going to present and which may be called a summary of this speech. I said the other afternoon that to establish monarchical institutions it was necessary to possess monarchical faith and sentiment. One must have the poetry and the traditions of monarchy. I said this because I know that, although the Assembly, and the official authorities can make laws, they cannot decree ideas or sentiments, those real and solid foundations of institutions. Formerly, in other times, kings were representative of the national dignity, and now from those same benches we have heard that they sold their native soil to a foreigner and even prostrated themselves at his feet, the people in the meantime answering the enemy with the 2d of May and the siege of Saragossa.

Formerly art sketched the apotheosis of Charles V with Titian's brush, or the ladies-in-waiting of Philip VI with the brush of Velasquez. Now it sketches the image of the communists of Paris, of the victims of Charles V or the ship in which the Puritans took the soul of a republic to the bosom of virgin America. Formerly, the gala days of the people were the birthdays of kings and the anniversaries of the beginning of their reigns. Now, the great days of celebration are the 10th of August, the 30th of July, the 24th of February, and the 29th of September—days which mark the expulsion of kings. Formerly, when a navigator landed in America, or an explorer went into the interior of a new country, the purest piece of gold, the largest pearl, the clearest diamond was reserved for the king. Now, your minister of the treasury claims from the king even the clasp which holds the royal mantle about his shoulders.

As there is no possibility of establishing the monarchy, as no candidate acceptable to all can be found, it is necessary, it is indispensable to get rid of the suspense, and I say that we should establish a republic. Have you not said that the forms of government are accidental? Gentlemen, you know the republic I want. It is a federal republic. I shall always defend the federal republic. I am a federal, but, deputies, understand one thing: the republic is a form of government which admits many conditions, and which has many grades. From the Republic of Venice to that of Switzerland there is an immense scale. Adjoining Mexico, where Church and State are separated, there is Guatemala, where the clergy have great power. Close to the decentralized and federal Argentine Republic is the Chilean Republic, another decentralized country enjoying great prosperity, its paper money being quoted in all the markets of Europe as high as that of England.

Consequently, amid this great affliction, this trouble, this unstable equilibrium, which surrounds you, you can establish a form of government which is of the people and for the people, a form in harmony with the institutions you have proclaimed, and with the sentiment which all of you guard in the bottom of your hearts.

Have you not observed in history the inability of an assembly or any other power to establish a form of government in conflict with great ideas? Remember the eighteenth century. Never had a monarchy attained more power, never was absolutism so strong, never was the destruction of obstacles in the way of kings more complete. Philosophy ascended the throne with them, ascended with Charles III. and Aranda and Tombal. It ascended with Joseph I., with Frederick the Great, with Leopold of Tuscany. All seemed to conspire to establish the same idea, the idea of a philosophy and a liberalism. And did they succeed? No, they were the Baptists of the Revolution. They repented late, and the philosophy they had thrown at the feet of the thrones came to naught.

And what happened? Some were sentenced by the Assembly. The crowns of divine right were melted into cannon balls by the soldiers of the Revolution. What does this signify? That great powers can not place absolutism above philosophy any more than you can build monarchical institutions on individual rights. Therefore, I beseech you to establish the republic. You are assured of our patriotism, our great interest in the country, our abnegation. Cato committed suicide because he found a Caesar. Radicals of Spain, do not commit suicide because you cannot find a monarch.

AN ADDRESS AT THE CONGRESS OF ANGOSTURA, FEB. 15, 1819

Simon Bolivar

(1783-1830)

Simon Bolivar, Liberator of South America, was born in aristocracy and wealth at Caracas, Venezuela; was educated in law at Madrid, Spain; travelled extensively on the continent, where he studied the effects of the French Revolution, visited the United States in 1809 where he became an ardent admirer of republican institutions; and returned to Venezuela determined to free his country from foreign despotism. It was the spectacle of the French Revolution, and his impressions gleaned of the United States through his travels, together with the influence of the personality of General Miranda, leader of the Venezuelan revolutionary movement against the policies of Spanish colonial government, which inspired Bolivar to join the revolutionary forces of South America. As a soldier and statesman Bolivar led the revolutions which resulted in the independence from Spain of what today are known as the republics of Venezuela, Colombia, Ecuador, Peru, Panama, and Bolivia. It was in all of these countries that he became known as the "Liberator," being the hero in his lifetime of over 200 bloody battles fought in the cause of South American independence. From three of these rebelling colonies he organized "Greater Colombia." With keen foresight, Bolivar saw the trend of the struggle for democracy in the Old Spanish Empire of South America. He it was who charted the course for other military leaders; yet his life was a medley of tragedy and success. His own personal fortune he lost in the cause of the revolution and his farewell address to the people of Colombia was a bitter complaint of ingratitude for aspersions cast on his own character by the people for whose liberty he had so sincerely fought. Forceful in speech, Bolivar was a prophet and preacher of new Americanism.

GENTLEMEN: Happy is the citizen who under the protection of the army of his command has convoked National Sovereignty to exercise its absolute will! I, therefore, count myself among those most favored by Divine Providence since I have had the honor to gather the Representatives of the People of Venezuela in this August Congress, the source of legitimate authority, depository of sovereign will and the arbiter of the Destiny of the Nation.

In transferring to the Representatives of the People the Supreme Power with which I have been entrusted, I fulfill the wishes of my own heart, those of my fellow citizens and those of our future generations which expect everything from your wisdom, uprightness and prudence. In discharging this sweet duty, I free myself from the overburdening of immense authority and the unlimited responsibility weighing upon my weak shoulders! Only a compelling necessity coupled with the commanding will of the People could have made me assume the tremendous and dangerous charge of Dictator Supreme Chief of the Republic. But I can breathe easier now in handing back to you that authority, which I have succeeded in maintaining with so much risk, difficulty and hardships amid the most awful tribulations that could ever afflict any social political body. . . .

Legislators! I deposit in your hands the supreme command of Venezuela. Yours is now the august duty of devoting yourselves to achieving the happiness of the Republic; you hold in your hands the scales of our destinies, the measure of our glory; your hands will seal the decrees insuring our Liberty. At this moment the Supreme Chief of the Republic is nothing but a plain citizen, and such he wishes to remain until death. I will serve, however, in the career of a soldier while there are enemies in Venezuela. The country has a multitude of most worthy sons capable of guiding her; talents, virtues, experience, and all that is required to direct free men, are the patrimony of many of those who are representing the people here; and outside of this Sovereign Body, there are citizens, who at all times have shown their courage in facing danger, prudence in avoiding it, and the art, in short, to govern themselves and of governing others. These illustrious men undoubtedly merit the vote of Congress, and they will be entrusted with the Government that I have just resigned so cordially and sincerely and forever.

The continuation of authority in the same person has frequently proved the undoing of democratic governments. Repeated elections are essential to the system of popular government, because there is nothing so dangerous as to suffer Power to be vested for a long time in one citizen. The people become accustomed to obeying him, and he becomes accustomed to commanding, hence the origin of usurpation and tyranny. A proper zeal is the guarantee of republican liberty, and our citizens must very justly fear that the same Magistrate who has governed them for a long time, may continue to rule them forever. . . .

By casting a glance over the past, we shall see what is the basic element of the Republic of Venezuela.

America, on becoming separated from the Spanish monarchy, found itself like the Roman Empire, when that enormous mass fell to pieces in the midst of the ancient world. Each dismembered portion formed then an independent nation in accordance with its situation or its interests, the difference being that those members established anew their former associations. We do not even preserve the vestiges of what once we were; we are not Europeans, we are not Indians, but an intermediate species between the aborigines and the Spaniards—Americans by birth and Europeans in right, we are placed in the dilemma of disputing with the natives our titles of possession and maintaining ourselves in the country where we were born, against the opposition of the invaders. Thus, ours is a most extraordinary and complicated case. Moreover, our part has always been a purely passive one; our political existence has always been null, and we find ourselves in greater difficulties in attaining our liberty than we ever had when we lived on a plane lower than servitude, because we had been robbed not only of liberty but also of active and domestic tyranny. . . .

Nature, in truth, endows us at birth with the instinctive desire for liberty; but whether because of negligence, or because of an inclination inherent in humanity, it remains still under the bonds imposed on it. And as we see it in such a state of debasement we seem to have reason to be persuaded that the majority of men hold as a truth the humiliating principle that it is harder to maintain the balance of liberty than to endure the weight of tyranny. Would to God that this principle, contrary to the morals of Nature, were false! Would to God that this principle were not sanctioned by the indolence of man as regards his most sacred rights!

Many ancient and modern nations have cast off oppression; but those which have been able to enjoy a few precious moments of liberty are most rare, as they soon relapsed into their old political vices; because it is the people more often than the government, that bring on tyranny. The habit of suffering domination makes them insensible to the charms of honor and national prosperity, and leads them to look with indolence upon the bliss of living in the midst of liberty, under the protection of laws framed by their own free will. The history of the world proclaims this awful truth!

Only democracy, in my opinion, is susceptible of absolute freedom. But where is there a democratic government that has united at the same time power, prosperity and permanence? Have we not seen, on the contrary, aristocracy, monarchy rearing great and powerful empires for centuries and centuries? What government is there older than that of China? What republic has exceeded in duration that of Sparta, that of Venice?

The Roman Empire, did it not conquer the world? Does not France count fourteen centuries of monarchy? Who is greater than England? These nations, however, have been, or still are, aristocracies and monarchies.

Notwithstanding such bitter reflections, I am filled with unbounded joy because of the great strides made by our republic since entering upon its noble career. Loving that which is most useful, animated by what is most just and aspiring to what is most perfect, Venezuela in separating from the Spanish Nation has recovered her independence, her freedom, her equality, her national sovereignty. In becoming a democratic republic, she proscribed monarchy, distinctions, nobility, franchises and privileges; she declared the rights of man, the liberty of action, of thought, of speech, of writing. These preeminently liberal acts will never be sufficiently admired for the sincerity by which they are inspired. The first Congress of Venezuela has impressed upon the annals of our legislation with indelible characters the majesty of the people, so fittingly expressed in the consummation of the social act best calculated to develop the happiness of a Nation. . . .

And passing now from ancient to modern times, we find England and France attracting the attention of all nations, and teaching them eloquent lessons of all sorts in the matter of government. The revolution of these two great peoples, like a brilliant meteor, has flooded the world with such a profusion of political light that now all thinking men have learned what are the rights of men, what are their duties, what constitutes the excellency of a government and what its vices. All know how to appreciate the intrinsic value of the speculative theories of modern philosophers and lawmakers. In fine, that star, in its luminous career, has even inflamed the heart of the apathetic Spaniards, who have also entered the political whirlwind, have made ephemeral attempts at liberty, have acknowledged their incapacity to live under the gentle rule of law, and have gone back to their immemorial dungeons and the stake.

This is the proper time, Legislators, to repeat what the eloquent Volney says in the dedication of his Ruins of Palmyra: "To the rising peoples of the Spanish Indies, to the generous men who lead them to liberty. May the errors and misfortunes of the Old World teach wisdom and happiness to the New World." Let us not lose, then, the benefit of the lessons drawn from experience, and may the schools of Greece, Rome, France, England and America instruct us in the difficult science of creating and maintaining the nations under proper laws, just, legitimate and above all useful. We must never forget that the superiority of a government does not consist in its theories, or in its form, or in its mechanism, but in its being appropriate to the nature and character of the nation for which it has been instituted. . . .

The merging of New Granada and Venezuela into one Great State has been the unanimous wish of the peoples and the government of both republics. The fortunes of war have effected this union so earnestly desired by all Colombians; in fact, we are incorporated. These sister countries have already entrusted to you their interests, their rights and their destinies. In contemplating the union of these countries my soul rises to the heights demanded by the colossal perspective of such a wonderful picture. Soaring among the coming ages my imagination rests on the future centuries, and seeing from afar with admiration and amazement the prosperity, the splendor and the life which have come to this vast region, I feel myself carried away, and I see her in the very heart of the universe, stretching along her lengthy shores between two oceans which Nature has separated, but which our country unites through long wide channels. I can see her as the bond, as the center, as the emporium of the human family. I can see her sending to all the corners of the globe the treasure hidden in her mountains of silver and gold; I see her sending broadcast, by means of her divine plants, health and life to the sufferers of the old world; I see her confiding her precious secrets to the learned who do not know how much her store of knowledge is superior to the store of wealth bestowed by Nature upon her; I can see her sitting on the throne of liberty, the scepter of justice in her hand, crowned by glory, showing the old world the majesty of the modern world.

Deign, Legislators, to accept with indulgence the profession of my political faith, the highest wishes of my heart and the fervent prayer which on behalf of the people I dare address you: Deign to grant to Venezuela a government preeminently popular, preeminently just, preeminently moral, which will hold in chains oppression, anarchy and guilt. A government which will allow righteousness, tolerance, peace to reign; a government which will cause equality and liberty to triumph under the protection of inexorable laws.

Gentlemen, commence your duties; I have finished mine.

Translated by Francisco Javier Yánes.

Reprinted by permission of the Pan-American Union, Washington, D.C.

BIBLIOGRAPHY OF THE FRENCH
REVOLUTIONARY PERIOD

Aulard, F. Alphonse, ed: *L'Éloquence Parliementaire pendant la Révolution Française,* Hachette et Cie, Paris, 1882.

Aulard, F. Alphonse, ed: *Les Orateurs de la Législative et de la Convention,* 2nd ed., E. Cornely, Paris, 1905.

Blair, Hugh: *Lectures on Rhetoric and Belles-lettres,* J. I. Kay Company, Philadelphia, 1833.

Bryan, William Jennings, ed: *World's Famous Orations,* Funk & Wagnalls Company, New York, 1906.

Cambridge Modern History, The: The Macmillan Company, New York, 1907.

Carlyle, Thomas: *The French Revolution,* Harper & Brothers, New York, 1859.

Coppens, Charles: *The Art of Oratorical Composition,* Schwartz, Kirwin and Fauss, New York, 1885.

De Cormenin, Timon, ed: *Orators of France,* Belford, Clarke and Company, New York, 1884.

Dickinson, G. L.: *The Revolution and Reaction in Modern France,* Brentano's, New York, 1927.

Duclaux, Mme.: *A Short History of France,* G. P. Putnam's Sons, New York, 1918.

Elton, Godfrey: *The Revolutionary Idea in France,* Edward Arnold and Company, London, 1923.

Encyclopedia Britannica, "The French Revolution," Encyclopedia Britannica Company, Ltd., London, 1929.

Garnier-Pages: *Histoire de la Révolution de 1848,* 8 vols., Pagnerre, Paris, 1860-62.

Gershoy, Leo: *The French Revolution,* Henry Holt and Company, Inc., New York, 1932.

Hamel, Ernest: *Histoire de France depuis la Révolution,* Jouvet et Cie, Paris, 1887-97.

Hamel, Ernest: *Vie de Robespierre,* A. Lacroix, Paris, 1865.

Lamartine, Alphonse de: *History of the Girondist Speeches,* George Bell and Sons, Ltd., London, 1899.

Lamartine, Alphonse de: *History of the Restoration of Monarchy in France,* Vizetelly and Company, London, 1851-53.

Lee, Carleton, ed: *The World's Orators,* G. P. Putnam's Sons, New York, 1901.

McCarthy, Justin: *French Revolution, II,* Simpkin, Marshall, Hamilton, Kent and Company, Ltd., London, 1884.

Madelin, Louis: *The French Revolution,* G. P. Putnam's Sons, New York, 1928.

Mathews, Shailer: *The French Revolution,* 1789-1815, Longmans, Green and Company, New York, 1927.

Morris, Charles, ed: *The World's Great Orators and Their Orations,* The John C. Winston Company, Philadelphia, 1902.

Murry, J. Middleton: *Problems of Style,* Oxford University Press, New York, 1930.

Platz, Mabel: *The History of Public Speaking,* Noble and Noble. New York, 1935.

Schultz, Albert: *Bibliographie de la Commune,* H. le Soudier, Paris, 1886.

Sears, Lorenzo: *History of Oratory,* S. C. Griggs and Company, Chicago, 1896.

Thiers, Louis Adolphe: *History of the French Revolution,* Bentley and Sons, London, 1881.

Thorndike, E. Ashley, ed: *Modern Eloquence,* Modern Eloquence Corporation, New York, 1928.

Tocqueville, A. C.: *L'Ancien Régime et la Révolution,* G. W. Headlam, Oxford University Press, London, 1859.

Vallee, Leon, ed: *Orations of Foreign Orators,* Fifth Avenue Press, New York, 1900.

THE BRITISH PERIOD

INTRODUCTION

The emergence of the British Empire as a democratic state was largely accomplished in her Houses of Parliament. Within the halls of this ancient institution standing on the banks of the Thames River in London the struggles for political and religious freedom were debated by England's greatest statesmen and orators. So potent was this parliamentary oratory that it established a precedent for the control of government which has influenced subsequent history. Today the British nation is representative of the efficacy of deliberative arbitration and debate in affairs of state and in international relations.

The first important event in the history of British oratory occurred in the thirteenth century when the Magna Charta was wrung from the reluctant pen of King John. The rise of Parliament started at this date as the agent through which the people's demands for certain rights inherent in the structure of a democratic free state were accomplished.

During the reign of the Stuarts English secular oratory acquired preeminence. The people, rising against tyranny, challenged royal power and demanded reform. During the reign of King James powerful speakers arose in Parliament as spokesmen of the people's rights, and eventually, when the storm of revolution had broken, hereditary tyranny was replaced by parliamentary protection. The early Parliament of Charles I was marked by eloquence of a superior quality, and the Petition of Right stands as an indication of the efficacy of that eloquence. It marks the yielding of the divine right of Kings, monarchy, and absolutism to the principles of democracy.

It was in 1689, after the accession of William and Mary, that Parliament passed the significant act known as the Bill of Rights affirming freedom of debate in Parliament, the freedom of elections, and the freedom of petitions. This great document ranks with the Magna Charta and the Petition of Right as the embodiment of the fundamental principles of political freedom in England. In 1689 was also passed the Toleration Act allowing people who did not agree with the established system of the Church in England to worship after their own fashion. These two acts—The Bill of Rights and the Toleration Act—were the greatest triumphs for freedom of speech of the 17th century, and the controversies exercised in their adoption are most significant to the history of oratory in England.

Again in the eighteenth century British platform oratory took new life, and ecclesiastical oratory, stimulated by the religious revivals of Wesley and Whitefield, paved the way for a period of British oratory so prominent by reason of the masters of eloquence who represented it that it has frequently been alluded to as the Golden Age of British Oratory. This period of parliamentary excellence in speech lasted nearly 100 years. Dominant issues instigating the oratory were the Reform Bills of Parliament, the controversies with the Established Church, and the Industrial Revolution. The names of the leaders of these movements are familiar to every student of 19th century history.

Orations representative of the great men of eloquence who shaped Britain's history are included here. Sir John Eliot, John Pym, and Sir Edward Coke, who fought for the Petition of Right; Oliver Cromwell, the spokesman of the Protectorate; the Earl of Chatham and Lord Mansfield, who first gave to British oratory the distinctly literary flavor which prevailed throughout the 18th century; John Wesley and George Whitefield, leaders of the great Revival of the eighteenth century; the great parliamentary orators, Edmund Burke, Charles Fox, Richard Sheridan, William Pitt, and their colleagues, the great men of eloquence whose oratory gave to their period the name of the Golden Age of British Oratory; Gladstone and Disraeli, the leading spokesmen of the Victorian era. To these are added a group of forensic orators and ecclesiasts who rose to prominence at the bar and in the pulpit, a roster of Irish men of eloquence who fought for Home Rule in Ireland, and the leading spokesmen of the great British possession, the Dominion of Canada—Sir John MacDonald and Sir Wilfrid Laurier.

ON THE PETITION OF RIGHT

Sir John Eliot

(1592-1632)

Among the earliest orators to fight in Parliament for the rights of the people was Sir John Eliot, most prominent for his agitation in behalf of the Petition of Right. His remarkable independence and fluent oratory in Parliament were directed against the encroachment on the rights of the House of Commons, which he considered the backbone of the national government. He was imprisoned for a time in the Tower of London as a result of a powerful speech which procured the impeachment of the Duke of Buckingham. Eliot constantly opposed leniency to Catholicism and ever supported constitutional rights. In 1628 he with Coke promoted the Petition of Right which was signed by Charles on June 7, 1628. At last his continued remonstrances against the royal acts of tyranny brought about a second imprisonment which broke his health.

Eliot's oratory was earnest and animated. He possessed some of the highest qualities as a speaker—"a singular power of statement, clearness, and facility in handling details, pointed classical allusions, keen and logical argument, forcible and rich declamation." Included here is a speech delivered by Eliot on June 3, 1628, before the House of Commons which was instrumental in procuring the ratification of the Petition of Right.

We sit here as the great Council of the King, and, in that capacity, it is our duty to take into consideration the state and affairs of the kingdom, and, when there is occasion, to give a true representation of them by way of counsel and advice, with what we conceive necessary or expedient to be done.

In this consideration, I confess many a sad thought hath affrighted me, and that not only in respect of our dangers from abroad (which yet I know are great, as they have often been pressed and dilated to us), but in respect of our disorders here at home, which do enforce those dangers and by which they are occasioned. For I believe I shall make it clear to you that both at first the cause of these dangers were our disorders, and our disorders now are yet our greatest dangers—that not so much the potency of our enemies, as the weakness of ourselves, doth threaten us: so that the saying of one of the Fathers may be assumed by us, "Non tam potentia sua quam negligentia nostra" (not so much by their power as by our neglect). Our want of true devotion to Heaven—our insincerity and doubting in religion—our want of councils—our precipitate actions—the insufficiency or unfaithfulness of our generals abroad—the ignorance or corruption of our ministers at home—the impoverishing of the sovereign —the oppression and depression of the subject—the exhausting of our treasures—the waste of our provisions—consumption of our ships—destruction of our men—these make the advantage to our enemies, not the reputation of their arms; and if in these there be not reformation, we need no foes abroad: Time itself will ruin us.

To show this more fully, I believe you will hold it necessary that what I say should not seem an aspersion on the State or imputation on the Government, as I have known such motives misinterpreted. But far is this from me to propose, who have none but clear thoughts of the excellency of the King; nor can I have other ends than the advancement of his Majesty's glory. I shall desire a little of your patience extraordinary as I lay open the particulars, which I shall do with what brevity I may, answerable to the importance of the cause and the necessity now upon us; yet with such respect and observation to the time, as I hope it shall not be thought troublesome.

For the first, then, our insincerity and doubting in religion is the greatest and most dangerous disorder of all others. This hath never been unpunished; and of this we have many strong examples of all States and in all times to awe us. What testimony doth it want? Will you have authority of books? Look on the collections of the Committee for Religion; there is too clear an evidence. See there the commission procured for composition with the Papists of the North! Mark the proceedings thereupon, and you will find them to little less amounting than a toleration in effect; the slight payments, and the easiness of them, will likewise show the favor that is intended. Will you have proofs of men? Witness the hopes, witness the presumptions, witness the reports of all the Papists generally. Observe the dispositions of commanders, the trust of officers, the confidence in secretaries to employments in this kingdom, in Ireland, and elsewhere. These will all show that it hath too great a certainty. And to this add but the incontrovertible evidence of that All-powerful Hand, which we have felt so sorely, that gave it full assurance; for as the heavens oppose themselves to our impiety, so it is we first opposed the heavens.

For the second, our want of councils, that great disorder in a State under which there can not be stability. If effects may show their causes (as they are often a perfect demonstration of them), our misfortunes, our disasters, serve to prove our deficiencies in council and the consequences they draw with them. If reason be allowed in this dark age, the judgment of dependencies and foresight of contingencies in affairs do confirm my position. For, if we view ourselves at home, are we in strength, are we in reputation, equal to our ancestors? If we view ourselves abroad, are our friends as many? Are our enemies no more? Do our friends retain their safety and possessions? Do not our enemies enlarge themselves, and gain from them and us? To what council owe we the loss of the Palatinate, where we sacrificed both our honor and our men sent thither, stopping those greater powers appointed for the service, by which it might have been defended? What council gave direction to the late action, whose wounds are yet bleeding—I mean the expedition to Rhé, of which there is yet so bad a memory in all men? What design for us, or advantage to our State, could that impart?

You know the wisdom of your ancestors, and the practice of their times, how they preserved their safeties. We all know, and have as much cause to doubt as they had, the greatness and ambition of the kingdom, which the Old World would not satisfy. Against this greatness and ambition, we likewise know the proceedings of the princess, that never-to-be-forgotten, excellent Queen Elizabeth, whose name, without admiration, falls not into mention even with her enemies. You know how she advanced herself, and how she advanced the nation in glory and in state; how she depressed her enemies, and how she upheld her friends; how she enjoyed a full security, and made those our scorn who now are made our terror.

Some of the principles she built on were these: and if I mistake, let reason and our statesmen contradict me.

First, to maintain, in what she might, a unity in France, that the kingdom, being at peace with itself, might be a bulwark to keep back the power of Spain by land.

Next, to preserve an amity and league between that State and us, that so we might come in aid of the Low Countries, and by that means receive their ships and help them by sea.

This triple cord, so working between France, the States, and England, might enable us, as occasion should require, to give assistance unto others. And by this means, as the experience of that time doth tell us, we were not only free from those fears that now possess and trouble us, but then our names were fearful to our enemies. See now what correspondency our action had with this. Try our conduct by these rules. It did induce, as a necessary consequence, a division in France between the Protestants and their King, of which there is too woeful and lamentable experience. It hath made an absolute breach between that State and us, and so entertains us against France, and France in preparation against us, that we have nothing to promise to our neighbors, nay hardly to ourselves. Next, observe the time in which it was attempted, and you shall find it not only varying from those principles, but directly contrary and opposite to those ends; and such as, from the issue and success, rather might be thought a conception of Spain than begotten here with us.

You know the dangers of Denmark, and how much they concern us; what in respect of our alliance and the country; what in the importance of the Sound; what an advantage to our enemies the gain thereof would be! What loss, what prejudice to us by this disunion; we breaking in upon France, France enraged by us, and the Netherlands at amazement between both! Neither could we intend to aid that luckless King, whose loss is our disaster.

Can those that express their trouble at the hearing of these things, and have so often told us in this place of their knowledge in the conjunctures and disjunctures of affairs—can they say they advised in this? Was this an act of council, Mr. Speaker? I have more charity than to think it; and unless they make confession of it themselves, I cannot believe it.

For the next, the insufficiency and unfaithfulness of our generals (that great disorder abroad), what shall I say? I wish there were not cause to mention it; and, but for the apprehension of the danger that is to come, if the like choice hereafter be not prevented, I could willingly be silent. But my duty to my Sovereign, my service to this House, and the safety and honor of my country, are above all respects; and what so nearly trenches to the prejudice of these, must not, shall not be forborne.

At Cadiz, then, in that first expedition we made, when we arrived and found a conquest ready—the Spanish ships, I mean, fit for the satisfaction of a voyage, and of which some of the chiefest then there themselves have since assured me that the satisfaction would have been sufficient, either in point of honor or in point of profit—why was it neglected? Why was it not achieved, it being granted on all hands how feasible it was?

Afterwards, when, with the destruction of some of our men and the exposure of others, who (though their fortune since has not been such) by chance came off safe—when, I say, with the loss of our serviceable men, that serviceable fort was gained, and the whole army landed, why was there nothing done? Why was there nothing attempted? If nothing was intended, wherefore did they land? If there was a service, wherefore were they shipped again? Mr. Speaker, it satisfies me too much in this case—when I think of their dry and hungry march into that drunken quarter (for so the soldiers termed it), which was the period of their journey—that divers of our men being left as a sacrifice to the enemy, that labor was at an end.

For the next undertaking, at Rhé, I will not trouble you much; only this, in short. Was not that whole action carried against the judgment and opinion of those officers that were of the council? Was not the first, was not the last, was not all in the landing—in the

intrenching—in the continuance there—in the assault—in the retreat—
without their assent? Did any advice take place of such as were of
the council? If there should be made a particular inquisition thereof,
these things will be manifest and more. I will not instance the manifesto that was made, giving the reason of these arms; nor by whom,
nor in what manner, nor on what grounds it was published, nor what
effects it hath wrought, drawing, as it were, almost the whole world
into league against us. Nor will I mention the leaving of the wines,
the leaving of the salt, which were in our possession, and of a value,
as it is said, to answer much of our expense. Nor will I dwell on
that great wonder (which no Alexander or Caesar ever did), the enriching of the enemy by courtesies when our soldiers wanted help; nor
the private intercourse and parleys with the fort, which were continually
held. What they intended may be read in the success; and upon due
examination thereof, they would not want their proofs.

For this last voyage to Rochelle, there need be no observations, it is
so fresh in memory; nor will I make an inference or corollary on all.
Your own knowledge shall judge what truth or what sufficiency they
express.

For the next, the ignorance and corruption of our ministers, where
can you miss of instances? If you survey the court, if you survey the
country; if the Church, if the city be examined; if you observe the
bar, if the bench, if the ports, if the shipping, if the land, if the seas—
all these will render you variety of proofs; and that in such measure
and proportion as show the greatness of our disease to be such that,
if there be not some speedy application for remedy, our case is almost
desperate.

Mr. Speaker, I fear I have been too long in these particulars that
are past, and am unwilling to offend you; therefore in the rest I shall
be shorter; and as to that which concerns the impoverishing of the
King, no other argument will I use than such as all men grant.

The exchequer, you know, is empty, and the reputation thereof gone;
the ancient lands are sold; the jewels pawned; the plate engaged; the
debts still great; almost all charges, both ordinary and extraordinary,
borne up by projects! What poverty can be greater? What necessity
so great? What perfect English heart is not almost dissolved into
sorrow for this truth?

For the oppression of the subject, which, as I remember, is the next
particular I proposed, it needs no demonstration. The whole kingdom
is a proof; and for the exhausting of our treasures, that very oppression
speaks it. What waste of provisions, what consumption of ships, what
destruction of our men there hath been; witness the expedition to
Algiers—witness that with Mansfeldt—witness that to Cadiz—witness
the next—witness that to Rhé—witness the last (I pray God we may
never have more such witnesses)—witness, likewise, the Palatinate—
witness Denmark—witness the Turks—witness the Dunkirkers—witness

all! What losses we have sustained! How we are impaired in munitions, in ships, in men!

It is beyond contradiction that we were never so much weakened, nor ever had less hope how to be restored.

These, Mr. Speaker, are our dangers, these are they who do threaten us; and these are, like the Trojan horse, brought in cunningly to surprise us. In these do lurk the strongest of our enemies, ready to issue on us; and if we do not speedily expel them, these are the signs, these the invitations to others! These will so prepare their entrance that we shall have no means left of refuge or defence; for if we have these enemies at home, how can we strive with those that are abroad? If we be free from these, no other can impeach us. Our ancient English virtue (like the old Spartan valor), cleared from these disorders— our being in sincerity of religion and once made friends with Heaven; having maturity of councils, sufficiency of generals, incorruption of officers, opulency in the King, liberty in the people, repletion in treasure, plenty of provisions, reparation of ships, preservation of men—our ancient English virtue, I say, thus rectified, will secure us; and, unless there be a speedy reformation in these, I know not what hopes or expectations we can have.

These are the things, Sir, I shall desire to have taken into consideration: that as we are the great council of the kingdom, and have the apprehension of these dangers, we may truly represent them unto the King; which I conceive we are bound to do by a triple obligation— of duty to God, of duty to his Majesty, and of duty to our country.

And therefore I wish it may so stand with the wisdom and judgment of the House, that these things may be drawn into the body of a remonstrance, and in all humility expressed, with a prayer to his Majesty that, for the safety of himself, for the safety of the kingdom, and for the safety of religion, he will be pleased to give us time to make perfect inquisition thereof, or to take them into his own wisdom, and there give them such timely reformation as the necessity and justice of the case doth import.

And thus, Sir, with a large affection and loyalty to his Majesty, and with a firm duty and service to my country, I have suddenly (and with a firm duty and service to my country) expressed the weak apprehensions that I have; wherein if I have erred, I humbly crave your pardon, and so submit myself to the censure of the House.

ON GRIEVANCES IN THE REIGN OF CHARLES I

John Pym

(1584-1643)

Supporting Sir John Eliot in his debates on the Petition of Right was Sir John Pym, who also during the reign of Charles I was one of the forceful leaders of the opposition to the arbitrary acts of tyranny. As a Puritan he directed his speeches against the political views of Catholicism. Pym opened the Short Parliament of 1640 with a speech two hours in length on the question of parliamentary privilege and in the Long Parliament, which met the same year, he conducted the impeachment of the Earl of Strafford, prime minister of Charles I. In this cause he was ably supported by John Hampden, who though not an orator was ever tireless in his efforts for the liberty of the English people. In 1641 Pym agitated for the Grand Remonstrance and later carried out the union with the Scots and the rather reluctant acceptance of the Covenant and the introduction of the Presbyterian form of church government. Pym was so eloquent a speaker that James I decried him as "King Pym," a name which clung to him until the day he was buried with great pomp in Westminster Abbey.

Included here is an abridgment of his speech delivered before the Short Parliament April 17, 1640.

Never Parliament had greater business to dispatch, nor more difficulties to encounter; therefore we have reason to take all advantages of order and address, and hereby we shall not only do our own work, but dispose and enable ourselves for the better satisfaction of his Majesty's desire of supply. The grievances being removed, our affections will carry us with speed and cheerfulness, to give his majesty that which may be sufficient both for his honor and support. Those that in the very first place shall endeavor to redress the grievances, will be found not to hinder, but to be the best furtherers of his majesty's service. He that taketh away weights, doth as much advantage motion, as he that addeth wings.

He [that is, the speaker, Pym] said he would labor to contract those manifold affairs both of the Church and State, which did so earnestly require the wisdom and faithfulness of this house, into a double method of grievances and cures. And because there wanted not some who pretended that these things, wherewith the commonwealth is now grieved, are much for the advantage of the king, and that the redress of them will be to his majesty's great disadvantage and loss, he doubted not but to make it appear, that in discovering the present great distempers and disorders, and procuring remedy for them, we should be no less serviceable to his majesty, who has summoned us to this great council, than useful to those whom we do here represent. For the better effecting whereof, he propounded three main branches of his discourse: In the first, he would offer them the several heads of some principal grievances, under which the kingdom groaned. In the second, he undertook to prove that the disorders from whence those grievances issued, were as hurtful to the king as to the people. In the third, he would advise such a way of healing, and removing those grievances, as might be equally effectual to maintain the honor and greatness of the king, and to procure the prosperity and contentment of the people.

The greatest liberty of the kingdom is religion; thereby we are freed from spiritual evils, and no impositions are so grievous as those that are laid upon the soul.

The next great liberty is justice, whereby we are preserved from injuries in our persons and estates; from this is derived into the commonwealth, peace, and order, and safety; and when this is interrupted, confusion and danger are ready to overwhelm all.

The third great liberty consists in the power and privilege of parliaments; for this is the fountain of law, the great council of the kingdom, the highest court; this is enabled by the legislative and conciliary power, to prevent evils to come; by the judiciary power, to suppress and remove evils present. If you consider these three great liberties in the order of dignity, this last is inferior to the end; but, if you consider them in the order of necessity and use, this may justly claim the first place in our care, because the end can not be obtained without the means; and if we do not preserve this, we can not long hope to enjoy either of the others. Therefore, being about to speak of those grievances which lie upon the kingdom, he would observe this order.

The privileges of Parliament were not given for the ornament or advantage of those who are the members of Parliament: They have a real use and efficacy toward that which is the end of parliaments. We are free from suits that we may the more entirely addict ourselves to the public services; we have, therefore, liberty of speech, that our counsels may not be corrupted with fear, or our judgments perverted with self-respect. Those three great faculties and functions of Parliament, the legislative, judiciary, and conciliary power, can not be well exercised without such privileges as these. The wisdom of our laws, the faithfulness of our counsels, the righteousness of our judgments, can hardly be kept pure and untainted if they proceed from distracted and restrained minds.

Then he propounded divers particular points wherein the privileges of Parliament had been broken. First, in restraining the members of the House from speaking. Secondly, in forbidding the Speaker to put any question.

These two were practised the last day of the last Parliament (and, as was alleged, by his majesty's command), both of them trench upon the very life and being of parliaments; for if such a restraining power as this should take root, and be admitted, it will be impossible for us to bring any resolution to perfection in such matters as shall displease those about the king.

Thirdly, by imprisoning divers members of the House, for matters done in Parliament. Fourthly, by indictments, informations, and judgments in ordinary and inferior courts, for speeches and proceedings in parliaments. Fifthly, by the disgraceful order of the king's bench, whereby some members of this House were enjoined to put in security of their good behavior; and for refusal thereof, were continued in prison divers years, without any particular allegation against them. One of them was freed by death. Others were not dismissed till his majesty had declared his intention to summon the present Parliament. And this he noted not only as a breach of privilege, but as a violation of the common justice of the kingdom. Sixthly, by the sudden and abrupt dissolution of parliaments, contrary to the law and custom.

Often hath it been declared in parliaments, that the Parliament should not be dissolved till the petitions be answered. This (he said) was a great grievance because it doth prevent the redress of other grievances. It were a hard case that a private man should be put to death without being heard. As this representative body of the Commons receives a being by the summons, so it receives a civil death by the dissolution. Is it not a much more heavy doom by which we lose our being, to have this civil death inflicted on us in displeasure, and not to be allowed time and liberty to answer for ourselves? That we should not only die, but have this mark of infamy laid upon us? to be made intestables, disabled to make our wills, to dispose of our business, as this House hath always used to do before adjournments or dissolutions? Yet this hath often been our case! We have not been permitted to pour out our last sighs and groans into the bosom of our dear sovereign. The words of dying men are full of piercing affections; if we might be heard to speak, no doubt we should so fully express our love and faithfulness to our prince, as might take off the false suggestions and aspersions of others; at least we should in our humble supplications recommend some such things to him in the name of his people, as would make for his own honor, and the public good of his kingdom.

Thus he concluded the first sort of grievances, being such as were against the privilege of Parliament, and passed on to the next, concerning religion; all which he conveyed under these four heads. The first was the great encouragement given to popery, of which he produced these particular evidences. A suspension of all laws against papists, whereby they enjoy a free and almost public exercise of that religion. Those good statutes which were made for restraint of idolatry and superstition, are now a ground of security to them in the practise of both; being used to no other end but to get money into the king's purse; which as it is clearly against the intentions of the law, so it is full of mischief to the kingdom. By this means a dangerous party is cherished and increased, who are ready to close with any opportunity of disturbing the peace and safety of the state. Yet he did not desire any new laws against popery, or any rigorous courses in the execution of those already in force; he was far from seeking the ruin of their persons or estates, only he wished they might be kept in such a condition as should restrain them from doing hurt.

A second encouragement is their admission into places of power and trust in the Commonwealth, whereby they get many dependents and adherents, not only of their own, but even of such as make profession to be Protestants.

A third, their freedom of resorting to London and the court, whereby they have opportunity, not only of communicating their counsels and designs, one to another, but of diving into his majesty's counsels, by the frequent access of those who are active men among them, to the tables and company of great men; and under subtle pretenses and disguises they want not means of cherishing their own projects and of endeavoring to mold and bias the public affairs to the great advantage of that party.

A fourth, that as they have a congregation of cardinals at Rome, to consider of the aptest ways and means of establishing the pope's authority and religion in England, so they have a nuncio here, to act and dispose that party to the execution of those counsels, and, by the assistance of such cunning and Jesuitical spirits as swarm in this town, to order and manage all actions and events, to the furtherance of that main end.

Having despatched these several points, he proceeded to the third kind of grievances, being such as are against the common justice of the realm, in the liberty of our persons, and propriety of our estates, of which he had many to propound; in doing whereof, he would rather observe the order of time, wherein they were acted, than of consequence; but when he should come to the cure, he should then persuade the House to begin with those which were of much importance, as being now in execution, and very much pressing and exhausting the common-wealth.

Since the breach of the last Parliament, his majesty hath, by a new book of rates, very much increased the burden upon merchandise, and now tonnage, and poundage, old and new impositions, are all taken by prerogative, without any grant in Parliament, or authority of law, as we conceive; from whence divers inconveniences and mischiefs are produced. The danger of the precedent, that a judgment in one court, and in one case, is made binding to all the kingdom. Men's goods are seized, their legal suits are stopped, and justice denied to those that desire to take the benefit of the law. The great sums of money received upon these impositions, intended for the guard of the seas, claimed and defended upon no ground but of public trust, for protection of merchants and defense of the ports, are dispersed to other uses, and a new tax raised for the same purposes.

These burdens are so excessive, that trade is thereby very much hindered, the commodities of our own growth extremely abased, and those imported much enhanced; all which lies not upon the merchant alone, but upon the generality of the subjects; and by this means the stock of the kingdom is much diminished, our exportation being less profitable, and our importation more changeable. And if the wars and troubles in the neighbor parts had not brought almost the whole stream of trade into this kingdom, we should have found many more prejudicial effects of these impositions, long before this time, than yet we have done. Especially they have been insupportable to the poor plantations, whither many of his majesty's subjects have been transported, in divers parts of the Continent and islands of America, in furtherance of a design to enlarge his majesty's dominions. The adventurers in this noble work have for the most part no other support but tobacco, upon which such a heavy rate is set that the king receives twice as much as the true value of the commodity to the owner. Whereas these great burdens have caused divers merchants to apply themselves to a way of traffic abroad by transporting goods from one country to another, without bringing them home into England. But now it hath been lately en-deavored to set an imposition upon this trade, so that the king will have a duty even out of those commodities which never come within his dominions, to the great discouragement of such active and industrious men.

The third general head of civil grievances was, the great inundation of monopolies, whereby heavy burdens are laid, not only upon foreign, but also native commodities. These began in the soap patent. The principal undertakers in this were divers popish recusants, men of estate and quality, such as in likelihood did not only aim at their private gain, but that by this open breach of law, the king and his people might be more fully divided, and the ways of Parliament men more thoroughly obstructed. Among the infinite inconveniences and mischiefs which this did produce, these few may be observed: The impairing the goodness, and enhancing the price of most of the commodities and manufactures of the realm, yea, of those which are of most necessary and common use, as salt, soap, beer, coals, and infinite others. That, under color of licenses, trades and manufactures are restrained to a few hands, and many of the subjects deprived of their ordinary way of livelihood. That, upon such illegal grants, a great number of persons had been unjustly vexed by pursuivants, imprisonments, attendance upon the council table, forfeiture of goods, and many other ways.

The fourth head of civil grievances was that great and unparalleled grievance of the ship money, which, tho it may seem to have more warrant of law than the rest, because there hath been a judgment passed for it, yet in truth it is thereby aggravated, if it be considered that the judgment is founded upon the naked opinion of some judges without any written law, without any custom, or authority of law books, yea, without any one precedent for it. Many express laws, many declarations in parliaments, and the constant practise and judgment at all times are against it! Yea, in the very nature of it, it will be found to be disproportionable to the case of "necessity" which is pretended to be the ground of it! Necessity excludes all formalities and solemnities. It is no time then to make levies and taxes to build and prepare ships. Every man's person, every man's ships are to be employed for the resisting of an invading enemy. The right on the subject's part was so clear, and the pretenses against it so weak, that he thought no man would venture his reputation or conscience in the defense of that judgment, being so contrary to the grounds of the law, to the practise of former times, and so inconsistent in itself. . . .

The seventh great civil grievance hath been the military charges laid upon the several counties of the kingdom—sometimes by warrant under his majesty's signature, sometimes by letters from the council table, and sometimes (such has been the boldness and presumption of some men) by the order of the lord lieutenants, or deputy lieutenant alone. This is a growing evil; still multiplying and increasing from a few particulars to many, from small sums to great. It began first to be practised as a loan, for supply of coat and conduct money; and for this it hath some countenance from the use in Queen Elizabeth's time, when the lords of the council did often desire the deputy lieutenants to procure so much money to be laid out in the country as the service did require, with a promise to pay it again in London; for which purpose there was a constant warrant in the exchequer. This was the practise in her time, and in a great part of King James'. But the payments were then so certain, as it was little otherwise than taking up money upon bills of exchange. At this day they follow these precedents in the manner of the demand (for it is with a promise of a repayment), but not in the certainty and readiness of satisfaction.

The first particular brought into a tax (as he thought) was the muster master's wages, at which many repined; but being for small sums, it began to be generally digested; yet, in the last Parliament, this House was sensible of it, and to avoid the danger of the precedent that the subjects should be forced to make any payments without consent in Parliament they thought upon a bill that might be a rule to the lieutenants what to demand, and to the people what to pay. But the hopes of this bill were dashed in the dissolution of that Parliament. Now of late divers other particulars are growing into practise, which make the grievance much more heavy. Those mentioned were these: 1. Pressing men against their will, and forcing them which are rich or unwilling to serve, to find others in their place. 2. The provision of public magazines for powder, and other munitions, spades and pick-axes. 3. The salary of divers officers besides the muster master. 4. The buying of cart horses and carts, and hiring of carts for carriages.

The next head of civil grievances was comprised in the high court of star chamber, which some think succeeded that which in the parliament rolls is called magnum concilium, and to which parliaments were wont so often to refer those important matters which they had no time to determine. But now this court, which in the late restoration or erection of it in Henry VII's time, was especially designed to restrain the oppression of great men, and to remove the obstructions and impediments of the law—this, which is both a court of counsel and a court of justice, hath been made an instrument of erecting, and defending monopolies and other grievances; to set a face of right upon those things which are unlawful in their own nature, a face of public good upon such as are pernicious in their use and execution. The soap patent and divers other evidences thereof may be given, so well known as not to require a particular relation. And as if this were not enough, this court hath lately intermeddled with the ship money! Divers sheriffs have been questioned for not levying and collecting such sums as their counties have been charged with; and if this beginning be not prevented, the star chamber will become a court of revenue, and it shall be made a crime not to collect or pay such taxes as the State shall require!

The eleventh head of civil grievances was now come to. He said, he was gone very high, yet he must go a little higher. That great and most eminent power of the king, of making edicts and proclamations, which are said to be "leges temporis," and by means of which our princes have used to encounter with such sudden and unexpected danger, as would not endure so much delay, as assembling the great council of the kingdom—this, which is one of the most glorious beams of majesty, most rigorous in commanding reverence and subjection, has, to our unspeakable grief, been often exercised of late for the enjoining and maintaining sundry monopolies and other grants—exceeding burdensome and prejudicial to the people.

The twelfth next. Now, altho he has come as high as he could upon earth, yet the presumption of evil men did lead him one step higher—even as high as heaven—as high as the throne of God! It was now (he said) grown common for ambitious and corrupt men of the clergy to abuse the truth of God and the bond of conscience; preaching down the laws and liberties of the kingdom, and pretending Divine authority for an absolute power in the king, to do what he would with persons and goods. This hath been so often published in sermons and printed books, that it is now the highway to preferment!

The thirteenth head of civil grievances he would thus express: The long intermission of parliaments, contrary to the two statutes yet in force, whereby it is appointed there should be parliaments once a year, at the least; and most contrary to the public good of the kingdom, since, this being well remedied, it would generate remedies for all the rest.

Having gone through the several heads of grievances, he came to the second main branch propounded in the beginning: that the disorders from whence these grievances issued were as hurtful to the king as to the people, of which he gave divers reasons.

As to the interruption of the sweet communion which ought to be betwixt the king and his people, in matters of grace and supply. They have need of him by his general pardon—to be secured from projectors and informers, to be freed from absolute laws, from the subtle devices of such as seek to restrain the prerogative to their own private advantage, and the public hurt; and he hath need of them for counsel and support in great and extraordinary occasions. This mutual intercourse, if indeed sustained, would so weave the affections and interests of his subjects into his actions and designs that their wealth and their persons would be his; his own estate would be managed to most advantage; and public undertakings would be prosecuted at the charge and adventure of the subject. The victorious attempts in Queen Elizabeth's time upon Portugal, Spain, and the Indies, were for the greatest part made upon the subjects' purses, and not upon the queen's; tho the honor and profit of the success did most accrue to her.

Those often breaches and discontentments betwixt the king and the people are apt to diminish his reputation abroad, and disadvantage his treaties and alliances.

The apprehension of the favor and encouragement given to popery hath much weakened his majesty's party beyond the sea, and impaired that advantage which Queen Elizabeth and his royal father have heretofore made, of being heads of the Protestant union.

The innovations in religion and rigor of ecclesiastical courts have forced a great many of his majesty's subjects to forsake the land; whereby not only their persons and their posterity, but their wealth and their industry are lost to this kingdom, much to the reduction, also, of his majesty's customs and subsidies. And, among other inconveniences of such a sort, this was especially to be observed, that divers clothiers, driven out of the country, had set up the manufacture of cloth beyond the seas; whereby this state is like to suffer much by abatement of the price of wools, and by want of employment for the poor; both which likewise tend to his majesty's particular loss.

The differences and discontents betwixt his majesty and the people at home, have in all likelihood diverted his royal thoughts and counsels from those great opportunities which he might have, not only to weaken the House of Austria, and to restore the Palatinate, but to gain himself a higher pitch of power and greatness than any of his ancestors. For it is not unknown how weak, how distracted, how discontented the Spanish colonies are in the West Indies. There are now in those parts in New England, Virginia, and the Caribbean Islands, and in the Bermudas, at least 60,000 able persons of this nation, many of them well armed and their bodies seasoned to that climate, which with a very small charge, might be set down in some advantageous parts of these pleasant, rich, and fruitful countries, and easily make his majesty master of all that treasure, which not only foments the war, but is the great support of popery in all parts of Christendom.

Having thus passed through the two first general branches, he was now come to the third, wherein he was to set down the ways of healing and removing those grievances which consisted of two main branches: first, in declaring the law where it was doubtful; the second, in better provision for the execution of law, where it is clear. But (he said) because he had already spent much time, and begun to find some confusion in his memory, he would refer the particulars to another opportunity, and for the present only move that which was general to all, and which would give weight and advantage to all the particular ways of redress. That is, that we should speedily desire a conference with the lords, and acquaint them with the miserable condition wherein we find the Church and State; and as we have already resolved to join in a religious seeking of God, in a day of fast and humiliation, so to entreat them to concur with us in a parliamentary course of petitioning the king, as there should be occasion, and in searching out the causes and remedies of these many insupportable grievances under which we lie. That so, by the united wisdom and authority of both Houses, such courses may be taken as (through God's blessing) may advance the honor and greatness of his majesty, and restore and establish the peace and prosperity of the kingdom.

This, he said, we might undertake with comfort and hope of success; for tho there be a darkness upon the land, a thick and palpable darkness, like that of Egypt, yet, as in that, the sun had not lost his light, nor the Egyptians their sight (the interruption was only in the medium), so with us, there is still (God be thanked!) light in the sun—wisdom and justice in his majesty—to dispel this darkness; and in us there remains a visual faculty, whereby we are enabled to apprehend, and moved to desire, light. And when we shall be blessed in the enjoying of it, we shall thereby be incited to return his majesty such thanks as may make it shine more clearly in the world, to his own glory, and in the hearts of his people, to their joy and contentment.

THE CHARGES IN RALEIGH'S CASE

Sir Edward Coke

(1552-1633)

As chief justice of the Court of James I, Sir Edward Coke proposed and framed the famous Petition of Right, the most explicit declaration of English liberty of his day. Coke's legal ability and learning supplemented by his tact and courage had early in his life secured for him a large clientele in his practice of law. In 1593 he was chosen speaker of the House of Commons; in 1594 as Attorney General he conducted the prosecution in the trials of Essex, Southampton, and Raleigh (to the latter of whom he showed brutal rancor and bitterness). Appointed Chief Justice in 1606 he fulfilled that office with dignity and honor and constantly opposed the encroachment of royalty. His ardent support of liberal measures in Parliament, particularly the right of freedom in debate, imprisoned him in the Tower of London. His last act was the framing of the celebrated Petition of Right. Coke's utterances throughout his lifetime aided greatly in the struggle for parliamentary freedom, and his law reports are valuable even today in the legal profession. It has been said that Samuel Adams and Thomas Jefferson are largely indebted to Coke for views which did much to shape American institutions.

Included here is a portion of his prosecution of Sir Walter Raleigh, conducted November 17, 1603, Coke being the King's Attorney General against Raleigh, who was accused of conspiracy against the king. Although unfair to Raleigh, the portion presented here shows the strength of Coke's style.

My speech shall chiefly touch these three points: imitation, supportation, and defence. The imitation of evil ever exceeds the precedent; as, on the contrary, imitation of good ever comes short. Mischief cannot be supported but by mischief; yea, it will so multiply that it will bring all to confusion. Mischief is ever underpropped by falsehood or foul practices; and because all these things did occur in this treason, you shall understand the ruin, as before ye did the bye.

The treason of the bye consisteth in these points: First, that the Lords Grey, Brooks, Markham, and the rest intended by force in the night to surprise the King's Court, which was a rebellion in the heart of the realm,—yea, in the heart of the heart, in the Court. They intended to take him that is a sovereign to make him subject to their power; purposing to open the doors with muskets and cavaliers, and to take also the Prince and the Council; then, under the King's authority, to carry the King to the Tower, and to make a stale of the Admiral.

When they had the King there to extort three things from him: First, a pardon for all their treasons; second, a toleration of the Roman superstition—which their eyes shall sooner fall out than they shall ever see; for the King has spoken these words in the hearing of many: "I will lose the crown and my life before ever I will alter religion." And, third, to remove counselors.

In the room of the Lord Chancellor they would have placed one Watson, a priest, absurd in humanity and ignorant in divinity. Brook, of whom I will speak nothing, was to be Lord Treasurer. The Great Secretary must be Markham, oculus patriae. A hole must be found in my Lord Chief-Justice's coat. Grey must be Earl-Marshal and Master of the Horse, because he would have a table in the Court; marry, he would advance the Earl of Worcester to a higher place.

All this cannot be done without a multitude; therefore, Watson, the priest, tells a resolute man that the King was in danger of Puritans and Jesuits, so as to bring him in blindfold into the action, saying, "That the King is no king until he be crowned; therefore, every man might right his own wrongs." But he is "rex natus," his dignity descends as well as yours, my lords.

Then Watson imposeth a blasphemous oath, that they should swear to defend the King's person; to keep secret what was given them in charge; and seek all ways and means to advance the Catholic religion. Then they intend to send for the Lord Mayor and the alderman, in the King's name, to the Tower, lest they should make any resistance, and then to take hostages of them, and to enjoin them to provide for them victuals and munition. Grey, because the King removed before midsummer, had a further reach; to get a company of swordsmen to assist the action; therefore he would stay till he had obtained a regiment from Ostend or Austria. So you see these treasons were like Samson's foxes, which were joined in their tails though their heads were severed.

AT THE OPENING OF PARLIAMENT UNDER THE PROTECTORATE

Oliver Cromwell
(1599-1658)

Oliver Cromwell was the leader and spokesman of the Commonwealth. He was a man of action rather than of words and his own energy of character over-weighed any elegance of language or grace of delivery, for he was rough and almost uncouth in his speech; yet he dominated his audiences and won points by conviction rather than by persuasion. Vehement and militant on the rostrum as on the field of battle, he carried both situations with a high hand. Carlyle said of him "His speeches excel all human belief in their unlikeness to all other speeches, in their utter disregard of all the standards of oratory and logical sequence of thought, but in their day they had as much weight in England as the most polished orations of Demosthenes in Athens."

Included here is part of his speech delivered on September 4, 1654, on the occasion of his installation as Lord Protector of England.

GENTLEMEN:—You are met here on the greatest occasion that, I believe, England ever saw; having upon your shoulders the interests of three great nations with the territories belonging to them; and truly, I believe I may say without any hyperbole, you have upon your shoulders the interests of all the Christian people in the world. And the expectation is that I should let you know, as far as I have cognizance of it, the occasion of your assembling together at this time.

It hath been very well hinted to you this day that you come hither to settle the interests above mentioned: for your work here, in the issue and consequences of it, will extend so far, even to all Christian people. In the way and manner of my speaking to you, I shall study plainness, and to speak to you what is truth, and what is upon my heart, and what will in some measure reach to these great concernments.

After so many changes and turnings which this nation hath labored under, to have such a day of hope as this is, and such a door of hope opened by God to us, truly I believe, some months since, would have been beyond all our thoughts! I confess it would have been worthy of such a meeting as this is, to have remembered that which was the rise of, and gave the first beginning to, all these troubles which have been upon this nation: and to have given you a series of the transactions,—not of men, but of the providence of God, all along unto our late changes: as also the ground of our first undertaking to oppose that usurpation and tyranny which was upon us, both in civils and spirituals; and the several grounds particularly applicable to the several changes that have been. . . .

The government hath had some things in desire; and it hath done some things actually. It hath desired to reform the laws. I say to reform them: and for that end it hath called together persons—without offense be it spoken—of as great ability and as great interest as are in these nations, to consider how the laws might be made plain and short and less chargeable to the people; how to lessen expense for the good of the nation. And those things are in preparation, and bills prepared, which in due time, I make no question, will be tendered to you. In the meanwhile there hath been care taken to put the administration of the laws into the hands of just men; men of the most known integrity and ability. The Chancery hath been reformed—hath been reformed, I hope, to the satisfaction of all good men: and as for the things, or causes, depending there, which made the burden and work of the honorable persons entrusted in those services too heavy for their ability, it hath referred many of them to those places where Englishmen love to have their rights tried, the courts of law at Westminster.

This government hath, farther, endeavored to put a stop to that heady way (likewise touched of in our sermon this day) of every man making himself a minister and preacher. It hath endeavored to settle a method for the approving and sanctioning of men of piety and ability to discharge that work. And I think I may say it hath committed the business to the trust of persons, both of the Presbyterian and Independent judgments, of as known ability, piety, and integrity as any, I believe this nation hath. And I believe also that, in that care they have taken, they have labored to approve themselves to Christ, to the nation and to their own consciences. And indeed I think, if there be anything of quarrel against them,—tho I am not here to justify the proceedings of any,—it is that they, in fact, go upon such a character as the Scripture warrants: To put men into that great employment, and to approve men for it, who are men that have "received gifts from Him that ascended up on high, and gave gifts" for the work of the ministry and for the edifying of the body of Christ. The government hath also taken care, we hope, for the expulsion of all those who may be judged any way unfit for this work; who are scandalous, and the common scorn and contempt of that function.

One thing more this government hath done: it hath been instrumental to call a free Parliament, which, blessed be God, we see here this day! I say, a free Parliament. And that it may continue so, I hope is in the heart and may continue so, I hope is in the heart and spirit of every good man in England, save such discontented persons as I have formerly mentioned. It is that which, as I have desired above my life, so I shall desire to keep it above my life.

I did before mention to you the plunges we were in with respect to foreign States; by the war with Portugal, France, the Dutch, the Danes, and the little assurance we had from any of our neighbors round about. I perhaps forgot, but indeed it was a caution upon my mind, and I desire now it may be so understood, that if any good hath been done, it was the Lord, not we, His poor instruments.

I did instance the wars, which did exhaust your treasure, and put you into such a condition that you must have sunk therein if it had continued but a few months longer: this I can affirm, if strong probability may be a fit ground. And now you have, tho it be not the first in time, peace with Swede-land; an honorable peace; through the endeavors of an honorable person here present as the instrument. I say you have an honorable peace with a kingdom which, not many years since, was much a friend to France, and lately perhaps inclinable enough to the Spaniard. And I believe you expect not much good from any of your Catholic neighbors; nor yet that they would be very willing you should have a good understanding with your Protestant friends. Yet, thanks be to God, that peace is concluded; and as I said before, it is an honorable peace.

You have a peace with the Danes—a State that lay contiguous to that part of this island which hath given us the most trouble. And certainly if your enemies abroad be able to annoy you, it is likely they will take their advantage (where it best lies) to give you trouble from that country. But you have a peace there, and an honorable one. Satisfaction to your merchants' ships; not only to their content, but to their rejoicing. I believe you will easily know it is so—an honorable peace. You have the Sound open; which used to be obstructed. That which was and is the strength of this nation, the shipping, will now be supplied thence. And whereas you were glad to have anything of that kind at second hand, you have now all manner of commerce there, and at as much freedom as the Dutch themselves, who used to be the carriers and venders of it to us; and at the same rates and tolls; and I think, by that peace, the said rates now fixed upon can not be raised to you in future.

You have a peace likewise with the crown of Portugal; which peace, tho it hung long in hand, yet is lately concluded. It is a peace which, your merchants make us believe, is of good concernment to their trade; the rate of insurance to that country having been higher, and so the profit which could bear such rate, than to other places. And one thing hath been obtained in this treaty which never before was since the Inquisition was set up here—that our people which trade thither have liberty of conscience—liberty to worship in chapels of their own.

Indeed, peace is, as you were well told today, desirable with all men, as far as it may be had with conscience and honor! We are upon a treaty with France. And we may say this, that if God gave us honor in the eyes of the nations about us, we have reason to bless Him for it, and so to own it. And I dare say that there is not a nation in Europe but is very willing to ask a good understanding with you.

I am sorry I am thus tedious: but I did judge that it was somewhat necessary to acquaint you with these things. And things being so, I hope you will not be unwilling to hear a little again of the sharp as well as of the sweet! And I should not be faithful to you, nor to the interest of these nations which you and I serve, if I did not let you know all.

As I said before, when this government was undertaken, we were in the midst of those domestic diversions and animosities and scatterings; engaged also with those foreign enemies round about us at such a vast charge—£120,000 a month for the very fleet, which sum was the very utmost penny of your assessments. Aye; and then all your treasure was exhausted and spent when this government was undertaken: all accidental ways of bringing in treasure were, to a very inconsiderable sum, consumed,—the forfeited lands sold; the sums on hand spent; rents, fee-farms, delinquents' lands, king's, queen's, bishops', dean-and-chapters' lands, sold. These were spent when this government was undertaken. I think it is my duty to let you know so much. And that is the reason why the taxes do yet lie so heavy upon the people—of which we have abated £30,000 a month for the next three months. Truly I thought it my duty to let you know, that tho God hath dealt thus bountifully with you, yet these are but entrances and doors of hope, whereby, through the blessing of God, you may enter into rest and peace. But you are not yet entered!

You were told to-day of a people brought out of Egypt toward the land of Canaan; but through unbelief, murmuring, repining, and other temptations and sins wherewith God was provoked, they were fain to come back again, and linger many years in the wilderness before they came to the place of rest. We are thus far, through the mercy of God. We have cause to take notice of it that we are not brought into misery, not totally wrecked, but have, as I said before, a door of hope open. And I may say this to you: If the Lord's blessing and His presence go along with the management of affairs at this meeting, you will be enabled to put the top-stone to the work and make the nation happy. But this must be by knowing the true state of affairs! You are yet like the people under circumcision, but raw. Your peaces are but newly made. And it is a maxim not to be despised, "Tho peace be made, yet it is interest that keeps peace";—and I hope you will not trust such peace except so far as you see interest upon it. But all settlement grows stronger by mere continuance. And therefore I wish that you may go forward and not backward; and in brief that you may have the blessing of God upon your endeavors! It is one of the great ends of calling this Parliament that the ship of the commonwealth may be brought into a safe harbor; which, I assure you, it will not be, without your counsel and advice.

You have great works upon your hands. You have Ireland to look unto. There is not much done to the planting thereof, tho some things leading and preparing for it are. It is a great business to settle the government of that nation upon fit terms, such as will bear that work through. You have had laid before you some considerations intimating your peace with several foreign states. But yet you have not made peace with all. And if they should see we do not manage our affairs with that wisdom which becomes us,—truly we may sink under disadvantages, for all that is done. And our enemies will have their eyes open, and be revived, if they see animosities among us; which indeed will be their great advantage.

I do therefore persuade you to a sweet, gracious, and holy understanding of one another and of your business, concerning which you had so good counsel this day; which as it rejoiced my heart to hear, so I hope the Lord will imprint it upon your spirits,—wherein you shall have my prayers.

Having said this, and perhaps omitted many other material things through the frailty of my memory, I shall exercise plainness and freeness with you; and say that I have not spoken these things as one who assumes to himself dominion over you; but as one who doth resolve to be a fellow servant with you to the interest of these great affairs and of the people of these nations. I shall trouble you no longer; but desire you to repair to your House, and there exercise your own liberty in the choice of a Speaker, that so you may lose no time in carrying on your work.

THE DEFENSE OF WALPOLE

Sir Robert Walpole

(1676-1745)

Robert Walpole entered Parliament in 1700 and distinguished himself at once through his practical powers of debate until he became a leader of the Whig party and Secretary of War in 1708. He was expelled from Parliament in 1712 and sent to the Tower of London but returned to his seat in Parliament in 1713. His service as Prime Minister from 1715 to 1717 and again from 1721 to 1742 has been characterized by Burke as "intelligent, prudent, and safe." Walpole was the first English statesman to adopt the easy, colloquial style of speech before Parliament, a style imitative of the simplicity and purity of diction used by Addison and Steele. He was at his best in satire and invective and gifted as a debater rather than an orator. Included here is a speech delivered before the House of Commons in February, 1741, against his removal from the office of Prime Minister. Walpole with Bolingbroke ranks as the leading orator of the early 18th century, but of Bolingbroke's speeches unfortunately there are none extant.

It has been observed by several gentlemen, in vindication of this motion, that if it should be carried, neither my life, liberty, nor estate will be affected. But do the honorable gentlemen consider my character and reputation as of no moment? Is it no imputation to be arraigned before this House, in which I have sat forty years, and to have my name transmitted to posterity with disgrace and infamy? I will not conceal my sentiments that to be named in Parliament as a subject of inquiry is to me a matter of great concern. But I have the satisfaction, at the same time, to reflect that the impression to be made depends upon the consistency of the charge and the motives of the prosecutors.

My great and principal crime is my long continuance in office; or, in other words, the long exclusion of those who now complain against me. This is the heinous offense which exceeds all others. I keep from them the possession of that power, those honors, and those emoluments, to which they so ardently and pertinaciously aspire. I will not attempt to deny the reasonableness and necessity of a party war; but in carrying on that war all principles and rules of justice should not be departed from. The Tories must confess that the most obnoxious persons have felt few instances of extra-judicial power. Wherever they have been arraigned, a plain charge has been exhibited against them. They have had an impartial trial and have been permitted to make their defense. And will they, who have experienced this fair and equitable mode of proceeding, act in direct opposition to every principle of justice and establish this fatal precedent of parliamentary inquisition? Whom would they conciliate by a conduct so contrary to principle and precedent?

Gentlemen have talked a great deal of patriotism. A venerable word, when duly practised. But I am sorry to say that of late it has been so much hackneyed about that it is in danger of falling into disgrace. The very idea of true patriotism is lost, and the term has been prostituted to the very worst of purposes. A patriot, sir! Why, patriots spring up like mushrooms! I could raise fifty of them within the four-and-twenty hours. I have raised many of them in one night. It is but refusing to gratify an unreasonable or an insolent demand, and up starts a patriot. I have never been afraid of making patriots; but I disdain and despise all their efforts. This pretended virtue proceeds from personal malice and disappointed ambition. There is not a man among them whose particular aim I am not able to ascertain, and from what motive they have entered into the lists of opposition.

I shall now consider the articles of accusation which they have brought against me, and which they have not thought fit to reduce to specific charges; and I shall consider these in the same order as that in which they were placed by the honorable member who made the motion: first, in regard to foreign affairs; secondly, to domestic affairs; and, thirdly, to the conduct of the war.

As to foreign affairs, I must take notice of the uncandid manner in which the gentlemen on the other side have managed the question by blending numerous treaties and complicated negotiations into one general mass.

To form a fair and candid judgment of the subject it becomes necessary not to consider the treaties merely insulated, but to advert to the time in which they were made, to the circumstances and situation of Europe when they were made, to the peculiar situation in which I stand, and to the power which I possessed. I am called repeatedly and insidiously prime and sole minister of all Europe. Am I answerable for the conduct of other countries as well as for that of my own? Many words are not wanting to show that the particular view of each court occasioned the dangers which affected the public tranquillity; yet the whole is charged to my account. Nor is this sufficient. Whatever was the conduct of England, I am equally arraigned. If we maintained ourselves in peace, and took no share in foreign transactions, we were reproached for tameness and pusillanimity. If, on the contrary, we interfered in these disputes, we were called Don Quixotes, and dupes to all the world. If we contracted guarantees, it was asked why is the nation wantonly burdened? If guarantees were declined, we were reproached with having no allies.

I now come, sir, to the second head—the conduct of domestic affairs. And here a most heinous charge is made, that the nation has been burdened with unnecessary expenses for the sole purpose of preventing the discharge of our debts and the abolition of taxes. But this attack is more to the dishonor of the whole cabinet council than to me. If there is any ground for this imputation, it is a charge upon king, lords and commons, as corrupted or imposed upon. And they have no proof of these allegations, but affect to substantiate them by common fame and public notoriety!

No expense has been incurred but what has been approved of and provided for by Parliament. The public treasure has been duly applied to the uses to which it was appropriated by Parliament, and regular accounts have been annually laid before Parliament, of every article of expense. If by foreign accidents, by the disputes of foreign states among themselves, or by their designs against us, the nation has often been put to an extraordinary expense, that expense can not be said to have been unnecessary; because, if by saving it we had exposed the balance of power to danger, or ourselves to an attack, it would have cost, perhaps, a hundred times that sum before we could recover from that danger or repel that attack.

In all such cases there will be a variety of opinions. I happened to be one of those who thought all these expenses necessary, and I had the good fortune to have the majority of both houses of Parliament on my side. But this, it seems, proceeded from bribery and corruption. Sir, if any one instance had been mentioned, if it had been shown that I ever offered a reward to any member of either House, or ever threatened to deprive any member of his office or employment, in order to influence his vote in Parliament, there might have been some ground for this charge. But when it is so generally laid I do not know what I can say to it unless it be to deny it as generally and as positively as it has been asserted. And, thank God! till some proof be offered, I have the laws of the land as well as the laws of charity in my favor.

Some members of both Houses have, it is true, been removed from their employments under the Crown; but were they ever told, either by me or by any other of his majesty's servants, that it was for opposing the measures of the administration in Parliament? They were removed because his majesty did not think fit to continue them longer in his service. His majesty had a right so to do; and I know no one that has a right to ask him, "What doest thou?" If his majesty had a mind that the favors of the crown should circulate, would not this of itself be a good reason for removing any of his servants? Would not this be approved of by the whole nation, except those who happen to be the present possessors? I can not, therefore, see how this can be imputed as a crime, or how any of the king's ministers can be blamed for his doing what the public has no concern in; for if the public be well and faithfully served it has no business to ask him by whom.

I shall now advert to the third topic of accusation—the conduct of the war. I have already stated in what manner and under what circumstances hostilities commenced; and as I am neither general nor admiral— as I have nothing to do either with our navy or army—I am sure that I am not answerable for the prosecution of it. But were I to answer for everything no fault could, I think, be found with my conduct in the prosecution of the war. It has from the beginning been carried on with as much vigor and as great care of our trade as was consistent with our safety at home and with the circumstances we were in at the beginning of the war. If our attacks upon the enemy were too long delayed, or if they have not been so vigorous or so frequent as they ought to have been, those only are to blame who have for many years been haranguing against standing armies; for, without a sufficient number of regular troops in proportion to the numbers kept up by our neighbors, I am sure we can neither defend ourselves nor offend our enemies. On the supposed miscarriages of the war, so unfairly stated and so unjustly imputed to me, I could, with great ease, frame an incontrovertible defense. But as I have trespassed so long on the time of the House I shall not weaken the effect of that forcible exculpation so generously and disinterestedly advanced by the right honorable gentleman who so meritoriously presides at the admiralty.

If my whole administration is to be scrutinized and arraigned, why are the most favorable parts to be omitted? If facts are to be accumulated on one side, why not on the other? And why may not I be permitted to speak in my own favor? Was I not called by the voice of the king and the nation to remedy the fatal effects of the South Sea project and to support declining credit? Was I not placed at the head of the treasury when the revenues were in the greatest confusion? Is credit revived, and does it now flourish? Is it not at an incredible height, and if so, to whom must that circumstance be attributed? Has not tranquillity been preserved both at home and abroad, notwithstanding a most unreasonable and violent opposition? Has the true interest of the nation been pursued, or has trade flourished? Have gentlemen produced one instance of this exorbitant power; of the influence which I extend to all parts of the nation; of the tyranny with which I oppress those who oppose, and the liberality with which I reward those who support me? But having first invested me with a kind of mock dignity, and styled me a prime minister, they impute to me an unpardonable abuse of that chimerical authority which they only have created and conferred.

If they are really persuaded that the army is annually established by me, that I have the sole disposal of posts and honors, that I employ this power in the destruction of liberty and the diminution of commerce, let me awaken them from their delusion. Let me expose to their view the real condition of the public weal. Let me show them that the crown has made no encroachments, that all supplies have been granted by Parliament, that all questions have been debated with the same freedom as before the fatal period in which my counsels are said to have gained the ascendency—an ascendency from which they deduce the loss of trade, the approach of slavery, the preponderance of prerogative, and the extension of influence. But I am far from believing that they feel those apprehensions which they so earnestly labor to communicate to others; and I have too high an opinion of their sagacity not to conclude that, even in their own judgment, they are complaining of grievances that they do not suffer, and promoting rather their private interest than that of the public.

What is this unbounded sole power which is imputed to me? How has it discovered itself, or how has it been proved? What have been the effects of the corruption, ambition, and avarice with which I am so abundantly charged?

Have I ever been suspected of being corrupted? A strange phenomenon, a corrupter himself not corrupt! Is ambition imputed to me? Why then do I still continue a commoner?—I, who refused a white staff and a peerage. I had, indeed, like to have forgotten the little ornament about my shoulders (the Garter), which gentlemen have so repeatedly mentioned in terms of sarcastic obloquy. But surely, tho this may be regarded with envy or indignation in another place, it can not be supposed to raise any resentment in this House, where many may be pleased to see those honors which their ancestors have worn, restored again to the Commons.

Have I given any symptoms of an avaricious disposition? Have I obtained any grants from the crown since I have been placed at the head of the treasury? Has my conduct been different from that which others in the same station would have followed? Have I acted wrong in giving the place of auditor to my son and in providing for my own family? I trust that their advancement will not be imputed to me as a crime unless it shall be proved that I placed them in offices of trust and responsibility for which they were unfit.

But while I unequivocally deny that I am sole and prime minister, and that to my influence and direction all the measures of the government must be attributed, yet I will not shrink from the responsibility which attaches to the post I have the honor to hold; and should, during the long period in which I have sat upon this bench, any one step taken by the government be proved to be either disgraceful or disadvantageous to the nation, I am ready to hold myself accountable.

To conclude, sir, tho I shall always be proud of the honor of any trust or confidence from his majesty, yet I shall always be ready to remove from his councils and presence when he thinks fit; and therefore I should think myself very little concerned in the event of the present question if it were not for the encroachment that will thereby be made upon the prerogatives of the crown. But I must think that an address to his majesty to remove one of his servants, without so much as alleging any particular crime against him, is one of the greatest encroachments that was ever made upon the prerogatives of the crown. And therefore, for the sake of my master, without any regard for my own, I hope all those that have a due regard for our constitution and for the rights and prerogatives of the crown, without which our constitution can not be preserved, will be against this motion.

AGAINST THE GIN BILL

Earl of Chesterfield

(1694-1773)

Lord Chesterfield, representative of the royalists of the Stuart dynasty, came from a noble line of statesmen, soldiers, and men of letters. At the death of his father in 1726 he succeeded to the earldom and took his seat in the House of Lords. Later he was Ambassador to the Hague and was knighted into the order of the Garter. He aligned himself against Walpole and joined the Pelham ministry in 1744. In 1746 he became Secretary of State and the following year was appointed Lord Lieutenant of Ireland. Chesterfield's ability as an orator was marked by his graceful manners, peculiar wit, and brilliant sarcasm. His speeches *Against the Licensing Act* of 1737 and *Against the Gin Bill* of 1743 are perhaps the best examples of his oratory. A portion of the latter speech is included here. It was delivered before the House of Lords February 21, 1743, against a measure proposing to increase the revenue by licensing the sale of gin.

Luxury, my lords, is to be taxed, but vice prohibited, let the difficulties in executing the law be what they will. Would you lay a tax on the breach of the Ten Commandments? Would not such a tax be wicked and scandalous; because it would imply an indulgence to all those who could pay the tax? Is not this a reproach most justly thrown by the Protestants upon the Church of Rome? Was it not the chief cause of the Reformation? And will you follow a precedent which brought reproach and ruin upon those that introduced it? This is the very case now before you. You are going to lay a tax, and consequently to indulge a sort of drunkenness, which almost necessarily produces a breach of every one of the Ten Commandments. Can you expect the reverend bench will approve of this? I am convinced they will not; and therefore I wish I had seen it full upon this occasion.

We have already, my lords, several sorts of funds in this nation, so many that a man must have a good deal of learning to be master of them. Thanks to his Majesty, we have now among us the most learned man of the nation in this way. I wish he would rise up and tell us what name we are to give this new fund. We have already the Civil List Fund, the Sinking Fund, the Aggregate Fund, the South Sea Fund, and God knows how many others. What name we are to give this new fund I know not, unless we are to call it the Drinking Fund. It may, perhaps, enable the people of a certain foreign territory [Hanover] to drink claret, but it will disable the people of this kingdom from drinking anything else but gin; for when a man has, by gin drinking, rendered himself unfit for labor or business, he can purchase nothing else; and then the best thing for him to do is to drink on till he dies.

Surely, my lords, men of such unbounded benevolence as our present ministers deserve such honors as were never paid before; they deserve to bestride a butt upon every signpost in the city, or to have their figures exhibited as tokens where this liquor is to be sold by the license which they have procured. They must be at least remembered to future ages as the "happy politicians" who, after all expedients for raising taxes had been employed, discovered a new method of draining the last relics of the public wealth, and added a new revenue to the Government. Nor will those who shall hereafter enumerate the several funds, now established among us, forget, among the benefactors of their country, the illustrious authors of the Drinking Fund. . . .

The noble lord has been pleased kindly to inform us that the trade of distilling is very extensive; that it employs great numbers; and that they have arrived at an exquisite skill, and therefore—note well the consequence—the trade of distilling is not to be discouraged.

Once more, my lords, allow me to wonder at the different conceptions of different understandings. It appears to me that since the spirits which the distillers produce are allowed to enfeeble the limbs and vitals of the blood, to pervert the heart and obscure the intellect, that the number of distillers should be no argument in their favor; for I never heard that a law against theft was repealed or delayed because thieves were numerous. It appears to me, my lords, that if so formidable a body are confederated against the virtue or the lives of their fellow-citizens, it is time to put an end to the havoc, and to interpose while it is yet in our power to stop the destruction.

So little, my lords, am I afflicted with the merit of this wonderful skill which the distillers are said to have attained, that it is, in my opinion, no faculty of great use to mankind to prepare palatable poison; nor shall I ever contribute my interest for the reprieve of a murderer, because he has, by long practice, obtained great dexterity in his trade.

If their liquors are so delicious that the people are tempted to their own destruction, let us at length, my lords, secure them from these fatal draughts by bursting the vials that contain them. Let us crush at once these artists in slaughter, who have reconciled their countrymen to sickness and to ruin, and spread over the pitfalls of debauchery such baits as cannot be resisted.

This bill, therefore, appears to be designed only to thin the ranks of mankind, and to disburden the world of the multitudes that inhabit it; and is perhaps the strongest proof of political sagacity that our new ministers have yet exhibited. They well know, my lords, that they are universally detested, and that, whenever a Briton is destroyed, they are freed from an enemy; they have therefore opened the flood gates of gin upon the nation, that, when it is less numerous, it may be more easily governed.

Other ministers, my lords, who had not attained to so great a knowledge in the art of making war upon their country, when they found their enemies clamorous and bold, used to awe them with prosecutions and penalties, or destroy them like burglars, with prisons and with gibbets. But every age, my lords, produces some improvement; and every nation, however degenerate, gives birth, at some happy period of time, to men of great and enterprising genius. It is our fortune to be witnesses of a new discovery in politics. We may congratulate ourselves upon being contemporaries with those men who have shown that hangmen and halters are unnecessary in a State, and that ministers may escape the reproach of destroying their enemies by inciting them to destroy themselves.

ON THE WAR IN AMERICA

Earl of Chatham

(1708-1778)

"The Great Commoner," as Chatham was called by the idolizing populace, was a virulent opponent of Walpole and the Court Party. He entered Parliament in 1735; was Secretary of State from 1756-61; and Prime Minister in 1766. In his day Chatham was recognized as England's greatest Parliamentary orator. By nature and training alike Chatham was a dignified and powerful orator. He had imagination and passion, and his enthusiasm for the national honor of his country made him intolerant of any acts of its rulers which might detract from the glory of England. His diction was forcible yet delicate, and in debate his brilliant wit and utter fearlessness made him invincible. The historian, Hazlitt, has attributed Chatham's power of oratory to sympathy—a deep understanding of his cause which made him instinctively eloquent in every tone and gesture. It was Chatham who gave English oratory the distinctly literary flavor which became characteristic of the nineteenth century and opened thereby a new era of oratory.

Chatham staunchly supported the cause of the American colonies against the policies of the king, and some of his most famous speeches were delivered in behalf of the colonists. In January, 1775, Chatham in a powerful speech before the House denounced the quartering of troops in Boston. In January, 1766, was delivered before the House of Commons his celebrated speech *On the Right to Tax America.* In November, 1777, just a few months before his death, he made his notable speech *On the War in America* which has been preserved as his greatest oration, the report of which was corrected by Chatham himself. On April 7, 1778, Chatham, then in his seventieth year, made his last speech in Parliament protesting against the acknowledgment of American independence since it would dismember the British Empire. This speech so exhausted him that he had to be carried from the House. He died on May 11, 1778, and was buried in Westminster Abbey.

Included here is his speech of November 18, 1777, *On the War in America.* The amendment proposed by Chatham in this speech was lost by a vote of 97 to 24. The alliance between America and France was made, and the triumph of the colonies became an accomplished fact.

I rise, my lords, to declare my sentiments on this most solemn and serious subject. It has imposed a load upon my mind, which, I fear, nothing can remove, but which impels me to endeavor its alleviation, by a free and unreserved communication of my sentiments.

In the first part of the address, I have the honor of heartily concurring with the noble earl who moved it. No man feels sincerer joy than I do; none can offer more genuine congratulations on every accession of strength to the Protestant succession. I therefore join in every congratulation on the birth of another princess, and the happy recovery of her majesty.

But I must stop here. My courtly complaisance will carry me no farther. I will not join in congratulation on misfortune and disgrace. I can not concur in a blind and servile address, which approves and endeavors to sanctify the monstrous measures which have heaped disgrace and misfortune upon us. This, my lords, is a perilous and tremendous moment! It is not a time for adulation. The smoothness of flattery can not now avail—can not save us in this rugged and awful crisis. It is now necessary to instruct the Throne in the language of truth. We must dispel the illusion and the darkness which envelop it, and display, in its full danger and true colors, the ruin that is brought to our doors.

This, my lords, is our duty. It is the proper function of this noble assembly, sitting, as we do, upon our honors in this House, the hereditary council of the Crown. Who is the minister—where is the minister, that has dared to suggest to the Throne the contrary, unconstitutional language this day delivered from it? The accustomed language from the Throne has been application to Parliament for advice, and a reliance on its constitutional advice and assistance. As it is the right of Parliament to give, so it is the duty of the Crown to ask it. But on this day, and in this extreme momentous exigency, no reliance is reposed on our constitutional counsels! no advice is asked from the sober and enlightened care of Parliament! but the Crown, from itself and by itself, declares an unalterable determination to pursue measures—and what measures, my lords. The measures that have produced the imminent perils that threaten us; the measures that have brought ruin to our doors.

Can the minister of the day now presume to expect a continuance of support in this ruinous infatuation? Can Parliament be so dead to its dignity and its duty as to be thus deluded into the loss of the one and the violation of the other? To give an unlimited credit and support for the steady perseverance in measures not proposed for our parliamentary advice, but dictated and forced upon us—in measures, I say, my lords, which have reduced this late flourishing empire to ruin and contempt! "But yesterday, and England might have stood against the world: now none so poor to do her reverence." I use the words of a poet; but, tho it be poetry, it is no fiction. It is a shameful truth, that not only the power and strength of this country are wasting away and expiring, but her well-earned glories, her true honor, and substantial dignity are sacrificed.

France, my lords, has insulted you; she has encouraged and sustained America; and, whether America be wrong or right, the dignity of this country ought to spurn the officious insult of French interference. The ministers and ambassadors of those who are called rebels and enemies are in Paris;[1] in Paris they transact the reciprocal interests of America and France. Can there be a more mortifying insult? Can even our ministers sustain a more humiliating disgrace? Do they dare to resent it? Do they presume even to hint a vindication of their honor, and the dignity of the State, by requiring the dismission of the plenipotentiaries of America? Such is the degradation to which they have reduced the glories of England! The people whom they affect to call contemptible rebels, but whose growing power has at last obtained the name of enemies; the people with whom they have engaged this country in war, and against whom they now command our implicit support in every measure of desperate hostility— this people, despised as rebels, or acknowledged as enemies, are abetted against you, supplied with every military store, their interests consulted, and their ambassadors entertained, by your inveterate enemy!—and our ministers dare not interpose with dignity or effect. Is this the honor of a great kingdom? Is this the indignant spirit of England, who "but yesterday" gave law to the house of Bourbon?

My lords, the dignity of nations demands a decisive conduct in a situation like this. Even when the greatest prince that perhaps this country ever saw filled our Throne, the requisition of a Spanish general, on a similar subject, was attended to and complied with; for, on the spirited remonstrance of the Duke of Alva, Elizabeth found herself obliged to deny the Flemish exiles all countenance, support, or even entrance into her dominions, and the Count Le Marque, with his few desperate followers, were expelled from the kingdom. Happening to arrive at the Brille, and finding it weak in defense, they made themselves masters of the place; and this was the foundation of the United Provinces.

[1] Referring to Franklin, Lee, and Dean.

My lords, this ruinous and ignominious situation, where we can not act with success, nor suffer with honor, calls upon us to remonstrate in the strongest and loudest language of truth, to rescue the ear of majesty from the delusions which surround it. The desperate state of our arms abroad is in part known. No man thinks more highly of them than I do. I love and honor the English troops. I know their virtues and their valor. I know they can achieve any thing except impossibilities; and I know that the conquest of English America is an impossibility. You cannot, I venture to say it, you cannot conquer America. Your armies in the last war effected every thing that could be effected; and what was it? It cost a numerous army, under the command of a most able general (Lord Amherst), now a noble lord in this House, a long and laborious campaign, to expel five thousand Frenchmen from French America. My lords, you cannot conquer America. What is your present situation there? We do not know the worst; but we know that in three campaigns we have done nothing and suffered much. Besides the sufferings, perhaps total loss of the Northern force, the best appointed army that ever took the field, commanded by Sir William Howe, has retired from the American lines. He was obliged to relinquish his attempt, and with great delay and danger to adopt a new and distant plan of operations. We shall soon know, and in any event have reason to lament, what may have happened since.

As to conquest, therefore, my lords, I repeat, it is impossible. You may swell every expense and every effort still more extravagantly; pile and accumulate every assistance you can buy or borrow; traffic and barter with every little pitiful German prince that sells and sends his subjects to the shambles of a foreign prince; your efforts are forever vain and impotent—doubly so from this mercenary aid on which you rely; for it irritates, to an incurable resentment, the minds of your enemies, to overrun them with the mercenary sons of rapine and plunder, devoting them and their possessions to the rapacity of hireling cruelty! If I were an American, as I am an Englishman, while a foreign troop was landing in my country, I never would lay down my arms—never—never—never.

Your own army is infected with the contagion of these illiberal allies. The spirit of plunder and of rapine is gone forth among them. I know it; and, notwithstanding what the noble earl [Lord Percy] who moved the address has given as his opinion of the American army, I know from authentic information, and the most experienced officers, that our discipline is deeply wounded. While this is notoriously our sinking situation, America grows and flourishes; while our strength and discipline are lowered, hers are rising and improving.

But, my lords, who is the man [2] that, in addition to these disgraces and mischiefs of our army, has dared to authorize and associate to our arms the tomahawk and scalping-knife of the savage; to call into civilized alliance the wild and inhuman savage of the woods; to delegate to the

[2] Lord George Germaine of the ministry.

merciless Indian the defense of disputed rights, and to w.ge the horrors
of his barbarous war against our brethren? My lords, these enormities
cry aloud for redress and punishment. Unless thoroughly done away,
it will be a stain on the national character. It is a violation of the Constitution. I believe it is against law.

It is not the least of our national misfortunes that the strength and
character of our army are thus impaired. Infected with the mercenary
spirit of robbery and rapine; familiarized to the horrid scenes of savage
cruelty, it can no longer boast of the noble and generous principles which
dignify a soldier; no longer sympathize with the dignity of the royal
banner, nor feel the pride, pomp, and circumstance of glorious war, "that
make ambition virtue!" What makes ambition virtue? The sense of
honor. But is the sense of honor consistent with a spirit of plunder, or
the practice of murder? Can it flow from mercenary motives, or can
it prompt to cruel deeds? Besides these murderers and plunderers, let
me ask our ministers, What other allies have they acquired? What other
powers have they associated in their cause? Have they entered into
alliance with the king of the gipsies? Nothing, my lords, is too low or
too ludicrous to be consistent with their counsels.

The independent views of America have been stated and asserted as
the foundation of this address. My lords, no man wishes for the due
dependence of America on this country more than I do. To preserve
it, and not confirm that state of independence into which your measures
hitherto have driven them, is the object which we ought to unite in
attaining. The Americans, contending for their rights against arbitrary
exactions, I love and admire. It is the struggle of free and virtuous
patriots. But, contending for independency and total disconnection from
England, as an Englishman, I can not wish them success; for in a due
constitutional dependency, including the ancient supremacy of this country
in regulating their commerce and navigation, consists the mutual happiness and prosperity both of England and America. She derived
assistance and protection from us; and we reaped from her the most
important advantages. She was, indeed, the fountain of our wealth, the
nerve of our strength, the nursery and basis of our naval power. It is
our duty, therefore, my lords, if we wish to save our country, most
seriously to endeavor the recovery of these most beneficial subjects; and
in this perilous crisis, perhaps the present moment may be the only one
in which we can hope for success.

For in their negotiations with France, they have, or think they have,
reason to complain; tho it be notorious that they have received from that
power important supplies and assistance of various kinds, yet it is certain
they expected it in a more decisive and immediate degree. America is in
ill humor with France; on some points they have not entirely answered
her expectations.

Let us wisely take advantage of every possible moment of reconciliation. Besides, the natural disposition of America herself still leans

toward England, to the old habits of connection and mutual interest that united both countries. This was the established sentiment of all the Continent; and still, my lords, in the great and principal part, the sound part of America, this wise and affectionate disposition prevails. And there is a very considerable part of America yet sound—the middle and the southern provinces. Some parts may be factious and blind to their true interests; but if we express a wise and benevolent disposition to communicate with them, those immutable rights of nature and those constitutional liberties to which they are equally entitled with ourselves, for the mutual benefit and preservation of every part, to constitute and conciliate the adverse.

I say, my lords, the rights and liberties to which they are equally entitled with ourselves, but not more. I would participate to them every enjoyment and freedom which the colonizing subjects of a free state can possess, or wish to possess; and I do not see why they should not enjoy every fundamental right in their property, and every original substantial liberty, which Devonshire, or Surrey, or the county I live in, or any other county in England, can claim; reserving always, as the sacred right of the mother country, the due constitutional dependency of the colonies. The inherent supremacy of the state in regulating and protecting the navigation and commerce of all her subjects, is necessary for the mutual benefit and preservation of every part, to constitute and preserve the prosperous arrangement of the whole empire.

The sound parts of America, of which I have spoken, must be sensible of these great truths and of their real interests. America is not in that state of desperate and contemptible rebellion which this country has been deluded to believe. It is not a wild and lawless banditti, who, having nothing to lose, might hope to snatch something from public convulsions. Many of their leaders and great men have a great stake in this great contest. The gentleman who conducts their armies, I am told, has an estate of four or five thousand pounds a year; and when I consider these things, I can not but lament the inconsiderate violence of our penal acts, our declaration of treason and rebellion, with all the fatal effects of attainder and confiscation.

As to the disposition of foreign powers which is asserted to be pacific and friendly, let us judge, my lords, rather by their actions and the nature of things than by interested assertions. The uniform assistance supplied to America by France suggests a different conclusion. The most important interests of France in aggrandizing and enriching herself with what she most wants, supplies of every naval store from America, must inspire her with different sentiments. The extraordinary preparations of the House of Bourbon, by land and by sea, from Dunkirk to the Straits, equally ready and willing to overwhelm these defenseless islands, should rouse us to a sense of their real disposition and our own danger. Not five thousand troops in England! hardly three thousand in Ireland! What can we oppose to the combined force of our enemies? Scarcely twenty ships of the line so fully or sufficiently manned, that any admiral's reputation would permit him to take the command of. The river of Lisbon in the possession of our enemies! The seas swept by American privateers! Our Channel trade torn to pieces by them! In this complicated crisis of danger, weakness at home, and calamity abroad, terrified and insulted by the neighboring powers, unable to act in America, or acting only to be destroyed, where is the man with the forehead to promise or hope for success in such a situation, or from perseverance in the measures that have driven us to it? Who has the forehead to do so? Where is that man? I should be glad to see his face.

You cannot conciliate America by your present measures. You cannot subdue her by your present or by any measures. What, then, can you do? You cannot conquer; you cannot gain; but you can address; you can lull the fears and anxieties of the moment into an ignorance of the danger that should produce them. But, my lords, the time demands the language of truth. We must not now apply the flattering unction of servile compliance or blind complaisance. In a just and necessary war, to maintain the rights of honor of my country, I would strip the shirt from my back to support it. But in such a war as this, unjust in its principle, impracticable in its means, and ruinous in its consequences, I would not contribute a single effort nor a single shilling. I do not call for vengeance on the heads of those who have been guilty; I only recommend to them to make their retreat. Let them walk off; and let them make haste, or they may be assured that speedy and condign punishment will overtake them.

My lords, I have submitted to you, with the freedom and truth which I think my duty, my sentiments on your present awful situation. I have laid before you the ruin of your power, the disgrace of your reputation, the pollution of your discipline, the contamination of your morals, the complication of calamities, foreign and domestic, that overwhelm your sinking country. Your dearest interests, your own liberties, the Constitution itself, totters to the foundation. All this disgraceful danger, this multitude of misery, is the monstrous offspring of this unnatural war. We have been deceived and deluded too long. Let us now stop short. This is the crisis—the only crisis of time and situation, to give us a possibility of escape from the fatal effects of our delusions. But if, in an obstinate and infatuated perseverance in folly, we slavishly echo the peremptory words this day presented to us, nothing can save this devoted country from complete and final ruin. We madly rush into multiplied miseries, and "confusion worse confounded."

Is it possible, can it be believed, that ministers are yet blind to this impending destruction? I did hope, that instead of this false and empty vanity, this overweening pride, engendering high conceits and presumptuous imaginations, ministers would have humbled themselves in their errors, would have confessed and retracted them, and by an active, tho a late, repentance, have endeavored to redeem them. But, my lords, since they had neither sagacity to foresee, nor justice nor humanity to shun these oppressive calamities—since not even severe experience can make them feel, nor the imminent ruin of their country awaken them from their stupefaction, the guardian care of Parliament must interpose.

I shall, therefore, my lords, propose to you an amendment of the address to his majesty, to be inserted immediately after the two first paragraphs of congratulation on the birth of a princess, to recommend an immediate cessation of hostilities, and the commencement of a treaty to restore peace and liberty to America, strength and happiness to England, security and permanent prosperity to both countries. This, my lords, is yet in our power; and let not the wisdom and justice of your lordships neglect the happy, and, perhaps, the only opportunity. By the establishment of irrevocable law, founded on mutual rights, and ascertained by treaty, these glorious enjoyments may be firmly perpetuated. And let me repeat to your lordships, that the strong bias of America, at least of the wise and sounder parts of it, naturally inclines to this happy and constitutional reconnection with you. Notwithstanding the temporary intrigues with France, we may still be assured of their ancient and confirmed partiality to us. America and France cannot be congenial. There is something decisive and confirmed in the honest American, that will not assimilate to the futility and levity of Frenchmen.

My lords, to encourage and confirm that innate inclination to this country, founded on every principle of affection, as well as consideration of interest; to restore that favorable disposition into a permanent and powerful reunion with this country; to revive the mutual strength of the empire; again to awe the House of Bourbon, instead of meanly truckling, as our present calamities compel us, to every insult of French caprice and Spanish punctilio; to reestablish our commerce; to reassert our rights and our glories for ever—a consummation most devoutly to be endeavored! and which, I trust, may yet arise from reconciliation with America— I have the honor of submitting to you the following amendment, which I move to be inserted after the two first paragraphs of the address:

And that this House does most humbly advise and supplicate his majesty to be pleased to cause the most speedy and effectual measures to be taken for restoring peace in America; and that no time may be lost in proposing an immediate opening of a treaty for the final settlement of the tranquillity of these invaluable provinces, by a removal of the unhappy causes of this ruinous civil war, and by a just and adequate security against the return of the like calamities in times to come. And this House desire to offer the most dutiful assurances to his majesty, that they will, in due time, cheerfully cooperate with the magnanimity and tender goodness of his majesty for the preservation of his people, by such explicit and most solemn declarations, and provisions of fundamental and irrevocable laws, as may be judged necessary for the ascertaining and fixing forever the respective rights of Great Britain and her colonies.

At this point Lord Suffolk undertook to defend the employment of Indians in the war, contending that the measure was allowable on principle, for "it was perfectly justifiable to use all the means that God and nature put into our hands!" Chatham then rose and said:

I am astonished, shocked! to hear such principles confessed—to hear them avowed in this House, or in this country; principles equally unconstitutional, inhuman, and unchristian!

My lords, I did not intend to have encroached again upon your attention, but I cannot repress my indignation. I feel myself impelled by every duty. My lords, we are called upon as members of this House, as men, as Christian men, to protest against such notions standing near the Throne, polluting the ear of majesty. "That God and nature put into our hands!" I know not what ideas that lord may entertain of God and nature, but I know that such abominable principles are equally abhorrent to religion and humanity. What! to attribute the sacred sanction of God and nature to the massacres of the Indian scalping-knife—to the cannibal savage, torturing, murdering, roasting, and eating—literally, my lords, eating the mangled victims of his barbarous battles! Such horrible notions shock every precept of religion, divine or natural, and every generous feeling of humanity. And, my lords, they shock every sentiment of honor; they shock me as a lover of honorable war, and a detester of murderous barbarity.

These abominable principles, and this more abominable avowal of them, demand the most decisive indignation. I call upon that right reverend bench, those holy ministers of the Gospel, and pious pastors of our Church—I conjure them to join in the holy work, and vindicate the religion of their God. I appeal to the wisdom and the law of this learned bench, to defend and support the justice of their country. I call upon the Bishops to interpose the unsullied sanctity of their lawn; upon the learned judges, to interpose the purity of their ermine, to save us from this pollution. I call upon the honor of your lordships, to reverence the dignity of your ancestors, and to maintain your own. I call upon the spirit and humanity of my country to vindicate the national character. I invoke the genius of the Constitution. From the tapestry that adorns these walls, the immortal ancestor [3] of this noble lord frowns with indignation at the disgrace of his country.

In vain he led your victorious fleets against the boasted Armada of Spain; in vain he defended and established the honor, the liberties, the religion—the Protestant religion—of this country, against the arbitrary cruelties of popery and the Inquisition, if these more than popish cruelties

[3] Lord Howard, High Admiral of England, who commanded the fleet which conquered the Spanish Armada in 1588. The tapestries represented the battle.

and inquisitorial practises are let loose among us—to turn forth into our settlements, among our ancient connections, friends, and relations, the merciless cannibal, thirsting for the blood of man, woman and child; to send for the the infidel savage—against whom? against your Protestant brethren; to lay waste their country, to desolate their dwellings and extirpate their race and name with these horrible hell-hounds of savage war—hell-hounds, I say, of savage war! Spain armed herself with bloodhounds to extirpate the wretched natives of America, and we improve on the inhuman example of Spanish cruelty; we turn loose these savage hell-hounds against our brethren and countrymen in America, of the same language, laws, liberties, and religion, endeared to us by every tie that should sanctify humanity.

My lords, this awful subject, so important to our honor, our Constitution, and our religion, demands the most solemn and effectual inquiry. And I again call upon your lordships, and the united powers of the State, to examine it thoroughly and decisively, and to stamp upon it an indelible stigma of the public abhorrence. And I again implore those holy prelates of our religion to do away these iniquities from among us. Let them perform a lustration; let them purify this House, and this country, from this sin.

My lords, I am old and weak, and at present unable to say more; but my feelings and indignation were too strong to have said less. I could not have slept this night in my bed, nor reposed my head on my pillow, without giving this vent to my eternal abhorrence of such preposterous and enormous principles.

ON THE RIGHT TO TAX AMERICA

Lord Mansfield

(1703-1793)

Lord Mansfield was the greatest jurist who sat on the English bench in the 18th century. He was called to the bar in 1730 and won recognition through his Scottish appeal cases which made him a great favorite throughout Scotland. A single speech in a jury trial in England in 1737 placed him at the head of the English bar and in 1742 he was appointed Solicitor-General. During the next fourteen years Mansfield was one of the most conspicuous figures in parliamentary history. In 1754-1756 he was Attorney-General, and from 1756-1788 he served as Chief Justice of the King's Bench.

Mansfield was an able, calm, and logical debater. His style of oratory differed from that of Chatham in that he was serene and unemotional; yet he did perpetuate the literary style of speech first introduced by Chatham, but he avoided oratorical flights and sought to win his hearers by judgment rather than by artifice. His moral qualities as well as his dignity made him exemplary of all a great judge should be.

Included here is a speech delivered in the British House of Lords, February 3, 1766, in reply to Lord Camden, just two weeks after Chatham had spoken on the same subject.

I shall speak to the question strictly as a matter of right, for it is a proposition in its nature so perfectly distinct from the expediency of the tax, that it must necessarily be taken separate, if there is any true logic in the world; but of the expediency or inexpediency I will say nothing. It will be time enough to speak upon that subject when it comes to be a question.

I shall also speak to the distinctions which have been taken, without any real difference, as to the nature of the tax; and I shall point out, lastly, the necessity there will be of exerting the force of the superior authority of government, if opposed by the subordinate part of it.

I am extremely sorry that the question has ever become necessary to be agitated, and that there should be a decision upon it. No one in this House will live long enough to see an end put to the mischief which will be the result of the doctrine which has been inculcated; but the arrow is shot and the wound already given. I shall certainly avoid personal reflections. No one has had more cast upon him than myself; but I never was biased by any consideration of applause from without, in the discharge of my public duty, and in giving my sentiments according to what I thought law, I have relied upon my own consciousness. It is with great pleasure I have heard the noble lord who moved the resolution express himself in so manly and sensible a way when he recommended a dispassionate debate, while at the same time he urged the necessity of the House coming to such a resolution, with great dignity and propriety of argument.

I shall endeavor to clear away from the question all that mass of dissertation and learning displayed in arguments which have been fetched from speculative men who have written upon the subject of government, or from ancient records, as being little to the purpose. I shall insist that these records are no proofs of our present constitution. A noble lord has taken up his argument from the settlement of the constitution at the revolution; I shall take up my argument from the constitution as it now is.

The constitution of this country has been always in a moving state, either gaining or losing something; and with respect to the modes of taxation, when we get beyond the reign of Edward the First or of King John, we are all in doubt and obscurity. The history of those times is full of uncertainties. In regard to the writs upon record, they were issued some of them according to law, and some not according to law; and such (that is, of the latter kind) were those concerning ship-money, to call assemblies to tax themselves, or to compel benevolences. Other taxes were raised from escuage, fees for knights' service, and by other means arising out of the feudal system. Benevolences are contrary to law; and it is well known how people resisted the demands of the Crown in the case of ship-money and were persecuted by the court; and if any set of men were to meet now to lend the king money, it would be contrary to law, and a breach of the rights of Parliament.

I shall now answer the noble lord particularly upon the cases he has quoted. With respect to the Marches of Wales, who were the borderers, privileged for assisting the king in his war against the Welsh in the mountains, their enjoying this privilege of taxing themselves was but of a short duration, and during the life of Edward the First, till the Prince of Wales came to be the king; and then they were annexed to the Crown and became subject to taxes like the rest of the dominions of England; and from thence came the custom, tho unnecessary, of naming Wales and the town of Monmouth in all proclamations and in acts of Parliament. Henry the Eighth was the first who issued writs for it to return two members to Parliament. The Crown exercised this right "ad libitum," from whence arises the inequality of representation in our constitution at this day. Henry the Eighth issued a writ to Calais to send one burgess to Parliament.

One of the counties palatine (I think he said Durham) was taxed fifty years to subsidies before it sent members to Parliament. The clergy were at no time unrepresented in Parliament. When they taxed themselves, it was done with the concurrence and consent of Parliament, who permitted them to tax themselves upon their petition, the convocation sitting at the same time with the Parliament. They had, too, their representatives always sitting in this House, bishops and abbots, and in the other House they were at no time without a right of voting singly for the election of members; so that the argument fetched from the case of the clergy is not an argument of any force, because they were at no time unrepresented here.

The reasoning about the colonies of Great Britain, drawn from the colonies of antiquity, is a mere useless display of learning; for the colonies of the Tyrians in Africa, and of the Greeks in Asia, were totally different from our system. No nation before ourselves formed any regular system of colonization but the Romans; and their system was a military one, and of garrisons placed in the principal towns of the conquered provinces. The states of Holland were not colonies of Spain; they were states dependent upon the house of Austria in a feudal dependence. Nothing could be more different from our colonies than that flock of men, as they have been called, who came from the North and poured into Europe. Those emigrants renounced all laws, all protection, all connection with their mother countries. They chose their leaders, and marched under their banners to seek their fortunes and establish new kingdoms upon the ruins of the Roman Empire.

But our colonies, on the contrary, emigrated under the sanction of the Crown and Parliament. They were modeled gradually into their present forms, respectively, by charters, grants, and statutes; but they were never separated from the mother country or so emancipated as to become *sui juris*. There are several sorts of colonies in British America: the charter colonies, the proprietary governments, and the king's colonies. The first colonies were the charter colonies, such as the Virginia Company; and these companies had among their directors members of the privy council and of both Houses of Parliament; they were under the authority of the privy council, and had agents resident here, responsible for their proceedings.

So much were they considered as belonging to the Crown, and not to the king personally (for there is a great difference, tho few people attend to it), that when the two Houses, in the time of Charles the First, were going to pass a bill concerning the colonies, a message was sent to them by the king that they were the king's colonies, and that the bill was unnecessary, for that the privy council would take order about them; and the bill never had the royal assent. The Commonwealth Parliament, as soon as it was settled, were very early jealous of the colonies separating themselves from them; and passed a resolution or act (and it is a question whether it is not in force now) to declare and establish authority of England over its colonies.

But if there was no express law, or reason founded upon any necessary inference from an express law, yet the usage alone would be sufficient to support that authority; for have not the colonies submitted ever since their first establishment to the jurisdiction of the mother country? In all questions of property the appeals from the colonies have been to the privy council here; and such causes have been determined, not by the law of the colonies, but by the law of England.

At present the several forms of their constitution are very various, having been produced, as all governments have been originally, by accident and circumstances. The forms of government in every colony were adopted, from time to time, according to the size of the colony; and so have been extended again, from time to time, as the numbers of their inhabitants and their commercial connections outgrew the first model. In some colonies at first there was only a governor assisted by two or three counsel; then more were added; afterward courts of justice were erected; then assemblies were created.

Some things were done by instructions from the secretaries of state; other things were done by order of the king and council; and other things by commissions under the great seal. It is observable that in consequence of these establishments from time to time, and of the dependency of these governments upon the supreme legislature at home, the lenity of each government in the colonies has been extreme toward the subject; and a great inducement has been created for people to come and settle in them. But if all those governments which are now independent of each other should become independent of the mother country, I am afraid that the inhabitants of the colonies are very little aware of the consequences. They would feel in that case very soon in the hand of power more heavy upon them in their own governments, than they have yet done or have ever imagined.

The constitutions of the different colonies are thus made up of different principles. They must remain dependent, from the necessity of things and their relation to the jurisdiction of the mother country; or they must be totally dismembered from it and form a league of union among themselves against it, which could be effected without great violences. No one ever thought the contrary till the trumpet of sedition was blown.

Acts of Parliament have been made, not only without a doubt of their legality, but with universal applause, the great object of which has been ultimately to fix the trade of the colonies so as to center in the bosom of that country from whence they took their original. The Navigation Act shut up their intercourse with foreign countries. Their ports have been made subject to customs and regulations which have cramped and diminished their trade. And duties have been laid, affecting the very inmost parts of their commerce, and among others, that of the post; yet all these have been submitted to peaceably, and no one ever thought till now of this doctrine that the colonies are not to be taxed, regulated, or bound by Parliament.

A few particular merchants were then, as now, displeased at restrictions which did not permit them to make the greatest possible advantages of their commerce in their own private and peculiar branches. But tho these few merchants might think themselves losers in articles which they had no right to gain, as being prejudicial to the general and national system, yet I must observe that the colonies, upon the whole, were benefited by these laws. For these restrictive laws, founded upon principles of the most solid policy, flung a great weight of naval force into the hands of the mother country, which was to protect its colonies.

Without a union with her the colonies must have been entirely weak and defenseless; but they thus became relatively great, subordinately, and in proportion as the mother country advanced in superiority over the rest of the maritime powers in Europe, to which both mutually contributed, and of which both have reaped a benefit equal to the natural and just relation in which they both stand reciprocally, of dependency on one side and protection on the other.

There can be no doubt, my lords, but that the inhabitants of the colonies are as much represented in Parliament as the greatest part of the people of England are represented; among nine millions of whom there are eight which have no votes in electing members of Parliament. Every objection, therefore, to the dependency of the colonies upon Parliament, which arises to it upon the ground of representation, goes to the whole present constitution of Great Britain; and I suppose it is not meant to new-model that, too.

People may form speculative ideas of perfection and indulge their own fancies or those of other men. Every man in this country has his particular notion of liberty; but perfection never did and never can exist in any human institution. To what purpose, then, are arguments drawn from a distinction, in which there is no real difference, of a virtual and actual representation?

A member of Parliament chosen for any borough represents not only the constituents and inhabitants of that particular place, but he represents the inhabitants of every other borough in Great Britain. He represents the city of London, and all the other commons of this land, and the inhabitants of all the colonies and dominions of Great Britain; and is, in duty and conscience, bound to take care of their interests.

With respect to what has been said or written upon this subject I differ from the noble lord who spoke of Mr. Otis and his book [4] with

[4] James Otis. *The Rights of The Colonies Asserted and Proved.* Published in London, 1765.

contempt, tho he maintained the same doctrine in some points, while in others he carried it farther than Otis himself, who allows everywhere the supremacy of the Crown over the colonies. No man, on such a subject, is contemptible. Otis is a man of consequence among the people there. They have chosen him for one of their deputies at the Congress and general meeting from the respective governments. It was said the man is mad. What then? One madman often makes many. Masaniello was mad. Nobody doubts it; yet for all that he overturned the government of Naples. Madness is catching in all popular assemblies and upon all popular matters. The book is full of wildness. I never read it till a few days ago, for I seldom look into such things. I never was actually acquainted with the contents of the Stamp Act, till I sent for it on purpose to read it before the debate was expected.

I am far from bearing any ill will to the Americans; they are a very good people, and I have long known them. I began life with them and owe much to them, having been much concerned in the plantation causes before the privy council; and so I became a good deal acquainted with American affairs and people. I dare say their heat will soon be over when they come to feel a little the consequences of their opposition to the legislature. Anarchy always cures itself; but the ferment will continue so much the longer while hotheaded men there find that there are persons of weight and character to support and justify them here.

I am satisfied, notwithstanding, that time and a wise and steady conduct may prevent those extremities which would be fatal to both. I remember well when it was the violent humor of the times to decry standing armies and garrisons as dangerous, and incompatible with the liberty of the subject. Nothing would do but a regular militia. The militia are embodied; they march; and no sooner was the militia law thus put into execution but it was then said to be an intolerable burden upon the subject, and that it would fall, sooner or later, into the hands of the Crown. That was the language, and many counties petitioned against it.

This may be the case with the colonies. In many places they begin already to feel the effects of their resistance to government. Interest very soon divides mercantile people; and, altho there may be some mad, enthusiastic, or ill-designing people in the colonies, yet I am convinced that the greatest bulk, who have understanding and property, are still well affected to the mother country. You have, my lords, many friends still in the colonies; and take care that you do not, by abdicting your own authority, desert them and yourselves and lose them for ever.

In all popular tumults the worst men bear the sway at first. Moderate and good men are often silent for fear or modesty, who in good time may declare themselves. Those who have any property to lose are sufficiently alarmed already at the progress of these public violences and violations to which every man's dwelling, person, and property are hourly exposed. Numbers of such valuable men and good subjects are ready and willing to declare themselves for the support of government in due time, if government does not fling away its own authority.

My lords, the Parliament of Great Britain has its rights over the colonies; but it may abdicate its rights.

But, my lords, I shall make this application of it. You may abdicate your rights over the colonies. Take care, my lords, how you do so, for such an act will be irrevocable. Proceed, then, my lords, with spirit and firmness; and, when you shall have established your authority, it will then be a time to show your lenity. The Americans, as I said before, are a very good people, and I wish them exceedingly well; but they are heated and inflamed. The noble lord who spoke before ended with a prayer. I can not end better than by saying to it Amen; and in the words of Maurice, Prince of Orange, concerning the Hollanders: "God bless this industrious, frugal, and well-meaning, but easily deluded people."

ON CONCILIATION WITH AMERICA [5]

Edmund Burke

(1729-1797)

Edmund Burke was born in Ireland of Norman parentage. His mother was a Catholic, but Burke adopted the religion of his Protestant father; yet always retained a tolerance for Catholicism. Before he was elected to Parliament Burke had a varied career. He travelled extensively in England and on the Continent; delved into literature and philosophy; frequented the theatres and debating clubs, gleaning everywhere valuable experience for his colorful career as an orator. In Parliament he expressed a sincere zeal in the cause of the oppressed and delivered his most famous orations in behalf of the American colonists and the slaves in India.

Burke's oratorical ability has been the subject of dispute. Macaulay said of him "that in aptitude of comprehension and richness of imagination he was superior to every orator ancient and modern." Yet his gestures have been described as clumsy, and his voice somewhat harsh and with a strong Irish brogue; nevertheless his brilliance was such that his orations are even more effective when read than when delivered. One of Burke's most brilliant and impressive speeches was that delivered at the trial of Warren Hastings, an East Indian official accused of corruption while in office. Again he was distinguished for his fervid opposition to the French Revolution; but most significant to Americans is his speech *On Conciliation with America* delivered in the House of Commons March 22, 1775 in support of 13 resolutions favoring conciliation. On this occasion Burke spoke for three hours; at the close of his speech the Earl of Chatham remarked that so powerful had been his attack there

[5] Abridged.

was nothing left to be said on the subject. Had his conciliatory measures been accepted the war might have been averted and England would have saved for herself the American colonies.

America, gentlemen say, is a noble object. It is an object well worth fighting for. Certainly it is, if fighting a people be the best way of gaining them. Gentlemen in this respect will be led to their choice of means by their complexions and their habits. Those who understand the military art will, of course, have some predilection for it. Those who wield the thunder of the State may have more confidence in the efficacy of arms. But I confess, possibly for want of this knowledge, my opinion is much more in favor of prudent management than of force, considering force not as an odious, but a feeble, instrument for preserving a people so numerous, so active, so growing, so spirited as this, in a profitable and subordinate connection with us.

First, sir, permit me to observe, that the use of force alone is but temporary. It may subdue for a moment, but it does not remove the necessity of subduing again; and a nation is not governed which is perpetually to be conquered.

My next objection is its uncertainty. Terror is not always the effect of force; and an armament is not a victory. If you do not succeed you are without resource, for conciliation failing, force remains, but force failing, no further hope of reconciliation is left. Power and authority are sometimes brought by kindness, but they can never be begged as alms by an improverished and defeated violence.

A further objection to force is, that you impair the object by your very endeavors to preserve it. The thing you fought for is not the thing which you recover; but depreciated, sunk, wasted, and consumed in the contest. Nothing less will content me than whole America. I do not choose to consume its strength along with our own, because in all parts it is the British strength that I consume. I do not choose to be caught by a foreign enemy at the end of this exhausting conflict, and still less in the midst of it. I may escape; but I can make no insurance against such an event. Let me add, that I do not choose wholly to break the American spirit, because it is the spirit that has made the country.

Lastly, we have no sort of experience in favor of force as an instrument in the rule of our colonies. Their growth and their utility have been owing to methods altogether different. Our ancient indulgence has been said to be pursued to a fault. It may be so; but we know, if feeling is evidence, that our fault was more tolerable than our attempt to mend it, and our sin far more salutary than our penitence.

These, sir, are my reasons for not entertaining that high opinion of untried force, by which many gentlemen, for whose sentiments in other particulars I have great respect, seem to be so greatly captivated.

But there is still behind a third consideration concerning this object, which serves to determine my opinion on the sort of policy which ought to be pursued in the management of America, even more than its population and its commerce,—I mean its temper and character. In this character of the Americans a love of freedom is the predominating feature, which marks and distinguishes the whole; and, as an ardent is always a jealous affection, your colonies become suspicious, restive, and untractable, whenever they see the least attempt to wrest from them by force, or shuffle from them by chicane, what they think the only advantage worth living for. This fierce spirit of liberty is stronger in the English colonies, probably, than in any other people of the earth, and this from a variety of powerful causes, which, to understand the true temper of their minds, and the direction which this spirit takes, it will not be amiss to lay open somewhat more largely.

First, the people of the colonies are descendants of Englishmen. England, sir, is a nation which still, I hope, respects, and formerly adored, her freedom. The colonists emigrated from you when this part of your character was most predominant; and they took this bias and direction the moment they parted from your hands. They are, therefore, not only devoted to liberty, but to liberty according to English ideas and on English principles. Abstract liberty, like other mere abstractions, is not to be found. Liberty inheres in some sensible object, and every nation has formed to itself some favorite point which, by way of eminence, becomes the criterion of their happiness. It happened you know, sir, that the great contests for freedom in this country were, from the earliest times, chiefly upon the question of taxing. Most of the contests in the ancient commonwealths turned primarily on the right of election of magistrates, or on the balance among the several orders of the State. The question of money was not with them so immediate. But in England it was otherwise. On this point of taxes the ablest pens and most eloquent tongues have been exercised; the greatest spirits have acted and suffered. In order to give the fullest satisfaction concerning the importance of this point, it was not only necessary for those who in argument defended the excellence of the English constitution to insist on this privilege of granting money as a dry point of fact and to prove that the right had been acknowledged in ancient parchments and blind usages to reside in a certain body called the House of Commons. They went much further: they attempted to prove—and they succeeded—that in theory it ought to be so, from the particular nature of a House of Commons, as an immediate representative of the people, whether the old records had delivered this oracle or not. They took infinite pains to inculcate, as a fundamental principle, that, in all monarchies, the people must, in effect, themselves, mediately or immediately, possess the power of granting their own money, or no shadow of liberty could subsist. The colonies draw from you, as with their lifeblood, those ideas and principles, their love of liberty, as with you, fixed and attached on this specific point of taxing. Liberty might be safe or might be endangered in twenty other particulars, without their being much pleased or alarmed. Here they felt its pulse; and, as they found that beat, they thought themselves sick or sound. I do not say whether they were right or wrong in applying your general arguments to their own case. It is not easy, indeed, to make a monopoly of theorems and corollaries. The fact is, that they did thus apply those general arguments; and your mode of governing them, whether through lenity or indolence, through wisdom or mistake, confirmed them in the imagination that they, as well as you, had an interest in these common principles.

They were further confirmed in these pleasing errors by the form of their provincial legislative assemblies. Their governments are popular in a high degree; some are merely popular; in all, the popular representative is the most weighty; and this share of the people in their ordinary government never fails to inspire them with lofty sentiments and with a strong aversion from whatever tends to deprive them of their chief importance.

If anything were wanting to this necessary operation of the form of Government, religion would have given it a complete effect. Religion, always a principle of energy, in this new people is in no way worn out or impaired; and their mode of professing it is also one main cause of this free spirit. The people are Protestants, and of that kind which is most averse to all implicit submission of mind and opinion. This is a persuasion not only favorable to liberty, but built upon it. I do not think, sir, that the reason of this averseness in the dissenting churches from all that looks like absolute government is so much to be sought in their religious tenets as in their history. Every one knows that the Roman Catholic religion is at least coeval with most of the governments where it prevails, that it has generally gone hand in hand with them, and received great favor and every kind of support from authority. The Church of England, too, was formed from her cradle under the nursing care of regular government. But the dissenting interests have sprung up in direct opposition to all the ordinary powers of the world, and could justify that opposition only on a strong claim to natural liberty. Their very existence depended on the powerful and unremitted assertion of that claim. All Protestantism, even the most cold and passive, is a kind of dissent. But the religion most prevalent in our northern colonies is a refinement on the principle of resistance; it is the dissidence of dissent, and the protestantism of the Protestant religion. This religion, under a variety of denominations, agreeing in nothing but in the communion of the spirit of liberty, is predominant in most of the northern provinces, where the Church of England, notwithstanding its legal rights, is in reality no more than a sort of private sect, not composing most probably, the tenth of the people. The colonists left England when this spirit was high, and in the emigrants was the highest of all; and even that stream of foreigners which has been constantly flowing into these colonies has, for the greatest part, been composed of dissenters from the establishments of their several countries, and have brought with them a temper and character far from alien to that of the people with whom they mixed.

Sir, I can perceive by their manner that some gentlemen object to the latitude of this description, because in the southern colonies the Church of England forms a large body and has a regular establishment. It is certainly true. There is, however, a circumstance attending these colonies, which, in my opinion, fully counterbalances this difference, and makes the spirit of liberty still more high and haughty than in those to the northward. It is that in Virginia and the Carolinas they have a vast multitude of slaves. Where this is the case in any part of the world, those who are free are by far the most proud and jealous of their freedom. Freedom is to them not only an enjoyment, but a kind of rank and privilege. Not seeing there that freedom, as in countries where it is a common blessing, and as broad and general as the air, may be united with much abject toil, with great misery, with all the exterior of servitude, liberty looks, among them, like something that is more noble and liberal. I do not mean, sir, to commend the superior morality of this sentiment, which has at least as much pride as virtue in it; but I cannot alter the nature of man. The fact is so; and these people of the southern colonies are much more strongly, and with a higher and more stubborn spirit, attached to liberty than those to the northward. Such were all the ancient commonwealths; such were our Gothic ancestors; such, in our days, were the Poles, and such will be all masters of slaves, who are not slaves themselves. In such a people the haughtiness of domination combines with the spirit of freedom, fortifies it, and renders it invincible.

Permit me, sir, to add another circumstance in our colonies, which contributes no mean part toward the growth and effect of this untractable spirit—I mean their education. In no country perhaps in the world is the law so general a study. The profession itself is numerous and powerful; and in most provinces it takes the lead. The greater number of the deputies sent to Congress were lawyers. But all who read, and most do read, endeavor to obtain some smattering in that science. I have been told by an eminent bookseller, that in no branch of his business, after tracts of popular devotion, were so many books as those on the law exported to the plantations. The colonists have now fallen into the way of printing them for their own use. I hear that they have sold nearly as many of Blackstone's "Commentaries" in America as in England. General Gage marks out this disposition very particularly in a letter on your table. He states that all the people in his government are lawyers, or smatterers in law, and that in Boston they have been enabled, by successful chicane, wholly to evade many parts of one of your capital penal constitutions. The smatterers of debate will say that this knowledge ought to teach them more clearly the rights of legislature, their obligations to obedience, and the penalties of rebellion. All this is mighty well. But my honorable and learned friend on the floor, who condescends to mark what I say for animadversion, will disdain that ground. He has heard, as well as I, that when great honors and great emoluments do not win over this knowledge to the service of the State, it is a formidable adversary to government. If the spirit be not tamed and broken by these happy methods, it is stubborn and litigious. "Abeunt studia in mores." This study renders men acute, inquisitive, dexterous, prompt in attack, ready in defense, full of resources. In other countries, the people, more simple and of a less mercurial cast, judge of an ill principle in government only by an actual grievance. Here they anticipate the evil, and judge of the pressure of the grievance by the badness of the principle. They augur misgovernment at a distance, and snuff the approach of tyranny in every tainted breeze.

The last cause of this disobedient spirit in the colonies is hardly less powerful than the rest, as it is not merely moral, but laid deep in the natural constitution of things. Three thousand miles of ocean lie between you and them. No contrivance can prevent the effect of this distance in weakening government. Seas roll and months pass between the order and the execution, and the want of a speedy, explanation of a single point is enough to defeat the whole system. You have, indeed, "winged ministers" of vengeance, who carry your bolts in their pouches to the remotest verge of the sea. But there a power steps in that limits the arrogance of raging passion and furious elements, and says: "So far shalt thou go, and no farther." Who are you, that should fret and rage, and bite the chains of nature? Nothing worse happens to you than does to all nations who have extensive empire; and it happens in all the forms into which empire can be thrown. In large bodies the circulation of power must be less vigorous at the extremities. Nature has said it. The Turk cannot govern Egypt and Arabia and Koordistan as he governs Thrace, nor has he the same dominion in Crimea and Algiers which he has at Brussa and Smyrna. Despotism itself is obliged to truck and huckster. The Sultan gets such obedience as he can. He governs with a loose rein, that he may govern at all, and the whole of the force and vigor of his authority in his centre is derived from a prudent relaxation in all his borders. Spain, in her provinces, is, perhaps, not so well obeyed as you are in yours. She complies too; she submits; she watches times. This is the immutable condition, the eternal law, of extensive and detached empire.

Then, sir, from these six capital sources of descent, of form of government, of religion in the northern provinces, of manners in the southern, of education, of the remoteness of situation from the first mover of government—from all these causes a fierce spirit of liberty has grown up. It has grown with the growth of the people in your colonies, and increased with the increase of their wealth; a spirit that, unhappily, meeting with an exercise of power in England, which, however lawful, is not reconcilable to any ideas of liberty, much less with theirs, has kindled this flame that is ready to consume us. . . .

But, sir, in wishing to put an end to pernicious experiments, I do not mean to preclude the fullest inquiry. Far from it. Far from deciding on a sudden or partial view, I would patiently go round and round the subject and survey it minutely in every possible aspect. Sir, if I were capable of engaging you to an equal attention, I would state that, as far as I am capable of discerning, there are but three ways of proceeding relative to this stubborn spirit which prevails in your colonies and disturbs your government. These are, to change that spirit, as inconvenient, by removing the causes; to prosecute as criminal; or to comply with it as necessary. I would not be guilty of an imperfect enumeration. I can think of but these three. Another has, indeed, been started—that of giving up the colonies; but it met so slight a reception that I do not think myself obliged to dwell a great while upon it. . . .

Mr. Burke then proceeded in detail to build up his argument in behalf of the colonists, closing his speech as follows:

The Americans will have no interest contrary to the grandeur and glory of England, when they are not oppressed by the weight of it; and they will rather be inclined to respect the acts of a superintending legislature, when they see them the acts of that power which is itself the security, not the rival, of their secondary importance. In this assurance my mind most perfectly acquiesces, and I confess I feel not the least alarm from the discontents which are to arise from putting people at their ease; nor do I apprehend the destruction of this empire from giving, by an act of free grace and indulgence, to two millions of my fellow-citizens, some share of the rights upon which I have always been taught to value myself. . . .

My hold of the colonies is in the close affection which grows from common names, from kindred blood, from similar privileges, and equal protection. These are the ties which, though light as air, are as strong as links of iron. Let the colonies always keep the idea of their civil rights associated with your government; they will cling and grapple to you, and no force under heaven will be of power to tear them from their allegiance. But let it be once understood that your government may be one thing and their privileges another; that these two things may exist without any mutual relation; the cement is gone; the cohesion is loosened; and everything hastens to decay and dissolution. As long as you have the wisdom to keep the sovereign authority of this country as the sanctuary of liberty, the sacred temple consecrated to our common faith, wherever the chosen race and sons of England worship freedom, they will turn their faces toward you. The more they multiply, the more friends you will have. The more ardently they love freedom, the more perfect will be their obedience. Slavery they can have anywhere. It is a weed that grows in every soil. They may have it in Spain; they may have it from Prussia; but, until you become lost to all feeling of your true interest and your natural dignity, freedom they can have from none but you. This is the commodity price of which you have the monopoly. This is the true Act of Navigation, which binds to you the commerce of the colonies, and through them secures to you the wealth of the world. Deny them this participation of freedom, and you break the sole bond which originally made, and must still preserve, the unity of the empire. . . .

All this, I know well enough, will sound wild and chimerical to the profane herd of those vulgar and mechanical politicians, who have no place among us; a sort of people who think that nothing exists but what is gross and material, and who, therefore, far from being qualified to be directors of the great movement of the empire are not fit to turn a wheel in the machine. But to men truly initiated and rightly taught, these ruling master principles, which in the opinion of such men as I have mentioned have no substantial existence, are, in truth, everything and all in all. Magnanimity in politics is not seldom the truest wisdom; and a great empire and little minds go ill together. If we are conscious of our situation, and glow with zeal to fill our place as becomes our station and ourselves, we ought to auspicate all our public proceeding in America with the warning of the church, *sursum corda.* We ought to elevate our minds to the greatness of that trust to which the order of providence has called us. By adverting to the dignity of this high calling, our ancestors have turned a savage wilderness into a glorious temple, and have made the most extensive and only honorable conquests not by destroying but by promoting the wealth, the number, the happiness of the human race. Let us get an American revenue as we have got an American empire. English privileges have made it all that it is; English privileges will make it all it can be.

In full confidence of this unalterable truth, I now, *quod felix faustumque sit,* lay the first stone in the temple of peace: and I move you,

That the colonies and plantations of Great Britain in North America, consisting of fourteen separate governments and containing two millions and upwards of free inhabitants, have not had the liberty and privilege of electing and sending knights and burgesses, or others, to represent them in the high court of Parliament.

THE TYRANNY OF THE EAST INDIA COMPANY [6]

Charles Fox

(1749-1806)

Charles Fox, a descendant of noble lineage, was educated at Eton and Oxford and after travelling on the Continent entered Parliament at the age of 19. From 1770 to 1774 he was in Lord North's ministry, but on his dismissal became a Whig and led the opposition to William Pitt. He strenuously opposed the war with France, advocating non-intervention. He was also one of the able prosecutors of Warren Hastings for his misrule of India and aided Wilberforce in his efforts to abolish the slave trade. His sympathy with the American colonies in the Revolutionary War distinguished him for Americans. He advocated complete separation of the colonies, and his greatest oratory was that in defence of the colonists against the injustice and greed of the King's party in England.

Fox had great fluency in extemporaneous speech and his colleague, Burke, said of him that he was the greatest debater the world had ever seen, while the critic, Mackintosh, described him as the most Demosthenian speaker since Demosthenes. Undoubtedly Fox was one of the most brilliant figures of the 18th century. His personal appearance was most striking. He had all the vices of his day, but he had also an unfailing honesty and a genial kindly disposition and was devoid of malignant feelings toward his opponents. Included here is his speech on *The Tyranny of the East India Company*, delivered December 1, 1783, a speech which paved the way for the trial of Warren Hastings.

[6] Abridged.

Sir, the necessity of my saying something upon the present occasion is so obvious that no apology will, I hope, be expected from me for troubling the House, even at so late an hour (two o'clock in the morning). I shall not enter much into a detailed or minute defense of the particulars of the bill before you, because few particular objections have been made, the opposition to it consisting only of general reasonings, some of little application, and others totally distinct from the point in question.

This bill has been combated through its past stages upon various principles; but to this moment the House has not heard it canvassed upon its own intrinsic merits. The debate this night has turned chiefly upon two points—violation of charter, and increase of influence; and upon both these points I shall say a few words.

The honorable gentleman who opened the debate (Mr. Powys) first demands my attention, not indeed for the wisdom of the observations which fell from him this night (acute and judicious as he is upon most occasions), but from the natural weight of all such characters in this country, the aggregate of whom should, in my opinion, always decide upon public measures; but his ingenuity was never, in my opinion, exerted more ineffectually, upon more mistaken principles, and more inconsistently with the common tenor of his conduct, than in this debate.

The honorable gentleman charges me with abandoning that cause, which, he says, in terms of flattery, I had once so successfully asserted. I tell him in reply, that if he were to search the history of my life, he would find that the period of it, in which I struggled most for the real, substantial cause of liberty, is this very moment that I am addressing you. Freedom, according to my conception of it, consists in the safe and sacred possession of a man's property, governed by laws defined and certain; with many personal privileges, natural, civil, and religious, which he cannot surrender without ruin to himself; and of which to be deprived by any other power is despotism. This bill, instead of subverting, is destined to give stability to these principles; instead of narrowing the basis of freedom, it tends to enlarge it; instead of suppressing, its object is to infuse and circulate the spirit of liberty.

What is the most odious species of tyranny? Precisely that which this bill is meant to annihilate. That a handful of men, free themselves, should execute the most base and abominable despotism over millions of their fellow-creatures; that innocence should be the victim of oppression; that industry should toil for rapine; that the harmless laborer should sweat, not for his own benefit, but for the luxury and rapacity of tyrannic depredation; in a word, that thirty millions of men, gifted by Providence with the ordinary endowments of humanity, should groan under a system of despotism unmatched in all the histories of the world.

What is the end of all government? Certainly the happiness of the governed. Others may hold other opinions, but this is mine, and I proclaim it. What are we to think of a government whose good fortune is supposed to spring from the calamities of its subjects, whose aggrandizement grows out of the miseries of mankind? This is the kind of government exercised under the East India Company upon the natives of Hindostan; and the subversion of that infamous government is the main object of the bill in question. But in the progress of accomplishing this end, it is objected that the charter of the company should not be violated; and upon this point, sir, I shall deliver my opinion without disguise. A charter is a trust to one or more persons for some given benefit. If this trust be abused, if the benefit be not obtained, and its failure arise from palpable guilt, or (what in this case is full as bad) from palpable ignorance or mismanagement, will any man gravely say that that trust should not be resumed and delivered to other hands, more especially in the case of the East India Company, whose manner of executing this trust,—whose laxity and languor have produced, and tend to produce consequences diametrically opposite to the ends of confiding that trust, and of the institution for which it was granted? I beg the gentlemen to be aware of the lengths to which their arguments upon the intangibility of this charter may be carried. Every syllable virtually impeaches the establishment by which we sit in this House, in the enjoyment of this freedom, and of every other blessing of our Government. These kinds of arguments are batteries against the main pillar of the British Constitution. Some men are consistent with their own private opinions, and discover the inheritance of family maxims, when they question the principles of the Revolution; but I have no scruple in subscribing to the articles of that creed which produced it. Sovereigns are sacred, and reverence is due to every king; yet, with all my attachments to the person of a first magistrate, had I lived in the reign of James II., I should most certainly have contributed my efforts, and borne part in those illustrious struggles which vindicated an empire from hereditary servitude, and recorded this valuable doctrine, "that trust abused is revocable."

No man, sir, will tell me that a trust to a company or merchants stands upon the solemn and sanctified ground by which a trust is committed to a monarch; and I am at a loss to reconcile the conduct of men who approve that resumption of violated trust, which rescued and re-established our unparalleled and admirable Constitution with a thousand valuable improvements and advantages at the Revolution, and who, at this moment, rise up the champions of the East India Company's charter, although the incapacity and incompetency of that company to a due and adequate discharge of the trust deposited in them by that charter are themes of ridicule and contempt to the world; and although, in consequence of their mismanagement, connivance, and imbecility, combined with the wickedness of their servants, the very name of an Englishman is detested, even to a proverb, through all Asia, and the national character is become degraded and dishonored. To rescue that name from odium and redeem this character from disgrace are some of the objects of the present bill; and, gentlemen should, indeed, gravely weigh their opposition to a measure which, with a thousand other points not less valuable, aims at the attainment of these objects.

Those who condemn the present bill as a violation of the chartered rights of the East India Company, condemn, on the same ground, I say again, the Revolution as a violation of the chartered rights of King James II. He, with as much reason, might have claimed the property of dominion; but what was the language of the people? "No; you have no property in dominion; dominion was vested in you, as it is in every chief magistrate, for the benefit of the community to be governed; it was a sacred trust delegated by compact; you have abused that trust; you have exercised dominion for the purposes of vexation and tyranny— not of comfort, protection, and good order; and we, therefore, resume the power which was originally ours; we recur to the first principles of all government—the will of the many, and it is our will that you shall no longer abuse your dominion." The case is the same with the East India Company's government over a territory, as it has been said by my honorable friend (Mr. Burke), of two hundred and eighty thousand square miles in extent, nearly equal to all Christian Europe, and containing thirty millions of the human race. It matters not whether dominion arise from conquest or from compact. Conquest gives no right to the conqueror to be a tyrant; and it is no violation of right to abolish the authority which is misused. . .

THE ARRAIGNMENT OF
WARREN HASTINGS

Richard Brinsley Sheridan

(1751-1816)

Richard Sheridan, Britain's brilliant dramatist, wit, statesman, and orator, entered Parliament in 1780 as a Whig and held his seat in that body for 32 years. He was Secretary of the Treasury in 1783; Treasurer of the Navy in 1806. It was in 1787 at the trial of Warren Hastings that he established his fame as an orator. The occasion at which this speech was delivered was before the Parliament sitting as a High Court in Westminister Hall when as much as fifty pounds was paid for a seat. The reports of these speeches are not altogether adequate or reliable, but enough may be gleaned from the extract of the arraignment included here to judge the ironical and classical power of Sheridan's speech. It is reported that after five hours, when Sheridan had spoken his final words, "My Lords, I have done" he was caught in the arms of Burke and embraced with the energy of generous admiration; but Macaulay states that Sheridan contrived with a knowledge of stage effect which his father might have envied to sink back as if exhausted into the arms of Burke. Nevertheless the Begum speech is still regarded as one of the most splendid examples of eloquence extant. Sheridan, himself, only once again reached the same height of eloquence in a speech delivered in 1794 supporting the French Revolution.

I trust your Lordships will not believe that, because something is necessary to retrieve the British character, we call for an example to be made without due and solid proof of the guilt of the person whom we pursue:—no, my Lords, we know well that it is the glory of this Constitution, that not the general fame or character of any man; not the weight or power of any prosecutor; no plea of moral or political expediency; nor even the secret consciousness of guilt which may live in the bosom of the Judge; can justify any British court in passing any sentence to touch a hair of the head, or an atom, in any respect, of the property, of the fame, of the liberty of the poorest or meanest subject that breathes the air of this just and free land. We know, my Lords, that there can be no legal guilt without legal proof, and that the rule which defines the evidence is as much the law of the land as that which creates the crime. It is upon that ground we mean to stand.

Major Scott comes to your Bar; describes the shortness of time; represents Mr. Hastings as it were contracting for a character, putting his memory into commission, making departments for his conscience. A number of friends meet together, and he, knowing (no doubt) that the accusation of the Commons had been drawn up by a committee, thought it necessary, as a point of punctilio, to answer it by a committee also. One furnishes the raw material of fact, the second spins the argument, and the third twines up the conclusion, while Mr. Hastings, with a master's eye, is cheering and looking over this loom. He says to one, "You have got my good faith in your hands; you, my veracity to manage. Mr. Shore, I hope you will make me a good financier. Mr. Middleton, you have my humanity in commission." When it is done, he brings it to the House of Commons, and says, "I was equal to the task. I knew the difficulties, but I scorn them; here is the truth, and if the truth will convict me, I am content myself to be the channel of it!" His friends hold up their heads, and say, "What noble magnanimity! This must be the effect of conscious and real innocence." Well, it is so received, it is so argued upon; but it fails of its effect.

Then says Mr. Hastings: "That my defence! no, mere journeyman work—good enough for the Commons, but not fit for your Lordships' consideration." He then calls upon his counsel to save him: "I fear none of my accusers' witnesses. I know some of them well; I know the weakness of their memory, and the strength of their attachment; I fear no testimony but my own—save me from the peril of my own panegyric; preserve me from that, and I shall be safe." Then is this plea brought to your Lordship's Bar, and Major Scott gravely asserts that Mr. Hastings did, at the Bar of the House of Commons, vouch for facts of which he was ignorant, and for arguments of which he had never read.

After such an attempt, we certainly are left in doubt to decide to which set of his friends Mr. Hastings is the least obliged, those who assisted him in making his defence, or those who advised him to deny it.

I am perfectly convinced that there is one idea which must arise in your Lordships' minds as a subject of wonder: how a person of Mr. Hastings' reputed abilities can furnish such matter of accusation against himself. He knows that truth must convict him, and concludes a converso, that falsehood will acquit him; forgetting that there must be some connection, some system, some co-operation, or, otherwise, his host of falsities fall without an enemy, self-discomfited and destroyed.

But of this he never seems to have had the slightest apprehension. He falls to work, and artificer of fraud, against all the rules of architecture; he lays his ornamental work first, and his massy foundation at the top of it; and thus his whole building tumbles upon his head. Other people look well to their ground, choose their position, and watch whether they are likely to be surprised there; but he, as if in the ostentation of his heart, builds upon a precipice, and encamps upon a mine, from choice. He seems to have no one actuating principle, but a steady, persevering resolution not to speak the truth or to tell the fact.

It is impossible, almost, to treat conduct of this kind with perfect seriousness; yet I am aware that it ought to be more seriously accounted for; because I am sure it has been a sort of paradox, which must have struck your Lordships, how any person having so many motives to conceal; having so many reasons to dread detection; should yet go to work so clumsily upon the subject. It is possible, indeed, that it may raise this doubt, whether such a person is of sound mind enough to be a proper object of punishment; or at least it may give a kind of confused notion that the guilt cannot be of so deep and black a grain, over which such a thin veil was thrown, and so little trouble taken to avoid detection. I am aware that, to account for this seeming paradox, historians, poets, and even philosophers—at least of ancient times—have adopted the superstitious solution of the vulgar, and said that the gods deprive men of reason whom they devote to destruction or to punishment. But to unassuming or unprejudiced reason there is no need to resort to any supposed supernatural interference; for the solution will be found in the eternal rules that formed the mind of man, and gave a quality and nature to every passion that inhabits it.

An honorable friend of mine, who is now, I believe, near me, has told you that Prudence, the first of virtues, never can be used in the cause of vice. But I should doubt whether we can read the history of a Philip of Macedon, a Caesar, or a Cromwell, without confessing that there have been evil purposes, baneful to the peace and to the rights of men, conducted—if I may not say, with prudence or with wisdom—yet with awful craft and most successful and commanding subtlety. If, however, I might make a distinction, I should say that it is the proud attempt to mix a variety of lordly crimes that unsettles the prudence of the mind and breeds this distraction of the brain. One master-passion, domineering in the breast, may win the faculties of the understanding to advance its purpose, and to direct to that object everything that thought or human knowledge can effect; but, to succeed, it must maintain a solitary despotism in the mind—each rival profligacy must stand aloof, or wait in abject vassalage upon its throne. For the Power that has not forbade the entrance of evil passions into man's mind, has, at least, forbade their union;—if they meet they defeat their object; and their conquest, or their attempt at it, is tumult. To turn to the Virtues—how different the decree! Formed to connect, to blend, to associate, and to co-operate;

bearing the same course, with kindred energies and harmonious sympathy; each perfect in its own lovely sphere; each moving in its wider or more contracted orbit with different, but concentering powers; guided by the same influence of reason, and endeavoring at the same blessed end—the happiness of the individual, the harmony of the species, and the glory of the Creator. In the Vices, on the other hand, it is the discord that insures the defeat; each clamorous to be heard in its own barbarous language; each claims the exclusive cunning of the brain; each thwarts and reproaches the other; and even while their full rage assails with common hate the peace and virtue of the world, the civil war among their own tumultuous legions defeats the purpose of the foul conspiracy. These are the Furies of the mind, my Lords, that unsettle the understanding; these are the Furies that destroy the virtue, Prudence; while the distracted brain and shivered intellect proclaim the tumult that is within, and bear their testimonies, from the mouth of God himself to the foul condition of the heart.

ON THE REFUSAL TO NEGOTIATE WITH FRANCE

William Pitt

(1759-1806)

William Pitt, the son of the Earl of Chatham, was elected to Parliament in 1780 and on the occasion of his maiden speech demonstrated, as Burke remarked, that "he was not a chip of the old block, but the old block itself." His first prominent speech was in favor of Edmund Burke's scheme of economic reform. When only 24 years of age he was made Chancellor of the Exchequer and in 1783 Prime Minister, a position which he retained for 17 years. Throughout his ministry he was idolized by his country as his father had been. His lofty patriotism, keen statesmanship, sympathy with civil and religious freedom, and his unusual eloquence aided him in steering his country through most perilous times. It is also to be credited to Pitt's ministry that industrial reforms were accomplished, and his work did much to bring about the ultimate downfall of Napoleon.

The style of oratory which the younger Pitt adopted differed from his father's in that where Chatham was impassioned, the younger Pitt was stately. Lord Brougham remarked of his work that "while he lacked somewhat rhetoric and variety and grace of manner he could sieze the attention of his audience and hold it till he chose to let it go; yet that the last effect of the highest eloquence was lacking, for the speaker was seldom forgot in his work."

Among the prominent speeches of Pitt are his maiden speech, the speech delivered before the House of Commons in June, 1781, denouncing the war in America, and the speech on refusing to negotiate with France delivered in the House of Commons February 3, 1800, which is considered his most elaborate oration and, as a parliamentary discourse which both informs and inspires, has rarely been equalled. An abridgement of this speech is included here.

I will enlarge no further on the origin of the war. I have read and detailed to you a system which was in itself a declaration of war against all nations; which was so intended, and which has been so applied; which has been exemplified in the extreme peril and hazard of almost all who for a moment have trusted to treaty and which has not at this hour overwhelmed Europe in one indiscriminate mass of ruin, only because we have not indulged, to a fatal extremity, that disposition which we have, however, indulged too far—because we have not consented to trust to profession and compromise, rather than to our own valor and exertion, for security against a system from which we never shall be delivered till either the principle is extinguished or its strength is exhausted.

I might, sir, if I found it necessary, enter into much detail upon this part of the subject. You cannot look at the map of Europe and lay your hand upon that country against which France has not either declared an open and aggressive war, or violated some positive treaty, or broken some recognized principle of the law of nations.

For the express purpose of producing the war they excited a popular tumult in Paris; they insisted and obtained the dismissal of M. Delessart. A new minister was appointed in his room; the tone of the negotiation was immediately changed, and an ultimatum was sent to the emperor, similar to that which was afterward sent to this country, affording him no satisfaction on his just grounds of complaint, and requiring him, under those circumstances, to disarm. The first events of the contest proved how much more France was prepared for war than Austria, and afford a strong confirmation of the proposition which I maintain, that no offensive intention was entertained on the part of the latter power.

War was then declared against Austria, a war which I state to be a war of aggression on the part of France. The king of Prussia has declared that he should consider war against the emperor or empire as war against himself. He had declared that as a coestate of the empire he was determined to defend their rights; that as an ally to the emperor he would support him to the utmost against any attack; and that for the sake of his own dominions he felt himself called upon to resist the progress of French principles and to maintain the balance of power in Europe. With this notice before them, France declared war upon the emperor, and the war with Prussia was the necessary consequence of this aggression, both against the emperor and the empire.

It was not till a considerably later period that almost all the other nations of Europe found themselves equally involved in actual hostility; but it is not a little material to the whole of my argument, compared with the statement of the learned gentleman and with that contained in the French note, to examine at what period this hostility extended itself. It extended itself, in the course of 1796, to the states of Italy which had hitherto been exempted from it. In 1797 it had ended in the destruction of most of them; it had ended in the virtual deposition of the king of Sardinia; it had ended in the conversion of Genoa and Tuscany into democratic republics; it had ended in the revolution of Venice, in the violation of treaties with the new Venetian republic; and finally, in transferring that very republic, the creature and vassal of France, to the dominion of Austria.

I observe from the gestures of some honorable gentlemen that they think we are precluded from the use of any argument founded on this last transaction. I already hear them saying that it was as criminal in Austria to receive as it was in France to give. I am far from defending or palliating the conduct of Austria upon this occasion. But because Austria, unable at last to contend with the arms of France, was forced to accept an unjust and insufficient indemnification for the conquests France had made from it, are we to be debarred from stating what, on the part of France, was not merely an unjust acquisition, but an act of the grossest and most aggravated perfidy and cruelty, and one of the most striking specimens of that system which has been uniformly and indiscriminately applied to all the countries which France has had within its grasp?

Let us look at the conduct of France. She had spurned the offers of Great Britain; she had reduced her Continental enemies to the necessity of accepting a precarious peace; she had (in spite of those pledges repeatedly made and uniformly violated) surrounded herself by new conquests on every part of her frontier but one. That one was Switzerland. The first effect of being relieved from the war with Austria, of being secured against all fears of Continental invasion on the ancient territory of France, was their unprovoked attack against this unoffending and devoted country.

The country they attacked was one which had long been the faithful ally of France; which, instead of giving cause of jealousy to any other power, had been for ages proverbial for the simplicity and innocence of its manners, and which had acquired and preserved the esteem of all the nations of Europe; which had almost, by the common consent of mankind, been exempted from the sound of war, and marked out as a land of Goshen, safe and untouched in the midst of surrounding calamities.

Look, then, at the fate of Switzerland, at the circumstances which led to its destruction. Add this instance to the catalogue of aggression against all Europe, and then tell me whether the system I have described has not been prosecuted with an unrelenting spirit which can not be subdued in adversity, which can not be appeased in prosperity, which neither solemn professions, nor the general law of nations, nor the obligation of treaties (whether previous to the revolution of subsequent to it) could restrain from the subversion of every state into which, either by force or fraud, their arms could penetrate.

Then tell me, whether the disasters of Europe are to be charged upon the provocation of this country and its allies, or on the inherent principle of the French Revolution, of which the natural result produced so much misery and carnage in France and carried desolation and terror over so large a portion of the world.

After this, it remains only shortly to remind gentlemen of the aggression against Egypt, not omitting, however, to notice the capture of Malta in the way to Egypt. Inconsiderable as that island may be thought, compared with the scenes we have witnessed, let it be remembered that it is an island of which the government had long been recognized by every state of Europe, against which France pretended no cause of war, and whose independence was as dear to itself and as sacred as that of any country in Europe. It was in fact not unimportant, from its local situation to the other powers of Europe; but in proportion as any man may diminish its importance the instance will only serve the more to illustrate and confirm the proposition which I have maintained.

The all-searching eye of the French Revolution looks to every part of Europe and every quarter of the world in which can be found an object either of acquisition or plunder. Nothing is too great for the temerity of its ambition, nothing too small or insignificant for the grasp of its rapacity. From hence Bonaparte and his army proceeded to Egypt.

The attack was made; pretenses were held out to the natives of that country in the name of the French king whom they had murdered. They pretended to have the approbation of the grand seignior whose territory they were violating; their project was carried on under the profession of a zeal for Mohammedanism; it was carried on by proclaiming that France had been reconciled to the Mussulman faith, had abjured that of Christianity, or, as he in his impious language termed it, of the sect of the Messiah.

The only plea which they have since held out to color this atrocious invasion of a neutral and friendly territory is that it was the road to attack the English power in India. It is most unquestionably true that this was one and a principal cause of this unparalleled outrage; but another and an equally substantial cause (as appears by their own statements) was the division and partition of the territories of what they thought a falling power. It is impossible to dismiss this subject without observing that this attack against Egypt was accompanied by an attack upon British possessions in India, made on true revolutionary principles. In Europe the propagation of the principles of France had uniformly prepared the way for the progress of its arms.

What, then, was the nature of this system? Was it anything but what I have stated it to be—an insatiable love of aggrandizement, and implacable spirit of destruction against all the civil and religious institutions of every country? This is the first moving and acting spirit of the French Revolution; this is the spirit which animated it at its birth, and this is the spirit which will not desert it till the moment of its dissolution, "which grew with its growth, which strengthened with its strength," but which has not abated under its misfortunes nor declined in its decay. It has been invariably the same in every period, operating more or less, according as accident or circumstances might assist it; but it has been inherent in the Revolution in all stages; it has equally belonged to Brissot, to Robespierre, to Tallien, to Reubel, to Barras, and to every one of the leaders of the Directory, but to none more than to Bonaparte, in whom now all their powers are united.

Its first fundamental principle was to bribe the poor against the rich, by proposing to transfer into new hands, on the delusive notion of equality, and in breach of every principle of justice, the whole property of the country. The practical application of this principle was to devote the whole of that property to indiscriminate plunder, and to make it the foundation of a revolutionary system of finance, productive in proportion to the misery and desolation which it created.

It has been accompanied by an unwearied spirit of proselytism, diffusing itself over all the nations of the earth: a spirit which can apply itself to all circumstances and all situations, which can furnish a list of grievances and hold out a promise of redress equally to all nations; which inspired the teachers of French liberty with the hope of alike recommending themselves to those who live under the feudal code of the German Empire; to the various States of Italy, under all their different institutions; to the old republicans of Holland, and to the new republicans of America; to the Catholics of Ireland, whom it was to deliver from Protestant usurpation; the Protestant of Switzerland, whom it was to deliver from popish superstition; and to the Mussulman of Egypt, whom it was to deliver from Christian persecution; to the remote Indian, blindly bigoted to his ancient institutions; and to the natives of Great Britain, enjoying the perfection of practical freedom, and justly attached to their Constitution, from the joint result of habit, of reason, and of experience.

The last and distinguishing feature is a perfidy which nothing can bind, which no tie of treaty, no sense of the principles generally received among nations, no obligation, human or divine, can restrain. Thus qualified, thus armed for destruction, the genius of the French Revolution marched forth, the terror and dismay of the world. Every nation has in its turn been the witness, many have been the victims of its principles; and it is left for us to decide whether we will compromise with such a danger while we have yet resources to supply the sinews of war, while the heart and spirit of the country is yet unbroken, and while we have the means of calling forth and supporting a powerful cooperation in Europe.

In examining this part of the subject let it be remembered that there is one other characteristic of the French Revolution as striking as its dreadful and destructive principles: I mean the instability of its government, which has been of itself sufficient to destroy all reliance, if any such reliance could at any time have been placed on the good faith of any of its rulers. Such has been the incredible rapidity with which the revolutions in France have succeeded each other, that I believe the names of those who have successively exercised absolute power under the pretense of liberty are to be numbered by the years of the revolution, and by each of the new constitutions, which, under the same pretense, has in its turn been imposed by force on France: all of which alike were founded upon principles which professed to be among all the nations of the earth. Each of these will be found, upon an average, to have had about two years as the period of its duration.

Having taken a view of what it was, let us now examine what it is. In the first place we see, as has been truly stated, a change in the description and form of the sovereign authority. A supreme power is placed at the head of this nominal republic, with a more open avowal of military despotism than at any other period; with a more open and undisguised abandonment of the names and pretenses under which that despotism long attempted to conceal itself. The different institutions, republican in their form and appearance, which were before the instruments of that despotism, are now annihilated; they have given way to the absolute power of one man, concentrating in himself all the authority of the State, and differing from other monarchs only in this, that (as my honorable friend, Mr. Canning, truly stated it) he wields a sword instead of a scepter. What, then, is the confidence we are to derive either from the frame of the government or from the character and past conduct of the person who is now the absolute ruler of France?

Had we seen a man of whom we had no previous knowledge suddenly invested with the sovereign authority of the country; invested with the power of taxation, with the power of the sword, the power of war and peace, the unlimited power of commanding the resources, of disposing of the lives and fortunes of every man in France; if we had seen at the same moment all the inferior machinery of the revolution, which, under the variety of successive shocks had kept the system in motion, still remaining entire, all that, by requisition and plunder, had given activity to the revolutionary system of finance, and had furnished the means of creating an army, by converting every man who was of age to bear arms into a soldier, not for the defense of his own country, but for the sake of carrying the war into the country of the enemy; if we had seen all the subordinate instruments of Jacobin power subsisting in their full force, and retaining (to use the French phrase) all their original organizations, and had then observed this single change in the conduct of their affairs that there was now one man, with no rival to thwart his measures, no colleague to divide his powers, no council to control his operations, no liberty of speaking or writing, no expression of public opinion to check or influence his conduct; under such circumstances should we be wrong to pause, or wait for the evidence of facts and experience, before we consented to trust our safety to the forbearance of a single man, in such a situation, and to relinquish those means of defense which have hitherto carried us safe through all the storms of the Revolution? If we were to ask what are the principles and character of this stranger to whom fortune has suddenly committed the concerns of a great and powerful nation?

But is this the actual state of the present question? Are we talking of a stranger of whom we have heard nothing? No, sir, we have heard of him; we, and Europe, and the world, have heard both of him and of the satellites by whom he is surrounded, and it is impossible to discuss fairly the propriety of any answer which could be returned to his overtures of negotiation without taking into consideration the inferences to be drawn from his personal character and conduct.

If we carry our views out of France and look at the dreadful catalogue of all the breaches of treaty, which are precisely commensurate with the number of treaties which the republic has made (for I have sought in vain for any one which it has made and which it has not broken), if we trace the history of them all from the beginning of the Revolution to the present time, or if we select those which have been accompanied by the most atrocious cruelty and marked the most strongly with the characteristic features of the Revolution, the name of Bonaparte will be found allied to more of them than that of any other that can be handed down in the history of the crimes and miseries of the last ten years.

It is unnecessary to say more with respect to the credit due to his professions or the reliance to be placed on his general character. But it will perhaps be argued that whatever may be his character or whatever has been his past conduct, he has now an interest in making and observing peace. That he has an interest in making peace is at best but a doubtful proposition, and that he has an interest in preserving it is still more uncertain. That it is his interest to negotiate I do not indeed deny. It is his interest, above all, to engage this country in separate negotiation in order to loosen and dissolve the whole system of the confederacy on the Continent, to palsy at once the arms of Russia, or of Austria, or of any other country that might look to you for support; and then either to break off his separate treaty, or, if he should have concluded it, to apply the lesson which is taught in his school of policy in Egypt, and to revive at his pleasure those claims of indemnification which may have been reserved to some happier period.

This is precisely the interest which he has in negotiation. But on what grounds are we to be convinced that he has an interest in concluding and observing a solid and permanent pacification? Under all the circumstances of his personal character, and his newly acquired power, what other security has he for retaining that power but the sword? His hold upon France is the sword, and he has no other. Is he connected with the soil, or with the habits, the affections, or the prejudices of the country? He is a stranger, a foreigner, and a usurper. He unites in his own person everything that a pure republican must detest; everything that an enraged Jacobin has abjured; everything that a sincere and faithful royalist must feel as an insult. If he is opposed at any time in his career, what is his appeal? He appeals to his fortune—in other words, to his army and his sword. Placing, then, his whole reliance upon military support, can he afford to let his military renown pass away, to let his laurels wither, to let the memory of his trophies sink in obscurity? Is it certain that, with his army confined within France, and restrained from inroads upon her neighbors, he can maintain at his devotion a force sufficiently numerous to support his power? Having no object but the possession of absolute dominion, no passion but military glory, is it to be reckoned as certain that he can feel such an interest in permanent peace as would justify us in laying down our arms, reducing our expense, and relinquishing our means of security, on the faith of his engagements?

Do we believe that, after the conclusion of peace, he would not still sigh over the lost trophies of Egypt, wrested from him by the celebrated victory of Aboukir and the brilliant exertions of that heroic band of British seamen whose influence and example rendered the Turkish troops invincible at Acre? Can he forget that the effect of these exploits enabled Austria and Russia in one campaign to recover from France all which she had acquired by his victories, to dissolve the charm which for a time fascinated Europe, and to show that their generals, contending in a just cause, could efface even by their success and their military glory the most dazzling triumphs of his victorious and desolating ambition?

Can we believe, with these impressions on his mind, that if, after a year, eighteen months, or two years of peace had elapsed, he should be tempted by the appearance of fresh insurrection in Ireland, encouraged by renewed and unrestrained communication with France, and fomented by the fresh infusion of Jacobin principles; if we were at such a moment without a fleet to watch the ports of France or to guard the coasts of Ireland, without a disposable army or an embodied militia capable of supplying a speedy and adequate reinforcement, and that he had suddenly the means of transporting thither a body of twenty or thirty thousand French troops; can we believe that at such a moment his ambition and vindictive spirit would be restrained by the recollection of engagements or the obligation of treaty? Or if, in some new crisis of difficulty and danger to the Ottoman empire, with no British navy in the Mediterranean, no confederacy formed, no force collected to support it, an opportunity should present itself for resuming the abandoned expedition to Egypt, for renewing the avowed and favorite project of conquering and colonizing that rich and fertile country, and of opening the way to wound some of the vital interests of England and to plunder the treasures of the East in order to fill the bankrupt coffers of France? Would it be the interests of Bonaparte under such circumstances, or his principles, his moderation, his love of peace, his aversion to conquest, and his regard for the independence of other nations—would it be all or any of these that would secure us against an attempt which would leave us only the option of submitting without a struggle to certain loss and disgrace, or of renewing the contest which we had prematurely terminated, without allies, without preparation, with diminished means, and with increased difficulty and hazard?

Hitherto I have spoken only of the reliance which we can place on the professions, the character, and the conduct of the present first consul; but it remains to consider the stability of his power. The revolution has been marked throughout by a rapid succession of new depositaries of public authority, each supplanting its predecessor. What grounds have we to believe that this new usurpation, more odious and more undisguised than all that preceded it, will be more durable? Is it that we rely on the particular provisions contained in the code of the pretended constitution, which was proclaimed as accepted by the French people as soon as the garrison of Paris declared their determination to exterminate all its enemies, and before any of its articles could be known to half the country whose consent was required for its establishment?

I will not pretend to inquire deeply into the nature and effects of a constitution which can hardly be regarded but as a farce and a mockery. If, however, it could be supposed that its provisions were to have any effect, it seems equally adapted to two purposes—that of giving to its founder for a time an absolute and uncontrolled authority, and that of laying the certain foundation of disunion and discord which, if they once prevail, must render the exercise of all the authority under the constitution impossible and leave no appeal but to the sword.

Is, then, military despotism that which we are accustomed to consider as a stable form of government? In all ages of the world it has been attained with the least stability to the persons who exercised it, and with the most rapid succession of changes and revolutions. In the outset of the French Revolution its advocates boasted that it furnished a security forever, not to France only, but to all countries in the world, against military despotism; that the force of standing armies was vain and delusive; that no artificial power could resist public opinion; and that it was upon the foundation of public opinion alone that any government could stand. I believe that in this instance, as in every other, the progress of the French Revolution has belied its professions; but, so far from its being a proof of the prevalence of public opinion against military force, it is, instead of the proof, the strongest exception from that doctrine which appears in the history of the world.

If, then, I am asked how long are we to persevere in the war, I can only say that no period can be accurately assigned. Considering the importance of obtaining complete security for the objects for which we contend, we ought not to be discouraged too soon; but, on the contrary considering the importance of not impairing and exhausting the radical strength of the country, there are limits beyond which we ought not to persist, and which we can determine only by estimating and comparing fairly from time to time the degree of security to be obtained by treaty, and the risk and disadvantage of continuing the contest.

But, sir, there are some gentlemen in the House who seem to consider it already certain that the ultimate success to which I am looking is unattainable. They suppose us contending only for the restoration of the French monarchy, which they believe to be impracticable, and deny to be desirable for this country. We have been asked in the course of this debate: Do you think you can impose monarchy upon France against the will of the nation? I never thought it, I never hoped it, I never wished it. I have thought, I have hoped, I have wished, that the time might come when the effect of the arms of the allies might so far overpower the military force which keeps France in bondage as to give vent and scope to the thoughts and actions of its inhabitants.

On the question, sir, how far the restoration of the French monarchy, if practicable, is desirable, I shall not think it necessary to say much. Can it be supposed to be indifferent to us or to the world whether the throne of France is to be filled by a prince of the house of Bourbon or by him whose principles and conduct I have endeavored to develop? Is it nothing, with a view to influence and example, whether the fortune of this last adventurer in the lottery of revolutions shall appear to be permanent? Is it nothing whether a system shall be sanctioned which confirms, by one of its fundamental articles, that general transfer of property from its ancient and lawful possessors, which holds out one of the most terrible examples of national injustice, and which has furnished the great source of revolutionary finance and revolutionary strength against all the powers of Europe?

In the exhausted and impoverished state of France it seems for a time impossible that any system but that of robbery and confiscation, anything but the continued torture which can be applied only by the engines of the revolution, can extort from its ruined inhabitants more than the means of supporting in peace the yearly expenditure of its government. Suppose, then, the heir of the house of Bourbon reinstated on the throne; he will have sufficient occupation in endeavoring, if possible, to heal the wounds and gradually to repair the losses of ten years of civil convulsion—to reanimate the drooping commerce, to rekindle the industry, to replace the capital, and to revive the manufactures of the country.

Under such circumstances there must probably be a considerable interval before such a monarch, whatever may be his views, can possess the power which can make him formidable to Europe; but while the system of the Revolution continues the case is quite different. It is true indeed that even the gigantic and unnatural means by which that Revolution has been supported are so far impaired, the influence of its principles and the terror of its arms so far weakened, and its power of action so much contracted and circumscribed, that against the embodied force of Europe, prosecuting a vigorous war, we may justly hope that the remnant and wreck of this system can not long oppose an effectual resistance.

Can we forget that in the ten years in which that power has subsisted it has brought more misery on surrounding nations and produced more acts of aggression, cruelty, perfidy, and enormous ambition than can be traced in the history of France for the centuries which have elapsed since the foundation of its monarchy, including all the wars which in the course of that period have been waged by any of those sovereigns whose projects of aggrandizement and violations of treaty afford a constant theme of general reproach against the ancient government of France? And if not, can we hesitate whether we have the best prospect of permanent peace, the best security for the independence and safety of Europe, from the restoration of the lawful governmnt or from the continuance of revolutionary power in the hands of Bonaparte?

In compromise and treaty with such a power, placed in such hands as now exercise it, and retaining the same means of annoyance which it now possesses, I see little hope of permanent security. I see no possibility at this moment of such a peace as would justify that liberal intercourse which is the essence of real amity; no chance of terminating the expenses or the anxieties of war, or of restoring to us any of the advantages of established tranquillity; and, as a sincere lover of peace, I cannot be content with its nominal attainment. I must be desirous of pursuing that system which promises to attain in the end the permanent enjoyment of its solid and substantial blessings for this country and for Europe. As a sincere lover of peace I will not sacrifice it by grasping at the shadow when the reality is not substantially within my reach.

ABOLITION OF THE SLAVE TRADE

William Wilberforce

(1759-1833)

William Wilberforce, the advocate of freedom for the slaves, was even as a student at Cambridge affected by "the odious traffic in human flesh." He entered Parliament in 1780 where he at once became an inseparable friend of Pitt, although he himself remained independent of party affiliations. In 1787 he began his great agitation against the slave trade to which he dedicated his life. His most famous speech in the cause was that delivered on May 12, 1789, in support of his own resolution condemning the slave trade, which with the help of Pitt, Burke, and Fox was carried without division.

In opening, concerning the nature of the slave trade, I need only observe that it is found by experience to be just such as every man who uses his reason would infallibly conclude it to be. For my own part, so clearly am I convinced of the mischiefs inseparable from it, that I should hardly want any further evidence than my own mind would furnish, by the most simple deductions. Facts, however, are now laid before the House. A report has been made by his majesty's privy council, which, I trust, every gentleman has read, and which ascertains the slave trade to be just as we know. What should we suppose must naturally be the consequence of our carrying on a slave trade with Africa? With a country vast in its extent, not utterly barbarous, but civilized in a very small degree? Does any one suppose a slave trade would help their civilization? Is it plain that she must suffer from it; that civilization must be checked; that her barbarous manners must be made more barbarous; and that the happiness of her millions of inhabitants must be prejudiced with her intercourse with Britain? Does not every one see that a slave trade carried on around her coasts must carry violence and desolation to her very center? That in a continent just emerging from barbarism, if a trade in men is established, if her men are all converted into goods, and become commodities that can be bartered, it follows they must be subject to ravage just as goods are; and this, too, at a period of civilization, when there is no protecting legislature to defend this, their only sort of property, in the same manner as the rights of property are maintained by the legislature of every civilized country.

We see then, in the nature of things, how easily the practises of Africa are to be accounted for. Her kings are never compelled to war, that we can hear of, by public principles, by national glory, still less by the love of their people. In Europe it is the extension of commerce, the maintenance of national honor, or some great public object, that is ever the motive to war with every monarch; but, in Africa, it is the personal avarice and sensuality of their kings. These two vices of avarice and sensuality, the most powerful and predominant in natures thus corrupt, we tempt, we stimulate in all these African princes, and we depend upon these vices for the very maintenance of the slave trade. Does the king of Barbessin want brandy? He has only to send his troops, in the night-time, to burn and desolate a village; the captives will serve as commodities, that may be bartered with the British trader.

The slave trade, in its very nature, is the source of such kind of tragedies; nor has there been a single person, almost, before the privy council, who does not add something by his testimony to the mass of evidence upon this point. Some, indeed, of these gentlemen, and particularly the delegates from Liverpool, have endeavored to reason down this plain principle; some have palliated it; but there is not one, I believe, who does not more or less admit it. Some, nay most, I believe, have admitted the slave trade to be the chief cause of wars in Africa.

Having now disposed of the first part of this subject, I must speak of the transit of the slaves to the West Indies. This, I confess, in my own opinion, is the most wretched part of the whole subject. So much misery condensed in so little room is more than the human imagination had ever before conceived. I will not accuse the Liverpool merchants. I will allow them, nay, I will believe them, to be men of humanity; and I will therefore believe, if it were not for the multitude of these wretched objects, if it were not for the enormous magnitude and extent of the evil which distracts their attention from individual cases, and makes them think generally, and therefore less feelingly on the subject, they never would have persisted in the trade. I verily believe, therefore, if the wretchedness of any one of the many hundred negroes stowed in each ship could be brought before their view, and remain within the sight of the African merchant, that there is no one among them whose heart would bear it.

Let anyone imagine to himself six or seven hundred of these wretches chained two and two, surrounded with every object that is nauseous and disgusting, diseased, and struggling under every kind of wretchedness! How can we bear to think of such a scene as this? One would think it had been determined to heap on them all the varieties of bodily pain, for the purpose of blunting the feelings of the mind; and yet, in this very point (to show the power of human prejudice), the situation of the slaves has been described by Mr. Norris, one of the Liverpool delegates, in a manner which I am sure will convince the House how interest can draw a film over the eyes, so thick that total blindness could do no more; and how it is our duty therefore to trust not to the reasonings of interested men, nor to their way of coloring a transaction.

"Their apartments," says Mr. Norris, "are fitted up as much for their advantage as circumstances will admit. The right ankle of one, indeed, is connected with the left ankle of another by a small iron fetter, and if they are turbulent, by another on their wrist. They have several meals a day—some of their own country provisions, with the best sauces of African cookery; and by the way of variety, another meal of pulse, etc., according to European taste. After breakfast they have water to wash themselves, while their apartments are perfumed with frankincense and lime juice. Before dinner they are amused after the manner of their country. The song and the dance are promoted," and, as if the whole were really a scene of pleasure and dissipation, it is added that games of chance are furnished. "The men play and sing, while the women and girls make fanciful ornaments with beads, with which they are plentifully supplied." Such is the sort of strain in which the Liverpool delegates, and particularly Mr. Norris, gave evidence before the privy council. What will the House think, when, by the concurring testimony of other witnesses, the true history is laid open? The slaves, who are sometimes described as rejoicing at their captivity, are so wrung with misery at leaving their country, that it is the constant practise to set sail in the night, lest they should be sensible of their departure. The pulse which Mr. Norris talks of are horse beans; and the scantiness of both water and provision was suggested by the very legislature of Jamaica, in the report of their committee, to be a subject that called for the interference of Parliament.

Mr. Norris talks of frankincense and lime juice: when the surgeons tell you the slaves are stored so close that there is not room to tread among them; and when you have it in evidence from Sir George Young, that even in a ship which wanted two hundred of her complement, the stench was intolerable. The song and dance are promoted, says Mr. Norris. It had been more fair, perhaps, if he had explained that word "promoted." The truth is, that for the sake of exercise, these miserable wretches, loaded with chains, oppressed with disease and wretchedness, are forced to dance by the terror of the lash, and sometimes by the actual use of it. "I," says one of the other evidences, "was employed to dance to men, while another person danced to women." Such, then, is the meaning of the word "promoted"; and it may be observed, too, with respect to food, that an instrument is sometimes carried out in order to force them to eat, which is the same sort of proof how much they enjoy themselves in that instance also.

As to their singing, what shall we say when we are told that their songs are of lamentation upon their departure which, while they sing, are always in tears, insomuch that one captain (more humane as I should conceive him, therefore, than the rest) threatened one of the women with a flogging, because the mournfulness of her song was too painful for his feelings. In order, however, not to trust too much to any sort of description, I will call the attention of the House to one species of evidence, which is absolutely infallible. Death, at least, is a sure ground of evidence, and the proportion of deaths will not only confirm, but, if possible, will even aggravate our suspicion of their misery in the transit. It will be found, upon an average of all ships of which evidence has been given at the privy council, that exclusive of those who perish before they sail, not less than twelve and one-half per cent, perish in the passage. Besides these, the Jamaica report tells you that not less than four and one-half per cent die on shore before the day of sale, which is only a week or two from the time of landing. One-third more die in the seasoning, and this in a country exactly like their own, where they are healthy and happy, as some of the evidences would pretend. The diseases, however, which they contract on shipboard, the astringent washes which are to hide their wounds, and the mischievous tricks used to make them up for sale, are, as the Jamaica report says—a most precious and valuable report, which I shall often have to advert to—one principal cause of this mortality. Upon the whole, however, here is a mortality of about fifty per cent, and this among negroes who are not bought unless quite healthy at first, and unless (as the phrase is with cattle) they are sound in wind and limb.

When we consider the vastness of the continent of Africa; when we reflect how all other countries have for some centuries past been advancing in happiness and civilization; when we think how in this same period all improvement in Africa has been defeated by her intercourse with Britain; when we reflect that it is we ourselves that have degraded them to that wretched brutishness and barbarity which we now plead as the justification of our guilt; how the slave trade has enslaved their minds, blackened their character, and sunk them so low in the scale of animal beings that some think the apes are of a higher class, and fancy the orang-outang has given them the go-by. What a mortification must we feel at having so long neglected to think of our guilt, or attempt any reparation! It seems, indeed, as if we had determined to forbear from all interference until the measure of our folly and wickedness was so full and complete; until the impolicy which eventually belongs to vice was become so plain and glaring that not an individual in the country should refuse to join in the abolition; it seems as if we had waited until the persons most interested should be tired out with the folly and nefariousness of the trade, and should unite in petitioning against it.

Let us then make such amends as we can for the mischiefs we have done to the unhappy continent; let us recollect what Europe itself was no longer ago than three or four centuries. What if I should be able to show this House that in a civilized part of Europe, in the time of our Henry VII., there were people who actually sold their own children?

What if I should tell them that England itself was that country? What if I should point out to them that the very place where this inhuman traffic was carried on was the city of Bristol? Ireland at that time used to drive a considerable trade in slaves with these neighboring barbarians; but a great plague having infested the country, the Irish were struck with a panic, suspected (I am sure very properly) that the plague was a punishment sent from heaven for the sin of the slave trade, and therefore abolished it. All I ask, therefore, of the people of Bristol is, that they would become as civilized now as Irishmen were four hundred years ago. Let us put an end at once to this inhuman traffic—let us stop this effusion of human blood.

The true way to virtue is by withdrawing from temptation; let us then withdraw from these wretched Africans those temptations to fraud, violence, cruelty, and injustice, which the slave trade furnishes. Wherever the sun shines, let us go round the world with him, diffusing our benevolence; but let us not traffic, only that we may set kings against their subjects, subjects against their kings, sowing discord in every village, fear and terror in every family, setting millions of our fellow creatures a-hunting each other for slaves, creating fairs and markets for human flesh through one whole continent of the world, and, under the name of policy, concealing from ourselves all the baseness and iniquity of such a traffic.

It will appear from everything which I have said, that it is not regulation, it is not mere palliatives, that can cure this enormous evil. Total abolition is the only possible cure for it. The Jamaica report, indeed, admits much of the evil, but recommends it to us so to regulate the trade that no persons should be kidnapped or made slaves contrary to the custom of Africa. But may they not be made slaves unjustly, and yet by no means contrary to the custom of Africa? I have shown they may, for all the customs of Africa are rendered savage and unjust through the influence of this trade; besides, how can we discriminate between the slaves justly and unjustly made? Or, if we could, does any man believe that the British captains can, by any regulation in this country, be prevailed upon to refuse all such slaves as have not been fairly, honestly, and uprightly enslaved? But granting even that they should do this, yet how would the rejected slaves be recompensed? They are brought, as we are told, from three or four thousand miles off, and exchanged like cattle from one hand to another, until they reach the coast. We see then that it is the existence of the slave trade that is the spring of all this infernal traffic, and that the remedy can not be applied without abolition.

And, sir, when we think of eternity, and of the future consequences of all human conduct, what is there in this life that should make any man contradict the dictates of his conscience, the principles of justice, the laws of religion, and of God? Sir, the nature and all the circumstances of this trade are now laid open to us; we can no longer plead ignorance, we can

not evade it; it is now an object placed before us, we can not pass it;
we may spurn it, we may kick it out of our way, but we can not turn
aside so as to avoid seeing it; for it is brought now so directly before
our eyes that this House must decide, and must justify to all the world,
and to their own consciences, the rectitude of the grounds and principles
of their decision.

DISABILITIES OF THE JEWS

Sir Robert Peel

(1788-1850)

It is largely as the champion of free trade in England that Peel won recognition in Parliament. His election to Parliament in 1809 was as a Tory. He was Secretary for Ireland in 1812-18; Prime-Minister in 1834 and 1841, and in 1846 became the staunch champion of free trade, and although he was at first in the opposition he was instrumental in securing the repeal of the Corn Laws.

In the popular sense Peel was not eloquent, but he was earnest, and his personal sincerity coupled with his ability in argument and the exposition and presentation of facts made him effective in securing his ends. On June 28, 1850, Peel spoke with great eloquence in the debate on Lord Palmerston's Greek policy, but the following day was thrown from his horse and injured so severely that he died that evening.

The speech which follows was made on the occasion of an attempt to postpone a bill relieving the disabilities of the Jews. The bill was one to place the Jew on the same footing, so far at least as civil rights, as the Christian. The speech is on the side of tolerance and justice and displays the measured diction and pointed reasoning of the great minister.

MR. SPEAKER: I must in the first place disclaim altogether any concurrence in the doctrine that to us, in our legislative capacity, religion is a matter of indifference. I am deeply impressed with the conviction that it is our paramount duty to promote the interests of religion and its influence on the human mind. I am impressed by a conviction that the spirit and precepts of Christianity ought to influence our deliberations; nay, more, that, if our legislation be at variance with the precepts and spirit of Christianity, we cannot expect the blessings of God upon them. I may indeed say with truth that whether my decision on this question be right or wrong, it is influenced much less by consideration of political expediency than by a deep sense of religious obligation.

Between the tenets of the Jew and the Christian there is, in my opinion, a vital difference. The religion of the Christian and the religion of the Jew are opposed in essentials. Between them there is complete antagonism. I do not consider that the concurrence of the Jew with the Christian in recognizing the historical truths and divine origin of the moral precepts of the Old Testament can avail to reconcile their differences in respect to those doctrines which constitute the vital principle and foundation of Christianity. If, as a legislature, we had authority to determine religious error and a commission to punish religious error, it might be our painful duty to punish the Jews. But we have no such commission. If the Jews did commit an inexpiable crime nearly two thousand years ago, we have had no authority given us—even if we could determine who were the descendants of the persons guilty of that crime—to visit the sins of the fathers upon the children, not unto the third or fourth, but unto the three hundredth or four hundredth generation. That awful power is not ours. "Vengeance is mine; I will repay, saith the Lord."

I cannot, therefore, admit the right of the legislature to inflict a penalty for mere religious error. I consider civil disability to partake of the nature of a penalty. I speak of religious error simply and abstractly. If you can certainly infer from that religious error dangerous political opinions, and if you have no other mode of guarding against those political opinions except by the administration of a test for the purpose of ascertaining the religious opinions, in that case you may have a right to impose the penalty of exclusion from certain trusts. In the case of the Roman Catholic, you did not exclude him because he maintained the worship of the Virgin Mary or the doctrine of Transubstantiation, but because you thought he was a dangerous subject, in consequence of his acknowledging the supremacy of a foreign power and his allegiance to another sovereign. You excluded him from political power because you believed he would abuse it. You did not inflict civil disability for mere religious error. If you can show, in this case, the maintenance of certain religious opinions by the Jews is a decisive proof of their civil unworthiness, you may have a right to exclude them from power; but the *onus* of showing this is imposed upon you. The presumption is in their favor. The presumption is that a Jew, as a subject of the British crown, is entitled to all the qualifications and the privileges of a British subject. You may defeat that claim by proof of danger to the State from admitting it; but the *onus* of proof lies upon you.

The claims of the Jews, as British-born subjects, is for entire and complete qualification for office. You do not diminish the force of that claim by their partial qualification. You allow the Jew to fill municipal offices—you conceed to him the elective franchise; but the obligation to assign a reason for withdrawing from him what remains is precisely the same. Nay, after you admit the qualifications for the privileges of franchise which you have entrusted him, it becomes the more incumbent upon you to assign a reason for withholding a complete qualification.

A noble lord, who has spoken with so much good feeling upon the question,—the member for Bath,—quoted an authority entitled to much weight, a distinguished man, now no more. I wish to speak of the late Dr. Arnold with the utmost respect. The noble lord read an extract from the works of Dr. Arnold, which appeared to make a considerable impression upon the House—a passage in which Mr. Arnold says: "For the Jews I see no plea of justice whatever; they are voluntary strangers here, and have no claim to become citizens but by conforming to our moral law, which is the Gospel."

We are to reject the claim of the Jews now living—born in this country and owing entire allegiance to the British Crown—to the privileges of British subjects, because their ancestors were voluntary strangers here. The descendants of an ancient Briton, of the pure blood, may be entitled to urge this objection to a Jew; but the descendant of a Norman, or a Roman, or a Saxon, or a Dane can hardly insist upon it. His ancestors, I apprehend, were not invited here; they were "voluntary strangers"; with this difference between them and the Jews, that the Jews were content to submit to the laws and the institutions which they found established, and that the others subverted them. Dr. Arnold proceeds: "I would give the Jews the honorary citizenship which was so often given by the Romans, namely the private rights of citizens, *jus commercii et jus connubii,* but not the public rights, *jus suffragii et jus honorum.*"

I contend that the British law recognizes no such distinction; that, after conferring upon the Jew *jus commercii,* the *onus* of assigning satisfactory reasons for withholding from the Jew the remaining rights of citizenship continues undiminished. Unless you can show that there is something *politically hostile in the character and conduct of the Jew in relation to the State; that in times of civil discord and discontent there is reason to apprehend his disaffection; or that, for some good cause or other he is unworthy of confidence,* you cannot defeat his equitable claim to the entire rights of citizenship.

To the opinion of Dr. Arnold I oppose the opinion of a still higher authority, that of Lord Bacon. In his argument upon the rights of the *post nati* of Scotland, Lord Bacon has the following remarkable observations: "It seemeth admirable unto me to consider with what measured hand, and with how true proportions, our law doth impart and confer the several degrees of the benefits of civilization. The first degree is an alien enemy. The second is an alien friend. The third is a denizen. To this person the law giveth an ability and capacity abridged, not in matter but in time. The fourth and last degree is a natural-born citizen—he is 'complete and entire.' " . . .

The Jew is a subject natural-born; and I contend that he has a right, as such, to be qualified for all civil trusts—that he has a "capacity or ability to all benefits whatever," unless you show a reason to the contrary—a reason not founded upon a mere religious error, but upon some good cause for political disqualification. . . .

It is well known that Jews have been selected by the Crown for civil distinctions; that, under the late government, the baronetcy was conferred by the Queen upon Sir Moses Montefiore; under the present, upon Mr. Rothschild. It is also well known that the Jews are, by a recent act of Parliament, qualified for all municipal offices. But it is not generally known that all civil and military appointments, with very few exceptions, are tenable by a Jew. . . .

If the Jews were debased or inferior in moral worth to Christians, could that debasement and inferiority—the natural result of oppression—be assigned with any semblance of justice as an impediment to the grant of equal rights to the Jews? Could the Christian rulers of Europe justly reproach the Jews for continuing a separate people, and for being deficient in ardent patriotism and devoted attachment to the institutions under which such wrongs had been inflicted? Could they be astonished if, vexed by repeated persecutions, the Jews permitted the past, the distant, and the future, to predominate over the present? . . .

But, according to your own acknowledgment, the Jews have not been debased. In point of courage, of moral worth, of intellectual power, of mental acquirements, they yield preference to none. They have been faithful subjects of the Crown; in the times of severe trial, at home or abroad, their loyalty has never wavered. On what ground, then, do you justify their exclusion from any privilege of a Protestant subject? Are they not so far entitled to our confidence that they may be qualified for a trust which they cannot exercise through good will of Christian constituencies?. . . .

It is for these reasons—because I believe it to be in conformity with the enlarged comprehension of the British Constitution that these disqualifications should no longer exist; because I rejoice in the opportunity of making reparation for the injuries and persecutions of former times; because I think the Jew has fairly earned the privileges which it is proposed to extend to him, by patience and forbearance, by tried fidelity and loyalty; but above all, because I am one of a Christian people, because I am a member of a Christian legislature, I will perform an act I believe to be in strict conformity with the spirits and precepts of the Christian religion. We are commended by that religion, as the condition of our own forgiveness, to forgive those who have trespassed against us. That duty is not in this case imposed upon us; but there is another duty, as sacred in point of moral obligation, and more trying to human pride, namely, that we should forgive those against whom we have trespassed. Sir, I shall give my cordial support to the bill before the House.

ON GRANTING AID TO PORTUGAL

George Canning
(1770-1827)

As a child Canning, who was reared by his wealthy uncle, had the advantage of associating with men like Burke, Sheridan, and Fox. Later, while at school at Eton and Oxford, he distinguished himself as a wit and orator of consequence. His contributions to the "Anti-Jacobin", a famous series of political satires, reflected his earlier ability. When, in 1794, he entered Parliament under the sponsorship of Pitt his brilliant wit again attracted attention. At this time he opposed parliamentary reform and peace with France but later aided Wilberforce in abolishing the slave trade. From 1807-1809 he was foreign secretary and again from 1822-27; when in 1827 he became Prime Minister, he asserted the universal right of self-government and opposed an invasion of Portugal by Spain in 1826. Under Canning's ministry Great Britain stood against the "Holy Alliance" of the despots of Europe and favored the American Monroe Doctrine; recognized the independence of the South American republics and aided in Catholic emancipation. In his capacity as Foreign Minister Canning advocated the policy toward South America which he described as "calling the new world into existence to adjust the balance of the old", a policy which later took shape in the Monroe Doctrine.

The speech included here *On Granting Aid to Portugal* was delivered in the House of Commons December, 1826, following an effort of the Portuguese who favored absolutism to overthrow the existing constitutional government in Portugal.

Among the alliances by which, at different periods of our history, this country has been connected with the other nations of Europe, none is so ancient in origin, and so precise in obligation—none has continued so long, and been observed so faithfully—of none is the memory so intimately interwoven with the most brilliant records of our triumphs, as that by which Great Britain is connected with Portugal. It dates back to distant centuries; it has survived an endless variety of fortunes. Anterior in existence to the accession of the House of Braganza to the throne of Portugal—it derived, however, fresh vigor from that event; and never from that epoch to the present hour, has the independent monarchy of Portugal ceased to be nurtured by the friendship of Great Britain. This alliance has never been seriously interrupted, but it has been renewed by repeated sanctions. It has been maintained under difficulties by which the fidelity of other alliances was shaken, and has been vindicated in fields of blood and of glory.

That the alliance with Portugal has been always unqualifiedly advantageous to this country—that is has not been sometimes inconvenient and sometimes burdensome—I am not bound nor prepared to maintain. But no British statesman, so far as I know, has ever suggested the expediency of shaking it off; and it is assuredly not in a moment of need that honor and what I may be allowed to call national sympathy would permit us to weigh, with an overscrupulous exactness, the amount of difficulties and dangers attendant upon its faithful and steadfast observance. What feelings of national honor would forbid, is forbidden alike by the plain dictates of national faith.

It is not at distant periods of history, and in bygone ages only, that the traces of the union between Great Britain and Portugal are to be found. In the last compact of modern Europe, the compact which forms the basis of its present international law—I mean the treaty of Vienna of 1815—this country, with its eyes open to the possible inconveniences of the connection, but with a memory awake to its past benefits, solemnly renewed the previously existing obligations of alliance and amity with Portugal.

In order to appreciate the force of this stipulation—recent in point of time, recent, also, in the sanction of Parliament—the House will, perhaps, allow me to explain shortly the circumstances in reference to which it was contracted. In the year 1807, when, upon the declaration of Bonaparte that the House of Braganza had ceased to reign, the King of Portugal, by the advice of Great Britain, was induced to set sail for the Brazils; almost at the very moment of his most faithful majesty's embarkation, a secret convention was signed between his majesty and the king of Portugal, stipulating that, in the event of his most faithful majesty's establishing the seat of his government in Brazil, Great Britain would never acknowledge any other dynasty than that of the House of Braganza on the throne of Portugal. That convention, I say, was contemporaneous with the migration to the Brazils—a step of great importance at the time, as removing from the grasp of Bonaparte the sovereign family of Braganza. Afterward, in the year 1810, when the seat of the king of Portugal's government was established at Rio de Janeiro, and when it seemed probable, in the then apparently hopeless condition of the affairs of Europe, that it was likely long to continue there, the secret convention of 1807, of which the main object was accomplished by the fact of the emigration to Brazil, was abrogated, and a new and public treaty was concluded, into which was transferred the stipulation of 1807, binding Great Britain, so long as his faithful majesty should be compelled to reside in Brazil, not to acknowledge any other sovereign of Portugal than a member of the House of Braganza. That stipulation, which had hitherto been secret, thus became patent, and part of the known law of nations.

In the year 1814, in consequence of the happy conclusion of the war, the option was afforded to the king of Portugal of returning to his European dominions. It was then felt that, as the necessity of his most faithful majesty's absence from Portugal had ceased, the ground for the obligation originally contracted in the secret convention of 1807, and afterward transferred to the patent treaty of 1810, was removed. The treaty of 1810 was, therefore, annulled at the Congress of Vienna; and in lieu of the stipulation not to acknowledge any other sovereign of Portugal than a member of the House of Braganza, was substituted that which I have just read to the House.

Annulling the treaty of 1810, the treaty of Vienna renews and confirms (as the House will have seen) all former treaties between Great Britain and Portugal, describing them as "ancient treaties of alliance, friendship, and guarantee"; as having "long and happily subsisted between the two Crowns"; and as being allowed, by the two high contracting parties, to remain "in full force and effect."

What, then, is the force—what is the effect of those ancient treaties? I am prepared to show to the House what it is. But before I do so, I must say, that if all the treaties to which this article of the treaty of Vienna refers, had perished by some convulsion of nature, or had by some extraordinary accident been consigned to total oblivion, still it would be impossible not to admit, as an incontestable inference from this article of the treaty of Vienna alone, that, in a moral point of view, there is incumbent on Great Britain a decided obligation to act as the effectual defender of Portugal. If I could not show the letter of a single antecedent stipulation, I should still contend that a solemn admission, only ten years old, of the existence at that time of "treaties of alliance, friendship, and guarantee," held Great Britain to the discharge of the obligations which that very description implies. But fortunately there is no such difficulty in specifying the nature of those obligations. All of the preceding treaties exist—all of them are of easy reference—all of them are known to this country, to Spain, to every nation of the civilized world.

This, sir, being the state, morally and politically, of our obligations toward Portugal, it is obvious that when Portugal, in apprehension of the coming storm, called on Great Britain for assistance, the only hesitation on our part could be, not whether that assistance was due, supposing the occasion for demanding it to arise, but simply whether that occasion—in other words, whether the *casus foederis*—had arisen.

The main question, however, is this: Was it obligatory upon us to comply with that requisition? In other words, had the *casus foederis* arisen? In our opinion it had. Bands of Portuguese rebels, armed, equipped, and trained in Spain, had crossed the Spanish frontier, carrying terror and devastation into their own country, and proclaiming sometimes the brother of the reigning sovereign of Portugal, sometimes a Spanish princess, and sometimes even Ferdinand of Spain, as the rightful occupant of the Portuguese throne. These rebels crossed the frontier, not at one point only, but at several points; for it is remarkable that the aggression, on which the original application to Great Britain for succor was founded, is not the aggression with reference to which that application has been complied with.

If a single company of Spanish soldiers had crossed the frontier in hostile array, there could not, it is presumed, be a doubt as to the character of that invasion. Shall bodies of men, armed, clothed, and regimented by Spain, carry fire and sword into the bosom of her unoffending neighbor, and shall it be pretended that no attack, no invasion has taken place, because forsooth, these outrages are committed against Portugal by men to whom Portugal had given birth and nurture? What petty quibbling would it be to say that an invasion of Portugal from Spain was not a Spanish invasion, because Spain did not employ her own troops, but hired mercenaries to effect her purpose? And what difference is it, except as an aggravation, that the mercenaries in this instance were natives of Portugal.

I have already stated, and now repeat, that it never has been the wish or the pretension of the British government to interfere in the internal concerns of the Portuguese nation. Questions of that kind the Portuguese nation must settle among themselves. But if we were to admit that hordes of traitorous refugees from Portugal, with Spanish arms, or arms furnished or restored to them by Spanish authorities, in their hands, might put off their country for one purpose, and put it on again for another— put it off for the purpose of attack, and put it on again for the purpose of impunity—if, I say, we were to admit this juggle, and either pretend to be deceived by it ourselves, or attempt to deceive Portugal, into a belief that there was nothing of external attack, nothing of foreign hostility, in such a system of aggression—such pretense and attempt would, perhaps, be only ridiculous and contemptible, if they did not require a much more serious character from being employed as an excuse for infidelity to ancient friendship, and as a pretext for getting rid of the positive stipulations of treaties.

This, then, is the case which I lay before the House of Commons. Here is, on the one hand, an undoubted pledge of national faith—not taken in a corner, not kept secret between the parties, but publicly recorded among the annals of history, in the face of the world. Here are, on the other hand, undeniable acts of foreign aggression, perpetrated, indeed, principally through the instrumentality of domestic traitors, but supported with foreign means, instigated by foreign councils, and directed to foreign ends. Putting these facts and this pledge together, it is impossible that his majesty should refuse the call that has been made upon him; nor can Parliament, I am convinced, refuse to enable his majesty to fulfil his undoubted obligations. I am willing to rest the whole question of tonight, and to call for the vote of the House of Commons upon this simple case, divested altogether of collateral circumstances; from which I especially wish to separate it, in the minds of those who hear me, and also in the minds of others, to whom what I now say will find its way. If I were to sit down this moment, without adding another word, I have no doubt but that I should have the concurrence of the House in the address which I mean to propose.

When I state this, it will be obvious to the House that the vote for which I am about to call upon them is a vote for the defense of Portugal, not a vote for war against Spain. I beg the House to keep these two points entirely distinct in their consideration. For the former I think I have said enough. If, in what I have now further to say, I should bear hard upon the Spanish government, I beg that it may be observed, that, unjustifiable as I shall show their conduct to have been—contrary to the law of nations, contrary to the law of good neighborhood, contrary, I might say, to the laws of God and man—with respect to Portugal, still I do not mean to preclude a *locus poenitentiae,* a possibility of redress and reparation. It is our duty to fly to the defense of Portugal, be the assailant who he may. And, be it remembered, that, in thus fulfilling the stipulation of ancient treaties, of the existence and obligation of which all the world are aware, we, according to the universally admitted construction of the law of nations, neither make war upon that assailant, nor give to that assailant, much less to any other power, just cause of war against ourselves.

Sir, I set out with saying that there were reasons which entirely satisfied my judgment that nothing short of a point of national faith or national honor would justify, at the present moment, any voluntary approximation to the possibility of war. Let me be understood, however, distinctly as not meaning to say that I dread war in a good cause (and in no other way may it be the lot of this country ever to engage!) from a distrust of the strength of the country to commence it, or of her resources to maintain it. I dread it, indeed—but upon far other grounds: I dread it from an apprehension of the tremendous consequences which might arise from any hostilities in which we might now be engaged.

Some years ago, in the discussion of the negotiations respecting the French war against Spain, I took the liberty of adverting to this topic. I then stated that the position of this country in the present state of the world was one of neutrality, not only between contending nations, but between conflicting principles; and that it was by neutrality alone that we could maintain that balance, the preservation of which I believe to be essential to the welfare of mankind. I then said that I feared that the next war which should be kindled in Europe would be a war not so much of armies as of opinions. Not four years have elapsed, and behold my apprehension realized! It is, to be sure, within narrow limits that this war of opinion is at present confined; but it is a war of opinion that Spain (whether as government or as nation) is now waging against Portugal; it is a war which has commenced in hatred of the new institutions of Portugal. How long is it reasonable to expect that Portugal will abstain from retaliation? If into that war this country shall be compelled to enter, we shall enter into it with a sincere and anxious desire to mitigate rather than exasperate—and to mingle only in the conflict of arms, not in the more fatal conflict of opinions.

The consequence of letting loose the passions at present chained and confined, would be to produce a scene of desolation which no man can contemplate without horror; and I should not sleep easy on my couch if I were conscious that I had contributed to precipitate it by a single moment.

This, then, is the reason—a reason very different from fear, the reverse of a consciousness of disability—why I dread the recurrence of hostilities in any part of Europe; why I would bear much, and would forbear long; why I would (as I have said) put up with almost anything that did not touch national faith and national honor, rather than let slip the furies of war, the leash of which we hold in our hands—not knowing whom they may reach, or how far their ravages may be carried. Such is the love of peace which the British government acknowledges; and such the necessity for peace which the circumstances of the world inculcate. I will push these topics no further.

I return, in conclusion, to the object of the address. Let us fly to the aid of Portugal, by whomsoever attacked, because it is our duty to do so; and let us cease our interference where the duty ends. We go to Portugal not to rule, not to dictate, not to prescribe constitutions, but to defend and to preserve the independence of an ally. We go to plant the standard of England on the well-known heights of Lisbon. Where that standard is planted, foreign dominion shall not come.

A PLEA FOR FREE SPEECH

Sir James Mackintosh

(1765-1832)

Although he was educated in medicine Sir James Mackintosh renounced that profession to study law and in 1895 was called to the bar where he soon attained high eminence as a forensic lawyer. In 1799 he delivered a series of very successful lectures at Lincoln's Inn, London, on the law of nature and of nations.

His defense of Peltier, who was charged with libel against Napoleon, was delivered before the Court of the King's Bench in 1803, and is termed Mackintosh's greatest performance. It was translated into French by Madame de Staël and broadcast over the entire Continent. The introduction to this address is presented here.

The time is now come for me to address you in behalf of the unfortunate gentleman who is the defendant on this record. The charge which I have to defend is surrounded with the most invidious topics of discussion; but they are not of my seeking. The case and the topics which are inseparable from it are brought here by the prosecutor. Here I find them, and here it is my duty to deal with them, as the interests of Mr. Peltier seem to me to require. He, by his choice and confidence, has cast on me a very arduous duty, which I could not decline, and which I can still less betray. He has a right to expect from me a faithful, a zealous, and a fearless defense; and this his just expectation, according to the measure of my humble abilities, shall be fulfilled. I have said a fearless defense. Perhaps that word was unnecessary in the place where I now stand. Intrepidity in the discharge of professional duty is so common a quality at the English bar, that it has, thank God, long ceased to be a matter of boast or praise. If it had been otherwise, gentlemen, if the bar could have been silenced or overawed by power, I may presume to say that an English jury would not this day have been met to administer justice. Perhaps I need scarce say that my defense shall be fearless, in a place where fear never entered any heart but that of a criminal. But you will pardon me for having said so much when you consider who the real parties before you are.

Gentlemen, the real prosecutor is the master of the greatest empire the civilized world ever saw. The defendant is a defenseless, proscribed exile. He is a French royalist, who fled from his country in the autumn of 1792, at the period of that memorable and awful emigration, when all the proprietors and magistrates of the greatest civilized country in Europe were driven from their homes by the daggers of assassins; when our shores were covered, as with the wreck of a great tempest, with old men, and women, and children, and ministers of religion, who fled from the ferocity of their countrymen as before an army of invading barbarians.

You will not think unfavorably of a man who stands before you as the voluntary victim of his loyalty and honor. If a revolution (which God avert) were to drive us into exile, and to cast us on a foreign shore, we should expect, at least, to be pardoned by generous men, for stubborn loyalty and unseasonable fidelity to the laws and government of our fathers.

This unfortunate gentleman had devoted a great part of his life to literature. It was the amusement and ornament of his better days. Since his own ruin and the desolation of his country, he has been compelled to employ it as a means of support. For the last ten years he has been engaged in a variety of publications of considerable importance; but since the peace he has desisted from serious political discussion, and confined himself to the obscure journal which is now before you; the least calculated, surely, of any publication that ever issued from the Press, to rouse the alarms of the most jealous government; which will not be read in England, because it is not written in our language; which can not be read in France, because its entry into that country is prohibited by a power whose mandates are not very supinely enforced, nor often evaded with impunity; which can have no other object than that of amusing the companions of the author's principles and misfortunes, by pleasantries and sarcasms on their victorious enemies. There is, indeed, gentlemen, one remarkable circumstance in this unfortunate publication; it is the only, or almost the only, journal which still dares to espouse the cause of that royal illustrious family which but fourteen years ago was flattered by every Press and guarded by every tribunal in Europe. Even the court in which we are met affords an example of the vicissitudes of their fortune. My learned friend has reminded you that the last prosecution tried in this place, at the instance of a French government, was for a libel on that magnanimous princess, who has since been butchered in sight of her palace.

There is another point of view in which this case seems to me to merit your most serious attention. I consider it as the first of a long series of conflicts between the greatest power in the world and the only free Press remaining in Europe. No man living is more thoroughly convinced than I am that my learned friend, Mr. Attorney-General, will never degrade his excellent character, that he will never disgrace his high magistracy by mean compliances, by an immoderate and unconscientious exercise of power; yet I am convinced, by circumstances which I shall now abstain from discussing, that I am to consider this as the first of a long series of conflicts between the greatest power in the world and the only free Press now remaining in Europe. Gentlemen, this distinction of the English Press is new; it is a proud and melancholy distinction. Before the great earthquake of the French Revolution had swallowed up all the asylums of free discussion on the continent, we enjoyed that privilege, indeed, more fully than others; but we did not enjoy it exclusively.

Unfortunately for the repose of mankind, great States are compelled by regard to their own safety, to consider the military spirit and martial habits of their people as one of the main objects of their policy. Frequent hostilities seem almost the necessary condition of their greatness; and, without being great, they can not long remain safe. Smaller States exempted from this cruel necessity—a hard condition of greatness, a bitter satire on human nature—devoted themselves to the arts of peace, to the cultivation of literature, and the improvement of reason. They became places of refuge for free and fearless discussion; they were the impartial spectators and judges of the various contests of ambition which from time to time disturbed the quiet of the world. They thus became peculiarly qualified to be the organs of that public opinion which converted Europe into a great republic, with laws which mitigated, tho they could not extinguish, ambition; and with moral tribunals to which even the most despotic sovereigns were amenable. If wars of aggrandizement were undertaken, their authors were arraigned in the face of Europe. If acts of internal tyranny were perpetrated, they resounded from a thousand presses throughout all civilized countries. Princes, on whose will there were no legal checks, thus found a moral restraint which the most powerful of them could not brave with absolute impunity. They acted before a vast audience, to whose applause or condemnation they could not be utterly indifferent. The very constitution of human nature, the unalterable laws of the mind of man, against which all rebellion is fruitless, subjected the proudest tyrants to this control. No elevation of power, no depravity however consummate, no innocence however spotless, can render man wholly independent of the praise or blame of his fellow men.

One asylum of free discussion is still inviolate. There is still one spot in Europe where men can freely exercise his reason on the most important concerns of society, where he can boldly publish his judgment on the acts of the proudest and most powerful tyrants. The Press of England is still free. It is guarded by the free Constitution of our forefathers. It is guarded by the heart and arms of Englishmen, and I trust I may venture to say that if it be to fall, it will fall only under the ruins of the British Empire.

It is an awful consideration, gentlemen. Every other monument of European liberty has perished. That ancient fabric which has been gradually reared by the wisdom and virtue of our fathers still stands. It stands, thanks be to God! solid and entire; but it stands alone, and it stands amid ruins.

In these extraordinary circumstances, I repeat that I must consider this as the first of a long series of conflicts between the greatest power in the world and the only free Press remaining in Europe. And I trust that you will consider yourselves as the advanced guard of liberty, as having this day to fight the first battle of free discussion against the most formidable enemy that it ever encountered.

THE ABOLITION OF SLAVERY [7]

Lord Brougham

(1778-1868)

A native of Edinburgh and a founder of the *Edinburgh Review,* Lord Brougham had chosen law as his profession and had won fame in that profession before he entered Parliament in 1810. It was in 1820 that he presented his defense of Queen Caroline, the injured spouse of George IV who was accused of indecorous conduct, which brought him great popularity. In 1828 he won his greatest triumph when he spoke for six hours on the question of law reform. Brougham's active career may be said to extend from the time of the revolutionary furor in France to the era of Gladstone and Disraeli, for he ended his public activities about 1848. Although his appearance was rather grotesque, Brougham's voice, which was full and powerful, and his oratorical skill aided him in becoming one of the greatest liberal orators of his day. Included here is his speech on *The Abolition of Slavery* which was delivered in the House of Lords in February, 1838.

I do not think, my lords, that ever but once before in the whole course of my public life have I risen to address either House of Parliament with the anxiety under which I labor at this moment.

I rush at once into the midst of this great argument—I drag before you once more, but I trust for the last time, the African slave trade, which I lately denounced here, and have so often elsewhere. On this we are all agreed. Whatever difference of opinion may exist on the question of slavery, on the slave traffic there can be none. I am now furnished with a precedent which may serve for an example to guide us. On slavery we have always held that the colonial legislature could not be trusted; that, to use Mr. Canning's expression, you must beware of allowing the masters of slaves to make laws upon slavery. But upon the detestable traffic in slaves I can show you the proceeding of a

[7] Abridged.

colonial assembly which we should ourselves do well to adopt after their example. These masters of slaves, not to be trusted on that subject, have acted well and wisely on this. The legislature of Jamaica, owners of slaves, and representing all other slave owners, feel that they also represent the poor negroes, themselves; and they approach the throne, expressing themselves thankful—tardily thankful, no doubt—that the traffic has been for thirty years put down in our own colonies, and beseeching the sovereign to consummate the great work by the only effectual means—of having it declared piracy by the law of nations, as it is robbery and piracy and murder by the law of God!

I knew that this abominable law of our evil nature was not confined to different races, contrasted hues, and strange features, but prevailed also between white man and white—for I never yet knew any one hate me but those whom I had served, and those who had done me some grievous injustice. Why then should I expect other feelings to burn within the planter's bosom, and govern his conduct toward the unhappy beings who had suffered so much and so long at his hands? But, on the part of the slaves, I was not without some anxiety when I considered the corrupting effects of that degrading system under which they had for ages groaned, and recognized the truth of the saying in the first and the earliest of profane poets, that "the day which makes a man a slave robs him of half of his value."

I might well think that the West Indian slave offered no exception to this maxim, that the habit of compulsory labor might have incapacitated him from voluntary exertion; that overmuch toil might have made all work his aversion; that never having been accustomed to provide for his own wants, while all his supplies were furnished by others, he might prove unwilling or unfit to work for himself, the ordinary inducements to industry never having operated on his mind.

Let us now see the results of their sudden though partial liberation, and how far those fears have been realized; for upon this must entirely depend the solution of the present question—whether or not it is safe now to complete the emancipation, which, if it only be safe, we have not the shadow of right any longer to withhold.

Well, then, let us see. The first of August came, the object of so much anxiety and so many predictions—that day so joyously expected by the poor slaves, as sorely dreaded by their hard taskmasters; and surely, if there ever was a picture interesting, ever fascinating, to look upon, if there ever was a passage in a people's history that redounded to their eternal honor, if ever triumphant answer was given to all the scandalous calumnies for ages heaped upon an oppressed race, as if to justify the wrongs done them—that picture, and that passage, and that answer were exhibited in the uniform history of that auspicious day all over the islands of the Western Sea. Instead of the horizon being lit up with the lurid fires of rebellion, kindled by a sense of natural though lawless revenge, and the just resistance to intolerable oppression, the whole of that widespread scene was mildly illuminated with joy, contentment, peace, and good will toward men.

No civilized nation, no people of the most refined character, could have displayed, after gaining a sudden and signal victory, more forbearance, more delicacy, in the enjoyment of their triumph, than these poor untutored slaves did upon the great consummation of all their wishes which they had just attained. Not a gesture or a look was seen to scare the eye; not a sound or a breath from the negro's lips was heard to grate on the ear of the planter. All was joy, congratulation, and hope. Everywhere were to be seen groups of these harmless folks assembled to talk over their good fortunes, to communicate their mutual feelings of happiness, to speculate on their future prospects. Finding that they were now free in name, they hoped soon to taste the reality of liberty. Feeling their fetters loosened, they looked forward to the day which would see them fall off, and the degrading marks which they left be effaced from their limbs.

But all this was accomplished with not a whisper that could give offense to the master by reminding him of the change. This delicate, calm, tranquil joy was alone to be marked on that day over all the chain of the Antilles. Amusements there were none to be seen on that day—not even their simple pastimes by which they had been wont to beguile the hard hours of bondage, and which reminded that innocent people of the happy land of their forefathers, whence they had been torn by the hands of Christian and civilized men. The day was kept sacred as the festival of their liberation, for the negroes are an eminently pious race. Every church was crowded from early dawn with devout and earnest worshipers. Five or six times in the course of that memorable Friday were all those churches filled and emptied in succession by multitudes who came, not to give mouth-worship or eye-worship, but to render humble and hearty thanks to God for their freedom at length bestowed. In countries where the bounty of nature provokes the passions, where the fuel of intemperance is scattered with a profuse hand, I speak the fact when I tell that not one negro was seen in a state of intoxication. Three hundred and forty thousand slaves in Jamaica were at once set free on that day, and the peaceful festivity of those simple men was disturbed only on a single estate, in one parish, by the irregular conduct of three or four persons, who were immediately kept in order, and tranquillity was in one hour restored.

But the termination of slavery was to be an end of all labor; no man would work unless compelled, much less would any one work for hire. The cartwhip was to resound no more, and no more could exertion be obtained from the indolent African. The prediction is found to have been ridiculously false; the negro peasantry is as industrious as our own, and wages furnish more effectual stimulus than the scourge.

Oh, but, said the men of colonial experience—the true practical men—this may do for some kinds of produce. Cotton may be planted, coffee may be picked, indigo may be manufactured—all these kinds of work the negro may probably be got to do; but at least the cane will cease to grow, the cane piece can no longer be hoed, nor the plant be hewn down, nor the juice boiled, and sugar will utterly cease out of the land.

Now let the man of experience stand forward,—the practical man, the inhabitant of the colonies,—I require that he now come forth with his prediction, and I meet him with the fact; let him but appear, and I answer for him, we shall hear him prophesy no more. Put to silence by the past, which even these confident men have not the courage to deny, they will at length abandon this untenable ground.

Twice as much sugar by the hour was found, on my noble friend's inquiry, to be made since the apprenticeship, as under the slave system, and of a far better quality; and one planter on a vast scale has said that with twenty free laborers he could do the work of a hundred slaves.

But linger not on the islands where the gift of freedom has been but half bestowed. Look at Antigua and Bermuda, where the wisdom and the virtue have been displayed of at once giving complete emancipation. To Montserrat the same appeal might have been made, but for the folly of the upper House, which threw out the bill passed in the Assembly by the representatives of the planters. But in Antigua and in Bermuda, where for the last three years and a half there has not even been an apprentice—where all have been made at once as free as the peasantry of this country—the produce has increased, not diminished, and increased notwithstanding the accidents of bad seasons, droughts, and fires.

Whether we look to the noble-minded colonies which have at once freed their slaves, or to those who will still retain them in a middle and half-free condition, I have shown that the industry of the negro is undeniable, and that it is constant and productive in proportion as he is the director of its application and the master of its recompense. But I have gone a great deal further—I have demonstrated, by a reference to the same experience, the same unquestioned facts, that a more quiet, peaceful, inoffensive, innocent race is not to be found on the face of this earth than the Africans, not while dwelling in their own happy country, and enjoying freedom in a natural state under their own palm-trees and by their native streams, but after they have been torn away from it, enslaved, and their nature perverted in your Christian land, barbarized by the policy of civilized states; their whole character disfigured, if it were possible to disfigure it; all their feelings corrupted, if you could have corrupted them. Every effort has been made to spoil the poor African, every source of wicked ingenuity exhausted to deprave his nature, all the incentives of misconduct placed around him by the fiend-like artifice of Christian civilized men, and his excellent nature has triumphed over all your arts; your unnatural culture has failed to make it bear the poisonous fruit that might well have been expected from such abominable husbandry, though enslaved and tormented, degraded and debased, as far as human industry could effect its purpose of making him bloodthirsty and savage, his gentle spirit has prevailed and preserved, in spite of all your prophecies, aye, and of all your efforts, unbroken tranquillity over the whole Caribbean chain!

My lords, I cannot better prove the absolute necessity of putting an immediate end to the state of apprenticeship than by showing what the victims of it are daily fated to endure. The punishments inflicted are of monstrous severity. The law is wickedly harsh; its execution is committed to hands that exasperate that cruelty. For the vague, undefined, undefinable offense of insolence, thirty-nine lashes; the same number for carrying a knife in the pocket; for cutting the shoot of a cane-plant, fifty lashes, or three months' imprisonment in that most loathsome of all dungeons, a West Indian jail.

There seems to have prevailed at all times among the lawgivers of the slave colonies a feeling of which I grieve to say those of the mother country have partaken: that there is something in the nature of a slave, something in the disposition of the African race, something in the habits of those hapless victims of our crimes our cruelties, and frauds, which requires a peculiar harshness of treatment from their rulers, and makes what in other men's cases we call justice and mercy cruelty to society, and injustice to the law in theirs, inducing us to visit with the extremity of rigor in the African what, if done by our own tribes, would be slightly visited, or not at all, as though there were in the negro nature something so obdurate that no punishment with which they can be punished would be too severe.

If some carpicious despot were, in the career of ordinary tyranny, to tax his pampered fancy to produce something more monstrous, more unnatural than himself; were he to graft the thorn upon the vine, or place the dove among vultures to be reared, much as we might marvel at this freak of a perverted appetite, we should marvel still more if we saw tyranny, even its own measure of proverbial unreasonableness, and complain because the grape was not gathered from the thorn, or because the dove so trained had a thirst for blood. Yet this is the unnatural caprice, this the injustice, the gross, the foul, the outrageous, the monstrous, the incredible injustice of which we are daily and hourly guilty toward the whole of the ill-fated African race.

My lords, we fill up the measure of this injustice by executing laws wickedly conceived, in a yet more atrocious spirit of cruelty. Our whole punishments smell of blood. Let the treadmill stop, from the weary limbs and exhausted frames of the sufferers no longer having the power to press it down the requisite number of turns in a minute, the lash instantly resounds through the mansion of woe! Let the stone spread out to be broken not crumble fast enough beneath the arms already scarred, flayed, and wealed by the whip, again the scourge tears afresh the half-healed flesh! . . .

I hasten to a close. There remains little to add. It is, my lords, with a view to prevent such enormities as I have feebly pictured before you, to correct the administration of justice, to secure the comforts of the negroes, to restrain the cruelty of the tormentors, to amend the discipline of the prisons, to arm the governors with local authority over the police; it is with those views that I have formed the first five of the resolutions now upon your table, intending they should take effect during the very short interval of a few months which must elapse before the sixth shall give complete liberty to the slave.

From the instant that glad sound is wafted across the ocean, what a blessed change begins; what an enchanting prospect unfolds itself! The African, placed on the same footing with other men, becomes in reality our fellow citizen—to our feelings, as well as in his own nature, our equal, our brother. No difference of origin or color can now prevail to keep the two castes apart. The negro, master of his own labor—only induced to lend his assistance if you make it his interest to help you, yet that aid being absolutely necessary to preserve your existence—becomes an essential portion of the community, nay, the very portion upon which the whole must lean for support.

So now the fulness of time is come for at length discharging our duty to the African captive. I have demonstrated to you that everything is ordered—every previous step taken—all safe, by experience shown to be safe, for the long-desired consummation. The time has come, the trial has been made, the hour is striking; you have no longer a pretext for hesitation, or faltering, or delay. The slave has shown, by four years' blameless behavior and devotion to the pursuits of peaceful industry, that he is as fit for his freedom as any English peasant, aye, or any lord whom I now address.

I demand his rights; I demand his liberty without stint. In the name of justice and of law, in the name of reason, in the name of God, who has given you no right to work injustice. I demand that your brother be no longer trampled upon as your slave! I make my appeal to the Commons, who represent the free people of England, and I require at their hands the performance of that condition for which they paid so enormous a price—that condition which all their constituents are in breathless anxiety to see fulfilled! I appeal to this House! Hereditary judges of the first tribunal in the world, to you I appeal for justice! Patrons of all the arts that humanize mankind, under your protection I place humanity herself! To the merciful sovereign of a free people, I call aloud for mercy to the hundreds of thousands for whom half a million of her Christian sisters have cried out; I ask their cry may not have risen in vain. But, first, I turn my eye to the Throne of all justice, and, devoutly humbling myself before Him who is of purer eyes than to behold such vast iniquities, I implore that the curse hovering over the head of the unjust and the oppressor be averted from us, that your hearts may be turned to mercy, and that over all the earth His will may at length be done!

THE ROTTEN BOROUGHS OF ENGLAND

John, Lord Russell

(1792-1878)

Lord Russell was educated at Westminster School and the Edinburgh University. Upon his entrance into Parliament as a Whig in 1813 he became an ardent advocate of parliamentary reform and was the principal author of the Reform Bill of 1830, which after an almost revolutionary fight, became a law in 1832. He also agitated for the repeal of the Corn Laws. From 1846 to 1852 Russell served as Prime Minister of England.

As an orator Russell was somewhat affected, but as a debater he was most effective, successful, and admirable. A fragment of the speech on *The Rotten Boroughs of England* delivered by Russell in 1831 to correct the prevailing corruption in the distribution of seats in Parliament shows his strength of purpose.

A stranger—who was told that this country was unparalleled in wealth and industry, and more civilized and enlightened than any country was before it, that it is a country which prides itself upon its freedom, and which once in seven years elects representatives from its population to act as the guardians and preservers of that freedom—would be anxious and curious to see how that representation is formed, and how the people choose their representatives.

Such a person would be very much astonished if he were to be taken to a ruined mound, and told that that mound sent two representatives to Parliament; if he were taken to a stone wall, and told that these niches in it sent two representatives to Parliament; if he were taken to a park, where no houses were to be seen, and told that that park sent two representatives to Parliament. But he would be still more astonished if he were to see large and opulent towns, full of enterprise and industry, and intelligence, containing vast magazines of every species of manufacture, and were then told that those towns sent no representatives to Parliament. Such a person would be still more astonished if he were taken to Liverpool, where there is a large constituency, and told, "Here you will have a fine example of a popular election." He would see bribery employed to the greatest extent, and in the most unblushing manner; he would see every voter receiving a number of guineas in a bag as the price of his corruption; and after such a spectacle he would be, no doubt, much astonished that a nation, whose representatives are thus chosen, could perform the functions of legislation at all, or enjoy respect in any degree.

REPEAL OF THE CORN LAWS

Richard Cobden

(1804-1865)

Cobden, the Apostle of Free Trade, began his agitation in 1838 in the Anti-Corn Association. He had a rare gift for popular oratory and a tremendous enthusiasm, so that he could be combined campaign manager, press bureau, and stump speaker. He was plain, simple, and direct in his appeal and his honesty of purpose and his sincere interest in the cause of the oppressed made him capable of moving his audiences to action.

On March 13, 1845, Cobden delivered before the House of Commons the most powerful speech of his career on the *Repeal of the Corn Laws*. At the close of the speech, Peel is said to have muttered "Those may answer him who can; I cannot do it." The following year Peel, himself, campaigned in the cause, and was instrumental in securing the repeal of the laws.

Sir, the object of this motion is to appoint a select committee to inquire into the present condition of the agricultural interests; and, at the same time, to ascertain how the laws regulating the importation of agricultural produce have affected the agriculturists of this country. As regards the distress among farmers, I presume we can not go to a higher authority than those honorable gentlemen who profess to be the farmers' friends and protectors. I find it stated by those honorable gentlemen who recently paid their respects to the prime minister, that the agriculturists are in a state of great embarassment and distress. I find that one gentleman from Norfolk (Mr. Hudson) stated that the farmers in the country are paying their rents, but paying them out of capital, and not profits. I find Mr. Turner of Upton, in Devonshire, stating that one-half of the smaller farmers in that county are insolvent, and that the others are rapidly falling into the same condition; that the farmers with larger holdings are quitting their farms with a view of saving the rest of their property; and that, unless some remedial measures be adopted by this House, they will be utterly ruined.

The accounts which I have given you of those districts are such as I have had from many other sources. I put it to the honorable gentlemen opposite, whether the condition of the farmers in Suffolk, Wiltshire, and Hampshire, is better than that which I have described in Norfolk and Devonshire? I put it to county members, whether— taking the whole of the south of England, from the confines of Nottinghamshire to the Land's End—whether, as a rule, the farmers are not now in a state of the greatest embarassment; There may be exceptions; but I put it to them whether, as a rule, that is not their condition in all parts?

The distress of the farmers being admitted, the next question which arises is, What is its cause? I feel a greater necessity to bring forward this motion for a committee of inquiry, because I find great discrepancies of opinion among honorable gentlemen opposite as to what is the cause of the distress among the farmers. In the first place there is a discrepancy as to the generality or locality of the existing distress. I find the right honorable baronet at the head of the government (Sir Robert Peel) saying that the distress is local; and he moreover says it does not arise from the legislation of this House. The honorable member for Dorsetshire declares, on the other hand, that the distress is general, and that it does not arise from legislation.

Now, there are these very different opinions on the other side of the House; but there are members upon this side representing very important interests, who think that farmers are suffering because they have this legislative protection. There is all this difference of opinion. Now, is not that a fit and proper subject for your inquiry? I am prepared to go into a select committee, and to bring forward evidence to show that the farmers are laboring under great evils—evils that I would connect with the legislation of this House, tho they are evils which appear to be altogether dissociated from it. The first great evil under which the farmer labors is the want of capital. No one can deny that. I do not mean at all to disparage the farmers. The farmers of this country are just the same race as the rest of us; and, if they were placed in a similar position, theirs would be as good a trade—I mean that they would be as successful men of business—as others; but it is notorious, as a rule, that the farmers of this country are deficient in capital; and I ask: How can any business be carried on successfully where there is a deficiency of capital?

I take it that honorable gentlemen opposite, acquainted with farming, would admit that £10 an acre, on an arable farm, would be a sufficient amount of capital for carrying on the business of farming successfully. I will take it, then, £10 an acre would be a fair capital for an arable farm. I have made many inquiries upon this subject in all parts of the kingdom, and I give it you as my decided conviction, that at this present moment farmers do not average £5 an acre capital on their farms. I speak of England, and I take England south of the Trent, though, of course, there are exceptions in every country; there are men of large capital in all parts—men farming their own land; but, taking it as a rule, I hesitate not to give my opinion—and I am prepared to back that opinion by witnesses before your committee—that, as a rule, farmers have not, upon an average, more than £5 an acre capital for their arable land. I have given you a tract of country to which I may add all Wales; probably 20,000,000 of acres of cultivable land. I have no doubt whatever that there are £100,000,000 of capital wanting upon that land. What is the meaning of farming capital? There are strange notions about the word "capital." It means more manure, a greater amount of labor, a greater number of cattle, and larger crops. Picture a country in which you can say there is a deficiency of one-half of all those blessings which ought to, and might, exist there, and then judge what the condition of laborers wanting employment and food is.

But you will say, capital would be invested if it could be done with profit. I admit it; that is the question I want you to inquire into. How is it that in a country where there is a plethora of capital, where every other business and pursuit is overflowing with money, where you have men going to France for railways and to Pennsylvania for bonds, embarking in schemes for connecting the Atlantic with the Pacific by canals, railways in the valley of the Mississippi, and sending their money to the bottom of the Mexican mines; while you have a country rich and overflowing, ready to take investments in every corner of the globe, how is it, I say, that this capital does not find its employment in the most attractive of all forms—upon the soil of this country? The cause is notorious—it is admitted by your highest authorities; the reason is, there is not security for capital in land. Capital shrinks instinctively from insecurity of tenure; and you have not in England that security which would warrant men of capital investing their money in the soil.

Now, is it not a matter worthy of consideration, how far this insecurity of tenure is bound up with that protection system of which you are so enamored? Suppose it can be shown that there is a vicious circle; that you have made politics of Corn Laws, and that you want voters to maintain them; that you very erroneously think that the Corn Laws are your great mine of wealth, and, therefore, you must have a dependent tenantry, that you may have their votes at elections to maintain this law in Parliament. Well, if you will have dependent voters, you cannot have men of spirit and capital. Then your policy reacts upon you. If you have not men of skill and capital, you cannot have improvements and employment for your laborers. Then comes around that vicious termination of the circle—you have pauperism, poor-rates, county-rates, and all other evils of which you are now speaking and complaining.

Now, sir, not only does the want of security prevent capital flowing into the farming business, but it actually deters from the improvement of the land those who are already in the occupation of it. There are many men, tenants of your land, who could improve their farms if they had a sufficient security, and they have either capital themselves or their friends could supply it; but with the absence of leases, and the want of security, you are actually deterring them from laying out their money on your land. They keep everything the same from year to year. You know that it is impossible to farm your estates properly unless a tenant has an investment for more than one year. A man ought to be able to begin a farm with at least eight years before him, before he expects to see a return for the whole of the outlay of his money. You are, therefore, keeping your tenants-at-will at a yearly kind of cultivation, and you are preventing them carrying on their businesses in a proper way. Not only do you prevent the laying out of capital upon your land, and disable the farmers from cultivating it, but your policy tends to make them servile and dependent; so that they are actually disinclined to improvement, afraid to let you see that they can improve, because they are apprehensive that you will pounce upon them for an increase of rent.

Now, I do not know why we should not in this country have leases for land upon similar terms to the leases of manufactories, or any "plant" or premises. I do not think that farming will ever be carried on as it ought to be until you have leases drawn up in the same way as a man takes a manufactory, and pays perhaps a thousand pounds a year for it. I know people who pay four thousand pounds a year for manufactories to carry on their business, and at fair rents. There is an honorable gentleman near me who pays more than four thousand pounds a year for the rent of his manufactory. What covenants do you think he has in his lease? What would he think if it stated how many revolutions there should be in a minute of the spindles, or if they prescribed the construction of the straps or the gearing of the machinery? Why, he takes his manufactory with a schedule of its present state—bricks, mortar, and machinery—and when the lease is over, he must leave it in the same state, or else pay a compensation for the dilapidation. (The chancellor of the exchequer: "Hear, hear!")

The right honorable gentleman, the chancellor of the exchequer, cheers that statement. I want to ask his opinion respecting a similar lease for a farm. I am rather disposed to think that the Anti-Corn-Law Leaguers will very likely form a joint-stock association, having none but free-traders in the body, that we may purchase an estate and have a model farm; taking care that it shall be in one of the rural counties, one of the most purely agricultural parts of the country, where we think there is the greatest need of improvement—perhaps in Buckingham-shire—and there shall be a model farm, homestead, and cottages; and I may tell the noble lord, the member for Newark, that we shall have a model garden, and he will not make any boast about it. But the great object will be to have a model lease. We will have as the farmer a man of intelligence and capital.

I am not so unreasonable as to tell you that you ought to let your land to men who have not a competent capital, or are not sufficiently intelligent; but I say, select such a man as that, let him know his business and have a sufficient capital, and you can not give him too wide a scope. We will find such a man, and will let him our farm; there shall be a lease precisely such as that upon which my honorable friend takes his factory. There shall be no clause inserted in it to dictate to him how he shall cultivate his farm; he shall do what he likes with the old pasture. If he can make more by plowing it up he shall do so; if he can grow white crops every year—which I know there are people doing at this moment in more places than one in this country—or if he can make any other improvement or discovery, he shall be free to do so. We will let him the land, with a schedule of the state of tillage and the condition of the homestead, and all we will bind him to will be this: "You shall leave the land as good as when you entered upon it. If it be in an inferior state it shall be valued again, and you shall compensate us; but if it be in an improved state it shall be valued, and we, the landlords, will compensate you." We will give possession of everything upon the land, whether it be wild or tame animals; he shall have the absolute control.

Take as stringent precautions as you please to compel the punctual payment of the rent; take the right of reentry as summarily as you like if the rent be not duly paid, but let the payment of rent duly be the sole test as to the well-doing of the tenant; and so long as he can pay the rent, and do it promptly, that is the only criterion you need have that the farmer is doing well; and if he is a man of capital, you have the strongest possible security that he will not waste your property while he has possession of it.

Now, sir, I do not stop to connect the cause and effect in this matter, and inquire whether your Corn Laws or your protective system have caused the want of leases and capital. I do not stop to make good my proof, and for this reason, that you have adopted a system of legislation in this House by which you profess to make the farming trade prosperous. I show you, after thirty years' trial, what is the depressed condition of the agriculturists; I prove to you what is the impoverished state of farmers, and also of laborers, and you will not contest any one of those propositions. I say it is enough, having had thirty years' trial of your specific with no better results than these, for me to ask you to go into committee to see if something better can not be devised. I am going to contend that free trade in grain would be more advantageous to farmers—and with them I include laborers—than restriction; to oblige the honorable member for Norfolk, I will take with them also the landlords; and I contend that free trade in corn and grain of every kind would be more beneficial to them than to any other class of the community. I should have contended the same before the passing of the late tariff, but now I am prepared to do so with tenfold more force. . . .

You admit that the farmer's capital is sinking from under him, and that he is in a worse state than ever. Have you distinctly provided some plan to give confidence to the farmer, to cause an influx of capital to be expended upon his land, and so bring increased employment to the laborer? How is this to be met? I can not believe you are going to make this a political game. You must set up some specific object to benefit the agricultural interest. It is well said that the last election was an agricultural triumph. There are two hundred county members sitting behind the prime minister who prove that it was so.

What, then, is your plan for this distressing state of things? That is what I want to ask you. Do not, as you have done before, quarrel with me because I have imperfectly stated my case; I have done my best, and I again ask you what you have to propose? I tell you that this "Protection," as it has been called, is a failure. It was so when you had the prohibition up to 80 s. You know the state of your farming tenantry in 1821. It was a failure when you had a protection price of 60 s., for you know what was the condition of your farm tenantry in 1835. It is a failure now with your last amendment, for you have admitted and proclaimed it to us; and what is the condition of your agricultural population at this time?

I ask, what is your plan? I hope it is not a pretense—a mere political game that has been played throughout the last election, and that you have not all come up here as mere politicians. There are politicians in the House—men who look with an ambition—probably a justifiable one—to the honors of office. There may be men who—with thirty years of continuous service, having been pressed into a groove from which they can neither escape nor retreat—may be holding office, high office, maintained there probably at the expense of their present convictions which do not harmonize very well with their early opinions. I make allowances for them; but the great body of the honorable gentlemen opposite came up to this House, not as politicians, but as the farmers' friends, and protectors of the agricultural interests. Well, what do you propose to do? You have heard the prime minister declare that, if he could restore all the protection which you have had, that protection would not benefit agriculturists. Is that your belief? If so, why not proclaim it? And if it is not your conviction, you will have falsified your mission in this House by following the right honorable baronet out into the lobby, and opposing inquiry into the condition of the very men who sent you here.

With mere politicians I have no right to expect to succeed in this motion. But I have no hesitation in telling you that, if you give me a committee of this House, I will explode the delusion of agricultural protection! I will bring forward such a mass of evidence, and give you such a preponderance of talent and of authority, that when the blue book is published and sent forth to the world, as we can now send it, by our vehicles of information, your system of protection shall not live in public opinion for two years afterward. Politicians do not want that. The cry of protection has been a very convenient handle for politicians. The cry of protection carried the counties at the last election, and politicians gained honors, emoluments, and place by it. But is that old tattered flag of protection, tarnished and torn as it is already, to be kept hoisted still in the counties for the benefit of politicians; or will you come forward honestly and fairly to inquire into this question? I can not believe that the gentry of England will be made mere drumheads to be sounded upon by a prime minister to give forth unmeaning and empty sounds, and to have no articulate voice of their own. No! You are the gentry of England who represent the counties. You are the aristocracy of England. Your fathers led our fathers; you may lead us if you will go the right way. But, altho you have retained your influence with this country longer than any other aristocracy, it has not been by opposing popular opinion, or by setting yourselves against the spirit of the age.

In other days, when the battle and the hunting-fields were the tests of manly vigor, your fathers were first and foremost there. The aristocracy of England were not like the noblesse of France, the mere minions of a court; nor were they like the hidalgos of Madrid, who dwindled into pigmies. You have been Englishmen. You have not shown a want of courage and firmness when any call has been made upon you. This is a new era. It is the age of improvement; it is the age of social advancement, not the age for war or for feudal sports. You live in a mercantile age, when the whole wealth of the world is poured into your lap. You can not have the advantages of commercial rents and feudal privileges; but you may be what you always have been, if you will identify yourselves with the spirit of the age. The English people look to the gentry and aristocracy of their country as their leaders. I, who am not one of you, have no hesitation in telling you that there is a deep-rooted, and hereditary prejudice, if I may so call it, in your favor in this country. But you never got it, and you will not keep it, by obstructing the spirit of the age. If you are indifferent to enlightened means of finding employment to your own peasantry; if you are found obstructing that advance which is calculated to knit nations more together in the bonds of peace by means of commercial intercourse; if you are found fighting against the discoveries which have almost given breath and life to material nature, and setting up yourselves as obstructives of that which destiny has decreed shall go on—why, then, you will be the gentry of England no longer, and others will be found to take your place.

And I have no hesitation in saying that you stand just now in a very critical position. There is a wide-spread suspicion that you have been tampering with the best feelings and with the honest confidence of your constituents in this cause. Everywhere you are doubted and suspected. Read your own organs, and you will see that this is the case. Well, then, this is the time to show that you are not the mere party politicians which you are said to be. I have said that we shall be opposed in this measure by politicians; they do not want inquiry. But I ask you to go into this committee with me. I will give you a majority of county members. You shall have a majority of the Central Society in that committee. I ask you only to go into a fair inquiry as to the causes of the distress of your own population. I only ask that this matter may be fairly examined. Whether you establish my principle or yours, good will come out of the inquiry; and I do, therefore, beg and entreat the honorable independent country gentlemen of this House that they will not refuse, on this occasion, to go into a fair, a full, and an impartial inquiry.

ON PEACE

John Bright

(1811-1889)

John Bright was the son of a Quaker cotton spinner, and the influence of this environment affected him deeply in his work for the peaceful extension of industrial helpfulness and cooperation throughout the world. He was preeminently a business man, but in 1835 became prominent in the educational movement and later in 1841 in the political agitation over the Corn Laws. In 1843 he was elected to Parliament and cast his influence there into the movement for Corn Law repeal. Bright was also active in peace movements and in his speeches stressed arbitration as a substitute for war. He always defended the American institutions and sympathized with the Union in the American Civil War. He dissented with Gladstone on the Irish Home Rule question and labored for the extension of the franchise. Bright's oratory is lucid yet forcible. He was a logical and forceful speaker and rarely used satire, but when he did it was stinging. His own life of unselfish service made him convincing in his public speeches. The speech *On Peace* included here was made at the Conference of the Peace Society on the occasion of threat of war with Russia.

What is war? I believe that half the people that talk about war have not the slightest idea what it is. In a short sentence it may be summed up to be the combination and concentration of all the horrors, atrocities, crimes, and sufferings of which human nature on this globe is capable. But what is even a rumor of war? Is there anybody here who has anything in the funds, or who is the owner of any railway stock, or anybody who has a large stock of raw material or manufactured goods? The funds have recently gone down ten per cent. I do not say that the fall is all on account of this danger of war; but a great proportion of it undoubtedly is. A fall of ten per cent in the funds is nearly eighty million pounds sterling of value, and railway stock having gone down twenty per cent makes a difference of sixty million pounds in the value of the railway property of this country. Add the two—one hundred and forty million pounds—and take the diminished prosperity and value of manufactures of all kinds during the last few months, and you will understand the actual loss to the country now if you put it down at two hundred million pounds sterling. But that is merely a rumor of war. That is war a long way off—the small cloud no bigger than a man's hand; what will it be if it comes nearer and becomes a fact? And surely sane men ought to consider whether the case is a good one, the ground fair, the necessity clear, before they drag a nation of nearly thirty millions of people into a long and bloody struggle for a decrepit and tottering Empire which all the nations in Europe cannot long sustain. And, mind, war now would take a different aspect from what it did formerly. It is not only that you send out men who submit to be slaughtered, and that you pay a large amount of taxes—the amount of taxes would be but a feeble indication of what you would suffer. Our trade is now much more extensive than it was; our commerce is more expanded, our undertakings are more vast, and war will find you all out at home by withering up the resources of the prosperity enjoyed by the middle and working classes of the country. You would find out that war in 1853 would be infinitely more perilous and destructive to our country than it has ever yet been at any former period of our history. There is another question which comes home to my mind with a gravity and seriousness which I can scarcely hope to communicate to you. You who lived during the period from 1815 to 1822 may remember that this country was probably never in a more uneasy position. The sufferings of the working classes were beyond description; and the difficulties, and struggles, and bankruptcies of the middle classes were such as few persons have a just idea of. There was scarcely a year in which there was not an incipient insurrection in some parts of the country, arising from the sufferings which the working classes endured. You know very well that the Government of the day employed spies to create plots and to get ignorant men to combine to take unlawful oaths; and you know that, in the town of Sterling, two men who, but for this diabolical agency, might have lived good and honest citizens, paid the penalty of their lives for their connection with unlawful combinations of this kind.

Well, if you go into war now you will have more banners to decorate your cathedrals and churches. Englishmen will fight now as well as they ever did, and there is ample power to back them, if the country can be but sufficiently excited and deluded. You may raise up great generals. You may have another Wellington, and another Nelson too; for this country can grow men capable for every enterprise. Then there may be titles, and pensions, and marble monuments to eternize the men who have thus become great; but what becomes of you, and your children? For there is more than this in store. That seven years to which I have referred was a period dangerous to the existence of government in this country, for the whole substratum, the whole foundation of society were disconnected, suffering intolerable evils, and hostile in the bitterest degree to the institutions and the Government of the country.

Precisely the same things will come again. Rely on it that injustice of any kind, be it bad laws, or be it bloody, unjust, and unnecessary war, of necessity creates perils to every institution in the country. If the Corn-Law had continued, if it had been impossible, by peaceful agitation, to abolish it, the monarchy itself would not have survived the ruin and disaster that it must have wrought. And if you go into a war now, with a doubled population, with a vast commerce, with extended credit, and a wider diffusion of partial education among the people, let there ever come a time like the period between 1815 and 1822, when the whole basis of society is upheaving with a sense of intolerable suffering—I ask you how many years' purchase would you give even for the venerable and mild monarchy under which you have the happiness to live? I confess, when I think of the tremendous perils into which unthinking men—men who do not intend to fight themselves—are willing to drag or to hurry this country, I am amazed how they can trifle with interests so vast and consequences so much beyond their calculation.

But, speaking here in Edinburgh to such an audience—an audience probably for its numbers as intelligent and as influential as ever was assembled within the walls of any hall in this kingdom—I think I may put before you higher considerations even than those of property and the institutions of your country. I may remind you of duties more solemn, and of obligations more imperative. You profess to be a Christian nation. You make it your boast even—though boasting is somewhat out of place in such questions—you make it your boast that you are a Protestant people, and that you draw your rule of doctrine and practice, as from a well pure and undefiled, from the living oracles of God, and from the direct revelation of the Omnipotent. You have even conceived the magnificent project of illuminating the whole earth, even to its remotest and darkest recesses, by the dissemination of the volume of the New Testament, in whose every page are written forever the words of peace. Within the limits of this island alone, on every Sabbath, twenty thousand, yes, far more than twenty thousand temples are thrown open, in which devout men and women assemble that they may worship Him who is the "Prince of Peace."

Is this a reality? Or is your Christianity a romance? is your profession a dream? No, I am sure that your Christianity is not a romance, and I am equally sure that your profession is not a dream. It is because I believe this that I appeal to you with confidence, and that I have hope and faith in the future. I believe that we shall see, and at no very distant time, sound economic principles spreading much more widely amongst the people; a sense of justice growing up in a soil which hitherto has been deemed unfruitful; and, which will be better than all, the churches of the United Kingdom, the churches of Britain, awaking, as it were, from their slumbers, and girding up their loins to more glorious work, when they shall not only accept and believe in the prophecy, but labor earnestly for its fulfilment, that there shall come a time—a blessed time, a time which shall last forever—when "nation shall not lift up sword against nation, neither shall they learn war any more."

WARFARE AND COLONIZATION

William Gladstone

(1809-1898)

William Gladstone ranks foremost among the great orators of his century. As a student at Eton and Christ College, Oxford, Gladstone was distinguished for his prowess in oratory and debate; he was the leader of the Oxford Debating Union and in that society delivered a powerful oration against the Reform Bill of 1831. In 1832 Gladstone entered Parliament under Sir Robert Peel as a staunch Whig and maintained a seat in that body continuously, with the exception of a year and a half, from 1832 to 1895. He served as President of the Board of Trade in 1843; as Colonial Secretary in 1846; as Chancellor of the Exchequer in 1852, 1855, and 1859; and in 1868 became Prime Minister alternating terms with his great rival, Disraeli, subsequently until 1894.

Gladstone's career as Premier of England has been unparalleled. It was as a reformer in finance and as a defender of the liberty of all classes of the English people that Gladstone exerted his greatest eloquence. Free trade, equal taxation, popular education, manhood suffrage were the causes he agitated. He also supported the persecuted Bulgarians and Armenians in the Ottoman Wars. His Irish Home Rule bill, however, in spite of the great speech with which he introduced it, was ill received in his day. His public addresses and debates in Parliament grew to be such an integral part of that organization that when he died its members said that the House of Commons no longer seemed the same.

The charm and grace which marked Gladstone's youth were supplanted by dignity and grandeur in his old age. His voice never lost completely its vibrating quality, and his fluency of speech, although verbose at times, never tired his hearers. He richly adorned his speeches with the profundity of his classical knowledge, yet maintained the power of popular conviction. Undoubtedly Gladstone ranks as England's great orator of the 19th century, for he made more speeches and better ones on a greater variety of subjects than any Englishman of his generation. His speech on *Warfare and Colonization* illustrates not only the style of his eloquence but the principles for which he stood throughout his lifetime. Considered the most representative of his speeches, it was delivered at Glasgow November 1, 1865, on the presentation of the freedom of that city to Mr. Gladstone.

It is quite unnecessary before this audience—I may venture to say it is unnecessary before any audience of my countrymen—to dwell at this period of our experience upon the material benefits that have resulted from free trade, upon the enormous augmentation of national power which it has produced, or even upon the increased concord which it has tended so strongly to promote throughout the various sections of the community. But it is the characteristic of the system which we so denominate, that while it comes forward with homely pretensions, and professes, in the first instance, to address itself mainly to questions of material and financial interests, yet, in point of fact, it is fraught and charged throughout with immense masses of moral, social, and political results. I will not now speak of the very large measure of those results which are domestic, but I would ask you to consider with me for a few moments the effect of the system of unrestricted intercourse upon the happiness of the human family at large.

Now, as far as that happiness is connected with the movements of nations, war has been its great implement. And what have been the great causes of wars? They do not come upon the world by an inevitable necessity, or through a providential visitation. They are not to be compared with pestilences and famines even—in that respect, though, we have learned, and justly learned, that much of what we have been accustomed to call providential visitation is owing to our neglect of the wise and prudent means which man ought to find in the just exercise of his faculties for the avoidance of calamity—but with respect to wars, they are the direct and universal consequence of the unrestricted, too commonly of the unbridled, passions and lusts of men.

If we go back to a very early period of society, we find a state of things in which, as between one individual and another, no law obtained; a state of things in which the first idea almost of those who desired to better their condition was simply to better it by the abstraction of their neighbor's property. In the early periods of society, piracy and unrestrained freebooting among individuals were what wars, for the most part, have been in the more advanced periods of human history. Why, what is the case with a war? It is a case in which both cannot be right, but in which both may be wrong. I believe if the impartiality of the historian survey a very large proportion of the wars that have desolated the world—some, indeed, there may be, and undoubtedly there have been, in which the arm of valor has been raised simply for the cause of freedom and justice—that the most of them will be found to belong to that less satisfactory category in which folly, passion, greediness, on both sides, have led to effects which afterwards, when too late, have been so much deplored.

We have had in the history of the world religious wars. The period of these wars I trust we have now outlived. I am not at all sure that there was not quite as much to be said for them as for a great many other wars which have been recorded in the page of history. The same folly which led to the one led, in another form, to the other. We have had dynastic wars—wars of succession, in which, for long periods of years, the heads of rival families have fought over the bleeding persons of their people, to determine who should govern them. I trust we have overlived the period of wars of that class. Another class of wars, of a more dangerous and yet a more extensive description, have been territorial wars. No doubt it is a very natural, though it is a very dangerous and a very culpable sentiment, which leads nations to desire their neighbors' property, and I am very sorry to think that we have had examples—perhaps we have an example even at this moment before our eyes—to show that even in the most civilized parts of the world, even in the midst of the oldest civilization upon the continent of Europe, that thirst for territorial acquisition is not yet extinct.

But I wish to call your attention to a peculiar form in which, during the latter part of human history, this thirst for territorial acquisition became an extensive cause of bloodshed. It was when the colonizing power took possession of the European nations. It seems that the world was not wide enough for them. One would have thought, upon looking over the broad places of the earth, and thinking how small a portion of them is even now profitably occupied, and how much smaller a portion of them a century or two centuries ago, one would have thought there would have been ample space for all to go and help themselves; but, notwithstanding this, we found it necessary, in the business of planting colonies, to make those colonies the cause of bloody conflicts with our neighbors; and there was at the bottom of that policy this old lust of territorial aggrandizement. When the state of things in Europe had become so far settled that that lust could not be as freely indulged as it might in barbarous times, we then carried our armaments and our passions across the Atlantic, and we fought upon American and other distant soils for the extension of our territory.

That was one of the most dangerous and plausible, in my opinion, of all human errors; it was one to which a great portion of the wars of the last century was due; but had our forefathers then known, as we now know, the blessings of free commercial intercourse, all that bloodshed would have been spared. For what was the dominant idea that governed that policy? It was this, that colonizing, indeed, was a great function of European nations, but the purpose of that colonization was to reap the profits of extensive trade with the colonies which were founded, and, consequently, it was not the error of one nation or another—it was the error of all nations alike. It was the error of Spain in Mexico, it was the error of Portugal in Brazil, it was the error of France in Canada and Louisiana, it was the error of England in her colonies in the West Indies, and her possessions in the East; and the whole idea of colonization, all the benefits of colonization, were summed up in this, that when you had planted a colony on the other side of the ocean, you were to allow that colony to trade exclusively and solely with yourselves. But from that doctrine flowed immediately all those miserable wars, because if people believed, as they then believed, that the trade with colonies must, in order to be beneficial, necessarily be exclusive, it followed that at once there arose in the mind of each country a desire to be possessed of the colonies of other countries, in order to secure the extension of this exclusive trade.

In fact, my Lord Provost, I may say, such was the perversity of the misguided ingenuity of man, that during the period to which I refer he made commerce itself, which ought to be the bond and link of the human race, the cause of war and bloodshed, and wars were justified both here and elsewhere—justified when they were begun, and gloried in when they had ended—upon the ground that their object and effect had been to obtain from some other nation a colony which previously had been theirs, but which now was ours, and which, in our folly, we regarded as the sole means of extending the intercourse and the industry of our countrymen. Well, now, my Lord Provost, that was a most dangerous form of error, and for a very reason that it seemed to abandon the old doctrine of the unrestricted devastation of the world, and to contemplate a peaceful end; but I am thankful to say that we have entirely escaped from that delusion. It may be that we do not wisely when we boast ourselves over our fathers. The probability is that as their errors crept in unperceived upon them, they did not know their full responsibility; so other errors in directions as yet undetected may be creeping upon us. Modesty bids us in our comparison, whether with other ages or with other countries, to be thankful—at least, we ought to be—for the downfall of every form of error; and determined we ought to be that nothing shall be done by us to give countenance to its revival, but that we will endeavor to assist those less fortunate than ourselves in emancipating themselves from the like delusions. I need not say that as respects our colonies, they have ceased to be—I would almost venture to say a possible—at any rate, they have ceased to be a probable cause of war, for now we believe that the greatness of our country is best promoted in its relations with our colonies by allowing them freely and largely to enjoy every privilege that we possess ourselves; and so far from grudging it, if we find that there are plenty of American ships trading with Calcutta, we rejoice in it! because it contributes to the wealth and prosperity of our Indian empire, and we are perfectly assured that the more that wealth and prosperity are promoted, the larger will be the share of it accruing to ourselves through the legitimate operation of the principles of trade.

THE DANGERS OF DEMOCRACY

Benjamin Disraeli

(1804-1881)

Disraeli, born in London of Jewish parentage, succeeded in conquering the English aristocracy; was elected to Parliament in 1837; was Chancellor of the Exchequer in 1852, 1858, 1859 and 1866; and Prime Minister in 1868 and again in 1874-1880. In 1876 he achieved an earldom and in 1878 represented England in the Congress of Berlin.

Disraeli was in everything the opposite of his great adversary, William Gladstone. Where Gladstone was vigorous, Disraeli was sarcastic; where Gladstone was eloquent, Disraeli was analytical; Gladstone refused the peerage, Disraeli contrived for an earldom. Disraeli was an imperialist; Gladstone was called "the Great Commoner."

Disraeli's maiden speech in Parliament was a failure in delivery and was greeted with jibes and jeers; whereat Disraeli remarked, "I shall sit down, now, but the time will come when you will hear me." Thereafter he studied for a conversational effect in his speeches which aimed to convince rather than to persuade. He became the master of stinging invective and sarcasm, lightened somewhat by a pointed wit. In his style he set the pattern for future parliamentary address which was an unemotional presentation of matter entirely subordinated to manner. Staid simplicity in delivery became the fashion of parliamentary speech as introduced by Disraeli.

Included here is an address delivered by Disraeli in 1864 on the question of suffrage. Gladstone suggested the bill while Disraeli in this speech on *The Dangers of Democracy* presented his reasons for opposing it. Later, in 1867, when Disraeli realized the seriousness of the situation, he changed his politics and supported a suffrage reform bill granting the right of the vote as Gladstone had originally desired it.

That tremendous reckless opposition to the right honorable gentleman, which allowed the bill to be read the second time, seems to have laid the Government prostrate. If he had succeeded in throwing out the bill, the right honorable gentleman and his friends would have been relieved from great embarrassment. But the bill, having been read a second time, the Government were quite overcome, and it appears they never have recovered from the paralysis up to this time. The right honorable gentleman was good enough to say that the proposition of his Government was rather coldly received upon his side of the House, but he said "nobody spoke against it." Nobody spoke against the bill on this side, but I remember some most remarkable speeches from the right honorable gentleman's friends. There was the great city of Edinburgh, represented by acute eloquence of which we never weary, and which again upon the present occasion we have heard; there was the great city of Bristol, represented on that occasion among the opponents, and many other constituencies of equal importance.

But the most remarkable speech, which "killed cock robin," was absolutely delivered by one who might be described as almost a member of the Government—the chairman of ways and means (Mr. Massey,) who I believe, spoke from immediately behind the Prime Minister. Did the Government express any disapprobation of such conduct? They have promoted him to a great post, and have sent him to India with an income of fabulous amount. And now they are astonished they cannot carry a Reform Bill. If they removed all those among their supporters who oppose such bills by preferring them to posts of great confidence and great lucre, how can they suppose that they will ever carry one? Looking at the policy of the Government, I am not at all astonished at the speech which the right honorable gentleman, the Secretary of State, has made this evening. Of which speech I may observe, that although it was remarkable for many things, yet there were two conclusions at which the right honorable gentleman arrived. First, the repudiation of the rights of man, and next, the repudiation of the £6 franchise. The first is a great relief; and—remembering what the feeling of the House was only a year ago, when, by the dangerous but fascinating eloquence of the Chancellor of the Exchequer, we were led to believe that the days of Tom Paine had returned, and that Rousseau was to be rivaled by a new social contract—it must be a great relief to every respectable man here to find that not only are we not to have the rights of man, but we are not even to have the 1862 franchise. . . .

But I think it is possible to increase the electoral body of the country by the introduction of voters upon principles in unison with the principles of the constitution, so that the suffrage should remain a privilege, and not a right—a privilege to be gained by virtue, by intelligence, by industry, by integrity, and to be exercised for the common good of the country. I think if you quit that ground; if you once admit that every man has a right to vote whom you cannot prove to be disqualified; you would change the character of the constitution, and you would change it in a manner which will tend to lower the importance of this country. Between the scheme we brought forward, and the measure brought forward by the honorable member of Leeds, and the inevitable conclusion which its principal supporters acknowledge it must lead to, it is a question between an aristocratic government in the proper sense of the term—that is, a government by the best men of all classes—and a democracy. I doubt very much whether a democracy is a government that would suit this country; and it is just as well that the House, when coming to a vote on this question, should really consider if that be the real issue between retaining the present constitution—not the present constitutional body,—but between the present constitution and a democracy.

It is just as well for the House to recollect that what is of issue is of some price. You must remember, not to use the word profanely, that we are dealing really with a peculiar people. There is no country at the present moment that exists under the circumstances and under the same conditions as the people of this realm. You have, for example, an ancient, powerful, richly-endowed Church; and perfect religious liberty. You have unbroken order and complete freedom. You have estates as large as the Romans. You have a commercial system of enterprise such as Carthage and Venice united never equalled. And you must remember that this peculiar country, with these strong contrasts, is governed not by force; it is not governed by standing armies; it is governed by a most singular series of traditionary influences, which generation after generation cherishes and preserves because they know that they embalm customs and represent the law. And, with this, what have you done? You have created the greatest empire that ever existed in modern times. You have amassed a capital of fabulous amount; you have devised and sustained a system of credit still more marvelous; and, above all, you have established and maintained a scheme so vast and complicated, of labor and industry, that the history of the world offers no parallel to it. And all these mighty creations are out of all proportion to the essential and indigenous elements and resources of the country. If you destroy that state of society, remember this—England cannot begin again.

There are countries which have been in great peril and gone through great suffering. There are the United States, which in our own immediate day have had great trials. You have had—perhaps even now in the States of America you have—a protracted and fratricidal civil war which has lasted for four years. But if it lasted for four years more, vast as would be the disaster and desolation, when ended the United

States might begin again, because the United States would be only in the same condition that England was at the end of the War of the Roses, when probably she had not even 3,000,000 of population, with vast tracts of virgin soil and mineral treasures, not only undeveloped, but undiscovered. Then you have France. France had a real revolution in our days and those of our predecessors—a real revolution, not merely a political and social revolution. You had the institutions of the country uprooted, the orders of society abolished—you had even the landmarks and local names removed and erased. But France could begin again. France had the greatest spread of the most exuberant soil in Europe; she had, and always had, a very limited population, living in a most simple manner. France, therefore, could begin again. But England— the England we know, the England we live in, the England of which we are proud—could not begin again. I don't mean to say that after great troubles England would become a howling wilderness. No doubt the good sense of the people would to some degree prevail, and some fragments of the national character would survive; but it would not be the old England—the England of power and tradition, of credit and capital, that now exists. That is not in the nature of things, and, under these circumstances, I hope the House will, when the question before us is one impeaching the character of our constitution, sanction no step that has a preference for democracy, but that they will maintain the ordered state of free England in which we live.

GOD'S LOVE TO FALLEN MAN

John Wesley

(1703-1791)

It was at Oxford University in England in the year 1729 that a group of students of whom John Wesley was the leader organized an association ridiculed at first as the "Holy Club," and later as "Methodists" because of their strict methodical habits of living. In 1735 John Wesley and his brother, Charles, who was also a member of the Oxford group, joined General Oglethorpe as missionaries to Georgia, but the mission was not altogether successful. On his return to England, John broke with the Established Church because of their ceremonious ritual and founded the sect known as Methodists. For nearly fifty years John Wesley's preaching was done largely in the open air, sometimes to groups of 10,000 to 20,000 people. It is reported that he travelled nearly 250,000 miles about the country and preached in all some 40,000 sermons during his lifetime. Wesley, himself, was a mild, grave man, venerable in his old age, for he lived to be 88 years of age. His sermons were direct appeals to audiences composed mostly of humble working people and were altogether without oratorical embellishment.

How exceedingly common and how bitter is the outcry against our first parent for the mischief which he not only brought upon himself, but entailed upon his latest posterity! It was by his wilful rebellion against God "that sin entered into the world." "By one man's disobedience," as the Apostle observes, the many, as many as were then in the loins of their forefathers were made, or constituted sinners: not only deprived of the favor of God but also of His image, of all virtue, righteousness, and true holiness, and sunk partly into the image of the devil, in pride, malice, and all other diabolical tempers; partly into the image of the brute, being fallen under the dominion of brutal passions and groveling appetites. Hence also death entered into the world with all its forerunners and attendants—pain, sickness, and a whole train of uneasy as well as unholy passions and tempers. "For all this we may thank Adam" has been echoed down from generation to generation.

It were well if the charge rested here: but it is certain it does not. It can not be denied that it frequently glances from Adam to his Creator. Have not thousands, even of those that are called Christians, taken the liberty to call His mercy, if not His justice also, into question, on that very account? Some indeed have done this a little more modestly, in an oblique and indirect manner, but others have thrown aside the mask and asked, "Did not God foresee that Adam would abuse his liberty? And did He not know the baneful consequences which this must naturally have on all his posterity? And why then did He permit that disobedience? Was it not easy for the Almighty to have prevented it?" He certainly did foresee the whole. This cannot be denied.

Mankind in general have gained by the fall of Adam a capacity of attaining more holiness and happiness on earth than it would have been possible for them to attain if Adam had not fallen. For if Adam had not fallen Christ had not died. Nothing can be more clear than this: nothing more undeniable: the more thoroughly we consider the point, the more deeply shall we be convinced of it. Unless all the partakers of human nature had received that deadly wound in Adam it would not have been needful for the Son of God to take our nature upon Him. Do you not see that this was the very ground of His coming into the world? "By one man sin entered into the world, and death by sin. And thus death passed upon all" through him "in whom all men sinned." Was it not to remedy this very thing that "the Word was made flesh?" that "as in Adam all died, so in Christ all might be made alive?"

Unless, then, many had been made sinners by the disobedience of one, by the obedience of one many would not have been made righteous. So there would have been no room for that amazing display of the Son of God's love to mankind. There would have been no occasion for His "being obedient unto death, even the death of the cross." It could not then have been said, to the astonishment of all the hosts of heaven, "God so loved the world," yea, the ungodly world, which had no thought or desire of returning to Him, "that He gave His Son" out of His bosom, His only-begotten Son, "to the end that whosoever believeth on Him should not perish, but have everlasting life."

What is the necessary consequence of this? It is this: There could then have been no such thing as faith in God, thus loving the world, giving His only Son for us men and for our salvation. There could have been no such thing as faith in the Son of God "as loving us and giving Himself for us." There could have been no faith in the Spirit of God as renewing the image of God in our hearts, as raising us from the death of sin unto the life of righteousness. Indeed, the whole privilege of justification by faith could have no existence; there could have been no redemption in the blood of Christ: neither could Christ have been made of God unto us, either "wisdom, righteousness, sanctification, or redemption."

And the same grand point which was in our faith must likewise have been in our love. We might have loved the Author of our being, the Father of angels and men, as our Creator and Preserver: we might have said, "O Lord, our Governor, how excellent is Thy name in all the earth!" But we could not have loved Him under the nearest and dearest relation "as delivering up His Son for us all." We might have loved the Son of God as being the "Brightness of His Father's glory, the express image of His person" (altho this ground seems to belong rather to the inhabitants of heaven than earth). But we could not have loved Him as "bearing our sins in His own body on the tree," and "by that one oblation of Himself once offered, making a full oblation, sacrifice, and satisfaction for the sins of the whole world." We could not have been "made conformable to His death," not "have known the power of His resurrection."

And as our faith, both in God the Father and the Son, receives an unspeakable increase, if not its very being, from this grand event, as does also our love both of the Father and the Son; so does also our love of our neighbor also, our benevolence to all mankind, which cannot but increase in the same proportion with our faith and love of God. For who does not apprehend the force of that inference drawn by the loving Apostle, "Beloved, if God so loved us, we ought also to love one another."

Such gainers may we be by Adam's fall, with regard both to the love of God and of our neighbor. But there is another grand point, which, tho little adverted to, deserves our deepest consideration. By this one act of our first parent, not only "sin entered the world," but pain also, and was alike entailed on his whole posterity. And herein appeared, not only the justice, but the unspeakable goodness of God. For how much good does He continually bring out of this evil! How much holiness and happiness out of pain!

How innumerable are the benefits which God conveys to the children of men through the channel of sufferings, so that it might well be said, "What are termed afflictions in the language of men are in the language of God styled blessings." Indeed, had there been no suffering in the world, a considerable part of religion, yea, and in some respects, the most excellent part, could have had no place therein: since the very existence of it depends on our suffering: so that had there been no pain it could have had no being. Upon this foundation, even our suffering, it is evident all our passive graces are built; yea, the noblest of all Christian graces, love enduring all things.

What room could there be for trust in God if there was no such thing as pain or danger? Who might not say then, "The cup which my Father had given me, shall I not drink it?" It is by sufferings that our faith is tried, and, therefore, made more acceptable to God. It is in the day of trouble that we have occasion to say, "Tho He slay me, yet will I trust in Him." This is well pleasing to God; that we own Him in the face of danger, in defiance of sorrow, sickness, pain, or death.

Again: Had there been neither natural nor moral evil in the world, what must have become of patience, meekness, gentleness, long-suffering? It is manifested they could have had no being, seeing all these have evil for their object. If therefore evil had never entered into the world, neither could these have had any place in it. For who could have returned good for evil, had there been no evil-doer in the universe? How had it been possible, on that supposition, to overcome evil with good?

It is then we shall be enabled fully to comprehend, not only the advantages which accrue at the present time to the sons of men by the fall of their first parent, but the infinitely greater advantages which they may reap from it in eternity. In order to form some conception of this we may remember the observation of the Apostle, "As one star differeth from another star in glory, so also is the resurrection of the dead." The most glorious stars will undoubtedly be those who are the most holy; who bear most of that image of God wherein they were created. The next in glory to these will be those who have been most abundant in good works; and next to them, those that have suffered most, according to the will of God.

But what advantages in every one of these respects will the children of God receive in heaven by God's permitting the introduction of pain upon earth in consequence of sin? By occasion of this they attained many holy tempers which otherwise could have had no being: resignation to God, confidence in Him in times of trouble and danger, patience, meekness, gentleness, long-suffering, and the whole train of passion virtues. And on account of this superior holiness they will then enjoy superior happiness.

There is one advantage more that we reap from Adam's fall, which is not unworthy our attention. Unless in Adam all had died, being in the lions of their first parent, every descendant of Adam, every child of man, must have personally answered for himself to God: it seems to be a necessary consequence of this, that if he had once fallen, once violated any command of God, there would have been no possibility of his rising again; there was no help, but he must have perished without remedy. For that covenant knew not to show mercy: the word was, "The soul that sinneth, it shall die." Now who would not rather be on the footing he is now, under a covenant of mercy? Who would wish to hazard a whole eternity upon one stake? Is it not infinitely more desirable to be in a state wherein, tho encompassed with infirmities, yet we do not run such a desperate risk, but if we fall we may rise again?

See then, upon the whole, how little reason we have to repine at the fall of our first parent, since herefrom we may derive such unspeakable advantages both in time and eternity. See how small pretense there is for questioning the mercy of God in permitting that event to take place, since, therein, mercy, by infinite degrees, rejoices over judgment! Where, then, is the man that presumes to blame God for not preventing

Adam's sin? Should we not rather bless Him from the ground of the heart, for therein laying the grand scheme of man's redemption and making way for that glorious manifestation of His wisdom, holiness, justice, and mercy? If, indeed, God had decreed, before the foundation of the world, that millions of men should dwell in everlasting burnings because Adam sinned hundreds or thousands of years before they had a being, I know not who could thank him for this, unless the devil and his angels: seeing, on this supposition, all those millions of unhappy spirits would be plunged into hell by Adam's sin without any possible advantage from it. But, blessed be God, this is not the case. Such a decree never existed. On the contrary, every one, born of woman may be unspeakable gainer thereby: none ever was or can be loser but by choice.

ON THE METHOD OF GRACE

George Whitefield

(1714-1770)

George Whitefield was also a member of Wesley's student "Holy Club" at Oxford University. It was he who originated the open-air method of preaching. He became associated with Wesley in the great revival of the 18th century, but they parted ways on the question of the Calvinistic doctrine of Predestination. Much of Whitefield's preaching was done in the American Colonies which he visited on seven different occasions. He also toured Scotland, Wales, and Ireland, where he was welcomed with enthusiasm. Whitefield's voice was so clear and powerful that it has been stated he could reach 20,000 people. In all he preached more than 18,000 sermons. His power appears to have been due to his delivery more than to the content of his sermons. He was not an organizer, so his congregations scattered and many joined the Methodists.

As God can send a nation or people no greater blessing than to give them faithful, sincere, and upright ministers, so the greatest curse that God can possibly send upon a people in this world is to give them over to blind, unregenerate, carnal, lukewarm, and unskilful guides. And yet, in all ages, we find that there have been many wolves in sheep's clothing, many that daubed with untempered mortar, that prophesied smoother things than God did allow. As it was formerly, so it is now; there are many that corrupt the Word of God and deal deceitfully with it. It was so in a special manner in the prophet Jeremiah's time; and he, faithful to his Lord, faithful to that God who employed him, did not fail from time to time to open his mouth against them, and to bear a noble testimony to the honor of that God in whose name he from time to time spake. If you will read his prophecy, you will find that none spake more against such ministers than Jeremiah. In the words of the text, in a more special manner, he exemplifies how they had dealt falsely, how they had behaved treacherously to poor souls: says he, "They have healed also the hurt of the daughter of my people slightly, saying, Peace,

peace, when there is no peace." The prophet, in the name of God, had been denouncing war against the people; he had been telling them that their house should be left desolate, and that the Lord would certainly visit the land with war. "Therefore," says he, in the eleventh verse, "I am full of the fury of the Lord; I am weary with holding in; I will pour it out upon the children abroad, and upon the assembly of young men together; for even the husband with the wife shall be taken, the aged with him that is full of days. And their houses shall be turned unto others, with their fields and wives together; for I will stretch out My hand upon the inhabitants of the land, saith the Lord."

The prophet gives a thundering message, that they might be terrified and have some convictions and inclinations to repent; but it seems that the false prophets, that the false priests, went about stifling people's convictions, and when they were hurt or a little terrified, they were for daubing over the wound, telling them that Jeremiah was but an enthusiastic preacher, that there could be no such thing as war among them, and saying to people, "Peace, peace, be still," when the prophet told them there was no peace.

How many of us cry, "Peace, peace," to our souls, when there is no peace! How many are there who are now settled upon their lees, that now think they are Christians, that now flatter themselves that they have an interest in Jesus Christ; whereas if we come to examine their experiences we shall find that their peace is but a peace of the devil's making—it is not a peace of God's giving—it is not a peace that passeth human understanding.

It is a matter, therefore, of great importance, my dear hearers, to know whether we may speak peace to our hearts. We are all desirous of peace; peace is an unspeakable blessing; how can we live without peace? And, therefore, people from time to time must be taught how far they must go and what must be wrought in them before they can speak peace to their hearts. This is what I design at present, that I may deliver my soul, that I may be free from the blood of all those to whom I preach—that I may not fail to declare the whole counsel of God. I shall, from the words of the text, endeavor to show you what you must undergo and what must be wrought in you before you can speak peace to your hearts.

But before I come directly to this give me leave to premise a caution or two. And the first is, that I take it for granted you believe religion to be an inward thing; you believe it to be work in the heart, a work wrought in the soul by the power of the Spirit of God. If you do not believe this, you do not believe your Bibles. If you do not believe this, tho you have got your Bibles in your hand, you hate the Lord Jesus Christ in your heart; for religion is everywhere represented in Scripture as the work of God in the heart. "The kingdom of God is within us," says our Lord! and, "he is not a Christian who is one outwardly; but he is a Christian who is one inwardly." If any of you place religion in outward things, I shall not perhaps please you this morning; you will understand me no more when I speak of the work of God upon a poor sinner's heart than if I were talking in an unknown tongue.

First, then, before you can speak peace to your hearts, you must be made to see, made to feel, made to weep over, made to bewail, your actual transgressions against the law of God. According to the covenant of works, "the soul that sinneth it shall die"; cursed is that man, be he what he may, be he who he may, that continueth not in all things that are written in the book of the law to do them.

We are not only to do some things, but we are to do all things, and we are to continue so to do, so that the least deviation from the moral law, according to the covenant of works, whether in thought, word, or deed, deserves eternal death at the hand of God. And if one evil thought, if one evil word, if one evil action deserves eternal damnation, how many hells, my friends, do every one of us deserve whose whole lives have been one continued rebellion against God! Before ever, therefore, you can speak peace to your hearts, you must be brought to see, brought to believe, what a dreadful thing it is to depart from the living God.

And now, my dear friends, examine your hearts, for I hope you came hither with a design to have your souls made better. Give me leave to ask you, in the presence of God, whether you know the time, and if you do know exactly the time, do you know there was a time when God wrote bitter things against you, when the arrows of the Almighty were within you? Was ever the remembrance of your sins grievous to you? Was the burden of your sins intolerable to your thoughts? Did you ever see that God's wrath might justly fall upon you, on account of your actual transgressions against God? Were you ever in all your life sorry for your sins? Could you ever say, My sins are gone over my head as a burden too heavy for me to bear? Did you ever experience any such thing as this? Did ever any such thing as this pass between God and your soul? If not, for Jesus Christ's sake, do not call yourselves Christians; you may speak peace to your hearts, but there is no peace. May the Lord awaken you, may the Lord convert you, may the Lord give you peace, if it be His will, before you go home!

Did you ever feel and experience this, any of you—to justify God in your damnation—to own that you are by nature children of wrath, and that God may justly cut you off, tho you never actually had offended Him in all your life? If you were ever truly convicted, if your hearts were ever truly cut, if self were ever truly taken out of you, you would be made to see and feel this. And if you have never felt the weight of original sin, do not call yourselves Christians. I am verily persuaded original sin is the greatest burden of a true convert; this ever grieves the regenerate soul, the sanctified soul. The indwelling of sin in the heart is the burden of a converted person; it is the burden of a true Christian. He continually cries out: "Oh! who will deliver me from this body of death, this indwelling corruption in my heart?" This is that which disturbs a poor soul most. And, therefore, if you never felt this inward corruption, if you never saw that God might justly curse you for it, indeed, my dear friends, you may speak peace to your hearts, but I fear, nay, I know, there is no true peace.

After we are renewed, yet we are renewed but in part, indwelling sin continues in us, there is a mixture of corruption in every one of our duties; so that after we are converted, were Jesus Christ only to accept us according to our works, our works would damn us, for we cannot put up a prayer but it is far from perfection which the moral law requireth. I do not know what you may think, but I can say that I cannot pray but I sin—I cannot preach to you or to any others but I sin— I can do nothing without sin; as one expresseth it, my repentance wants to be repented of, and my tears to be washed in the precious blood of my dear Redeemer.

Our best duties are as so many splendid sins. Before you can speak peace to your heart you must not only be sick of your original and actual sin, but you must be made sick of your righteousness, of all your duties and performances. There must be a deep conviction before you can be brought out of your self-righteousness; it is the last idol taken out of our heart. The pride of our heart will not let us submit to the righteousness of Jesus Christ. But if you never felt that you had no righteousness of your own, if you never felt the deficiency of your own righteousness, you can not come to Jesus Christ.

But then, before you can speak peace to your souls, there is one particular sin you must be greatly troubled for, and yet I fear there are few of you think what it is; it is the reigning, the damning sin of the Christian world, and yet the Christian world seldom or never think of it.

And pray what is that? It is what most of you think you are not guilty of—and that is, the sin of unbelief. Before you can speak peace to your heart, you must be troubled for the unbelief of your heart. But can it be supposed that any of you are unbelievers here in this churchyard, that are born in Scotland, in a reformed country, that go to church every Sabbath? Can any of you that receive the sacrament once a year—oh, that it were administered oftener!—can it be supposed that you who had tokens for the sacrament, that you who keep up family prayer, that any of you do not believe in the Lord Jesus Christ?

My friends, we mistake a historical faith for a true faith, wrought in the heart by the Spirit of God. You fancy you believe because you believe there is such a book as we call the Bible, because you go to church—all this you may do and have no true faith in Christ; merely to believe there was such a person as Christ, merely to believe there is a book called the Bible, will do you no good, more than to believe there was such a man as Caesar or Alexander the Great. The Bible is a sacred depository. What thanks have we to give to God for these lively oracles! But yet we may have these and not believe in the Lord Jesus Christ.

My dear friends, there must be a principle wrought in the heart by the Spirit of the living God. Did I ask you how long it is since you believed in Jesus Christ? I suppose most of you would tell me you believed in Jesus Christ as long as ever you remember—you never did misbelieve. Then, you could not give me a better proof that you never yet believed in Jesus Christ, unless you were sanctified early, as from the womb; for they that otherwise believe in Christ know there was a time when they did not believe in Jesus Christ.

You say you love God with all your heart, soul, and strength. If I were to ask you how long it is since you loved God, you would say, as long as you can remember; you never hated God, you know no time when there was enmity in your heart against God. Then, unless you were sanctified very early, you never loved God in your life.

My dear friends, I am more particular in this, because it is a most deceitful delusion, whereby so many people are carried away, that they believe already. Therefore it is remarked of Mr. Marshall, giving account of his experiences, that he had been working for life, and he had ranged all his sins under the ten commandments, and then, coming to a minister, asked him the reason why he could not get peace. The minister looked to his catalogue. Away, says he, I do not find one work of the sin of unbelief in all your catalogue. It is the peculiar work of the Spirit of God to convince us of our unbelief—that we have got no faith. Says Jesus Christ, "I will send the Comforter; and when He is come, He will reprove the world" of the sin of unbelief; "of sin," says Christ, "because they believe not on Me."

I am now talking of the invisible realities of another world, of inward religion, of the work of God upon a poor sinner's heart. I am now talking of a matter of great importance, my dear hearers; you are all concerned in it, your souls are concerned in it, your eternal salvation is concerned in it. You may be all at peace, but perhaps the devil has lulled you asleep into a carnal lethargy and security, and will endeavor to keep you there till he get you to hell, and there you will be awakened; but it will be dreadful to be awakened and find yourselves so fearfully mistaken, when the great gulf is fixed, when you will be calling to all eternity for a drop of water to cool your tongue and shall not obtain it.

THE EVILS OF MONEY-GETTING

Cardinal Newman

(1801-1890)

At first as a leader of the Established Church of England and later as a Roman Catholic Newman was a leading spiritual and literary force of the 19th century in England. There is a chastity of beauty in his sermons akin to the spiritual beauty of his life. This elevated style may be attributed also to his familiarity with the authorized version of the Bible. He aimed to bring the simplicity of the early church fathers into the life of the church. A sermon from his series of Oxford sermons is included here.

I say, then, that it is a part of Christian caution to see that our engagements do not become pursuits. Engagements are our portion, but pursuits are for the most part of our own choosing. We may be engaged in worldly business without pursuing worldly objects. "Not slothful in business," yet "serving the Lord." In this, then, consists the danger of the pursuit of gain, as by trade and the like. It is the most common and widely spread of all excitements. It is one in which everyone almost may indulge, nay, and will be praised by the world for indulging. And it lasts through life—in that differing from the amusements and pleasures of the world, which are short-lived and succeed one after another. Dissipation of mind, which these amusements create, is itself, indeed, miserable enough; but far worse than this dissipation is the concentration of mind upon some worldly object which admits of being constantly pursued; and such is the pursuit of gain. Nor is it a slight aggravation of the evil that anxiety is almost sure to attend it. A life of money-getting is a life of care. From the first there is a fretful anticipation of loss in various ways to depress and unsettle the mind, nay, to haunt it, till a man finds he can think about nothing else, and is unable to give his mind to religion from the constant whirl of business in which he is involved. It is well this should be understood. You may hear men talk as if the pursuit of wealth was the business of life. They will argue that, by the law of nature, a man is bound to gain a livelihood for his family, and that he finds a reward in doing so—an innocent and honorable satisfaction—as he adds one sum to another, and counts up his gains. And, perhaps, they go on to argue that it is the very duty of man, since Adam's fall, "in the sweat of his face," by effort and anxiety, "to eat bread." How strange it is that they do not remember Christ's gracious promise, repealing that original curse and obviating the necessity of any real pursuit after "the meat that perisheth." In order that we might be delivered from the bondage of corruption, He has expressly told us that the necessaries of life shall never fail His faithful follower any more than the meal and oil the widow woman of Sarepta; that while he is bound to labor for his family, he need not be engrossed by his toil; that while he is busy, his heart may be at leisure for the Lord. "Be not anxious, saying: What shall we eat, or what shall we drink, or wherewithal shall we be clothed? For after all these things do the Gentiles seek; and your Heavenly father knoweth that ye have need of these things."

I have now given the main reason why the pursuit of gain, whether in a large or a small way, is prejudicial to our spiritual interests—that it fixes the mind upon an object of this world. Yet others remain behind. Money is a sort of creation, and gives the acquirer even more than the possessor an imagination of his own power, and tends to make him idolize self. Again, what we have hardly won, we are unwilling to part with; so that a man who has himself made his wealth will commonly be penurious, or at least will not part with it except in exchange for what will reflect credit on himself and increase his importance. Even when his conduct is most disinterested and amiable (as in spending for the comfort of those who depend on him), still this indulgence of self, of pride, and worldliness, insinuates itself. Very unlikely, therefore, is it that he should be liberal towards God; for religious offerings are an expenditure without sensible return, and that upon objects for which the very pursuit of wealth has indisposed his mind.

Moreover, if it may be added, there is a considerable tendency in occupations connected with gain to make a man unfair in his dealings; that is, in a subtle way. There are so many conventional deceits and prevarications in the details of the world's business, so much intricacy in the management of accounts, so many perplexed questions about justice and equity, so many plausible subterfuges and fictions of law, so much confusion between the distinct yet approximating outlines of honesty and civil enactment, that it requires a very straightforward mind to keep firm hold of strict conscientiousness, honor, and truth, and to look at matters in which he is engaged as he would have looked on them supposing he now came upon them all at once as a stranger.

And if such be the effect of the pursuit of gain on an individual, doubtless it will be the same on a nation. Only let us consider the fact that we are a money-making people, with our Saviour's declaration before us against wealth, and trust in wealth, and we shall have abundant matter for serious thought.

WAR AND TRUTH [8]

Thomas Chalmers

(1780-1847)

The great Scottish divine, Thomas Chalmers, was considered the first preacher of Scotland in his day. Because of "rare and singular qualities" he was ordained at the early age of 19. In 1810 grief and illness brought to him a spiritual revitalization which gave him the extraordinary power which he later exerted over the moral and spiritual life of Scotland. A group of sermons delivered in 1815 in the Trom Church at Glasgow brought all of Scotland under the spell of his preaching, and even in London folk were talking about the wondrous oratory of the Scottish divine. In 1828 he was elected to the Chair of Divinity at the University of Edinburgh, but left that chair later to become the founder of the Free Church of Scotland.

On every side of me I see causes at work which go to spread a most delusive coloring over war and to remove its shocking barbarities to the background of our contemplations altogether. I see it in the history which tells me of the superb appearance of the troops and the brilliancy of their successive charges. I see it in the poetry which lends the magic of its numbers to the narrative of blood, and transports its many admirers, as by its images and its figures and its nodding plumes of chivalry it throws its treacherous embellishments over a scene of legalized slaughter. I see it in the music which represents the progress of the battle, and where, after being inspired by the trumpet-notes of preparation, the whole beauty and tenderness of a drawing-room are seen to bend over the sentimental entertainment; nor do I hear the utterance of a single sigh to interrupt the death-tones of the thickening contest and the moans of the wounded men, as they fade away upon the ear and sink into lifeless silence.

All, all, goes to prove what strange and half-sighted creatures we are. Were it not so, war could never have been seen in any other aspect than that of unmingled hatefulness; and I can look to nothing

[8] Abridged.

but to the progress of Christian sentiment upon earth to arrest the strong current of the popular and prevailing partiality for war. Then only will an imperious sense of duty lay the check of severe principle on all the subordinate tastes and faculties of our nature. Then will glory be reduced to its right estimate, and the wakeful benevolence of the Gospel, chasing away every spell, will be turned by the treachery of no delusion whatever from its simple but sublime enterprises for the good of the species. Then the reign of truth and quietness will be ushered into the world, and war—cruel, atrocious, unrelenting war— will be stripped of its many and its bewildering fascinations.

ROME THE ETERNAL

Cardinal Henry Edward Manning

(1808-1892)

One of the most notable figures of the Catholic Church in the 19th century was Henry Manning. A graduate of Oxford, he was ordained to the Church of England but later turned to the Roman Catholic faith and in 1875 became a Cardinal of the Church. He did much to bring the Roman Catholic Church out of the obscurity of the centuries of repression and was zealous in charitable and temperance works.

Cardinal Manning had an unusual gift of persuasive eloquence and theological attainments of a superior order.

I know of no point of view in which the glory of Rome is more conspicuous than in its civil mission to the races of the world. When the seat of empire was translated from Rome to Constantinople, all the culture and civilization of Italy seemed to be carried away to enrich and adorn the East. It seemed as if God had decreed to reveal to the world what His Church could do without the world, and what the world could not do without the Church. A more melancholy history than that of the Byzantine Empire is nowhere to be read. It is one long narrative of the usurpation and insolent dominion of the world over the Church, which, becoming schismatical and isolated, fell easily under its imperial masters. With all its barbaric splendor and imperial power, what has Constantinople accomplished for the civilization or the Christianity of the East? If the salt had kept its savor, it would not have been cast out and trodden under the feet of the Eastern Antichrist.

While this was accomplished in the East, in the West a new world was rising, in order, unity, and fruitfulness, under the action of the Pontiffs. Even the hordes which inundated Italy were changed by them from the wildness of nature to the life of Christian civilization. From St. Leo to St. Gregory the Great, Christian Europe may be said not to exist! Rome stood alone under the rule of its pontiffs, while as yet empires and kingdoms had no existence. Thus, little by little, and one by one, the nations which now make up the unity of Christendom were created, trained and formed into political societies. First Lombardy, then Gaul, then Spain, then Germany, then Saxon England; then the first germs of lesser States began to appear. But to whom did they owe the laws, the principles, and the influences which made their existence possible, coherent, and mature? It was to the Roman Pontiffs that they owed the first rudiments of their social and political order. It was the exposition of the Divine law by the lips of the Vicar of Jesus Christ that founded the Christian policy of the world.

Thus, the Church has been able to do without the world, and even in spite of it. Nothing can be conceived more isolated, more feeble, or more encompassed with peril, than the line of the Roman Pontiffs; nevertheless, they have maintained inviolate their independence with their sacred deposit of faith and of jurisdiction, through all the ages and through all conflicts, from the beginning to this hour. It seemed as if God willed to remove the first Christian emperor from Rome in the early fervor of his conversion, lest it should seem as if the sovereignty of the Church were in any way the creation of his power. God is jealous of His own kingdom and will not suffer any unconsecrated hand to be laid upon His ark, even for its support.

The "stone cut without hands," which became a great mountain and filled the whole earth, is typical, not only of the expansion and universality of the Church, but of its mysterious and supernatural character. No human hand has accomplished its greatness. The hand of God alone could bring it to pass.

What is there in the history of the world parallel to the Rome of the Christians? The most warlike and imperial people of the world gave place to a people unarmed and without power. The pacific people arose from the Catacombs and entered upon the possession of Rome as their inheritance. The existence of Christian Rome, both in its formation, and next in its perpetuity, is a miracle of Divine power. God alone could give it to His people; God alone could preserve it to them, and them to it. What more wonderful sight than to see a Franciscan monk leading the *Via Crucis* in the Flavian Amphitheatre, or the Passionist missionaries conversing peacefully among the ilexes and the vaults where the wild beasts from Africa thirsted for the blood of the Christians? Who has prevailed upon the world for one thousand five hundred years to fall back as Attilla did from Christian Rome? Who has persuaded its will, and paralyzed its ambitions and conflicting interests? Such were my thoughts the other day when the Sovereign Pontiff, surrounded by the princes and pastors of the Church, was celebrating the festival of the Resurrection over the Confession of St. Peter. I thought of the ages past, when, in the amphitheatre of Nero, within which we stood, thousands of martyrs fell beneath the arms of the heathen. And now, the Rex Pacificus, the Vicar of the Prince of Peace, there holds his court and offers over the tomb of the Apostle the unbloody sacrifice of our redemption. The legions of Rome have given way before a people who have never lifted a hand in war. They have taken the city of the Caesars, and hold it to this day. The more than imperial court which surrounded the Vicar of Jesus Christ surpassed the glories of the Empire. "This is the victory which overcometh the world, even our faith." The noblest spectacle upon earth is an unarmed man whom all the world cannot bend by favor or by fear. Such a man is essentially above all worldly powers. And such, eminent among the inflexible, is he, the Pontiff and King, who, in the midst of the confusions and rebellions of the whole earth, bestowed that day his benediction upon the city and the world.

THE CONDESCENSION OF CHRIST

Charles Spurgeon

(1834-1892)

In the later 19th century Charles Spurgeon, a dissenter from the Church of England, was drawing enormous crowds of people in London under the spell of his preaching. The large Metropolitan Tabernacle with a seating capacity of 6000 was finally erected to hold the throngs of people who came to hear his sermons. To this Tabernacle was later added an orphanage and almshouses. His sermons in print had an enormous circulation and were translated into many languages.

Think not that our Savior began to live when he was born of the Virgin Mary; imagine not that he dates his existence from the manger of Bethlehem; remember he is the Eternal, he is before all things, and by him all things consist. There was never a time in which there was not God. And just so there was never a period in which there was not Christ Jesus our Lord. He is self-existent, has no beginning of days, neither end of years; he is the immortal, invisible, the only wise God, our Savior. Now, in the past eternity which had elapsed before his mission to this world, we are told that Jesus Christ was rich; and to those of us who believe his glories and trust in his divinity it is not hard to see how he was so. Jesus was rich in possessions. Lift up thine eye, believer, and for a moment review the riches of my Lord Jesus before he condescended to become poor for thee. Behold his sitting upon his throne and declaring his own all-sufficiency. "If I were hungry, I would not tell thee, for the cattle on a thousand hills are mine. Mine are the hidden treasures of gold; mine are the pearls that the diver can not reach; mine every precious thing that earth has seen."

Up to the summit, Christian, and survey thine inheritance; and when thou hast surveyed it all, when thou hast seen thy present possessions, thy promised possessions, thine entailed possessions, then remember that all these were bought by the poverty of thy Savior! Look thou upon all thou hast and say, "Christ bought them for me." Look thou on every promise and see the bloodstains on it; yea, look, too, on the harps and crowns of heaven and read the bloody purchase! Remember, thou couldst never have been anything but a damned sinner unless Christ had bought thee!

Remember, if he had remained in heaven thou wouldst forever have remained in hell; unless he had shrouded and eclipsed his own honor thou wouldst never have had a ray of light to shine upon thee.

Therefore bless his dear name, extol him, trace every stream to the fountain; and bless him who is the source and the fountain of everything thou hast. Brethren, "Ye know the grace of our Lord Jesus Christ, that, tho he was rich, yet for our sakes he became poor, that ye through his poverty might be rich."

Remember, Christ came to make those rich that have nothing of their own. My Savior is a physician; if you can heal yourself he will have nothing to do with you. Remember, my Savior came to clothe the naked. He will clothe you if you have not a rag of your own; but unless you let him do it from head to foot he will have nothing to do with you. Christ says he will never have a partner; he will do all or none. Come, then, hast thou given up all to Christ? Hast thou no reliance and trust save in the cross of Jesus? Then thou hast answered the question well. Be happy, be joyous; if death should surprise thee the next hour, thou art secure. Go on thy way and rejoice in the hope of the glory of God.

Remember, Christ will not reject thee; thou mayest reject him. Remember now, there is the cup of mercy put to thy lip by the hand of Jesus. I know, if thou feelest thy need, Satan may tempt thee not to drink, but he will not prevail; thou wilt put thy lip feebly and faintly, perhaps, to it. But oh! do but sip it; and the first draught shall give thee bliss; and the deeper thou shalt drink the more heaven shalt thou know.

Sinner, believe on Jesus Christ; hear the whole gospel preached to thee. It is written in God's Work, "He that believeth and is baptized shall be saved." Hear me translate it: He that believeth and is immersed shall be saved. Believe thou, trust thyself on the Savior, make a profession of thy faith in baptism, and then thou mayest rejoice in Jesus, that he hath saved thee. But remember not to make a profession till thou hast believed; remember, baptism is nothing until thou hast faith. Remember, it is a farce and a falsehood until thou hast first believed; and afterward it is nothing but the profession of thy faith.

THE GREATEST THING IN THE WORLD

Henry Drummond

(1851-1897)

Probably the most widely circulated religious publication of the 19th century in England was Henry Drummond's *The Greatest Thing in the World*.

Drummond was born in Scotland and in college had come in contact with the great evolutionists, Spencer and Huxley. In this noted sermon Drummond seeks to reconcile the scientific with the religious concept of life, for he considered the central thought of evolution to be in completest harmony with the central thought of religion. Consequently his sermon pacified a religious world apprehensive of the encroachments of what was known as "Darwinism."

Every one has asked himself the great question of antiquity as of the modern world: What is the summum bonum—the supreme good? You have life before you. Once only you can live it. What is the noblest object of desire, the supreme gift to covet?

We have been accustomed to be told that the greatest thing in the religious world is Faith. That great word has been the keynote for centuries of the popular religion, and we have easily learned to look upon it as the greatest thing in the world. Well, we are wrong. If we have been told that, we may miss the mark. I have taken you, in the chapter which I have just read, to Christianity at its source, and there we have seen "The greatest of these is love." It is not an oversight. Paul was speaking of faith just a moment before. He says: "If I have all faith, so that I can remove mountains, and have not love, I am nothing." So far from forgetting, he deliberately contrasts them, "Now abideth Faith, Hope, Love," and without a moment's hesitation the decision falls: "The greatest of these is Love." . . .

Can you tell me anything that is going to last? Many things Paul did not condescend to name. He did not mention money, fortune, fame; but he picked out the great things of his time, the things the best men thought had something in them, and brushed then peremptorily aside. Paul had no charge against these things in themselves. All he said about them was that they would not last. They were great things, but not supreme things. There were things beyond what we possess. Many things that men denounce as sins are not sins; but they are temporary. And that is a favorite argument of the New Testament. John says of the world, not that it is wrong, but simply that it "passeth away." There is a great deal in the world that is delightful and beautiful; there is a great deal in it that is great and engrossing; but it will not last. All that is in the world, the lust of the eye, the lust of the flesh, and the pride of life, are but for a little while. Love not the world therefore. Nothing that it contains is worth the life and consecration of an immortal soul. The immortal soul must give itself to something that is immortal. And the only immortal things are these: "Now abideth faith, hope, love, but the greatest of these is love."

Some think the time may come when two of these three things will also pass away—faith into sight, hope into fruition. Paul does not say so. We know but little now about the conditions of the life that is to come. But what is certain is that love must last. God, the eternal God, is Love. Covet, therefore, that everlasting gift, that one thing which it is certain is going to stand, that one coinage which will be current in the universe when all the other coinages of all the nations of the world shall be useless and unhonored. You will give yourselves to many things, give yourself first to Love. Hold things in their proportion. Hold things in their proportion. Let at least the first great object of our lives be to achieve the character defended in these words, the character— and it is the character of Christ—which is built round Love.

I have said this thing is eternal. Did you ever notice how continually John associates love and faith with eternal life? I was not told when I was a boy that "God so loved the world that he gave his only-begotten Son that whosoever believeth in him should have everlasting life." What I was told, I remember, was, that God so loved the world that if I trusted in him I was to have a thing called peace, or I was to have rest, or I was to have joy, or I was to have safety. But I had to find out for myself that whosoever trusteth in him—that is—whosoever loveth him, for trust is only the avenue to Love—hath everlasting life. The Gospel offers a man life. Never offer men a thimbleful of Gospel. Do not offer them merely joy, or merely peace, or merely rest, or merely safety; tell them how Christ came to give men a more abundant life than they have, a life abundant in love, and therefore abundant in salvation for themselves, and large in enterprise for the alleviation and redemption of the world. Then only can the Gospel take hold of the whole of a man, body, soul, and spirit, and give to each part of his nature its exercise and reward. Many of the current Gospels are addressed only to a part of man's nature. They offer peace, not life; faith, not Love; justification, not regeneration. And men slip back again from such religior because it has never really held them. Their nature was not all in it. It offered no deeper and gladder life-current than the life that was lived before. Surely it stands to reason that only a fuller love can compete with the love of the world.

To love abundantly is to live abundantly, and to love forever is to live forever. Hence, eternal life is inextricably bound up with Love. We want to live forever for the same reason that we want to live to-morrow. Why do you want to live to-morrow? It is because there is some one who loves you, and whom you want to see to-morrow, and be with, and love back, there is no other reason why we should live on than that we love and are beloved. It is when a man has no one to love him that he commits suicide. So long as he has friends, those who love him and whom he loves, he will live, because to live is to love. Be it but the love of a dog, it will keep him in life; but let that go and he has no contact with life, no reason to live. He dies by his own hand. Eternal life also is to know God, and God is Love. This is Christ's own definition. Ponder it. "This is life eternal, that they might know thee, the only true God, and Jesus Christ whom thou hast sent." Love must be eternal. It is what God is. On the last analysis, then, Love is life. Love never faileth, and life never faileth, so long as there is Love. That is the philosophy of what Paul is showing us; the reason why, in the nature of things, Love should be the supreme thing—because it is going to last; because, in the nature of things, it is an eternal life. It is a thing that we are living now, not that we get when we die; that we shall have a poor chance of getting when we die, unless we are living now. No worse fate can befall a man in this world than to live and grow old alone, unloving and unloved. To be lost is to live in an unregenerate condition, loveless and unloved; and to be saved is to love; and he that dwelleth in love dwelleth already in God. For God is Love.

In the book of Matthew, where the Judgment Day is depicted for us in the imagery of One seated upon a throne and dividing the sheep from the goats, the test of a man then is not, "How have I believed?" but "How have I loved?" The test of religion, the final test of religion, is not religiousness, but Love. I say, the final test of religion at that great day is not religiousness, but Love; not what I have done, not what I have believed, not what I have achieved, but how I have discharged the common charities of life. Sins of commission in that awful indictment are not even referred to. By what we have not done, by sins of omission, we are judged. It could not be otherwise. For the withholding of love is the negation of the spirit of Christ, the proof that we never knew him, that for us he lived in vain. It means that he suggested nothing in all our thoughts, that he inspired nothing in all our lives, that we were not once near enough to him to be seized with the spell of his compassion for the world. It means that—

"I lived for myself, I thought for myself,
    For myself, and none beside—
Just as if Jesus had never lived,
    As if he had never died."

It is the Son of Man before whom the nations of the world shall be gathered. It is in the presence of Humanity that we shall be charged. And the spectacle itself, the mere sight of it, will silently judge each one. Those will be there whom we have met and helped; or there, the unpitied multitude whom we neglected or despised. No other witness need be summoned. No other charge than lovelessness shall be preferred. Be not deceived. The words which all of us shall one day hear sound not of theology, but of life; not of churches and saints, but of the hungry and the poor; not of creeds and doctrines, but of shelter and clothing; not of Bibles and prayer-books, but of cups of cold water in the name of Christ. Thank God the Christianity of to-day is coming nearer the world's need. Live to help that on. Thank God, men know better, by a hair's breadth, what religion is, what God is, who Christ is, where Christ is. Who is Christ? He who fed the hungry, clothed the naked, visited the sick. And where is Christ? Where?—whoso shall receive a little child in my name receiveth men. And who are Christ's? Every one that loveth is born of God.

LIBERTY AS AN INALIENABLE RIGHT

Henry Grattan

(1746-1791)

Henry Grattan, the great Irish statesman and orator, the eloquent advocate of Irish self-government and Catholic Emancipation, was graduated from Trinity College in 1767 and was called
to the bar in 1772. It was in 1775 that Grattan joined the opposition in the Irish Parliament and started his agitation for a
free independent parliament. This was accomplished in 1782
by the repeal of Poyning's Law. In 1800 Grattan was again
prominent in his speeches against the union of the Irish and
English legislatures, and in 1805 entered the English Parliament,
where he remained until his death ever fighting for the interests
of Ireland and for Catholic emancipation.

Lecky has said of Grattan that no British orator except
Chatham had an equal power of firing an educated audience
with an intense enthusiasm or of animating and inspiring a
nation. His thoughts were often epigramatic and his argument
condensed, yet so clear and forceful was the effect that it appeared
axiomatic. Through his speeches were interspersed flashes of
poetic beauty which seemed almost inspired. Grattan was a
born orator who had a natural ear for the music of language
which with study made him the organ of liberty and progress
for Ireland. He overcame natural handicaps of a defective voice
and a clumsy figure, and the purity of his own life glowed
through every statement. One of Grattan's greatest speeches was
that delivered on April 19, 1780, on *Liberty as an Inalienable
Right*, of which critics have said that nothing equal to it had
ever been heard in Ireland nor probably was its superior ever
delivered in the British House of Commons.

Sir, I have entreated an attendance on this day that you might, in the most public manner, deny the claim of the British Parliament to make law for Ireland, and with one voice lift up your hands against it.

If I had lived when William took away the woolen manufacture, or when George I declared this country to be dependent and subject to laws to be enacted by the Parliament of England, I should have made a covenant with my own conscience to seize the first moment of rescuing my country from the ignominy of such acts of power; or, if I had a son, I should have administered to him an oath that he would consider himself a person separate and set apart for the discharge of so important a duty; upon the same principle I am now come to move a Declaration of Right, the first moment occurring, since my time, in which such a declaration could be made with any chance of success, and without aggravation of oppression. Sir, it must appear to every person that, notwithstanding the import of sugar and export of woolens, the people of this country are not satisfied—something remains; the greater work is behind; the public heart is not well at ease. To promulgate our satisfactions; to stop the throats of millions with the votes of Parliament; to preach homilies to the volunteers; to utter invectives against the people, under pretense of affectionate advice, is an attempt, weak, suspicious and inflammatory.

You can not dictate to those whose sense you are intrusted to represent; your ancestors, who sat within these walls, lost to Ireland trade and liberty; you, by the assistance of the people, have recovered trade; you still owe the kingdom liberty; she calls upon you to restore it.

The ground of public discontent seems to be:

"We have gotten commerce, but no freedom"; the same power which took away the export of woolens and the export of glass may take them away again; the repeal is partial, and the ground of repeal is upon a principle of expediency.

Sir, "expedient" is a word of appropriated and tyrannical import; "expedient" is an ill-omened word, selected to express the reservation of authority, while the exercise is mitigated; "expedient" is the ill-omened expression of the Repeal of the American Stamp Act. England thought it "expedient" to repeal that law; happy had it been for mankind, if, when she withdrew the exercise, she had not reversed the right! To that reservation she owes the loss of her American empire, at the expense of millions, and America the seeking of liberty through a sea of bloodshed. The repeal of the Woolen Act, similarly circumstanced, pointed against the principle of our liberty—a present relaxation, but tyranny in reserve—may be a subject for illumination to a populace, or a pretense for apostasy to a courtier, but cannot be the subject of settled satisfaction to a freeborn, intelligent, and injured community.

Nor are we only prompted to this when we consider our strength, we are challenged to it when we look to Great Britain. The people of that country are now waiting to hear the Parliament of Ireland speak on the subject of their liberty; it begins to be made a question in England whether the principal persons wish to be free; it was the delicacy of former Parliaments to be silent on the subject of commercial restrictions, lest they should show a knowledge of the fact, and not a sense of the violation; you have spoken out, you have shown a knowledge of the fact, and not a sense of the violation.   On the contrary, you have returned thanks for a partial repeal made on a principle of power; you have returned thanks as for a favor, and your exultation has brought your characters, as well as your spirit, into question, and tends to shake to her foundation your title to liberty; thus you do not leave your rights where you found them.   You have done too much not to do more; you have gone too far not to go on; you have brought yourselves into that situation in which you must silently abdicate the rights of your country, or publicly restore them.   It is very true you may feed your manufacturers, and landed gentlemen may get their rents, and you may export woolen, and may load a vessel with baize, serges, and kerseys, and you may bring back again directly from the plantations sugar, indigo, speckle-wood, beetle-root, and panellas.   But liberty, the foundation of trade, the charters of the land, the independency of Parliament, the securing, crowning, and the consummation of everything are yet to come.   Without them the work is imperfect, the foundation is wanting, the capital is wanting, trade is not free, Ireland is a colony without the benefit of a charter, and you are a provincial synod without the privilege of a Parliament.

The British minister mistakes the Irish character: had he intended to make Ireland a slave, he should have kept her a beggar; there is no middle policy; win her heart by the restoration of her right, or cut off the nation's right hand; greatly emancipate, or fundamentally destroy it.   We may talk plausibly to England, but so long as she exercises a power to bind this country, so long are the nations in a state of war; the claims of the one go against the liberty of the other, and the sentiments of the latter go to oppose these claims to the last drop of her blood.   The English Opposition, therefore, are right; mere trade will not satisfy Ireland —they judge of us by other great nations, by the nation whose political life has been a struggle for liberty; they judge of us with a true knowledge of, and just deference for, our character—that a country enlightened as Ireland, chartered as Ireland, armed as Ireland, and injured as Ireland, will be satisfied with nothing less than liberty.

There is no objection to this resolution, except fears; I have examined your fears; I pronounce them to be frivolous.   I might deny that the British nation was attached to the idea of binding Ireland; I might deny that England was a tyrant at heart; and I might call to witness the odium of North and the Popularity of Chatham, her support of Holland, her contributions to Corsica, and her charters communicated to Ireland; but ministers have traduced England to debase Ireland; and politicians, like priests, represent the power they serve as diabolical, to possess with superstitious fears the victim whom they design to plunder.   If England is a tyrant, it is you who have made her so; it is the slave that makes the tyrant, and then murmurs at the master whom he himself has constituted.

I do allow, on the subject of commerce, England was jealous in the extreme, and I do say it was commercial jealousy, it was the spirit of monopoly (the woolen trade and the Act of Navigation had made her tenacious of a comprehensive legislative authority), and having now ceded that monopoly, there is nothing in the way of your liberty except your own corruption and pusillanimity; and nothing can prevent your being free except yourselves. It is not in the disposition of England; it is not in the interest of England; it is not in her arms. What! can 8,000,000 of Englishmen opposed to 20,000,000 of French, to 7,000,000 of Spanish, to 3,000,000 of Americans, reject the alliance of 3,000,000 in Ireland? Can 8,000,000 of British men, thus outnumbered by foes, take upon their shoulders the expense of an expedition to enslave you? Will Great Britain, a wise and magnanimous country, thus tutored by experience and wasted by war, the French Navy riding her Channel, send an army to Ireland, to levy no tax, to enforce no law, to answer no end whatsoever, except to spoliate the charters of Ireland and enforce a barren oppression? What? has England lost thirteen Provinces? has she reconciled herself to this loss, and will she not be reconciled to the liberty of Ireland? Take notice that the very constitution which I move you to declare Great Britain herself offered to America; it is a very instructive proceeding in the British history. In 1778 a commission went out, with powers to cede to the thirteen Provinces of America, totally and radically, the legislative authority claimed over her by the British Parliament, and the commissioners, pursuant to their powers, did offer to all or any of the American States the total surrender of the legislative authority of the British Parliament.

What? has England offered this to the resistance of America, and will she refuse it to the loyalty of Ireland? Your fears, then, are nothing but a habitual subjugation of mind; that subjugation of mind which made you, at first, tremble at every measure of safety; which made the principal men among us conceive the commercial association would be a war; that fear, which made them imagine the military association had a tendency to treason; which made them think a short money bill would be public convulsion; and yet these measures have not only proved to be useful, but are held to be moderate, and the Parliament that adopted them, is praised, not for its unanimity only, but for its temper also. You now wonder that you submitted for so many years to the loss of the woolen trade and the deprivation of the glass trade; raised above your former abject state in commerce, you were ashamed at your past pusillanimity; so when you have summoned a boldness which shall assert the literties of your country—raised by the act, and reinvested, as you should be, in the glory of your ancient rights and privileges, you will be surprised at yourselves, who have so long submitted to their violation. Moderation is but the relative term; for nations, like men, are only safe in proportion to the spirit they put forth, and the proud contemplation with which they survey themselves. Conceive yourselves a plantation, ridden by an oppressive government, and everything you have done is but a fortunate frenzy; conceive yourselves to be what you are, a great, a growing, and a proud nation, and a declaration of right is no more than the safe exercise of your indubitable authority.

I shall hear of ingratitude! I name the argument to despise it and the men who make use of it; I know the men who use it are not grateful, they are insatiate; they are public extortioners, who would stop the tide of public prosperity and turn it to the channel of their own emolument; I know of no species of gratitude which should prevent my country from being free, no gratitude which should oblige Ireland to be the slave of England. In cases of robbery and usurpation, nothing is an object of gratitude except the thing stolen, the charter spoliated. A nation's liberty can not, like her treasures, be meted and parceled out in gratitude; no man can be grateful or liberal of his conscience, nor woman of her honor, nor nation of her liberty; there are certain unimpartable, inherent, invaluable properties, whether body politic or body natural. With the same contempt do I treat that charge which says that Ireland is insatiable; saying that Ireland asks nothing but that which Great Britain has robbed her of, her rights and privileges; to say that Ireland will not be satisfied with liberty, because she is not satisfied with slavery, is folly. I laugh at that man who supposes that Ireland will not be content with a free trade and a free constitution; and would any man advise her to be content with less?

The same laws, the same charters, communicate to both kingdoms, Great Britain and Ireland, the same rights and privileges; and one privilege above them all is that communicated by Magna Charta, by the 25th of Edward III, and by a multitude of other statutes, "not to be bound by any act except made with the arch-bishops, bishops, earls, barons, and freemen of the commonalty," namely, of the Parliament of the realm. On this right of exclusive legislation are founded the Petition of Right, Bill of Rights, Revolution, and Act of Settlement. The king has no other title to his crown than that which you have to your liberty; both are founded, the throne and your freedom, upon the right vested in the subject to resist by arms, notwithstanding the oaths of allegiance, any authority attempting to impose acts of power as laws, whether that authority be one man or a host, the second James, or the British Parliament!

Every argument for the House of Hanover is equally an argument for the liberties of Ireland; the Act of Settlement is an act of rebellion, or the declaratory statute of the 6th of George I, an act of usurpation; for both can not be law.

I do not refer to doubtful history, but to living record; to common charters; to the interpretation England has put upon these charters— an interpretation not made by words only, but crowned by arms; to the revolution she had formed upon them, to the king she has deposed, and to the king she has established; and, above all, to the oath of allegiance solemnly plighted to the House of Stuart, and afterward set aside, in the instance of a grave and moral people absolved by virtue of these very charters.

And as anything less than liberty is inadequate to Ireland, so is it dangerous to Great Britain. We are too near the British nation, we are too conversant with her history, we are too much fired by her example, to be anything less than her equal; anything less, we should be her bitterest enemies—an enemy to that power which smote us with her mace, and to that Constitution from whose blessings we were excluded: to be ground as we have been by the British nation, bound by her Parliament, plundered by her Crown, threatened by her enemies, insulted with her protection, while we return thanks for her condescension, or a system of meanness and misery which has expired in our determination, as I hope it has in her magnanimity.

There in no policy left for Great Britain but to cherish the remains of her Empire, and do justice to a country who is determined to do justice to herself, certain that she gives nothing equal to what she received from us when we gave her Ireland.

Do not tolerate that power which blasted you for a century, that power which shattered your loom, banished your manufacturers, dishonored your peerage, and stopped the growth of your people; do not, I say, be bribed by an export of woolen, or an import of sugar, and permit that power which has thus withered the land to remain in your country and have existence in your pusillanimity.

Do not suffer the arrogance of England to imagine a surviving hope in the fears of Ireland; do not send the people to their own resolves for liberty, passing by the tribunals of justice and the high court of Parliament; neither imagine that, by any formation of apology, you can palliate such a commission to your hearts, still less to your children, who will sting you with their curses in your grave for having interposed between them and their Maker, robbing them of an immense occasion, and losing an opportunity which you did not create, and can never restore.

Hereafter, when these things shall be history, your age of thraldom and poverty, your sudden resurrection, commercial redress, and miraculous armament, shall the historian stop at liberty, and observe that here the principal men among us fell into mimic trances of gratitude—they were awed by a weak ministry, and bribed by an empty treasury—and when liberty was within their grasp, and the temple opened her folding-doors, and the arms of the people clanged, and the zeal of the nation urged and encouraged them on, that they fell down and were prostituted at the threshold?

I might, as a constituent, come to your bar, and demand my liberty. I do call upon you, by the laws of the land and their violation, by the instruction of eighteen counties, by the arms, inspiration, and providence of the present moment, tell us the rule by which we shall go—assert the law of Ireland—declare the liberty of the land.

I will not be answered by a public lie, in the shape of an amendment; neither, speaking for the subject's freedom, am I to hear of faction. I wish for nothing but to breathe, in this our island, in common with my fellow subjects, the air of liberty. I have no ambition, unless it be the ambition to break your chain and contemplate your glory. I never will be satisfied so long as the meanest cottager in Ireland has a link of the British chain clanking to his rage—he may be naked, he shall not be in iron; and I do see the time is at hand, the spirit is gone forth, the declaration is planted; and tho great men shall apostatize, yet the cause will live; and tho the public speaker should die, yet the immortal fire shall outlast the organ which conveyed it, and the breath of liberty, like the word of the holy man, will not die with the prophet, but survive him.

IN BEHALF OF ROWAN AND FREE SPEECH [9]

John Philpot Curran
(1750-1817)

John Curran, Ireland's great legal orator and wit, was born in County Cork, educated at Trinity College, Dublin, and called to the Irish Bar in 1775. Here his eloquence and humor brought him an extensive practice. He defended his countrymen against charges of sedition and treason brought against them in their struggle for Irish nationality, particularly during the Insurrections of 1798. In 1784, when Curran entered the Irish Parliament, he at once joined Grattan in the defense of the cause of Ireland.

As a boy Curran had a stuttering in his speech which he overcame by arduous practice, and he later acquired an eloquence so copious, rapid, and ornate that he has been pronounced the greatest advocate of Ireland. The last years of his life, which were overshadowed by the desertion of his wife and the death of his daughter whose heart was broken by the execution of her lover, the patriotic Robert Emmet, were spent in London where he enjoyed the friendship of Thomas More, Erskine, and William Godwin.

There is included here an extract from his famous defense of Archibald Rowan, which although 25 pages long was delivered by Curran from a dozen "catch words" on the back of his brief. Rowan, President of the United Irishmen of Dublin, had been brought before the Court of the King's Bench for libel. Curran spoke for the defence—not so much to seek an acquittal as to defend the principles of free speech.

The peculiarity of the British Constitution (to which, in its fullest extent, we have an undoubted right, however distant we may be from

* Abridged.

the actual enjoyment, and in which it surpasses every known government in Europe) is this: that its only professed object is the general good, and its only foundation the general will. Hence the people have a right, acknowledged from time immemorial, fortified by a pile of statutes, and authenticated by a revolution that speaks louder than them all, to see whether abuses have been committed, and whether their properties and their liberties have been attended to as they ought to be. This is a kind of subject which I feel myself overawed when I approach. There are certain fundamental principles which nothing but necessity should expose to a public examination. They are pillars the depth of whose foundation you can not explore without endangering their strength; but let it be recollected that the discussion of such topics should not be condemned in me nor visited upon my client. The blame, if any there be, should rest only with those who have forced them into discussion. I say, therefore, it is the right of. the people to keep an eternal watch upon the conduct of their rulers; and in order to do that, the freedom of the Press has been cherished by the law of England. In private defamation let it never be tolerated; in wicked and wanton aspersion upon a good and honest administration let it never be supported—not that a good government can be exposed to danger by groundless accusation, but because a bad government is sure to find in the detected falsehood of a licentious Press a security and a credit which it could never otherwise obtain.

Gentlemen, without any observation of mine, you must see that this indictment contains a direct charge upon Mr. Rowan; namely, that he did, with the intents set forth in the information, publish this paper so that here you have, in fact, two or three questions for your decision: first, the matter of fact of the publication; namely, did Mr. Rowan publish that paper? If Mr. Rowan did not, in fact, publish that paper, you have no longer any question on which to employ your minds. If you think that he was in fact the publisher, then, and not till then, arises the great and important subject to which your judgments must be directed. And that comes shortly and simply to this: Is the paper a libel; and did he publish it with the intent charged in the information?

But whatever you may think of the abstract question, whether the paper be libelous or not, and of which paper it has not even been insinuated that he is the author, there can be no ground for a verdict against him unless you also are persuaded that what he did was done with a criminal design. I wish, gentlemen, to simplify, and not to perplex; I therefore say again, if these three circumstances conspire—that he published it, that it was a libel, and that it was published with the purposes alleged in the information—you ought unquestionably to find him guilty; if, on the other hand, you do not find that all these circumstances concurred; if you can not, upon your oaths, say that he published it; if it be not in your opinion a libel; and if he did not publish it with the intention alleged; I say upon the failure of any one of these points my client is entitled, in justice and upon your oaths, to a verdict of acquittal.

I speak in the spirit of the British law, which makes liberty commensurate with and inseparable from the British soil; which proclaims, even to the stranger and the sojourner, the moment he sets foot upon British earth, that the ground on which he treads is holy and consecrated by the genius of universal emancipation.

No matter in what language his doom may have been pronounced; no matter what complexion incompatible with freedom an Indian or an African sun may have burned upon him; no matter in what disastrous battle his liberty may have been cloven down; no matter with what solemnities he may have been devoted upon the altar of slavery; the first moment he touches the sacred soil of Britain the altar and the god sink together in the dust; his soul walks abroad in her own majesty; his body swells beyond the measure of his chains that burst from around him, and he stands, redeemed, regenerated, and disenthraled by the irresistible genius of universal emancipation.

ON CATHOLIC RELIEF [10]

Lord William Conyngham Plunkett
(1765-1854)

Lord Plunkett was the most eloquent Protestant pleader for Catholic emancipation. Graduating from Dublin University in 1784 he studied law in London and was called to the Irish bar in 1787; entered the Irish Parliament in 1798 and was denounced as a renegade when he became Solicitor-General in 1803; subsequently he became Attorney-General. He was raised to the peerage in 1827 and served as Lord Chancellor of Ireland 1830-1834 and again 1835-1841. It was Lord Plunkett who conducted the prosecution for Robert Emmet on an accusation of treason.

Plunkett had an imposing physical appearance and a commanding height, but his voice was rather cold, harsh, and metallic and his delivery was almost immobile.

Included here is a speech *On Catholic Relief* which Plunkett delivered in the House of Commons February 28, 1821. Peel accredited the speech as standing nearly the highest in point of ability of any ever heard in the House.

And now, sir, I shall proceed, without further preface, to the main argument. The question presents itself in three distinct points of view: as a question of religion, as a question of constitutional principle, and as a question of policy and expediency, in reference to the stability of our existing establishments.

In the first place, it appears obvious that the requiring a religious pledge to the State, as a qualification for civil rights, makes religion an affair of state; because you cannot lay it down as a rule to be applied only in a case of true religion, for every religion is the true one in the opinion of its own professors; and therefore, if the position is true in our instance, it must be equally true that, in every State, Protestant or Catholic, Christian or Pagan, the interests of true religion require a pledge to the State that the person admitted to its privileges is of the

[10] Abridged.

religion of that State. All this leads to the unavoidable inference that, in the opinion of those who so argue, there is no truth in any religion, and no criterion other than its adoption by the State. I do not say that such a principle may not be taken on trust by an honest man, and hotly insisted on by him, if he happens to be a zealous man, but I say it can not be deliberately and rationally maintained by any person who believes that there is any absolute trust in any religion.

Again, if religion is to be an affair of state, why not require some positive profession of faith as a qualification? Such as that he is a Christian, or that he believes in God, or in a future state, or that he has an immortal soul? Why does the declaration sound only in horror, and antipathy, and denunciation of another religion? If the law is to be put into a state of electricity by the Church, why not of positive electricity?

Again; if we are to denounce, why denounce only one particular sect of Christians? Why not Socinians? Why not those who deny the divine nature of our Lord? Why select those who believe all that we do, merely because they believe something more? Why not Jews, Mohammedans, Pagans? Any one of these may safely make the declaration, provided he is willing to commit the breach of good manners which it requires. He may not only deny our God and our Redeemer, but he may worship Jupiter or Osiris, an ape or a crocodile, the host of heaven or the creeping things of the earth; let him only have a statutable horror of the religion of others, and agree to brand with the name of idolatry the religion of the greater part of the Christian world. But further, if the Roman Catholic religion is to be singled out as that, by the common bond of hatred to which we are all to be united in the ties of brotherly love and Christian charity, why select only one particular article of their faith, and say that the sacrifice of the Mass is impious and idolatrous? Why leave them their seven sacraments, their auricular confession, their purgatory; all equally badges of superstition, evidences of contumacy and causes of schism? Why make war exclusively upon this one article? We all declare solemnly that we consider the sacrifice of the Mass as superstitious and idolatrous. Now I entreat each member of this House to suppose that I am asking him individually, and as a private gentleman, does he know what is said, or meant, or done in the sacrifice of the Mass; or how it differs from our own mode of celebrating the Communion, so as to render it superstitious and idolatrous? If I could count upon the vote of every member, who must answer me that upon his honor he does not know, I should be sure of carrying, by an overwhelming majority, this or any other question I might think it proper to propose. Were I now to enter on a discussion of the nature of these doctrines, every member would complain that I was occupying the time of statesmen with subjects utterly unconnected with the business of the House or the policy of the country. Can there be a more decisive proof of its unsuitableness as a test?

By the Constitution of England, every liege subject is entitled, not merely to the protection of the laws, but is admissable to all the franchises and all the privileges of the State. For the argument I have now to deal with is this: "That by some principle of the Constitution, independent of the positive law, the Roman Catholic is necessarily excluded." What, then, is this principle of exclusion? Merely this, "that the Roman Catholics acknowledge the spiritual supremacy of the pope." Why then if, independently of the positive law, this acknowledgment deprives them of the privileges which belong to the liege subjects of the realm, the exclusive principle must have been in force before the law. If so, there did not exist in England a liege man entitled to the privileges of the Constitution before the time of Henry the Eighth; for till then all acknowledged the spiritual supremacy of the pope. Magna Charta was established by outlaws from the State. Those gallant barons, whose descendants have been so feelingly alluded to by my noble friend, though they were indeed permitted to achieve, yet were not entitled to share the liberties of their country. They might not dare to open the great charter which had been won by their hardihood and patriotism. Nay, more; if this principle be true, there is not, at this moment, a liege subject in any Catholic country in Europe. Sir, such trash as this shocks our common sense, and sets all argument at defiance. . . .

One word more and I have done. It has been asked, where is concession to stop? I say, precisely where necessity, arising from public good, requires the continuance of the restriction. Exclusion is like war: *justum quibus necessarium.* Beyond this it would be folly to proceed. Short of this it is folly and injustice to stop. By this test let the claim be tried. If there is any office the possession of which by a Roman Catholic would be dangerous or injurious to our establishments, let him be excluded from it. If there is any franchise, whose exercise can be attended with real danger, let it be withheld. Such exclusion, or withholding, is not an anomaly, or inconsistency, in our system of conciliation, because, when the exclusion is not arbitrary and gratuitous, there is no insult. Such an exclusion forms no link of the chain, and the Roman Catholic will submit to it cheerfully; just as it would be the duty of the Protestant if, for similar reasons, a similar sacrifice were required from him. Let him know, in intelligible terms, the reason and the necessity, and he is satisfied. But do not, in so momentous a concern, give him words, and think to reconcile him. Talk to him of the Protestant establishment, and he understands you; he bows to it; he sees it engraved in capitals on the front of the political fabric. But if you tell him of Protestant ascendency, or Protestant exclusion, he asks in vain for it in the elements of our law or its traditions, in the commentaries of its sage expositors, in the Reformation, the Revolution, or the Union—he sees in it nothing but insult and contumacy; and he demands, in the name of the laws, and in the spirit of the Constitution, that he may be no longer its victim.

A PATRIOT'S PLEA [11]

Robert Emmet

(1778-1803)

Robert Emmet, the flaming young patriot of Ireland, who was hanged in the cause of the Irish Revolution when he was only twenty-five years of age, is one of the most romantic figures of the Irish struggle for freedom. As one of the "United Irishmen," Emmet with the impassioned nature of youth, had led an Irish rabble in Dublin and was held responsible for the death of those slain in the insurrection. While his accomplices escaped to the mountains, Emmet lingered in Dublin to bid farewell to his fiancée, Sara Curran. His speech in his own defense at the trial for treason had a tremendous influence on the Home Rule agitation in Ireland, for in his burst of eloquence he was fighting for his country as well as for his own life. It is included here as a masterpiece of extemporaneous eloquence.

I am charged with being an emissary of France! An emissary of France! And for what end? It is alleged that I wished to sell the independence of my country! And for what end? Was this the object of my ambition? And is this the mode by which a tribunal of justice reconciles contradictions? No, I am no emissary; and my ambition was to hold a place among the deliverers of my country—not in power, not in profit, but in the glory of the achievement! Sell my country's independence to France! And for what? Was it for a change of masters? No! But for ambition! O my country, was it personal ambition that could influence me? Had it been the soul of my actions, could I not by my education and fortune, by the rank and consideration of my family, have placed myself among the proudest of my oppressors? My country was my idol; to it I sacrificed every selfish, every endearing sentiment; and for it, I now offer up my life. O God! No, my lord; I acted as an Irishman, determined on delivering my country from the yoke of a foreign and unrelenting tyranny, and from the more galling yoke of a domestic faction, which is its joint partner and perpetrator in

[11] Abridged.

the parricide, for the ignominy of existing with an exterior of splendor and of conscious depravity. It was the wish of my heart to extricate my country from this doubly riveted despotism.

Let no man dare, when I am dead, to charge me with dishonor; let no man attaint my memory by believing that I could have engaged in any cause but that of my country's liberty and independence; or that I could have become the pliant minion of power in the oppression or the miseries of my countrymen. The proclamation of the provisional government speaks for our views; no inference can be tortured from it to countenance barbarity or debasement at home, or subjection, humiliation, or treachery from abroad; I would not have submitted to a foreign oppressor for the same reason that I would resist the foreign and domestic oppressor; in the dignity of freedom I would have fought upon the threshold of my country, and its enemy should enter only by passing over my lifeless corpse. Am I, who lived but for my country, and who have subjected myself to the dangers of the jealous and watchful oppressor, and the bondage of the grave, only to give my countrymen their rights, and my country her independence, and am I to be loaded with calumny, and not suffered to resent or repel it—no, God forbid!

If the spirits of the illustrious dead participate in the concerns and cares of those who are dear to them in this transitory life—oh, ever dear and venerated shade of my departed father, look down with scrutiny upon the conduct of your suffering son; and see if I have even for a moment deviated from those principles of morality and patriotism which it was your care to instill into my youthful mind, and for which I am now to offer up my life!

My lords, you are impatient for the sacrifice—the blood which you seek is not congealed by the artificial terrors which surround your victim; it circulates warmly and unruffled, through the channels which God created for noble purposes, but which you are bent to destroy, for purposes so grievous, that they cry to heaven. Be yet patient! I have but a few words more to say. I am going to my cold and silent grave: my lamp of life is nearly extinguished: my race is run: the grave opens to receive me, and I sink into its bosom! I have but one request to ask at my departure from this world—it is the charity of its silence! Let no man write my epitaph: for as no man who knows my motives dare now vindicate them, let not prejudice or ignorance asperse them. Let them and me repose in obscurity and peace, and my tomb remain uninscribed, until other times, and other men, can do justice to my character; when my country takes her place among the nations of the earth, then, and not till then, let my epitaph be written. I have done.

THE CHARMS OF KILDARE [12]

Daniel O'Connell

(1775-1847)

Daniel O'Connell was the lion of the Irish rostrum. From County Kerry, O'Connell was called to the Irish bar in 1798. In his twenty-two years of practice he fought for the rights of the Catholics and on his entrance into the English Parliament in 1828 he fought for the repeal of the Union of Ireland with Great Britain.

O'Connell was a man of royal aspect and his voice was seductively musical—"the most musical," Disraeli said, "ever heard in the House of Commons—deep, sonorous, and flexible." He had flashing expressive eyes. It is said he could "whine and wheedle and wink with one eye while he wept with the other." O'Connell was also a master of characterization and could be colloquial one moment and regal the next—could convulse the people with laughter and immediately drive them to tears.

His constant friction with the English conservatives resulted at last in O'Connell's arrest and conviction for treason, but he was released the following year. During the campaign for the freedom of Ireland in 1843 O'Connell delivered the following speech on the Hill of Tara in County Kildare to over 150,000 people.

I wish to live long enough to have perfect justice administered to Ireland and liberty proclaimed throughout the land. It will take me some time to prepare my plan for the formation of the new Irish House of Commons; that plan which we will yet submit to her Majesty for her approval, when she gets rid of her present paltry Administration [13] and has one which I can support. . . . You may be sure of this—and

---

[12] Abridged.

[13] Disraeli, whom O'Connell once designated as "heir-at-law of the blasphemous thief who died upon the cross."

I say it in the presence of Him who will judge me—that I never will willfully deceive you. I have but one wish under heaven, and that is for the liberty and prosperity of Ireland. I am for leaving England to the English, Scotland to the Scotch, but we must have Ireland for the Irish. I will not be content until I see not a single man in any office, from the lowest constable to the lord chancellor, but Irishmen. This is our land, and we must have it. We will be obedient to the Queen, joined to England by the golden link of the crown, but we must have our own parliament, our own bench, our own magistrates, and we will give some of the *shoneens* who now occupy the bench leave to retire, such as those lately appointed by Sugden. He is a pretty boy, sent here from England; but I ask, did you ever hear such a name as he has got? I remember, in Wexford, a man told me he had a pig at home of which he was so fond of that he would call it Sugden.

No; we will get judicial independence for Ireland. It is for this purpose we are assembled here to-day, as every countenance I see around me testifies. If there is any one here who is not for the Union let him say so. Is there anybody here for the repeal? (Cries of "All, all!")

Yes, my friends, the Union was begot in iniquity, it was perpetuated in fraud and cruelty. It was no compact, no bargain, but it was an act of the most decided tyranny and corruption that was ever yet perpetrated. Trial by jury was suspended; the right of personal protection was at an end; courts-martial sat throughout the land, and the country of Kildare, among others, flowed with blood. Oh, my friends, listen now to the man of peace, who will never expose you to the power of your enemies. In 1798 there were some brave men, some valiant men, at head of the people at large; but there were many traitors, who left the people in the power of their enemies. The Curragh of Kildare afforded an instance of the fate which Irishmen were to expect, who confided in their Saxon enemies. Oh, it was an ill-organized, a premature, a foolish, and an absurd insurrection; but you have a leader now who never will allow you to commit any act so foolish or so destructive.

How delighted do I feel with the thorough conviction which has come over the minds of the people, that they could not gratify your enemies more than by committing a crime. No; our ancestors suffered for confiding in the English, but we never will confide in them. They suffered for being divided among themselves. There is no division among us. They suffered for their own dissensions—for not standing man to man by each other's side. We shall stand peaceably side by side in the face of every enemy. Oh, how delighted was I in the scenes which I witnessed as I came along here to-day! How my heart throbbed, how my spirit was elevated, how my bosom swelled with delight at the multitude which I beheld, and which I shall behold, of the stalwart and strong men of Kildare! I was delighted at the activity and force that I saw around me: and my old heart grew warm again in admiring the beauty of the dark-eyed maids and matrons of Kildare. Oh, there is a starlight sparkling from the eye of a Kildare beauty, that is scarcely equaled, and could not be excelled, all over the world. And remember that you are the sons, the fathers, the brothers, and the husbands of such women, and a traitor or a coward could never be connected with any of them.

Yes, I am in a county remarkable in the history of Ireland for its bravery and its misfortune, for its credulity in the faith of others, for its people judged of the Saxon by the honesty of its own natures. I am in a country celebrated for the sacredness of its shrines and fanes. I am in a country where the lamp of Kildare's holy shrine burned with its sacred fire, through ages of darkness and storm; that fire which for six centuries burned before the high altar without being extinguished, being fed contiuously, without the slightest interruption; and it seemed to me to have been not an inapt representation of the continuous fidelity and religious love of country of the men of Kildare. Yes, you have those high qualities—religious fidelity, continuous love of country. Even your enemies admit that the world has never produced any people that exceeded the Irish in activity and strength. The Scottish philosopher has declared, and the French philosopher has confirmed it, that number one in the human race is, blessed by Heaven! the Irishman. In moral virtue, in religion, in perseverance, and in glorious temperance, you excel. Have I any teetotalers here? Yes, it is teetotalism that is repealing the Union. I could not afford to bring you together, I would not dare to bring you together, but that I had the teetotalers for my police.

Yes, among the nations of the earth, Ireland stands number one in the physical strength of her sons and in the beauty and purity of her daughters. Ireland, land of my forefathers, how my mind expands, and my spirit walks abroad in something of majesty, when I contemplate the high qualities, inestimable virtues, and true purity and piety and religious fidelity of the inhabitants of our green fields and productive mountains. Oh, what a scene surrounds us! It is not only the countless thousands of brave and active and peaceable and religious men that are here assembled, but Nature herself has written her character with the finest beauty in the verdant plains that surround us. Let any man run round the horizon with his eye, and tell me if created Nature ever produced anything so green and so lovely, so undulating, so teeming with production. The richest harvests that any land can produce are those reaped in Ireland; and then here are the sweetest meadows, the greenest fields, the loftiest mountains, the purest streams, the noblest rivers, the most capacious harbors, and her water-power is equal to turn the machinery of the whole world.

Oh, my friends, it is a country worth fighting for; it is a country worth dying for; but above all, it is a country worth being tranquil, determined, submissive, and docile for; disciplined as you are in obedience to those who are breaking the way, and trampling down the barriers between you and your constitutional liberty, I will see every man of you having a vote, and every man protected by the ballot from the agent or landlord. I will see labor protected, and every title to possession recognized, when you are industrious and honest. I will see prosperity again throughout your land; the busy hum of the shuttle and the tinkling of the smithy shall be heard again. We shall see the nailer employed even until the middle of the night, and the carpenter covering himself with his chips. I will see prosperity in all its gradations spreading through a happy, contented religious land. I will hear the hymn of a happy people go forth at sunrise, to God in praise of His mercies, and I will see the evening sun set amongst the uplifted hands of a religious and free population. Every blessing that man can bestow and religion can confer upon the faithful heart shall spread throughout the land. Stand by me—join with me—I will say be obedient to me, and Ireland shall be free.

THE SWORD SPEECH [14]

Thomas Meagher
(1823-1867)

The Irish-American orator and soldier, Thomas Meagher, dedicated his entire life to the cause of liberty. After making an enduring reputation as an orator in the cause of Irish independence Meagher was arrested by the English government and banished as a convict, but made his escape to New York City where he set up a practice of law and became editor of the *Irish News*. Later he fought valiantly in the American Civil War.

Meagher's famous *Sword Speech* delivered in Constitution Hall, Dublin, July 28, 1846, when he was scarcely 23 years of age, as a protest against "trafficking with the Whigs" scintillated over all of Europe and took its place among the classics of the English language. Meagher was a master of denunciation and had a remarkable sense of rhythm and a vivid imagination which made it natural for him to employ word pictures.

A good government may, indeed, redress the grievances of an injured people; but a strong people can alone build up a great nation. To be strong, a people must be self-reliant, self-ruled, self-sustained. The dependence of one people upon another, even for the benefits of legislation, is the deepest source of national weakness.

By an unnatural law it exempts a people from their just duties—their just responsibilities. When you exempt a people from these duties, from these responsibilities, you generate in them a distrust in their own powers. Thus you enervate, if you do not utterly destroy, that spirit which a sense of these responsibilities is sure to inspire, and which the fulfilment of these duties never fails to invigorate. Where this spirit does not actuate, the country may be tranquil—it will not be prosperous. It may exist—it will not thrive. It may hold together—it will not advance. Peace it may enjoy—for peace and serfdom are

14 Abridged.

compatible. But, my lord, it will neither accumulate wealth, nor win a character. It will neither benefit mankind by the enterprise of its merchants, nor instruct mankind by the examples of its statesmen. I make these observations, for it is the custom of some moderate politicians to say, that when the Whigs have accomplished the "pacification" of the country, there will be little or no necessity for Repeal.

But the Whigs will enrich as well as pacify! Grant it, my lord. Then do I conceive that the necessity for Repeal will augment. Great interests demand great safeguards. The prosperity of a nation requires the protection of a senate. Hereafter a national senate may require the protection of a national army.

So much for the extraordinary affluence with which we are threatened; and which, it is said by gentlemen on the opposite shore of the Irish Sea, will crush this association and clamor for Irish nationality, in a sepulcher of gold. This prediction, however, is feebly sustained by the ministerial program that has lately appeared. After that most consulatory announcement, my lord, let those who have the patience of Job and the poverty of Lazarus, continue in good faith "to wait on Providence and the Whigs"—continue to entertain "some kind of hope" that if not "a complete and immediate remedy," at least "some remedy," "some improvement" will place this country in "a far better state" than it is at present, "some ten or twelve years hence." After that, let those who prefer the periodical boons of a Whig government to that which would be the abiding blessing of an Irish Parliament—let those who deny to Ireland what they assert for Poland—let those who would inflict, as Henry Grattan said, an eternal disability upon this country, to which Providence has assigned the largest facilities for power—let those who would ratify the "base swap," as Mr. Sheil once stigmatized the Act of Union, and would stamp perfection upon that deed of perfidy—let such men

> "—Plod on in sluggish misery,
> Rotting from sire to sire, from age to age,
> Proud of their trampled nature."

But we, my lord, who are assembled in this hall, and in whose hearts the Union has not bred the slave's disease—we who have not been imperialized— we are here, with the hope to undo that work, which, forty-six years ago, dishonored the ancient peerage, and subjugated the people of our country.

My lord, to assist the people of Ireland to undo that work, I came to this hall. I came to repeal the Act of Union; I came here for nothing else. Upon every other question, I feel myself at perfect liberty to differ from each and every one of you. Upon questions of finance, questions of religious character, questions of an educational character, questions of municipal policy, questions that may arise from the proceedings of the legislature; upon all these questions, I feel myself at perfect liberty to differ from each and every one of you.

Yet more, my lord, I maintain that it is my right to express my opinion upon each of these questions, if necessary. The right of free discussion I have here upheld. In the exercise of that right I have differed, sometimes, from the leader of this association, and would do so again. That right I will not abandon—I shall maintain it to the last. In doing so, let me not be told that I seek to undermine the influence of the leader of this association and am insensible to his services. My lord, I am grateful for his services, and will uphold his just influence. This is the first time I have spoken in these terms of that illustrious man, in this hall. I did not do so before—I felt it was unnecessary. I hate unnecessary praise—I scorn to receive it, I scorn to bestow it.

No, my lord, I am not ungrateful to the man [15] who struck the fetters off my arms while I was yet a child, and by whose influence, my father—the first Catholic who did so for two hundred years—sat, for the last two years, in the civic chair of an ancient city. But, my lord, the same God who gave to that great man the power to strike down an odious ascendency in this country, and enable him to institute in this land the glorious law of religious equality; the same God gave to me a mind that is my own—a mind that has not been mortgaged to the opinions of any man or any set of men; a mind that I was to use, and not surrender. My lord, in the exercise of that right, which I have here endeavored to uphold—a right which this association should preserve inviolate, if it desires not to become a despotism—in the exercise of that right, I have differed from Mr. O'Connell on previous occasions, and differ from him now.

In the existing circumstances of the country an excitement to arms would be senseless and wicked because irrational. To talk nowadays of repealing the Act of Union by force of arms would be to rhapsodize. If the attempt were made it would be a decided failure. There might be a riot in the street—there would be no revolution in the country. The secretary, Mr. Crean, will far more effectually promote the cause of repeal, by registering votes in Green Street than registering firearms in the head police office. Conciliation Hall on Burg Quay is more impregnable than a rebel camp on Vinegar Hill. The hustings at Dundalk will be more successfully stormed than the magazine in the park. The registry club, the reading-room, the polling booths—these are the only positions in the country we can occupy. Voters' certificates, books, pamphlets, newspapers—these are the only weapons we can employ. Therefore, my lord, I cast my vote in favor of the peaceful policy of this association. It is the only policy we can adopt. If that policy be pursued with truth, with courage, with fixed determination of purpose, I firmly believe it will succeed.

[15] Daniel O'Connell.

But, my lord, I dissented from the resolutions before us for other reasons. I stated the first; I now come to the second. I dissented from them, for I felt that, by assenting to them, I should have pledged myself to the unqualified repudiation of physical force in all countries, at all times, and under every circumstance. This I could not do. For, my lord, I do not abhor the use of arms in the vindication of national rights. There are times when arms will alone suffice, and when political ameliorations call for a drop of blood, and many thousand drops of blood. Opinion, I admit, will operate against opinion. But, as the honorable member for Kilkenny has observed, force must be used against force. The soldier is proof against a bullet. The man that will listen to reason, let him be reasoned with; but it is the weaponed arm of the patriot that can alone prevail against battalioned despotism.

Then, my lord, I do not condemn the use of arms as immoral, nor do I conceive it profane to say that the King of Heaven—the Lord of Hosts! the God of Battles! bestows His benediction upon those who unsheathe the sword in the hour of a nation's peril.

From that evening on which, in the valley of Bethulia, He nerved the arm of the Jewish girl to smite the drunken tyrant in his tent, down to this day, in which He has blessed the insurgent chivalry of the Belgian priest, His Almighty hand hath ever been stretched forth from His throne of light, to consecrate the flag of freedom, to bless the patriot's sword! Be it in the defense, or be it in the assertion of a people's liberty, I hail the sword as a sacred weapon; and if, my lord, it has sometimes taken the shape of the serpent and reddened the shroud of the oppressor with too deep a dye, like the anointed rod of the high priest, it has at other times, and as often, blossomed into celestial flowers to deck the freeman's brow.

Abhor the sword—stigmatize the sword? No, my lord, for, in the passes of the Tyrol, it cut to pieces the banner of the Bavarian, and, through those cragged passes, struck a path to fame for the peasant insurrectionist of Insprück! Abhor the sword—stigmatize the sword? No, my lord, for at its blow, a giant nation started from the waters of the Atlantic, and by its redeeming magic, and in the quivering of its crimson light, the crippled colony sprang into the attitude of a proud Republic—prosperous, limitless, and invincible! Abhor the sword—stigmatize the sword? No, my lord, for it swept the Dutch marauders out of the fine old town of Belgium, scourged them back to their own phlegmatic swamps, and knocked their flag and scepter, their laws and bayonets, into the sluggish waters of the Scheldt.

My lord, I learned that it was the right of a nation to govern herself, not in this hall, but upon the ramparts of Antwerp. This, the first article of a nation's creed, I learned upon those ramparts, where freedom was justly estimated, and the possession of the precious gift was purchased by the effusion of generous blood. My lord, I honor the Belgians, I admire the Belgians, I love the Belgians, for their enthusiasm, their courage, their success, and I, for one, will not stigmatize, for I do not abhor, the means by which they obtained a citizen king, a chamber of deputies. . . . [16]

[16] The speech was never completed for Meagher was expelled from the hall at this point.

AT THE BAR OF THE HOUSE OF LORDS [17]

Isaac Butt

(1813-1879)

The words "Home Rule" may be said to have been given
to the vocabulary of the British Isles by Isaac Butt, for it was
he who created the Home Rule party, renewed the drooping
hope of the Irish patriots, and compelled the English statesmen
to reckon again with Ireland. He blazed the trail for the more
militant Parnell who trod it with more spectacular triumph. As
a professor of political economy in his alma mater, Trinity College, Dublin, Butt first projected his political views. He became
a member of the Irish bar in 1838 and in 1852 entered Parliament. From 1836 to 1838 he was editor of *The Dublin Magazine*.

Butt was a lovable, brainy, charming character and a pure
patriot, politician, and gentleman. In his speech he was fluent,
clear and persuasive. Few Irish leaders were so eloquent and
none more lovable than Isaac Butt. Included here is a speech
which he delivered before the bar of the House of Lords, May 15,
1840.

Now, my lords, the point we have urged in our petition is, that
Dublin ought to be exempt, as you have exempted London; that, whatever
regulations you may hereafter apply to us, you can not deal with Dublin
upon the principle of establishing a purely democratic corporation. In
our petition we state our willingness to acquiesce in any measure of
reform that your lordships can adopt that will not compromise the
safety of the Protestant religion or violate our charters; but, my lords,
by adopting this measure you will do grievous injustice to the population
of a metropolitan city. Why subject us to the control of a democratic
corporation, with which we have no sympathy, no unity of sentiment,
no connection, no influence? Why place the bar, the professional
classes, the gentry of Ireland, under the control of the populace of its

[17] Abridged.

chief city? The principle has never been carried into effect in England. I do not merely urge that London has been exempted; but what would your lordships say if it was proposed to incorporate into one vast corporation the whole of this immense metropolis, so that Finsbury Square should give law to St. James? Is it because the professional classes and gentry of Dublin are distant, because they are unprotected, that you will inflict upon them a grievance and tyranny which you would not endure in London? I may be told that you must give the same Bill to Ireland that you have given to England, no matter how differently circumstanced the two countries. I take the argument. I say, if you give us all the evil, give us the one solitary good. London has been exempted—exempt Dublin. You have respected the Magna Charta of John in London; why not respect the Magna Charta of Henry in Dublin? Am I to be told that, because on the faith of England we gave up our independent Parliament, that you are to disregard us? On the faith of the legislative union, my lords, we demand that our rights should be held in the same respect as those of London. In our own Parliament they were so. Once, indeed, in that Parliament, in a debate upon the privileges of the City of Dublin, it was pleaded that some similar rights of the City of London had been respected by the English legislature. Some one dared to hint that the privileges of Dublin stood on lower and less sacred grounds. Who was the man who rose with prompt indignation to resent this insult to the Constitution of Ireland?—a man, my lords, whose memory is still held in honor in our country—the illustrious Henry Grattan! He it was who, in the spirit of a true Irishman, indignantly denounced the attempt to place the privileges of Dublin below those of London. It was no part of that great man's patriotism to vilify and bring into contempt the institutions of his country.

There is, indeed, my lords, a people who look with intense anxiety to your decision on this question—the people to whom these charters were granted, the Protestant people of Ireland. They contemplate this Bill with alarm and dismay; they believe that it will place them under a tyranny intolerant and intolerable—that it will hand over their country to the control of Jacobin clubs, but Jacobinism on which will be engrafted the worst elements of national antipathy and religious hate; which will present to the world the spectacle of the extraordinary influence of civil anarchy and religious despotism, uniting in an anomalous combination all the evils of democracy and of superstition. They implore of your lordships to protect them from this tyranny. One argument they have against this measure which your lordships will not disregard. In this the highest court of judicature in the realm, where the errors of every inferior tribunal are corrected—in this most solemn and most honorable of all tribunals, they appeal with confidence to your lordships, and say that this measure ought not to pass because it is unjust.

My lords, I have done. For myself I have no words strong enough to express my gratitude for the patience and indulgence with which you have heard me. If in any thing I may have wandered beyond the limits which my situation imposed, I implore of your lordships to attribute it to the embarrassment and novelty of my position—my inexperience in the forms and usages of your lordships' House.

IN DEFENCE OF IRISH CATHOLICS [18]

Richard L. Sheil

(1791-1851)

Richard Sheil, Irish dramatist, lawyer, essayist and orator, became a colleague of O'Connell in Parliament in the fight for Catholic emancipation. From the year 1830 to 1839 his eloquence often electrified the House of Commons.

Sheil's enunciation was quick and impetuous; his gestures rapid and continuous. It is said that he produced his effects in speech by short quick electric sentences which came like bolts from a thundercloud.

The speech included here is one delivered in defense of the Irish Catholics in the House of Commons, February 23, 1837, at a debate on the Irish Municipal Bill in reply to a remark made by Lord Lyndhurst that the Irish were aliens in blood and religion.

I should be surprised, indeed, if, while you are doing us wrong, you did not profess your solicitude to do us justice. From the day on which Strongbow set his foot upon the shore of Ireland, Englishmen were never wanting in protestations of their deep anxiety to do us justice. Even Strafford, the deserter of the people's cause—the renegade Wentworth, who gave evidence in Ireland of the spirit of instinctive tyranny which predominated in his character—even Strafford, while he trampled upon our rights, and trod upon the heart of the country, protested his solicitude to do justice to Ireland! What marvel is it, then, that gentlemen opposite should deal in such vehement protestations?

There is, however, one man of great abilities—not a member of this House, but whose talents and whose boldness have placed him in the topmost place in his party—who, disdaining all imposture, and thinking it the best course to appeal directly to the religious and national antipathies of the people of this country—abandoning all reserve, and flinging off the slender veil by which his political associates affect to cover, altho they can not hide, their motives—distinctly and audaciously tells the Irish people that they are not entitled to the same privileges

[18] Abridged.

as Englishmen; and pronounces them, in any particular which could enter his minute enumeration of the circumstances by which fellow citizenship is created, in race, identity and religion, to be aliens—to be aliens in race, to be aliens in country, to be aliens in religion! Aliens! good God! was Arthur, Duke of Wellington, in the House of Lords— and did he not start up and exclaim, "Hold, I have seen the aliens do their duty!"

The Duke of Wellington is not a man of an excitable temperament. His mind is of a cast too martial to be easily moved; but, notwithstanding his habitual inflexibility, I can not help thinking that, when he heard his Roman Catholic countrymen (for we are his countrymen) designated by a phrase as offensive as the abundant vocabulary of his eloquent confederate could supply—I can not help thinking that he ought to have recollected the many fields of fight in which we have been contributors to his renown. "The battles, sieges, fortunes that he has passed," ought to have come back upon him. He ought to have remembered that, from the earliest achievement in which he displayed that military genius which has placed him foremost in the annals of modern warfare, down to that last and surpassing combat which has made his name imperishable—from Assaye to Waterloo—the Irish soldiers, with whom your armies are filled, were the inseparable auxiliaries to the glory with which his unparalleled successes have been crowned.

Whose were the arms that drove your bayonets at Vimiéra through the phalanxes that never reeled in the shock of war before? What desperate valor climbed the steeps and filled the moats at Badajos? All his victories should have rushed and crowded back upon his memory—Vimiéra, Badajos, Salamanca, Albuéra, Toulouse, and, last of all, the greatest——. Tell me—for you were there—I appeal to the gallant soldier before me (Sir Henry Harding), from whose opinions I differ, but who bears, I know, a generous heart in an intrepid breast— tell me—for you must needs remember—on that day when the destinies of mankind were trembling in the balance, while death fell in showers, when the artillery of France was leveled with a precision of the most deadly science, when her legions, incited by the voice and inspired by the example of their mighty leader, rushed again and again to the onset—tell me if, for an instant, when to hesitate for an instant was to be lost, the "aliens" blenched?

And when, at length, the moment for the last and decided movement had arrived, and the valor which had so long been wisely checked was, at last, let loose—when, with words familiar, but immortal, the great captain commanded the great assault—tell me if Catholic Ireland with less heroic valor than the natives of this your own glorious country precipitated herself upon the foe? The blood of England, Scotland, and of Ireland, flowed in the same stream, and drenched the same field. When the chill morning dawned, their dead lay cold and stark together

—in the same deep pit their bodies were deposited; the green corn of spring is now breaking from their commingled dust; the dew falls from Heaven upon their union in the grave. Partakers in every peril, in the glory shall we not be permitted to participate; and shall we be told, as a requittal, that we are estranged from the noble country for whose salvation our life-blood was poured out?

THE TREATY OF WASHINGTON

Sir John Alexander Macdonald

(1815-1891)

The history of Sir John A. Macdonald, the first prime minister of the Dominion of Canada, is practically that of his country, for no man played so great a part in Canadian political life both before and after the confederation of its provinces. The great purpose of his life was to make Canada a mighty and powerful state by the union of her provinces, a purpose which he succeeded in accomplishing.

Born in Glasgow, Scotland, Macdonald came to Ontario, Canada, with his parents and at the early age of 15 entered a law office. By the year 1836, when he was only 19 years of age, he was called to the bar, and set up his practice of law in Kingston. In 1844 he was elected conservative member of the Legislative Assembly and from this date to the end of his life was the most conspicuous figure in the Ontario Assembly and the Dominion Parliament. The united Canada of today is largely the fruit of his labors.

The first government of the Dominion was formed by Macdonald in 1867 and from that time until his death (with an intermission of only five years) he retained the premiership. The Canadian Pacific Railway, completed in 1885, which did much to cement the war-separated members of the Dominion confederacy, was constructed through Macdonald's efforts.

Although not an eminent orator, Macdonald had rare skill as a parlimentarian and dominated the Dominion debates. He had a striking personal magnetism. Included here is an extract of his speech on *The Treaty of Washington*. This treaty of 1871 was one of the greatest triumphs of Macdonald's life, for it settled questions of dispute in regard to the boundaries of the

United States and Canada.   To win his point on this occasion
Macdonald had not only to persuade the Washington diplomats
but also his British colleagues.

I shall now move the first reading of this bill, and I shall simply
sum up my remarks by saying that with respect to the treaty I consider
that every portion of it is unobjectionable to the country, unless the
articles connected with the fisheries may be considered objectionable.
With respect to those articles, I ask this House fully and calmly to
consider the circumstances, and I believe, if they fully consider the
situation, that they will say it is for the good of Canada that those
articles should be ratified.   Reject the treaty, and you do not get re-
ciprocity; reject the treaty, and you leave the fishermen of the Maritime
Provinces at the mercy of the Americans; reject the treaty, and you will
leave the merchants engaged in that trade cut off from the American
market: reject the treaty, and you will have a large annual expenditure in
keeping up a marine police force to protect those fisheries, amounting to
about $84,000 per annum; reject the treaty, and you will have to call upon
England to send her fleet and give you both her moral and physical
support, although you will not adopt her policy; reject the treaty, and
you will find that the bad feeling which formerly and until lately
existed in the United States against England will be transferred to
Canada; that the United States will say, and say justly: "Here, where
two great nations like England and the United States have settled all
their differences and all their quarrels upon a perpetual basis, these
happy results are to be frustrated and endangered by the Canadian people,
because they have not got the value of their fish for ten years."

It has been said by the honorable gentleman on my left (Mr. Howe),
in his speech to the Young Men's Christian Association, that England
had sacrificed the interests of Canada.   If England has sacrificed the
interests of Canada, what sacrifice has she not made in the cause of
peace?   Has she not, for the sake of peace between these two great
nations, rendered herself liable, leaving out all indirect claims, to pay
millions out of her own treasury?   Has she not made all this sacrifice,
which only Englishmen and English statesmen know, for the sake of
peace—and for whose sake has she made it?   Has she not made it
principally for the sake of Canada?   Let Canada be severed from England, let England not be responsible to us, and for us, and what could
the United States do to England?   Let England withdraw herself into
her shell, and what can the United States do?   England has got the
supremacy of the sea—she is impregnable in every point but one, and
that point is Canada; and if England does call on us to make a financial
sacrifice; does find it for the good of the empire that we, England's
first colony, should sacrifice something; I say that we would be unworthy
of our proud position if we were not prepared to do so.

I hope to live to see the day, and if I do not that my son may be spared to see Canada the right arm of England, to see Canada a powerful auxiliary to the empire—not as now a cause of anxiety and a source of danger. And I think that if we are worthy to hold that position as the right arm of England, we should not object to a sacrifice of this kind when so great an object is attained, and the object is a great and lasting one. It is said that amities between nations cannot be perpetual; but I say that this treaty, which has gone through so many difficulties and dangers, if it is carried into effect, removes almost all possibility of war. If ever there was an irritating cause of war, it was from the occurrences arising out of the escape of those vessels, and when we see the United States people and Government forget this irritation, forget those occurrences, and submit such a question to arbitration, to the arbitration of a disinterested tribunal, they have established a principle which can never be forgotten in this world. No future question is ever likely to arise that will cause such irritation as the escape of the Alabama did, and if they could be got to agree to leave such a matter to the peaceful arbitrament of a friendly power, what future cause of quarrel can, in the imagination of man, occur that will not bear the same pacific solution that is sought for in this? I believe that this treaty is an epoch in the history of civilization; that it will set an example to the wide world that must be followed; and with the growth of the great Anglo-Saxon family, and with the development of that mighty nation to the south of us, I believe that the principle of arbitration will be advocated as the sole principle of settlement of differences between the English-speaking peoples, and that it will have a moral influence on the world.

CANADA, ENGLAND, AND THE UNITED STATES IN 1899 [19]

Sir Wilfrid Laurier

(1841-1919)

Sir Wilfrid Laurier, the great liberal reformer of Canada, was born of French Roman Catholic parentage in Quebec, Canada. He studied law at McGill University and at his graduation delivered the valedictory address in which he pleaded for sympathy and union between the French and English races of Canada, a cause which he supported throughout his lifetime. Laurier was elected to the Quebec legislature in 1871. His first speech in this body aroused attention because of its literary qualities and the appealing manner and logical method of the speaker. In 1874 Laurier entered the Dominion House of Commons where in his speeches he supported Riel and the French half-breeds during the Red River Rebellion. In 1887 he became the leader of the Liberal Party of Canada as the first French-Canadian to assume that role since the confederation. He was also the first French-Canadian to become premier, and held that position from 1896 to 1911. In 1897 he was knighted and thereafter was prominent at Queen Victoria's Jubilee in England (1897); and at the Coronations of Edward VII in 1902, and George V in 1911. When the World War was declared in 1914 Sir Wilfrid, then in his 73d year, delivered in the Canadian House of Commons a speech entitled *Ready, Aye, Ready* which retained the same eloquence with which he swayed courts and parliaments throughout his lifetime.

By many, Laurier is considered Canada's ablest orator of all time "not more by the finished grace of his oratory than by the boldness and authority with which he handled the deepest

[19] Abridged.

political problems in the Dominion's House of Commons." He belonged always to the Liberal English school of Charles Fox, Daniel O'Connell, and William Gladstone.

There are no two nations today on the face of the globe so united as Great Britain and the United States of America. The Secretary of State told us some few months ago that there was no treaty of alliance between Great Britain and the United States of America. It is very true, there is between the United States of America and Great Britain today no treaty of alliance which the pen can write and which the pen can unmake, but there is between Great Britain and the United States of America a unity of blood, of blood which is thicker than water, and I appeal to recent history when I say that whenever our nation has had to face an emergency—a greater emergency than usual—forthwith the sympathies of the other nation go to her sister.

In the month of June last I spoke on the floor of the House of Commons on the question of Alaska, and I enunciated the very obvious truism that international problems can be settled in one of two ways only, either by arbitration or by war. And although I proceeded to say immediately that war between Great Britain and the United States would be criminal and would not be thought of for a moment, still the very word "war" created quite an excitement in this country. For that causeless excitement, although I was indirectly the cause of it, I do not at this moment find any fault, because it convinced me to an absolute certainty that between your country and my country the relations have reached such a degree of dignity and respect and affection that even the word "war" is never to be mentioned in a British assembly or in an American assembly. The word is not to be pronounced, not even to be predicted. It is not to be pronounced at all. The very idea is abhorrent to us.

I repeat what I then stated, that war between Great Britain and the United States would be criminal—in my estimation and judgment, just as criminal as the Civil War which desolated your country some thirty years ago. Whatever may have been the mistaken views of the civilized world at the time, the civilized world has come to the conclusion that it was a benefit to mankind that this rebellion did not succeed and that the Government of the people, by the people, and for the people, did not perish from the earth. . . .

Sirs, there was another civil war. There was a civil war in the last century. There was a war with England then and her colonies. The union which existed between England and her colonies was severed. If it was severed, American citizens, as you know it was, through no fault of your fathers, the fault was altogether the fault of the British government of that day. If the British government of that day had treated the American colonies as the British government for the last fifty years has treated its colonies; if Great Britain had given you then the same degree of liberty which it gives to Canada, my country; if it had given you, as it has given us, legislative independence absolute, the result would have been different—the course of victory, the course of history, would have been very different.

But what has been done cannot be undone. You cannot expect that the union which was then severed shall ever be restored; but can we not escape—can we not hope that if the union cannot be restored under the law, at least there can be a union of hearts? Can we not hope that the banners of England and the banners of the United States shall never, never again meet in conflict, except those conflicts provided by the arts of peace, such as we see today in the harbor of New York in the contest between the Shamrock and the Columbia for the supremacy of naval architecture and naval prowess? Can we not hope that if ever the banners of England and the banners of the United States are again to meet on the battlefield, they shall meet entwined together in the defense of some holy cause, in the defense of holy justice, for the defense of the oppressed, for the enfranchisement of the downtrodden, for the advancement of liberty, progress, and civilization?

FIRST SPEECH IN AMERICA

Charles Stuart Parnell
(1846-1891)

It has been said that Parnell ran contrary to the Irish temperament. He was born in Avondale, Ireland, was educated at Cambridge in England, entered the English Parliament in 1875; was President of the Irish Free Land League in 1879 and visited the United States in the interests of Home Rule for Ireland. In these respects he seems to have run much the same course as his fellow-countrymen who were leaders in the cause of Irish independence, but in his nature he was taciturn, calculating, and retiring rather than jovial and warm hearted as were his colleagues. Yet he was idolized in Ireland while he was feared in England. Upsetting ministries, defying governments, obstructing legislation, threatening revolution, establishing boycotts, skirting sedition he turned Parliament into bedlam and made Ireland a vital force in the affairs of the Empire. He never compromised; he never conciliated; he never trusted his enemy—he *fought.*

Parnell lacked the rhetorical eloquence, the richness of voice and the dramatic effect common to his fellow countrymen, but when he spoke the silence which crept over the house was painful in its intensity. His expression was almost Attic in its severity.

Among his best speeches are those delivered during his visit to the United States in 1880. Included here is his reply to an address of welcome on his arrival in St. Louis, March 4, 1880.

I thank you for this magnificent meeting—a splendid token of your sympathy and appreciation for the cause of suffering Ireland. It is a remarkable fact that, while America, throughout the length and breadth of her country, does her very utmost to show her sympathy and send her practical help to our people; while there is scarcely any hand save America's between the starvation of large masses of the western peasantry; England alone of almost all the civilized nations does scarcely anything, although close behind Ireland, to help the terrible suffering and famine which now oppress that country. I speak a fact when I say that if it had not been for the help which has gone from America during the last two months among these, our people would have perished ere now of starvation. . . .

We are asked: "Why do you not recommend emigration to America?" and we are told that the lands of Ireland are too crowded. They are less thickly populated than those of any civilized country in the world; they are far less thickly populated—the rich lands of Ireland—than any of your western States. It is only on the barren hillsides of Connemara and along the west Atlantic coast that we have too thick a population, and it is only on the unfertile lands that our people are allowed to live. They are not allowed to occupy and till the rich lands; these rich lands are retained and preserved for landlords, and as vast grazing tracts for cattle. And although emigration might be a temporary alleviation of the trouble in Ireland, it would be a cowardly step on our part; it would be running away from our difficulties in Ireland, and it would be acknowledgment of the complete conquest of Ireland by England, an acknowledgment which, please God, Ireland shall never make.

No! we will stand by our country, and whether we are exterminated by famine to-day, or decimated by English bayonets to-morrow, the people of Ireland are determined to uphold the God-given right of Ireland to take her place among the nations of the world. Our tenantry are engaged in a struggle of life and death with the Irish landlords. It is no use to attempt to conceal the issues which have been made there. The landlords say that there is not room for both tenants and landlords, and that the people must go. But it may—it may, and it undoubtedly will—happen in this struggle that some of our gallant tenantry will be driven from their homes and evicted. In that case we will use some of the money you are entrusting us with in this country for the purpose of finding happier homes in this far western land for those of our expatriated people, and it will place us in a position of great power, and give our people renewed confidence in their struggle, if they are assured that any of them who are evicted in their attempts to stand by their rights will get one hundred and fifty good acres of land in Minnesota, Illinois, or some of your fine Western States.

Now the cable announces to us to-day that the Government is about to attempt to renew the famous Irish Coercion Acts which expired this year. Let me explain to you what these Coercion Acts are. Under them the Lord-Lieutenant of Ireland is entitled to proclaim at any time, in any Irish county, forbidding any inhabitant of that county to go outside of his door after dark, and subjecting him to a long term of imprisonment with hard labor, if he is found outside his door after dark.

No man is permitted to carry a gun, or to handle arms in his house, and the farmers of Ireland are not even permitted to shoot at the birds when they eat the seed corn on their freshly-sowed land. Under these acts it is also possible for the Lord-Lieutenant of Ireland to have any man arrested and consigned to prison without charge, and without bringing him to trial; to keep him in prison as long as he pleases; and circumstances have been known where the Government has arrested prisoners under these Coercion Acts, and has kept them in solitary confinement for two years, and not allowed them to see a single relative or to communicate with a friend during all that period, and has finally forgotten the existence of the helpless prisoners. And this is the infamous code which England is now seeking to re-enact.

I tell you, when I read this dispatch, strongly impressed as I am with the magnitude and vast importance of the work in which we are engaged in this country, that I felt strongly tempted to hurry back to Westminster in order to show this English Government whether it shall dare, in this year 1880, to renew this odious code with as much facility as it has done in former years. We shall then be able to put to a test the newly-forged gagging rules that they have invented for the purpose of depriving the Irish members of freedom of speech. And I wish to express my belief, my firm conviction, that if the Irish members do their duty, it will be impossible that this infamous statute can be re-enacted; and if it again finds its place upon the statute-book, I say that the day upon which the royal assent is given to that Coercion Act will sound the knell of the political future of the Irish people.

BIBLIOGRAPHY OF THE BRITISH PERIOD

Bagehot, Walter: *The British Constitution*, D. Appleton and Company, New York, 1911.

Blair, Hugh: *Lecture on Rhetoric and Belles-lettres*, J. I. Kay and Company, Philadelphia, 1833.

Bowers, Claude G.: *Irish Orators*, Bobbs-Merrill Company, Indianapolis, 1916.

Brewer, D. J.: *The World's Best Orators*, 10 v., Kaiser Company, New York, 1899.

Browning, W. E.: *Wit and Wisdom of Lord Chesterfield*, R. Bentley and Sons, London, 1875.

Bryan, William Jennings: *The World's Famous Orations*, Funk and Wagnalls Company, New York, 1906.

Bryce, James: *William Edward Gladstone*, The Century Company, New York, 1899.

Campbell, John: *Lives of the Lord Chancellors*, 7 v., John Murray, London, 1848-50.

Campbell, John: *Lives of the Chief Justices of England*, John Murray, London, 1849.

Cody, Sherwin: *World's Great Orations*, A. C. McClurg and Company, Chicago, 1923.

Cormenin, Timon de: *Orators of France*, Belford, Clark and Company, New York, 1884.

Craig, W. H.: *Life of Lord Chesterfield*, John Lane, London, 1907.

Depew, Chauncey: *The Library of Oratory*, Colonial Press, New York, 1902.

Fulton, Robert: *British and American Eloquence*, Ginn and Company, Boston, 1912.

Garnett, R.: *Orations of British Orators*, Fifth Avenue Press, New York, 1900.

Goodrich, Chauncey A.: *Select British Eloquence*, Harper and Brothers, New York, 1852.

Hawthorne, Julian: *Orations of British Orators*, P. F. Collier and Son, New York, 1900.

Jepson, Henry: *The Platform, Its Rise and Progress*, 2 v., Macmillan and Company, London, 1892.

Kettle, T. M.: *Irish Orators*, Frederick A. Stokes Company, Dublin, 1915.

Lee, Carleton: *The World's Orators*, 10 v., G. P. Putnam's Sons, New York, 1900.

Mathews, William: *Oratory and Orators*, S. C. Griggs and Company, Chicago, 1882.

Morris, Charles: *The World's Orators and Their Orations*, The John C. Winston Company, Philadelphia, 1917.

Neilson, William A., and Thorndike, Ashley: *The History of English Literature*, Houghton, Mifflin Company, Boston, 1927.

Platz, Mabel: *The History of Public Speaking*, Noble and Noble, New York City, 1936.

Prothero, G.: *Select Statutes and other Constitutional Documents Illustrative of Reigns of Elizabeth and James I*, Oxford University Press, London, 1911.

Reed, B. Thomas: *Great Orations*, D. Appleton and Company, New York, 1899.

Robertson, Howard: *A History of Great Britain*, Houghton, Mifflin Company, Boston, 1927.

Trevelyan, George Macaulay: *History of England*, Longmans, Green and Company, London, 1929.

Tout, T. F.: *An Advanced History of Great Britain*, Longmans, Green and Company, London, 1927.

THE AMERICAN PERIOD

INTRODUCTION

America, because of her democratic institutions, is possessed of a quantity and quality of oratory unsurpassed by any other modern nation. The colonists who settled America were, in a way, products of the Reformation. Some, it is true, came to the new world in quest of wealth or adventure, but the majority were prompted by political and economic discontent and came in search of freedom of speech in government and religion.

The earliest form of American oratory was that of the clergy. Seeking a fundamental reform of the English Church, the Puritans had come to America, so that the clergy who led the migration considered themselves acting as the representatives of God. From the pulpit they ruled the early settlements with a self-confident, yet simple, speech. The pulpiteers of the north, represented here by Cotton Mather and Jonathan Edwards, were calm, stedfast, incisive and stern. Roger Williams, who pleaded for toleration, and John Winthrop, the first governor of Massachusetts, are also included in the colonial group.

The fiery, tempestuous eloquence of the southern orators did not assert itself until the Revolutionary agitation of 1765-1775. The struggle for political freedom which at that time swept the colonies was led, not so much by the clergy, as by the lawyers. This shift of power from the clergy to the lawyers brought with it a change in style which was more forceful than graceful because born under stress. From the Declaration of Independence to the adoption of the Constitution the young Republic of America was led by the voices of her orators such as Patrick Henry, James Otis, Alexander Hamilton, John Marshall and John Quincy Adams.

The establishment of a national government brought in even greater incentive to oratory. It was, therefore, in the days when the constitutional government was being formed that some

of the greatest oratory flourished.   The debates on the adoption
of the federal constitution were led by such men as Edmund
Randolph, Alexander Hamilton, Samuel Adams, and Benjamin
Franklin.   Following the adoption of the constitution there came
about results inevitable in republics.   Factionalism usurped the
place of patriotism and party spirit resulted.   From the bitter
discussions arising over this sectionalism sprang the congressional
oratory of Henry Clay, Daniel Webster, and John Calhoun.
Floridity may be used as descriptive of the style of this period,
for multiplicity of words was the key to oratorical success.

The next great cycle of American oratory was that concerned
with the questions of slavery and states rights, resulting in the
secession of the South from the Union, the bitter years of civil
warfare, and the arduous years of reconstruction.   Throughout
this period rang the voices of Edward Everett, Wendell Phillips,
Jefferson Davis, Robert Toombs, Charles Sumner, William
Seward, Henry Ward Beecher, Stephen A. Douglas, and Abraham
Lincoln.

With the Civil War the wordy style of Webster was exchanged
for one of directness and simplicity.   It was probably Wendell
Phillips with his manner of repose and Abraham Lincoln with
his brevity and clarity of language who set the standard for
the oratorical style of the period.

After the reconstruction period following the Civil War which
was illuminated by such oratory as that of Henry Grady, there
followed years of what may be termed Lyceum oratory centering
about reform movements.   Leaders in these movements were
William Jennings Bryan, the agitator for free silver, prohibition,
and international peace; Robert Ingersoll, the agnostic; Susan
B. Anthony, the woman's suffrage agitator; Francis E. Willard,
the leader of the temperance movement; and Theodore Roosevelt,
the great progressive reformer of the era.   It was the latter
orator who may be credited with setting the fashion for the
brusque, matter-of-fact style of the 20th century.   The orators
of this era are also linked closely with the problems of industrial
and social reconstruction preceding and attendant upon the World
War.

LITTLE SPEECH ON LIBERTY

John Winthrop
(1588-1649)

John Winthrop, colonial governor of Massachusetts, was born in Suffolk, England, in 1588. His education at Trinity College in England prepared him for the law. A Puritan by conviction Winthrop had been such a powerful influence both in England and the colonies that he was selected as governor of the Massachusetts Bay colony in 1629 and headed the voyage of a fleet of seven ships, carrying 900 colonists to the New World. On this voyage he started his journal of daily events in the colonies which he continued the rest of his life and which after his death was published as *The History of New England*.

Winthrop was governor of Massachusetts for a period of nearly twenty years and his learning, dignity, and self-command were a beneficent influence upon the colonists. We include here his *Little Speech,* the first consequential political speech recorded in Colonial America, delivered at his trial for impeachment arising from a trivial question of preferment in the militia. The dignity, wisdom, and piety of this speech were such that Winthrop was not only acquitted but recommended most highly to the esteem of the public. Few speeches of that period, or of any period, obtained wider celebrity in history.

I suppose something may be expected from me upon this charge that has befallen me, which moves me to speak now to you; yet I intend not to intermeddle in the proceedings of the court or with any of the persons concerned therein. Only I bless God that I see an issue of this troublesome business. I also acknowledge the justice of the court, and for mine own part I am well satisfied. I was publicly charged, and I am publicly and legally acquitted, which is all I did expect or desire. And though this be sufficient for my justification before men, yet not so before the God who hath seen so much amiss in my dispensations (and even in this affair) as calls me to be humble.

For to be publicly and criminally charged in this court is matter of humiliation (and I desire to make a right use of it), notwithstanding I be thus acquitted. If her father had spit in her face (saith the Lord concerning Miriam), should she not have been ashamed seven days? Shame had lien upon her, whatever the occasion had been. I am unwilling to stay you from your urgent affairs, yet give me leave (upon this special occasion) to speak a little more to this assembly. It may be of some good use to inform and rectify the judgments of some of the people, and may prevent such distempers as have arisen amongst us.

The great questions that have troubled the country are about the authority of the magistrates and the liberty of the people. It is yourselves who have called us to this office, and, being called by you, we have our authority from God, in way of an ordinance, such as hath the image of God eminently stamped upon it, the contempt and violation whereof hath been vindicated with examples of divine vengeance.

I entreat you to consider that, when you choose magistrates, you take them from among yourselves, men subject to like passions as you are. Therefore, when you see infirmities in us, you should reflect upon your own, and that would make you bear the more with us, and not be severe censurers of the failings of your magistrates, when you have continual experience of the like infirmities in yourselves and others.

We account him a good servant who breaks not his covenant. The covenant between you and us is the oath you have taken of us, which is to this purpose, that we shall govern you and judge your causes by the rules of God's laws and our own, according to our best skill. When you agree with a workman to build you a ship or house, etc., he undertakes as well for his skill as for his faithfulness; for it is his profession, and you pay him for both. But when you call one to be a magistrate he doth not profess or undertake to have sufficient skill for that office, nor can you furnish him with gifts, etc., therefore you must run the hazard of his skill and ability. But if he fails in faithfulness, which by his oath he is bound unto, that he must answer for. If it fall out that the case be clear to common apprehension, and the rule clear also, if he transgress here, the error is not in the skill, but in the evil of the will: it must be required of him. But if the case be doubtful, or the rule doubtful, to men of such understanding and parts as your magistrates are, if your magistrates should err here, yourselves must bear it.

For the other point concerning liberty, I observe a great mistake in the country about that. There is a twofold liberty, natural (I mean as our nature is now corrupt) and civil or federal. The first is common to man with beasts and other creatures. By this man, as he stands in relation to man simply, hath liberty to do what he lists: it is a liberty to evil as well as to good. This liberty is incompatible and inconsistent with authority, and cannot endure the least restraint of the most just authority. The exercise and maintaining of this liberty makes men grow more evil, and in time to be worse than brute beasts: *omnes sumus licentia deteriores*. This is that great enemy of truth and peace, that wild beast, which all the ordinances of God are bent against, to restrain and subdue it.

The other kind of liberty I call civil or federal; it may also be termed moral, in reference to the covenant between God and man in the moral law, and the politic covenants and constitutions amongst men themselves. This liberty is the proper end and object of authority, and cannot subsist without it; and it is a liberty to that only which is good, just, and honest. This liberty you are to stand for, with the hazard (not only of your goods, but) of your lives, if need be. Whatsoever crosseth this is not authority, but a distemper thereof. This liberty is maintained and exercised in a way of subjection to authority; it is of the same kind of liberty wherewith Christ hath made us free. The woman's own choice makes such a man her husband; yet, being so chosen, he is her lord, and she is to be subject to him, yet in a way of liberty, not of bondage; and a true wife accounts her subjection her honor and freedom, and would not think her condition safe and free but in her subjection to her husband's authority. Such is the liberty of the church under the authority of Christ, her king and husband; his yoke is so easy and sweet to her as a bride's ornaments; and if, through forwardness or wantonness, etc., she shake it off at any time, she is at no rest in her spirit until she take it up again; and whether her lord smiles upon her, and embraceth her in his arms, or whether he frowns, or rebukes, or smites her, she apprehends the sweetness of his love in all, and is refreshed, supported, and instructed by every such dispensation of his authority over her. On the other side, ye know who they are that complain of this yoke and say, let us break their bands, etc., we will not have this man to rule over us.

Even so, brethren, it will be between you and your magistrates. If you stand for your natural corrupt liberties, and will do what is good in your own eyes, you will not endure the least weight of authority, but will murmur, and oppose, and be always striving to shake off that yoke; but if you will be satisfied to enjoy such civil and lawful liberties, such as Christ allows you, then will you quietly and cheerfully submit unto that authority which is set over you, in all the administrations of it, for your good. Wherein, if we fail at any time, we hope we shall be willing (by God's assistance) to hearken to good advice from any of you, or in any other way of God; so shall your liberties be preserved, in upholding the honor and power of authority amongst you.

LIBERTY OF CONSCIENCE OR THE SOLE MEANS TO OBTAIN PEACE AND TRUTH

Roger Williams
(1604-1683)

Roger Williams, the exponent of toleration, was born in London and educated at Cambridge University. Thereafter he was ordained to the Established Church of England which he later forsook to become a Puritan. He migrated to America where he took an active part in the affairs of the Massachusetts Colony but was banished therefrom in 1635 because of his theories of toleration in matters of the religious practices of his day. He settled in the section of the country which became identified as Rhode Island; here he put into active practice his doctrines of toleration in matters of religion and state and was also of great service to the Indians, by studying their language and by defending their rights to the land.

The Quaker debate in which Roger Williams participated in 1672 was his opportunity to vindicate in public his principle of "free disputes, debates, writings, printings, etc." Into these debates Williams entered against George Fox, a leader of the Quaker pilgrimage, and his twelve disciples who had settled in Rhode Island in 1672. Roger Williams had been frequently molested by Quaker fanatics whom he considered rude, uncivil, and meddlesome. Therefore he challenged Fox to a public dispute based on fourteen charges. Unable to secure a shorthand writer, Williams reproduced from memory this spectacular series of debates in a book entitled *George Fox Digged Out of His Burrows.*

The speech a part of which is included in this volume is symbolic of Roger's attitude toward freedom of conscience in religion as well as in matters of state. It was printed in 1643.

I am not ignorant that the lawfulness of neutrality is much controverted both in policy and conscience, but men of moderation which endeavor to qualify or decline the precipice of extremes, ought not to be accounted neutrals or luke-warms. Neither is this complying with weak consciences, or the tolerating of several opinions any other sort of libertinism than what Paul practiced when he "suffered all things lest he should hinder the Gospel," and "was made all things to all that he might save some," at which time he professed himself notwithstanding "to live not without law to God but under law to Christ." And Peter tells us that "we must live as free, but not using our liberty for a cloak of maliciousness," but as the servants of God. . . You demand whether heretics then may not be reclaimed? . . Since heresies must needs be, though a woe betide the authors of them, how much more may we well think there should be a liberty of conscience? . . But some will say that the learned and wisest men have always been and are full of opinion, that it is no good policy to suffer so many feverish religions to be publicly professed in one and the same kingdom and jurisdiction, because that though many men may be able with scripture to defend their own religion, and others perhaps steadfast and obstinate enough in their opinions whatever they may be, yet if contrary tenets be debated freely and made profession of without control, some numbers more or less among such multitudes of people, either by importunity, worldly advantages, or in that their ignorance or little knowledge in spiritual matters, is not able to withstand the arguments which are urged against them, must needs be seduced and led away from the religion established by law: wherefore I answer that the advice of wise and learned men, if they be otherwise also as well qualified, is to be far preferred to that of ignorant and less wise, but such whose affections and carnal lusts are mortified, and whose gifts are sanctified, these men's counsels ought to take place before the law of the gospel: worldly wisdom and learning are both useful and expedient when they concur with the Scripture, not against it. . . .

And if it be objected, that there then must be no true church amongst Christians, and that all of them do persecute one another more or less, it will notwithstanding follow, that such Christian states and churches which persecute most are most corrupted, and I could hope for their sakes which still retain it with less rigour, that every smaller degree of persecuting Christians which differ from them in opinion, they may not hinder to be true Christians. . . .

Evidence of the Scriptures is that only which should be our guide in what we do or say, our supreme rule or touchstone to make trial of what we hear or see; according whereunto if we proceed, whatsoever be alleged to the contrary, we may clearly find, that "persecution for matters of religion does plainly cross so many places of Scripture, murders so many of God's saints, and so much hinders the propagation of the Gospel, as no other erroneous tenet or heresie whatsoever": for if the Gospel had but a free passage, and the true professors liberty to teach and publish it, this only as a sovereign remedy and counter-poison, would prevail against all heresies, unless you grant that error may possibly vanquish truth.

Abridged by the compiler of this volume
from the original manuscript.

AT THE SOUND OF THE TRUMPET

Cotton Mather

(1663-1728)

Cotton Mather, the great pulpit orator of Colonial America, was born in Boston, Massachusetts, and educated at Harvard University of which his father, Increase Mather, a preacher of great influence in his day, was President.

Cotton Mather had a propensity to stammer when a youth but conquered this defect by adopting methods of deliberative speech, and at the early age of seventeen occupied the pulpit at North Church in Boston as his father's assistant. He distinguished himself in the affairs of the Puritans and became widely celebrated as a scholar and writer, his published works numbering three hundred eighty-two.

Mather's unfortunate connection with the witchcraft persecutions and his publication *The Wonders of the Invisible World* have somewhat obscured for posterity his better qualities. Puritan Colonial America knew no more powerful speaker than Cotton Mather in spite of his egotistic and pedantic nature and a tendency to use euphonious combinations of words, which at times seem almost puerile.

Included here is a sermon illustrative of Cotton Mather's style.

There was a direction given and taken in the old Church of Israel, "Make thee two trumpets of silver, that thou mayst use them for the calling of the assembly." By the sound of such silver trumpets, the people of God were called unto the employments and enjoyments of their sacred solemnities. And was this the joyful sound, for which the people that heard it are now pronounced a blessed people? I deny not the reference hereunto, which may be here supposed. But then we will suppose a further intent of the Holy Spirit, by whom the Psalm was dictated. He may intend the joyful sound, which in the Gospel and the institutions thereof his people are blessed withal. And, accordingly, it will be no wrong unto the text, if we put it unto the use of supporting this doctrine.

Glorious is the blessedness of the people who truly know the joyful sound, which in and with the glorious Gospel of the blessed God, and the institutions thereof, arrives unto us.

In the Gospel, and the ordinances of it, there is a joyful sound, which we are made partakers of. A true knowledge of this joyful sound will render the people that have it a blessed people. . . .

In order to blessedness, it is requisite, not only that we have, but also that we know the joyful sound which is brought into us in the Gospel, and in the ordinances of it. Indeed, in a larger sense, to have the joyful sound is to know it. A people that have the Gospel, and know the joyful sound, in the external enjoyment of it, these do enjoy a rich favor of God. The places which enjoy the Scriptures and have the Church state, with the faith and order of the Gospel, are therein highly favored of the Lord.

Gideon's fleece, wet with the dews of heaven, when the ground all about is dry, has a singular token for good upon it. The sound of the trumpets which proclaim the kingdom of God is heard in some happy lands, while others are left unacquainted with it. Even so, righteous Father, because it pleases thee! And so far they have a singular happiness. It may be said unto them: "Blessed are your eyes, for they see, and your ears, for they hear." Such a people are in some degree the favorites of heaven. They have the kingdom in some essay of it among them. Where the trumpets of the Gospel are sounding, we may say: "The Lord is near." Yea, the name of that city, that country, is Jehovah Shammah, "the Lord is there." A people who so far know the joyful sound are after a peculiar manner known by the King of Heaven. He may say to such: "You only have I known." But alas, many who so far know the joyful sound may, after all, come to "lie down in sorrow." They that are so far lifted up to heaven may be thrown down to hell after all. In such a knowledge of the joyful sound as will render a people a blessed people, there is more implied than a mere hearing of it. To know the joyful sound, as it should be known, is to know the meaning of it, the value of it, the credit of it, and the power of it. . . .

O blessed people, who so know the joyful sound! It is one of the notes in the silver trumpets. If ye know these things, happy are ye if ye do them. And one of the Divine heralds that carried the silver trumpets through the world has assured us, "the doer of the word, this man shall be blessed in his deed."

The blessedness of the people who thus know this joyful sound is a very glorious blessedness.

A most considerable article of the blessedness attending a people who hear the silver trumpets of the Gospel, and pay due regard unto them, is this: they shall walk, O Lord, in the light of thy countenance. A gracious preference of the blessed God among a people accompanies the joyful sound. The silver trumpets are heard nowhere but where the king of heaven keeps his court. There are those whose office it is to blow in the silver trumpets. Unto those our Savior has engaged himself: "Lo, I am with you always." Will health and wealth and rest among a people make a blessed people? 'Tis commonly thought so. But what will God have among a people? Oh, blessed that people whose god is the Lord, and who have a gracious preference of God among them. Even such are the people who know the joyful sound! Where the Gospel, with the ordinances of it are well settled, maintained, respected, and the silver trumpets well sounded among a people, it may be said, as in Numbers XXIII: 21: "The Lord their God is with them, and the shout of a king is among them." In one word the ordinances of the Gospel furnish us with opportunities for communion with God. "In them I will commune with you," saith the Lord. We may herein draw near to God, God will herein draw near to us. The voice of the silver trumpets is, draw near to God, and he will draw near to you! Can any blessedness be more glorious?

But more particularly, first, in the joyful sound, we have the guide to blessedness. The silver trumpets put us into the way, unto the "rest that remaineth for the people of God." We are ignorant of the way to blessedness; and the way of peace we have not known. But where the trumpets of the Gospel sound, there is a fulfillment of that word: "Thine ears shall hear a word behind thee, saying: This is the way, walk in it." They reveal to us what we are to think, what we are to do, what we are to wish for; they lead us in the way wherein we should go.

Second, in the joyful sound we have the cause of blessedness. The silver trumpets are like the golden pipes in Zachariah, which convey the golden oil of grace into the souls of men. 'Tis by them that God fetches men out of the graves, in which they lie sinfully and woefully putrefying; and infuses a principle of piety into them; and inclines them to the things that are holy, and just, and good. That effectual calling which brings men into blessedness, 'tis in the trumpets of the Gospel that the spirit of God gives it unto his chosen ones; men hear the word of the Gospel and believe.

But let us now make some improvements of these instructions.

I. Blessed the people who know the joyful sound; then wretched the people, forlorn the people, undone the people, who are strangers to the joyful sound. Oh! the pity that is due unto them!

The Jewish nation have now lost their silver trumpets for these many ages. And in their long dispersion how pathetical is their cry unto us! Have pity on me, O ye, my friends, have pity on me, for the hand of the Lord hath touched me. Yea, and how many Protestant Churches have in our days had their silver trumpets forced from them; and instead thereof heard the "enemies roaring in the midst of the congregations"! Yea, how many nations are there that never heard the joyful sound! That lie buried in Paganizing or in Mohammedan infidelity! And is it not a lamentable thing that so near unto ourselves there should be so many ungospelized plantations! Our pity for those ought certainly to put us upon prayer for them; upon study for them. Oh! what shall be done for them who lie in wickedness, and have this epitaph upon them: If our Gospel be hid, it is hid unto them that be lost.

II. Blessed the people who know the joyful sound; then we are a blessed people; and at the same time we are to be taught how to continue so. My brethren, we have the joyful sound at such a rate, that it may almost be said of us in Deuteronomy: "What nation is there who hath God so nigh unto them?" For the silver trumpets to be heard sounding as they are in the American regions—verily 'tis the Lord's doings, and marvelous in our eyes! May we ever account these our precious and our pleasant things!

Oh! how thankful ought we to be unto our God for his Gospel and the ordinances of it! When the silver trumpets were of old going to sound, the angels of God were heard making those acclamations thereupon, "Glory to God in the highest." And shall not we give glory to the most High God on the occasion? O Gospelized people, God hath showed his statutes and his judgments unto us. Praise ye the Lord. When the trumpets of God are sounding, shall not our trumpets be sounding too? His trumpets are in his ordinances; our trumpets are in our thanksgivings, we are so called upon: "With trumpets make a joyful noise before the Lord."

Such a blessed people should be thankful people. But, verily, our God will not look on us as a thankful people, if we are not also a fruitful people. A barren people; oh! what a fearful doom are they threatened with! What a fearful fate are they warned of! "It is nigh unto cursing." Sirs, be fruitful in every good work; fruitful and always abounding in the work of the Lord.

In the midst of these cares you will use all due means, that you may see no intermission of the joyful sound. You will provide seasonably for the succession that shall be needful, by all due cares about the means of education in our land, without which the land becomes a Scythian desert. But when you make this provision, oh! look up to the gracious Lord, that you may be blessed with truly silver trumpets; never have any but men of worth; such as will be of good metal; and such as in the cause of God will always "life up their voice like a trumpet."

But this is that which is most of all to be urged upon you: Hearken to the joyful sound. Hearken to it, and comply with it. The joyful sound is that: "Let the wicked forsake his way, and return to the Lord, who will have mercy on him." Hearken to it, and with echoes of devotion reply: "My God, I return unto thee!" The joyful sound is that: "Come to me, all ye that labor and are heavy laden, and I will give you rest." Hearken to it, and with echoes of devotion reply: "My Savior, I come unto thee!" That grace of God which bringeth salvation has the joyful sound of the silver trumpet in it. Now, your echoes to the trumpet must be these: Lord, I desire, I resolve to lead a godly, a sober, a righteous life before thee!

My friends, the last trumpet that is to sound at the appearance of the glorious Lord, who is to judge the world, will ere long summon you to give an account of your compliance with the silver trumpets of God. You that now hear the joyful sound of these trumpets must ere long hear the awful sound of that amazing trumpet. A loud and a shrill trumpet will sound: "Arise, ye dead, and come to judgment!" Oh! may our compliance with the joyful sound of the silver trumpets now be such that we may find mercy in that day. So comply with it now that the joyful sound of a "Come, ye blessed," may be heard by you in the day when "the times of refreshing shall come from the presence of the Lord."

SINNERS IN THE HANDS OF AN ANGRY GOD

Jonathan Edwards

(1703-1758)

Jonathan Edwards was the leader of the Great Awakening, a religious revival in America extending from the year 1735 to 1741. Born into a minister's family Edwards was precocious as a child; was graduated from Harvard when only 17 years of age and began his preaching career. His theology although tinctured at times with mysticism was strongly Calvanistic. He was a thinker of great power and his treatise on *The Freedom of the Will* still remains one of the great theological books of America. Edwards' powers as a preacher were undisputed, for he practically hypnotized his audiences. "His sermons were moral inquisitions in which sinners were placed upon argumentative racks and beneath screws and with an awful revolution of the great truth in hand evenly and steadily screwed down and crushed."

Included here is a part of his famous sermon, *Sinners in the Hands of an Angry God,* which so affected his hearers that they groaned and shrieked convulsively.

The God that holds you over the pit of hell much as one holds a spider or some loathsome insect over the fire abhors you, and is dreadfully provoked. His wrath toward you burns like fire; he looks upon you as worthy of nothing else but to be cast into the fire; he is of purer eyes than to bear you in his sight; you are ten thousand times as abominable in his eyes as the most hateful and venomous serpent is in ours. You have offended him infinitely more than ever a stubborn rebel did his prince, and yet it is nothing but his hand that holds you from falling into the fire every moment; it is ascribed to nothing else that you did not go to hell the last night; that you were suffered to awake again in this world after you closed your eyes in sleep; and there is no other reason to be given why you have not dropped into hell since you arose in the morning, but that God's hand has held you up; there is no other reason to be given why you have not gone to hell since you have sat here in the house of God provoking his pure eye by your sinful, wicked manner of attending his solemn worship; yea, there is nothing else that is to be given as a reason why do you not this very moment drop down into hell.

O sinner! consider the fearful danger you are in; it is a great furnace of wrath, a wide and bottomless pit, full of the fire of wrath that you are held over in the hands of that God whose wrath is provoked and incensed as much against you as against many of the damned in hell; you hang by a slender thread, with the flames of Divine wrath flashing about it and ready every moment to singe it and burn it asunder, and you have no interest in any mediator and nothing to lay hold of to save yourself, nothing to keep off the flames of wrath, nothing of your own, nothing that you have ever done, nothing that you can do to induce God to spare you one moment. . . .

It would be dreadful to suffer this fierceness and wrath of Almighty God one moment; but you must suffer it to all enternity: there will be no end to this exquisite, horrible misery: when you look forward you shall see along forever a boundless duration before you, which will swallow up your thoughts and amaze your soul, and you will absolutely despair of ever having any deliverance, any end, any mitigation, any rest at all; you will know certainly that you must wear out long ages, millions of millions of ages in wrestling and conflicting with this Almighty, merciless vengeance; and then when you have done so, when so many ages have actually been spent by you in this manner, you will know that all is but a point to what remains, so that your punishment will indeed be infinite. Oh! Who can express what the state of a soul in such circumstances is! All that we can possibly say about it gives but a very feeble, faint representation of it; it is inexpressible and inconceivable: for "who knows the power of God's anger!"

How dreadful is the state of those that are daily and hourly in danger of this great wrath and infinite misery! But this is the dismal case of every soul in this congregation that has not been born again, however moral and strict, sober and religious they may otherwise be. Oh, that you would consider it, whether you be young or old! There is reason to think that there are many in this congregation now hearing this discourse that will actually be the subjects of this very misery to all eternity. We know not who they are, or in what seats they sit, or what thoughts they now have—it may be they are now at ease and hear all these things without much disturbance, and are now flattering themselves that they are not the persons, promising themselves that they shall escape. If we knew that there was one person, and but one in the whole congregation, that was to be the subject of misery, what an awful thing it would be to think of! If we knew who it was, what an awful sight it would be to see such a person! How might all the rest of the congregation lift up a lamentable and bitter cry over him! But, alas! instead of one, how many is it likely will remember this discourse in hell! And it would be a wonder if some that are now present should not be in hell in a very short time, before this year is out. And it would be no wonder if some persons that now sit here in some seats of this meeting-house, in health, and quiet and secure, should be there before to-morrow morning!

THE CALL TO ARMS

Patrick Henry

(1736-1799)

Patrick Henry, the orator who heralded the American Revolution, was a Virginian. Lack of perseverance and knowledge made Henry's youth a series of failures in farming and business. It was the Reverend Samuel Davies, known as the apostle of Virginia, later President of Princeton University, who was the first to kindle the fire in Patrick Henry and afforded the model of his subsequent eloquence.

As a child Patrick sat under the pulpit oratory of this minister on the Sabbath day. Returning from church his mother would make Patrick give the text and a recapitulation of the discourse. In later years Henry remarked that Davies was the greatest orator he had ever heard.

When in later life Patrick Henry applied himself to the study of law, he realized a sensational success in a case known as *The Parson's Cause* in consequence of which he secured an enormous practice and assured prosperity for himself.

In 1765 Patrick Henry became a member of the House of Burgesses where he attracted attention by his fiery resolutions against the obnoxious Stamp Act. In the midst of the debate following the introduction of these resolutions Patrick Henry flung out a thunderbolt of defiant eloquence in the words: "Caesar had his Brutus, Charles the First his Cromwell, and George the Third" (interrupted here by shouts of "Treason, Treason," from all sides, he waited for silence and continued) "and George the Third may profit by their example. If this be treason, make the most of it." The resolutions were adopted.

In 1774 and 1775 when Patrick Henry represented Virginia in the First and Second Continental Congresses he again electrified the colonies with his statement, "The distinctions between Virginians, New Yorkers, and New Englanders are no more. I am not a Virginian, but an American."

It was in the Revolutionary Convention in 1775 that Patrick Henry delivered his greatest speech, *The Call to Arms,* supporting the resolution that the colonies be put into a "state of defense," a speech recognized as the most brilliant of the Revolutionary period. Patrick Henry was elected Governor of Virginia in 1776 and in 1784, and was a member of the Convention which ratified the Constitution in 1788. Before this Convention Patrick Henry spoke tirelessly for hours "in the language of his soul" on the side of the opposition; but he most manfully accepted his defeat, and thereafter directed his efforts to securing the amendments to the Constitution known as the Bill of Rights.

Twice thereafter Henry attracted attention by his eloquence— once before the Federal Court of Richmond in 1791 at the *Trial of a British Debts Case* and again in 1799 just before his death in defense of Washington's policies against disunion. Patrick Henry's chief characteristic as a speaker was enthusiasm, and moments of crisis called forth his most effective eloquence.

Presented here is Henry's famous *The Call to Arms,* a speech which turned the tide preceding the American Revolution. So powerful was the effect of his speech, which has become known as "Patrick Henry's personal Declaration of War against Great Britain," that the convention passed the resolutions for defense against further aggression by the British.

MR. PRESIDENT:—No man thinks more highly than I do of the patriotism, as well as abilities, of the very worthy gentlemen who have just addressed the House. But different men often see the same subject in different lights; and, therefore, I hope that it will not be thought disrespectful to those gentlemen if, entertaining as I do opinions of a character very opposite to theirs, I shall speak forth my sentiments freely and without reserve. This is no time for ceremony. The question before the House is one of awful moment to this country. For my own part, I consider it as nothing less than a question of freedom or slavery; and in proportion to the magnitude of the subject ought to be the freedom of the debate. It is only in this way that we can hope to arrive at truth and fulfil the great responsibility which we hold to God and our country. Should I keep back my opinions at such a time through fear of giving offence, I should consider myself as guilty of treason toward my country and of an act of disloyalty toward the majesty of Heaven, which I revere above all earthly kings.

Mr. President, it is natural to man to indulge in the illusions of hope. We are apt to shut our eyes against a painful truth and listen to the song of that siren, till she transforms us into beasts. Is this the part of wise men, engaged in a great and arduous struggle for liberty? Are we disposed to be of the number of those who, having eyes, see not, and having ears, hear not the things which so nearly concern their temporal salvation? For my part, whatever anguish of spirit it may cost, I am willing to know the whole truth—to know the worst and provide for it.

I have but one lamp by which my feet are guided, and that is the lamp of experience. I know of no way of judging the future but by the past. And, judging by the past, I wish to know what there has been in the conduct of the British ministry for the last ten years to justify those hopes with which gentlemen have been pleased to solace themselves and the House? It is that insidious smile with which our petition has been lately received? Trust it not, Sir; it will prove a snare to your feet. Suffer not yourselves to be betrayed with a kiss. Ask yourselves how this gracious reception of our petition comports with those warlike preparations which cover our waters and darken our land. Are fleets and armies necessary to a work of love and reconciliation? Have we shown ourselves so unwilling to be reconciled that force must be called in to win back our love? Let us not deceive ourselves, Sir. These are the implements of war and subjugation—the last arguments to which kings resort. I ask gentlemen, Sir, what means this martial array, if its purpose be not to force us to submission? Can gentlemen assign any other possible motives for it? Has Great Britain any enemy in this quarter of the world to call for all this accumulation of navies and armies? No, Sir, she has none. They are meant for us; they can be meant for no other. They are sent over to bind and rivet upon us those chains which the British ministry have been so long forging. And what have we to oppose to them? Shall we try argument? Sir, we have been trying that for the last ten years. Have we anything new to offer on the subject? Nothing. We have held the subject up in every light of which it is capable; but it has been all in vain. Shall we resort to entreaty and humble supplication? What terms shall we find which have not been already exhausted? Let us not, I beseech you, Sir, deceive ourselves longer. Sir, we have done everything that could be done to avert the storm which is now coming on. We have petitioned; we have remonstrated; we have supplicated; we have prostrated ourselves before the Throne, and have implored its interposition to arrest the tyrannical hands of the ministry and Parliament. Our petitions have been slighted; our remonstrances have produced additional violence and insult; our supplications have been disregarded; and we have been spurned with contempt from the foot of the Throne. In vain, after these things, may we indulge the fond hope of peace and reconciliation. There is no longer room for hope. If we wish to be free—if we mean to preserve inviolate those inestimable privileges for which we have been so long contending—if we mean not basely to abandon the noble struggle in which we have been so long engaged, and which we have pledged ourselves never to abandon until the glorious object of our contest shall be obtained, we must fight! I repeat it, Sir, we must fight! An appeal to arms and to the God of Hosts is all that is left us!

They tell us, Sir, that we are weak; unable to cope with so formidable an adversary. But when shall we be stronger? Will it be the next week, or the next year? Will it be when we are totally disarmed, and when a British guard shall be stationed in every house? Shall we gather strength by irresolution and inaction? Shall we acquire the means of effectual resistance by lying supinely on our backs and hugging the delusive phantom of hope, until our enemies shall have bound us hand and foot? Sir, we are not weak, if we make a proper use of the means which the God of nature hath placed in our power. Three millions of people, armed in the holy cause of liberty and in such a country as that which we possess, are invincible by any force which our enemy can send against us. Besides, Sir, we shall not fight our battles alone. There is a just God who presides over the destinies of nations, and who will raise up friends to fight our battles for us. The battle, Sir, is not to the strong alone; it is to the vigilant, the active, the brave. Besides, Sir, we have no election. If we were base enough to desire it, it is now too late to retire from the contest. There is no retreat but in submission and slavery! Our chains are forged; their clanking may be heard on the plains of Boston! The war is inevitable; and let it come! I repeat it, Sir, let it come!

It is in vain, Sir, to extenuate the matter. Gentlemen may cry Peace! peace! but there is no peace. The war is actually begun. The next gale that sweeps from the North will bring to our ears the clash of resounding arms. Our brethren are already in the field; why stand we here idle? What is it that the gentlemen wish? What would they have? Is life so dear, or peace so sweet, as to be purchased at the price of chains and slavery? Forbid it, Almighty God! I know not what course others may take; but as for me, give me liberty, or give me death!

THE WRITS OF ASSISTANCE [1]

James Otis
(1725-1783)

James Otis was a native of Massachusetts and was a most diligent student as a youth, graduating from Harvard in 1743. In 1748, when he was admitted to the bar, he went to Boston to set up his practice. When opposition to the tyranny of the King and Parliament began in Massachusetts, Otis was selected to defend the merchants against the Crown lawyers on the legality of the Writs of Assistance. These writs were search warrants which permitted customs officials to search any man's house which they thought might contain smuggled goods. This tyrannous right of search was bitterly resisted and incited Otis's brilliant attack considered the boldest, most treasonable ever delivered in the colonies. It was President John Adams who said that "American independence was then and there born." Afterward Otis remained active in the legislature for ten years. An accusation for treason brought against him by the English customs in 1769 resulted in a brawl in which Otis was so severely injured in his head that he never completely recovered from subsequent fits of insanity.

The famous speech on *The Writs of Assistance* included here shows his power as a speaker, his close logic and pleasing diction, and his absolute fearlessness.

May it please your Honors: I was desired by one of the court to look into the books, and consider the question now before them concerning Writs of Assistance. I have accordingly considered it, and now appear not only in obedience to your order, but likewise in behalf of the inhabitants of this town, who have presented another petition, and out of regard to the liberties of the subject. And I take this opportunity to declare that whether under a fee or not (for in such a cause as this I

[1] Abridged.

despise a fee) I will to my dying day oppose, with all the powers and faculties God has given me, all such instruments of slavery on the one hand and villainy on the other as this Writ of Assistance is.

It appears to me the worst instrument of arbitrary power, the most destructive of English liberty and the fundamental principles of law, that ever was found in an English law-book. I must therefore beg your Honors' patience and attention to the whole range of an argument that may perhaps appear uncommon in many things, as well as to points of learning that are more remote and unusual, that the whole tendency of my design may the more easily be perceived, the conclusions better descend, and the force of them be better felt. I shall not think much of my pains in this cause, as I engaged in it from principle. I was solicited to argue this cause as Advocate-General; and, because I would not, I have been charged with desertion from my office. To this charge I can give a very sufficient answer. I renounced that office and I argue this cause from the same principle; and I argue it with the greater pleasure, as it is in favor of British liberty, at a time when we hear the greatest monarch upon earth declaring from his throne that he glories in the name of Briton and that the privileges of his people are dearer to him than the most valuable prerogatives of his crown; and as it is in opposition to a kind of power, the exercise of which in former periods of history cost one king of England his head and another his throne. I have taken more pains in this cause than I ever will take again, although my engaging in this and another popular cause has raised much resentment. But I think I can sincerely declare that I cheerfully submit myself to every odious name for conscience' sake; and from my soul I despise all those whose guilt, malice, or folly has made them my foes. Let the consequences be what they will, I am determined to proceed. The only principles of public conduct that are worthy of a gentleman or a man are to sacrifice estate, ease, health, and applause, and even life, to the sacred calls of his country.

These manly sentiments, in private life, make good citizens; in public life, the patriot and the hero. I do not say that, when brought to the test, I shall be invincible. I pray God I may never be brought to the melancholy trial; but, if ever I should, it will then be known how far I can reduce to practice principles which I know to be founded in truth. In the meantime I will proceed to the subject of this writ.

Your Honors will find in the old books concerning the office of a justice of the peace precedents of general warrants to search suspected houses. But in more modern books you will find only special warrants to search such and such houses, specially named, in which the complainant has before sworn that he suspects his goods are concealed; and will find it adjudged that special warrants only are legal. In the same manner I will rely on it, that the writ prayed for in this petition, being general, is illegal. It is a power that places the liberty of every man in the hands of every petty officer. I say I admit that special Writs of Assistance, to search special places, may be granted to certain persons on oath; but I deny that the writ now prayed for can be granted, for I beg leave to make some observations on the writ itself, before I proceed to other Acts of Parliament. In the first place, the writ is universal, being directed "to all and singular justices, sheriffs, constables, and all other officers and subjects"; so that, in short, it is directed to every subject in the King's dominions. Every one with this writ may be a tyrant; if this commission be legal, a tyrant in a legal manner, also, may control, imprison, or murder any one within the realm. In the next place, it is perpetual; there is no return. A man is accountable to no person for his doings. Every man may reign secure in his petty tyranny, and spread terror and desolation around him, until the trump of the Archangel shall excite different emotions in his soul. In the third place, a person with this writ, in the daytime, may enter all houses, shops, etc., at will, and command all to assist him. Fourthly, by this writ not only deputies, etc., but even their menial servants, are allowed to lord it over us. What is this but to have the curse of Canaan with a witness on us: to be the servants of servants, the most despicable of God's creation? Now one of the most essential branches of English liberty is the freedom of one's house. A man's house is his castle; and whilst he is quiet, he is as well guarded as a prince in his castle. This writ, if it should be declared legal, would totally annihilate this privilege. Customhouse officers may enter our houses when they please; we are commanded to permit their entry. Their menial servants may enter, may break locks, bars, and everything in their way; and whether they break through malice or revenge, no man, no court can inquire. Bare suspicion without oath is sufficient. This wanton exercise of this power is not a chimerical suggestion of a heated brain. I will mention some facts. Mr. Pew had one of these writs, and, when Mr. Ware succeeded him, he endorsed this writ over to Mr. Ware; so that these writs are negotiable from one office to another; and so your Honors have no opportunity of judging the persons to whom this vast power is delegated. Another instance is this: Mr. Justice Walley had called this same Mr. Ware before him, by a constable, to answer for a breach of the Sabbath-day Acts, or that of profane swearing. As soon as he had finished, Mr. Ware asked him if he had done. He replied, "Yes." "Well then," said Mr. Ware, "I will show you a little of my power. I command you to permit me to search your house for uncus- tomed goods"—and went on to search the house from the garret to the cellar; and then served the constable in the same manner! But to show another absurdity in this writ: if it should be established, I insist upon it every person, by the 14th Charles Second, has this power as well as the custom-house officers. The words are: "It shall be lawful for any person or persons authorized," etc. What a scene does this open! Every man prompted by revenge, ill-humor, or wantonness to inspect the inside of his neighbor's house, may get a Writ of Assistance. Others will ask it from self defense; one arbitrary exertion will provoke another, until society be involved in tumult and in blood.

THE FIRST INAUGURAL ADDRESS

George Washington

(1732-1799)

George Washington, the first President of the United States of America, in early youth showed a marked aptitude for military life. When only 19 years of age he was appointed an adjutant of the Virginia troops to protect the colony from the forays of the Indians. In 1753 he was sent on an expedition to the French on the Ohio river where he displayed unusual judgment and coolness in his handling of the situation. Two years later he was promoted to the command of the provincial troops and in 1763 was elected to the House of Burgesses and there urged the right of the colonies to self-government, although he asserted that arms should be the last resort. It was in 1774 that he made one of the few impulsive speeches of his life in behalf of the Bostonians suffering from the Boston Port Bill. That same year he was appointed delegate to the Continental Congress and the following year became Commander-in-Chief of the Continental Army, a post for which he was remarkably equipped by nature and experience. After the war in 1789 he was unanimously chosen by the Convention as the first President of the United States in which position he most ably served his country until 1797.

Washington was a man of action—a statesman and a soldier rather than an orator, but his good judgment and his earnestness of purpose gave conviction to all his public utterances. His *First Inaugural Address* is included here. It was delivered in Federal Hall, Wall Street, New York City, on April 30, 1789.

Among the vicissitudes incident to life no event could have filled me with greater anxieties than that of which the notification was transmitted by your order, and received on the fourth day of the present month. On the one hand, I was summoned by my country, whose voice I can never hear but with veneration and love, from a retreat which I had chosen with the fondest predilection, and, in my flattering hopes, with an immutable decision, as the asylum of my declining years; a retreat which was rendered every day more necessary as well as more dear to me by the addition of habit to inclination, and of frequent interruptions in my health to the gradual waste committed on it by time; on the other hand, the magnitude and difficulty of the trust to which the voice of my country called me being sufficient to awaken, in the wisest and most experienced of her citizens, a distrustful scrutiny into his qualifications, could not but overwhelm with despondence one who, inheriting inferior endowments from nature, and unpractised in the duties of civil administration, ought to be peculiarly conscious of his own deficiencies.

In this conflict of emotions all I dare aver is that it has been my faithful study to collect my duty from a just appreciation of every circumstance by which it might be affected. All I dare hope is that if, in executing this task, I have been too much swayed by a grateful remembrance of former instances, or by an affectionate sensibility to this transcendent proof of the confidence of my fellow citizens, and have thence too little consulted my incapacity as well as disinclination for the weighty and untried cares before me, my error will be palliated by the motives which misled me, and its consequences be judged by my country with some share of the partiality in which they originated.

Such being the impression under which I have, in obedience to the public summons, repaired to the present station, it would be peculiarly improper to omit, in this first official act, my fervent supplications to that Almighty Being who rules over the universe, who presides in the councils of nations, and whose providential aids can supply every human defect, that His benediction may consecrate to the liberties and happiness of the people of the United States a government instituted by themselves for these essential purposes, and may enable every instrument employed in its administration to execute, with success, the functions allotted to his charge. In tendering this homage to the Great Author of every public and private good, I assure myself that it expresses your sentiments not less than my own nor those of my fellow citizens at large less than either.

No people can be bound to acknowledge and adore the Invisible Hand which conducts the affairs of men more than the people of the United States. Every step by which they have advanced to the character of an independent nation seems to have been distinguished by some token of providential agency. And, in the important revolution just accomplished, in the system of their united government, the tranquil deliberations and voluntary consent of so many distinct communities, from which the event has resulted, can not be compared with the means by which most governments have been established, without some return of pious gratitude, along with a humble anticipation of the future blessings which the past seems to presage. These reflections, arising out of the present crisis, have forced themselves too strongly on my mind to be suppressed. You will join with me, I trust, in thinking that there are none under the influence of which the proceedings of a new and free government can more auspiciously commence.

By the Article establishing the executive department it is made the duty of the president "to recommend to your consideration such measures as he shall judge necessary and expedient." The circumstances under which I now meet you will acquit me from entering into that subject further than to refer you to the great constitutional charter under which we are assembled; and which, in defining your powers, designates the objects to which your attention is to be given. It will be more consistent with those circumstances and far more congenial with the feelings which actuate me, to substitute, in place of a recommendation of particular measures, the tribute that is due to the talents, the rectitude, and the patriotism which adorn the characters selected to devise and adopt them. In these honorable qualifications, I behold the surest pledges, that as, on one side, no local prejudices or attachments, no separate views nor party animosities, will misdirect the comprehensive and equal eye which ought to watch over this great assemblage of communities and interests—so, on another, that the foundations of our national policy will be laid in the pure and immutable principles of private morality; and the preeminence of a free government be exemplified by all the attributes which can win the affections of its citizens and command the respect of the world.

I dwell on this prospect with every satisfaction which an ardent love for my country can inspire; since there is no truth more thoroughly established than that there exists, in the economy and course of nature, an indissoluble union between virtue and happiness—between duty and advantage—between the genuine maxims of an honest and magnanimous policy and the solid rewards of public prosperity and felicity; since we ought to be no less persuaded that the propitious smiles of heaven can never be expected on a nation that disregards the eternal rules of order and right which heaven itself has ordained; and since the preservation of the sacred fire of liberty, and the destiny of the republican model of government, are justly considered as deeply, perhaps as finally staked, on the experiment intrusted to the hands of the American people.

Besides the ordinary objects submitted to your care, it will remain with your judgment to decide how far an exercise of the occasional power delegated by the fifty articles of the Constitution is rendered expedient, at the present juncture, by the nature of objections which have been urged against the system, or by the degree of inquietude which has given birth to them. Instead of undertaking particular recommendations on this subject, in which I could be guided by no lights derived from official opportunities, I shall again give way to my entire confidence in your discernment and pursuit of the public good. For I assure myself that, while you carefully avoided every alteration which might endanger the benefits of a united and effective government, or which ought to await the future lessons of experience, a reverence for the characteristic rights of freemen and a regard for the public harmony will sufficiently influence your deliberations on the question how far the former can be more impregnably fortified, or the latter be safely and more advantageously promoted.

To the preceding observation I have one to add, which will be most properly addressed to the House of Representatives. It concerns myself, and will therefore be as brief as possible.

When I was first honored with a call into the service of my country, then on the eve of an arduous struggle for its liberties, the light in which I contemplated my duty required that I should renounce every pecuniary compensation. From this resolution I have in no instance departed. And being still under the impressions which produced it, I must decline, as inapplicable to myself, any share in the personal emoluments which may be indispensably included in a permanent provision for the executive department; and must accordingly pray that the pecuniary estimates for the station in which I am placed may, during my continuation in it, be limited to such actual expenditures as the public good may be thought to require.

Having thus imparted to you my sentiments, as they have been awakened by the occasion which brings us together, I shall take my present leave, but not without resorting once more to the benign Parent of the human race, in humble supplication that, since He has been pleased to favor the American people with opportunities for deliberating in perfect tranquillity, and dispositions for the deciding with unparalleled unanimity, on a form of government for the security of their union and the advancement of their happiness, so His divine blessings may be equally conspicuous in the enlarged views, the temperate consultations, and the wise measures on which the success of this government must depend.

ON THE FEDERAL CONSTITUTION

Benjamin Franklin

(1706-1790)

Benjamin Franklin, though primarily a philosopher, statesman, scientist and author, was on occasion an effective speaker. It was at his instigation that the debating society for the "Discussion of Morals, Politics, and Natural Philosophy" which later developed into the American Philosophical Society was started in 1743. In 1757 he was sent to England to represent the colonies and became involved in an examination before the House of Commons as to the effects of the Stamp Act. Although Franklin preferred to see America grow and develop within the British Empire until she became free, and opposed bloody revolution, yet he offered all his wealth to Congress when the war began. During the Revolution Franklin represented American interests in Europe, particularly in France where his dignity of character, charm of manner, and scientific reputation made him extremely popular. It was this skill in diplomacy which made Franklin most valuable to his country, and he must have possessed no small amount of persuasiveness in speech to accomplish his ends. On many occasions it became necessary for Franklin to make public addresses, and this he always accomplished with finesse and dignity. In spite of advancing age Franklin was active as a member of the Convention which formed a national constitution in 1787. The speech included here was delivered before that Convention and very ably shows Franklin's diplomacy.

I confess that I do not entirely approve of this Constitution at present; but, sir, I am not sure I shall never approve of it, for, having lived long, I have experienced many instances of being obliged, by better information or fuller consideration, to change opinions even on important subjects, which I once thought right, but found to be otherwise. It is therefore that, the older I grow, the more apt I am to doubt my own judgment of others. Most men, indeed, as well as most sects in religion, think themselves in possession of all truth, and that wherever others differ from them, it is so far error. Steele, a Protestant, in a dedication, tells the Pope that the only difference between our two churches in their opinions of the certainty of their doctrine is, the Romish Church is infallible, and the Church of England is never in the wrong. But, though many private persons think almost as highly of their own infallibility as of that of their sect, few express it so naturally as a certain French lady, who, in a little dispute with her sister, said: "But I meet with nobody but myself that is always in the right."

In these sentiments, sir, I agree to this Constitution with all its faults—if they are such—because I think a general government necessary for us, and there is no form of government but what may be a blessing to the people, if well administered; and I believe, further, that this is likely to be well administered for a course of years, and can only end in despotism, as other forms have done before it, when the people shall become so corrupted as to need despotic government, being incapable of any other. I doubt, too, whether any other convention we can obtain may be able to make a better Constitution; for, when you assemble a number of men, to have the advantage of their joint wisdom, you inevitably assemble with those men all their prejudices, their passions, their errors of opinion, their local interests, and their selfish views. From such an assembly can a perfect production be expected?

It therefore astonishes me, sir, to find this system approaching so near to perfection as it does; and I think it will astonish our enemies, who are waiting with confidence to hear that our counsels are confounded like those of the builders of Babel, and that our States are on the point of separation, only to meet hereafter for the purpose of cutting one another's throats. Thus I consent, sir, to this Constitution, because I expect no better, and because I am not sure that it is not the best. The opinions I have had of its errors I sacrifice to the public good. I have never whispered a syllable of them abroad. Within these walls they were born, and here they shall die. If every one of us, in returning to our constituents, were to report the objections he has had to it, and endeavor to gain partizans in support of them, we might prevent its being generally received, and thereby lose all the salutary effects and great advantages resulting naturally in our favor among foreign nations, as well as among ourselves, from our real or apparent unanimity. Much of the strength and efficiency of any government, in procuring and securing happiness to the people, depends on opinion, on the general opinion of the goodness of that government, as well as of the wisdom and integrity of its governors. I hope, therefore, for our own sakes, as a part of the people, and for the sake of our posterity, that we shall act heartily and unanimously in recommending this Constitution wherever our influence may extend, and turn our future thoughts and endeavors to the means of having it well administered.

On the whole, sir, I can not help expressing a wish that every member of the Convention who may still have objections to it, would, with me, on this occasion, doubt a little of his own infallibility, and, to make manifest our unanimity, put his name to this instrument.

ON AMERICAN INDEPENDENCE [2]

Samuel Adams

(1722-1803)

Samuel Adams was a leader of the Boston patriots in the American Revolution. Born in Boston of the aristocratic Adams family, Samuel attended Harvard as was the family custom and later practiced law. He was early engaged in the activities of town politics where he became known as "The Man of the Town Meeting" because of his frequent participation in the discussions. He was the leading spirit of the celebrated "Boston Tea Party." Later he became a member of the Continental Congress where he distinguished himself as an orator and statesman earning the title of colossus of debate, and labored unflinchingly for the Declaration of Independence. It was at the signing of the Declaration that Adams delivered the speech included here which is the only oration of his we have today.

Although he lacked oratorical fluency, Samuel Adams had the power of stirring the heart as well as appealing to the intellect. His short speeches were his most forceful. He was close and logical in his reasoning, and his shrewdness, adroitness, and adeptness in the art of handling men made him a powerful leader in molding and directing public opinion in the colonies.

No man had once a greater veneration for Englishmen than I entertained. They were dear to me as branches of the same parental trunk, and partakers of the same religion and laws; I still view with respect the remains of the Constitution as I would a lifeless body which had once been animated by a great and heroic soul. But when I am aroused by the din of arms; when I behold legions of foreign assassins paid by Englishmen to imbrue their hands in our blood; when I tread over the uncoffined bodies of my countrymen, neighbors, and friends; when I see the locks of a venerable father torn by savage hands, and a feeble

[2] Abridged.

mother, clasping her infants to her bosom, and on her knees imploring their lives from her own slaves, whom Englishmen have allured to treachery and murder; when I behold my country, once the seat of industry, peace, and plenty, changed by Englishmen to a theater of blood and misery, Heaven forgive me if I cannot root out those passions which it has implanted in my bosom, and detest submission to a people who have either ceased to be human, or have not virtue enough to feel their own wretchedness and servitude! . . . .

Who amongst you, my countrymen, that is a father, would claim authority to make your child a slave because you had nourished him in infancy?

'Tis a strange species of generosity which requires a return infinitely more valuable than anything it could have bestowed; that demands as a reward for a defence of our property a surrender of those inestimable privileges to the arbitrary will of vindictive tyrants, which alone give value to that very property.

Courage, then, my countrymen; our contest is not only whether we ourselves shall be free, but whether there shall be left to mankind an asylum on earth for civil and religious liberty. Dismissing, therefore, the justice of our cause as incontestable, the only question is, What is best for us to pursue in our present circumstances?

The doctrine of dependence on Great Britain is, I believe, generally exploded; but as I would attend to the honest weakness of the simplest of men, you will pardon me if I offer a few words on that subject.

We are now on this continent, to the astonishment of the world, three millions of souls united in one cause. We have large armies, well disciplined and appointed, with commanders inferior to none in military skill, and superior in activity and zeal. We are furnished with arsenals and stores beyond our most sanguine expectations, and foreign nations are waiting to crown our success by their alliances. There are instances of, I would say, an almost astonishing providence in our favor; our success has staggered our enemies, and almost given faith to infidels; so we may truly say it is not our own arm which has saved us.

The hand of Heaven appears to have led us on to be, perhaps, humble instruments and means in the great providential dispensation which is completing.

To unite the supremacy of Great Britain and the liberty of America is utterly impossible. So vast a continent and of such a distance from the seat of empire will every day grow more unmanageable. The motion of so unwieldy a body can not be directed with any despatch and uniformity without committing to the Parliament of Great Britain powers inconsistent with our freedom. The authority and force which would be absolutely necessary for the preservation of the peace and good order of this continent would put all our valuable rights within the reach of that nation.

If there is any man so base or so weak as to prefer a dependence on Great Britain to the dignity and happiness of living a member of a free and independent nation, let me tell him that necessity now demands what the generous principle of patriotism should have dictated.

We have no other alternative than independence, or the most ignominious and galling servitude. The legions of our enemies thicken on our plains; desolation and death mark their bloody career, while the mangled corpses of our countrymen seem to cry to us as a voice from heaven.

Our Union is now complete; our Constitution composed, established, and approved. You are now the guardians of your own liberties. We may justly address you as the *decemviri* did the Romans, and say: "Nothing that we propose can pass into a law without your consent. Be yourselves, O Americans, the authors of those laws on which your happiness depends."

You have now in the field armies sufficient to repel the whole force of your enemies and their base and mercenary auxiliaries. The hearts of your soldiers beat high with the spirit of freedom; they are animated with the justice of their cause, and while they grasp their swords can look up to Heaven for assistance. Your adversaries are composed of wretches who laugh at the rights of humanity, who turn religion into derision, and would, for higher wages, direct their swords against their leaders or their country. Go on, then, in your generous enterprise with gratitude to Heaven for past success, and confidence of it in the future. For my own part I ask no greater blessing than to share with you the common danger and common glory. If I have a wish dearer to my soul than that my ashes may be mingled with those of a Warren and Montgomery, it is that these American States may never cease to be free and independent.

THE FEDERAL CONSTITUTION

Alexander Hamilton

(1757-1804)

Alexander Hamilton, brilliant soldier, statesman, lawyer, and financier, has been ranked with Fox and Napoleon as one of the three greatest men of his day. As a lad Hamilton came to the United States from his birthplace in the West Indies, and when only seventeen years of age he made his debut as a revolutionary orator in an eloquent speech in New York City in which he denounced Great Britain and called upon the colonies to resist British aggression. At the outbreak of the war he volunteered and instantly won recognition which placed him as aide-de-camp to General Washington. After the war Hamilton prepared for the practice of law but in 1782 was elected to the Continental Congress; in 1787 he was a member of the General Convention for framing the Federal Constitution and delivered there one of his ablest speeches in which he sought for centralization. When the time came to ratify, Hamilton, in his own state of New York, presented a series of eloquent speeches in behalf of the new instrument of government. One of Hamilton's greatest contributions was as Secretary of the Treasury under Washington when, as Daniel Webster later stated, "he touched the dead corpse of public credit and it sprang upon its feet."

Throughout the latter part of his life Hamilton was the undisputed head of the New York bar, where in 1804 he delivered what is often considered his greatest forensic speech in defense of Henry Croswell in a libel suit—a speech whose power moved even the austere bench of judges to tears. In the same year Hamilton became involved in a political dispute with Aaron Burr resulting in a duel in which Hamilton was fatally wounded. Among the famous eulogies written on Hamilton are one by Gouverneur Morris and one by Eliphalet Nott.

In all his speeches Hamilton shows his indisputable right
to rank as one of America's most able statesmen and orators.
His establishment of the financial system, his aid to Washington in devising a foreign policy, his cooperation with John
Marshall in establishing a doctrine of liberal interpretation of the
Constitution and his efforts to lay the foundations of nationalism
as opposed to states rights were his contributions to his country.
"The Little Lion," a term bestowed upon him by his fellow
officers in the Revolutionary War, applied also to him as an
orator.

The speech included here was delivered before the Constitutional Convention of New York on June 24, 1788, urging the
adoption of the Constitution.

I am persuaded, Mr. Chairman, that I in my turn shall be indulged
in addressing the committee. We all in equal sincerity profess to be
anxious for the establishment of a republican government on a safe
and solid basis. It is the object of the wishes of every honest man in
the United States, and I presume that I shall not be disbelieved when
I declare that it is an object of all others the nearest and most dear
to my own heart. The means of accomplishing this great purpose
become the most important study which can interest mankind. It is
our duty to examine all those means with peculiar attention and to
choose the best and most effectual. It is our duty to draw from nature,
from reason, from examples, the best principles of policy, and to pursue
and apply them in the formation of our government. We should contemplate and compare the systems which in this examination come under
our view; distinguish with a careful eye the defects and excellencies of
each, and, discarding the former, incorporate the latter, as far as circumstances will admit, into our Constitution. If we pursue a different course
and neglect this duty we shall probably disappoint the expectations of
our country and of the world.

In the commencement of a revolution which received its birth from
the usurpations of tyranny, nothing was more natural than that the
public mind should be influenced by an extreme spirit of jealousy. To
resist these encroachments and to nourish this spirit was the great object
of all our public and private institutions. The zeal for liberty became
predominant and excessive. In forming our Confederation this passion
alone seemed to actuate us, and we appear to have had no other view
than to secure ourselves from despotism. The object certainly was a
valuable one, and deserved our utmost attention. But, sir, there is
another object equally important and which our enthusiasm rendered

us little capable of regarding; I mean a principle of strength and stability in the organization of our government, and vigor in its operations. This purpose can never be accomplished but by the establishment of some select body formed peculiarly upon this principle. There are few positions more demonstrable than that there should be in every republic some permanent body to correct the prejudices, check the intemperate passions, and regulate the fluctuations of a popular assembly. It is evident that a body instituted for these purposes must be so formed as to exclude as much as possible from its own character those infirmities and that mutability which it is designed to remedy. It is therefore necessary that it should be small, that it should hold its authority during a considerable period, and that it should have such an independence in the exercise of its powers as will divest it as much as possible of local prejudices. It should be so formed as to be the center of political knowledge, to pursue always a steady line of conduct, and to reduce every irregular propensity to system. Without this establishment we may make experiments without end, but shall never have an efficient government.

It is an unquestionable truth that the body of the people in every country desire sincerely its prosperity; but it is equally unquestionable that they do not possess the discernment and stability necessary for systematic government. To deny that they are frequently led into the grossest errors by misinformation and passion would be a flattery which their own good sense must despise. That branch of administration especially which involves our political relations with foreign states, a community will ever be incompetent to [administer]. These truths are not often held up in public assemblies, but they cannot be unknown to any who hear me. From these principles it follows that there ought to be two distinct bodies in our government: one, which shall be immediately constituted by and peculiarly represent the people and possess all the popular features; another, formed upon the principle and for the purposes before explained. Such considerations as these induced the Convention who formed your State Constitution to institute a Senate upon the present plan. The history of ancient and modern republics had taught them that many of the evils which these republics had suffered arose from the want of a certain balance and mutual control indispensable to a wise administration. They were convinced that popular assemblies are frequently misguided by ignorance, by sudden impulses, and the intrigues of ambitious men, and that some firm barrier against these operations was necessary; they therefore instituted your Senate, and the benefits we have experienced have fully justified their conceptions.

Gentlemen in their reasoning have placed the interests of the several States and those of the United States in contrast; this is not a fair view of the subject: they must necessarily be involved in each other. What we apprehend is that some sinister prejudice or some prevailing passion may assume the form of a genuine interest. The influence of these is as powerful as the most permanent conviction of the public good, and against this influence we ought to provide. The local interests of a State ought in every case to give way to the interests of the Union; for when a sacrifice of one or the other is necessary, the former becomes only an apparent, partial interest, and should yield on the principle that the small good ought never to oppose the great one. When you assemble from your several counties in the Legislature, were every member to be guided only by the apparent interests of his county, government would be impracticable. There must be a perpetual accommodation and sacrifice of local advantages to general expediency; but the spirit of a mere popular assembly would rarely be actuated by this important principle. It is therefore absolutely necessary that the Senate should be so formed as to be unbiased by false conceptions of the real interests or undue attachment to the apparent good of their several States.

Gentlemen indulge too many unreasonable apprehensions of danger to the State governments; they seem to suppose that the moment you put men into a national council, they become corrupt and tyrannical and lose all their affection for their fellow citizens. But can we imagine that the Senators will ever be so insensible of their own advantage as to sacrifice the genuine interests of their constituents? The State governments are essentially necessary to the form and spirit of the general system. As long, therefore, as Congress has a full conviction of this necessity, they must even upon principles purely national, have as firm an attachment to the one as to the other. This conviction can never leave them, unless they become madmen. While the Constitution continues to be read and its principle known the States must by every rational man be considered as essential, component parts of the Union; and therefore the idea of sacrificing the former to the latter is wholly inadmissible.

The objectors do not advert to the natural strength and resources of State governments, which will ever give them an important superiority over the general government. If we compare the nature of their different powers, or the means of popular influence which each possesses, we shall find the advantage entirely on the side of the States. This consideration, important as it is, seems to have been little attended to. The aggregate number of representatives throughout the States may be two thousand. Their personal influence will, therefore, be proportionably more extensive than that of one or two hundred men in Congress. The State establishments of civil and military officers of every description, infinitely surpassing in number any possible correspondent establishments in the general government, will create such an extent and complication of attachments as will ever secure the predilection and support of the people. Whenever, therefore, Congress shall meditate any infringement of the State Constitutions, the great body of the people will naturally take part with their domestic representatives. Can the general government withstand such a united opposition? Will the people suffer themselves to be stripped of their privileges? Will they suffer their Legislatures to be reduced to a shadow and a name? The idea is shocking to common sense.

From the circumstances already explained and many others which might be mentioned, results a complicated, irresistible check, which must ever support the existence and importance of the State governments. The danger, if any exists, flows from an opposite source, the probable evil is that the general government will be too dependent on the State Legislatures, too much governed by their prejudices, and too obsequious to their humors, that the States, with every power in their hands, will make encroachments on the national authority till the Union is weakened and dissolved.

Every member must have been struck with an observation of a gentleman from Albany. Do what you will, says he, local prejudices and opinions will go into the government. What! shall we then form a Constitution to cherish and strengthen these prejudices? Shall we confirm the distemper instead of remedying it? It is undeniable that there must be a control somewhere. Either the general interest is to control the particular interests, or the contrary. If the former, then certainly the government ought to be so framed as to render the power of control efficient to all intents and purposes; if the latter, a striking absurdity follows; the controlling powers must be as numerous as the varying interests, and the operations of the government must therefore cease; for the moment you accommodate these different interests, which is the only way to set the government in motion, you establish a controlling power. Thus, whatever constitutional provisions are made to the contrary, every government will be at last driven to the necessity of subjecting the partial to the universal interest. The gentlemen ought always in their reasoning to distinguish between the real, genuine good of a State and the opinions and prejudices which may prevail respecting it; the latter may be opposed to the general good, and consequently ought to be sacrificed; the former is so involved in it that it never can be sacrificed.

There are certain social principles in human nature from which we may draw the most solid conclusions with respect to the conduct of individuals and of communities. We love our families more than our neighbors; we love our neighbors more than our countrymen in general. The human affections, like the solar heat, lose their intensity as they depart from the center and become languid in proportion to the expansion of the circle on which they act. On these principles, the attachment of the individual will be first and forever secured by the State governments; they will be a mutual protection and support. Another source of influence, which has already been pointed out, is the various official connections in the States. Gentlemen endeavor to evade the force of this by saying that these offices will be insignificant. This is by no means true. The State officers will ever be important, because they are necessary and useful. Their powers are such as are extremely interesting to the people; such as affect their property, their liberty, and life. What is more important than the administration of justice and the execution of the civil and criminal laws? Can the State governments become insignificant while they have the power of raising money independently and without control? If they are really useful, if they are calculated to promote the essential interests of the people, they must have their confidence and support. The States can never lose their powers till the whole people of America are robbed of their liberties. These must go together; they must support each other, or meet one common fate. On the gentleman's principle we may safely trust the State governments, though we have no means of resisting them; but we can not confide in the national government, though we have an effectual constitutional guard against every encroachment. This is the essence of their argument, and it is false and fallacious beyond conception.

With regard to the jurisdiction of the two governments I shall certainly admit that the Constitution ought to be so formed as not to prevent the States from providing for their own existence; and I maintain that it is so formed, and that their power of providing for themselves is sufficiently established. This is conceded by one gentleman, and in the next breath the concession is retracted. He says Congress has but one exclusive right in taxation—that of duties on imports; certainly, then, their other powers are only concurrent. But to take off the force of this obvious conclusion, he immediately says that the laws of the United States are supreme and that where there is one supreme there can not be a concurrent authority; and further, that where the laws of the Union are supreme those of the States must be subordinate, because there can not be two supremes. This is curious sophistry. That two supreme powers can not act together is false. They are inconsistent only when they are aimed at each other or at one indivisible object. The laws of the United States are supreme as to all their proper constitutional objects; the laws of the States are supreme in the same way. These supreme laws may act on different objects without clashing, or they may operate on different parts of the same common object with perfect harmony. Suppose both governments should lay a tax of a penny on a certain article; has not each an independent and uncontrollable power to collect its own tax? The meaning of the maxim, there cannot be two supremes, is simply this—two powers cannot be supreme over each other. This meaning is entirely perverted by the gentlemen. But, it is said, disputes between collectors are to be referred to the Federal courts. This is again wandering in the field of conjecture. But suppose the fact is certain, is it not to be presumed that they will express the true meaning of the Constitution and the laws? Will they not be bound to consider the concurrent jurisdiction; to declare that both the taxes shall have equal operation; that both the powers, in that respect, are sovereign and coextensive? If they transgress their duty we are to hope that they will be punished. Sir, we can reason from probabilities alone. When we leave common sense and give ourselves up to conjecture, there can be no certainty, no security in our reasonings.

THE TREATY WITH GREAT BRITAIN [3]

Fisher Ames

(1758-1808)

Fisher Ames was the foremost orator during the first decade of the new American Republic. He was born in Massachusetts, educated at Harvard College, and in the year 1781 entered the practice of law. By the time the Massachusetts Convention for the adoption of the Constitution met in 1788, Ames, as a leading member of the bar, was chosen as a delegate. Later he was elected to the state legislature and in 1789 to Congress in the House of Representatives, where he remained until ill health obliged him to withdraw.

Ames is particularly famous for two speeches—one *On Jay's Treaty*, delivered in 1796 in favor of appropriations to carry out the Jay Treaty with England. For this speech Ames received recognition as the greatest orator in Congress; and the second, usually called his *Tomahawk Speech*, because it included references to the Indian massacres. Another oratorical distinction was granted to Ames when he was selected to pronounce the congressional *Address to Washington* on the latter's retirement.

The Treaty with Great Britain included here was delivered by Ames in the House of Representatives on April 28, 1796. The Jay Treaty aimed to settle disputes with Great Britain which arose as an aftermath of the American Revolution relative to the treatment of the Tories, British merchants, and the seizure of American vessels at sea. There was intense excitement over the Treaty at the time when Ames earnestly spoke in its behalf in a speech which Priestly proclaimed as the most bewitching piece of parliamentary oratory to which he had ever listened. It shook the nation as no other speech since Patrick Henry's

[3] Abridged.

Call to Arms. By this speech Ames won the vote for the Treaty, saved his country's faith, and probably averted war with England.

It would be strange that a subject which has aroused in turn all the passions of the country should be discussed without the interference of any of our own. We are men, and, therefore, not exempt from those passions; as citizens and representatives we feel the interests that must excite them. The hazard of great interests can not fail to agitate strong passions. We are not disinterested; it is impossible we should be dispassionate. The warmth of such feelings may becloud the judgment and for a time pervert the understanding. But the public sensibility, and our own, has sharpened the spirit of inquiry and given an animation to the debate. The public attention has been quickened to mark the progress of the discussion, and its judgment, often hasty and erroneous on first impressions, has become solid and enlightened at last. Our result will, I hope, on that account be safer and more mature, as well as more accordant with that of the nation. The only constant agents in political affairs are the passions of men. Shall we complain of our nature—shall we say that man ought to have been made otherwise? It is right already, because He, from whom we derive our nature, ordained it so; and because thus made and thus acting, the cause of truth and the public good is more surely promoted.

The treaty is bad, fatally bad, is the cry. It sacrifices the interest, the honor, the independence of the United States and the faith of our engagements to France. If we listen to the clamor of party intemperance, the evils are of a number not to be counted, and of a nature not to be borne, even in idea. The language of passion and exaggeration may silence that of sober reason in other places; it has not done it here. The question here is, whether the treaty be really so very fatal as to oblige the nation to break its faith. I admit that such a treaty ought not to be executed. I admit that self-preservation is the first law of society as well as of individuals. It would, perhaps, be deemed an abuse of terms to call that a treaty which violates such a principle. I waive, also, for the present, any inquiry what departments shall represent the nation and annul the stipulations of a treaty.

I content myself with pursuing the inquiry whether the nature of this compact be such as to justify our refusal to carry it into effect. A treaty is the promise of a nation. Now, promises do not always bind him that makes them. But I lay down two rules which ought to guide us in this case. The treaty must appear to be bad, not merely in the petty details, but in its character, principle, and mass. And in the next place, this ought to be ascertained by the decided and general concurrence of the enlightened public.

I confess there seems to be something very like ridicule thrown over the debate by the discussion of the articles in detail. The undecided point is, shall we break our faith? And while our country and enlightened Europe await the issue with more than curiosity, we are enployed to gather piecemeal, and article by article, from the instrument, a justification for the deed by trivial calculations of commercial profit and loss. This is little worthy of the subject, of this body, or of the nation. If the treaty is bad it will appear to be so in its mass. Evil to a fatal extreme, if that be its tendency, requires no proof; it brings it. Extremes speak for themselves and make their own law. What if the direct voyage of American ships to Jamaica with horses or lumber might net one or two *per centum* more than the present trade to Surinam; would the proof of the fact avail anything in so grave a question as the violation of the public engagements?

What is patriotism? Is it a narrow affection for the spot where a man was born? Are the very clods where we tread entitled to this ardent preference because they are greener? No, sir, this is not the character of the virtue, and it soars higher for its object. It is an extended self-love, mingling with all the enjoyments of life, and twisting itself with the minutest filaments of the heart. It is thus we obey the laws of society, because they are the laws of virtue. In their authority we see not the array of force and terror, but the venerable image of our country's honor. Every good citizen makes that honor his own and cherishes it not only as precious, but as sacred. He is willing to risk his life in its defense, and is conscious that he gains protection while he gives it. For, what rights of a citizen will be deemed inviolable when a State renounces the principles that constitute their security? Or if his life should not be invaded, what would its enjoyments be in a country odious in the eyes of strangers and dishonored in his own? Could he look with affection and veneration to such a country as his parent? The sense of having one would die within him; he would blush for his patriotism, if he retained any, and justly, for it would be a vice. He would be a banished man in his native land.

I see no exception to the respect that is paid among nations to the law of good faith. If there are cases in this enlightened period when it is violated, there are none when it is decried. It is the philosophy of politics, the religion of governments. It is observed by barbarians—a whiff of tobacco smoke, or a string of beads gives not merely binding force but sanctity to treaties. Even in Algiers a truce may be bought for money, but when ratified even Algiers is too wise, or too just, to disown and annul its obligation. Thus we see, neither the ignorance of savages, nor the principles of an association for piracy and rapine, permit a nation to despise its engagements. If, sir, there could be a resurrection from the foot of the gallows, if the victims of justice could live again, collect together and form a society, they would, however loath, soon find themselves obliged to make justice, that justice under which they fell, the fundamental law of their State. They would perceive it was their interest to make others respect, and they would, therefore, soon pay some respect themselves to the obligations of good faith.

It is painful, I hope it is superfluous, to make even the supposition that America should furnish the occasion of this opprobrium. No, let me not even imagine that a republican government, sprung as our own is from a people enlightened and uncorrupted, a government whose origin is right, and whose daily discipline is duty, can, upon solemn debate, make its option to be faithless—can dare to act what despots dare not avow, what our own example evinces, the States of Barbary are unsuspected of.

No, let me rather make the supposition that Great Britain refuses to execute the treaty, after we have done everything to carry it into effect. Is there any language of reproach pungent enough to express your commentary of the fact? What would you say, or, rather, what could you not say? Would you not tell them, wherever an Englishman might travel, shame would stick to him—he would disown his country. You would exclaim: England, proud of your wealth, and arrogant in the possession of power—blush for these distinctions which become the vehicles of your dishonor. Such a nation might truly say to corruption, thou art my father, and to the worm, thou are my mother and my sister. We would say of such a race of men, their name is a heavier burden than their debt.

On this theme my emotions are unutterable. If I could find words for them, if my powers bore any proportion of my zeal, I would swell my voice to such a note of remonstrance it should reach every log house beyond the mountains. I would say to the inhabitants: Wake from your false security; your cruel dangers, your more cruel apprehensions are soon to be renewed; the wounds, yet unhealed are to be torn open again; in the daytime your path through the woods will be ambushed; the darkness of midnight will glitter with the blaze of your dwellings. You are a father—the blood of your sons shall fatten your cornfield; you are a mother—the war-whoop shall wake the sleep of the cradle.

On this subject you need not suspect any deception on your feelings. It is a spectacle of horror which can not be overdrawn. If you have nature in your hearts, it will speak a language compared with which all I have said or can say will be poor and frigid.

Will it be whispered that the treaty has made me a new champion for the protection of the frontiers? It is known that my voice as well as my vote have been uniformly given in conformity with the ideas I have expressed. Protection is the right of the frontiers; it is our duty to give it.

Who will accuse me of wandering out of the subject? Who will say that I exaggerate the tendencies of our measures? Will any one answer by a sneer that all this is idle preaching? Will anyone deny that we are bound, and I would hope to good purpose, by the most solemn sanctions of duty for the vote we give? Are despots alone to be reproached for unfeeling indifference to the tears and blood of their subjects? Have the principles on which you ground the reproach upon cabinets and kings no practical influence, no binding force? Are they merely themes of idle declamation introduced to decorate the morality of a newspaper essay or to furnish petty topics of harang from the windows of that State House? I trust it is neither too presumptuous nor too late to ask. Can you put the dearest interest of society at risk without guilt and without remorse?

By rejecting the posts we light the savage fires—we bind the victims. This day we undertake to render account to the widows and orphans whom our decision will make, to the wretches that will be roasted at the stake, to our country, and I do not deem it too serious to say, to conscience and to God. We are answerable, and if duty be anything more than a word of imposture, if conscience be not a bugbear, we are preparing to make ourselves as wretched as our country.

There is no mistake in this case—there can be none. Experience has already been the prophet of events, and the cries of future victims have already reached us. The Western inhabitants are not a silent and uncomplaining sacrifice. The voice of humanity issues from the shade of their wilderness. It exclaims that, while one hand is held up to reject this treaty, the other grasps a tomahawk. It summons our imagination to the scenes that will open. It is no great effort of the imagination to conceive that events so near are already begun. I can fancy that I listen to the yells of savage vengeance and the shrieks of torture. Already they seem to sigh in the west wind—already they mingle with every echo from the mountains.

Let me cheer the mind, weary, no doubt, and ready to despond on this prospect, by presenting another, which it is yet in our power to realize. Is it possible for a real American to look at the prosperity of this country without some desire for its continuance—without some respect for the measures which, many will say, produce, and all will confess, have preserved it? Will he not feel some dread that a change of system will reverse the scene? The well-grounded fears of our citizens in 1794 were removed by the treaty, but are not forgotten. Then they deemed war nearly inevitable, and would not this adjustment have been considered at that day as a happy escape from the calamity? The great interest and the general desire of our people were to enjoy the advantages of neutrality. This instrument, however misrepresented, affords America that inestimable security. The causes of our disputes are either cut up by the roots or referred to a new negotiation after the end of the European war. This was gaining everything, because it confirmed our neutrality by which our citizens are gaining everything. This alone would justify the engagements of the government. For, when the fiery vapors of the war lowered in the skirts of our horizon, all our wishes were concentrated in this one, that we might escape the desolation of the storm.   This treaty, like a rainbow on the edge of the cloud, marked to our eyes the space where it was raging and afforded at the same time the sure prognostic of fair weather.   If we reject it the vivid colors will grow pale—it will be a baleful meteor portending tempest and war.

I rose to speak under the impressions that I would have resisted if I could.   Those who see me will believe that the reduced state of my health has unfitted me almost equally for much exertion of body or mind.   Unprepared for debate, by careful reflection in my retirement or by long attention here, I thought the resolution I had taken to sit silent was imposed by necessity, and would cost me no effort to maintain.   With a mind thus vacant of ideas and sinking, as I really am, under a sense of weakness, I imagined the very desire of speaking was extinguished by the persuasion that I had nothing to say.   Yet, when I come to the moment of deciding the vote I start back with dread from the edge of the pit into which we are plunging.   In my view even the minutes I have spent in expostulation have their value, because they protract the crisis and the short period in which alone we may resolve to escape it.

I have thus been led by my feelings to speak more at length than I intended.   Yet I have, perhaps, as little personal interest in the event as any one here.   There is, I believe, no member who will not think his chance to be a witness of the consequences greater than mine.   If, however, the vote shall pass to reject, and a spirit should rise, as it will, with the public disorders, to make confusion worse confounded, even I, slender and almost broken as my hold upon life is, may outlive the government and Constitution of my country.

THE TARIFF AND THE CONSTITUTION [4]

John Randolph

(1773-1833)

John Randolph, branded "The Son of Satan" by his opponents, occupied a most unique position in American history. Descended from an old and wealthy Virginia family and the Indian princess, Pocahontas, educated at Princeton, Columbia University, and the College of William and Mary, Randolph seemed a child of fortune. His personality was startling. In voice, feature, and figure he possessed eccentric peculiarities. At times he was intensely malignant and again kind and loving (his will at his death gave freedom to his 300 slaves). As a member of Congress for over twenty-five years Randolph threw his influence on the side of states rights. In 1820 he voted against the Missouri Compromise because it limited the South in slavery and he stigmatized the northern supporters of the bill as "doughfaces." He directed a series of violent speeches against Madison and Jefferson in the Yazoo land-fraud cases. In 1808 he delivered his famous speech against the Gregg Resolution which pointed toward war with England and in 1811 opposed the Militia Bill which was the forerunner of the War of 1812. Two of his most remarkable speeches were delivered in 1824 before the House of Representatives *On Internal Revenue* and *On the Tariff* in which he became a prophet of the Civil War. Before the Senate in 1826 Randolph delivered an insulting speech (entitled *Bilfil and Black George*) which was aimed against Clay and President Adams and was so filled with rancour and malignancy that Clay challenged him to a duel. During Jackson's administration Randolph was sent as minister to Russia in return for his services during the presidential election, but on his return to America he again reentered his verbal warfare with Clay over the southern situation and continued his attacks until his death.

[4] Abridged.

Randolph's wit and genius were acknowledged by all. He probably spoke to more listeners than any other man of his day, riveting their attention by the force and pungency of his language, the beauty and ease of his diction, and his emphatic manner. He was always strongest in aggressive debate, for there he could exert sarcasm and invective to the greatest advantage. He was indeed a veritable fire-brand. Included here is a portion of his speech on the tariff of 1816 in which he supported the South in the desire for free trade as suited to its cotton farming industries.

I am very glad, Mr. Speaker, that old Massachusetts Bay and the province of Maine and Sagadahock, by whom we stood in the days of the Revolution, now stand by the South, and will not aid in fixing on us this system of taxation, compared with which the taxation of Mr. Grenville and Lord North was as nothing. I speak with knowledge of what I say, when I declare that this bill is an attempt to reduce the country south of Mason and Dixon's line, and east of the Alleghany mountains, to a state of worse than colonial bondage; a state to which the domination of Great Britain was, in my judgment, far preferable; and I trust I shall always have the fearless integrity to utter any political sentiment which the head sanctions and the heart ratifies; for the British Parliament never would have dared to lay such duties on our imports, or their exports to us, either "at home" or here, as is now proposed to be laid upon the imports from abroad. At that time we had the command of the market of the vast dominions then subject, and we should have had those which have since been subjected to the British empire; we enjoyed a free trade eminently superior to anything we can enjoy if this bill shall go into operation. It is a sacrifice of the interests of a part of this nation to the ideal benefit of the rest. It marks us out as the victims of a worse than Egyptian bondage. It is a barter of so much of our rights, of so much of the fruits of our labor, for political power to be transferred to other hands. It ought to be met, and I trust it will be met, in the southern country as was the Stamp Act, and all those measures which I will not detain the House by recapitulating, which succeeded the Stamp Act, and produced the final breach with the mother country, which it took about ten years to bring about; as I trust, in my conscience, it will not take as long to bring about similar results from this measure, should it become a law.

All policy is very suspicious, says an eminent statesman, that sacrifices the interest of any part of a community to the ideal good of the whole; and those governments only are tolerable where, by the necessary construction of the political machine, the interests of all the parts are obliged to be protected by it. Here is a district of country extending from the Patapsco to the Gulf of Mexico, from the Alleghany to the Atlantic; a district which, taking in all that part of Maryland lying south of the Patapsco and east of Elk river, raises five-sixths of all the exports of this country that are of home growth. I have in my hand the official statements which prove it—but which I will not weary the House by reading—in all this country, yes, sir, and I bless God for it; for with all the fantastical and preposterous theories about the rights of man (the theories, not the rights themselves, I speak of), there is nothing but power that can restrain power. I bless God that, in this insulted, oppressed, and outraged region, we are, as to our counsels in regard to this measure, but as one man; that there exists on the subject but one feeling and one interest. We are proscribed and put to the bar; and if we do not feel, and, feeling, do not act, we are bastards to those fathers who achieved the revolution; then shall we deserve to make our bricks without straw. There is no case on record in which a proposition like this, suddenly changing the whole frame of a country's polity, tearing asunder every ligature of the body politic, was ever carried by a lean majority of two or three votes, unless it be the usurpation of the septennial act, which passed the British Parliament by, I think, the majority of one vote, the same that laid the tax on cotton bagging. I do not stop here, sir, to argue about the constitutionality of this bill; I consider the Constitution a dead letter. I consider it to consist at this time of the power of the General Government and the power of the States; that is the Constitution. I have no faith in parchment, sir; I have no faith in the "abracadabra" of the Constitution; I have faith in the power of that commonwealth of which I am an unworthy son; in the power of those Carolinas, and of that Georgia, in her ancient and utmost extent, to the Mississippi, which went with us through the valley of the shadow of death in the war of our independence. I have said that I shall not stop to discuss the constitutionality of this question, for that reason and for a better; that there never was a constitution under the sun in which, by an unwise exercise of the powers of the government, the people may not be driven to the extremity of resistance by force. "For it is not, perhaps, so much by the assumption of unlawful powers as by the unwise or unwarrantable use of those which are most legal, that governments oppose their true end and object; for there is such a thing as tyranny as well as usurpation." If under a power to regulate trade you prevent exportation; if, with the most approved spring lancets, you draw the last drop of blood from our veins; if, *secundum artem*, you draw the last shilling from our pockets, what are the checks of the Constitution to us? A fig for the Constitution! When the scorpion's sting is probing us to the quick, shall we stop to chop logic? Shall we get some learned and cunning clerk to say whether the power to do this is to be found in the Constitution, and then if he, from whatever motive, shall maintain the affirmative, like the animal whose fleece forms so material a portion of this bill, quietly lie down and be shorn?

. . . . . .

THE EVILS OF THE EMBARGO ACT

Josiah Quincy

(1772-1864)

Josiah Quincy, Jr., whose father had been an eloquent exponent of patriotism and justice in his day, came into prominence under the administration of Thomas Jefferson. Although President Jefferson, himself, was not an orator and his only public utterances were his inaugural speeches, his administration was marked by the oratorical clashes of the Federalists and Antifederalist or Jeffersonian Republicans. As John Randolph was the leading exponent of the Federalists, so Josiah Quincy was the ablest orator of the administration. His life span covered both the Revolutionary and Civil Wars. Some of his ablest speeches were against the Embargo Act of 1807; against the Admission of Louisiana in 1811. He was also one of the first to denounce slavery in Congress. After his years in Congress (1804-1813) Mr. Quincy was active as a judge, as mayor of Boston during 1823-29, and as President of Harvard University 1829-1845. His speeches are marked by sound argument and his declamation was always fervid and manly.

Included here is an extract from Quincy's speech on *The Evils of the Embargo Act*. In consequence of the Napoleonic Wars in Europe and the bitter conflict between the British and French in ocean trade, the United States passed the Embargo Act forbidding American intercourse in foreign trade. Josiah Quincy saw the danger to American commerce in this act and produced his eloquent speech in opposition to it on November 28, 1808.

When I enter on the subject of the embargo, I am struck with wonder at the very threshold. I know not with what words to express my astonishment. At the time I departed from Massachusetts, if there was an impression which I thought universal, it was that, at the commencement of this session, an end would be put to this measure. The opinion was not so much that it would be terminated, as that it was then at an end. Sir, the prevailing sentiment, according to my apprehension, was stronger than this—even that the pressure was so great that it could not possibly be endured; that it would soon be absolutely insupportable. And this opinion, as I then had reason to believe, was not confined to any one class, or description, or party; that even those who were friends of the existing administration, and unwilling to abandon it, were yet satisfied that a sufficient trial had been given to this measure. With these impressions I arrive in this city. I hear the incantations of the great enchanter. I feel his spell. I see the legislative machinery begin to move. The scene opens. And I am commanded to forget all my recollections, to disbelieve the evidence of my senses, to contradict what I have seen, and heard, and felt. I hear, that all this discontent is mere party clamor—electioneering artifice; that the people of New England are able and willing to endure this embargo for an indefinite, unlimited period; some say for six months; some a year; some two years. The gentleman from North Carolina (Mr. Macon) told us, that he preferred three years of embargo to a war. And the gentleman from Virginia (Mr. Clopton) said expressly, that he hoped we should never allow our vessels to go upon the ocean again, until the orders and decrees of the belligerents were rescinded; in plain English, until France and Great Britain should, in their great condescension, permit. Good heavens! Mr. Chairman, are men mad? Is this House touched with that insanity which is the neverfailing precursor of the intention of Heaven to destroy? The people of New England, after eleven months' deprivation of the ocean, to be commanded still longer to abandon it, for an undefined period; to hold their unalienable rights at the tenure of the will of Britain or of Bonaparte! A people, commercial in all aspects, in all their relations, in all their hopes, in all their recollections of the past, in all their prospects of the future; a people whose first love was the ocean, the choice of their childhood, the approbation of their manly years, the most precious inheritance of their fathers; in the midst of their success, in the moment of the most exquisite perception of commercial prosperity, to be commanded to abandon it, not for a time limited, but for a time unlimited; not until they can be prepared to defend themselves there (for that is not pretended), but until their rivals recede from it; not until their necessities require, but until foreign nations permit! I am lost in astonishment, Mr. Chairman. I have not words to express the matchless absurdity of this attempt. I have no tongue to express the swift and headlong destruction which a blind perseverance in such a system must bring upon this nation.

But men from New England, representatives on this floor, equally with myself the constitutional guardians of her interests, differ from me in these opinions. My honorable colleague (Mr. Bacon) took occasion, in secret session, to deny that there did exist all that discontent and distress, which I had attempted, in an humble way, to describe. He told us he had traveled in Massachusetts, that the people were not thus dissatisfied, that the embargo had not produced any such tragical effects. Really, sir, my honorable colleague has traveled—all the way from Stockbridge to Hudson; from Berkshire to Boston; from inn to inn; from county court to county court; and doubtless he collected all that important information which an acute intelligence never fails to retain on such occasions. He found tea, sugar, salt, West India rum and molasses dearer; beef, pork, butter and cheese cheaper. Reflection enabled him to arrive at this difficult result, that in this way the evil and the good of the embargo equalize one another. But has my honorable colleague traveled on the seaboard? Has he witnessed the state of our cities? Has he seen our ships rotting at our wharves, our wharves deserted, our stores tenantless, our streets bereft of active business; industry forsaking her beloved haunts, and hope fled away from places where she had from earliest time been accustomed to make and fulfil her most precious promises? Has he conversed with the merchant, and heard the tale of his embarrassments—his capital arrested in his hands; forbidden by your laws to resort to a market; with property four times sufficient to discharge all his engagements, necessitated to hang on the precarious mercy of moneyed institutions for that indulgence which preserves him from stopping payment, the first step towards bankruptcy? Has he conversed with our mechanics? That mechanic, who, the day before this embargo passed, the very day that you took this bit, and rolled it like a sweet morsel under your tongue, had more business than he had hands, or time, or thought to employ in it, now soliciting, at reduced prices, that employment which the rich, owing to the uncertainty in which your laws have involved their capital, cannot afford? I could heighten this picture. I could show you laboring poor in the almshouse, and willing industry dependent upon charity. But I confine myself to particulars which have fallen under my own observation, and of which ten thousand suffering individuals on the seaboard of New England are living witnesses that here is nothing fictitious. . . .

It is in vain to say that if the embargo was raised there would be no market. The merchants understand that subject better than you; and the eagerness with which preparations to load were carried on previous to the commencement of this session, speaks, in a language not to be mistaken, their opinion of the foreign markets. But it has been asked in debate, "Will not Massachusetts, the cradle of liberty, submit to such privations?" An embargo liberty was never cradled in Massachusetts. Our liberty was not so much a mountain as a sea-nymph. She was free as air. She could swim, or she could run. The ocean was her cradle. Our fathers met her as she came, like the goddess of beauty, from the waves. They caught her as she was sporting on the beach. They courted her whilst she was spreading her nets upon the rocks. But an embargo liberty; a hand-cuffed liberty; a liberty in fetters; a liberty traversing between the four sides of a prison and beating her head against the walls, is none of our offspring. We abjure the monster. Its parentage is all inland. . . .

However, suppose that the payment of this duty is inevitable, which it certainly is not, let me ask—Is embargo independence? Deceive not yourselves. It is palpable submission. Gentlemen exclaim, Great Britain "smites us on one cheek." And what does administration? "It turns the other also." Gentlemen say "Great Britain is a robber; she takes our cloak." And what say administration? "Let her take our coat also." France and Great Britain require you to relinquish a part of your commerce, and you yield it entirely. Sir, this conduct may be the way to dignity and honor in another world, but it will never secure safety and independence in this.

EMANCIPATION OF SOUTH AMERICA [5]

Henry Clay

(1777-1852)

The Great Pacificator, Henry Clay, was the idol of the American public in the nineteenth century when the agitations over tariff and slavery were disrupting the country. Clay was born on a Virginia farm, the son of a Baptist clergyman and as a youth was known as "The mill boy of the slashes." At the age of fourteen he was employed in a retail house, but he studied law at night so that at twenty years of age he was admitted to the bar, and because of his phenomenal skill in debate by the time he was thirty he was a member of the United States Senate. In his subsequent public life Clay served terms in both the House and Senate, was three times nominated and defeated for the presidency, served as Secretary of State, and as Peace Commissioner to Ghent.

For a period of forty years Henry Clay was America's foremost statesman and held command through his captivating powers of oratory, his magnetic personality, and his generosity of heart and mind. His three greatest triumphs for his country were the adoption of the Missouri Compromise in 1820; the Tariff Compromise of 1833, which undermined the nullification project of Calhoun; and the Territorial Compromise of 1850, which postponed the Civil War for a decade. Among his greatest speeches are those on the *New Army Bill* in 1813; the *Emancipation of South America* in 1818, in which he stood for a united America against the Holy Alliance; *The Seminole War* in 1818; *The Greek Revolution* in 1824, in which he attacked Andrew Jackson for military despotism; *On the American System* in behalf of a high protective tariff; his *Valedictory to the Senate* in 1842; and his *Speech on the Compromise Measures of 1850.*

[5] Abridged.

In spite of a lack of early education Clay's natural abilities, rich voice, graceful manners, and fluency in speech made him a matchless orator in his day. He sought always to win through mild measures rather than through violence; where other orators made themselves admired, Clay made himself loved. He was ever intelligent, frank, and candid. His speeches when read today suffer from the lack of charm of his delivery, but contemporaries so esteemed him for his gentleness and courtesy that it has been stated his name alone evoked cheers so hearty, distinct, and ringing that as he progressed from place to place the hurrahs of one town scarcely died away as those of the next were heard. It was Lincoln who called Clay the "beau ideal" of a statesman.

Included here is a portion of Clay's speech on the *Emancipation of South America* delivered before the House of Representatives, March 24, 1818.

Spain has undoubtedly given us abundant and just cause for war. But it is not every cause of war that should lead to war. War is one of those dreadful scourges that so shakes the foundation of society, overturns or changes the character of governments, interrupts or destroys the pursuits of private happiness, brings, in short, misery and wretchedness in so many forms, and at last is, in its issue, so doubtful and hazardous that nothing but dire necessity can justify an appeal to arms. If we are to have war with Spain, I have, however, no hesitation in saying that no mode of bringing it about could be less fortunate than that of seizing, at this time, upon her adjoining province. There was a time, under certain circumstances, when we might have occupied East Florida with safety; had we then taken it, our posture in the negotiation with Spain would have been totally different from what it is.

But we have permitted that time, not with my consent, to pass by unimproved. If we were now to seize upon Florida after a great change in those circumstances, and after declaring our intention to acquiesce in the procrastination desired by Spain, in what light should we be viewed by foreign powers—particularly Great Britain? We have already been accused of inordinate ambition, and of seeking to aggrandize ourselves by an extension, on all sides, of our limits. Should we not, by such an act of violence, give color to the accusation? No, Mr. Chairman; if we are to be involved in a war with Spain, let us have the credit of disinterestedness. Let us put her yet more in the wrong.

Let us command the respect which is never withheld from those who act a noble and generous part. I hope to communicate to the committee the conviction which I so strongly feel, that the adoption of the amendment which I intend to propose would not hazard, in the slightest degree, the peace of the country. But if that peace is to be endangered, I would infinitely rather it should be for our exerting the right appertaining to every State, of acknowledging the independence of another State, than for the seizure of a province, which sooner or later we must acquire.

In contemplating the great struggle in which Spanish America is now engaged, our attention is fixed first by the immensity and character of the country which Spain seeks again to subjugate. Stretching on the Pacific Ocean from about the fortieth degree of north latitude to about the fifty-fifth degree of south latitude, and extending from the mouth of the Rio del Norte (exclusive of East Florida), around the Gulf of Mexico and along the South Atlantic to near Cape Horn, it is nearly five thousand miles in length, and in some places nearly three thousand in breadth. Within this vast region we behold the most sublime and interesting objects of creation, the richest mines of the precious metals, and the choicest productions of the earth. We behold there a spectacle still more interesting and sublime—the glorious spectacle of eighteen millions of people struggling to burst their chains and to be free. When we take a little nearer and more detailed view, we perceive that nature has, as it were, ordained that this people and this country shall ultimately constitute several different nations.

Leaving the United States on the north, we come to New Spain, or the viceroyalty of Mexico on the south; passing by Guatemala, we reach the viceroyalty of New Granada, the late captain-generalship of Venezuela, and Guiana, lying on the east side of the Andes. Stepping over the Brazils, we arrive at the united provinces of La Plata, and crossing the Andes we find Chili on their west side, and, further north, the viceroyalty of Lima, or Peru. Each of these several parts is sufficient in itself in point of limits to constitute a powerful state; and, in point of population, that which has the smallest contains enough to make it respectable. Throughout all the extent of that great portion of the world which I have attempted thus hastily to describe, the spirit of revolt against the dominion of Spain has manifested itself. The Revolution has been attended with various degrees of success in the several parts of Spanish America. In some it has been already crowned, as I shall endeavor to show, with complete success, and in all I am persuaded that independence has struck such deep root, that the power of Spain can never eradicate it. What are the causes of this great movement?

Three hundred years ago, upon the ruins of the thrones of Montezuma and the Incas of Peru, Spain erected the most stupendous system of colonial despotism that the world has ever seen—the most vigorous, the most exclusive. The great principle and object of this system has been to render one of the largest portions of the world exclusively subservient, in all its faculties, to the interests of an inconsiderable spot in Europe. To effectuate this aim of her policy, she locked up Spanish America from all the rest of the world, and prohibited, under the severest penalties, any foreigner from entering any part of it. To keep the natives themselves ignorant of each other and of the strength and resources of the several parts of her American possessions, she next prohibited the inhabitants of one viceroyalty or government from visiting those of another; so that the inhabitants of Mexico, for example, were not allowed to enter the viceroyalty of New Granada. The agriculture of those vast regions was so regulated and restrained as to prevent all collision with the agriculture of the peninsula. Where nature, by the character and composition of the soil, has commanded, the abominable system of Spain has forbidden the growth of certain articles. Thus the olive and the vine, to which Spanish America is so adapted, are prohibited wherever their culture can interfere with the olive and the vine peninsula.

The commerce of the country, in the direction and objects of the exports and imports, is also subjected to the narrow and selfish views of Spain, and fettered by the odious spirit of monopoly existing in Cadiz. She has sought, by scattering discord among the several castes of her American population, and by a debasing course of education, to perpetuate her oppression. Whatever concerns public law or the science of government, all writings upon political economy, or that tend to give vigor and freedom and expansion of the intellect, are prohibited. Gentlemen would be astonished by the long list of distinguished authors whom she proscribes, to be found in Depon's and other works. A main feature in her policy is that which constantly elevates the European and depresses the American character. Out of upward of seven hundred and fifty viceroys and captains-general, whom she has appointed since the conquest of America, about eighteen only have been from the body of her American population. On all occasions, she seeks to raise and promote her European subjects, and to degrade and humiliate the Creoles. Wherever in America her sway extends, everything seems to pine and wither beneath its baneful influence. The richest regions of the earth, man, his happiness and his education, all the fine faculties of his soul, are regulated and modified and molded to suit the execrable purposes of an inexorable despotism.

Such is the brief and imperfect picture of the state of things in Spanish America in 1808, when the famous transactions of Bayonne occurred. The king of Spain and the Indies (for Spanish America has always constituted an integral part of the Spanish Empire) abdicated his throne and became a voluntary captive. Even at this day one does not know whether he should most condemn the baseness and perfidy of the one party, or despise the meanness and imbecility of the other. If the obligation of obedience and allegiance existed on the part of the Colonies to the king of Spain, it was founded on the duty of protection which he owed them. By disqualifying himself for the performance of this duty, they became released from that obligation. The monarchy was dissolved, and each integral part had a right to seek its own happiness by the institution of any new government adapted to its wants. Joseph Bonaparte, the successor *de facto* of Ferdinand, recognized this right on the part of the Colonies, and recommended them to establish their independence.

Thus upon the ground of strict right, upon the footing of a mere legal question, governed by forensic rules, the Colonies, being absolved by the acts of the parent country from the duty of subjection to it, had an indisputable right to set up for themselves. But I take a broader and a bolder position. I maintain that an oppressed people are authorized, whenever they can, to rise and break their fetters. This was the great principle of the English Revolution. It was the great principle of our own. Vattel, if authority were wanting, expressly supports this right. We must pass sentence of condemnation upon the founders of our liberty, say that you were rebels, traitors, and that we are at this moment legislating without competent powers, before we can condemn the cause of Spanish America. Our Revolution was mainly directed against the mere theory of tyranny. We had suffered but comparatively little; we had, in some respects, been kindly treated; but our intrepid and intelligent fathers saw, in the usurpation of the power to levy an inconsiderable tax, the long train of oppressive acts that were to follow. They rose; they breasted the storm; they achieved our freedom. Spanish America for centuries has been doomed to the practical effects of an odious tyranny. If we were justified, she is more than justified.

In the establishment of the independence of Spanish America, the United States have the deepest interest. I have no hesitation in asserting my firm belief that there is no question in the foreign policy of this country, which has ever arisen, or which I can conceive as ever occurring, in the decision of which we have had or can have so much at stake. This interest concerns our politics, our commerce, our navigation. There cannot be a doubt that Spanish America, once independent, whatever may be the form of government established in its several parts, these governments will be animated by an American feeling, and guided by an American policy. They will obey the laws of the system of the new world, of which they will compose a part, in contradistinction to that of Europe. Without the influence of that vortex in Europe, the balance of power between its several parts, the preservation of which has often drenched Europe in blood, America is sufficiently remote to contemplate the new wars which are to afflict that quarter of the globe, as a calm if not a cold and indifferent spectator. In relation to those wars, the several parts of America will generally stand neutral. And as, during the period when they rage, it will be important that a liberal system of neutrality should be adopted and observed, all America will be interested in maintaining and enforcing such a system. The independence of Spanish America, then, is an interest of primary consideration.

But it is sometimes said that they are too ignorant and too superstitious to admit of the existence of free government. This charge of ignorance is often urged by persons themselves actually ignorant of the real condition of that people. I deny the alleged fact of ignorance; I deny the inference from that fact, if it were true, that they want capacity for free government. And I refuse assent to the further conclusion if the fact were true, and the inference just, that we are to be indifferent to their fate. All the writers of the most established authority, Depons, Humboldt, and others, concur in assigning to the people of Spanish America great quickness, genius, and particular aptitude for the acquisition of the exact sciences, and others which they have been allowed to cultivate. In astronomy, geology, mineralogy, chemistry, botany, and so forth, they are allowed to make distinguished proficiency. They justly boast of their Abzate, Velasques, and Gama, and other illustrious contributors to science. They have nine universities, and in the City of Mexico, it is affirmed by Humboldt, there are more solid scientific establishments than in any city even of North America. I would refer to the message of the supreme director of La Plata, which I shall hereafter have occasion to use for another purpose, as a model of fine composition of a State paper, challenging a comparison with any, the most celebrated, that ever issued from the pens of Jefferson or Madison.

It is the doctrine of thrones that man is too ignorant to govern himself. Their partizans assert his incapacity, in reference to all nations; it they can not command universal assent to the proposition, it is then demanded to particular nations; and our pride and our presumption too often make converts of us. I contend, that it is to arraign the disposition of Providence Himself, to suppose that He has created beings incapable of governing themselves, and to be trampled on by kings. Self-government is the natural government of man, and for proof I refer to the aborigines of our own land. Were I to speculate in hypotheses unfavorable to human liberty, my speculations should be founded rather upon the vices, refinements, or density of population. Crowded together in compact masses, even if they were philosophers, the contagion of the passions is communicated and caught, and the effect too often, I admit, is the overthrow of liberty. Dispersed over such an immense space as that on which the people of Spanish America are spread, their physical, and I believe, also, their moral condition, both favor their liberty.

With regard to their superstition, they worship the same God with us. Their prayers are offered up in their temples to the same Redeemer whose intercession we expect to save us. Nor is there anything in the Catholic religion unfavorable to freedom. All religions united with government are more or less inimical to liberty. All, separated from government, are compatible with liberty. If the people of Spanish America have not already gone as far in religious toleration as we have, the difference in their condition from ours should not be forgotten. Everything is progressive; and, in time, I hope to see them imitating in this respect our example. But grant that the people of Spanish America are ignorant and incompetent for free government, to whom is that ignorance to be ascribed? Is it not to the execrable system of Spain, which she seeks again to establish and to perpetuate? So far from chilling our hearts, it ought to increase our solicitude for unfortunate brethren. It ought to animate us to desire the redemption of the minds and bodies of unborn millions from the brutifying effects of a system whose tendency is to stifle the faculties of the soul and to degrade man to the level of beasts. I would invoke the spirits of our departed fathers. Was it for yourselves only that you nobly fought? No, no! It was the chains that were forging for your posterity that made you fly to arms, and, scattering the elements of these chains to the winds, you transmitted to us the rich inheritance of liberty.

ON THE CLAY COMPROMISE MEASURES [6]

John C. Calhoun
(1782-1850)

The Great Nullifier, John C. Calhoun, the virulent South Carolinian who advocated states rights, ranks with Clay and Webster as one of the three leading orators of America's Golden Age. This Great Triumvirate ruled the American rostrum for a period of nearly forty years. Of this group Calhoun excelled in parliamentary debate. He had studied law at Yale and Charleston and in 1807 was admitted to the bar. After serving a period in the South Carolinian legislature, Calhoun appeared in Congress in 1811, where he at once displayed his superior eloquence in debates connected with the War of 1812. During 1817-1824, Calhoun served as Secretary of War, and in 1824 and 1828 was elected Vice-President of the United States. During his years in Congress Calhoun became the most bitter adversary of Daniel Webster on the question of the Union and States Rights and in connection with the slavery question. Calhoun never gained the popularity of Clay and Webster, but he did gain a reputation as an able orator, a logical and forceful debater, and a genuinely profound political philosopher. The eloquence of Calhoun is defined by his contemporary, Daniel Webster, as part of his intellectual character—plain, strong, terse, condensed, concise; sometimes impassioned, but always severe.

Among Calhoun's most famous speeches are: *On the Militia Bill*, delivered in 1811 relative to the War of 1812; *On the Tariff of 1816*; *On States Rights*, delivered in 1833; *The Force Bill* in 1833; *On the Oregon Question* in 1846; and his last great speech *On the Slavery Question* in 1850.

[6] Abridged.

Included here is his last speech read before the Senate March 4, 1850, which is probably his most significant speech. Calhoun, then aged and ill, was unable to deliver the speech himself but in a hushed gallery "as if for a funeral ceremony" he sat and listened as it was read by another. A few weeks later Calhoun died.

I have, Senators, believed from the first that the agitation of the subject of slavery would, if not prevented by some timely and effective measure, end in disunion. Entertaining this opinion, I have, on all proper occasions, endeavored to call the attention of both the two great parties which divide the country to adopt some measure to prevent so great a disaster, but without success. The agitation has been permitted to proceed with almost no attempt to resist it, until it has reached a point when it can no longer be disguised or denied that the Union is in danger. You have thus had forced upon you the greatest and gravest question that can ever come under your consideration: How can the Union be preserved?

To give a satisfactory answer to this mighty question, it is indispensable to have an accurate and thorough knowledge of the nature and the character of the cause by which the Union is endangered. Without such knowledge it is impossible to pronounce with any certainty, by what measure it can be saved; just as it would be impossible for a physician to pronounce in the case of some dangerous disease, with any certainty, by what remedy the patient could be saved, without similar knowledge of the nature and character of the cause which produces it. The first question, then, presented for consideration in the investigation I propose to make in order to obtain such knowledge is: What is it that has endangered the Union?

To this question there can be but one answer,—that the immediate cause is the almost universal discontent which pervades all the States composing the Southern section of the Union. This widely extended discontent is not of recent origin. It commenced with the agitation of the slavery question and has been increasing ever since. The next question, going one step further back, is: What has caused this widely diffused and almost universal discontent?

It is a great mistake to suppose, as is by some, that it originated with demagogues who excited the discontent with the intention of aiding their personal advancement, or with the disappointed ambition of certain politicians who resorted to it as the means of retrieving their fortunes. On the contrary, all the great political influences of the section were arrayed against excitement, and exerted to the utmost to keep the people quiet. The great mass of the people of the South were divided, as in the other section, into Whigs and Democrats. The leaders and the presses of both parties in the South were very solicitous to prevent excitement and to preserve quiet; because it was seen that the effects of the former would necessarily tend to weaken, if not destroy, the political ties which united them with their respective parties in the other section.

Those who know the strength of party ties will readily appreciate the immense force which this cause exerted against agitation and in favor of preserving quiet. But, great as it was, it was not sufficient to prevent the widespread discontent which now pervades the section.

No; some cause far deeper and more powerful than the one supposed must exist, to account for discontent so wide and deep. The question then recurs: What is the cause of this discontent? It will be found in the belief of the people of the Southern States, as prevalent as the discontent itself, that they cannot remain, as things now are, consistently with honor and safety, in the Union. The next question to be considered is: What has caused this belief?

One of the causes is, undoubtedly, to be traced to the long-continued agitation of the slave question on the part of the North, and the many aggressions which they have made on the rights of the South during the time. I will not enumerate them at present, as it will be done hereafter in its proper place.

There is another lying back of it—with which this is intimately connected—that may be regarded as the great and primary cause. This is to be found in the fact that the equilibrium between the two sections in the government as it stood when the Constitution was ratified and the government put in action has been destroyed. At that time there was nearly a perfect equilibrium between the two, which afforded ample means to each to protect itself against the aggression of the other; but, as it now stands, one section has the exclusive power of controlling the government, which leaves the other without any adequate means of protecting itself against its encroachment and oppression.

The result of the whole is to give the Northern section a predominance in every department of the government, and thereby concentrate in it the two elements which constitute the federal government: a majority of States, and a majority of their population, estimated in federal numbers. Whatever section concentrates the two in itself possesses the control of the entire government.

But we are just at the close of the sixth decade and the commencement of the seventh. The census is to be taken this year, which must add greatly to the decided preponderance of the North in the House of Representatives and in the Electoral College. The prospect is, also, that a great increase will be added to its present preponderance in the Senate, during the period of the decade, by the addition of new States. Two Territories, Oregon and Minnesota, are already in progress, and strenuous efforts are making to bring in three additional States from the Territory recently conquered from Mexico; which, if successful, will add three other States in a short time to the Northern section, making five States, and increasing the present number of its States from fifteen to twenty, and of its senators from thirty to forty.

On the contrary, there is not a single Territory in progress in the Southern section, and no certainty that any additional State will be added to it during the decade. The prospect then is, that the two sections in the Senate, should the efforts now made to exclude the South from the newly acquired Territories succeed, will stand, before the end of the decade, twenty Northern States to fourteen Southern (considering Delaware as neutral), and forty Northern senators to twenty-eight Southern. This great increase of senators, added to the great increase of members of the House of Representatives and the Electoral College on the part of the North, which must take place under the next decade, will effectually and irretrievably destroy the equilibrium which existed when the government commenced.

Had this destruction been the operation of time without the interference of government, the South would have had no reason to complain; but such was not the fact. It was caused by the legislation of this government, which was appointed as the common agent of all and charged with the protection of the interests and security of all.

The legislation by which it has been effected may be classed under three heads: The first is that series of acts by which the South has been excluded from the common territory belonging to all the States as members of the federal Union—which have had the effect of extending vastly the portion allotted to the Northern section, and restricting within narrow limits the portion left the South. The next consists in adopting a system of revenue and disbursements by which an undue proportion of the burden of taxation has been imposed upon the South, and an undue proportion of its proceeds appropriated to the North. And the last is a system of political measures by which the original character of the government has been radically changed. I propose to bestow upon each of these, in the order they stand, a few remarks, with the view of showing that it is owing to the action of this government that the equilibrium between the two sections has been destroyed, and the whole powers of the system centered in a sectional majority.

I have not included the territory recently acquired by the treaty with Mexico. The North is making the most strenuous efforts to appropriate the whole to herself, by excluding the South from every foot of it. If she should succeed, it will add to that from which the South has already been excluded 526,078 square miles, and would increase the whole which the North has appropriated to herself to 1,764,023, not including the portion that she may succeed in excluding us from in Texas. To sum up the whole, the United States, since they declared their independence, have acquired 2,373,046 square miles of territory, from which the North will have excluded the South, if she should succeed in monopolizing the newly-acquired Territories, about three-fourths of the whole, leaving to the South but about one-fourth. Such is the first and great cause that has destroyed the equilibrium between the two sections in the government.

The next is the system of revenue and disbursements which has been adopted by the government. It is well known that the government has derived its revenue mainly from duties on imports. I shall not undertake to show that such duties must necessarily fall mainly on the exporting portion of the states, and that the South, as the great exporting portion of the Union, has in reality paid vastly more than her due proportion of the revenue; because I deem it unnecessary, as the subject has on so many occasions been fully discussed. Nor shall I, for the same reason, undertake to show that a far greater portion of the revenue has been disbursed in the North, than its due share; and that the joint effect of these causes has been to transfer a vast amount from South to North, which, under an equal system of revenue and disbursements, would not have been lost to her. If to this be added that many of the duties were imposed, not for revenue but for protection—that is, intended to put money, not in the Treasury, but directly into the pocket of the manufacturers—some conception may be formed of the immense amount which in the long course of sixty years has been transferred from South to North. There are no data by which it can be estimated with any certainty; but it is safe to say that it amounts to hundreds of millions of dollars. Under the most moderate estimate it would be sufficient to add greatly to the wealth of the North, and thus greatly increase her population by attracting immigration from all quarters to that section.

This, combined with the great primary cause, amply explains why the North has acquired a preponderance in every department of the government by its disproportionate increase of population and States. The former, as has been shown, has increased, in fifty years, 2,400,000 over that of the South. This increase of population during so long a period is satisfactorily accounted for by the number of immigrants, and the increase of their descendants, which have been attracted to the Northern section from Europe and the South, in consequence of the advantages derived from the causes assigned. If they had not existed— if the South had retained all the capital which has been extracted from her by the fiscal action of the government; and if it had not been excluded by the Ordinance of 1787 and the Missouri Compromise, from the region lying between the Ohio and the Mississippi Rivers, and between the Mississippi and the Rocky Mountains north of 36° 30′—it scarcely admits of a doubt that it would have divided the immigration with the North, and by retaining her own people would have at least equaled the North in population under the census of 1840, and probably under that about to be taken. She would also, if she had retained her equal rights in those territories, have maintained an equality in the number of States with the North, and have preserved the equilibrium between the two sections that existed at the commencement of the government. The loss, then, of the equilibrium is to be attributed to the action of this government.

There is a question of vital importance to the Southern section, in reference to which the views and feelings of the two sections are as opposite and hostile as they can possibly be. I refer to the relation between the two races in the Southern section, which constitutes a vital portion of her social organization. Every portion of the North entertains views and feelings more or less hostile to it. Those most opposed and hostile regard it as a sin, and consider themselves under the most sacred obligation to use every effort to destroy it.

Indeed, to the extent that they conceive that they have power, they regard themselves as implicated in the sin, and responsible for not suppressing it by the use of all and every means. Those less opposed and hostile regard it as a crime—an offense against humanity, as they call it and, although not so fanatical, feel themselves bound to use all efforts to effect the same object; while those who are least opposed and hostile regard it as a blot and a stain on the character of what they call the "nation," and feel themselves accordingly bound to give it no countenance or support. On the contrary, the Southern section regards the relation as one which can not be destroyed without subjecting the two races to the greatest calamity, and the section to poverty, desolation, and wretchedness; and accordingly they feel bound by every consideration of interest and safety to defend it.

Unless something decisive is done, I again ask, What is to stop this agitation before the great and final object at which it aims—the abolition of slavery in the States—is consummated? Is it, then, not certain that if something is not done to arrest it, the South will be forced to choose between abolition and secession? Indeed, as events are now moving, it will not require the South to secede in order to dissolve the Union. Agitation will of itself effect it, of which its past history furnishes abundant proof—as I shall next proceed to show.

It is a great mistake to suppose that disunion can be effected by a single blow. The cords which bind these States together in one common Union are far too numerous and powerful for that. Disunion must be the work of time. It is only through a long process, and successively, that the cords can be snapped until the whole fabric falls asunder. Already the agitation of the slavery question has snapped some of the most important, and has greatly weakened all the others.

If the agitation goes on, the same force, acting with increased intensity, as has been shown, will finally snap every cord, when nothing will be left to hold the States together except force. But surely that can with no propriety of language be called a Union when the only means by which the weaker is held connected with the stronger portion is force. It may, indeed, keep them connected; but the connection will partake much more of the character of subjugation on the part of the weaker to the stronger than the union of free, independent, and sovereign

States in one confederation, as they stood in the early stages of the government, and which only is worthy of the sacred name of Union.

Having now, Senators, explained what it is that endangers the Union, and traced it to its cause, and explained its nature and character, the question again recurs, How can the Union be saved? To this I answer, there is but one way by which it can be, and that is by adopting such measures as will satisfy the States belonging to the Southern section that they can remain in the Union consistently with their honor and their safety. There is, again, only one way by which this can be effected, and that is by removing the causes by which this belief has been produced. Do this, and discontent will cease, harmony and kind feelings between the sections be restored, and every apprehension of danger to the Union removed. The question, then, is, How can this be done? There is but one way by which it can with any certainty; and that is by a full and final settlement, on the principle of justice of all the questions at issue between the two sections. The South asks for justice, simple justice, and less she ought not to take. She has no compromise to offer but the Constitution, and no concession or surrender to make. She has already surrendered so much that she has little left to surrender. Such a settlement would go to the root of the evil, and remove all cause of discontent, by satisfying the South that she could remain honorably and safely in the Union, and thereby restore the harmony and fraternal feelings between the sections which existed anterior to the Missouri agitation. Nothing else can, with any certainty, finally and forever settle the question at issue, terminate agitation, and save the Union.

But can this be done? Yes, easily; not by the weaker party, for it can of itself do nothing—not even protect itself—but by the stronger. The North has only to will it to accomplish it—to do justice by conceding to the South an equal right in the acquired territory, and to do her duty by causing stipulations relative to fugitive slaves to be faithfully fulfilled—to cease the agitation of the slave question, and to provide for the insertion of a provision in the Constitution, by an amendment, which will restore to the South, in substance, the power she possessed of protecting herself before the equilibrium between the sections was destroyed by the action of this government. There will be no difficulty in devising such a provision—one that will protect the South, and which at the same time will improve and strengthen the government instead of impairing and weakening it.

But will the North agree to this? It is for her to answer the question. But, I will say, she can not refuse if she has half the love of the Union which she professes to have, or without justly exposing herself to the charge that her love of power and aggrandizement is far greater than her love of the Union. At all events, the responsibility of saving the Union rests on the North, and not on the South. The South can not save it by any act of hers, and the North may save it without any sacrifice whatever, unless to do justice and to perform her duties under the Constitution should be regarded by her as a sacrifice.

It is time, Senators, that there should be an open and manly avowal on all sides as to what is intended to be done. If the question is not now settled, it is uncertain whether it ever can hereafter be; and we, as the representatives of the States of this Union regarded as governments, should come to a distinct understanding as to our respective views, in order to ascertain whether the great questions at issue can be settled or not. If you who represent the stronger portion, can not agree to settle them on the broad principle of justice and duty, say so; and let the States we both represent agree to separate and part in peace.

If you are unwilling we should part in peace, tell us so; and we shall know what to do when you reduce the question to submission or resistance. If you remain silent, you will compel us to infer by your acts what you intend. In that case California will become the test question. If you admit her under all the difficulties that oppose her admission, you compel us to infer that you intend to exclude us from the whole of the acquired Territories, with the intention of destroying irretrievably the equilibrium between the two sections. We should be blind not to perceive in that case that your real objects are power and aggrandizement, and infatuated, not to act accordingly.

I have now, Senators, done my duty in expressing my opinions fully, freely, and candidly on this solemn occasion. In doing so I have been governed by the motives which have governed me in all the stages of the agitation of the slavery question since its commencement. I have exerted myself during the whole period to arrest it, with the intention of saving the Union if it could be done; and if it could not, to save the section where it has pleased providence to cast my lot, and which I sincerely believe has justice and the Constitution on its side. Having faithfully done my duty to the best of my ability, both to the Union and my section, throughout this agitation, I shall have the consolation, let what will come, that I am free from all responsibility.

THE BUNKER HILL MONUMENT ORATION

Daniel Webster

(1782-1852)

Daniel Webster, America's consummate orator, statesman, and lawyer, was the bulwark of the Union in the perilous days preceding the Civil War. Born in New Hampshire of Scotch parentage, Webster tutored to pay his way through Dartmouth College. Upon graduation he entered the profession of law and had obtained a reputation in Boston for his legal powers by the time he entered Congress in 1813.

In Congress he at once made two notable speeches before the House which established his reputation. He strengthened his oratorical position in 1818 by a speech before the Supreme Court on the celebrated Dartmouth College case and in 1820 by his *Plymouth Rock Address,* delivered on the 200th anniversary of the landing of the Pilgrims. Again in 1825 at the laying of the cornerstone of the Bunker Hill monument on the 50th anniversary of the battle he confirmed his standing as America's foremost orator. On this occasion General Lafayette was present and Webster spoke to one of the greatest multitudes ever assembled to hear an orator. His speech was both forceful and pathetic as suited the occasion. In the following year on the 50th anniversary of the signing of the Declaration of Independence Webster delivered in Faneuil Hall his great commemorative address on Adams and Jefferson, a high-water mark in his oratorical career. It was Webster, also, who was selected to deliver the address at the laying of the corner-stone of the United States capitol. When Webster again appeared in Congress in 1824, he delivered an eloquent speech on *The Greek*

Revolution, which was translated into several European languages and was circulated throughout South America.

It was Webster's career in the Senate, however, which marked his greatest achievements in oratory. Here in 1830 he delivered his *Reply to Hayne,* the most eloquent parliamentary address of his era including a statement of the constitutional sanctions of the Union as opposed to nullification and the doctrine of states rights. In this same year Webster appeared in the White murder case and distinguished himself as the leading criminal lawyer of his day. Again three years later he met Calhoun in a verbal combat on the Constitution in a speech of remarkable statesmanship and logic. Finally, when confronted with a choice between slavery or a dissolution of the Union, Webster chose the former evil and delivered what became his greatest address before the Senate on March 7, 1850, on *The Clay Compromise Measure.* Webster's support of these measures, although they postponed for a decade the bloodshed of the Civil War, caused Webster the loss of the presidency as well as his personal contemporary popularity.

Webster's style may seem florid to a modern audience and his earlier oratory somewhat bombastic, but he still remains a king of the American rostrum. Throughout all his oratory runs the absorbing theme of the perpetuation of the Constitution and the preservation of the Union. "He was a grand figure— a parliamentary Hercules", as Carlyle designated him, "in appearance, in voice, in gesture, and in personality. He ranks with the great orators of all ages—Demosthenes, Cicero, Chrysostom, Bossuet, Chatham, and Burke."

Included here are portions of Webster's first *Bunker Hill Monument Oration* and the great *Reply to Hayne.* Of the latter speech Webster had no written copy, but he is reported to have said that his whole life-time had been a preparation for this reply to Hayne.

This uncounted multitude before me and around me proves the feeling which the occasion has excited. These thousands of human faces, glowing with sympathy and joy, and from the impulses of a common gratitude turned reverently to heaven in this spacious temple of the firmament, proclaim that the day, the place, and the purpose of our assembling have made a deep impression on our hearts.

. . . .

We still have among us some of those who were active agents in the scenes of 1775, and who are now here, from every quarter of New England, to visit once more, and under circumstances so affecting—I had almost said so overwhelming—this renowned theater of their courage and patriotism.

VENERABLE MEN! you have come down to us from a former generation. Heaven has bounteously lengthened out your lives, that you might behold this joyous day. You are now where you stood fifty years ago, this very hour, with your brothers and your neighbors, shoulder to shoulder, in the strife for your country. Behold, how altered! The same heavens are indeed over your heads; the same ocean rolls at your feet; but all else, how changed! You hear now no roar of hostile cannon; you see no mixed volumes of smoke and flame rising from burning Charlestown. The ground strewed with the dead and the dying; the impetuous charge; the steady and successful repulse; the loud call to repeated assault; the summoning of all that is manly to repeated resistance; a thousand bosoms freely and fearlessly bared in an instant to whatever of terror there may be in war and death—all these you have witnessed, but you witness them no more.

All is peace. The heights of yonder metropolis, its towers and roofs, which you then saw filled with wives and children and countrymen in distress and terror, and looking with unutterable emotions for the issue of the combat, have presented you to-day with the sight of its whole, happy population, come out to welcome and greet you with a universal jubilee. Yonder proud ships, by a felicity of position appropriately lying at the foot of this mount, and seeming fondly to cling around it, are not means of annoyance to you, but your country's own means of distinction and defense. All is peace; and God has granted you this sight of your country's happiness, ere you slumber in the grave. He has allowed you to behold and to partake the reward of your patriotic toils; and he has allowed us, your sons and countrymen, to meet you here, and in the name of the present generation, in the name of your country, in the name of liberty, to thank you!

. . . .

VETERANS! you are the remnant of many a well-fought field. You bring with you marks of honor from Trenton and Monmouth, from Yorktown, Camden, Bennington, and Saratoga. VETERANS OF HALF A CENTURY! when in your youthful days you put everything at hazard in your country's cause, good as that cause was, and sanguine as youth is, still your fondest hopes did not stretch onward to an hour like this! At a period to which you could not reasonably have expected to arrive, at a moment of national prosperity such as you could never have foreseen, you are now met here to enjoy the fellowship of old soldiers, and to receive the overflowings of a universal gratitude.

But your agitated countenances and your heaving breasts inform me that even this is not an unmixed joy. I perceive that a tumult of contending feelings rushes upon you. The images of the dead, as well as the persons of the living, present themselves before you. The scene overwhelms you, and I turn from it. May the Father of all mercies smile upon your declining years and bless them! And when you shall here have exchanged your embraces, when you shall once more have pressed the hands which have been so often extended to give succor in adversity, or grasped in the exultation of victory, ther. look abroad upon this lovely land which your young valor defended, and mark the happiness with which it is filled; yea, look abroad upon the whole earth, and see what a name you have contributed to give to your country, and what a praise you have added to freedom, and then rejoice in the sympathy and gratitude which beam upon your last days from the improved condition of mankind!

Information of these events, circulating throughout the world, at length reached the ears of one [7] who now hears me. He has not forgotten the emotion which the fame of Bunker Hill, and the name of Warren, excited in his youthful breast.

Sir, we are assembled to commemorate the establishment of great public principles of liberty and to do honor to the distinguished dead. The occasion is too severe for eulogy of the living. But, sir, your interested relation to this country, the peculiar circumstances which surround you and surround us, call on me to express the happiness which we derive from your presence and aid in this solemn commemoration.

Fortunate, fortunate man! with what measure of devotion will you not thank God for the circumstances of your extraordinary life! You are connected with both hemispheres and with two generations. Heaven saw fit to ordain that the electric spark of liberty should be conducted, through you, from the New World to the Old· and we, who are now here to perform this duty of patriotism, have all of us long ago received it in charge from our fathers to cherish your name and your virtues. You will account it an instance of your good fortune, sir, that you crossed the seas to visit us at a time which enables you to be present at this solemnity. You now behold the field, the renown of which reached you in the heart of France, and caused a thrill in your ardent bosom. You see the lines of the little reboubt thrown up by the incredible diligence of Prescott; defended, to the last extremity, by his lion-hearted valor, and within which the corner-stone of our monument has now taken its position. You see where Warren fell, and where Parker, Gardner, McClary, Moore, and other early patriots fell with him. Those who survived that day, and whose lives have been prolonged to the present hour, are now around you. Some of them you have known in

[7] Lafayette who had come from France for the occasion

the trying scenes of the war. Behold! they now stretch forth their feeble arms to embrace you. Behold! they raise their trembling voices to invoke the blessing of God on you and yours forever.

.   .   .   .

And now, let us indulge an honest exultation in the conviction of the benefit which the example of our country has produced, and is likely to produce, on human freedom and human happiness. Let us endeavor to comprehend in all its magnitude, and to feel in all its importance, the part assigned to us in the great drama of human affairs. We are placed at the head of the system of representative and popular governments. Thus far our example shows that such governments are compatible, not only with respectability and power, but with repose, with peace, with security of personal rights, with good laws, and a just administration.

We are not propagandists. Wherever other systems are preferred, either as being thought better in themselves, or as better suited to existing conditions, we leave the preference to be enjoyed. Our history hitherto proves, however, that the popular form is practicable, and that with wisdom and knowledge men may govern themselves; and the duty incumbent on us is to preserve the consistency of this cheering example, and take care that nothing may weaken its authority with the world. If, in our case, the representative system ultimately fail, popular governments must be pronounced impossible. No combination of circumstances more favorable to the experiment can ever be expected to occur. The last hopes of mankind, therefore, rest with us; and if it should be proclaimed that our example had become an argument against the experiment, the knell of popular liberty would be sounded throughout the earth.

These are excitements to duty; but they are not suggestions of doubt. Our history and our condition, all that is gone before us, and all that surrounds us, authorize the belief, that popular governments, though subject to occasional variations, in form perhaps not always for the better, may yet, in their general character, be as durable and permanent as other systems. We know, indeed, that in our country any other is impossible. The principle of free government adheres to the American soil. It is bedded in it, immovable as its mountains.

And let the sacred obligations which have devolved on this generation, and on us, sink deep into our hearts. Those who established our liberty and our government are daily dropping from among us. The great trust now descends to new hands. Let us apply ourselves to that which is presented to us, as our appropriate object. We can win no laurels in a war for independence. Earlier and worthier hands have gathered them all. Nor are there places for us by the side of Solon, and Alfred, and other founders of states. Our fathers have filled them. But there remains to us a great duty of defense and preservation; and there is opened to us, also, a noble pursuit, to which the spirit of the times strongly invites us. Our proper business is improvement. Let our age be the age of improvement. In a day of peace, let us advance the arts of peace and the works of peace. Let us develop the resources of our land, call forth its powers, build up its institutions, promote all its great interests, and see whether we also, in our day and generation, may not perform something worthy to be remembered. Let us cultivate a true spirit of union and harmony. In pursuing the great objects which our condition points out to us, let us act under a settled conviction, and an habitual feeling, that these twenty-four states are one country. Let our conceptions be enlarged to the circle of our duties. Let us extend our ideas over the whole of the vast field in which we are called to act. Let our object be, OUR COUNTRY, OUR WHOLE COUNTRY, AND NOTHING BUT OUR COUNTRY. And, by the blessing of God, may that country itself become a vast and splendid monument, not of oppression and terror, but of wisdom, of peace, and of liberty, upon which the world may gaze with admiration forever!

REPLY TO HAYNE [8]

Daniel Webster

(1782-1852)

The eulogium pronounced on the character of the State of South Carolina, by the honorable gentleman, for her revolutionary and other merits, meets my hearty concurrence. I shall not acknowledge that the honorable member goes before me in regard for whatever of distinguished talent, or distinguished character, South Carolina has produced. I claim part of the honor, I partake in the pride, of her great names. I claim them for countrymen, one and all: the Laurenses, the Rutledges, the Pinckneys, the Sumpters, the Marions—Americans all—whose fame is no more to be hemmed in by State lines than their talents and patriotism were capable of being circumscribed within the same narrow limits. In their day and generation they served and honored the country, and the whole country, and their renown is of the treasures of the whole country. Him, whose honored name the gentleman himself bears—does he esteem me less capable of gratitude for his patriotism, or sympathy for his sufferings, than if his eyes had first opened upon the light of Massachusetts instead of South Carolina? Sir, does he suppose it in his power to exhibit a Carolina name so bright as to produce envy in my bosom? No, sir, increased gratification and delight, rather. I thank God, that, if I am gifted with little of the spirit which is able to raise mortals to the skies, I have yet none, as I trust, of that other spirit which would drag angels down. When I shall be found, sir, in my place here in the Senate, or elsewhere, to sneer at public merit, because it happens to spring up beyond the little limits of my own State or neighborhood; when I refuse, for any such cause, or for any cause, the homage due to American talent, to elevated patriotism, to sincere devotion to liberty and the country; or, if I see an uncommon endowment of Heaven, if I see extraordinary capacity and virtue in any son of the South, and if, moved by local prejudice, or gangrened by State jealousy, I get up here to abate a tithe of a hair from his just character and just fame, may my tongue cleave to the roof of my mouth!

Sir, let me recur to pleasing recollections—let me indulge in refreshing remembrances of the past—let me remind you that in early times no States cherished greater harmony, both of principle and feeling, than Massachusetts and South Carolina. Would to God that harmony might again return! Shoulder to shoulder they went through the Revolution; hand in hand they stood round the administration of Washington, and

[8] Abridged.

felt his own great arm lean on them for support. Unkind feeling, if it exist, alienation and distrust, are the growth, unnatural to such soils, of false principles since sown. They are weeds, the seeds of which that same great arm never scattered.

Mr. President, I shall enter on no encomium upon Massachusetts— she needs none. There she is—behold her, and judge for yourselves. There is her history; the world knows it by heart. The past, at least, is secure. There is Boston, and Concord, and Lexington, and Bunker Hill—and there they will remain forever. The bones of her sons, falling in the great struggle for Independence, now lie mingled with the soil of every State from New England to Georgia; and there they will lie forever. And, sir, where American Liberty raised its first voice, and where its youth was nurtured and sustained, there it still lives, in the strength of its manhood and full of its original spirit. If discord and disunion shall wound it, if party strife and blind ambition shall hawk at and tear it, if folly and madness—if uneasiness, under salutary and necessary restraint—shall succeed to separate it from that Union, by which alone its existence is made sure; it will stand, in the end, by the side of that cradle in which its infancy was rocked; it will stretch forth its arm, with whatever of vigor it may still retain, over the friends who gather round it; and it will fall at last, if fall it must, amidst the proudest monuments of its own glory, and on the very spot of its origin.

. . . .

Let it be remembered that the Constitution of the United States is not unalterable. It is to continue in its present form no longer than the people who established it shall choose to continue it. If they shall become convinced that they have made an injudicious or inexpedient partition and distribution of power between the State governments and the general government, they can alter that distribution at will.

If anything be found in the national Constitution, either by original provision, or by subsequent interpretation, which ought not to be in it, the people know how to get rid of it. If any construction be established, unacceptable to them, so as to become, practically, a part of the Constitution, they will amend it, at their own sovereign pleasure; but while the people choose to maintain it, as it is; while they are satisfied with it, and refuse to change it; who has given, or who can give, to the State legislatures a right to alter it, either by interference, construction, or otherwise? Gentlemen do not seem to recollect that the people have any power to do anything for themselves; they imagine there is no safety for them any longer than they are under the close guardianship of the State legislatures. Sir, the people have not trusted their safety, in regard to the general Constitution, to these hands. They have required other security, and taken other bonds. They have chosen to trust themselves; first, to the plain words of the instrument, and to such construction as the government itself, in doubtful cases, should put on its own powers, under their oaths of office, and subject to their responsibility to them—just as the people of a State trust their own State governments with a similar power. Secondly, they have reposed their trust in the efficacy of frequent elections, and in their own power to remove their own servants and agents, whenever they see cause. Thirdly, they have reposed trust in the judicial power; which, in order that it might be trustworthy, they have made as respectable, as disinterested, and as independent as was practicable. Fourthly, they have seen fit to rely, in case of necessity, or high expediency, on their known and admitted power to alter or amend the Constitution, peaceably and quietly, whenever experience shall point out defects or imperfections. And, finally, the people of the United States have, at no time, in no way, directly or indirectly, authorized any State legislature to construe or interpret their high instrument of government; much less to interfere, by their own power, to arrest its course and operation.

If, sir, the people, in these respects, had done otherwise than they have done, their Constitution could neither have been preserved, nor would it have been worth preserving. And, if its plain provisions shall now be disregarded, and these new doctrines interpolated in it, it will become as feeble and helpless a being as its enemies, whether early or more recent, could possibly desire. It will exist in every State but as a poor dependent on State permission. It must borrow leave to be; and will be no longer than State pleasure, or State discretion, sees fit to grant the indulgence, and to prolong its poor existence.

But, sir, although there are fears, there are hopes also. The people have preserved this, their own chosen Constitution, for forty years, and have seen their happiness, prosperity, and renown grow with its growth, and strengthen with its strength. They are now, generally, strongly attached to it. Overthrown by direct assault, it cannot be; evaded, undermined, nullified it will not be, if we, and those who shall succeed us here, as agents and representatives of the people, shall conscientiously and vigilantly discharge the two great branches of our public trust—faithfully to preserve, and wisely to administer it.

Mr. President, I have thus stated the reasons of my dissent to the doctrines which have been advanced and maintained. I am conscious of having detained you and the Senate much too long. I was drawn into the debate, with no previous deliberation such as is suited to the discussion of so grave and important a subject. But it is a subject of which my heart is full, and I have not been willing to suppress the utterance of its spontaneous sentiments. I cannot, even now, persuade myself to relinquish it, without expressing, once more, my deep conviction that, since it respects nothing less than the Union of the States, it is of most vital and essential importance to the public happiness.

I profess, sir, in my career, hitherto, to have kept steadily in view the prosperity and honor of the whole country and the preservation of our Federal Union. It is to that Union we owe our safety at home and our consideration and dignity abroad. It is to that Union that we are chiefly indebted for whatever makes us most proud of our country. That Union we reached only by the discipline of our virtues in the severe school of adversity. It had its origin in the necessities of disordered finance, prostrate commerce and ruined credit. Under its benign influences these great interests immediately awoke as from the dead and sprang forth with newness of life. Every year of its duration has teemed with fresh proofs of its utility and its blessings; and although our territory has stretched out wider and wider, and our population spread farther and farther, they have not outrun its protection or its benefits. It has been to us all a copious fountain of national, social and personal happiness.

I have not allowed myself, sir, to look beyond the Union to see what might be hidden in the dark recess behind. I have not coolly weighed the chances of preserving liberty when the bonds that unite us together shall be broken asunder. I have not accustomed myself to hang over the precipice of disunion to see whether, with my short sight, I can fathom the depth of the abyss below; nor could I regard him as a safe counsellor in the affairs of this government whose thoughts should be mainly bent on considering, not how the Union should be best preserved, but how tolerable might be the condition of the people when it shall be broken up and destroyed.

While the Union lasts we have high, exciting, gratifying prospects spread out before us, for us and our children. Beyond that I seek not to penetrate the veil. God grant that, in my day at least, that curtain may not rise. God grant that on my vision never may be opened what lies behind. When my eyes shall be turned to behold, for the last time, the sun in heaven, may I not see him shining on the broken and dishonored fragments of a once glorious Union; on States dissevered, discordant, belligerent; on a land rent with civil feuds or drenched, it may be, in fraternal blood! Let their last feeble and lingering glance, rather, behold the gorgeous ensign of the republic, now known and honored throughout the earth, still full high advanced, its arms and trophies streaming in their original lustre, not a stripe erased or polluted, nor a single star obscured, bearing for its motto no such miserable interrogatory as, What is all this worth? nor those other words of delusion and folly, Liberty first and Union afterwards,—but everywhere, spread all over in characters of living light, blazing on all its ample folds, as they float over the sea and over the land, and in every wind under the whole heavens, that other sentiment, dear to every true American heart— Liberty and Union, now and forever, one and inseparable!

ORATION ON LIBERTY

Edward Everett

(1794-1865)

Edward Everett of Massachusetts, one of the most literary of all American orators, through his tolerance, integrity, and sincerity influenced the South as well as the North in the perilous days preceding the Civil War. He was graduated from Harvard at the early age of 17, studied for and was ordained to the ministry but resigned his pastorate in Boston to assume duties as a professor of Greek at Harvard University. He received his Ph.D. in Europe at Göttingen and after extensive travel returned to take up his work at Harvard. For ten years (1824-34) Everett sat in Congress, resigning his post there at the end of that period to become governor of Massachusetts. In 1841 he was appointed Minister to Great Britain, an office which he filled with distinguished success.

Everett was a conservative by nature and favored conciliatory policy between the North and the South, but when the war was finally in progress he strongly supported the government. He died at the close of the war.

Of his addresses, the best known are *On George Washington* delivered for the Mt. Vernon Association which Everett supported in the endeavor to preserve Washington's home; his eloquent *Oration at the Dedication of the National Cemetery at Gettysburg;* and the *Oration on Liberty* delivered at Cambridge as a Fourth of July speech on the 50th anniversary of the independence of the United States. The charm of Everett's oratory is its scholarly finish and symmetry. His wide reading and extensive travel gave him a fluency and aptness of quotation together with a poetic forcefulness. There is a classic elegance to the *Oration on Liberty* whose peroration is here given.

In that unceasing march of things, which calls forward the successive generations of men to perform their part on the stage of life, we are at length summoned to appear. Our fathers have passed their hour of visitation—how worthily, let the growth and prosperity of our happy land and the security of our firesides attest. Or, if this appeal be too weak to move us, let the eloquent silence of yonder famous heights— let the column which is there rising in simple majesty—recall their venerable forms, as they toiled in the hasty trenches through the dreary watches of that night of expectation, heaving up the sods, where many of them lay in peace and honor before the following sun had set. The turn has come to us. The trial of adversity was theirs; the trial of prosperity is ours. Let us meet it as men who know their duty and prize their blessings. Our position is the most enviable, the most responsible, which men can fill. If this generation does its duty, the cause of constitutional freedom is safe. If we fail—if we fail, not only do we defraud our children of the inheritance which we received from our fathers, but we blast the hopes of the friends of liberty throughout our continent, throughout Europe, throughout the world to the end of time.

History is not without her examples of hard-fought fields where the banner of liberty has floated triumphantly on the wildest storm of battle. She is without her examples of a people by whom the dear-bought treasure has been wisely employed and safely handed down. The eyes of the world are turned for that example to us. It is related by an ancient historian, of that Brutus who slew Caesar, that he threw himself on his sword, after the disastrous battle of Philippi, with the bitter exclamation that he had followed virtue as a substance, but found it a name. It is not too much to say that there are, at this moment, noble spirits in the elder world, who are anxiously watching the practical operation of our institutions, to learn whether liberty, as they have been told, is a mockery, a pretense, a curse—or a blessing, for which it became them to brave the scaffold and the scimitar.

Let us then, as we assemble on the birthday of the nation, as we gather upon the green turf, once wet with precious blood—let us devote ourselves to the sacred cause of Constitutional Liberty! Let us abjure the interests and passions which divide the great family of American freemen! Let the rage of party spirit sleep to-day! Let us resolve that our children shall have cause to bless the memory of their fathers as we have cause to bless the memory of ours!

EULOGY ON WEBSTER AT DARTMOUTH [9]

Rufus Choate

(1799-1859)

Rufus Choate, one of America's ablest jurists, was born in Massachusetts, graduated from Dartmouth College in 1819, and was admitted to the bar in 1823. In 1830 he was elected to Congress and took Webster's place in the Senate in 1841 when the latter became Secretary of State. Here he made speeches on the questions of the tariff, the bank bill, the Oregon boundary, the Smithsonian Institution, and the annexation of Texas.

Choate was by nature endowed with a commanding figure, expressive features, a rich and musical voice, forcible gestures, and a fertile imagination. These combined assets he threw into full force when presenting a case. He is reported to have watched his jury like a hawk and could read their every thought so that he would never close his appeal until he was certain of every juryman. His speeches were seasoned with humor and literary allusions although his argument was cumulative. His sentences, at times direct and terse and at others long and involved, were carried along by his pleasing persuasive manner.

Included here is Choate's speech delivered at Dartmouth College on July 27, 1853, on the occasion of the death of Daniel Webster. It was while a student at Dartmouth College, following Webster's proceedings in the famous Dartmouth College case that Choate became inspired to follow in Webster's footsteps and thereafter became Webster's most intimate friend and political follower. He was therefore ably fitted to deliver this oration which is considered a supreme example of eulogistic prose.

[9] Abridged.

It would be a strange neglect of a beautiful and approved custom of the schools of learning, and of one of the most pious and appropriate of the offices of literature, if the college in which the intellectual life of Daniel Webster began, and to which his name imparts charm and illustration, should give no formal expression to her grief in the common sorrow; if she should not draw near, of the most sad, in the procession of the bereaved, to the tomb at the sea, nor find, in all her classic shades, one affectionate and grateful leaf to set in the garland with which they have bound the brow of her child, the mightiest departed. Others mourn and praise him by his more distant and more general titles to fame and remembrance; his supremacy of intellect, his statesmanship of so many years, his eloquence of reason and of heart, his love of country, incorruptible, conscientious, and ruling every hour and act; that greatness combined of genius, of character, of manner, of place, of achievement, which was just now among us, and is not, and yet lives still and ever more. You come, his cherished mother, to own a closer tie, to indulge an emotion more personal and more fond—grief and exultation contending for mastery, as in the bosom of the desolated parent, whose tears could not hinder him from exclaiming, "I would not exchange my dead son for any living one of Christendom."

Many places in our American world have spoken his eulogy. To all places the service was befitting, for "his renown, is it not of the treasures of the whole country?" To some it belonged, with a strong local propriety, to discharge it. In the halls of Congress, where the majestic form seems ever to stand, and the deep tones to linger, the decorated scene of his larger labors and most diffusive glory; in the courts of law, to whose gladsome light he loved to return,—putting on again the robes of that profession ancient as magistracy, noble as virtue, necessary as justice,—in which he found the beginning of his honors; in Faneuil Hall, whose air breathes and burns of him; in the commercial cities, to whose pursuits his diplomacy secured a peaceful sea; in the cities of the inland, around which his capacious public affections, and wise discernment, aimed ever to develop the uncounted resources of that other, and that larger, and that newer America; in the pulpit, whose place among the higher influences which exalt a state, our guide in life, our consolation in death, he appreciated profoundly, and vindicated by the weightiest argument and testimony, of whose offices it is among the fittest to mark and point the moral of the great things of the world, the excellency of dignity, and the excellency of power passing away as the pride of the wave,—passing from our eye to take on immortality,— in these places, and such as these, there seemed a reason beyond and other than the universal calamity, for such honors of the grave. But if so, how fit a place is this for such a service!

We are among the scenes where the youth of Webster awoke first and fully to the life of the mind. We stand, as it were, at the sources— physical, social, moral, intellectual—of that exceeding greatness. Some now here saw that youth; almost it was yours, *Nilum parvum videre.* Some one of his instructors certainly, some possibly of his classmates, or nearest college friends, some of the books he read, some of the apartments in which he studied are here. We can almost call up from their habitation in the past, or in the fancy, the whole spiritual circle which environed that time of his life. . . .

Still the same outward world is around you, and above you. The sweet and solemn flow of the river, gleaming through intervals here and there; margins and samples of the same old woods, but thinned and retiring; the same range of green hills yonder, tolerant of culture to the top, but shaded then by primeval forests, on whose crest the last rays of sunset lingered; the summit of Ascutney; the great northern light that never sets; the constellations that walk around and watch the pole; the same nature, undecayed, unchanging, is here. We stand at the fountain of a stream; we stand, rather, at the place where a stream, sudden, and from hidden springs, bursts to light; and whence we can follow it along and down, as we might our own Connecticut, and trace its resplendent pathway to the sea; and we venerate, and would almost build altars here.

If I may adopt the lofty language of one of the admirers of William Pitt, we come naturally to this place, as if we could thus recall every circumstance of splendid preparation which contributed to fit the great man for the scene of his glory. We could come, as if, better here than elsewhere, "we could watch, fold by fold, the bracing on of his Vulcanian panoply, and observe with pleased anxiety the leading forth of that chariot, which, borne on irresistible wheels, and drawn by steeds of immortal race, is to crush the necks of the mighty, and sweep away the serried strength of armies."

. . . . . .

In looking over the public remains of the oratory of Webster, it is striking to remark how, even in that sober and massive understanding and nature, you see gathered and expressed the characteristic sentiments and the passing time of our America. It is the strong old oak which ascends before you; yet our soil, our heaven, are attested in it as perfectly as if it were a flower that could grow in no other climate and in no other hour of the year or day. Let me instance in one thing only. It is a peculiarity of some schools of eloquence that they embody and utter, not merely the individual genius and character of the speaker, but a national consciousness—a national era, a mood, a hope, a dread, a despair—in which you listen to the spoken history of the time. There is an eloquence of an expiring nation, such as seems to sadden the glorious speech of Demosthenes; such as breathes grand and gloomy from the visions of the prophets of the last days of Israel and Judah; such as gave a spell to the expression of Grattan and of Kossuth—the sweetest, most mournful, most awful of the words which man may utter, or which man may hear—the eloquence of a perishing nation.

There is another eloquence, in which the national consciousness of a young or renewed and vast strength, of trust in a dazzling, certain, and limitless future, an inward glorying in victories yet to be won, sounds out as by voice of clarion, challenging to contest for the highest prize of earth; such as that in which the leader of Israel in its first days holds up to the new nation the Land of Promise; such as that in the well-imagined speeches scattered by Livy over the history of the "majestic series of victories" speaks the Roman consciousness of growing aggrandizement which should subject the world; such as that through which, at the tribunes of her revolution in the bulletins of her rising soldiers, France told to the world her dream of glory.

And of this kind somewhat is ours—cheerful, hopeful, trusting as befits youth and spring; the eloquence of a state beginning to ascend to the first class of power, eminence, and consideration, and conscious of itself. It is to no purpose that they tell you it is in bad taste; that it partakes of arrogance and vanity; that a true national good breeding would not know, or seem to know, whether the naiton is old or young; whether the tides of being are at their flow or ebb; whether these coursers of the sun are sinking slowly to rest, wearied with a journey of a thousand years, or just bounding from the Orient unbreathed. Higher laws than those of taste determine the general forms of the expression of that consciousness. Let the downward age of America find its orators and poets and artists to erect its spirit or grace and soothe its dying; be it ours to go up with Webster to the Rock, the Monument, the Capitol, and bid "the distant generations hail!"

AGAINST WAR WITH MEXICO [10]

Thomas Corwin

(1794-1865)

Thomas Corwin, a Kentuckian by birth, was admitted to the Ohio State bar in 1818, where he soon became famous for his eloquence. In 1830 he was elected to Congress and in 1840 became governor of Ohio; from 1845 to 1850 he was in the United States Senate, and in 1850 became Secretary of the Treasury; from 1861 to 1864 he was Minister to Mexico where he remained until ill health forced him to return home.

The two most famous speeches Corwin delivered were *The Reply to General Crary,* which was a defense of General Harrison against the charge of military incapacity, and *Against War with Mexico,* delivered in 1847, which ranks as one of the most memorable speeches ever delivered in America. This latter oration doomed Corwin's career, because, although it brought unlimited admiration from his supporters, it also brought unlimited denunciation from the opposition. Yet this one speech has placed Corwin in the foremost rank of American political orators.

Corwin had an easy and natural flow of words which were powerful although frequently veiled in sarcasm.

Mr. President, this uneasy desire to augment our territory has depraved the moral sense and blunted the otherwise keen sagacity of our people. What has been the fate of all nations who have acted upon the idea that they must advance! Our young orators cherish this notion with a fervid but fatally mistaken zeal. They call it by the mysterious name of "destiny." "Our destiny," they say, "is onward," and hence they argue, with ready sophistry, the propriety of seizing upon any territory and any people that may lie in the way of their fated advance. Recently these progressives have grown classical; some assiduous student of antiques has helped them to a patron saint. They have wandered back into the desolate Pantheon, and there, among the polytheistic relics of that "pale mother of dead empires," they have found a god whom these Romans, centuries gone by, baptized "Terminus."

[10] Abridged.

Sir, I have heard much and read somewhat of this gentleman, Terminus. Alexander, of whom I have spoken, was a devotee of this divinity. We have seen the end of him and his empire. It was said to be an attribute of this god that he must always advance and never recede. So both republican and imperial Rome believed. It was, as they said, their destiny. And for a while it did seem to be even so. Roman Terminus did advance. Under the eagles of Rome he was carried from his home on the Tiber to the farthest East on the one hand, and to the far West, among the then barbarous tribes of Western Europe, on the other.

But at length the time came when retributive justice had become "a destiny." The despised Gaul calls out the condemned Goth, and Attila with his Huns answers back the battle-shout to both. The "blue-eyed nations of the North," in succession or united, pour forth their countless hosts of warriors upon Rome and Rome's always advancing god Terminus. And now the battle-ax of the barbarian strikes down the conquering eagle of Rome. Terminus at last recedes, slowly at first, but finally he is driven to Rome, and from Rome to Byzantium. Whoever would know the further fate of this Roman deity, so recently taken under the patronage of American democracy, may find ample gratification of his curiosity in the luminous pages of Gibbon's *Decline and Fall*.

Such will find that Rome thought as you now think, that it was her destiny to conquer provinces and nations, and no doubt she sometimes said, as you say, "I will conquer a peace," where now is she, the mistress of the world? The spider weaves his web in her palaces; the owl sings his watch-song in her towers. Teutonic power now lords it over the servile remnant, the miserable memento of old and once omnipotent Rome.

Sad, very sad, are the lessons which time has written for us. Through and in them all I see nothing but the inflexible execution of that old law which ordains as eternal that cardinal rule, "Thou shalt not covet thy neighbor's goods, nor anything which is his." Since I have lately heard so much about the dismemberment of Mexico, I have looked back to see how, in the course of events, which some call "providence," it has fared with other nations who engaged in this work of dismemberment. I see that, in the latter half of the eighteenth century, three powerful nations, Russia, Austria, and Prussia, united in the dismemberment of Poland. They said, too, as you say, "It is our destiny." They "wanted room." Doubtless each of these thought, with his share of Poland, his power was too strong ever to fear invasion, or even insult. One had his California, another his New Mexico, and the third his Vera Cruz. Did they remain untouched and incapable of harm? Alas! no—far, very far, from it. Retributive justice must fulfill its destiny, too.

A very few years pass off, and we hear of a new man, a Corsican lieutenant, the self-named "armed soldier of democracy," Napoleon. He ravages Austria, covers her land with blood, drives the Northern

Caesar from his capital, and sleeps in his palace. Austria may now remember how her power trampled upon Poland. Did she not pay dear, very dear, for California?

But has Prussia no atonement to make? You see this same Napoleon, the blind instrument of providence, at work there. The thunders of his cannon at Jena proclaim the work of retribution for Poland's wrongs; and the successors of the great Frederick, the drill-sergeant of Europe, are seen flying across the sandy plain that surrounds their capital, right glad if they may escape captivity or death.

But how fares it with the autocrat of Russia? Is he secure in his share of the spoils of Poland? No. Suddenly we see, sir, six hundred thousand men marching to Moscow. Does his Vera Cruz protect him now? Far from it. Blood, slaughter, desolation spread abroad over the land, and finally the conflagration of the old commercial metropolis of Russia closes the retribution she must pay for her share in the dismemberment of her weak and impotent neighbor.

Mr. President, a mind more prone to look for the judgments of heaven in the doings of men than mine, can not fail in this to see the providence of God. When Moscow burned, it seemed as if the earth was lighted up that the nations might behold the scene. As that mighty sea of fire gathered and heaved and rolled upward and yet higher till its flames licked the stars and fired the whole heavens, it did seem as though the God of the nations was writing in characters of flame on the front of his throne that doom shall fall upon the strong nation which tramples in scorn upon the weak. And what fortune awaits him, the appointed executor of this work, when it was all done? He, too, conceived the notion that his destiny pointed onward to universal dominion. France was too small—Europe, he thought, should bow down before him.

But as soon as this idea took possession of his soul, he, too, becomes powerless. His Terminus must recede, too. Right there, while he witnessed the humiliation and doubtless meditated subjugation of Russia, He who holds the winds in His fist gathered the snows of the north and blew them upon his six hundred thousand men; they fled—they froze—they perished. And now the mighty Napoleon, who has resolved on universal dominion, he, too, is summoned to answer for the violation of that ancient law, "Thou shalt not covet anything which is thy neighbor's." How is the mighty fallen! He, beneath whose proud footstep Europe trembled, he is now an exile at Elba, and now finally a prisoner on the rock of St. Helena, and there, on a barren island, in an unfrequented sea, in the crater of an extinct volcano, there is the death-bed of the mighty conqueror. All his annexations have come to that! His last hour is now come, and he, the man of destiny, he who rocked the world as with the throes of an earthquake, is now powerless, still—even as a beggar, so he died. On the wings of a tempest that raged with unwonted fury, up to the throne of the only Power that controlled him while he lived, went the fiery soul of that wonderful warrior, another witness to the existence of that eternal decree that they who do not rule in righteousness shall perish from the earth. He has found "room" at last.

And France,—she, too, has found "room." Her "eagles" now no longer scream along the banks of the Danube, the Po, the Borysthenes. They have returned home, to their old eyrie, between the Alps, the Rhine, and the Pyrenees. So it shall be with yours. You may carry them to the loftiest peaks of the Cordilleras, they may wave with insolent triumph in the halls of the Montezumas, the armed men of Mexico may quail before them, but the weakest hand in Mexico, uplifted in prayer to the God of Justice, may call down against you a Power in the presence of which the iron hearts of your warriors shall be turned into ashes.

A EULOGY ON LAFAYETTE [11]

John Quincy Adams

(1767-1848)

John Quincy Adams, the son of John Adams, second President of the United States, had every advantage as a youth. While his father was ambassador abroad, John Quincy studied in Paris, The Hague, and London and travelled throughout Europe; returning to America, he completed his studies at Harvard and was admitted to the bar in 1791. Thereafter he was successively Minister to The Hague, Prussia, Russia, and England. He was appointed Secretary of State after the expiration of these duties and in this office originated the Monroe Doctrine. In 1825 he became the President of the United States.

John Quincy Adams was considered one of the most highly educated men of his day. The language of his speeches is most scholarly, at times heavy and ponderous. In his latter days he was indicated as "The Old Man Eloquent" because of his continued presentations to Congress of petitions for the abolition of slavery. Included here is Adams' *Eulogy on Lafayette* delivered on the death of the distinguished French nobleman who had endeared himself to all Americans and who passed away May 20, 1834. The rather peculiar and turgid phraseology employed by Adams was a characteristic of the speech of his day and was highly applauded.

Pronounce him one of the first men of his age, and you have not yet done him justice. Try him by that test to which he sought in vain to stimulate the vulgar and selfish spirit of Napoleon; class him among the men who, to compare and seat themselves, must take in the compass of all ages; turn back your eyes upon the records of time; summon from the creation of the world to this day the mighty dead of every age and every clime—and where, among the race of merely mortal men,

[11] Abridged.

shall one be found who, as the benefactor of his kind, shall claim to take precedence of Lafayette?

There have doubtless been in all ages men whose discoveries or inventions, in the world of matter or of mind, have opened new avenues to the dominion of man over the material creation; have increased his means or his faculties of enjoyment; have raised him in nearer approximation to that higher and happier condition, the object of his hopes and aspirations in his present state of existence.

Lafayette discovered no new principle of politics or morals. He invented nothing in science. He disclosed no new phenomenon in the laws of nature. Born and educated in the highest order of feudal nobility, under the most absolute monarchy of Europe, in possession of an affluent fortune, and master of himself and of all his capabilities at the moment of attaining manhood, the principle of republican justice and of social equality took possession of his heart and mind, as if by inspiration from above. He devoted himself, his life, his fortune, his hereditary honors, his towering ambition, his splendid hopes, all to the cause of liberty. He came to another hemisphere to defend her. He became one of the most effective champions of our independence; but, that once achieved, he returned to his own country, and thenceforward took no part in the controversies which have divided us. In the events of our Revolution, and in the forms of policy which we have adopted for the establishment and perpetuation of our freedom, Lafayette found the most perfect form of government. He wished to add nothing to it. He would gladly have abstracted nothing from it. Instead of the imaginary Republic of Plato, or the Utopia of Sir Thomas More, he took a practical existing model, in actual operation here, and never attempted or wished more than to apply it faithfully to his own country.

It was not given to Moses to enter the promised land; but he saw it from the summit of Pisgah. It was not given to Lafayette to witness the consummation of his wishes in the establishment of a republic, and the extinction of all hereditary rule in France. His principles were in advance of the age and hemisphere in which he lived. A Bourbon still reigns on the throne of France, and it is not for us to scrutinize the title by which he reigns. The principles of elective and hereditary power, blended in reluctant union in his person, like the red and white roses of York and Lancaster, may postpone to aftertime the last conflict to which they must ultimately come. The life of the patriarch was not long enough for the development of his whole political system. Its final accomplishment is in the womb of time.

The anticipation of this event is the more certain, from the consideration that all the principles for which Lafayette contended were practical. He never indulged himself in wild and fanciful speculations. The principle of hereditary power was, in his opinion, the bane of all republican liberty in Europe. Unable to extinguish it in the Revolution of 1830, so far as concerned the chief magistracy of the nation, Lafayette had the satisfaction of seeing it abolished with reference to the peerage. An hereditary Crown, stript of the support which it may derive from an hereditary peerage, however compatible with Asiatic despotism, is an anomaly in the history of the Christian world and in the theory of free government. There is no argument producible against the existence of an hereditary peerage, but applies with aggravated weight against the transmission, from sire to son, of an hereditary crown. The prejudices and passions of the people of France rejected the principle of inherited power, in every station of public trust, excepting the first and highest of them all; but there they clung to it, as did the Israelites of old to the savory deities of Egypt.

This is not the time or the place for a disquisition upon the comparative merits, as a system of government, of a republic, and a monarchy surrounded by republican institutions. Upon this subject there is among us no diversity of opinion; and if it should take the people of France another half century of internal and external war, of dazzling and delusive glories, of unparalleled triumphs, humiliating reverses, and bitter disappointments, to settle it to their satisfaction, the ultimate result can only bring them to the point where we have stood from the day of the Declaration of Independence—to the point where Lafayette would have brought them, and to which he looked as a consummation devoutly to be wished.

Then, too, and then only, will be the time when the character of Lafayette will be appreciated at its true value throughout the civilized world. When the principle of hereditary dominion shall be relinquished in all the institutions of France; when government shall no longer be considered as property transmissible from sire to son, but as a trust committed for a limited time, and then to return to the people whence it came; as a burdensome duty to be discharged, and not as a reward to be abused; when a claim, any claim, to political power by inheritance shall, in the estimation of the whole French people, be held as it now is by the whole people of the North American Union—then will be the time for contemplating the character of Lafayette, not merely in the events of his life, but in the full development of his intellectual conceptions, of his fervent aspirations, of the labors and perils and sacrifices of his long and eventful career upon earth; and thenceforward, till the hour when the trump of the Archangel shall sound to announce that time shall be no more, the name of Lafayette shall stand enrolled upon the annals of our race, high on the list of the pure and disinterested benefactors of mankind.

THE YOUNG AMERICAN [12]

Ralph Waldo Emerson
(1803-1882)

America's poet-philosopher, Ralph Waldo Emerson, was also an effective public speaker. He was born into a minister's family in Boston, Massachusetts, and received his education at Harvard, was ordained to the ministry, and occupied a Unitarian pulpit in Boston from 1829 to 1832. He was always considered an able, earnest, and altogether pleasing minister, but it was not until after extensive travels through Europe and his entrance into his long career as a lecturer in 1833 that he became nationally and internationally known. His language is homely and simple, redolent of the soil of New England, full of imagery but never crude. His was an eloquence of the ideal. Of his numerous lectures *The American Scholar,* a Phi Beta Kappa oration delivered at Cambridge Massachusetts August 31, 1837, and his *Lecture on the Times* have become most popularly known. We include here an abridgement of a lecture delivered on February 7, 1844, at Boston, entitled *The Young American* which seems almost as applicable to youth of the 20th century as it was to the New England youth to whom it was addressed.

We cannot look on the freedom of this country, in connection with its youth, without a presentiment that here shall laws and institutions exist on some scale of proportion to the majesty of nature. To men legislating for the area betwixt the two oceans, betwixt the snows and the tropics, somewhat of the gravity of nature will infuse itself into the code. A heterogeneous population crowding on all ships from all corners of the world to the great gates of North America, namely Boston, New York, and New Orleans, and thence proceeding inward to the prairie and the mountains, and quickly contributing their private thought to the public opinion, their toll to the treasury, and their vote to the election, it cannot be doubted that the legislation of this country

[12] Abridged.

should become more catholic and cosmopolitan than that of any other. It seems so easy for America to inspire and express the most expansive and humane spirit; new-born, free, healthful, strong, the land of the laborer, of the democrat, of the philanthropist, of the believer, of the saint, she should speak for the human race. It is the country of the future. From Washington, proverbially "the city of magnificent distances," through all its cities, states, and territories, it is a country of beginnings, of projects, of designs, of expectations. . . .

In consequence of the revolution in the state of society wrought by trade, Government in our times is beginning to wear a clumsy and cumbrous appearance. We have already seen our way to shorter methods. The time is full of good signs. Some of them shall ripen to fruit. All this beneficient socialism is a friendly omen, and the swelling cry of voices for the education of the people indicates that government has other offices than those of banker and executioner. Witness the new movements in the civilized world. . . .

These proceeded from a variety of motives, from an impatience of many usages in common life, from a wish for greater freedom than the manners and opinions of society permitted, but in great part from a feeling that the true offices of the State, the State had let fall to the ground; that in the scramble of parties for the public purse, the main duties of government were omitted,—the duty to instruct the ignorant, to supply the poor with work and with good guidance. . . .

Undoubtedly, abundant mistakes will be made by these first adventurers, which will draw ridicule on their schemes. I think for example that they exaggerate the importance of a favorite project of theirs, that of paying talent and labor at one rate, paying all sorts of service at one rate, say ten cents the hour. They have paid it so; but not an instant would a dime remain a dime. In one hand it became an eagle as it fell, and in another hand a copper cent. For the whole value of the dime is in knowing what to do with it. One man buys with it a land-title of an Indian, and makes his posterity princes; or buys corn enough to feed the world; or pen, ink, and paper, or a painter's brush, by which he can communicate himself to the human race as if he were fire; and the other buys barley candy. Money is of no value; it cannot spend itself. All depends on the skill of the spender.

. . . . . .

How can our young men complain of the poverty of things in New England, and not feel that poverty as a demand on their charity to make New England rich? Where is he who seeing a thousand men useless and unhappy, and making the whole region forlorn by their inaction, and conscious himself of possessing the faculty they want, does not hear his call to go and be their king?

. . . . . .

In every society some men are born to rule and some to advise. Let the powers be well directed, directed by love, and they would everywhere be greeted with joy and honor. . . .   It is only their dislike of the pretender, which makes men sometimes unjust to the accomplished man. If society were transparent, the noble would everywhere be gladly received and accredited, and would not be asked for his day's work, but would be felt as benefit, inasmuch as he was noble. That were his duty and stint,—to keep himself pure and purifying, the leaven of his nation. I think I see place and duties for a nobleman in every society; but it is not to drink wine and ride in a fine coach, but to guide and adorn life for the multitude by forethought, by elegant studies, by perseverance, self-devotion, and the remembrance of the humble old friend, by making his life secretly beautiful.

I call upon you, young men, to obey your heart and be the nobility of this land. In every age of the world there has been a leading nation, one of a more generous sentiment, whose eminent citizens were willing to stand for the interests of general justice and humanity, at the risk of being called, by the men of the moment, chimerical and fantastic. Which should be that nation but these States? Which should lead that movement, if not New England? Who should lead the leaders, but the Young American? The people, and the world, are now suffering from the want of religion and honor in its public mind. In America, out-of-doors all seems a market; in-doors an air-tight stove of conventionalism. Everybody who comes into our houses savors of these habits; the men, of the market; the women, of the custom. I find no expression in our state papers or legislative debate, in our lyceums or churches, especially in our newspapers, of a high national feeling, no lofty counsels that rightfully stir the blood. I speak of those organs which can be presumed to speak a popular sense. They recommend conventional virtues, whatever will earn and preserve property; always the capitalist; the college, the church, the hospital, the theatre, the hotel, the road, the ship, of the capitalist,—whatever goes to secure, adorn, enlarge these is good; what jeopardizes any of these is damnable. The "opposition" papers, so called, are on the same side. They attack the great capitalist, but with the aim to make a capitalist of the poor man. The opposition is against those who have money, from those who wish to have money. But who announces to us in journal, or in pulpit, or in the street, the secret of heroism?

> "Man alone
> Can perform the impossible."

. . . . . .

The timidity of our public opinion is our disease, or, shall I say, the publicness of opinion, the absence of private opinion. Good nature is plentiful, but we want justice, with heart of steel, to fight down the proud. The private mind has the access to the totality of goodness and truth that it may be a balance to a currupt society; and to stand for the private verdict against popular clamor is the office of the noble. If a humane measure is propounded in behalf of the slave, or of the

Irishman, or the Catholic, or for the succor of the poor; that sentiment, that project, will have the homage of the hero. That is his nobility, his oath of knighthood, to succor the helpless and oppressed; always to throw himself on the side of weakness, of youth, of hope; on the liberal, on the expansive side, never on the defensive, the conserving, the timorous, the lock-and-bolt system. More than our good-will we may not be able to give. We have our own affairs, our own genius, which chains each to his proper work. We cannot give our life to the cause of the debtor, of the slave, or the pauper, as another is doing; but to one thing we are bound, not to blaspheme the sentiment and the work of that man, not to throw stumbling-blocks in the way of the abolitionist, the philanthropist; as the organs of influence and opinion are swift to do. It is for us to confide in the beneficent Supreme Power, and not to rely on our money, and on the state because it is the guard of money. At this moment, the terror of old people and of vicious people is lest the Union of these states be destroyed: as if the Union had any other real basis than the good pleasure of a majority of the citizens to be united. But the wise and just man will always feel that he stands on his own feet; that he imparts strength to the State, not receives security from it; and that if all went down, he and such as he would quite easily combine in a new and better constitution. Every great and memorable community has consisted of formidable individuals, who, like the Roman or the Spartan, lent his own spirit to the State and made it great. Yet only by the supernatural is a man strong; nothing is so weak as an egotist. Nothing is mightier than we, when we are vehicles of a truth before which the State and the individual are alike ephemeral.

Gentlemen, the development of our American internal resources, the extension to the utmost of the commercial system, and the appearance of new moral causes which are to modify the State, are giving an aspect of greatness to the Future, which the imagination fears to open. One thing is plain for all men of common sense and common conscience, that here, here in America, is the home of man.

. . . .

Our houses and towns are like mosses and lichens, so slight and new; but youth is a fault of which we shall daily mend. This land too is as old as the Flood, and wants no ornament or privilege which nature could bestow. Here stars, here woods, here hills, here animals, here men abound, and the vast tendencies concur of a new order. If only the men are employed in conspiring with the designs of the Spirit who led us hither and is leading us still, we shall quickly enough advance out of all hearing of others' censures, out of all regrets of our own, into a new and more excellent social state than history has recorded.

MURDER OF LOVEJOY [12]

Wendell Phillips
(1911-1884)

Wendell Phillips, one of the great orators of the abolition movement in America, was the son of a wealthy and cultured New England family, graduated from Harvard University in 1831 where he had received high honors for his eloquence, and was admitted to the bar in 1834.

He became an ardent abolitionist and made one of the most brilliant speeches of his life at a mass meeting in Faneuil Hall in 1837 to protest the murder of the abolitionist Lovejoy, in Illinois, while defending the right to print anti-slavery literature. When John Brown's Insurrection at Harper's Ferry was stirring the country in 1859, Wendell Phillips eulogized John Brown as a patriot and martyr. In addition to these two speeches Phillips delivered many lyceum lectures, and a famous eulogy over Daniel O'Connell whom he had met in London.

Phillips differed from the contemporary orators because he had no party affiliation but attacked the slavery question before hostile and prejudiced audiences and won by sheer force of eloquence. Not until the 15th amendment to the Constitution was passed in 1870 did he cease his efforts. Thereafter he agitated for woman's suffrage, labor reform, and prohibition.

Wendell Phillips had the natural gift of eloquence. He had a tall handsome figure; his voice of a baritone register, was remarkably compelling for its timbre; in gesture he was sparing; he possessed a rare quality of wit and could tell an anecdote with infinite skill. Horace Greeley gave the most apt description of his manner when he stated that Phillips made one think it easy to be an orator. This air of comparative

[12] Abridged.

repose by its directness and simplicity influenced the speaking of his day, for Phillips was before the public longer than any of his contemporaries, and, although he never appeared in Congress, his influence through the lyceum and the academic platform was so far-reaching that he was unrivalled in his day.

Mr. Chairman: We have met for the freest discussion of these resolutions, and the events which gave rise to them. I hope I shall be permitted to express my surprise at the sentiments of the last speaker, surprise not only at such sentiments from such a man, but at the applause they have received within these walls.

A comparison has been drawn between the events of the Revolution and the tragedy at Alton. We have heard it asserted here, in Faneuil Hall, that Great Britain had a right to tax the colonies, and we have heard the mob at Alton, the drunken murderers of Lovejoy, compared to those patriot fathers who threw the tea overboard! Fellow-citizens, is this Faneuil Hall doctrine?

The mob at Alton were met to wrest from a citizen his just rights— met to resist the laws. We have been told that our fathers did the same; and the glorious mantle of Revolutionary precedent has been thrown over the mobs of our day.

To make out their title to such a defense, the gentleman says that the British Parliament had a right to tax these colonies. It is manifest that, without this, his parallel falls to the ground, for Lovejoy had stationed himself within constitutional bulwarks. He was not only defending the freedom of the press, but he was under his own roof, in arms with the sanction of the civil authority. The men who assailed him went against and over the laws.

The mob, as the gentleman terms it—mob, forsooth! certainly, we sons of the tea-spillers are a marvelously patient generation!—the "orderly mob" which assembled in the Old South to destroy the tea, were met to resist, not the laws, but illegal enactments. Shame on the American who calls the tea tax and the stamp act laws! Our fathers resisted, not the King's prerogative, but the King's usurpation.

To find any other account, you must read our Revolutionary history upside down. Our State archives are loaded with arguments of John Adams to prove the taxes laid by the British Parliament unconstitutional —beyond its power. It was not until this was made out that the men of New England rushed to arms. The arguments of the Council Chamber and the House of Representatives preceded and sanctioned the contest.

To draw the conduct of our ancestors into a precedent for mobs, for a right to resist laws we have ourselves enacted, is an insult to their memory. The difference between the excitements of those days and our own, which the gentleman, in kindness to the latter, has over-looked, is simply this: the men of that day went for the right, as secured by the laws. They were the people rising to sustain the laws and constitution of the Province. The rioters of our days go for their own wills, right or wrong.

Sir, when I heard the gentleman lay down principles which place the murderers of Alton side by side with Otis and Hancock, with Quincy and Adams, I thought those pictured lips (pointing to the portraits in the hall) would have broken into voice to rebuke the recreant American—the slanderer of the dead. The gentleman said that he should sink into insignificance if he dared to gainsay the principles of these resolutions. Sir, for the sentiments he has uttered, on soil consecrated by the prayers of Puritans and the blood of patriots, the earth should have yawned and swallowed him up.

Fellow-citizens, I cannot take back my words. Surely, the Attorney-General, so long and so well known here, needs not the aid of your hisses against one so young as I am—my voice never before heard within these walls!

The gentleman says Lovejoy was presumptuous and imprudent—he "died as the fool dieth." And a reverend clergyman of the city tells us that no citizen has a right to publish opinions disagreeable to the community! If any mob follows such publication, on him rests the guilt. He must wait, forsooth, till the people come up to it and agree with him!

This libel on liberty goes on to say that the want of right to speak as we think is an evil inseparable from republican institutions! If this be so, what are they worth? Welcome the despotism of the Sultan, where one knows what he may publish and what he may not, rather than the tyranny of this many-headed monster, the mob, where we know not what we may do or say, till some fellow-citizen has tried it, and paid for the lesson with his life.

This clerical absurdity chooses as a check for the abuses of the press, not the law, but the dread of a mob. By so doing it deprives not only the individual and the minority of their rights, but the majority also, since the expression of their opinion may sometimes provoke disturbances from the minority. A few men may make a mob as well as many. The majority, then, have no right, as Christian men, to utter their sentiments, if by any possibility it may lead to a mob! Shades of Hugh Peters and John Cotton, save us from such pulpits!

Imprudent to defend the liberty of the press! Why? Because the defense was unsuccessful? Does success gild crime into patriotism, and the want of it change heroic self-devotion to imprudence? Was Hampden imprudent when he drew the sword and threw away the scabbard? Yet he, judged by the single hour, was unsuccessful. After a short exile, the race he hated sat again upon the throne.

Imagine yourself present when the first news of Bunker Hill battle reached a New England town. The tale would have run thus: "The patriots are routed,—the redcoats victorious,—Warren lies dead upon the field." With what scorn would that Tory have been received, who should have charged Warren with imprudence! who should have said that, bred a physician, he was "out of place" in that battle, and "died as the fool dieth." How would the intimation have been received, that Warren and his associates should have waited a better time? But if success be indeed the only criterion of Prudence, *Respice finem*— wait till the end!

Presumptuous to assert the freedom of the press on American ground! Is the assertion of such freedom before the age? So much before the age as to leave one no right to make it, because it displeases the community? Who invents this libel on his country? It is this very thing which entitles Lovejoy to greater praise. The disputed right which provoked the Revolution—taxation without representation—is far beneath that for which he died.

One word, gentlemen. As much as thought is better than money, so much is the cause in which Lovejoy died nobler than a mere question of taxes. James Otis thundered in this hall when the King did but touch his pocket. Imagine, if you can, his indignant eloquence, had England offered to put a gag upon his lips.

I am glad, sir, to see this crowded house. It is good for us to be here. When liberty is in danger, Faneuil Hall has the right, it is her duty, to strike the key-note for these United States. I am glad, for one reason, that remarks such as those to which I have alluded have been uttered here. The passage of these resolutions, in spite of this opposition, led by the Attorney-General of the Commonwealth, will show more clearly, more decisively, the deep indignation with which Boston regards this outrage.

THE TRUE GRANDEUR OF NATIONS [13]

Charles Sumner
(1811-1874)

Charles Sumner was the great advocate of abolition in the Senate. A graduate of Harvard University, he entered the profession of law, studying the judicial practices of foreign countries on a visit to Europe in 1837. Sumner first attracted attention as an orator on 1845, when he delivered the traditional Fourth of July address in Boston with a remarkable oration entitled *The True Grandeur of Nations* in which he declared that this grandeur consisted in the achievement of peace rather than the glories of war. This speech brought criticism as well as extreme approval upon Sumner. In 1851 he took his seat in the Senate and became known as the champion of the anti-slavery cause. It was in 1854 that he made his virulent oratorical attack *The Crime Against Kansas* on the question of the Kansas-Nebraska bill. This speech so aroused the opposition that Sumner was severely caned in the Senate chamber by Brooks, a nephew of Senator Butler whom Sumner had attacked in his speech. Sumner never completely recovered from the effects of this brutal act, but although he was unable to resume his seat in the Senate for four years, his place remained vacant as a tribute to him.

Eloquence was not native to Sumner but rather acquired and his oratory is representative of the academic method. Yet his influence was far-reaching, particularly on the major questions of the war with Mexico and in the slavery agitation preceding the Civil War. Upon his death he was eulogized alike by the North and by the South as a statesman and an orator.

[13] Abridged.

In our age there can be no peace that is not honorable; there can be no war that is not dishonorable. The true honor of a nation is to be found only in deeds of justice, and in the happiness of its people, all of which are inconsistent with war. In the clear eye of Christian judgment vain are its victories; infamous are its spoils. He is the true benefactor and alone worthy of honor who brings comfort where before was wretchedness; who dries the tears of sorrow; who pours oil into the wounds of the unfortunate; who feeds the hungry and clothes the naked; who unlooses the fetters of the slave; who does justice; who enlightens the ignorant; who enlivens and exalts, by his virtuous genius, in art, in literature, in science, the hours of life; who, by words or actions, inspires a love for God and for man. This is the Christian hero; this is the man of honor in a Christian land. He is no benefactor, nor deserving of honor, whatever may be his worldly renown, whose life is passed in acts of force; who renounces the great law of Christian brotherhood; whose vocation is blood; who triumphs in battle over his fellow-men. Well may old Sir Thomas Browne exclaim: "The world does not know its greatest men;" for thus it has chiefly discerned the violent brood of battle, the armed men springing up from the dragon's teeth sown by Hate, and cared little for the truly good men, children of Love, Cromwells guiltless of their country's blood, whose steps on earth have been as noiseless as an angel's wing. . . .

Thus far mankind has worshipped in military glory an idol compared with which the colossal images of ancient Babylon or modern Hindostan are but toys; and we, in this blessed day of light, in this blessed land of freedom, are among the idolaters. The heaven-descending injunction, "Know thyself," still speaks to an ignorant world from the distant letters of gold at Delphi—know thyself; know thyself; know that the moral nature is the most noble part of man; transcending far that part which is the seat of passion, strife, and war; nobler than the intellect itself. Suppose war to be decided by force, where is the glory? Suppose it to be decided by chance, where is the glory? No; true greatness consists in imitating, as near as possible for finite man, the perfections of an Infinite Creator; above all, in cultivating those highest perfections, justice and love—justice, which like that of St. Louis, shall not swerve to the right hand or to the left; love, which like that of William Penn, shall regard all mankind of kin. "God is angry," says Plato, "when anyone censures a man like himself, or praises a man of an opposite character. And the Godlike man is the good man." And again, in another of those lovely dialogues, vocal with immortal truth, "Nothing resembles God more than that man among us who has arrived at the highest degree of justice." The true greatness of nations is in those qualities which constitute the greatness of the individual. It is not to be found in extent of territory, nor in vastness of population; nor in wealth; not in fortifications, or armies, or navies; not in the phosphorescent glare of fields of battle; not in Golgothas, though covered by monuments that kiss the clouds: for all these are the creatures and representatives of those qualities of our nature which are unlike anything in God's nature.

Nor is the greatness of nations to be found in triumphs of intellect alone; in literature, learning, science or art. The polished Greeks, the world's masters in the delights of language, and in range of thought; and the commanding Romans, overawing the earth with their power; were little more than splendid savages; and the age of Louis XIV of France, spanning so long a period of ordinary worldly magnificence, thronged by marshals bending under military laurels, enlivened by the unsurpassed comedy of Molière, dignified by the tragic genius of Corneille, illumined by the splendors of Bossuet, is degraded by immoralities that cannot be mentioned without a blush, by a heartlessness in comparison with which the ice of Nova Zembla is warm, and by a succession of deeds of injustice not to be washed out by the tears of all the recording angels of heaven.

The true greatness of a nation cannot be in triumphs of the intellect alone. Literature and art may widen the sphere of its influence; they may adorn it; but they are in their nature but accessories. The true grandeur of humanity is in moral elevation, sustained, enlightened, and decorated by the intellect of man. The truest tokens of this grandeur in a state are the diffusion of the greatest happiness among the greatest number, and that passionless, Godlike justice, which controls the relations of the state to other states, and to all the people who are committed to its charge. . . .

As we cast our eyes over the history of nations, we discern with horror the succession of murderous slaughters by which their progress had been marked. As the hunter traces the wild beast, when pursued to his lair, by the drops of blood on the earth; so we follow man, faint, weary staggering with wounds, through the black forest of the past, which he has reddened with his gore. Oh! let it not be in the future ages as in those which we now contemplate. Let the grandeur of man be discerned in the blessings which he has secured; in the good he has accomplished; in the triumphs of benevolence and justice; in the establishment of perpetual peace.

As the ocean washes every shore, and clasps with all-embracing arms every land, while it bears upon its heaving bosom the products of various climes; so peace surrounds, protects, and upholds all other blessings. Without it, commerce is vain, the ardor of industry is restrained, happiness is blasted, virtue sickens and dies.

And peace has its own peculiar victories, in comparison with which Marathon and Bannockburn and Bunker Hill, fields held sacred in the history of human freedom, shall lose their lustre. Our own Washington rises to a truly heavenly statue,—not when we follow him over the ice of the Delaware to the capture of Trenton; not when we behold him victorious over Cornwallis at Yorktown,—but when we regard him, in noble deference to justice, refusing the kingly crown which a faithless soldiery proffered, and at a later day upholding the peaceful neutrality of the country, while he received unmoved the clamor of the people wickedly crying for war. What glory of battle in England's annals will not fade by the side of that great act of justice, by which her legislature, at a cost of one hundred million dollars, gave freedom to eight hundred thousand slaves! And when the day shall come (may these eyes be gladdened by its beams!) that shall witness an act of greater justice still, the peaceful emancipation of three millions of our fellow-men, "guilty of a skin not colored as our own," now held in gloomy bondage, under the Constitution of our country, then shall there be a victory, in comparison with which that of Bunker Hill shall be as a farthing candle held up to the sun. That victory shall need no monument of stone. It shall be written on the grateful hearts of un-counted multitudes, that shall proclaim it to the latest generation. It shall be one of the links in the golden chain by which humanity shall connect itself with the throne of God.

As the cedars of Lebanon are higher than the grass of the valley; as the heavens are higher than the earth; as man is higher than the beasts of the field; as the angels are higher than man; as he that ruleth his spirit is higher than he that taketh a city; so are the virtues and victories of peace higher than the virtues and victories of war.

THE IRREPRESSIBLE CONFLICT

William H. Seward

(1801-1872)

William Seward was born in New York State where he pursued the study of law and was admitted to the bar in 1822. Although not a brilliant speaker Seward had a faculty of characterizing a situation by a few epigrammatical words which became memorable. Upon his election to the Senate in 1849 Seward in a debate on the occasion of the admission of California denounced slavery declaring that "there is a law higher than the constitution." This speech created a furor throughout the country. He also vigorously opposed the Kansas-Nebraska Bill. Again in October 1858 in a stump speech at Rochester, New York, he spoke of the antagonism between freedom and slavery as an "irrepressible conflict" which could only terminate by the United States becoming entirely a slave-holding nation or entirely free. This characterization was caught up and quoted far and wide. Upon the election of Lincoln to the presidency Seward became Secretary of State and filled that post for eight years supporting Lincoln throughout. After the war he entertained moderate views of reconstruction. Mr. Gladstone has called Seward's argument in the defense of the Negro in 1846 "the greatest forensic effort in the English language." We include here an abridgement of his speech, *The Irrepressible Conflict.*

The unmistakable outbreaks of zeal which occur all around me show that you are earnest men—and such a man am I. Let us, therefore, at least for a time, pass all secondary and collateral questions, whether of a personal or of a general nature, and consider the main subject of the present canvass.

Our country is a theater which exhibits in full operation two radically different political systems—the one resting on the basis of servile or slave labor, the other on the basis of voluntary labor of free-men.

The laborers who are enslaved are all negroes, or persons more or less purely of African derivation. But this is only accidental. The principle of the system is that labor in every society, by whomsoever performed, is necessarily unintellectual, groveling, and base; and that the laborer, equally for his own good and for the welfare of the State, ought to be enslaved. The white laboring man, whether native or foreigner, is not enslaved only because he cannot as yet be reduced to bondage.

You need not be told now that the slave system is the older of the two and that once it was universal. The emancipation of our own ancestors, Caucasians and Europeans as they were, hardly dates beyond a period of five hundred years. The great melioration of human society which modern times exhibit is mainly due to the incomplete substitution of the system of voluntary labor for the old one of servile labor which has already taken place. This African slave system is one which, in its origin and its growth, has been altogether foreign from the habits of the races which colonized these States and established civilization here. It was introduced on this new continent as an engine of conquest and for the establishment of monarchical power by the Portuguese and the Spaniards, and was rapidly extended by them all over South America, Central America, Louisiana, and Mexico. Its legitimate fruits are seen in the poverty, imbecility, and anarchy which now pervade all Portuguese and Spanish America.

The free-labor system is of German extraction, and it was established in our country by emigrants from Sweden, Holland, Germany, Great Britain and Ireland. We justly ascribe to its influences the strength, wealth, greatness, intelligence, and freedom which the whole American people now enjoy. One of the chief elements of the value of human life is freedom in the pursuit of happiness. The slave system is not only intolerable, unjust, and inhuman toward the laborer, whom, only because he is a laborer, it loads down with chains and converts into merchandise; but is scarcely less severe upon the freeman, to whom, only because he is a laborer from necessity, it denies facilities for employment and whom it expels from the community because it can not enslave and convert him into merchandise also. It is necessarily improvident and ruinous because, as a general truth, communities prosper and flourish, or droop and decline in just the degree that they practise or neglect to practise the primary duties of justice and humanity. The free-labor system conforms to the divine law of equality which is written in the hearts and consciences of men, and therefore is always and everywhere beneficent.

The slave system is one of constant danger, distrust, suspicion, and watchfulness. It debases those whose toil alone can produce wealth and resources for defense to the lowest degree of which human nature is capable—to guard against mutiny and insurrection; and thus wastes energies which otherwise might be employed in national development and aggrandizement.

Russia yet maintains slavery and is a despotism. Most of the other European states have abolished slavery and adopted the system of free labor. It was the antagonistic political tendencies of the two systems which the first Napoleon was contemplating when he predicted that Europe would ultimately be either all Cossack or all republican. Never did human sagacity utter a more pregnant truth. The two systems are at once perceived to be incongruous. But they are more than incongruous—they are incompatible. They never have permanently existed together in one country and they never can. It would be easy to demonstrate this impossibility from the irreconcilable contrast between their great principles and characteristics. But the experience of mankind has conclusively established it.

Slavery, as I have already intimated, existed in every State in Europe. Free labor has supplanted it everywhere except in Russia and Turkey. State necessities developed in modern times are now obliging even those two nations to encourage and employ free labor; and already, despotic as they are, we find them engaged in abolishing slavery. In the United States slavery came into collision with free labor at the close of the last century, and fell before it in New England, New York, New Jersey, and Pennsylvania, but triumphed over it effectually and excluded it for a period yet undetermined, from Virginia, the Carolinas, and Georgia. Indeed, so incompatible are the two systems that every new state which is organized within our ever-extending domain makes its first political act a choice of the one and the exclusion of the other, even at the cost of civil war if necessary. The slave state, without law, at the last national election successfully forbade, within their own limits, even the casting of votes for a candidate for president of the United States supposed to be favorable to the establishment of the free-labor system in new states.

Hitherto the two systems have existed in different states, but side by side within the American Union. This has happened because the Union is a confederation of states. But in another aspect the United States constitute only one nation. Increase of population, which is filling the states out to their very borders, together with a new and extended network of railroads and other avenues, and an internal commerce which daily becomes more intimate, is rapidly bringing the states into a higher and more perfect social unity or consolidation. Thus these antagonistic systems are continually coming into closer contact and collision results.

Shall I tell you what this collision means? They who think that it is accidental, unnecessary, the work of interested or fanatical agitators, and therefore ephemeral, mistake the case altogether. It is an irrepressible conflict between opposing and enduring forces, and it means that the United States must and will, sooner or later, become either entirely a slave-holding nation or entirely a free-labor nation. Either the cotton and rice fields of South Carolina and the sugar plantations of Louisiana will ultimately be tilled by free labor, and Charleston and New Orleans become marts for legitimate merchandise alone, or else the rye fields and wheat fields of Massachusetts and New York must again be surrendered by their farmers to slave culture and to the production of slaves, and Boston and New York become once more markets for trade in the bodies and souls of men.

It is the failure to apprehend this great truth that induces so many unsuccessful attempts at final compromise between the slave and free states, and it is the existence of this great fact that renders all such pretended compromises, when made, vain and ephemeral. Startling as this saying may appear to you, fellow citizens, it is by no means an original or even a modern one. Our forefathers knew it to be true, and unanimously acted upon it when they framed the Constitution of the United States. They regarded the existence of the servile system in so many of the States with sorrow and shame, which they openly confessed, and they looked upon the collision between them, which was then just revealing itself, and which we are now accustomed to deplore, with favor and hope. They knew that either the one or the other system must exclusively prevail.

Unlike too many of those who in modern time invoke their authority, they had a choice between the two. They preferred the system of free labor, and they determined to organize the government and so to direct its activity that that system should surely and certainly prevail. For this purpose, and no other, they based the whole structure of government broadly on the principle that all men are created equal, and therefore free—little dreaming that within the short period of one hundred years their descendants would bear to be told by any orator, however popular, that the utterance of that principle was merely a rhetorical rhapsody; or by any judge, however venerated, that it was attended by mental reservations which rendered it hypocritical and false. By the Ordinance of 1787 they dedicated all of the national domain not yet polluted by slavery to free labor immediately, thenceforth and forever; while by the new Constitution and laws they invited foreign free labor from all lands under the sun, and interdicted the importation of African slave labor, at all times, in all places, and under all circumstances whatsoever. It is true that they necessarily and wisely modified this policy of freedom by leaving it to the several states, affected as they were by differing circumstances, to abolish slavery in their own way and at their own pleasure, instead of confiding that duty to Congress; and that they secured to the slave states, while yet retaining the system of slavery, a three-fifths representation of slaves in the federal government, until they should find themselves able to relinquish it with safety. But the very nature of these modifications fortifies my position—that the fathers knew that the two systems could not endure within the Union, and expected that within a short period slavery would disappear forever. Moreover, in order that these modifications might not altogether defeat their grand design of a republic maintaining universal equality, they provided that two-third of the states might amend the Constitution.

ON SECESSION

Robert Toombs

(1810-1885)

Robert Toombs, the Mirabeau of the South, was born in Georgia, studied law at Union College, and was admitted to the bar by a special act of the legislature before he attained his majority. In 1844 he became a member of Congress and held his seat there until his resignation in 1861. He became a member of the first confederate congress; and served throughout the war as confederate secretary of war, senator, and brigadier-general. After the war he refused to take the oath of allegiance to the United States.

As an orator Toombs had remarkable fluency, fervor, and daring. He was the South's leader in the secession movement. A portion of his audacious and defiant farewell to Congress delivered in the United States Senate January 7, 1861, is presented here.

SENATORS, the Constitution is a compact. It contains all our obligations and the duties of the Federal Government. I am content, and have ever been content to sustain it. While I doubt its perfection, while I do not believe it was a good compact, and while I never saw the day that I would have voted for it as a proposition *de novo*, yet I am bound to it by oath and by that common prudence which would induce men to abide by established forms rather than to rush into unknown dangers. I have given to it, and intend to give to it, unfaltering support and allegiance; but I choose to put that allegiance on the true ground, not on the false idea that anybody's blood was shed for it. I say that the Constitution is the whole compact. All the obligations, all the chains that fetter the limbs of my people, are nominated in the bond, and they wisely excluded any conclusion against them by declaring "that the powers not granted by the Constitution to the United States, or forbidden by it to the States, belonged to the States respectively or the people." Now I will try it by that standard; I will subject it to that test. The law of nature, the law of justice, would say—and it is so expounded by the publicists—that equal rights in the common property shall be enjoyed. Even in a monarchy the king cannot prevent the subjects from enjoying equality in the disposition of the public property. Even in a despotic government this principle is recognized. It was the blood and the money of the whole people, says the learned Grotius, and say all the publicists, which acquired the public property, and therefore it is not the property of the sovereign. This right of equality being, then, according to justice and natural equity, a right belonging to all the States, when did we give it up? You say Congress has a right to pass rules and regulations concerning the territory and other property of the United States. Very well. Does that exclude those whose blood and money paid for it? Does "dispose of" mean to rob the rightful owners? You must show a better title than that, or a better sword than we have.

But, you say, try the right. I agree to it. But how? By our judgment? No, not until the last resort. What then? By yours? No, not until the same time. How then try it? The South has always said, by the Supreme Court. But that is in our favor, and Lincoln says he will not stand that judgment. Then each must judge for himself of the mode and manner or redress. But you deny us that privilege, and finally reduce us to accepting our judgment. The senator from Kentucky comes to your aid, and says he can find no constitutional right of secession. Perhaps not; but the Constitution is not the place to look for state rights. If that right belongs to independent states, and they did not cede it to the Federal Government, it is reserved to the states or to the people. Ask your new commentator where he gets the right to judge for us. Is it in the bond?

The northern doctrine was, many years ago, that the Supreme Court was the judge. That was their doctrine in 1800. They denounced Madison for the report of 1799 on the Virginia Resolutions; they denounced Jefferson for framing the Kentucky Resolutions, because they were presumed to impugn the decisions of the Supreme Court of the United States; and they declared that that court was made by the Constitution the ultimate and supreme arbiter. That was the universal judgment, the declaration of every free state in this Union, in answer to the Virginia Resolutions of 1798, or of all who did answer, even including the state of Delaware, then under Federal control.

The Supreme Court has decided that, by the Constitution, we have a right to go to the territories and be protected there with our property. You say, we cannot decide the compact for ourselves. Well, can the Supreme Court decide it for us? Mr. Lincoln says he does not care what the Supreme Court decides, he will turn us out anyhow. He says this in his debate with the honorable member from Illinois. I have it before me. He said he would vote against the decision of the Supreme Court. Then you did not accept that arbiter. You will not take my construction; you will not take the Supreme Court as an arbiter; you will not take the practice of the Government; you will not take the treaties under Jefferson and Madison; you will not take the opinion of Madison upon the very question of prohibition in 1820. What, then, will you take? You will take nothing but your own judgment; that is, you will not only judge for yourselves, not only discard the court, discard our construction, discard the practice of the Government, but you will drive us out, simply because you will it. Come and do it! You have sapped the foundations of society; you have destroyed almost all hope of peace. In a compact where there is no common arbiter, where the parties finally decide for themselves, the sword alone becomes at last the real, if not the constitutional arbiter. Your party says that you will not take the decision of the Supreme Court. You said so at Chicago; you said so in committee; every man of you in both Houses says so. What are you going to do? You say we shall submit to your construction. We shall do it, if you can make us; but not otherwise, or in any other manner. That is settled. You may call it secession, or you may call it revolution; but there is a big fact standing before you, ready to oppose you: that fact is, freemen with arms in their hands. The cry of the Union will not disperse them; we have passed that point; they demand equal rights; you had better heed the demand.

FAREWELL TO CONGRESS

Jefferson Davis

(1808-1889)

Jefferson Davis, president of the Confederate States of America, was a Kentuckian, a graduate of West Point, and a scholar of the highest order. He entered political life in 1843 and in 1845 was sent to Congress where he served in the House and Senate. In 1853 he became Secretary of War. John Quincy Adams upon hearing his first speech in the Senate remarked, "That young man, gentleman, is no ordinary man; he will make his mark yet." Later Davis became the South's able orator and leader on the question of states rights and secession and the guiding spirit in the formation of the confederacy. He was a polished speaker, for his education and literary taste gave him a choice and fluent diction. Included here is his *Farewell To Congress*, delivered in the United States Senate to a crowded audience on January 21, 1861.

I rise, Mr. President, for the purpose of announcing to the Senate that I have satisfactory evidence that the State of Mississippi, by a solemn ordinance of her people in convention assembled, has declared her separation from the United States. Under these circumstances, of course my functions are terminated here. It has seemed to me proper, however, that I should appear in the Senate to announce that fact to my associates, and I will say but very little more. The occasion does not invite me to go into argument, and my physical condition would not permit me to do so if it were otherwise; and yet it seems to become me to say something on the part of the State I here represent on an occasion so solemn as this.

It is known to senators who have served with me here that I have for many years advocated, as an essential attribute of State sovereignty, the right of a state to secede from the Union. Therefore, if I had not believed there was justifiable cause; if I had thought that Mississippi was acting without sufficient provocation, or without an existing necessity, I should still, under my theory of the government, because of my allegiance to the State of which I am a citizen, have been bound by her action. I, however, may be permitted to say that I do think that she has justifiable cause, and I approve of her act. I conferred with her people before the act was taken, counseled them then that if the state of things which they apprehended should exist when the convention met, they should take the action which they have now adopted.

I hope none who hear me will confound this expression of mine with the advocacy of the right of a State to remain in the Union, and to disregard its constitutional obligations by the nullification of the law. Such is not my theory. Nullification and secession, so often confounded, are indeed antagonistic principles. Nullification is a remedy which it is sought to apply within the Union, and against the agent of the States. It is only to be justified when the agent has violated his constitutional obligation, and a State, assuming to judge for itself, denies the right of the agent thus to act, and appeals to the other States of the Union for a decision; but when the States themselves, and when the people of the States, have so acted as to convince us that they will not regard our constitutional rights then, and then for the first time, arises the doctrine of secession in its practical application.

A great man who now reposes with his fathers, and who has been often arraigned for a want of fealty to the Union, advocated the doctrine of nullification because it preserved the Union. It was because of his deep-seated attachment to the Union, his determination to find some remedy for existing ills short of a severance of the ties which bound South Carolina to the other States, that Mr. Calhoun advocated the doctrine of nullification, which he proclaimed to be peaceful, to be within the limits of State power, not to disturb the Union, but only to be a means of bringing the agent before the tribunal of the States for their judgment.

Secession belongs to a different class of remedies. It is to be justified upon the basis that the States are sovereign. There was a time when none denied it. I hope the time may come again when a better comprehension of the theory of our government, and the inalienable rights of the people of the States, will prevent any one from denying that each State is a sovereign, and thus may reclaim the grants which it has made to any agent whomsoever.

I therefore say I concur in the action of the people of Mississippi, believing it to be necessary and proper, and should have been bound by their action if my belief had been otherwise; and this brings me to the important point which I wish on this last occasion to present to the Senate. It is by this confounding of nullification and secession that the name of the great man, whose ashes now mingle with his mother earth, has been invoked to justify coercion against a seceded State. The phrase "to execute the laws" was an expression which General Jackson applied to the case of a State refusing to obey the laws while yet a member of the Union. That is not the case which is now presented.

The laws are to be executed over the United States, and upon the people of the United States. They have no relation to any foreign country. It is a perversion of terms, at least it is a great misapprehension of the case, which cites that expression for application to a State which has withdrawn from the Union. You may make war on a foreign State. If it be the purpose of gentlemen, they may make war against a State which has withdrawn from the Union; but there are no laws of the United States to be executed within the limits of a seceded State. A State finding herself in the condition in which Mississippi has judged she is, in which her safety requires that she should provide for the maintenance of her rights out of the Union, surrenders all the benefits (and they are known to be many), deprives herself of the advantages (they are known to be great), severs all the ties of affection (and they are close and enduring), which have bound her to the Union; and thus divesting herself of every benefit, taking upon herself every burden, she claims to be exempt from any power to execute the laws of the United States within her limits.

I well remember an occasion when Massachusetts was arraigned before the bar of the Senate, and when then the doctrine of coercion was rife and to be applied against her because of the rescue of a fugitive slave in Boston. My opinion then was the same that it is now. Not in a spirit of egotism, but to show that I am not influenced in my opinion because the case is my own, I refer to that time and that occasion as containing the opinion which I then entertained, and on which my present conduct is based. I then said, if Massachusetts, following her through a stated line of conduct, chooses to take the last step which separates her from the Union, it is her right to go, and I will neither vote one dollar nor one man to coerce her back; but will say to her, Godspeed, in memory of the kind associations which once existed between her and the other States.

It has been a conviction of pressing necessity, it has been a belief that we are to be deprived in the Union of the rights which our fathers bequeathed to us, which has brought Mississippi into her present decision. She has heard proclaimed the theory that all men are created free and equal, and this made the basis of an attack upon her social institutions; and the sacred Declaration of Independence has been invoked to maintain the position of the equality of the races. That Declaration of Independence is to be construed by the circumstances and purposes for which it was made. The communities were declaring their independence; the people of those communities were asserting that no man was born— to use the language of Mr. Jefferson—booted and spurred to ride over the rest of mankind; that men were created equal—meaning the men of the political community; that there was no divine right to rule; that no man inherited the right to govern; that there were no classes by which power and place descended to families, but that all stations were equally within the grasp of each member of the body politic. These were the great principles they announced; these were the purposes for which they made their declaration; these were the ends to which their enunciation was directed. They have no reference to the slave, else how happened it that among the items of arraignment made against George III was that he endeavored to do just what the North had been endeavoring of late to do—to stir up insurrection among our slaves? Had the Declaration announced that the negroes were free and equal, how was the prince to be arraigned for stirring up insurrection among them? And how was this to be enumerated among the high crimes which caused the Colonies to sever their connection with the mother country? When our Constitution was formed the same idea was rendered more palpable, for there we find provision made for that very class of persons as property; they were not put upon the footing of equality with white men—not even upon that of paupers and convicts; but, so far as representation was concerned, were discriminated against as a lower caste, only to be represented in the numerical proportion of three-fifths.

Then, senators, we recur to the compact which binds us together; we recur to the principles upon which our government was founded; and when you deny them, and when you deny to us the right to withdraw from a government which, thus perverted, threatens to be destructive of our rights, we but tread in the path of our fathers when we proclaim our independence, and take the hazard.

I find in myself, perhaps, a type of the general feeling of my constituents toward yours. I am sure I feel no hostility to you senators from the North. I am sure there is not one of you, whatever sharp discussion there may have been between us, to whom I cannot now say, in the presence of my God, I wish you well; and such, I am sure, is the feeling of the people whom I represent toward those whom you represent. I therefore feel that I but express their desire when I say I hope, and they hope, for peaceful relations with you, though we must part. They may be mutually beneficial to us in the future, as they have been in the past, if you so will it. The reverse may bring disaster on every portion of the country; and if you will have it thus, we will invoke the God of our fathers, who delivered them from the power of the lion, to protect us from the ravages of the bear; and thus, putting our trust in God, and in our firm hearts and strong arms, we will vindicate the right as best we may.

In the course of my service here, associated at different times with a great variety of senators, I see now around me some with whom I have served long; there have been points of collision; but whatever of offense there has been to me, I leave here; I carry with me no hostile remembrance. Whatever offense I have given which has not been redressed, or for which satisfaction has not been demanded, I have, senators, in this hour of our parting, to offer you my apology for any pain which, in heat of discussion, I have inflicted. I go hence unencumbered of the remembrance of any injury received, and having discharged the duty of making the only reparation in my power for any injury offered.

Mr. President and senators, having made the announcement which the occasion seemed to me to require, it only remains for me to bid you a final adieu.

DISCOURSE ON THE DEATH OF DANIEL WEBSTER

Theodore Parker

(1810-1860)

Theodore Parker, one of the greatest pulpit orators of New England during the years of the slavery agitation, was not only a great orator but an ardent reformer. He was born in Lexington, Massachusetts; was graduated from Harvard University; and was ordained to the ministry, preaching his ordination sermon in the South Church at Boston in 1841 on *The Transient and Permanent in Christianity,* an epoch making sermon in the Unitarian faith. In his subsequent speeches Parker dwelt on subjects of theology, social reform, and slavery, becoming more and more virulent in his agitations for abolition. Parker's most famous speeches are his *Eulogy of John Quincy Adams* in 1848 and his *Discourse on the Death of Daniel Webster,* delivered in 1852. Portions of the latter address are included here.

Do men mourn for him, the great man eloquent? I put on sackcloth long ago. I mourned for him when he wrote the Creole letter which surprised Ashburton, Briton that he was. I mourned when he spoke the speech of the Seventh of March. I mourned when the Fugitive Slave Bill passed Congress, and the same cannon that had fired "minute guns" for him fired also one hundred rounds of joy for the forging of a new fetter for the fugitive's foot. I mourned for him, when the kidnappers first came to Boston—hated then—now respectable men, the companions of princes, enlarging their testimony in the courts. I mourned when my own parishioners fled from the "stripes" of New England to the "stars" of Old England. I mourned when Ellen Craft fled to my house for shelter and for succor, and for the first time in all my life, I armed this hand. I mourned when the courthouse was hung in chains, when Thomas Simms, from his dungeon, sent out his petition for prayers and the churches did not dare to pray. I mourned when I married William and Ellen Craft, and gave them a Bible for their soul, and a sword to keep that soul living, and in a living frame. I mourned when the poor outcast in yonder dungeon sent for me to visit him, and, when I took him by the hand that Daniel Webster was chaining in that house. I mourned for Webster when we prayed our prayer and sung our psalm on Long Wharf in the morning's gray. I mourned then, I shall not cease to mourn. The flags will be removed from the streets, the cannons will sound their other notes of joy, but for me I shall go mourning all my days. I shall refuse to be comforted, and at last I shall lay down my gray hairs with weeping and with sorrow in the grave. O, Webster! Webster! would God that I had died for thee!

He was a great man, a man of the largest mould, a great body and a great brain, he seemed made to last a hundred years. Since Socrates there has seldom been a head so massive, so huge—seldom such a face since the stormy features of Michael Angelo—he who sculptured day and night into such beautiful forms,—he looked them in his face before he chiselled them in stone. In the Senate of the United States, he looked an emperor in that council. Even the majestic Calhoun seemed common compared with him. Clay looked vulgar, and Van Buren but a box. What a mouth he had! It was a lion's mouth. Yet there was a sweet grandeur in his smile, and a woman's sweetness when he would. What a brow it was! What eyes! like charcoal fire in the bottom of a deep, dark well. His face was rugged with volcanic fires, great passions, and great thoughts.

You remember the last time he spoke in Boston—the procession last summer. You remember it well. What a sad and careworn countenance was that of the old man, welcomed with their mockery of applause! You remember when the orator, wise-headed and friendly hearted, came to thank him for his services, he said not a word of saving the Union, of the compromise measures, not a word; but for his own great services he thanked him.

And when Webster replied, he said: "Here in Boston I am not disowned—at least here I am not disowned." No, Daniel Webster! you were not disowned in Boston. So long as I have a tongue to teach, a heart to feel, you shall never be disowned. It was by our sin, by Boston's sin, that the great man fell! I pity his victims; you pity them too. But I pity him more; oh, far more. Pity the oppressed, will you? Will you not pity the oppressor in his sin?

Look there. See that face, so manly strong, so maiden meek. Hear that voice: "Neither do I condemn thee. Go, and sin no more." Listen to the last words of the crucified: "Father, forgive them, for they know not what they do."

The last time he was in Faneuil Hall—it was Faneuil Hall open; once it had been shut—it was last June, the sick old man—you remember the feeble look and the sad face. I felt then that it was his last time, and forebore to look upon that saddened countenance. The last time he was in the Senate, it was to hear his successor speak. He stayed an hour, and heard Charles Sumner demonstrate that the Fugitive Slave

Bill was not good religion, nor good morality, nor good constitution, nor good law.

He came home to Boston and went down to Marshfield to die. An old man, broken with the storms of state, went home—to die! To him, to die was gain; life was the only loss. His friends were about him; his dear ones—his wife, his son (the last of six children he had loved). Name by name he bade them all farewell, and all his friends, man by man. Two colored servants of his were there—men that he had bought out of slavery and had blessed with freedom and life. They watched over the bedside of the dying man. The kindly doctors thought to sweeten the bitterness of death with medicated skill, and when that failed, he gave the great man a little manna that fell down from heaven three thousand years ago, and the shepherd David gathered it up and kept it in a psalm:—

"The Lord is my shepherd. Though I walk through the valley of the shadow of death, I will fear no evil, Thy rod and thy staff they comfort me."

And the great man faltered out his last words: "That is what I want—thy rod, thy rod; thy staff, thy staff." That great heart had never renounced God. Oh, no! It had scoffed at his "higher law," but in the heart of hearts there was religion still!

Just four years after his great speech, on the twenty-fourth of October, the mortal Daniel Webster went down to the dust, and the soul to the motherly bosom of God! Men mourn for him; he heeds it not. He needs not pity. The great man has gone where the servant is free from his master; where the weary are at rest; where the wicked cease from troubling.

Massachusetts has lost her great adopted son. Has lost! Oh, no! "I still live" is truer than the sick man knew.

His memory will long live with us, still dear to many a loving heart. What honor shall we pay? Let the State go out mindful of his noblest services, yet tearful for his fate, sad that he would fain have filled him with the husks the swine do eat, and no man gave to him. Sad and tearful, let her remember the force of circumstance and dark temptation's secret power. Let her remember that while we know what he yielded to, and what his sin, God knows what also he resisted, and He alone knows who the sinner is. The dear old mother of us all! Oh, let her warn her children to fling away ambition, and let her charge them, every one, that there is a God who must, indeed, be worshipped and a higher law of God which must be kept though gold and Union fail. Then let her say to them: "Ye have dwelt long enough in this mountain; turn ye and take your journey into the land of Freedom, which the Lord your God giveth you!"

THE FORT SUMTER FLAG-RAISING ADDRESS

Henry Ward Beecher

(1813-1887)

Henry Ward Beecher, the great pulpit orator of Plymouth Church, Brooklyn, New York, was born in Connecticut, educated in New England and Lane Seminary in Ohio and ordained to the Presbyterian ministry. In 1847 he was called to the Plymouth Church in Brooklyn and occupied that pulpit for forty years, making his church a mecca for religious pilgrims from two continents and a shrine of patriotism for all Americans. His greatest agitation against slavery was on the Clay Compromise Measures of 1850. From the start he was a close adviser of Abraham Lincoln and his influence was apparent in the Emancipation Proclamation. In 1863 he took a three months' leave to visit Europe and there addressed large audiences on the subject of slavery and the Civil War. Until the close of the war he strongly supported Lincoln and afterward became active in the discussion of the problems of reconstruction.

Beecher was an extremely effective speaker. As a reformer, statesman, and orator he will stand forever in the foremost ranks while as a pulpiteer his name ranks with Chrysostom, Bernard, Luther, Whitefield, and Spurgeon. Among his famous speeches are his *Lectures to Young Men* (1841); *Lecture to the American and Foreign Anti-Slavery Society* (1851); *Liverpool Address* (1863); *The Fort Sumter Flag-Raising Address* (1865); *Memorial Sermon for Lincoln* (1865); and *Yale Lectures on Preaching* (1872).

On this solemn and joyful day we again lift to the breeze our fathers' flag, now again the banner of the United States, with the fervent prayer that God would crown it with honor, protect it from treason, and send it down to our children, with all the blessings of civilization, liberty, and religion. Terrible in battle, may it be beneficent in peace. Happily, no bird or beast of prey has been inscribed upon it. The stars that redeem the night from darkness, and the beams of red light that beautify the morning, have been united upon its folds. As long as the sun endures, or the stars, may it wave over a nation neither enslaved nor enslaving! Once, and but once, has treason dishonored it. In that insane hour when the guiltiest and bloodiest rebellion of all time hurled its fires upon this fort, you, sir (turning to General Anderson), and a small heroic band, stood within these now crumbled walls, and did gallant and just battle for the honor and defense of the nation's banner. In that cope with fire, that glorious flag still peacefully waved to the breeze above your head, unconscious of harm as the stars and skies above it. Once it was shot down. A gallant hand, in whose care this day it has been, plucked it from the ground, and reared it again—"cast down, but not destroyed." After a vain resistance, with trembling hand and sad heart, you withdrew it from its height, closed its wings, and bore it far away, sternly to sleep amid the tumults of rebellion and the thunder of battle. The first act of war had begun. The long night of four years had set it. While the giddy traitors whirled in a maze of exhilaration, dim horrors were already advancing, that were ere long to fill the land with blood. To-day you are returned again. We devoutly join with you in thanksgiving to Almighty God that He has spared your honored life, and vouchsafed to you the honors of this day. The heavens over you are the same, the same shores; morning comes, and evening, as they did. All else, how changed! What grim batteries crowd the burdened shores! What scenes have filled this air and disturbed these waters! These shattered heaps of shapeless stone are all that is left of Fort Sumter. Desolation broods in yonder sad city—solemn retribution hath avenged our dishonored banner! You have come back with honor, who departed hence four years ago, leaving the air sultry with fanaticism. The surging crowds that rolled up their frenzied shouts as the flag came down, are dead, or scattered, or silent, and their habitations are desolate. Ruin sits in the cradle of treason. Rebellion has perished. But there flies the same flag that was insulted. With starry eyes it looks all over this bay for the banner that supplanted it, and sees it not. You that then, for the day, were humbled, are here again, to triumph once and forever. In the storm of that assault this glorious ensign was often struck; but, memorable fact, not one of its stars was torn out by shot or shell. It was a prophecy. It said: "Not one state shall be struck from this nation by treason!" The fulfillment is at hand. Lifted to the air to-day, it proclaims that after four years of war, "not a state is blotted out." Hail to the flag of our fathers, and our flag! Glory to the banner that has gone through four years black with tempests of war, to pilot the nation back to peace without dismemberment! And glory be to God, who, above all hosts and banners, hath ordained victory, and shall ordain peace. Wherefore have we come hither, pilgrims from distant places? Are we come to exult that northern hands are stronger than southern? No, but to rejoice that the hands of those who defended a just and beneficent government are mightier than the hands that assaulted it. Do we exult over fallen cities? We exult that a nation has not fallen. We sorrow with the sorrowful. We sympathize with the desolate. We look upon this shattered fort and yonder dilapidated city with sad eyes, grieved that men should have committed such treason, and glad that God hath set such a mark upon treason that all ages shall dread and abhor it. We exult, not for a passion gratified, but for a sentiment victorious; not for temper, but for conscience; not, as we devoutly believe, that our will is done, but that God's will hath been done. We should be unworthy of that liberty entrusted to our care, if, on such a day as this, we sullied our hearts by feelings of aimless vengeance, and equally unworthy if we did not devoutly thank Him who hath said: "Vengeance is mine; I will repay saith the Lord," that He hath set a mark upon arrogant rebellion, ineffaceable while time lasts.

Since this flag went down on that dark day, who shall tell the mighty woes that have made this land a spectacle to angels and men? The soil has drunk blood and is glutted. Millions mourn for millions slain, or, envying the dead, pray for oblivion. Towns and villages have been razed. Fruitful fields have turned back to wilderness. It came to pass, as the prophet said: "The sun was turned to darkness, and the moon to blood." The course of law was ended. The sword sat chief magistrate in half the nation; industry was paralyzed; morals corrupted; the public weal invaded by rapine and anarchy; whole states ravaged by avenging armies. The world was amazed. The earth reeled. When the flag sank here, it was as if political night had come, and all beasts of prey had come forth to devour. That long night has ended. And for this returning day we have come from afar to rejoice and give thanks. No more war. No more accursed secession. No more slavery, that spawned them both. Let no man misread the meaning of this unfolding flag! It says: "Government hath returned hither." It proclaims, in the name of vindicated government, peace and protection to loyalty, humiliation and pains to traitors. This is the flag of sovereignty. The nation, not the states, is sovereign. Restored to authority, this flag commands, not supplicates. There may be pardon, but no concession. There may be amnesty and oblivion, but no honeyed compromises. The nation today has peace for the peaceful, and war for the turbulent. The only condition of submission is to submit! There is the Constitution, there are the laws, there is the government. They rise up like mountains of strength that shall not be moved. They are the conditions of peace. One nation, under one government, without slavery, has been ordained, and shall stand. There can be peace on no other basis. On this basis reconstruction is easy, and needs neither architect nor engineer. Without this basis no engineer or architect shall ever reconstruct these rebellious states. We do not want your cities nor your fields. We do not envy you your prolific soil, nor heavens full of perpetual summer. Let agriculture revel here; let manufacturers make every stream twice musical; build fleets in every port; inspire the arts of peace and genius second only to that of Athens, and we shall be glad in your gladness, and rich in your wealth. All that we ask is unswerving loyalty and universal liberty. And that, in the name of this high sovereignty of the United States of America, we demand; and that, with the blessing of Almighty God, we will have! We raise our fathers' banner that it may bring back better blessings than those of old; that it may cast out the devil of discord; that it may restore lawful government, and a prosperity purer and more enduring than that which it protected before; that it may win parted friends from their alienation; that it may inspire hope, and inaugurate universal liberty; that it may say to the sword, "Return to thy sheath"; and to the plow and sickle, "Go forth"; that it may heal all jealousies, unite all policies, inspire a new national life, compact our strength, purify our principles, ennoble our national ambitions, and make this people great and strong, not for aggression and quarrelsomeness, but for the peace of the world, giving to us the glorious prerogative of leading all nations to juster laws, to more humane policies, to sincerer friendship, to rational, instituted civil liberty, and to universal Christian brotherhood. Reverently, piously, in hopeful patriotism, we spread this banner on the sky, as of old the bow was painted on the cloud, and, with solemn fervor, beseech God to look upon it and make it a memorial of an everlasting covenant and decree that never again on this fair land shall a deluge of blood prevail. Why need any eye turn from this spectacle? Are there not associations which, overleaping the recent past, carry us back to times when, over North and South, this flag was honored alike by all? In all our colonial days we were one; in the long revolutionary struggle and in the scores of prosperous years succeeding. When the passage of the Stamp Act in 1765 aroused the colonies, it was Gadsden, of South Carolina, that cried, with prescient enthusiasm, "We stand on the broad common ground of those natural rights that we all feel and know as men. There ought to be no New England man, no New Yorker, known on this continent, but all of us," said he, "Americans." That was the voice of South Carolina. That shall be the voice of South Carolina. Faint is the echo; but it is coming. We now hear it sighing sadly through the pines; but it shall yet break in thunder upon the shore. No North, no West, no South, but one United States of America. There is scarcely a man born in the South who has lifted his hand against this banner but had a father who would have died for it. Is memory dead? Is there no historic pride? Has a fatal fury struck blindness or hate into eyes that used to look kindly toward each other, that read the same Bible, that hung over the historic pages of our national glory, that studied the same Constitution? Let this uplifting bring back all of the past that was good, but leave in darkness all that was bad. It was never before so wholly unspotted, so clear of all wrong, so purely and simply the sign of justice and liberty. Did I say that we brought back the same banner that you bore away, noble and heroic sir? It is not the same. It is more and better than it was. The land is free from slavery since that banner fell.

.   .   .   .   .

We have shown, by all that we have suffered in war, how great is our estimate of the importance of the Southern States of this Union; and we will measure that estimate, now, in peace, by still greater exertions for their rebuilding. Will reflecting men not perceive, then, the wisdom of accepting established facts, and, with alacrity of enterprise, begin to retrieve the past? Slavery cannot come back. It is the interest, therefore, of every man to hasten its end. Do you want more war? Are you not yet weary of contest? Will you gather up the unexploded fragments of this prodigious magazine of all mischief, and heap them up for continued explosions? Does not the South need peace? And, since free labor is inevitable, will you have it in its worst forms or in its best? Shall it be ignorant, impertinent, indolent, or shall it be educated, self-respecting, moral, and self-supporting? Will you have men as drudges, or will you have them as citizens? Since they have vindicated the government, and cemented its foundation stones with their blood, may they not offer the tribute of their support to maintain its laws and its policy? It is better for religion; it is better for political integrity; it is better for industry; it is better for money—if you will have that ground motive—that you should educate the black man, and, by education, make him a citizen. They who refuse education to the black man would turn the South into a vast poorhouse, and labor into a pendulum, incessantly vibrating between poverty and indolence. From this pulpit of broken stone we speak forth our earnest greeting to all our land. We offer to the President of these United States our solemn congratulations that God has sustained his life and health under the unparralleled burdens and sufferings of four bloody years, and permitted him to behold this auspicious consummation of that national unity for which he has waited with so much patience and fortitude, and for which he has labored with such disinterested wisdom. To the members of the government associated with him in the administration of perilous affairs in critical times; to the senators and representatives of the United States, who have eagerly fashioned the instruments by which the popular will might express and enforce itself, we tender our grateful thanks. To the officers and men of the army and navy, who have so faithfully, skillfully, and gloriously upheld their country's authority, by suffering, labor, and sublime courage, we offer here a tribute beyond the compass of words. Upon those true and faithful citizens, men and women, who have borne up with unflinching hope in the darkest hour, and covered the land with the labors of love and charity, we invoke the divinest blessing of Him whom they have so truly imitated. But chiefly, to Thee, God of our fathers, we render thanksgiving and praise for that wondrous providence that has brought forth from such a harvest of war the seed of so much liberty and peace. We invoke peace upon the North. Peace be to the West. Peace be upon the South! In the name of God we lift up our banner, and dedicate it to peace, union, and liberty, now and forevermore! Amen.

THE KANSAS-NEBRASKA BILL

Stephen A. Douglas

(1813-1860)

"The Little Giant," as Stephen Douglas was called by his followers, was born in Vermont, received but a scanty education due to poverty, but by perseverence gained admission to the bar in 1834 and by 1841 was elected Supreme Court judge in Illinois. This position he resigned to enter Congress in 1843. It was in the Senate that he supported Clay's Compromise Bill of 1850 and initiated the doctrine known as "popular sovereignty," often called "squatter sovereignty," because it advocated leaving to the people of each territory the decision of admission as a free or slave state. Douglas's name became most intimately associated with the passage of the Kansas-Nebraska Bill of 1854, which repealed the Missouri Compromise and by granting popular sovereignty created in opposition to the Democratic party a new Republican party. It was this party which elected Lincoln president and thus indirectly assumed responsibility for the Civil War. Quite paradoxically Douglas was on three successive occasions (1852-1856-1860) nominated for the presidency and in the last instance was defeated by Abraham Lincoln.

In 1858 Lincoln and Douglas entered into their famous oratorical combat in the campaign for a seat in the Senate from the state of Illinois. Douglas overthrew Lincoln in this battle, but two years later when the two rivals met again in competition this time for the presidency, Lincoln was victorious. It is to Douglas's credit that he nevertheless threw his energies into the support of the government although he died before the actual conflict of the war fully began.

As a speaker Douglas had great quickness of thought and a fluency of language which frequently discomfitted his opponent.

His diminutive stature was over-balanced by a great mental power and a forcefulness of delivery which was always at its best in debate. The joint debates with Lincoln are splendid examples of a homely but effective style of oratory, but his most brilliant exhibition of eloquence was that delivered in support of the Kansas-Nebraska Bill after midnight on March 3, 1854. The preoration of this speech is included here.

Mr. President: It has been urged in debate that there is no necessity for the organization of these Territorial governments; and I have been called upon to point out any public and national considerations which require action at this time.

Senators seem to forget that our immense and valuable possessions on the Pacific are separated from the States and organized Territories on this side of the Rocky Mountains by a vast wilderness, filled by hostile savages—that nearly a hundred thousand emigrants pass through this barbarous wilderness every year, on their way to California and Oregon—that the emigrants are American citizens, our own constituents, who are entitled to the protection of law and government, and that they are left to make their way, as best they may, without the protection or aid of law or government. The United States mails for New Mexico and Utah, and official communications between this government and the authorities of those Territories are required to be carried over these wild plains, and through the gorges of the mountains, where you have made no provisions for roads, bridges, or ferries to facilitate travel, or forts or other means of safety to protect life.

As often as I have brought forward and urged the adoption of measures to remedy these evils, and afford security against the damages to which our people are constantly exposed, they have been promptly voted down as not being of sufficient importance to command the favorable consideration of Congress. Now, when I propose to organize the Territories, and allow the people to do for themselves what you have so often refused to do for them, I am told that there are not white inhabitants enough permanently settled in the country to require and sustain a government. True; there is not a very large population there, for the very reason that your Indian code and intercourse laws exclude the settlers, and forbid their remaining there to cultivate the soil. You refuse to throw the country open to settlers, and then object to the organization of the Territories, upon the ground that there is not a sufficient number of inhabitants.

Mr. President, I should like to bring forward for your consideration the great principle involved in this bill, without omitting, however, to notice some of those extraneous matters which have been brought into this discussion with the view of producing another anti-slavery agitation.

The opponents of this measure wish to have people believe that the abrogation of what they call the Missouri Compromise was the main object and aim of the bill, and that the only question involved is, whether the prohibition of slavery north of thirty-six degrees thirty minutes shall be repealed or not? That which is a mere incident they choose to consider the principle. They make war on the means by which we propose to accomplish an object, instead of openly resisting the object itself. The principle which we propose to carry into effect by the bill is this: That Congress shall neither legislate slavery into any Territories or State, nor out of the same; but the people shall be left free to regulate their domestic concerns in their own way, subject only to the Constitution of the United States.

Now, sir, if opponents of this measure have entire confidence in the correctness of their own position, why do they not meet the issue boldly and fairly, and controvert the soundness of this great principle of popular sovereignty in obedience to the Constitution? They know full well that this was the principle upon which the colonies separated from the crown of Great Britain, the principle upon which the battles of the Revolution were fought, and the principle upon which our republican system was founded. They cannot be ignorant of the fact that the Revolution grew out of the assertion of the right on the part of the imperial government to interfere with the internal affairs and domestic concerns of the colonies.

The Declaration of Independence had its origin in the violation of that great fundamental principle which secured to the colonies the right to regulate their own domestic affairs in their own way; and the Revolution resulted in the triumph of that principle, and the recognition of the right asserted by it. Abolitionism proposes to destroy the right and extinguish the principle for which our forefathers waged a seven years' bloody war, and upon which our whole system of free government is founded. They not only deny the application of this principle to the Territories, but insist upon fastening the prohibition upon all the States to be formed out of those Territories.

The doctrine, therefore, of the Abolitionists—the doctrine of the opponents of the Nebraska and Kansas Bill, and the advocates of the Missouri restriction—demands Congressional interference with slavery not only in the Territories, but in all the new States to be formed therefrom. It is the same doctrine, when applied to the Territories and new States of this Union, which the British government attempted to enforce by the sword upon the American colonies.

The opponents of the bill tell us that agitation is no part of their policy; that their great desire is peace and harmony; and they complain bitterly that I should have disturbed the repose of the country by the introduction of this measure! Let me ask these professed friends of peace, and avowed enemies of agitation, how the issue could have been avoided. They tell me that I should have left the question alone; that is, that I should have left Nebraska unorganized, the people unprotected, and the Indian barrier in existence, until the swelling tide of emigration should burst through and accomplish by violence what it is the part of wisdom and statesmanship to direct and regulate by law. How long could you have postponed action with safety? How long could you maintain that Indian barrier, and restrain the onward march of civilization, Christianity, and free government by a barbarian wall? Do you suppose that you could keep that vast country a howling wilderness in all time to come, roamed over by hostile savages, cutting off all safe communication between our Atlantic and Pacific possessions? I tell you that the time for action has come, and cannot be postponed. It is a case in which the "let-alone" policy would precipitate a crisis which must inevitably result in violence, anarchy, and strife.

You cannot fix bounds to the onward march of this great and growing country. You cannot fetter the limbs of the young giant. He will burst all your chains. He will expand, and grow, and increase, and extend civilization, Christianity, and liberal principles. Then, sir, if you cannot check the growth of the country in that direction, is it not the part of wisdom to look the danger in the face, and provide for an event which you cannot avoid? I tell you, sir, you must provide for lines of continuous settlement from the Mississippi valley to the Pacific ocean. And in making this provision, you must decide upon what principles the Territories shall be organized; in other words, whether the people shall be allowed to regulate their domestic institutions in their own way, according to the provisions of this bill, or whether the opposite doctrine of Congressional interference is to prevail. Postpone it, if you will; but whenever you do act, this question must be met and decided.

GETTYSBURG ADDRESS

Abraham Lincoln
(1809-1865)

Abraham Lincoln, the Great Emancipator, was a child of the American frontier—tall, gaunt and lank was this rail-splitter lad of Illinois who lived in a rude log cabin and tramped miles to secure the books which he read by fire-light. It was on a trip to New Orleans on a flat-boat that Lincoln is reported to have been shocked by the slave-trader's auction block and to have declared, "If I ever get a chance to hit that institution I'll hit it hard." As a clerk in a country grocery store Lincoln developed his faculty as a droll story-teller, an art which remained his throughout his lifetime. Here also in the village store he studied "Blackstone's Commentaries" and prepared himself for the bar. In 1837 he took up the practice of law, a profession which he followed for ten years until his election to Congress in 1847. In 1855 he became famous over night when he entered the field of public debate at Peoria and Springfield, Illinois, with Douglas on the question of the admission of Kansas as a free or slave state. Again in 1858 he most creditably matched his eloquence against Douglas in a series of speeches which became known as the Lincoln-Douglas debates. In February, 1860 in New York City Lincoln secured the political backing of the East for the presidency by his *Cooper Arms Institute Address*. That year Lincoln became President of the United States just before the outbreak of the Civil War. In 1862 he issued the Emancipation Proclamation, was re-elected President in 1864 after having steered the nation through the Civil War, and was assassinated shortly after the fall of the Confederacy in April, 1865.

It was Lincoln's brevity and clarity of language which gave him his power in public address. He spoke directly to the point, discarding rhetoric and polish of diction for sincerity and fervor; yet the very sublimity and simplicity of his addresses have made them immortal. They are virtually prose-poems.

Lincoln displayed the acumen of his statesmanship and eloquence in his public debates with Douglas in 1858 and 1860, the most significant debates of American history, but his speeches, *The House Divided Against Itself,* delivered at the Illinois Republican Convention in 1858 when he was the candidate chosen to run against Stephen A. Douglas for the United States Senate; *The Cooper Arms Institute Speech* of 1860; *The Gettysburg Address* delivered at the dedication of the cemetery in Gettysburg in 1863 after Edward Everett had given the formal speech of the day; and his *Second Inaugural Address* in 1865 delivered just before his death have perpetuated the character and the oratory of this great man. There is little finer in the English language than these speeches from the simple, great-souled, kindly-hearted Abraham Lincoln. We include here two of his addresses.

Fourscore and seven years ago our fathers brought forth upon this continent a new nation, conceived in liberty, and dedicated to the proposition that all men are created equal.

Now we are engaged in a great civil war, testing whether that nation, or any nation so conceived and so dedicated, can long endure. We are met on a great battle-field of that war. We have come to dedicate a portion of that field as a final resting-place for those who here gave their lives that that nation might live. It is altogether fitting and proper that we should do this.

But in a larger sense, we can not dedicate—we can not consecrate—we can not hallow this ground. The brave men, living and dead, who struggled here, have consecrated it far above our poor power to add or detract. The world will little note, nor long remember, what we say here, but it can never forget what they did here. It is for us, the living, rather, to be dedicated here to the unfinished work which they who fought here have thus far so nobly advanced. It is rather for us to be here dedicated to the great task remaining before us—that from these honored dead we take increased devotion to that cause for which they gave the last full measure of devotion—that we here highly resolve that these dead shall not have died in vain—that this nation, under God, shall have a new birth of freedom and that government of the people, by the people, and for the people, shall not perish from the earth.

SECOND INAUGURAL ADDRESS

Abraham Lincoln

(1809-1865)

At this second appearing to take the oath of the presidential office, there is less occasion for an extended address than there was at first. Then a statement, somewhat in detail, of a course to be pursued seemed very fitting and proper. Now, at the expiration of four years, during which public declarations have been constantly called forth on every point and phase of the great contest which still absorbs the attention and engrosses the energies of the nation, little that is new could be presented.

The progress of our arms, upon which all else chiefly depends, is as well known to the public as to myself, and it is, I trust, reasonably satisfactory and encouraging to all. With high hope for the future, no prediction in regard to it is ventured.

On the occasion corresponding to this four years ago, all thoughts were anxiously directed to an impending civil war. All dreaded it; all sought to avoid it. While the inaugural address was being delivered from this place, devoted altogether to saving the Union without war, insurgent agents were in the city seeking to destroy it with war—seeking to dissolve the Union and divide the effects by negotiation. Both parties deprecated war, but one of them would make war rather than let the nation survive, and the other would accept war rather than let it perish, and the war came. One-eighth of the whole population were colored slaves, not distributed generally over the Union, but localized in the Southern part of it.

These slaves constituted a peculiar and powerful interest. All knew that this interest was somehow the cause of the war. To strengthen, perpetuate, and extend this interest was the object for which the insurgents would rend the Union by war, while the government claimed no right to do more than to restrict the Territorial enlargement of it.

Neither party expected for the war the magnitude or the duration which it has already attained. Neither anticipated that the cause of the conflict might cease when, or even before the conflict itself should cease. Each looked for an easier triumph, and a result less fundamental and astounding. Both read the same Bible and pray to the same God, and each invokes His aid against the other. It may seem strange that any men should dare to ask a just God's assistance in wringing their bread from the sweat of other men's faces, but let us judge not, that we be not judged. The prayer of both could not be answered. That of neither has been answered fully. The Almighty has His own purposes. "Woe unto the world because of offenses, for it must needs be that offenses come; but woe to that man by whom the offense cometh!"

If we shall suppose that American slavery is one of those offenses which, in the providence of God, must needs come, but which having continued through His appointed time, He now wills to remove, and that He gives to both North and South this terrible war as the woe due to those by whom the offense came, shall we discern there any departure from those divine attributes which the believers in a living God always ascribe to Him? Fondly do we hope, fervently do we pray, that this mighty scourge of war may speedily pass away. Yet if God wills that it continue until all the wealth piled by the bondsman's two hundred and fifty years of unrequited toil shall be sunk, and until every drop of blood drawn with the lash shall be paid by another drawn with the sword, as was said three thousand years ago, so still it must be said, that the judgments of the Lord are true and righteous altogether.

With malice toward none, with charity for all, with firmness in the right as God gives us to see the right, let us finish the work we are in, to bind up the nation's wounds, to care for him who shall have borne the battle, and for his widow and his orphans, to do all which may achieve and cherish a just and a lasting peace among ourselves and with all nations.

THE NEW SOUTH [14]

Henry Grady

(1851-1889)

Henry Grady was the orator of the New South in the days
of reconstruction following the Civil War. A Georgian by
birth, educated in universities of the South, and a journalist by
profession, Grady was little known outside his own state until the
occasion of an impromptu address before the New England Society of New York on December 21, 1886, on *The New South*.
This speech from the lips of the young southerner created a tremendous sensation throughout the entire country with its message
of mutual understanding and goodwill.

Ten days before his death on December 13, 1889, Grady
delivered at a banquet in Boston a speech on *The Race Problem,*
which some critics consider the best of his career and a high-
water mark of modern oratory. This, his last contribution, is
replete with the higher politics of his country—a politics above
partisanship and self-seeking.

Included here is his speech of 1886 on *The New South*.

There was a South of secession and slavery—that South is dead.
There is a South of union and freedom—that South is living, breathing,
growing every hour.

I accept the term, "the new South," as in no sense disparaging to
the old. Dear to me is the home of my childhood and the traditions
of my people. There is a new South, not through protest against the
old, but because of new conditions, new adjustments, and, if you please,
new ideas and aspirations. It is to this that I address myself. You have
just heard an eloquent description of the triumphant armies of the
North, and the grand review at Washington. I ask you, gentlemen, to
picture, if you can, the foot-sore soldier who, buttoning up in his faded
gray jacket the parole which was taken, testimony to his children of his
fidelity and faith, turned his face southward from Appomattox in April,

[14] Abridged.

1865. Think of him as ragged, half-starved, heavy-hearted, enfeebled by want and wounds. Having fought to exhaustion, he surrenders his gun, wrings the hands of his comrades, and, lifting his tear-stained and pallid face for the last time to the graves that dot the old Virginia hills, pulls his gray cap over his brow and begins the slow and painful journey. What does he find?—let me ask you, who went to your homes eager to find all the welcome you had justly earned, full payment for four years' sacrifice—what does he find, when he reaches the home he left four years before? He finds his home in ruins, his farm devastated, his slaves freed, his stock killed, his barns empty, his trade destroyed, his money worthless, his social system, feudal in its magnificence, swept away, his people without law or legal status, his comrades slain, and the burden of others heavy on his shoulders. Crushed by defeat, his very traditions gone, without money, credit, employment, material, or training; and, besides all this, confronted with the gravest problem that ever met human intelligence—the establishing of a status for the vast body of his liberated slaves.

What does he do—this hero in gray with a heart of gold—does he sit down in sullenness and despair? Not for a day. Surely, God, who had scourged him in his prosperity, inspired him in his adversity! As ruin was never before so overwhelming, never was restoration swifter.

The soldiers stepped from the trenches into the furrow; the horses that had charged upon General Sherman's line marched before the plow, and fields that ran red with human blood in April were green with the harvest in June. From the ashes left us in 1865, we have raised a brave and beautiful city; and, somehow or other, we have caught the sunshine in the bricks and mortar of our homes and have builded therein not one single ignoble prejudice or memory.

It is a rare privilege, sir, to have had part, however humble, in this work. Never was nobler duty confided to human hands than the uplifting and upbuilding of the prostrate South—misguided, perhaps, but beautiful in her suffering, and honest, brave, and generous always. On the record of her social, industrial, and political restoration we await with confidence the verdict of the world.

The old South rested everything on slavery and agriculture, unconscious that these could neither give nor maintain healthy growth. The new South presents a perfect democracy, the oligarchs leading in the popular movement—a social system compact and closely knitted, less splendid on the surface but stronger at the core—a hundred farms for every plantation, fifty homes for every palace; and a diversified industry that meets the complex needs of this complex age.

The new South is enamored of her work. Her soul is stirred with the breath of a new life. The light of a grander day is falling fair in her face. She is thrilling with the consciousness of growing power and prosperity.

As she stands full-statured and equal among the people of the earth, breathing the keen air and looking out upon an expanding horizon, she understands that her emancipation came because in the inscrutable wisdom of God her honest purpose was crossed and her brave armies were beaten. This is said in no spirit of time-serving and apology. The South has nothing to take back; nothing for which she has excuses to make. In my native town of Athens is a monument that crowns its central hills—a plain white shaft. Deep cut into its shining sides is a name dear to me above the names of men, that of a brave and simple man who died in brave and simple faith. Not for all the glories of New England, from Plymouth Rock all the way, would I exchange the heritage he left me in his patriot's death. But, sir, speaking from the shadow of that memory, which I honor as I do nothing else on earth, I say that the cause in which he suffered and for which he gave his life was adjudged by higher and fuller wisdom than his or mine, and I am glad that the omniscient God held the balance of battle in His almighty hand and that the American Union was saved from the wreck of war.

I stand here, Mr. President, to profess no new loyalty. When General Lee, whose heart was the temple of our hopes and whose arm was clothed with our strength, renewed his allegiance to the government at Appomattox, he spoke from a heart too great to be false, and he spoke for every honest man from Maryland to Texas. From that day to this, Hamilcar has nowhere in the South sworn young Hannibal to hatred and vengeance—but everywhere to loyalty and to love. Witness the soldier standing at the base of a Confederate monument above the graves of his comrades, his empty sleeve tossing in the April wind, adjuring the young men about him to serve as honest and loyal citizens the government against which their fathers fought. This message, delivered from that sacred presence, has gone home to the hearts of my fellows! And, sir, I declare here, if physical courage be always equal to human aspirations, that they would die, sir, if need be, to restore this republic their fathers fought to dissolve!

AT HIS BROTHER'S GRAVE

Robert Ingersoll

(1833-1899)

Robert Ingersoll, the Great Agnostic, was a powerful political and platform orator and a religious controversialist at a period of conflict in American history between the Republican and Democratic parties and a period of conflict over Darwin's theory of evolution. As the son of a Congregational minister Ingersoll was in youth thoroughly exposed to orthodox religion and rebelled against its creed and theology. He received his education in the common schools of Illinois, the state in which he was admitted to the bar. During the war he served as a colonel in the army then returned to his law practice. In 1876 Ingersoll first achieved fame as an orator by his speech nominating James Blaine for President. Thereafter Ingersoll was in frequent demand as a speaker and his reputation as an orator became even more fixed by a speech delivered at Indianapolis in 1876 to the veteran soldiers entitled *The Vision of War*. Again in 1877 his lecture on the *Liberty of Man, Woman and Child*, a declaration of independence for personal liberty of thought and action, both shocked and charmed his listeners. It was in 1879 that Ingersoll delivered his commemorative discourse, *At His Brother's Grave*, which is one of the rarest eulogies ever delivered in sublimity of thought, beauty of imagery and diction, and simplicity of pathos. On May 30, 1888, Chauncey Depew introduced Robert Ingersoll to the war veterans at the great Metropolitan Opera House in New York City as "the greatest living orator." On this occasion Ingersoll augmented his already famous address, *The Vision of War* with *A Vision of Peace* in language so exquisitely eloquent that it stirred men's souls to the depths.

My Friends:—I am going to do that which the dead oft promised he would do for me.

The loved and loving brother, husband, father, friend died where manhood's morning almost touches noon, and while the shadows still were falling toward the west.

He had not passed on life's highway the stone that marks the highest point, but, being weary for a moment, he lay down by the wayside, and, using his burden for a pillow, fell into that dreamless sleep that kisses down his eyelids still. While yet in love with life and raptured with the world he passed to silence and pathetic dust.

Yet, after all, it may be best, just in the happiest, sunniest hour of all the voyage, while eager winds are kissing every sail, to dash against the unseen rock, and in an instant hear the billows roar above a sunken ship. For, whether in midsea or 'mong the breakers of the farther shore, a wreck at last must mark the end of each and all. And every life, no matter if its hour is rich with love and every moment joy, will, at its close, become a tragedy as sad and deep and dark as can be woven of the warp and woof of mystery and death.

This brave and tender man in every storm of life was oak and rock, but in the sunshine he was vine and flower. He was the friend of all heroic souls. He climbed the heights and left all superstitions far below, while on his forehead fell the golden dawning of the grander day.

He loved the beautiful, and was with color, form, and music touched to tears. He sided with the weak, and with a willing hand gave alms; with loyal heart and with purest hands he faithfully discharged all public trusts.

He was a worshiper of liberty, a friend of the oppressed. A thousand times I have heard him quote these words: "For justice, all places a temple, and all seasons, summer." He believed that happiness was the only good, reason the only torch, justice the only worship, humanity the only religion, and love the only priest. He added to the sum of human joy; and were every one to whom he did some loving service to bring a blossom to his grave, he would sleep to-night beneath a wilderness of flowers.

Life is a narrow vale between the cold and barren peaks of two eternities. We strive in vain to look beyond the heights. We cry aloud, and the only answer is the echo of our wailing cry. From the voiceless lips of the unreplying dead there comes no word; but in the night of death hope sees a star, and listening love can hear the rustle of a wing.

He who sleeps here, when dying, mistaking the approach of death for the return of health, whispered with his latest breath: "I am better now." Let us believe, in spite of doubts and dogmas, and tears and fears, that these dear words are true of all the countless dead.

And now to you who have been chosen, from among the many men he loved, to do the last sad office for the dead, we give this sacred dust. Speech cannot contain our love. There was, there is, no greater, stronger, manlier man.

WOMAN'S RIGHT TO THE SUFFRAGE

Susan B. Anthony

(1820-1906)

Susan B. Anthony, prominent woman reformer of the 19th century, was born of Quaker parentage in Massachusetts. During the slavery agitation she became an ardent abolitionist. In 1858 she advocated co-education and thereafter devoted her energies to the emancipation of women, to higher wages for women, possession of their own earnings, and the guardianship of their children. Miss Anthony was also active in the Woman's Christian Temperance Union as a colleague of Frances E. Willard.

Susan B. Anthony was an eloquent speaker and lectured extensively both in the United States and abroad. Her last important public appearance was as a delegate to the International Council of Women in London in 1899. When arrested and fined $100 for voting in the presidential election of 1872, Miss Anthony delivered the speech included here.

FRIENDS AND FELLOW-CITIZENS: I stand before you to-night, under indictment for the alleged crime of having voted at the last presidential election, without having a lawful right to vote. It shall be my work this evening to prove to you that in thus voting, I not only committed no crime, but, instead, simply exercised my citizen's rights, guaranteed to me and all United States citizens by the national Constitution, beyond the power of any Senate to deny. . . .

The preamble of the Federal Constitution says: "We, the people of the United States, in order to form a more perfect union, establish justice, insure domestic tranquillity, provide for the common defence, promote the general welfare, and secure the blessings of liberty to ourselves and our posterity, do ordain and establish this Constitution for the United States of America."

It was we, the people; not we, the white male citizens; nor yet we, the male citizens; but we, the whole people, who formed the Union. And we formed it, not to give the blessings of liberty, but to secure them; not to the half of ourselves and the half of our posterity, but to the whole people—women as well as men. And it is a downright mockery to talk to women of their enjoyment of the blessings of liberty while they are denied the use of the only means of securing them provided by this democratic-republican government—the ballot.

The early journals of Congress show that when the committee reported to that body the original articles of confederation, the very first article which became the subject of discussion was that respecting equality of suffrage. Article IV. said: "The better to secure and perpetuate mutual friendship and intercourse between the people of the different States of the Union, the free inhabitants of each of the States (paupers, vagabonds and fugitives from justice excepted), shall be entitled to all the privileges and immunities of the free citizens of the several States."

Thus, at the very beginning, did the fathers see the necessity of the universal application of the great principle of equal rights to all; in order to produce the desired result—a harmonious union and a homogeneous people. . . . .

B. Gratz Brown, of Missouri, in the three days' discussion in the United States Senate in 1866, on Senator Cowan's motion to strike the word male from the District of Columbia suffrage bill, said:

Mr. President, I say here on the floor of the American Senate, I stand for universal suffrage; and, as a matter of fundamental principle, do not recognize the right of society to limit it on any ground of race or sex. . . ."

Charles Sumner, in his brave protests against the fourteenth and fifteenth amendments, insisted that, so soon as by the thirteenth amendment the slaves became free men, the original powers of the United States Constitution guaranteed to them equal rights—the right to vote and to be voted for. . . .

Article I of the New York State Constitution says: "No member of this State shall be disfranchised or deprived of the rights or privileges secured to any citizen thereof, unless by the law of the land or the judgment of his peers."

And so carefully guarded is the citizen's right to vote that the Constitution makes special mention of all who may be excluded. It says: "Laws may be passed excluding from the right of suffrage all persons who have been or may be convicted of bribery, larceny or any infamous crime. . . ."

"The law of the land" is the United States Constitution, and there is no provision in that document that can be fairly construed into a permission to the States to deprive any class of their citizens of their right to vote. Hence, New York can get no power from that source to disfranchise one entire half of her members. Nor has "the judgment of their peers" been pronounced against women exercising their right to vote; no disfranchised person is allowed to be judge or juror, and none but disfranchised persons can be women's peers; nor has the Legislature passed laws excluding them on account of idiocy or lunacy; nor yet the courts convicted them of bribery, larceny or any infamous crime.

Clearly, then, there is no constitutional ground for the exclusion of women from the ballot-box in the State of New York. No barriers whatever stand to-day between women and the exercise of their right to vote save those of precedent and prejudice. . . .

For any State to make sex a qualification that must ever result in the disfranchisement of one entire half of the people is to pass a bill of attainder, or an *ex post facto* law, and is therefore a violation of the supreme law of the land. By it the blessings of liberty are forever withheld from women and their female posterity. To them this government has no just powers derived from the consent of the governed. To them this government is not a democracy. It is not a republic. It is an odious aristocracy; a hateful oligarchy of sex; the most hateful aristocracy ever established on the face of the globe; an oligarchy of wealth, where the rich govern the poor. An oligarchy of learning, where the educated govern the ignorant, or even an oligarchy of race, where the Saxon rules the African, might be endured; but this oligarchy of sex, which makes father, brothers, husband, sons the oligarchs over the mother and sisters, the wife and daughters of every household; which ordains all men sovereigns, all women subjects; carries dissension, discord, and rebellion into every home of the nation. . . .

Webster, Worcester and Bouvier all define a citizen to be a person in the United States, entitled to vote and hold office.

The only question left to be settled now is: Are women persons? And I hardly believe any of our opponents will have the hardihood to say they are not. Being persons, then, women are citizens, and no State has a right to make any law, or to enforce any old law, that shall abridge their privileges or immunities. Hence, every discrimination against women in the constitutions and laws of the several States is to-day null and void, precisely as is every one against negroes.

WORK FOR HUMANITY

Frances E. Willard

(1839-1898)

Frances E. Willard, best known for her services in connection with temperance, was born in New York, educated at
Northwestern University in Illinois. After two years of travel in
Europe and the East, she became Dean of Women in the Woman's
College of her alma mater. It was in the year 1879 that she
became president of the Woman's Christian Temperance Union
a position which she held until her death. Not only was Miss
Willard active in the temperance movement, but she was also
interested in the woman's suffrage movement and aided both
of these reforms with her pen as well as with her voice throughout her lifetime. Included here is a portion of an address
delivered before the Convention of the Woman's Christian
Temperance Union at Atlanta, Georgia, in 1890.

I wish we were all more thorough students of the mighty past, for
we should thus be rendered braver prophets of the future, and more
cheerful workers in the present. History shows us with what tenacity
the human race survives. Earthquake, famine, and pestilence have
done their worst, but over them rolls a healing tide of years and they
are lost to view; on sweeps the great procession, and hardly shows a
scar. Rulers around whom clustered new forms of civilization pass
away; but greater men succeed them. Nations are rooted up; great
hopes seem blighted; revolutions rise and rivers run with the blood of
patriots; the globe itself seems headed toward the abyss; new patriots
are born; higher hopes bloom out like stars; humanity emerges from
the dark ages vastly ahead of what it was on entering that cave of gloom,
and ever the right comes uppermost; and now is Christ's kingdom nearer
than when we first believed.

Only those who have not studied history lose heart in great reforms;
only those unread in the biography of genius imagine themselves to be
original. Except in the realm of material invention, there is nothing
new under the sun. There is no reform which some great soul has

not dreamed of centuries ago; there is not a doctrine that some father of the Church did not set forth. The Greek philosophers and early Christian Fathers boxed the compass once for all; we may take our choice of what they have left on record. Let us then learn a wise humility, but at the same time a humble wisdom, as we remember that there are but two classes of men—one which declares that our times are the worst the world has seen, and another which claims our times as best—and he who claims this, all revelation, all science, all history witnesses is right and will be right forevermore.

The introspective is not the beautiful life. Suppose the eye should set out to see itself, the ear to hear itself! No, these organs are only in their normal use when applied to the outward world; and the soul is normal only when joined on to God and Humanity—its natural correlates, the atmosphere of its lungs, the air to its wings, the love for its heart. Introspection is the last infirmity of noble minds, it is repression's penalty and life's distemper; it reverses the soul's enginery and sets it grinding on itself. (Let us rather fling ourselves out into the thickening battle; let us live the life of action which is the only true and happy life.) Men tell us God is force—nay, He is that purposed force behind all forces, that combines head, hand, and heart; God is action—let us be like God. God's word constantly sets before us images of vigor, of action, of power. Women need to study this; they need translating out of the passive into the active voice; out of aimless reverie and into resolute aim. The Woman's Christian Temperance Union has no higher, holier mission than to help bring this about. The most perfect eye is the one of which its possessor is most unconscious except that he knows how well it sees. The most perfect ear is that of which its possessor is most unconscious except that he knows how well it hears. This which is true in detail is just as true in the wholeness of one's life. A morbid self-consciousness is the greatest hindrance to any heart. Man is like an engine—the greater and more perfect, the less conscious is it of its parts, but more conscious of its power. The Corliss engine swings its great levers and turns its mighty wheels a thousand times more quietly than the rattling little freight.

(The most normal and the most perfect human being is the one who most thoroughly addresses himself to the activity of his best powers, gives himself most thoroughly to the world around him, flings himself out into the midst of humanity, and is so preoccupied by his own beneficent reaction on the world that he is practically unconscious of a separate existence.) Introspection and retrospection were good for the cloister; but the uplook, the outlook and the onlook are alone worthy the modern Christian. To change the figure, a normal Christian stands in the midst of a great, beautiful and varied landscape. It is the landscape of beneficent work. Above him reach the boundless skies, brilliant with the stars of God and Heaven.

(Love and friendship form a beautiful rainbow over his landscape and reach up toward his sky) But the only two great environments of the soul are work for humanity and faith in God. Those wounded in love will find that affection, dear and vital as it is, comes to us not as the whole of life, not as its wide wondrous landscape of the earth, not as its beautiful vision of the sky, but as its beautiful embellishments, its rainbow fair and sweet. But were it gone there would still remain the two greatest and most satisfying pictures on which the soul can gaze— Humanity and God.

THE PRINCE OF PEACE [15]

William Jennings Bryan

(1860-1925)

The Silver-Tongued Orator, William Jennings Bryan, advocate of popular government, international peace, and prohibition, indelibly engraved his name on the roster of American orators. This great spokesman of the masses was the dominant personality of the Democratic Party between Grover Cleveland's and Woodrow Wilson's administrations. He was born in Illinois, was graduated from a Chicago law school in 1883, and began his long career in Congress in 1891. It was at the Democratic convention of 1896 that Bryan rose to the fore as an orator with his speech, *The Cross of Gold,* on the question of the coinage of silver, a speech which has never been equalled in convention oratory. Although he lost the election for the presidency in this and in two subsequent campaigns, Bryan nevertheless remained the idol of his party and the West. Later speeches which contributed to his oratorical fame were: *America's Mission* (1899); his acceptance speech of 1900 entitled *Imperialism*; his *Madison Square Speech,* delivered in 1900; and his famous lecture on *The Prince of Peace* which was delivered hundreds of times throughout the country on the lyceum platform.

As one of the foremost advocates of prohibition Bryan was influential in securing the passage of the Eighteenth Amendment to the United States Constitution. Toward the end of his life Bryan advocated orthodox religion and lectured against Darwin's theory of evolution. His sudden death came before he could deliver a speech which he had prepared as a summary of his case against the evolutionists.

Beyond doubt Bryan's eloquence was the source of his power, and through that power he influenced the politics of his day as no

[15] Abridged.

other man. The Great Commoner he always was; the foe of militarism and alcoholism; the champion of democracy; but above all he was an orator. Those who heard him never forgot the charm of his voice and the power of his personality, which often carried his point against the dictates of their own reason and logic.

Included here is his lecture on *The Prince of Peace* which he delivered in Canada, Mexico, Tokyo, Manila, Bombay, Cairo, and Jerusalem, as well as throughout the United States.

Man is a religious being; the heart instinctively seeks for a God. Whether he worships on the banks of the Ganges, prays with his face upturned to the sun, kneels toward Mecca or, regarding all space as a temple, communes with the Heavenly Father according to the Christian creed, man is essentially devout. . . .

Religion has been defined by Tolstoy as the relation which man fixes between himself and his God, and morality as the outward manifestation of this inward relation. Every one, by the time he reaches maturity, has fixed some relation between himself and God and no material change in this relation can take place without a revolution in the man, for this relation is the most potent influence that acts upon a human life.

Religion is the foundation of morality in the individual and in the group of individuals. . . .

Morality is the power of endurance in man; and a religion which teaches personal responsibility to God gives strength to morality. There is a powerful restraining influence in the belief that an all-seeing eye scrutinizes every thought and word and act of the individual.

There is a wide difference between the man who is trying to conform his life to a standard of morality about him and the man who seeks to make his life approximate to a divine standard. The former attempts to live up to the standard, if it is above him, and down to it, if it is below him—and if he is doing right only when others are looking he is sure to find a time when he thinks he is unobserved, and then he takes a vacation and falls. One needs the inner strength which comes with the conscious presence of a personal God. If those who are thus fortified sometimes yield to temptation, how helpless and hopeless must those be who rely upon their own strength alone! . . .

I do not carry the doctrine of evolution as far as some do; I am not yet convinced that man is a lineal descendant of the lower animals. I do not mean to find fault with you if you want to accept the theory; all I mean to say is that while you may trace your ancestry back to the monkey if you find pleasure or pride in doing so, you shall not connect me with your family tree without more evidence than has yet been produced. I object to the theory for several reasons. . . .

Go back as far as we may, we can not escape from the creative act, and it is just as easy for me to believe that God created man as he is as to believe that, millions of years ago, He created a germ of life and endowed it with power to develop into all that we see to-day. I object to the Darwinian theory, until more conclusive proof is produced, because I fear we shall lose the consciousness of God's presence in our daily life, if we must accept the theory that through all the ages no spiritual force has touched the life of man or shaped the destiny of nations.

But there is another objection. The Darwinian theory represents man as reaching his present perfection by the operation of the law of hate—the merciless law by which the strong crowd out and kill off the weak. If this is the law of our development then, if there is any logic that can bind the human mind, we shall turn backward toward the beast in proportion as we substitute the law of love. I prefer to believe that love rather than hatred is the law of development. How can hatred be the law of development when nations have advanced in proportion as they have departed from that law and adopted the law of love?

But, I repeat, while I do not accept the Darwinian theory I shall not quarrel with you about it; I only refer to it to remind you that it does not solve the mystery of life or explain human progress. . . .

Science has taught us so many things that we are tempted to conclude that we know everything, but there is really a great unknown which is still unexplored and that which we have learned ought to increase our reverence rather than our egotism. Science has disclosed some of the machinery of the universe, but science has not yet revealed to us the great secret—the secret of life. It is to be found in every blade of grass, in every insect, in every bird and in every animal, as well as in man. Six thousand years of recorded history and yet we know no more about the secret of life than they knew in the beginning. We live, we plan; we have our hopes, our fears; and yet in a moment a change may come over any one of us and this body will become a mass of lifeless clay. What is it that, having, we live, and having not, we are as the clod? The progress of the race and the civilization which we now behold are the work of men and women who have not yet solved the mystery of their own lives.

And our food, must we understand it before we eat it? If we refused to eat anything until we could understand the mystery of its growth, we would die of starvation. But mystery does not bother us in the dining-room; it is only in the church that it is a stumbling block. . . .

But there is something even more wonderful still—the mysterious change that takes place in the human heart when the man begins to hate the things he loved and to love the things he hated—the marvelous transformation that takes place in the man who, before the change, would have sacrificed a world for his own advancement but who, after

the change, would give his life for a principle and esteem it a privilege
to make sacrifice for his convictions! What greater miracle than this,
that converts a selfish, self-centered, human being into a center from
which good influences flow out in every direction! And yet this miracle
has been wrought in the heart of each one of us—or may be wrought—
and we have seen it wrought in the hearts and lives of those about us.
No, living a life that is a mystery, and living in the midst of mystery
and miracles, I shall not allow either to deprive me of the benefits of
the Christian religion. If you ask me if I understand everything in
the Bible, I answer, no, but if we will try to live up to what we do
understand, we will be kept so busy doing good that we will not have
time to worry about the passages which we do not understand.

Some of those who question the miracle also question the theory
of atonement; they assert that it does not accord with their idea of
justice for one to die for all. Let each one bear his own sins and the
punishments due for them, they say. The doctrine of vicarious suffering
is not a new one; it is as old as the race. That one should suffer for
others is one of the most familiar of principles and we see the principle
illustrated eveiy day of our lives. Take the family, for instance; from
the day the mother's first child is born, for twenty or thirty years her
children are scarcely out of her waking thoughts. Her life trembles
in the balance at each child's birth; she sacrifices for them, she surrenders
herself to them. Is it because she expects them to pay her back?
Fortunate for the parent and fortunate for the child if the latter has an
opportunity to repay in part the debt it owes. But no child can compensate a parent for a parent's care. In the course of nature the debt is
paid, not to the parent, but to the next generation, and the next—each
generation suffering, sacrificing for and surrendering itself to the generation that follows. This is the law of our lives.

Nor is this confined to the family. Every step in civilization has
been made possible by those who have been willing to sacrifice for
posterity. Freedom of speech, freedom of the press, freedom of conscience and freedom of government have all been won for the world
by those who were willing to labor unselfishly for their fellows. So
well established is this doctrine that we do not regard anyone as great
unless he recognizes how unimportant his life is in comparison with
the problems with which he deals.

I find proof that man was made in the image of his Creator in the
fact that, throughout the centuries, man has been willing to die, if necessary, that blessings denied to him might be enjoyed by his children, his
children's children and the world.

The seeming paradox: "He that saveth his life shall lose it and he
that loseth his life for my sake shall find it," has an application wider
than that usually given to it; it is an epitome of history. Those who
live only for themselves live little lives, but those who stand ready to
give themselves for the advancement of things greater than themselves

find a larger life than the one they would have surrendered. Wendell Phillips gave expression to the same idea when he said, "What imprudent men the benefactors of the race have been. How prudently most men sink into nameless graves, while now and then a few forget themselves into immortality." We win immortality, not by remembering ourselves, but by forgetting ourselves in devotion to things larger than ourselves.

Instead of being an unnatural plan, the plan of salvation is in perfect harmony with human nature as we understand it. Sacrifice is the language of love, and Christ, in suffering for the world, adopted the only means of reaching the heart. This can be demonstrated not only by theory but by experience, for the story of His life, His teachings, His sufferings and His death has been translated into every language and everywhere it has touched the heart.

But if I were going to present an argument in favor of the divinity of Christ, I would not begin with miracles or mystery or with the theory of atonement. I would begin as Carnegie Simpson does in his book entitled, "The Fact of Christ." Commencing with the undisputed fact that Christ lived, he points out that one can not contemplate this fact without feeling that in some way it is related to those now living. He says that one can read of Alexander, of Caesar or of Napoleon, and not feel that it is a matter of personal concern; but that when one reads that Christ lived, and how He lived and how He died, he feels that somehow there is a cord that stretches from that life to his. As he studies the character of Christ he becomes conscious of certain virtues which stand out in bold relief—His purity, His forgiving spirit, and His unfathomable love. . . .

The most difficult of all the virtues to cultivate is the forgiving spirit. Revenge seems to be natural with man; it is human to want to get even with an enemy. It has even been popular to boast of vindictiveness; it was once inscribed on a man's monument that he had repaid both friends and enemies more than he had received. This was not the spirit of Christ. He taught forgiveness and in that incomparable prayer which He left as a model for our petitions, He made our willingness to forgive the measure by which we may claim forgiveness. He not only taught forgiveness but He exemplified His teachings in His life. When those who persecuted Him brought Him to the most disgraceful of all deaths, His spirit of forgiveness rose above His sufferings and He prayed "Father, forgive them, for they know not what they do!"

What conclusion is to be drawn from the life, the teachings and the death of this historic figure? Reared in a carpenter shop; with no knowledge of literature, save Bible literature; with no acquaintance with philosophers living or with the writings of sages dead, when only about thirty years old He gathered disciples about Him, promulgated a higher code of morals than the world had ever known before, and proclaimed Himself the Messiah. He taught and performed miracles for a few brief months and then was crucified; His disciples were scattered and many of them put to death; His claims were disputed, His resurrection denied and His followers persecuted; and yet from this beginning His religion spread until hundreds of millions have taken His name with reverence upon their lips and millions have been willing to die rather than surrender the faith which He put into their hearts. How shall we account for Him? Here is the greatest fact of history; here is One who has with increasing power, for nineteen hundred years, molded the hearts, the thoughts and the lives of men, and He exerts more influence to-day than ever before. . . .

I was thinking a few years ago of the Christmas which was then approaching and of Him in whose honor the day is celebrated. I recalled the message, "Peace on earth, good will to men," and then my thoughts ran back to the prophecy uttered centuries before His birth, in which He was described as the Prince of Peace. To reinforce my memory I re-read the prophecy and I found immediately following a verse which I had forgotten—a verse which declares that of the increase of His peace and government there shall be no end. And Isaiah adds that He shall judge His people with justice and with judgment. I had been reading of the rise and fall of nations, and occasionally I had met a gloomy philosopher who preached the doctrine that nations, like individuals, must of necessity have their birth, their infancy, their maturity and finally their decay and death. But here I read of a government that is to be perpetual—a government of increasing peace and blessedness—the government of the Prince of Peace—and it is to rest on justice. I have thought of this prophecy many times during the last few years, and I have selected this theme that I might present some of the reasons which lead me to believe that Christ has fully earned the right to be called the Prince of Peace—a title that will in the years to come be more and more applied to Him. If he can bring peace to each individual heart, and if His creed when applied will bring peace throughout the earth, who will deny His right to be called the Prince of Peace?

All the world is in search of peace; every heart that ever beat has sought for peace, and many have been the methods employed to secure it. Some have thought to purchase it with riches and have labored to secure wealth, hoping to find peace when they were able to go where they pleased and buy what they liked. Of those who have endeavored to purchase peace with money, the large majority have failed to secure the money. But what has been the experience of those who have been eminently successful in finance? They all tell the same story, viz., that they spent the first half of their lives trying to get money from others and the last half trying to keep others from getting their money, and that they found peace in neither half. Some have even reached the point where they find difficulty in getting people to accept their money; and I know of no better indication of the ethical awakening in this country than the increasing tendency to scrutinize the methods of money-making. I am sanguine enough to believe that the time will yet come when respectability will no longer be sold to great criminals by helping them to spend their ill-gotten gains. A long step in advance will have been taken when religious, educational and charitable institutions refuse to condone conscienceless methods and leave the possessor of illegitimate accumulations to learn how lonely life is when one prefers money to morals.

Some have sought peace in social distinction, but whether they have been within the charmed circle and fearful lest they might fall out, or outside, and hopeful that they might get in, they have not found peace. Some have thought, vain thought, to find peace in political prominence; but whether office comes by birth, as in monarchies, or by election, as in republics, it does not bring peace. An office is not considered a high one if all can occupy it. Only when few in a generation can hope to enjoy an honor do we call it a great honor. I am glad that our Heavenly Father did not make the peace of the human heart to depend upon our ability to buy it with money, secure it in society, or win it at the polls, for in either case but few could have obtained it, but when He made peace the reward of a conscience void of offense toward God and man, He put it within the reach of all. The poor can secure it as easily as the rich, the social outcasts as freely as the leader of society, and the humblest citizen equally with those who wield political power.

. . . .

Christ promoted peace by giving us assurance that a line of communication can be established between the Father above and the child below. And who will measure the consolations of the hour of prayer?

And immortality! Who will estimate the peace which a belief in a future life has brought to the sorrowing hearts of the sons of men? You may talk to the young about death ending all, for life is full and hope is strong, but preach not this doctrine to the mother who stands by the death-bed of her babe or to one who is within the shadow of a great affliction. When I was a young man I wrote to Colonel Ingersoll and asked him for his views on God and immortality. His secretary answered that the great infidel was not at home, but enclosed a copy of a speech by Colonel Ingersoll which covered my question. I scanned it with eagerness and found that he had expressed himself about as follows: "I do not say that there is no God, I simply say I do not know. I do not say that there is no life beyond the grave, I simply say I do not know." And from that day to this I have asked myself the question and have been unable to answer it to my satisfaction, how could anyone find pleasure in taking from a human heart a living faith and substituting therefor the cold and cheerless doctrine, "I do not know."

. . . .

If the Father deigns to touch with divine power the cold and pulseless heart of the buried acorn and to make it burst forth from its prison walls, will he leave neglected in the earth the soul of man, made in the image of his Creator? If he stoops to give to the rose bush, whose withered blossoms float upon the autumn breeze, the sweet assurance of another springtime, will He refuse the words of hope to the sons of men when the frosts of winter come? If matter, mute and inanimate, though changed by the forces of nature into a multitude of forms, can never die, will the imperial spirit of man suffer annihilation when it has paid a brief visit like a royal guest to this tenement of clay? No, I am sure that He who, notwithstanding his apparent prodigality, created nothing without a purpose, and wasted not a single atom in all his creation, has made provision for a future life in which man's universal longing for immortality will find its realization. . . .

Again, Christ deserves to be called the Prince of Peace because He has given us a measure of greatness which promotes peace. When His disciples quarreled among themselves as to which should be greatest in the Kingdom of Heaven, He rebuked them and said: "Let him who would be chiefest among you be the servant of all." Service is the measure of greatness; it always has been true; it is true to-day, and it always will be true, that he is greatest who does the most of good. And how this old world will be transformed when this standard of greatness becomes the standard of every life! Nearly all of our controversies and combats grow out of the fact that we are trying to get something from each other—there will be peace when our aim is to do something for each other. Our enmities and animosities arise largely from our efforts to get as much as possible out of the world—there will be peace when our endeavor is to put as much as possible into the world. The human measure of a human life is its income; the divine measure of a life is its outgo, its overflow—its contribution to the welfare of all.

Christ also led the way to peace by giving us a formula for the propagation of truth. Not all of those who have really desired to do good have employed the Christian method—not all Christians even. In the history of the human race but two methods have been used. The first is the forcible method, and it has been employed most frequently. A man has an idea which he thinks is good; he tells his neighbors about it and they do not like it. This makes him angry; he thinks it would be so much better for them if they would like it, and, seizing a club, he attempts to make them like it. But one trouble about this rule is that it works both ways; when a man starts out to compel his neighbors to think as he does, he generally finds them willing to accept the challenge and they spend so much time in trying to coerce each other that they have no time left to do each other good.

The other is the Bible plan—"Be not overcome of evil but overcome evil with good." And there is no other way of overcoming evil. I am not much of a farmer—I get more credit for my farming than I should, and my little farm receives more advertising than it deserves. But I am farmer enough to know that if I cut down weeds they will spring

up again; and farmer enough to know that if I plant something there
which has more vitality than the weeds I shall not only get rid of the
constant cutting, but have the benefit of the crop besides.

In order that there might be no mistake in His plan of propagating
the truth, Christ went into detail and laid emphasis upon the value of
example—"So live that others seeing your good works may be constrained to glorify your Father which is in Heaven." There is no
human influence so potent for good as that which goes out from an
upright life. A sermon may be answered; the arguments presented in
a speech may be disputed, but no one can answer a Christian life—it
is the unanswerable argument in favor of our religion.

It may be a slow process—this conversion of the world by the
silent influence of a noble example but it is the only sure one, and the
doctrine applies to nations as well as to individuals. The Gospel of the
Prince of Peace gives us the only hope that the world has—and it is
an increasing hope—of the substitution of reason for the arbitrament
of force in the settlement of international disputes. And our nation
ought not to wait for other nations—it ought to take the lead and prove
its faith in the omnipotence of truth.

But Christ has given us a platform so fundamental that it can be
applied successfully to all controversies. We are interested in platforms;
we attend conventions, sometimes traveling long distances; we have
wordy wars over the phraseology of various planks, and then we wage
earnest campaigns to secure the endorsement of these platforms at the
polls. The platform given to the world by the Prince of Peace is more
far-reaching and more comprehensive than any platform ever written
by the convention of any party in any country. When He condensed
into one commandment those of the ten which relate to man's duty
toward his fellows and enjoined upon us the rule, "Thou shalt love thy
neighbor as thyself," He presented a plan for the solution of all the
problems that now vex society or may hereafter arise. Other remedies
may palliate or postpone the day of settlement, but this is all-sufficient
and the reconciliation which it effects is a permanent one.

My faith in the future—and I have faith—and my optimism—for
I am an optimist—my faith and my optimism rest upon the belief that
Christ's teachings are being more studied to-day than ever before, and
that with this larger study will come a larger application of those teachings to the everyday life of the world, and to the questions with which
we deal. In former times when men read that Christ came "to bring
life and immortality to light," they placed the emphasis upon immortality; now they are studying Christ's relation to human life. People
used to read the Bible to find out what it said of Heaven; now they read
it more to find what light it throws upon the pathway of to-day. In
former years many thought to prepare themselves for future bliss by a
life of seclusion here; we are learning that to follow in the footsteps
of the Master we must go about doing good. Christ declared that He

came that we might have life and have it more abundantly. The world is learning that Christ came not to narrow life, but to enlarge it—not to rob it of its joy, but to fill it to overflowing with purpose, earnestness and happiness. . . .

Only those who believe attempt the seemingly impossible, and, by attempting, prove that one, with God, can chase a thousand and that two can put ten thousand to flight. I can imagine that the early Christians who were carried into the Coliseum to make a spectacle for those more savage than the beasts, were entreated by their doubting companions not to endanger their lives. But, kneeling in the center of the arena, they prayed and sang until they were devoured. How helpless they seemed, and, measured by every human rule, how hopeless was their cause! And yet within a few decades the power which they invoked proved mightier than the legions of the emperor and the faith in which they died was triumphant o'er all the land. It is said that those who went to mock at their sufferings returned asking themselves, "What is it that can enter into the heart of man and make him die as these die?" They were greater conquerors in their death than they could have been had they purchased life by a surrender of their faith.

What would have been the fate of the church if the early Christians had had as little faith as many of our Christians have to-day? And if the Christians of to-day had the faith of the martyrs, how long would it be before the fulfilment of the prophecy that "every knee shall bow and every tongue confess"?

I am glad that He, who is called the Prince of Peace—who can bring peace to every troubled heart and whose teachings, exemplified in life, will bring peace between man and man, between community and community, between State and State, between nation and nation throughout the world—I am glad that He brings courage as well as peace so that those who follow Him may take up and each day bravely do the duties that to that day fall.

As the Christian grows older he appreciates more and more the completeness with which Christ satisfies the longings of the heart, and grateful for the peace which he enjoys and for the strength which he has received, he repeats the words of the great scholar, Sir William Jones:

"Before thy mystic altar, heavenly truth,
I kneel in manhood, as I knelt in youth,
Thus let me kneel, till this dull form decay
And life's last shade be brightened by thy ray."

THE NEW NEGRO

Booker T. Washington

(1858-1915)

Booker T. Washington, orator of the Negro race, was born a plantation slave, borrowed his name from the father of his country, and worked his way through Hampton Institute as a janitor, becoming upon graduation a teacher of the negroes. In 1881 Booker T. Washington was appointed, through an Alabama State appropriation, to establish a colored normal school at Tuskegee, Alabama. His numerous addresses in behalf of this institution gave him a national reputation as an eloquent and fluent as well as an earnest speaker. He sought the salvation of the Negro race through industrial education and material as well as moral elevation. His greatest speech, no doubt, was that delivered at the International Exposition in 1895 at Atlanta, Georgia, entitled *The New Negro*. This speech, which is included here, created at the time of its delivery a tremendous sensation in the press throughout the country.

Mr. President and Gentlemen of the Board of Directors and Citizens: One-third of the population of the South is of the Negro race. No enterprise seeking the material, civil, or moral welfare of this section can disregard this element of our population and reach the highest success. I but convey to you, Mr. President and Directors, the sentiment of the masses of my race when I say that in no way have the value and manhood of the American Negro been more fittingly and generously recognized than by the managers of this magnificent Exposition at every stage of its progress. It is a recognition that will do more to cement the friendship of the two races than any occurrence since the dawn of our freedom.

Not only this, but the opportunity here afforded will awaken among us a new era of industrial progress. Ignorant and inexperienced, it is not strange that in the first years of our new life we began at the top instead of at the bottom; that a seat in Congress or the State Legislature was more sought than real estate or industrial skill; that the political convention or stump speaking had more attractions than starting a dairy farm or truck garden.

A ship lost at sea for many days suddenly sighted a friendly vessel. From the mast of the unfortunate vessel was seen a signal, "Water, water; we die of thirst!" The answer from the friendly vessel at once came back, "Cast down your bucket where you are." A second time the signal, "Water, water; send us water!" ran up from the distressed vessel, and was answered, "Cast down your bucket where you are." And a third and fourth signal for water was answered, "Cast down your bucket where you are." The captain of the distressed vessel, at last heeding the injunction, cast down his bucket, and it came up full of fresh, sparkling water from the mouth of the Amazon River. To those of my race who depend on bettering their condition in a foreign land, or who underestimate the importance of cultivating friendly relations with the Southern white man, who is their next door neighbor, I will say: "Cast down your bucket where you are,"—cast it down in making friends in every manly way of the people of all races by whom we are surrounded.

Cast it down in agriculture, in mechanics, in commerce, in domestic service, and in the professions. And in this connection, it is well to bear in mind that whatever other sins the South may be called to bear, when it comes to business, pure and simple, it is in the South that the Negro is given a man's chance in the commercial world, and in nothing is this Exposition more eloquent than in emphasizing this chance. Our greatest danger is that in the great leap from slavery to freedom we may overlook the fact that the masses of us are to live by the productions of our hands, and fail to keep in mind that we shall prosper in proportion as we learn to dignify and glorify common labor, and put brains and skill into the common occupations of life; shall prosper in proportion as we learn to draw the line between the superficial and the substantial, the ornamental gewgaws of life and the useful. No race can prosper till it learns that there is as much dignity in tilling a field as in writing a poem. It is at the bottom of life we must begin, and not at the top. Nor should we permit our grievances to overshadow our opportunities. To those of the white race who look to the incoming of those of foreign birth and strange tongue and habits for the prosperity of the South, were I permitted I would repeat what I say to my own race, "Cast down your bucket where you are." Cast it down among the eight millions of negroes whose habits you know, whose fidelity and love you have tested in days when to have proved treacherous meant the ruin of your firesides. Cast down your bucket among those people who have, without strikes and labor wars, tilled your fields, cleared your forests, builded your railroads and cities, and brought forth treasures from the bowels of the earth, and helped make possible this magnificent representation of the progress of the South. Casting down your bucket among my people, helping and encouraging them as you are doing on these grounds, and in education of head, hand, and heart, you will find that they will buy your surplus land, make blossom the waste places in your fields, and run your factories.

While doing this, you can be sure in the future, as in the past, that you and your families will be surrounded by the most patient, faithful, law-abiding and unresentful people that the world has seen. As we have proved our loyalty to you in the past, in nursing your children, watching by the sick-bed of your mothers and fathers, and often following them with tear-dimmed eyes to their graves, so in the future, in our humble way, we shall stand by you with a devotion that no foreigner can approach, ready to lay down our lives, if need be, in defence of yours, interlacing our industrial, commercial, civil and religious life with yours in a way that shall make the interests of both races one. In all things that are purely social we can be as separate as the fingers, yet one as the hand in all things essential to mutual progress.

THE STRENUOUS LIFE [17]

Theodore Roosevelt
(1858-1919)

Theodore Roosevelt, America's great outstanding spokes-man of social progressive reform, was born in New York City, the son of a prosperous Dutch family. Because of frailty of body as a child, Roosevelt early applied himself to physical training until in later life he was distinguished as the famous leader of the Rough Riders and as a hunter. After his graduation from Harvard University at the age of seventeen Roosevelt toured Europe before studying law. It was in 1882 that he entered on his long political career as an assemblyman in the New York legislature, where he at once started his reform agitation by se-curing the impeachment for corruption of several state officials. In 1889 he was appointed National Civil Service Commissioner in Washington, D.C. During President McKinley's administra-tion Roosevelt was selected as Assistant Secretary of the Navy, but upon the outbreak of the war with Spain resigned to join the cavalry volunteers, known as "Roosevelt's Rough Riders." After the war he was elected Governor of New York State, and here again he inaugurated a program of reform in state politics; be-fore the expiration of his term of office he became the Republican Vice-President of the United States. Upon the assassination of President McKinley in 1901 Roosevelt became President and was re-elected in 1904. During his administration he carried further his civil reforms; settled a serious coal strike; secured the right to build the Panama Canal; purified the meat packing industry; inaugurated pure-food and drug legislation; and prosecuted "bad trusts." In his conduct of international relations he was in-strumental in securing the establishment of Pan-American good will and in terminating the Russo-Japanese War.

[17] Abridged.

After his retirement from the presidency Roosevelt went big-game hunting in Africa, obtaining many valuable specimens for American museums and making a triumphant tour of Europe on his return, lecturing before the universities of Europe. At the outbreak of war in Europe in 1914 Roosevelt strongly urged preparedness. His own participation in the war was frustrated, but he lived to see the sacrifice of his own son, Quentin, on the field of action, and the triumph of the Allies.

Roosevelt's brusque matter-of-fact style of delivery set a precedent for the speech of the 20th century. His emphatic gestures, clenched fist, flashing smile, revealing the much car-tooned rows of white teeth, his cutting sarcasm and bursts of humor all distinguished him before the American public.

Among his best known speeches are: *The Strenuous Life* (1899); *National and Industrial Peace* (1902); *The Right of the People to Rule* (1912); *Khartoum* and *Guildhall Speeches* (1910); *Columbia Speech* (1912); *Plattsburg Speech* (1915); *The Flag on the Firing Line* (1917).

Roosevelt's speech may well be classified as "something greater and higher than eloquence—as action, noble, sublime, god-like action."

Included here is his speech on *The Strenuous Life* delivered before the Hamilton Club in Chicago on April 10, 1899, which is itself an epitome of his own life.

GENTLEMEN: In speaking to you, men of the greatest city of the West, men of the State which gave to the country Lincoln and Grant, men who preeminently and distinctly embody all that is most American in the American character, I wish to preach not the doctrine of ignoble ease but the doctrine of the strenuous life; the life of toil and effort; of labor and strife; to preach that highest form of success which comes not to the man who desires mere easy peace but to the man who does not shrink from danger, from hardship, or from bitter toil, and who out of these wins the splendid ultimate triumph.

A life of ignoble ease, a life of that peace which springs merely from lack either of desire or of power to strive after great things, is as little worthy of a nation as of an individual. I ask only that what every self-respecting American demands from himself, and from his sons, shall be demanded of the American nation as a whole. Who among you would teach your boys that ease, that peace is to be the first consideration in your eyes—to be the ultimate goal after which they strive? You men of Chicago have made this city great, you men of Illinois have done your share, and more than your share, in making America great, because you neither preach nor practice such a doctrine. You work yourselves, and you bring up your sons to work. If you are rich, and are worth your salt, you will teach your sons that though they have leisure, it is not to be spent in idleness; for wisely used leisure merely means that those who possess it, being free from the necessity of working for their livelihood are all the more bound to carry on some kind of non-remunerative work in science, in letters, in art, in exploration, in historical research—work of the type we most need in this country, the successful carrying out of which reflects most honor upon the nation.

We do not admire the man of timid peace. We admire the man who embodies victorious effort; the man who never wrongs his neighbor; who is prompt to help a friend; but who has those virile qualities necessary to win in the stern strife of actual life. It is hard to fail; but it is worse never to have tried to succeed. In this life we get nothing save by effort. Freedom from effort in the present merely means that there has been stored up effort in the past. A man can be freed from the necessity of work only by the fact that he or his fathers before him have worked to good purpose. If the freedom thus purchased is used aright, and the man still does actual work, though of a different kind, whether as a writer or a general, whether in the field of politics or in the field of exploration and adventure, he shows he deserves his good fortune. But if he treats this period of freedom from the need of actual labor as a period not of preparation but of mere enjoyment, he shows that he is simply a cumberer of the earth's surface; and he surely unfits himself to hold his own with his fellows if the need to do so should again arise. A mere life of ease is not in the end a satisfactory life, and above all it is a life which ultimately unfits those who follow it for serious work in the world.

As it is with the individual so it is with the nation. It is a base untruth to say that happy is the nation that has no history. Thrice happy is the nation that has a glorious history. Far better it is to dare mighty things, to win glorious triumphs, even though checkered by failure, than to take rank with those poor spirits who neither enjoy much nor suffer much because they live in the gray twilight that knows neither victory nor defeat. If in 1861 the men who loved the Union had believed that peace was the end of all things and war and strife the worst of all things, and had acted up to their belief, we would have saved hundreds of thousands of lives, we would have saved hundreds of millions of dollars. Moreover, besides saving all the blood and treasure we then lavished, we would have prevented the heartbreak of many women, the dissolution of many homes; and we would have spared the country those months of gloom and shame when it seemed as if our armies marched only to defeat. We could have avoided all this suffering simply by shrinking from strife. And if we had thus avoided it we should have shown that we were weaklings and that we were unfit to stand among the great nations of the earth. Thank God for the iron in the blood of our fathers, the men who upheld the wisdom of Lincoln and bore sword or rifle in the armies of Grant! Let us, the children of the men who proved themselves equal to the mighty days—let us, the children of the men who carried the great Civil War to a triumphant conclusion, praise the God of our fathers that the ignoble counsels of peace were rejected, that the suffering and loss, the blackness of sorrow and despair, were unflinchingly faced and the years of strife endured; for in the end the slave was freed, the Union restored, and the mighty American Republic placed once more as a helmeted queen among nations.

We of this generation do not have to face a task such as that our fathers faced, but we have our tasks, and woe to us if we fail to perform them! We cannot, if we would, play the part of China, and be content to rot by inches in ignoble ease within our borders, taking no interest in what goes on beyond them; sunk in a scrambling commercialism; heedless of the higher life, the life of aspiration, of toil and risk; busying ourselves only with the wants of our bodies for the day; until suddenly we should find, beyond a shadow of question, what China has already found, that in this world the nation that has trained itself to a career of unwarlike and isolated ease is bound in the end to go down before other nations which have not lost the manly and adventurous qualities. If we are to be a really great people, we must strive in good faith to play a great part in the world. We cannot avoid meeting great issues. All that we can determine for ourselves is whether we shall meet them well or ill. Last year we could not help being brought face to face with the problem of war with Spain. All we could decide was whether we should shrink like cowards from the contest or enter into it as beseemed a brave and high-spirited people; and, once in, whether failure or success should crown our banners. So it is now. We cannot avoid the responsibilities that confront us in Hawaii, Cuba, Porto Rico, and the Philippines. All we can decide is whether we shall meet them in a way that will rebound to the national credit, or whether we shall make of our dealings with these new problems a dark and shameful page in our history. To refuse to deal with them at all merely amounts to dealing with them badly. We have a given problem to solve. If we undertake the solution there is, of course, always danger that we may not solve it aright, but to refuse to undertake the solution simply renders it certain that we cannot possibly solve it aright.

The timid man, the lazy man, the man who distrusts his country, the overcivilized man, who has lost the great fighting, masterful virtues, the ignorant man and the man of dull mind, whose soul is incapable of feeling the mighty lift that thrills "stern men with empires in their brains"—all these, of course, shrink from seeing the nation undertake its new duties; shrink from seeing us build a navy and army adequate to our needs; shrink from seeing us do our share of the world's work by bringing order out of chaos in the great, fair tropic islands from which the valor of our soldiers and sailors has driven the Spanish flag. These are the men who fear the strenuous life, who fear the only national life which is really worth leading. They believe in the cloistered life which saps the hardy virtues in a nation, as it saps them in the individual; or else they are wedded to that base spirit of gain and greed which recognizes commercialism as the be-all and end-all of national life, instead of realizing that, though an indispensable element, it is after all but one of the many elements that go to make up true national greatness. No country can long endure if its foundations are not laid deep in the material prosperity which comes from thrift, from business energy and enterprise, from hard unsparing effort in the fields of industrial activity; but neither was any nation ever yet truly great if it relied upon material prosperity alone. All honor must be paid to the architects of our material prosperity; to the great captains of industry who have built our factories and our railroads; to the strong men who toil for wealth with brain or hand; for great is the debt of the nation to these and their kind. But our debt is yet greater to the men whose highest type is to be found in a statesman like Lincoln, a soldier like Grant. They showed by their lives that they recognized the law of work, the law of strife; they toiled to win a competence for themselves and those dependent upon them; but they recognized that there were yet other and even loftier duties—duties to the nation and duties to the race.

We cannot sit huddled within our own borders and avow ourselves merely an assemblage of well-to-do hucksters who care nothing for what happens beyond. Such a policy would defeat even its own end; for as the nations grow to have ever wider and wider interests and are brought into closer and closer contact, if we are to hold our own struggle for naval and commercial supremacy, we must build up our power without our own borders. We must build the Isthmian Canal, and we must grasp the points of vantage which will enable us to have our say in deciding the destiny of the oceans of the East and the West.

So much for the commercial side. From the standpoint of international honor, the argument is even stronger. The guns that thundered off Manila and Santiago left us echoes of glory, but they also left us a legacy of duty. If we drove out a medieval tyranny only to make room for savage anarchy, we had better not have begun the task at all. It is worse than idle to say that we have no duty to perform and can leave to their fates the islands we have conquered. Such a course would be the course of infamy. It would be followed at once by utter chaos in the wretched islands themselves. Some stronger, manlier power would have to step in and do the work; and we would have shown ourselves weaklings, unable to carry to successful completion the labors that great and high-spirited nations are eager to undertake. The work must be done. We cannot escape our responsibility, and if we are worth our salt, we shall be glad of the chance to do the work—glad of the chance to show ourselves equal to one of the great tasks set modern civilization. But let us not deceive ourselves as to the importance of the task. Let us not be misled by vainglory into underestimating the strain it will put on our powers. Above all, let us face the responsibilities with proper seriousness, courage, and high resolve. We must demand the highest order of integrity and ability in our public men who are to grapple with these new problems. We must hold to a rigid accountability those public servants who show unfaithfulness to the interests of the nation or inability to rise to the high level of the new demands upon our strength and our resources. . . .

So at the present hour no small share of the responsibility for the blood shed in the Philippines, the blood of our brothers and the blood of their wild and ignorant foes, lies at the thresholds of those who by their worse than foolish words deliberately invited a savage people to plunge into a war fraught with sure disaster for them—a war, too, in which our own brave men must pay with their blood for the silly mock-humanitarianism of the prattlers who sit at home in peace.

The army and navy are the sword and the shield which this nation must carry if she is to do her duty among the nations of the earth— if she is not to stand merely as the China of the Western Hemisphere. Our proper conduct toward the tropic islands we have wrested from Spain is merely the form which our duty has taken at the moment. Of course, we are bound to handle the affairs of our own household well. We must see that there is civic honesty, civic cleanliness, civic good sense in our home administration of city, State, and Nation. We must strive for honesty in office, for honesty toward the creditors of the nation and of the individual; for the widest freedom of individual initiative where possible, and for the wisest control of individual initiative where it is hostile to the welfare of the many. But because we set our own household in order, we are not thereby excused from playing our part in the great affairs of the world. A man's first duty is to his own home, but he is not thereby excused from doing his duty to the State; for if he fails in this second duty it is under the penalty of ceasing to be a freeman. In the same way, while a nation's first duty is within its own borders, it is not thereby absolved from facing its duties in the world as a whole; and if it refuses to do so it merely forfeits its right to struggle for a place among the peoples that shape the destiny of mankind.

In the West Indies and the Philippines alike we are confronted by most difficult problems. It is cowardly to shrink from solving them in the proper way; for solved they must be, if not by us, then by some stronger and more manful race; if we are too weak, too selfish, or too foolish to solve them, some bolder and abler people must undertake the solution. Personally I am far too firm a believer in the greatness of my country and the power of my countrymen to admit for one moment that we shall ever be driven to the ignoble alternative.

So, if we do our duty aright in the Philippines, we will add to that national renown which is the highest and finest part of national life; will greatly benefit the people of the Philippine Islands; and, above all, we will play our part well in the great work of uplifting mankind. But to do this work, keep ever in mind that we must show in a high degree the qualities of courage, of honesty, and of good judgment. Resistance must be stamped out. The first and all-important work to be done is to establish the supremacy of our flag. We must put down armed resistance before we can accomplish anything else, and there should be no parleying, no faltering in dealing with our foe. As for those in our own country who encourage the foe, we can afford contemptuously to disregard them; but it must be remembered that their utterances are saved from being treasonable merely from the fact that they are despicable.

When once we have put down armed resistance, when once our rule is acknowledged, then an even more difficult task will begin, for then we must see to it that the islands are administered with absolute honesty and with good judgment. If we let the public service of the islands be turned into the prey of the spoils politician we shall have begun to tread the path which Spain trod to her own destruction. We must send out there only good and able men, chosen for their fitness and not because of their partisan service, and these men must not only administer impartial service to the natives and serve their own government with honesty and fidelity, but must show the utmost tact and firmness, remembering that with such people as those with whom we are to deal, weakness is the greatest of crimes, and that next to weakness comes lack of consideration for their principles and prejudices.

I preach to you, then, my countrymen, that our country calls not for the life of ease, but for the life of strenuous endeavor. The twentieth century looms before us big with the fate of many nations. If we stand idly by, if we seek merely swollen, slothful ease, and ignoble peace, if we shrink from the hard contests where men must win at hazard of their lives and at the risk of all they hold dear, then the bolder and stronger peoples will pass us by and will win for themselves the domination of the world. Let us therefore boldly face the life of strife, resolute to do our duty well and manfully; resolute to uphold righteousness by deed and by word; resolute to be both honest and brave, to serve high ideals, yet to use practical methods. Above all, let us shrink from no strife, moral or physical, within or without the nation, provided we are certain that the strife is without the nation, provided we are certain that the strife is justified; for it is only through strife, through hard and dangerous endeavor, that we shall ultimately win the goal of true national greatness.

CAPITAL AND LABOR

Thomas Talmadge

(1832-1902)

Thomas Talmadge, a Presbyterian clergyman, was graduated from New Brunswick Theological Seminary in 1856 and became successively pastor of the Reformed Dutch Church in Belleville, New Jersey; in Syracuse, New York; and in Philadelphia. During the Civil War he was a chaplain and following the war in 1869 became pastor of the Brooklyn Tabernacle in New York where he remained until 1894, when he became associate pastor of the First Presbyterian Church in Washington, D.C. Talmadge was very popular as an extemporaneous pulpit orator and lecturer and was a most fluent speaker. His Brooklyn Tabernacle sermons have been published; included here is a portion of one entitled *Capital and Labor.*

The greatest war the world has ever seen is between capital and labor. The strife is not like that which in history is called the Thirty Years' War, for it is a war of centuries, it is a war of the five continents, it is a war hemispheric. The middle classes in this country, upon whom the nation has depended for holding the balance of power and for acting as mediators between the two extremes, are diminishing; and if things go on at the same ratio as they are now going, it will not be very long before there will be no middle class in this country, but all will be very rich or very poor, princes or paupers, and the country will be given up to palaces and hovels.

The antagonistic forces are closing in upon each other. The telegraphic operators' strikes, the railroad employees' strikes, the Pennsylvania miners' strikes, the movements of the boycotters and the dynamiters are only skirmishes before a general engagement, or, if you prefer it, escapes through the safety-valves of an imprisoned force which promises the explosion of society. You may pooh-pooh it; you may say that this trouble, like an angry child, will cry itself to sleep; you may belittle it by calling it Fourierism, or Socialism, or St. Simonism, or Nihilism, or Communism; but that will not hinder the fact that it is the mightiest, the darkest, the most terrific threat of this century. All attempts at pacification have been dead failures, and monopoly is more arrogant, and the trades unions more bitter. "Give us more wages," cry the employees. "You shall have less," say the capitalists. "Compel us to do fewer hours of toil in a day." "You shall toil more hours," say the others. "Then, under certain conditions, we will not work at all," say these. "Then you shall starve," say those, and the workmen gradually use up that which they accumulated in better times. Unless there be some radical change, we shall have soon in this country three million hungry men and women. Now, three million hungry people can not be kept quiet. All the enactments of legislatures and all the constabularies of the cities, and all the army and navy of the United States cannot keep three million hungry people quiet. What then? Will this war between capital and labor be settled by human wisdom? Never. The brow of the one becomes more rigid, the fist of the other more clenched.

But that which human wisdom can not achieve will be accomplished by Christianity if it be given full sway. You have heard of medicines so powerful that one drop would stop a disease and restore a patient; and I have to tell you that one drop of my text properly administered will stop all these woes of society and give convalescence and complete health to all classes. "Whatsoever ye would that men should do to you, do ye even so to them." . . . .

In crossing the Alleghany Mountains, many years ago, the stage halted, and Henry Clay dismounted from the stage, went out on a rock at the very verge of the cliff, and as he stood there with his cloak wrapped about him, he seemed to be listening for something. Some one said to him, "What are you listening for?" Standing there, on the top of the mountain, he said: "I am listening to the tramp of the footsteps of the coming millions of this continent." A sublime posture for an American statesman! You and I to-day stand on the mountain-top of privilege, and on the Rock of Ages, and we look off, and we hear coming from the future the happy industries, and smiling populations, and the consecrated fortunes, and the innumerable prosperities of the closing nineteenth and the opening twentieth century.

While I speak this morning, there lies in state the dead author and patriot of France, Victor Hugo. The ten thousand dollars in his will he has given to the poor of the city are only a hint of the work he has done for nations and for all times. I wonder not that they allow eleven days to pass between his death and his burial, his body meantime kept under a triumphal arch, for the world can hardly afford to let go this man who for more than eight decades has by his unparalleled genius blessed it. His name shall be a terror to all despots, and an encouragement to all the struggling. He has made the world's burden lighter, and its darkness less dense, and its chain less galling, and its thrones of iniquity less secure. Farewell, patriot, genius of the century, Victor Hugo! But he was not the overtowering friend of mankind.

The greatest friend of capitalist and toiler, and the one who will yet bring them together in complete accord, was born one Christmas night while the curtains of heaven swung, stirring by the wings angelic. Owner of all things—all the continents, all worlds, and all the islands of light. Capitalist of immensity, crossing over to our condition. Coming into our world, not by gate of palace, but by door of barn. Spending His first night amid the shepherds. Gathering after around Him the fishermen to be His chief attendants. With adze, and saw, and chisel, and ax, and in a carpenter-shop showing himself brother with the tradesmen. Owner of all things, and yet on a hillock back of Jerusalem one day resigning everything for others, keeping not so much as a shekel to pay for His obsequies, by charity buried in the suburbs of a city that had cast Him out. Before the cross of such a capitalist, and such a carpenter, all men can afford to shake hands and worship. Here is the every man's Christ. None so high, but He was higher. None so poor, but He was poorer. At His feet the hostile extremes will yet renounce their animosities, and countenances which have glowered with the prejudices and revenge of centuries shall brighten with the smile of heaven as He commands: "Whatsoever ye would that men should do to you, do ye even so to them."

BIBLIOGRAPHY OF THE AMERICAN PERIOD

American Oratory, 1775-1826, comp. members Philadelphia Bar, E. C. and J. Biddle, Philadelphia, 1853.

Bancroft, George: *History of the United States,* D. Appleton and Company, New York, 1839.

Bassett, John A.: *A Short History of the United States,* The Macmillan Company, New York, 1930.

Beecher, Henry Ward: *Lectures and Orations,* Fleming H. Revell Company, New York, 1913.

Brown, S. G.: *Complete Works of Rufus Choate,* Little, Brown and Company, Boston, 1862.

Bryan, William Jennings: *Collected Works,* Funk and Wagnalls Company, New York, 1909.

Cass, Lewis: "The Ten Regiment Bill of 1848," *Congressional Globe,* 1848, First Session, 30th Congress, Appendix.

Depew, Chauncey: *The Library of Oratory,* Colonial Press, New York, 1902.

Dicey, Albert: *Law of the Constitution,* The Macmillan Company, New York, 1915.

Dunning, W. A.: *Reconstruction, Political and Economic,* Harper and Brothers, New York, 1907.

Elliot, Jonathan: *Debates on the Adoption of the Federal Constitution,* 5 vols., J. B. Lippincott and Company, Philadelphia, 1836-45.

Francis, G. H.: *Orators of the Age,* Harper and Brothers, New York, 1847.

Frothingham, Louis: *Brief History of the Constitution and Government of Massachusetts,* Houghton, Mifflin Company, Boston, 1925.

Garnett, Richard; Valee, Leon; and Billings, Shaw: *Masterpieces of Oratory,* Fifth Avenue Press, New York, 1900.

Graves, J. T.: *Eloquent Sons of the South,* 2 vols., The Chapple Publishing Company, Ltd., Boston, 1909.

Harding, Samuel Bannister: *Select Orations.* The Macmillan Company, New York, 1909.

Harris, A. M.: *Selected Orations,* Cokesbury Press, Nashville, 1924.

Hart, Albert Bushnell: *Epochs of American History,* Longmans, Green and Company, New York, 1931.

Hawthorne, Julian: *Orations of American Orators,* Colonial Press, New York, 1900.

Higginson, Francis: *American Orators and Oratory,* Imperial Press, Cleveland, 1901.

Ingersoll, Robert: *Works,* Ingersoll Publishers, Inc., New York, 1900.

Johnson, Alexander: *Representative American Orations,* G. P. Putnam's Sons, New York, 1884.

Lecky, W. E.: *The American Revolution,* D. Appleton and Company, New York, 1763-83.

Lecky, W. E.: *History of England in the Eighteenth Century.* D. Appleton and Company, New York, 1878-90.

Lee, Carleton: *The World's Orations,* "Orators of America," G. P. Putnam's Sons, New York, 1900.

McClure, Alexander: *Famous American Statesmen and Orators,* 6 vols., F. F. Lovell Company, New York, 1902.

Miller, M. M.: *Great Debates in American History,* 14 vols., Current Literature Publications, New York, 1913.

Nicolay, John George, and Hay, John: *Abraham Lincoln,* The Century Company, New York, 1923.

O'Neill, James M.: *Contemporary Speeches,* The Century Company, New York, 1930.

Pattee, Fred Lewis: *Century Readings in American Literature,* The Century Company, New York, 1919.

Peabody, S. H.: *American Patriotism,* American Book Company, New York, 1880.

Platz, Mabel: *The History of Public Speaking,* Noble and Noble, New York, 1935.

Reed, Thomas B.: *Modern Eloquence,* J. D. Morris and Company, Philadelphia, 1900.

Ringwalt, R. C.: *Modern American Oratory,* Henry Holt and Company, New York, 1898.

Shaw, Warren Choate: *History of American Oratory,* Bobbs-Merrill Company, Indianapolis, 1928.

Shurter, Edwin: *Oratory of the South,* Neale Publishing Company, New York, 1908.

Thorndike, Ashley: *Modern Eloquence,* Modern Eloquence Corporation, New York, 1928.

Thornton, J. Wingate: *The Pulpit of the American Revolution*, Sheldon and Company, New York, 1860.

West, Willis Mason: *A History of the American Nation*, Ronald Press, New York, 1929.

Wilson, Woodrow: *Selected Literary and Political Papers and Addresses*, 3 vols., Grosset and Dunlap, New York, 1921.

Woodson, C. A.: *Negro Orators and Their Orations*, Associated Publishers, Washington, D.C., 1925.

Webster, Daniel: *Works*, 5 vols., Little Brown and Company, Boston, 1869.

Van Doren, Carl: *Selections from the Works of Jonathan Edwards*, Charles Scribner's Sons, New York, 1926.

THE WORLD WAR PERIOD

INTRODUCTION

The agitations for social and industrial reforms which were engrossing orators of the world during the early decades of the 20th century were ruthlessly interrupted by the advent of the World War. To understand a situation which could martial the leading nations of the world into its ranks would require a study not only of the political, social, and economic relations of the world powers of the twentieth century but a study of the 18th and 19th century diplomatic history of Eurrope.

Before the war there were frequent public discussions on militarism, international relations, disarmament, and world peace. A study of these speeches reveals data of great interest alike to the student of public speaking and to the historian. It is not possible in a work of this size to include all the speeches which might throw light on the background of the World War. Since, however, militarism, imperialism, nationalism, and the system of secret alliances were dominant factors leading to the catastrophe, there are included here speeches by Otto von Bismarck and Emperor Wilhelm II, who were the preachers of these doctrines in Germany.

The declaration of war was an oratorical opportunity for the statesmen of the various countries as they successively took up arms in the conflict. The declaration as made by Raymond Poincaré, President of France, is selected here as representative of the call to arms.

While the war was in progress there were frequent eloquent exhortations to "carry on." In England David Lloyd George, England's Premier during the conflict, made a strong *Appeal to the Nation* on September 19, 1914; and in France Georges Clemenceau urged the people *On to Victory* as he took over the premiership of France. Both of these speeches are here included as representative of this phase of the war.

The Russian Revolution, paralleling the World War, gave birth to Soviet Russia under the leadership of Nikolai Lenin, a man so gifted with the power of speech, insight, and leadership that he became gradually the spokesman of the Russian proletariat.   Communism, which overthrew the aristocracy of Russia and placed the reins of the government in the hands of self-asserted leaders, grew out of Lenin's efforts.   On his death he passed on the leadership of communism to Joseph Stalin. A representative speech of Lenin is *A Dictatorship of the Proletariat.*

Following the Armistice of November 11, 1919, the terms of the peace treaty were the subject of national and international debates.   It was Woodrow Wilson, President of the United States, who presented the salient Fourteen Points which outlined the terms of the Peace of Paris and the League of Nations. The League especially became the principal subject of violent discussion throughout the United States and abroad.   It is the speech which Woodrow Wilson made on his Fourteen Points which has been included here as representative of the agitation.

Outstanding among subsequent international conferences following the war was the Conference on the Limitation of Armaments which met in Washington, D. C., in November of 1921.   On this occasion Charles Evans Hughes, as permanent chairman, delivered the opening address.   Again in 1927 the Briand-Kellogg Treaty was initiated with the purpose of renouncing war.   Aristide Briand, then Premier of France, presented the treaty to the plenipotentiaries who signed it at Paris in 1928.   These two speeches are presented as indicative of the discussions on world peace.

The most universal aftermath of the World War was felt in an international economic depression which engulfed all the countries of the world.   Seeking readjustment socially, economically, and politically, leaders everywhere were engaged in public discussions on world affairs.   In England Stanley Baldwin challenged the youth of Great Britain to protect democracies; in the United States President Roosevelt through an extensive program sought to alleviate the inevitable consequences of war; while from the pulpits of the world came such messages as that of Harry Emerson Fosdick delivered at the Assembly of the League of Nations on *A Christian Conscience About War* in an attempt to show the utter futility of war in solving the problems of the world. Speeches of these three orators have been selected for this volume as indicative of the post-war attitude.

There was a strong reaction to the World War felt throughout Europe. In Italy there grew up the fascist party under the dynamic leadership of Benito Mussolini, whose power as an orator was in no small way responsible for the sweeping success of the fascist movement as he strove to make Italy one of the leading world powers. In order to gain natural resources for the New Italy and to establish strong national defenses Mussolini invaded Ethiopia in 1938, although his conquest of this country was a violation of the covenants he was pledged to support. Included here is a speech delivered by Mussolini following the conquest of Ethiopia. The speech, entitled *The Absurdity of Eternal Peace,* is characteristic of the leader of fascism in Italy.

Following the World War in Turkey Kemal Ataturk undertook to bring about the recovery of Turkey and appealed by public speech for self-defense and international cooperation as a guarantee of peace. In this collection is an excerpt from the longest speech made by this Turkish leader in which he defined the purpose of the new Turkey which he had created.

In Japan Toyohiko Kagawa for many years went about preaching against the imperialistic policies of Japan. It was a huge task to which this speaker set himself. Although his doctrines seemed to be thwarted by the war into which the imperialistic policies of Japan flung the Orient, we record here a speech of this great reformer entitled *The New Social Order.*

Organized under her great leader, Chiang Kai-Shek, China has since the World War expressed national unity more than ever before in her history. Although vast areas of China have been devastated by Japanese aggression, there is significance in the speeches delivered by the spokesman of modern China.

It was in 1919, following the World War, that Mahatma Gandhi in India issued his famous pledge of passive resistance to Great Britain in an effort to relieve the condition of the Untouchables and establish dominion status for India. Because of the significance of his work a characteristic speech of this savior of India is presented.

Perhaps the most consequential aftermath of the World War was the birth of nazism in Germany, under the leadership of Adolph Hitler, spokesman of modern Germany. In the second decade following the World War, agitations on international relations resulting from the conflict precipitated another major European war, the extent of which is as yet unseen. Brewing under a system of secret alliances and international hatreds, the forces of naziism in Germany spurted into a new conflict of arms with the democracies of Europe.

Germany, resenting the terms of the Versailles Treaty, was led by her spokesman, Adolph Hitler, to regain for Germany her lost territories and to revive German nationalism. It was a system of organized propaganda under such spokesmen as Conrad Henlein, agitator of nazi policies in Czechoslovakia in 1938, which paved the way for the bloodless conquest of Austria and Czechoslovakia in 1939 by Adolph Hitler. Success in these ventures was followed by the invasion of Poland.

On September 3, 1939, England in order to guard her national prestige, preserve her own colonies, and defend her treaty obligations to Poland declared war on Germany and was joined by France in a declaration of war against nazi aggression.

The Americas "stood by" while the conflict which would inevitably also affect the fiber of their economic systems, raged. There was a strong belief on the part of many that "Europe had gone mad" by flinging itself into another major war so soon after the catastrophe of the World War. Others, recalling that Europe had always had her boundary disputes, said "Let us strive to maintain peace among ourselves."

Because of the significance of the declaration of war in Europe in 1939 there are included here the address of Adolph Hitler, Chancellor of Germany, made before the Reichstag on September 1, 1939, expressing the German point of view; the declaration of war on Germany as made by Neville Chamberlain, Prime Minister of England, before the House of Commons on September 1, 1939, expressing the British point of view; and that of Edouard Daladier, Premier of France, before the Chamber of Deputies on September 2, 1939. Accompanying these speeches is a radio address by the President of the United States, Franklin D. Roosevelt, *This Nation Will Remain Neutral,* delivered on September 4, 1939.

The World War may continue to throw its shadows down the years of the twentieth century; but, as the pages of the history of oratory reveal, there are always leaders who are striving to regenerate and save the best of civilization for posterity.

The radio may gradually become a factor in cementing together people of distant countries—as it may be a menace by spreading nationalistic propaganda. A series of Pan American peace broadcasts from the United States Office of Education at Washington, D. C., with the purpose of creating a Good Neighbor Policy between the countries of the Americas, is indicative of the work which the radio can do in breaking down national barriers and creating international goodwill and cooperation. The press and radio are mighty factors in molding public thought today. Hope for the future rests in leaders who will arise to use these agencies aright.

The world is indeed on the verge of a new social order. What that social order is to be will be determined to a great extent by the rights of the people to express their views. Leaders will be needed, but dictatorship—be it Nazist, Fascist, or Communist, where the voice of one individual speaks for the nation—cannot lead to an ultimately satisfactory social order. Freedom of speech must remain the prerogative of the people.

War appears a sordid note with which to close an anthology of world speeches, but therein may lie the greatest demonstration to posterity of the futility of force in the solution of international relations. There was never a more opportune time for the expression of social, national, and international reform from the platform than the present day. To the youth of the world is flung the challenge of keeping aglow the torch of free speech, one of the greatest safeguards of liberty and equality.

WAR AND ARMAMENTS

Otto von Bismarck

(1815-1898)

Otto von Bismarck, the German Chancellor who established the German militaristic policy which precipitated the World War, was born of a noble family, served in the army, and began his diplomatic career in 1851 as a member of the German Diet at Frankfurt. Here he started his agitations for the cause to which he devoted his life—the revival of the German Empire under the leadership of Prussia. Under Napoleon the Holy Roman Empire, which was under German supremacy, had expired; Bismarck wished to re-create an Empire confined to the German States. After a career as Ambassador to St. Petersburg and Paris, Bismarck was made Prime Minister of Germany in 1862 and set about to accomplish the unification of the German States under Prussia, with Austria counted out. To this end he brought about a war with Denmark in 1864 and with Austria in 1866, resulting in the alliance of Prussia with the German States and the North German Confederation of twenty-two states; and the war with France in 1870, followed by the union of all the German States under King Wilhelm of Prussia, who was crowned Emperor of Germany at Versailles in 1871. Thus the "man of blood and iron" accomplished his life's ambition. In 1866 Bismarck was made Prince and Chancellor and remained in this office until 1890 when he came into conflict with the new Wilhelm II over the question of the treatment of the laboring classes. Bismarck resigned and retired to his private estate until a reconciliation with the Kaiser took place in 1896 on Bismarck's 81st birthday, just two years before his death.

Bismarck may be credited with molding the German Empire, yet "his ideals of patriotism and foreign relations are marked by a sterling sense which were not found in the policies at the period of the declaration of the World War." It was Sir Wilfred Laurier who said of Bismarck, "He was the embodiment of resolute common sense, unflinching determination, relentless strength, moving onward to his end, and crushing everything in his way as unconcernedly as fate itself." Included here is his speech on *War and Armaments* which is representative of the militaristic policies which laid the foundations of the World War.

No man would attack us when we have such a powerful war machine as we wish to make of the German army. If I were to come before you to-day and say to you—supposing me to be convinced that the conditions are different from what they are—if I were to say to you, "We are strongly threatened by France and Russia; it is evident that we will be attacked; my conviction as a diplomat, considering the military necessities of the case, is that it is expedient for us to take the defensive by striking the first blow, as we are now in a position to do; an aggressive war is our advantage, and I beg the Reichstag for a milliard or half a milliard to begin it at once against both our neighbors"—indeed, gentlemen, I do not know that you would have sufficient confidence in me to consent. I hope you would not.

But if you were to do it, it would not satisfy me. If we, in Germany, should wish to wage war with the full exertion of our national strength, it must be a war in which all who engage in it, all who offer themselves as sacrifices in it—in short the whole nation, takes part as one man; it must be a people's war; it must be a war carried on with the enthusiasm of 1870, when we were ruthlessly attacked. I well remember the ear-splitting, joyful shouts at the Cologne railway station; it was the same from Berlin to Cologne; and it was the same here in Berlin. The waves of public feeling in favor of war swept us into it whether we wished or not. It must always be so if the power of a people such as ours is to be exerted to the full. It will be very difficult, however, to make it clear to the provinces and states of the confederation and to their people that war is now unavoidable and necessary. They would ask: "Are you sure of that? Who knows?" In short, when we came to actual hostilities, the weight of such imponderable considerations would be much heavier against us than the material opposition we would meet from our enemies. "Holy Russia" would be irritated; France would bristle with bayonets as far as the Pyrenees. It would be the same everywhere. A war which was not decreed by the popular will could be carried on if once the constituted authorities had finally decided on it as a necessity; it would be carried on vigorously, and perhaps successfully after the first fire and

sight of blood. But it would not be a finish fight in its spirit with
such fire and *élan* behind it as we would have in a war in which we
were attacked. Then all Germany from Memel to Lake Constance
would flame out like a powder mine; the country would bristle with
arms, and no enemy would be rash enough to join issues with the
"furor Teutonicus" thus roused by attack.

We must not lose sight of such considerations, even if we are now
superior to our future opponents, as many military critics beside our
own consider us to be. All our own critics are convinced of our
superiority. Naturally every soldier believes it. He would come very
near to being a failure as a soldier if he did not wish for war and
feel full assurance of victory. If our rivals sometimes suspect that it
is fear of the result which makes us peaceful, they are grievously in
error. We believe as thoroughly in the certainty of our victory in a
righteous cause as any lieutenant in a foreign garrison can believe in
his third glass of champagne—and perhaps we have more ground for
our assurance. It is not fear which makes us peaceful, but the consciousness of our strength—the consciousness that if we were attacked
at the most unfavorable time, we are strong enough for defense and
for keeping in view the possibility of leaving it to the providence of
God to remove in the meantime the necessity for war.

I am never for an offensive war, and if war can come only through
our initiative, it will not begin. Fire must be kindled by some one
before it can burn, and we will not kindle it. Neither the consciousness
of our strength, as I have just represented it, nor the trust in our
alliances, will prevent us from continuing with our accustomed zeal
our accustomed efforts to keep the peace. We will not allow ourselves
to be led by bad temper; we will not yield to prejudice. It is undoubtedly true that the threats, the insults, the provocations which have
been directed against us have aroused great and natural animosities on
our side. And it is hard to rouse such feelings in the Germans, for
they are less sensitive to the dislike of others toward them than any
other nation. We are taking pains, however, to soften these animosities,
and in the future, as in the past, we will strive to keep the peace with
our neighbors—especially with Russia. When I say "especially with
Russia," I mean that France offers us no security for the success of
our efforts, though I will not say that it does not help. We will never
seek occasion to quarrel. We will never attack France. In the many
small occasions for trouble which the disposition of our neighbors to
spy and to bribe has given us, we have made pleasant and amicable
settlements. I would hold it grossly criminal to allow such trifles either
to occasion a great national war or to make it probable. There are
occasions when it is true that the "more reasonable gives way." I name
Russia especially, and I have the same confidence in the result I had
a year ago, when my expression gave this "Liberal" paper here occasion
for black type. But I have it without running after—or, as a German

paper expressed it, "groveling before Russia." That time has gone by. We no longer sue for favor, either in France or in Russia. The Russian press and Russian public opinion have shown the door to an old powerful and attached friend, as we were. We will not force ourselves upon them. We have sought to regain the old confidential relationship, but we will run after no one. But this does not prevent us from observing—it rather spurs us on to observe with redoubled care—the treaty rights of Russia. Among these treaty rights are some which are not conceded by all our friends: I mean the rights which at the Berlin congress Russia won in the matter of Bulgaria.

In consequence of the resolution of the congress, Russia up to 1885 chose as prince a near relative of the Czar, concerning whom no one asserted or could assert that he was anything else than a Russian dependent. It appointed the minister of war and a greater part of the officials. In short, it governed Bulgaria. There is no possible doubt of it. The Bulgarians, or a part of them, or their prince—I do not know which—were not satisfied. There was a *coup d'état*, and there has been a defection from Russia. This has created a situation in which we have no call to change theoretically the rights which Russia gained from the conference. But if Russia should seek to establish its rights forcibly, I do not know what difficulties might arise, and it does not concern us to know. We will not support forcible measures and we will not advise them. I do not believe there is any disposition toward them. I am sure no such inclination exists. But if through diplomatic means, through the intervention of the sultan as the suzerain of Bulgaria, Russia seeks its right, then I assume that it is the province of loyal German statesmanship to give an unmistakable support to the provisions of the Berlin treaty, and to stand by the interpretation which, without exception, we gave it—an interpretation on which the voice of the Bulgarians cannot make me err. Bulgaria, the little state between the Danube and the Balkans, is certainly not of sufficient importance to justify plunging Europe into war from Moscow to the Pyrenees, from the North Sea to Palermo—a war the issue of which no one could foresee, at the end of which no one could tell what the fighting had been about.

So I can say openly that the position of the Russian press, the unfriendliness we have experienced from Russian public opinion, will not prevent us from supporting Russia in a diplomatic attempt to establish its rights as soon as it makes up its mind to assert them in Bulgaria. I say deliberately, "as soon as Russia expresses the wish." We have put ourselves to some trouble heretofore to meet the views of Russia on the strength of reliable hints; but we have lived to see the Russian press attacking, as hostile to Russia, the very things in German politics which were prompted by a desire to anticipate Russia's wishes. We did that at the congress, but it will not happen again. If Russia officially asks us to support measures for the restoration in

Bulgaria of the situation approved by the congress, with the sultan as suzerain, I would not hesitate to advise his Majesty, the emperor, that it should be done. This is the demand which the treaties make on our loyalty to a neighbor with whom, be the mood what it will, we have to maintain neighborly relations and defend great common interests of monarchy, such as the interests of order against its antagonists in all Europe—with a neighbor, I say, whose sovereign has a perfect understanding in this regard with the allied sovereigns. I do not doubt that when the Czar of Russia finds that the interests of his great empire of a hundred million people require war, he will make war. But his interests cannot possibly prompt him to war against us. I do not think it at all probable that such a question of interest is likely to present itself. I do not believe that a disturbance of the peace is imminent—if I may recapitulate—and I beg that you will consider the pending measure without regard to that thought or that apprehension, looking on it rather as a full restoration of the mighty power which God has created in the German people—a power to be used if we need it. If we do not need it we will not use it, and we will seek to avoid the necessity for its use. This attempt is made somewhat more difficult by threatening articles in foreign newspapers, and I may give special admonition to the outside world against the continuance of such articles. They lead to nothing. The threats made against us—not by the government, but in the newspapers—are incredibly stupid, when it is remembered that they assume that a great and proud power such as the German empire is capable of being intimidated by an array of black spots made by a printer on paper, a mere marshaling of words. If they give up that idea, we could reach a better understanding with both our neighbors. Every country is finally answerable for the wanton mischief done by its newspapers, and the reckoning is liable to be presented some day in the shape of a final decision from some other country. We can be bribed very easily—perhaps too easily—with love and good will. But with threats, never!

We Germans fear God, nothing else in the world.

It is the fear of God which makes us love peace and keep it. He who breaks it against us ruthlessly will learn the meaning of the warlike love of the Fatherland which in 1813 rallied to the standard the entire population of the then small and weak kingdom of Prussia; he will learn, too, that this patriotism is now the common property of the entire German nation, so that whoever attacks Germany will find it unified in arms, every warrior having in his heart the steadfast faith that God will be with us.

ADDRESS TO THE GERMAN PEOPLE

Emperor Wilhelm II

(1859-   )

Emperor William II, King of Prussia and Kaiser of Germany during the World War, received a thorough military training as a youth; from Bismarck he learned a type of statecraft which made a religion of militarism and imperialism. To this background was added an innate personal aggressiveness, an autocratic manner, and an absolute belief in the divine right of kings, which gave the Kaiser a peculiar power.

In 1888 Wilhelm II ascended the throne and set to work on the aggrandizement of Germany through colonial expansion, industrial and commercial supremacy, and primacy among the great world powers. His effort to gain world domination through the World War was frustrated by the combined forces of the Allies. After Germany's defeat in 1918, the Kaiser abdicated his throne and fled to Holland where he remained on his estate at Doorn as an exile.

Among other aspirations the Kaiser sought to be an orator and delivered in all over 170 public addresses throughout his lifetime, all of which were strongly tinctured with the confidence of his appoinment as "the instrument of God" and with the imperialistic doctrines which led to the World War.

Included here is Kaiser Wilhelm's address to the German people which was delivered on August 6, 1914, at the outbreak of the war.

Since the founding of the Empire, during a period of forty-three years, it has been my zealous endeavor and the endeavor of my ancestors to preserve peace to the world and in peace to promote our vigorous development. But our enemies envy us the success of our toil. All professed and secret hostility from East and West and from beyond the sea, we have till now borne in the consciousness of our responsibility and power. Now, however, our opponents desire to humble us. They demand that we look on with folded arms while our enemies gird themselves for treacherous attack. They will not tolerate that we support our ally with unshaken loyalty, who fights for its prestige as a great power, and with whose abasement our power and honor are likewise lost. Therefore the sword must decide. In the midst of peace the world attacks us. Therefore up! To arms! All hesitation, all delay were treachery to the fatherland. It is a question of the existence or non-existence of the Empire which our fathers founded anew. It is the question of the existence or the non-existence of German might and German culture. We shall defend ourselves to the last breath of man and beast. And we shall survive this fight, even though it were against a world of enemies. Never yet was Germany conquered when she was united. Then forward march with God! He will be with us as He was with our fathers.

DECLARATION OF WAR BY FRANCE

Raymond Poincaré

(1860-1934)

Raymond Poincaré, President of France during the World War, was born in Lorraine of a distinguished professional family; was educated in the French Lycée and completed his studies in law at the University of Paris with a brilliant record. At the age of 27 Poincaré was a member of the Chamber of Deputies as a moderate Republican. In 1893 he was made Minister of Public Instruction; in 1894 Minister of Finance and in 1903 was elected to the Senate. When he entered on his joint duties as Prime Minister and Minister of Foreign Affairs in 1912, Poincaré supported the alliance with Russia and the entente with England. Poincaré's election as President of the Republic of France in 1913 was a victory for military nationalism and his efforts resulted in the enactment of the three-year military service law as a check on Teutonic aggression.

When war was declared in 1914, Poincaré's able voice gave courage and patriotic enthusiasm to his countrymen, and he with Clemenceau steered the course of the war to Allied victory. Following the Armistice Poincaré served as Premier from 1922 to 1924 and as Prime Minister from 1928 to 1929 and in 1931 was elected leader of the French bar. Because of his brilliant oratory as well as his writings Poincaré was admitted to the French Academy.

Included here is the *Declaration of War by France* as made by Poincaré in the Parliament of France August 4, 1914.

Gentlemen: France has just been the object of a violent and premeditated attack, which is an insolent defiance of the law of nations. Before any declaration of war had been sent to us, even before the German Ambassador had asked for his passports, our territory has been violated. The German Empire has waited till yesterday evening to give at this late stage the true name to a state of things, which it had already created.

For more than forty years the French, in sincere love of peace, have buried at the bottom of their heart the desire for legitimate reparation.

They have given to the world the example of a great nation which, definitely raised from defeat by the exercise of will, patience and labor, has only used its renewed and rejuvenated strength in the interest of progress and for the good of humanity.

Since the ultimatum of Austria opened a crisis which threatened the whole of Europe, France has persisted in following and in recommending on all sides a policy of prudence, wisdom, and moderation.

To her there can be imputed no act, no movement, no word, which has not been peaceful and conciliatory.

At the hour when the struggle is beginning, she has the right, in justice to herself, of solemnly declaring that she has made, up to the last moment, supreme efforts to avert the war now about to break out, the crushing responsibility for which the German Empire will have to bear before history.

On the very morrow of the day when we and our allies were publicly expressing our hope of seeing negotiations which had been begun under the auspices of the London Cabinet carried to a peaceful conclusion, Germany suddenly declared war upon Russia, she has invaded the territory of Luxemburg, she has outrageously insulted the noble Belgian nation, our neighbor and our friend, and attempted treacherously to fall upon us while we were in the midst of diplomatic conversation.

But France was watching. As alert as she was peaceful, she was prepared; and our enemies will meet on their path our valiant covering troops, who are at their post and will provide the screen behind which the mobilization of our national forces will be methodically completed.

Our fine and courageous army, which France to-day accompanies with her maternal thought, has risen eager to defend the honor of the flag and the soil of the country.

The President of the Republic, interpreting the unanimous feeling of the country, expresses to our troops by land and sea the admiration and confidence of every Frenchman.

Closely united in a common feeling, the nation will persevere with the cool self-restraint of which, since the beginning of the crisis, she has given daily proof. Now, as always, she will know how to harmonize the most ardent enthusiasm with that self-control which is the sign of enduring energy and is the best guarantee of victory.

In the war which is beginning France will have Right on her side, the eternal power of which cannot with impunity be disregarded by nations any more than by individuals.

She will be heroically defended by all her sons; nothing will break their sacred union before the enemy; to-day they are joined together as brothers in a common indignation against the aggressor, and in a common patriotic faith.

She is faithfully helped by Russia, her ally; she is supported by the loyal friendship of England.

And already from every part of the civilized world sympathy and good wishes are coming to her. For to-day once again she stands before the universe for Liberty, Justice and Reason. *Haut les coeurs et vive la France!*

APPEAL TO THE NATION [2]

David Lloyd George
(1863-   )

David Lloyd George, England's Premier during the World War, born of Welsh parentage, was reared in a simple, frugal environment in the home of an uncle, who was a shoemaker. With this uncle he studied French to enable him to pass the examinations for the Law Society. In 1884 he was admitted as a solicitor and opened his office at Portmadoc. Here, as a member of the local debating society, he exhibited and cultivated his talent for platform oratory and learned the English language. As a solicitor he won a reputation as an industrious and reliable pleader and won his first important trial in the Llanfrothen Burial Case. Upon his entrance into the House of Commons as a Liberal in 1880, Lloyd George did not at first enter into the debates, but on the outbreak of the South African War he at once became an antagonist of the war policy. In 1905 he became President of the Board of Trade and there distinguished himself by being as capable in handling men as he had been adroit and effective in debate.

In spite of his pacifist tendencies before the great World War, Lloyd George in his speech delivered at Queen's Hall on September 19, 1914, at the declaration of the war entered heartily into the prosecution of the war. On the death of Lord Kitchener, June, 1916, he became Secretary of War and in December of that same year was made Prime Minister. Following the completion of the war Lloyd George was prominent in the discussions of the Peace Conference at Paris in 1919.

Lloyd George is regarded by his fellow countrymen as the personification of democracy. His oratory flamed through the

[2] Abridged.

years of the war and his driving force, enthusiasm, and courage in the face of reverses aided in securing the triumph of the Allies in 1918. His appearance is most impressive and he has the ability to stir the emotions.

Included here is the peroration of Lloyd George's *Appeal to the Nation* at Queen's Hall, London, September 19, 1914, delivered primarily to win Welsh recruits to the war.

I will not say a single word in disparagement of the German people. They are a great people, and have great qualities of head and hand and heart. I believe, in spite of recent events, that there is as great a store of kindliness in the German peasant as in any peasant in the world; but he has been drilled into a false idea of civilization. It is efficient, it is capable; but it is a hard civilization; it is a selfish civilization; it is a material civilization. They cannot comprehend the action of Britain at the present moment; they say so. They say, "France we can understand; she is out for vengeance; she is out for territory—Alsace and Lorraine." They say they can understand Russia, she is fighting for mastery—she wants Galicia. They can understand you fighting for vengeance—they can understand you fighting for mastery—they can understand you fighting for greed of territory; but they cannot understand a great empire pledging its resources, pledging its might, pledging the lives of its children, pledging its very existence, to protect a little nation that seeks to defend herself. God made man in His own image, high of purpose, in the region of the spirit; German civilization would recreate him in the image of a Diesel machine—precise, accurate, powerful, but with no room for soul to operate.

Have you read the Kaiser's speeches? If you have not a copy I advise you to buy one; they will soon be out of print, and you will not have many more of the same sort. They are full of the glitter and bluster of German militarism—"mailed fist," and "shining armor." Poor old mailed fist. Its knuckles are getting a little bruised. Poor shining armor! The shine is being knocked out of it. There is the same swagger and boastfulness running through the whole of the speeches. The extract which was given in the British Weekly this week is a very remarkable product as an illustration of the spirit we have to fight. It is the Kaiser's speech to his soldier on the way to the front.

Lunacy is always distressing, but sometimes it is dangerous; and when you get it manifested in the head of the State, and it has become the policy of a great Empire, it is about time that it should be ruthlessly put away. I do not believe he meant all these speeches; it was simply the martial straddle he had acquired. But there were men around him who meant every word of them. This was their religion. Treaties? They tangle the feet of Germany in her advance. Cut them with the sword. Little nations? They hinder the advance of Germany. Trample them in the mire under the German heel! The Russian Slav? He challenges the supremacy of Germany in Europe. Hurl your legions at him and massacre him! Christianity? Sickly sentimentalism about sacrifice for others! Poor pap for German digestion! We will have a new diet. We will force it upon the world. It will be made in Germany—a diet of blood and iron. What remains? Treaties have gone. The honor of nations has gone. Liberty has gone. What is left? Germany! Germany is left!—"Deutschland über alles!"

That is what we are fighting,—that claim to predominancy of a material, hard civilization, which if it once rules and sways the world, liberty goes, democracy vanishes. And unless Britain and her sons come to the rescue it will be a dark day for humanity.

Have you followed the German Junker in his doings? We are not fighting the German people. The German people are under the heel of this military caste, and it will be a day of rejoicing for the German peasant, artisan, and trader when the military caste is broken. You know its pretensions. They give themselves the airs of demigods. They walk the pavements, and civilians and their wives are swept into the gutter: they have no right to stand in the way of the great Prussian soldier. Men, women, nations—they all have to go. He thinks all he has to say is "We are in a hurry." That is the answer he gave Belgium—"Rapidity of action is Germany's greatest asset," which means, "I am in a hurry; clear out of my way." You know the type of motorist, the terror of the roads, with a 60-horse-power car; he thinks the roads are made for him and knocks down anybody who impedes the action of his car, by a single mile an hour. The Prussian Junker is the road-hog of Europe. Small nationalities in his way are hurled to the roadside, bleeding and broken. Women and children are crushed under the wheels of his cruel car and Britain is ordered out of his road. All I can say is this: if the old British spirit is alive in British hearts, that bully will be torn from his seat. Were he to win it would be the greatest catastrophe that has befallen democracy since the day of the Holy Alliance and its ascendancy.

They think we cannot beat them. It will not be easy. It will be a long job; it will be a terrible war; but in the end we shall march through terror to triumph. We shall need all our qualities—every quality that Britain and its people possess—prudence in counsel, daring in action, tenacity in purpose, courage in defeat, moderation in victory; in all things faith.

It has pleased them to believe and to preach the belief that we are a decadent and a degenerate people. They proclaim to the world through their professors that we are a non-heroic nation skulking behind our mahogany counters, whilst we egg on more gallant races to their destruction. This is a description given us in Germany—"a timorous, craven nation, trusting to its Fleet." I think they are beginning to find their mistake out already—and there are half a million young men of Britain who have already registered a vow to their King that they will cross the seas and hurl that insult to British courage against its perpetrators on the battlefields of France and Germany. We want half a million more; and we shall get them.

I envy you young people your opportunity. They have put up the age limit for the Army, but I am sorry to say I have marched a good many years even beyond that. It is a great opportunity, an opportunity that only comes once in many centuries to the children of men. For most generations sacrifice comes in drabness and weariness of spirit. It comes to you to-day, and it comes to-day to us all, in the form of the glow and thrill of a great movement for liberty, that impels millions throughout Europe to the same noble end. It is a great war for the emancipation of Europe from the thraldom of a military caste which has thrown its shadows upon two generations of men, and is now plunging the world into a welter of bloodshed and death. Some have already given their lives. There are some who have given more than their own lives; they have given the lives of those who are dear to them. I honor their courage, and may God be their comfort and their strength. But their reward is at hand; those who have fallen have died consecrated deaths. They have taken their part in the making of a new Europe—a new world. I can see signs of it coming in the glare of the battlefield.

The people will gain more by this struggle in all lands than they comprehend at the present moment. It is true they will be free of the greatest menace to their freedom. That is not all. There is something infinitely greater and more enduring which is emerging already out of this great conflict—a new patriotism, richer, nobler, and more exalted than the old. I see amongst all classes, high and low, shedding themselves of selfishness, a new recognition that the honor of the country does not depend merely on the maintenance of its glory in the stricken field, but also in protecting its homes from distress. It is bringing a new outlook for all classes. The great flood of luxury and sloth which had submerged the land is receding and a new Britain is appearing. We can see for the first time the fundamental things that matter in life, and that have been obscured from our vision by the tropical growth of prosperity.

May I tell you in a simple parable what I think this war is doing for us? I know a valley in North Wales, between the mountains and the sea. It is a beautiful valley, snug, comfortable, sheltered by the mountains from all the bitter blasts. But it is very enervating, and I remember how the boys were in the habit of climbing the hills above the village to have a glimpse of the great mountains in the distance, and to be stimulated and freshened by the breezes which came from the hill-tops, and by the great spectacle of their grandeur. We have been living in a sheltered valley for generations. We have been too comfortable and too indulgent, many, perhaps, too selfish, and the stern hand of fate has scourged us to an elevation where we can see the great everlasting things that matter for a nation—the great peaks we had forgotten, of Honor, of Duty, of Patriotism, and clad in glittering white, the great pinnacle of sacrifice pointing like a rugged finger to Heaven. We shall descend into the valleys again; but as long as the men and women of this generation last, they will carry in their hearts the image of those great mountain peaks whose foundations are not shaken, though Europe rock and sway in the convulsions of a great war.

ONE AIM: VICTORY

Georges Clemenceau
(1841-1929)

Clemenceau, the Tiger of France, had studied to become a physician, but while yet a youth he was thrown into jail for shouting "Vive la République" on the streets of Paris during an Imperial Anniversary celebration. Thereafter an exile, he came to America where he became an earnest student of American ideals, government, and language. Returning to France he was elected Mayor of Montmartre and had charge of clothing and feeding the army and the refugees during the war. At the end of the war he strove to gain "home rule" for Paris and became an enemy of the Commune.

In 1876 Clemenceau was chosen a Republican member of the Chamber of Deputies where he became a bitter opponent of the Royalist ministry and attracted attention by his pithy utterances and independent actions. His political career was enhanced by his journalistic activities. In both Clemenceau expressed a radical independence and followed no leader but his own principles. Gradually he grew away from reckless radicalism to the sane advocacy of a just and free democracy. In 1906 he was made Premier of France and executed a law separating Church and State. It was during the miners' strike that Clemenceau, then Premier, entered into his great debate with Jaurès, the socialist leader, which attracted international attention because of the brilliant attack and defense of the fundamental principles of socialism. Clemenceau, although not a socialist, believed in government ownership of monopolies and objected to the violent riots of the miners as he did also to the uprising of the wine growers in 1907, on which occasion his prompt action averted a revolution.

When the war of 1914 opened, Clemenceau entered the Viviani ministry and in 1917 was called to the premiership of France where he energetically prosecuted the war throughout its course. Following the war, he was made permanent chairman of the Peace Conference in Paris and was active in all its deliberations.

Clemenceau was a most brilliant speaker and wielded both his tongue and pen with a sharp, forceful incisiveness. Clearness, wit, and irony characterized his eloquence.

When I accepted the premiership offered to me by the President of the Republic I could not ignore the fact that we were at the most critical period of the War. I remember that I told you we should pass together through difficult and exacting times; I remember I spoke of "cruel hours." No one protested when I announced that they would come. They are coming and the only question is whether we can stand them.

When Russia's desertion occurred, when men who believed that it was only necessary to will a democratic peace to obtain it from William II, had given up their country, unwittingly I prefer to think, to the army of the invader, what one of you here could believe that the million German soldiers who were thus liberated would not be turned against us? This and more is what happened. For four years our forces have been wearing themselves out. Our front was guarded by a line of soldiers which was becoming thinner and thinner, with our allies who had themselves suffered enormous losses. And at that moment you saw arrive against you a fresh mass of German divisions in good condition when you were far from your best strength.

Is there any one of you who did not realize that under the shock of this enormous mass our lines had to give way at some points? Certainly not, for in all the conversations which I had with members of this assembly, the question asked me was, how much we had to give way.

The recoil was very serious for the English army, which had suffered formidable losses. It was grave and dangerous for the French army. I said dangerous, serious, but nothing more, and there is nothing in that to shake the confidence we should have in our soldiers.

Our men are engaged in the battle, a terrible one. They fought one against five without sleep for three and four days together. These soldiers, these great soldiers, have good and great leaders: worthy of them in every way. I have seen these leaders at work and some of them against whom I will not deny that I was prejudiced, struck me with admiration.

Is that saying that there are nowhere mistakes? I cannot maintain that. I know it too well; my duty is to discover these mistakes and correct them. In this I am supported by two great soldiers,—General Foch and General Pétain. General Foch enjoys the confidence of our allies to such a degree that yesterday at the conference of Versailles they wished to have their unanimous confidence in him expressed in the communiqué given to the press.

These men are at this moment fighting in the hardest battle of the war, fighting it with a heroism which I can find no phrase worthy to express. And it is we who for a mistake made in such and such a place, or which may not even have been made, demand explanations, on the field of battle of a man worn with fatigue. It is of this man that we demand to know whether on such and such a day he did such and such a thing! Drive me from this place if that is what you ask, for I will not do it.

I came here with the desire to find simple, brief and measured words, to express the sentiment of the French people at the front and at the rear, to show the world a state of mind which cannot be analyzed, but which at this moment is the admiration of all civilized people.

I accuse no one. I am the leader of these men and it is my duty to punish them if I consider it of general benefit to do so; but it is also my greater duty to protect them if they have been unjustly attacked.

The army is better than we could ever have expected and when I say "the army" I mean men of all ranks who are under fire. That is one of the elements of our confidence, the main element. Although faith in a cause is an admirable thing, it will not bring victory; men must die for their faith to assure victory and our men are dying. We have an army made up of our children and our brothers—what can we say against it? Their leaders too have come from among us; they too are our brothers, they too are good soldiers. They come back covered with wounds when they are not left on the field of battle. What can you say against them?

We have yielded ground, much more ground than either you or I should have wished. There are men without number who have paid for this with their blood, without reproach. I know of the deeds of a group of lost men, Bretons, surrounded in a wood all night. The next day, still resisting, they sent a carrier pigeon to their corps to say "We are here. We have promised not to yield. We shall fight to the end. If you can come to find us, come; we can hold out half a day longer." Those men make and safeguard the country of which you are so proud. They die for the greatest and most noble ideal—to continue a history which shall be the foremost among all the histories of civilized peoples.

Our own duty is very simple, very tame. We run no danger. We are at our posts, you here, I with my cabinet—posts which are not dangerous as are those of the soldiers, but which are nevertheless where the capital interests of the country are decided.

As long as you remain calm, confident in yourself, determined to hold out to the end of this hard struggle, victory is yours. It is yours because our enemies, who are not as intelligent as they are said to be, have only one method—to throw their whole force into the venture and risk everything. They tried it at Verdun and on the Yser, at Dunkirk and at Calais. They were checked—by whom? First by the English and then by the French. After that they appeared in Champagne; they advanced. Do you think it possible to make a war in which you never have to retreat? There is only one thing that matters, the victorious issue, the final success. Our men can only give their lives; but you through patience, firmness and determination can give them what they deserve—victory.

You have before you a government, which, as it told you at the very beginning, never conceived of the possibility of negotiating without victory. You know what you are doing. You can keep us in power or send us away; but as long as you keep us, whatever may happen, you can be sure that the country will be defended to the death and that no force will be spared to obtain success. We will never consent to anything but peace with victory. That is the watchword of our government.

The Germans are once more staking all. The "coup" which they are attempting is to terrorize you, to frighten you so that you will abandon the struggle. One must be ignorant of German tactics to doubt this. Why did they suddenly throw all their forces on the Yser? It was to gain Calais, to separate us from England and force us to surrender. For what was the dreadful march on Paris? To take Paris and through terror force us to surrender. Why are they beginning again to-day? To secure this effect of terror which they have never yet achieved.

The decision is in your hands for the simple reason that it is not a matter of mere reasoning but a question of action. The Americans are coming. The forces of the English and the French, as well as of our enemies, are worn out; but we have allies who are coming as a decisive factor. I have said from the beginning that American cooperation would decide the issue of the war. The point is this: events in Russia have allowed a million of the enemy's men to appear on the Franco-British front. We have allies, whom we did not have in 1870, when we yielded because we were alone. We have allies, who represent the foremost nations of the world, who have pledged themselves to continue the war to the end, to the success which we hold in our grasp, which we are on the point of achieving if we have the necessary tenacity.

I declare, and it must be my last word, that victory depends upon us. The civil forces must rise to the height of their duty; it is not necessary to make this demand of the soldiers. Send me away if I have been an unworthy servant; drive me out, condemn me, but at least take the trouble to formulate criticisms. As for me, I assert that the French people have in all ways done their full duty. Those who have fallen have not fallen in vain, for they have made French history great. It remains for the living to complete the magnificent work of the dead.

LAST SPEECH

Jean Jaurès
(1859-1914)

Jean Jaurès, French socialist leader, was born in Castres, became a professor at Toulouse, and in 1885 was elected to the French Chamber of Deputies as a moderate Republican. After his period of service he returned to Toulouse and founded an Academy of Medicine. It was at approximately this time that he became a socialist and was returned to the French Chamber in 1893, where his oratorical powers made him a leader of the socialist party.

Jaurès soon came to be considered the leading Socialist of France, sharing with August Bebel the leadership of international socialism. Through his moderation toward Captain Dreyfus, whom he defended as innocent, Jaurès conflicted with the revolutionary Marxian Socialists. He also supported the Socialist deputy, Millerand, as a member of the cabinet, and this led to a great debate between Bebel and Jaurès resulting in the formation of a Syndicate of Socialists.

In 1910 Jaurès championed the cause of the railroad workers in their strike. He was bitterly opposed to the war and favored an agreement with Germany to halt armaments and even a general strike to stop war. In 1913 he opposed the three-year military law and in 1914, just before the outbreak of the great World War, he made a notable speech against militarism at Brussels. This speech aroused so much agitation that on July 31 after Jaurès had had an interview with Premier Viviani he was assassinated in front of a café in Paris.

Jean Jaurès is almost universally regarded as one of the leading 20th century orators. Included here is his *Last Speech* delivered at Brussels July 29, 1914, at a meeting of the International Socialist Bureau.

The diplomats negotiate. It seems that they will be satisfied to take from Serbia a little of its blood. We have, therefore, a little rest to insure peace. But to what lessons is Europe submitted? After twenty centuries of Christianity, after one hundred years of the triumph of the rights of men, how is it possible that millions of persons, without knowing why, can kill each other?

And Germany? If she knew of the Austrian note it is inexcusable to have allowed such a step. And if official Germany did not know of the Austrian note what is her governmental wisdom? You have a contract which binds you and drags you into war and don't know why you have been dragged? I ask, what people have given such an example of anarchy?

Nevertheless the authorities hesitate. Let us profit thereby and organize. For us, Socialists, our duty is simple. We do not need to impose upon our government a policy of peace; our government is practising it. I, who have never hesitated to bring upon my head the hatred of our patriots by my obstinate will and by my desire to bring about a Franco-German understanding, have the right to say that the French government desires peace.

The French government is the best ally for peace of the English government which has taken the initiative in conciliation and gives Russia advice of prudence and patience. As for us, it is our duty to insist that the government shall speak to Russia with force so that she will refrain. If unfortunately Russia pays no heed, it is our duty to say, "We know of but one treaty; the treaty which binds us to the human race."

This is our duty, and in expressing it we find ourselves in accord with our German comrades who demand that their government see to it that Austria moderates her acts. It is possible that the telegram of which I spoke is due partly to that desire of the German workers. One cannot go against the wish of four millions of enlightened consciences.

Do you know what the proletarians are? They are the men who have collectively an affection for peace and a horror of war. The chauvinists, the nationalists, are men who have collectively a love for war and slaughter. When, however, they feel over their heads the menace of conflicts and wars which may put an end to their capitalistic existence, then they remind themselves that they have friends who seek to reduce the storm. But for the supreme masters, the ground is mined. In the darkness of the first battles they will succeed in pulling along the masses. But gradually as disease completes the work of the shells, as death and misery strike, these men will turn to German, French, Russian, Austrian and Italian authorities and demand what reasons they can give for all the corpses. And then revolution let loose will say, "Go and beg grace from God and man."

LABOR'S ATTITUDE

Samuel Gompers
(1850-1924)

In London, England, in the year 1850, was born a boy who was to become a leader of labor in the United States. When 13 years of age this lad, Samuel Gompers, left his native land to come to America with his parents; at 21 years of age he was an American citizen. Cigarmaking became his trade and as a member of the International Union of Cigarmakers he helped to organize the American Federation of Labor in 1881. In 1882 he became president of the Federation and held that office until his death in 1924 with an interim of two years when he was defeated by the Socialists, whom he opposed in their movements among the unions.

In 1894 Gompers was made editor of the *American Federationist,* official publication of the American Federation of Labor. The Clayton Anti-Trust Law of 1914 was a result of Gompers' agitations through this publication.

Although previous to the World War an ardent pacifist, Gompers swung over to the cause of the war, suppressed pacifist tendencies in the trade unions, and became a commissioner of the U.S. Council of National Defense in 1917. After the armistice Gompers represented the American Federation of Labor at the Peace Conference in Paris, 1918-1919. Later he became active in the organization of the Pan-American Federation of Labor. He fought the I.W.W. and compulsory arbitration of labor disputes.

A good public speaker, Gompers was prominent in agitating for labor for over forty years. The speech included here was delivered on February 22, 1918, in New York City, to rally the workingmen of the United States in support of the war. It indicates the prevalent attitude of leaders throughout the United States at that time. It is in the concise, almost epigrammatic style used by the advocates of war in times of stress.

I doubt if there existed, or now exists, in all the world a man who is so pronounced a pacifist as was I. I belonged to every peace society of which I knew anything. An officer in some form or other of each of them, a speaker of nearly all of them, within the sphere of my opportunities. In addition, as a union man, a labor man, an internationalist in spirit, I had believed, came to believe, that it would be impossible for such a war to have occurred at any time after the international understandings and pledge of the workers of nearly all the civilized countries; and I really believed in the pledge, in the spirit of it . . . I had permitted myself to live in a fool's paradise. I believed that when men solemnly pledged themselves and those in whose name they had the authority to speak, they would go to the limit in their own countries to prevent a rupture of international peace.

Almost out of a clear sky came this declaration of war, and I found the men who had pledged to me and mine, my fellows, flying to the colors of the greatest autocrat of all times, the modern buccaneer of the world, the type of the intellectual scientific murderer, to fly to the colors upon his order, to attack the brothers whose lives they vouched to protect. I awoke. From then until now and until the peace of the world is assured I count myself transformed from an ultrapacifist to a living, breathing, fighting man. No one who has known me fairly intimately has ever accused me of running away from an honorable contest. And it is not of much interest what any one man may believe or is, but that which he tries to inculcate upon his fellow-citizens. I believe that in our country we have the greatest opportunities existing of any country upon the face of the globe. America is not perfect; the Republic of the United States is not perfect; it has the imperfections of the human; and inasmuch as we are not perfect, we have not been able to make a perfect democratic republic; but it is the best country on the face of the earth.

America is not merely a name. It is not merely a land. It is not merely a country, nor is it merely a continent. America is a symbol; it is an ideal, the hopes of the world can be expressed in the ideal America. The man in America, with the opportunities afforded, with the right of expression, with the right of determination, with the right of creating a political revolution by well-ordered methods, who will not or does not appreciate that it is his duty to stand by such a country in such stress and in such a storm, who is unwilling to stand up and be counted as a man in this fight for the maintenance of these ideals—is unworthy of the privilege of living in this country. . . .

To me this war has quite a different meaning than almost any war in history of which I have read. It began through the machinations of the German Kaiser and in the splendid responses made by France, and England, and Belgium. In Prussia they were all exulting, but when the Republic of the United States entered into this world struggle it ceased to be a war and became at once a crusade for freedom and justice and liberty. I hold it to be the duty of every man to give every ounce of energy in fighting, in producing, in helping in any way that he can, that this crusade shall be a triumph for the world. If we may not be able to abolish war for all time, at least let us make the conditions such that a war of this character may never again occur, or at least shall be long deferred.

For years and years the workers of America, realizing the position in which we are placed in this most favored country of ours, pressed home upon the agencies of government, the agencies of industry, the agencies of all activities, that inasmuch as the workers performed so large a service for society and civilization, the human side of the workers should receive the highest consideration, and that no agency of government or of industry should be constituted without the representative of the workers as part of that agency.

I never have asked anything for myself. I have no favor to ask. I have no personal pleas to make. I speak for a cause. I speak for the masses of workers as well as the masses of all our people. For, no matter, the meanest of all of them, I consider it my duty and privilege to say a word for him, even when perhaps he might repudiate me. But, as the result of this war or crusade, this principle for which labor has been contending has found recognition in the department of government. . . .

Who is there in America today who looks back with regret on the sacrifices made when the Declaration of Independence was coined for the world and a new nation created? Who regrets that anyone belonging to them, no matter how near or how remote, sacrificed his life and his all that America should be born? The war of our civilized life, our Civil War, when the struggle was for the maintenance of the Union and the abolition of human slavery, who among the gallant men on both sides, or either side, now regrets that the fight was made and the sacrifices borne in order to make good that this nation is one and indivisible and that on its shores and under its flag slavery is forever abolished? Who doubts that? Our war with Spain, small though it was, meant sacrifices. It meant Cuba free and independent. Is there a man or woman in this audience or this country who regrets the sacrifice that was made that Cuba might be made free?

So the men and the women of the future will regard this struggle as we now look upon those struggles to which I have referred. They will call us blessed, every man and every woman, who has given something to this great cause of human justice and freedom, to feel the satisfaction, the exultation, the exaltation of youth and energy renewed in them in a great cause, the greatest that has ever been presented to the peoples of any country and in any time. It is a privilege to live in this time and to help in this common fight.

With all my heart and spirit I appeal to my fellow citizens, to my fellow workers, to make this one great slogan the watchword from now on until triumph shall perch upon our arms: "Unity, solidarity, energy, and the will to fight and to win."

THE FOURTEEN POINTS

Woodrow Wilson
(1856-1924)

Woodrow Wilson, President of the United States during the World War, was born at Staunton, Virginia. The son of a Presbyterian minister, he spent his childhood in Georgia, where the effects of the Civil War were evident. After his graduation from Princeton University in 1879 he studied law at the University of Virginia. In 1885 he received the degree of Ph.D. from Johns Hopkins University and began his teaching career as a lecturer there. He served successively on the faculties of Bryn Mawr, Wesleyan and Princeton, and in 1902 became president of Princeton. In 1910 he was elected Governor of New Jersey by the Democratic Party. His reforms in that state included the establishment of direct primaries, a public service commission, a state school system, widows' pensions, the incorporation of trusts and scientific poor relief.

When in 1912 Wilson was elected President of the United States he continued his efforts for reform, advocating the reduction of the tariff, the establishment of a federal trade commission, labor laws, the construction of an Alaskan railway, the establishment of a federal income tax and the promise of independence for the Philippines.

After making every effort to preserve neutrality, Wilson finally declared America's entrance into the World War in 1917, "to make the world safe for democracy." With this same ideal he became a member of the Peace Conference, where he urged the creation of the League of Nations. He was disappointed in his hope that the United States would enter the League, and shortly thereafter he suffered a stroke of paralysis which incapacitated him until his death.

Wilson's oratory was scholarly rather than popular in character. In his university teaching and in politics he tried to arouse and persuade the intellect of his audience. The orderly arrangement and logical content of his speeches was exceptional, while his humor and his well-modulated voice made him a most attractive speaker. Whatever the verdict of history may be upon Wilson as a statesman—inspired idealist or vacillating pacifist—the fact remains that he won the world's recognition for his eloquence in behalf of international peace and disarmament.

Included here is a speech on the famous Fourteen Points which Wilson delivered to Congress on January 8, 1918. This speech laid the foundation for the whole plan of the Peace of Paris in 1919 and for the League of Nations.

Gentlemen of the Congress: Once more, as repeatedly before, the spokesmen of the Central Empires have indicated their desire to discuss the objects of the war and the possible basis of a general peace. Parleys have been in progress at Brest-Litovsk between Russian representatives and representatives of the Central Powers to which the attention of all the belligerents has been invited for the purpose of ascertaining whether it may be possible to extend these parleys into a general conference with regard to terms of peace and settlement.

The Russian representatives presented not only a perfectly definite statement of the principles upon which they would be willing to conclude peace but also an equally definite program of the concrete application of those principles. The representatives of the Central Powers, on their part, presented an outline of settlement which, if much less definite, seemed susceptible of liberal interpretation until their specific program of practical terms was added. That program proposed no concessions at all either to the sovereignty of Russia or to the preferences of the populations with whose fortunes it dealt, but meant, in a word, that the Central Empires were to keep every foot of territory their armed forces had occupied—every province, every city, every point of vantage—as a permanent addition to their territories and their power.

It is a reasonable conjecture that the general principles of settlement which they at first suggested originated with the more liberal statesmen of Germany and Austria, the men who have begun to feel the force of their own people's thought and purpose, while the concrete terms of actual settlement came from the military leaders who have no thought but to keep what they have got. The negotiations have been broken off. The Russian representatives were sincere and in earnest. They cannot entertain such proposals of conquest and domination.

The whole incident is full of significance. It is also full of perplexity. With whom are the Russian representatives dealing? For whom are the representatives of the Central Empires speaking? Are they speaking for the majorities of their respective parliaments or for the minority parties, that military and imperialistic minority which has so far dominated their whole policy and controlled the affairs of Turkey and of the Balkan states which have felt obliged to become their associates in this war?

The Russian representatives have insisted, very justly, very wisely, and in the true spirit of modern democracy, that the conferences they have been holding with the Teutonic and Turkish statesmen should be held within open, not closed, doors, and all the world has been audience, as was desired. To whom have we been listening, then? To those who speak the spirit and intention of the resolutions of the German Reichstag of the 9th of July last, the spirit and intention of the Liberal leaders and parties of Germany, or to those who resist and defy that spirit and intention and insist upon conquest and subjugation? Or are we listening, in fact, to both, unreconciled and in open and hopeless contradiction? These are very serious and pregnant questions. Upon the answer to them depends the peace of the world.

But, whatever the results of the parleys at Brest-Litovsk, whatever the confusions of counsel and of purpose in the utterances of the spokesmen of the Central Empires, they have again attempted to acquaint the world with their objects in the war and have again challenged their adversaries to say what their objects are and what sort of settlement they would deem just and satisfactory. There is no good reason why that challenge should not be responded to, and responded to with the utmost candor. We did not wait for it. Not once, but again and again, we have laid our whole thought and purpose before the world, not in general terms only, but each time with sufficient definition to make it clear what sort of definite terms of settlement must necessarily spring out of them. Within the last week Mr. Lloyd George has spoken with admirable candor and in admirable spirit for the people and Government of Great Britain.

There is no confusion of counsel among the adversaries of the Central Powers, no uncertainty of principle, no vagueness of detail. The only secrecy of counsel, the only lack of fearless frankness, the only failure to make definite statement of the objects of the war, lies with Germany and her allies. The issues of life and death hang upon these definitions. No statesman who has the least conception of his responsibility ought for a moment to permit himself to continue this tragical and appalling outpouring of blood and treasure unless he is sure beyond a peradventure that the objects of the vital sacrifice are part and parcel of the very life of Society and that the people for whom he speaks think them right and imperative as he does.

There is, moreover, a voice calling for these definitions of principle and of purpose which is, it seems to me, more thrilling and more compelling than any of the many moving voices with which the troubled air of the world is filled. It is the voice of the Russian people. They are prostrate and all but helpless, it would seem, before the grim power of Germany, which has hitherto known no relenting and no pity. Their power, apparently, is shattered. And yet their soul is not subservient. They will not yield either in principle or in action. Their conception of what is right, of what is humane and honorable for them to accept, has been stated with a frankness, a largeness of view, a generosity of spirit, and a universal human sympathy which must challenge the admiration of every friend of mankind; and they have refused to compound their ideals or desert others that they themselves may be safe.

They call to us to say what it is that we desire, in what, if in anything, our purpose and our spirit differ from theirs; and I believe that the people of the United States would wish me to respond, with utter simplicity and frankness. Whether their present leaders believe it or not, it is our heartfelt desire and hope that some way may be opened whereby we may be privileged to assist the people of Russia to attain their utmost hope of liberty and ordered peace.

It will be our wish and purpose that the processes of peace, when they are begun, shall be absolutely open and that they shall involve and permit henceforth no secret understandings of any kind. The day of conquest and aggrandizement is gone by; so is also the day of secret covenants entered into in the interest of particular governments and likely at some unlooked-for moment to upset the peace of the world. It is this happy fact, now clear to the view of every public man whose thoughts do not still linger in an age that is dead and gone, which makes it possible for every nation whose purposes are consistent with justice and the peace of the world to avow now or at any other time the objects it has in view.

We entered this war because violations of right had occurred which touched us to the quick and made the life of our own people impossible unless they were corrected and the world secure once for all against their recurrence.

What we demand in this war, therefore, is nothing peculiar to ourselves. It is that the world be made fit and safe to live in; and particularly that it be made safe for every peace-loving nation which, like our own, wishes to live its own life, determine its own institutions, be assured of justice and fair dealing by the other peoples of the world as against force and selfish aggression.

All the peoples of the world are in effect partners in this interest, and for own part we see very clearly that unless justice be done to others it will not be done to us. The program of the world's peace, therefore, is our program; and that program, the only possible program, as we see it, is this:

1. Open covenants of peace, openly arrived at, after which there shall be no private international understandings of any kind, but diplomacy shall proceed always frankly and in the public view.

2. Absolute freedom of navigation upon the seas, outside territorial waters, alike in peace and in war, except as the seas may be closed in whole or in part by international action for the enforcement of international covenants.

3. The removal, so far as possible, of all economic barriers and the establishment of an equality of trade conditions among all the nations consenting to the peace and associating themselves for its maintenance.

4. Adequate guarantees given and taken that national armaments will be reduced to the lowest points consistent with domestic safety.

5. A free, open-minded, and absolutely impartial adjustment of all colonial claims, based upon a strict observance of the principle that in determining all such questions of sovereignty the interests of the populations concerned must have equal weight with the equitable claims of the government whose title is to be determined.

6. The evacuation of all Russian territory and such a settlement of all questions affecting Russia as will secure the best and freest co-operation of the other nations of the world in obtaining for her an unhampered and unembarrassed opportunity for the independent determination of her own political development and national policy and assure her of a sincere welcome into the society of free nations under institutions of her own choosing; and, more than a welcome, assistance also of every kind that she may need and may herself desire. The treatment accorded Russia by her sister nations in the months to come will be the acid test of their good will, of their comprehension of her needs as distinguished from their own interests, and of their intelligent and unselfish sympathy.

7. Belgium, the whole world will agree, must be evacuated and restored, without any attempt to limit the sovereignty which she enjoys in common with all other free nations. No other single act will serve as this will serve to restore confidence among the nations in the laws which they have themselves set and determined for the government of their relations with one another. Without this healing act the whole structure and validity of international law is forever impaired.

8. All French territory should be freed and the invaded portions restored, and the wrong done to France by Prussia in 1871 in the matter of Alsace-Lorraine, which has unsettled the peace of the world for nearly fifty years, should be righted, in order that peace may once more be made secure in the interest of all.

9. A readjustment of the frontiers of Italy should be effected along clearly recognizable lines of nationality.

10. The peoples of Austria-Hungary, whose place among the nations we wish to see safeguarded and assured, should be accorded the freest opportunity of autonomous development.

11. Rumania, Serbia, and Montenegro should be evacuated; occupied territories restored; Serbia accorded free and secure access to the sea; and the relations of the several Balkan states to one another determined by friendly counsel along historically established lines of allegiance and nationality; and international guarantees of the political and economic independence and territorial integrity of the several Balkan states should be entered into.

12. The Turkish portions of the present Ottoman Empire should be assured a secure sovereignty, but the other nationalities which are now under Turkish rule should be assured an undoubted security of life and an absolutely unmolested opportunity of autonomous development, and the Dardanelles should be permanently opened as a free passage to the ships and commerce of all nations under international guarantees.

13. An independent Polish state should be erected which should include the territories inhabited by indisputably Polish populations, which should be assured a free and secure access to the sea, and whose political and economic independence and territorial integrity should be guaranteed by international covenant.

14. A general association of nations must be formed under specific covenants for the purpose of affording mutual guarantees of political independence and territorial integrity to great and small states alike.

In regard to these essential rectifications of wrong and assertions of right we feel ourselves to be intimate partners of all the governments and peoples associated together against the imperialists. We cannot be separated in interest or divided in purpose. We stand together until the end.

For such arrangements and covenants we are willing to fight and to continue to fight until they are achieved; but only because we wish the right to prevail and desire a just and stable peace such as can be secured only by removing the chief provocations to war, which this program does remove.

We have no jealousy of German greatness, and there is nothing in this program that impairs it. We grudge her no achievement or distinction of learning or of pacific enterprise such as have made her record very bright and very enviable. We do not wish to injure her or to block in any way her legitimate influence or power. We do not wish to fight her either with arms or with hostile arrangements of trade if she is willing to associate herself with us and the other peace-loving nations of the world in covenants of justice and law and fair dealing.

We wish her only to accept a place of equality among the peoples of the world—the new world in which we now live—instead of a place of mastery.

Neither do we presume to suggest to her any alteration or modification of her institutions. But it is necessary, we must frankly say, and necessary as a preliminary to any intelligent dealings with her on our part, that we should know whom her spokesmen speak for when they speak to us, whether for the Reichstag majority or for the military party and the men whose creed is imperial domination.

We have spoken now, surely, in terms too concrete to admit of any further doubt or question. An evident principle runs through the whole program I have outlined. It is the principle of justice to all peoples and nationalities, and their right to live on equal terms of liberty and safety with one another, whether they be strong or weak.

Unless this principle be made its foundation no part of the structure of international justice can stand. The people of the United States could act upon no other principle; and to the vindication of this principle they are ready to devote their lives, their honor, and everything that they possess. The moral climax of this the culminating and final war for human liberty has come, and they are ready to put their own strength, their own highest purpose, their own integrity and devotion to the test.

SPEECH AT WASHINGTON ARMA-
MENT CONFERENCE [3]

Charles Evans Hughes
(1862-   )

Charles Evans Hughes was born in New York State, was graduated from the Columbia Law School in 1884, and was admitted to the bar and set up the practice of law in New York City in the same year. From 1891-95 he was professor and lecturer of law at Cornell University. In 1906 he defeated William Randolph Hearst in the election for the governorship of New York State, and was reelected in 1908. His administration as governor was progressive and impartial and one of the most efficient of its history. His fights for reform he accomplished largely by gaining popular support through speeches made over the State. Outstanding among these reforms were the creation of a State Probation Commission, a Public Service Commission, the Anti-Race Track Gambling Act, Direct Primary Elections, and the appointment of a State Highway Commission.

In 1910 Hughes was appointed Associate Justice of the United States Supreme Court, but he later resigned to accept the nomination to the presidency. During the war he aided President Wilson in the investigation of irregularities in airplane building in the United States army and navy. President Harding appointed Hughes Secretary of State in 1921 and he continued this service under President Coolidge until 1925. At the conference on the Limitation of Armaments which assembled in Continental Hall in Washington on November 12, 1921, with delegates from the United States, England, France, Italy, Japan, China, Holland, Belgium, and Portugal, Secretary Hughes was chosen as permanent chairman and delivered on that occasion the address included

[3] Abridged.

here. From 1926 to 1930 Hughes was a member of the International Court of Arbitration at the Hague and in 1930 he was appointed Chief Justice of the United States Supreme Court.

It is with a deep sense of privilege and responsibility that I accept the honor you have conferred.

Permit me to express the most cordial appreciation of the assurances of friendly cooperation, which have been generously expressed by the representatives of all the invited governments. The earnest desire and purpose, manifested in every step in the approach to this meeting, that we should meet the reasonable expectation of a watching world by effective action suited to the opportunity, is the best augury for the success of the conference.

The President invited the Governments of the British Empire, France, Italy and Japan to participate in a conference on the subject of limitation of armament, in connection with which Pacific and Far Eastern questions also would be discussed. It would have been most agreeable to the President to have invited all the powers to take part in this conference, but it was thought to be a time when other considerations should yield to the practical requirements of the existing exigency, and in this view the invitation was extended to the group known as the Principal Allied and Associated Powers, which, by reason of the conditions produced by the war, control in the main the armament of the world. The opportunity to limit armament lies within their grasp.

It was recognized, however, that the interest of other powers in the Far East made it appropriate that they should be invited to participate in the discussion of the Pacific and Far Eastern problems, and, with the approval of the five powers, an invitation to take part in the discussion of these questions has been extended to Belgium, China, The Netherlands, and Portugal.

The inclusion of the proposal for the discussion of Pacific and Far Eastern questions was not for the purpose of embarrassing or delaying an agreement for limitation of armament, but rather to support that undertaking by availing ourselves of this meeting to endeavor to reach a common understanding as to the principles and policies to be followed in the Far East and thus greatly to diminish and, if possible, wholly to remove, discernible sources of controversy. It is believed that by interchanges of views at this opportune time the governments represented here may find a basis of accord and thus give expression to their desire to assure enduring friendship.

In the public discussions which have preceded the conference, there have been apparently two competing views; one, that the consideration of armament should await the result of the discussion of Far Eastern questions, and another, that the latter discussion should be postponed until an agreement for limitation of armament has been reached. I am unable to find sufficient reason for adopting either of these extreme views. I think that it would be most unfortunate if we should disappoint the hopes which have attached to this meeting by a postponement of the consideration of the first subject.

The world looks to this conference to relieve humanity of the crushing burden created by competition in armament, and it is the view of the American Government that we should meet that expectation without any unnecessary delay. It is therefore proposed that the conference should proceed at once to consider the question of the limitation of armament.

This, however, does not mean we must postpone the examination of the Far Eastern questions. These questions of vast importance press for solution. It is hoped that immediate provision may be made to deal with them adequately, and it is suggested that it may be found to be entirely practicable through the distribution of the work among designated committees to make progress to the ends sought to be achieved without either subject being treated as a hindrance to the proper consideration and disposition of the other.

The proposal to limit armament by agreement of the powers is not a new one, and we are admonished by the futility of earlier effort. It may be well to recall the noble aspirations which were voiced twenty-three years ago in the imperial rescript of His Majesty the Emperor of Russia. It was then pointed out with clarity and emphasis that, "The intellectual and physical strength of the nations, labor, and capital are for the major part diverted from their natural application and unproductively consumed. Hundreds of millions are devoted to acquiring terrible engines of destruction, which, though today regarded as the last word of science, are destined tomorrow to lose all value in consequence of some fresh discovery in the same field. National culture, economic progress, and the production of wealth are either paralyzed or checked in their development. Moreover, in proportion as the armaments of each power increase, so do they less and less fulfill the object which the governments have set before themselves. The economic crisis, due in great part to the system of armaments *à l'outrance,* and the continual danger which lies in this massing of war materials, are transforming the armed peace of our days into a crushing burden, which the peoples have more and more difficulty in bearing. It appears evident, then, that if this state of things were prolonged it would inevitably lead to the calamity which it is desired to avert, and the horrors of which make every thinking man shudder in advance. To put an end to these incessant armaments and to seek the means of warding off the calamities which are threatening the whole world—such is the supreme duty which is to-day imposed on all States."

It was with this sense of obligation that His Majesty the Emperor of Russia proposed the conference which was "to occupy itself with this grave problem," and which met at The Hague in the year 1899.

Important as were the deliberations and conclusions of that Conference, especially with respect to the pacific settlement of international disputes, its results in the specific matter of limitation of armament went no further than the adoption of a final resolution setting forth the opinion "that the restrictions of military charges, which are at present a heavy burden on the world, is extremely desirable for the increase of the material and moral welfare of mankind," and the utterance of the wish that the governments "may examine the possibility of an agreement as to the limitation of armed forces by land and sea, and of war budgets."

It was seven years later that the Secretary of State of the United States, Mr. Elihu Root, in answering a note of the Russian Ambassador suggesting in outline a program of the Second Peace Conference, said: "The Government of the United States, therefore, feels it to be its duty to reserve for itself the liberty to propose to the Second Peace Conference, as one of the subjects for consideration, the reduction or limitation of armaments, in the hope that, if nothing further can be accomplished, some slight advance may be made toward the realization of the lofty conception which actuated the Emperor of Russia in calling the First Conference." It is significant that the Imperial German Government expressed itself as "absolutely opposed to the question of disarmament," and that the Emperor of Germany threatened to decline to send delegates if the subject of disarmament was to be discussed. In view, however, of the resolution which had been adopted at the First Hague Conference, the delegates of the United States were instructed that the subject of limitation of armament "should be regarded as unfinished business, and that the Second Conference should ascertain and give full consideration to the result of such examination as the Government may have given, to the possibility of an agreement pursuant to the wish expressed by the First Conference." But by reason of the obstacles which the subject had encountered, the Second Peace Conference at the Hague, although it made notable progress in provision for the peaceful settlement of controversies, was unable to deal with limitation of armament except by a resolution in the following general terms: "The Conference confirms the resolution adopted by the Conference of 1899 in regard to the limitation of military expenditure; and, inasmuch as military expenditure has considerably increased in almost every country since that time, the Conference declares that it is eminently desirable that the governments should resume the serious examination of this question."

This was the fruition of the efforts of eight years. Although the effect was clearly perceived, the race in preparation of armaments, wholly unaffected by these futile suggestions, went on until it fittingly culminated in the greatest war of history, and we are now suffering from the unparalleled loss of life, the destruction of hopes, the economic dislocations, and the widespread improverishment which measure the cost of the victory over the brutal pretensions of military force.

But if we are warned by the inadequacy of earlier endeavors for limitation of armament, we cannot fail to recognize the extraordinary opportunity now presented. We not only have the lessons of the past to guide us, not only do we have the reaction from the disillusioning experiences of war, but we must meet the challenge of imperative economic demands. What was convenient or highly desirable before is now a matter of vital necessity. If there is to be economic rehabilitation, if the longings for reasonable progress are not to be denied, if we are to be spared the uprising of peoples made desperate in the desire to shake off burdens no longer endurable, competition in armament must stop. The present opportunity not only derives its advantage from a general appreciation of this fact, but the power to deal with the exigency now rests with a small group of nations, represented here, who have every reason to desire peace and to promote amity.

The astounding ambition which lay athwart the promise of the Second Hague Conference no longer menaces the world, and the great opportunity of liberty-loving and peace-preserving democracies has come. Is it not plain that the time has passed for mere resolutions that the responsible powers should examine the question of limitation of armaments? We can no longer content ourselves with investigations, with statistics, with reports, with the circumlocution of inquiry. The essential facts are sufficiently known. The time has come, and this Conference has been called, not for general resolutions or mutual advice, but for action. We meet with full understanding that the aspirations of mankind are not to be defeated either by plausible suggestions of postponement or by impracticable counsels of perfection. Power and responsibility are here and the world awaits a practicable program which shall at once be put into execution.

ON THE ANTI-WAR TREATY

Aristide Briand

(1863-1932)

Aristide Briand, French Premier, was educated for the law and spent fifteen years of his life as a barrister and journalist. Early in life he identified himself with the cause of the proletariat and served for a time as General Secretary for the French Socialist Party. In 1902 Briand was elected to the Chamber of Deputies where he at once agitated for the separation of Church and State. This he accomplished and administered through his appointment in 1906 as Minister of Public Instruction and Worship; from 1909 to 1913 he was Prime Minister of France. It was at the outbreak of the World War that Briand rose to prominence when Viviani offered him the portfolio of justice. At the fall of Viviani's Cabinet Briand formed his own government and assumed the direction of foreign affairs. Following the war he was alternately in and out of the premiership, taking his tenth oath to that office in 1926.

In 1921 Briand was interested particularly in the Treaty of Versailles and was sent to Washington as the representative of the French government to the Conference on Naval Disarmament. He strove to direct the foreign policy of France toward European consolidation and reconstruction, and his services in behalf of peace as expressed in the Locarno Pact were recognized by the award of the Nobel Peace prize. It was Briand who in 1927 proposed a bilateral treaty to the United States to renounce war, which materialized as the Briand-Kellogg Treaty. This treaty was signed at Paris and by 1928 forty-four nations had accepted its terms. Again in 1930 Briand represented France at the London Naval Conference. The year before his death in 1932 he was the defeated candidate for the presidency of France.

It was his oratorical gifts which early distinguished Briand and won him widespread popularity with the masses. It has been stated that his voice was so penetrating that in its lowest tones it was audible to the most remote corner of the Chamber of Deputies. This ease and animation in speech, coupled with his parliamentary experience and ability in the conduct of foreign affairs, made him one of the outstanding statesmen of France. Included here is his speech delivered to the plenipotentiaries who signed the treaty renouncing war in Paris on August 27, 1928.

Gentlemen, I am fully conscious that silence would best befit such a solemn occasion. What I should like without any further words would be to let each of you simply rise from his seat to go and affix his signature in the name of his own country to the greatest collective deed born of peace. But I should be failing in my duty to my country if I did not tell you how deeply it feels the honor of welcoming the first signatories of a general pact for the renunciation of war.

If the honor has been left to France as acknowledgment of the moral standing she enjoys thanks to her constant effort in the cause of peace, I gladly accept such tribute on behalf of the Government of the French Republic and I express the gratification of the whole people, happy that the inmost recesses of their national psychology should at last be understood by the world.

While extending to you gentlemen a cordial welcome, let me rejoice at seeing gathered here, save those who were unavoidably prevented from coming by their state of health or by other duties, all the statesmen who, in their capacity as Ministers of Foreign Affairs, have taken a personal share in the conception, preparation and drafting of the new pact.

We owe special thanks to those who have undergone the fatigue of a long journey in order to be present at this manifestation.

I have no doubt that you are all ready to join with me in the same cordial impulse to one of our colleagues who did not hesitate to come himself and assert with the full moral authority attached to his name and the great country which he represents, the affirmation of his steady faith in the importance and scope of the deed which we are about to sign.

Seated today among us in this same hall where his illustrious forerunner, President Wilson, already gave earnest evidence by works of peace of his high consciousness of the role of his country, the Honorable Mr. Kellogg is able to measure with just pride all the roads covered in so short a time since the epoch when we examined, both of us, the possibilities of realization of this vast diplomatic enterprise.

None is better qualified to take part in the negotiations, today brought to a happy ending, a preponderant part of which was his, and which will always stand to his honor in the minds of men. His optimism and his tenacity have overcome human skepticism; his loyalty and his good faith, the good will he brought to dissipate by clear and precise explanations the legitimate misgivings, have won for him the confidence of all his collaborators; his clear-sightedness has shown him what one may expect from governments inspired by the deep yearnings of nations.

What greater lesson can be offered the world than the spectacle of a reunion where, for the signature of a pact against war, Germany of her own free will and on an even footing takes her place among the other signatories, her former adversaries?

The occasion is all the more striking when it is given to a representative of France to receive for the first time for more than a half century a German Foreign Minister on French soil and give him the same welcome as all his foreign colleagues. I would add, gentlemen, when this representative of Germany is named Stresemann, one can believe me particularly happy to render homage to the highness of mind and to the courage of this eminent statesman, who during more than three years has not hesitated to assume full responsibility in the work of European cooperation for the maintenance of peace.

Since I have gone so far as to mention names, you will not take it amiss—and certainly Lord Cushendun will approve—if I personally evoke among us with brotherly feeling the name of Sir Austen Chamberlain. Allow me to address to him all our wishes for a speedy and full return to health. When I think of the unwearying devotion that the cause of peace has always fostered in his noble soul, I can not help imagining the joy which so determined an enemy of war would have felt at the sight of a meeting such as this. As to ourselves, we must perforce believe that he is still with us, whether invisible or in the flesh, at any manifestation of peace.

It will be, I hope, no exaggeration to say that today's event marks a new date in history making.

For the first time, on general plans accessible to all nations in the universe, a congress of peace does something else than settle politically the immediate conditions of a particular peace such as are imposed in fact by the results of war. For the first time, on a comprehensive and absolute scale, a treaty is truly devoted to the very establishment of peace, initiating a new law and freed from all political contingencies. Such a treaty is a beginning and not an end unto itself.

Nor have we met to liquidate a war. The Pact of Paris, born of peace and drawn from a free juridical notion, can and must be a regular treaty of concord. That is, no doubt, why Mr. Kellogg, when he insisted on leaving to the French Government the privilege of receiving you in Paris, was so kind as to tell the French Ambassador that it seemed to him quite fitting that the neighborhood of the Place de la Concorde should be chosen for signing the pact.

The treaties of Locarno, after the Dawes plan, had already borne witness to this new spirit that now finds its full vent. All their signatories were quite familiar with the idea of the renunciation of war as an instrument of national policy, as I had the occasion of saying in my message to the American people on the 6th of April, 1927. But those practical agreements, calculated to create a political guarantee of peace in a definite section of Europe, could not, because of their very nature, assume that universal character from which a general pact against war derives all its value.

The League of Nations, deeply imbued with the same spirit, had likewise issued a declaration tending in fact to obtain eventually the same result as the new pact, but apart from the fact that the United States had no share in it, the formula and methods of the League could not be the same as those to which it has been possible for us to have recourse for such a general and absolute agreement as the pact provides. The League of Nations, a vast political undertaking of insurance against war and a powerful institution of organized peace where there is room to welcome all fresh contributions to the common work, can not but rejoice at the signing of an international contract whereby she is to benefit.

Far from being inconsistent with any of her obligations, this new act on the contrary offers her a kind of general reinsurance. Thus those of her members who will soon be able to ask the League to register today's contract will rightly feel that they are bringing her a precious token of their attachment and loyalty.

It may now be appropriate to explain what is finally the essential feature of this pact against war. It is this: For the first time in the face of the whole world, through a solemn covenant involving the honor of great nations which all have behind them a heavy past, of political conflict, war is renounced unreservedly as an instrument of national policy, that is to say in its most specific and dreaded form—selfish and wilful war. Considered of yore as of divine right and having remained in international ethics as an attribute of sovereignty, that form of war becomes at last juridically devoid of what constituted its most serious danger—its legitimacy.

Henceforth, branded with illegality, it is by mutual accord truly and regularly outlawed so that a culprit would incur the unconditional condemnation and probably the enmity of all its co-signatories. It is a direct blow at the institution of war, even at its very vitals. It is no longer a question of defensive organization against this scourge, but of attacking the evil at the root itself. Thus shall war as a means of arbitrary and selfish action no longer be deemed lawful. Thus its threat shall no longer hang over the economic, political, and social life of peoples. Thus shall the smaller nations henceforth enjoy real independence in international discussions. Freed from the old bondage, the nations that have signed the new contract will gradually foresake the habit of associating the idea of national prestige and national interest with the idea of force.   And this single psychological fact will not be the least important factor in the evolution that is needed to lead to the regular stabilization of peace.

Oh, but this is not realism, it has been said, and are not sanctions lacking?   It might be asked whether true realism consists in excluding from the realm of facts the moral forces, among which is that of public opinion.   In effect, a state which would act so as to incur the reprobation of all its partners would run the positive risk of seeing all of them gradually and freely gather against it with redoubtable consequences that would not be long in ensuing.   And where is the country, signatory to this pact, whose leaders would on their own responsibility expose it to such danger?   The modern law of interdependence between nations makes it incumbent upon every statesman to take up for himself those memorable words of President Coolidge: "An act of war in any part of the world is an act that injures the interests of my country."

Now we can realize how important it is to extend the scope of this wide range of international solidarity which tends, as an ideal end, to encompass the whole of the universe.

When on the 20th of June, 1927, I had the honor of proposing to the Honorable Mr. Kellogg the form of words which he decided to accept and embody in the draft of a multilateral pact, I never contemplated for one moment that the suggested engagement should only exist between France and the United States.   Indeed, I have always thought that in one way or another through multiplication or extension the proposed covenant would in itself possess an expanding force strong enough to reach rapidly all nations whose moral adhesion was indispensable.   It was, therefore, a source of gratification to me to see Mr. Kellogg from the beginning of the active negotiations that he was to lead with such a clear-sighted and persevering mind advocate extension of the pact and assign to it that universal character that fully answered the wishes of the French Government.

It may be said that this desirable universality that was at the origin of the pact has already found its application in actual practice, for the intentions expressed by many governments enable us even now to consider the spiritual community of the nations that are morally represented at this first signature as being much wider than it appears to the onlookers. All those peoples whose delegates have not been in a position to sit among us today must realize in this hour of complete union our unanimous regret that for purely technical reasons it was found imperative to adopt a procedure best calculated to insure and expedite, for the benefit of all, the success of this great undertaking.

Thus the mind's eye broadens this solemn assembly of first signatories to a general pact for renunciation of war and extends it beyond the walls of this room and even over all frontiers whether on land or on sea.   With this wide communion of men which we feel surrounding us, we sincerely are entitled to reckon that we are more than fifteen around this table. And well may you have noticed that the Government of the Republic has purposely ordered that the flags of all nations should be hoisted over the building which is sheltering us today.

Gentlemen, in a moment the awakening of a great hope will be signaled to the world along the wires. It will henceforth behoove us as a sacred duty to do all that can and must be done for that hope not to be disappointed. Peace is proclaimed. That is well, that is much, but it still remains necessary to organize it. In the solution of difficulties right and not might must prevail. That is to be the work of tomorrow.

At this unforgettable hour the conscience of peoples, pure and rid of any national selfishness, is sincerely endeavoring to attain those serene regions where human brotherhood can be felt in the beatings of one and the same heart. Let us seek a common ideal within which we can all merge our fervent hopes and give up any selfish thoughts.

As there is not one of the nations represented here that has not shed the blood of her children on the battlefields of the last war, I propose that we should dedicate to the dead, to all the dead of the Great War, the event which we are going to consecrate together by our signatures.

A CHRISTIAN CONSCIENCE ABOUT WAR

Harry Emerson Fosdick

(1878-   )

Harry Emerson Fosdick, American educator, pulpiteer, and author, was born in Buffalo, New York, where his father was a prominent educator. His brother Raymond Fosdick was active during the World War.

In 1900 Fosdick was graduated from Colgate University and in 1904 took his B.D. from Union Theological Seminary in New York City, where he became Morris Jesup professor of practical theology in 1915. It was while he was pastor of the First Presbyterian Church in New York City that Fosdick's plea for Christian fellowship regardless of credal belief brought about a bitter controversy in the Presbyterian Church. In 1925 the Park Avenue Baptist Church of New York agreed to open its membership to all Christians by waiving its traditional ordinance of baptism if Fosdick would accept its pastorate. From this has developed the Riverside Church of New York City, where Fosdick today preaches to capacity audiences.

Harry Emerson Fosdick has acquired an international reputation as an effective and eloquent speaker and is particularly popular in university circles where his books have had a wide circulation. In addition to his pastoral duties he has written many inspirational books on spiritual themes and has lectured widely on questions of educational and political import. He is an outstanding figure of statesmanlike stature in the American pulpit.

It has been Fosdick's privilege to be one of the annual speakers at the Cathedral of Geneva for the Assembly of the League of Nations. It was in this church, where John Calvin, the founder of the Presbyterian Church, preached, that Fosdick de-

livered the address here included on September 13, 1925, entitled
A Christian Conscience about War.

> "All they that take the sword shall perish with the sword."—
> Matthew 26:52.

One ought to read with awe these words spoken nearly two thousand
years ago and only now beginning to seem obviously true. Reliance
on violence is suicidal. Said Jesus, "All they that take the sword shall
perish with the sword."

When the Master said that, it could not possibly have seemed to be
true. Then it seemed evident that those who took the sword and knew
how to use it could rule the world. Reliance on violence did not seem
suicidal but necessary, salutary, and rich in its rewards. In these words
of Jesus we have one of those surprising insights where, far ahead of
the event, a seer perceives an obscure truth which only long afterward
will emerge clear, unmistakable, imperative, so that all men must
believe it.

Pythagoras in the sixth century B. C. had such a flare of insight
when he guessed that the sun did not go about the earth but that the
earth circled about a central fire. It was a surprising leap of intuition.
No one believed it. Long centuries had to pass before Copernicus and
Galileo came and people in general were convinced of what Pythagoras
with his inner eye had seen. So when the Master said that the sword
would destroy those who used it, that seemed incredible. War suicidal!
The world did not even note this strange thing that He said, and ever
since men have tried to explain it away or laugh it off as idealism too
lofty for this earth. But today that insight of the Master comes to its own.
Once more the seer is jusified of his vision. Reliance on violence is
self-defeating; war is suicidal; civilization itself cannot survive it. That
fact has been written in fire across the world until not seers alone, but
multitudes of plain people of every tongue, tribe, and nation under
heaven are beginning to see the truth once so incredible—"If mankind
does not end war, war will end mankind."

Today my plea is simple and direct. Of all the people on earth who
ought to take in earnest this unforeseeable confirmation of the Master's
insight, Christians come first. This question of war and its denial of
the method and spirit of Jesus is peculiarly their business. Speaking from
this historic Christian pulpit to Christians of many races and nations
gathered here, one finds himself inevitably concerned with that matter—
addressing, as it were, the conscience of Christendom about war. The
destinies of humankind depend upon the arousing of that conscience.
Here in Geneva you once more are setting your minds to the high task
of working out the technique of international co-operation. In this
sanctuary we set ourselves this morning to consider the dynamic without
which all technique will fail—the conscience of Christians about war.

Doubtless we represent here many different kinds of Christianity. We belong to different Churches, hold various theories about ecclesiastical polity, subscribe to diverse creeds. But one thing does unite us all. We all start with and include the Master Himself. To all of us He is the Lord and His way is the way of life. At the fountainhead of our Christianity is Jesus Christ. His life with the Father, His faith in the moral possibilities of man, His devotion to the Kingdom of Heaven on earth, His Good Samaritan, His Golden Rule, His Sermon on the Mount, His law of finding life by losing it, His insight into the self-defeating nature of violence, and His substitution of the way of love—all this is included in any special kind of Christianity we severally may profess. How, then, can any of us avoid the conviction that this colossal and ominous question of war, upon the answer to which the future of man depends, is in particular a crucial affair for Christianity? It has been said again and again that if another war befalls us and shakes civilization to its foundations, as it surely would, the Christians of the world will be to blame. Surely that is true. The continuance of war will advertise that the 576,000,000 professed Christians on earth have not had an earnest conscience about their Master's view of life; it will bear evidence that while they have called Him, "Lord, Lord," they have not been willing to do what He said. . . .

There may have been times when war could serve good ends, when armed conflict was a means of social progress. Of this war or that it may be claimed that the sword won benefactions lacking which mankind would be the poorer. At least, there is little use in arguing the contrary. For the conviction now growing strong in this generation's mind is that whatever may have been true about war in times past, modern war is futile to achieve any good or Christian thing.

To fight with the gigantic paraphernalia of modern science; to make war in our intimately interrelated and delicately balanced modern world, where our most indispensable means of existence already have become international; to fight, not with armies against armies as of old, but with entire populations massed against entire populations so that bombs rain indiscriminate destruction on whole cities and blockades mean indiscriminate starvation to millions of families; to make war now, when an average five hours of fighting, as in the last war, burns up the endowment of a great university; to fight, knowing that, agreements or no agreements to limit the weapons of war, demonic forces like gas and bacteria are certain to be used—this is obviously futile to achieve any good thing for which a Christian man might wish or pray.

The old appeals for war in the name of a good cause fall coldly now on the instructed ear and cease to carry conviction to thoughtful minds. "Would you not go to war to protect the weak?" men ask. The answer seems obvious. A modern war to protect the weak—that is a grim jest. See how modern war protects the weak: 10,000,000 known dead soldiers; 3,000,000 presumed dead soldiers; 13,000,000 dead civilians;

20,000,000 wounded; 3,000,000 prisoners; 9,000,000 war orphans; 5,000,000 war widows; 10,000,000 refugees. What can we mean— modern war protecting the weak? The conviction grows clear in increasing multitudes of minds that modern war is no way to protect the weak.

A World Court would protect the weak. A League of Nations would protect the weak. An international mind, backed by a Christian conscience, that would stop the race for armaments, provide co-operative substitutes for violence, forbid the nations to resort to force, and finally outlaw war altogether—that would protect the weak. But this is clear: war will not do it. It is the weak by millions who perish in every modern war.

As for Christianity, the dilemma which it faces in all this seems unmistakable. The war system as a recognized method of international action is one thing; Christianity with all its purposes and hopes is another; and not all the dialectic of the apologists can make the two lie down in peace together. We may have one or we may have the other, but we cannot permanently have both.

Another stake which Christianity has in this task of overpassing war and providing international substitutes for it lies in the new and ominous developments of nationalism. In our modern world nationalism, with its attendant patriotic emotions and loyalties, has increasingly taken a form which threatens to be the chief rival of Christianity. To be sure, passionate love of country is nothing modern or new. Its roots are deep in man's instincts and man's history. We here today are patriots. We intend to be patriots. We should think less of each other if we were not patriots. Love of fatherland is one of the oldest, deepest, most instinctive and most noble sentiments of man.

But within the last four hundred years nationalism has taken a new and startling form in our Western world. With the England of Elizabeth, the France of Louis XI, the Russia of Peter the Great, the development began which more and more has nationalized both the inner and the outer life of all of us. Our politics have become nationalized until the aggrandizement of one's own country in the competitive struggle with other nationalities has been the supreme aim of statesmanship. Our economic life has become nationalized; the powerful financial interests of each nation have wielded so enormous an influence over its statecraft that government, with its army and navy to back it, has frequently been a docile instrument for the furtherance of the country's economic aims. Our education has become nationalized; our children have been taught from infancy history all out of perspective, with national egoism for its organizing center and with hatred of other nations masquerading as patriotic training of the young. Even our religion has been nationalized; with state churches or without them, the center of loyalty in the religious life of the people has increasingly become the nation. Let Protestantism acknowledge its large responsibility for this in Western Christendom! In our fight for liberty we broke up the inclusive mother church into

national churches; we reorganized the worship of the people around
nationalistic ideals; we helped to identify religion and patriotism. And
so far has that identification gone that now, when war breaks, the one
God of all humanity, whom Christ came to reveal, is split up into tribal
deities, and before these pagan idols even Christians pray for the blood
of their enemies.

Never before has human life, its statecraft, its economics, its education, its religion, on so large a scale been organized on a nationalistic
basis, and the issue is obvious. The supreme object of devotion for
multitudes is the nation. In practical action they know no higher God.
They really worship Caesar. That is the limit of their loyalty. What
once was said of the king is said now of the nation: it can do no wrong.
And such sheer paganism is sometimes openly flaunted, at least in my
country, and I presume in yours, as, "Our country! . . . may she always
be in the right; but our country, right or wrong."

Nevertheless, at the same time that this nationalistic process has
been going on, another movement has been gathering headway. The
enlarging fellowship of human life upon this planet, which began with
the clan and tribe and has moved out through ever widening circles of
communication and contact, has now become explicitly and overwhelm-
ingly international, and it never can be crowded back again. Moreover,
within this unescapable internationalism of modern life, not yet adequately recognized in government, mankind has been learning one great
lesson from his social experiments. In area after area he has succeeded
in getting what he wanted, not by violence, but by overpassing violence
and substituting co-operation. That is what social progress consists in.
All social progress can be defined as carrying over one more realm of
human life from the regime of force to the regime of co-operation.
Wherever we have civilized any social group, the essential thing which
has happened is that in that group, not force, but co-operation has become
the arbiter.

That is true of the family. A household where men captured their
wives, exposed their children in infancy, relied for obedience on the
power of life and death over their offspring, would be recognizably
uncivilized. A civilized family, with all its faults, enters into marriage by
mutual consent, relies on reasonableness, not on force, for its coherence,
and from the beginning welcomes children into the democracy of the
household. At least we have learned that violence is no way to bring
up a good family. That same path of progress we have traveled in education. Once violence ruled our schools. It was said of an old
pedagogue, Rev. James Boyer, that "it was lucky the cherubim who took
him to heaven were nothing but wings and faces or he infallibly would
have flogged them by the way." But now our schools at their best would
be ashamed to rely on violence since reasonableness and cooperation so
plainly offer, not only a more ideal, but a more effective substitute. In
religion also, being civilized means traveling the road from violence to

cooperation. Once force was used to compel faith. If a man wished to be a Christian he could be a Christian, but if he did not wish to be a Christian he had to be a Christian, and the centuries are sad with the horrors of religious persecution. But social progress has largely left all that behind and what compelled its supersession was not sentimentality but the insight that violence is self-defeating, that force is no way to get religion. So, too, has government been carried over from violence to co-operation. The process is lamentably incomplete, but, so far as it has gone, it has furnished the indispensable background for all the civilization we possess. Still upon our Western clothes we wear the buttons, now decorative only, on which once our fathers' swordbelts hung. How impossible it would have seemed to them that the time would ever come when the common carrying of private weapons would be unnecessary because co-operative and peaceful government had provided a substitute!

In one realm after another the Master's insight has proved true. Violence defeats itself. It is no way to achieve family life or education or religion or stable government. Those who rely on it as their mainstay and effective instrument are sure to miss what they are seeking to achieve. Always progress has consisted in carrying over human life from violence to co-operation.

And now we face the next great step, the most momentous step in human history. Can we achieve a like result with our international relationships? Can we carry them over from brutality and organized slaughter to reasonableness and co-operation? How the best thinking and praying of our time center around that hope of superseding belligerent nationalism with co-operative international substitutes for war!

Here, then, we face one of the most crucial and dramatic conflicts of loyalty that men ever dealt with. On the one side our life has been organized as never before in history on a nationalistic basis. On the other hand, the one hope of humanity today, if it is to escape devastating ruin, lies in rising above and beyond this nationalism and organizing the world for peace. On the one side is a narrow patriotism saying, "My country against yours," on the other, a wider patriotism saying, "My country with yours for the peace of mankind." Is there any question where real Christianity must stand in that conflict? Is there any question that if she does not stand there she faces the most tragic and colossal moral failure of her history? One would like to cry so that all Christians should hear: Followers of Christ, so often straining at the gnat and swallowing the camel, tithing mint, anise, and cummin, and neglecting the weightier matters of the law, what do all the minutiae of creed and institution that distinguish us amount to in the presence of this gigantic problem in which one of the central meanings of Christ for the world is involved? A narrow belligerent nationalism is today the most explicit and thoroughgoing denial of Christianity, its thought of God and its love of man, that there is on earth.

How evident this central problem is when we try to discuss the real issues of the world today! Some still see those issues in terms of one nation against another. That is the level on which their thinking runs. America versus Japan or France versus Germany—so in a long list of nation against nation they see the world's affairs. How desperately real the problems are on that level no one needs to be told, but, after all, those are not the deepest issues. A clear conviction grows in the best thinking of today that mankind's realest conflict of interest is not between this nation and that, but between the forward-looking, progressive, open-minded people of all nations, who have caught a vision of humanity organized for peace, and the backward-looking, reactionary, militaristic people of the same nations. The deepest line of conflict does not run vertically between the nations; it runs horizontally through all the nations. The salvation of humanity from self-destruction depends on which side of that conflict wins.

What has happened thus to make a local, national patriotism, however sacred and beautiful in many of its forms, inadequate to meet our present need is clear. In unforgettable words the world has been told by a great patriot: "Patriotism is not enough." Why is it not enough? Well, patriotism once took men of little, local loyalties and expanded their outlook and allegiance. They had been citizens of a shire; patriotism made them citizens of a nation. Patriotism once called men to the widest imaginable outreach of their devotion; it broke down local provincialisms; it stretched human horizons; it demanded unaccustomed breadth of vision and unselfishness of life. To be a patriot for the nation meant a large loyalty as against the meanness and parochialism of a local mind. But the world has moved. Life has expanded and become international. Now it is possible for patriotism to fall from its high estate. Instead of calling men to wider horizons, it can keep them with narrow ones. Once the issue was patriotism versus a small parochialism; now the question may become patriotism versus a large care for humanity. Once patriotism was the great enemy of provincialism; now it can be made to mean provincialism and to sanctify the narrow mind.

This conflict of loyalties creates your difficult problems here in Geneva. You know how tenacious the adhesions of nationalism are, how difficult to entwine the thoughts and affections of men around new ideals and new methods of world peace. But this inner struggle between two loyalties goes deeper than the realm of statesmanship; it runs far down into the souls of men where the destinies of religion lie. How can a man be a follower of Jesus Christ and still be a belligerent nationalist, when once this better hope of a world organized for peace has dawned upon his view? Whatever else Christianity may believe in, it must believe in God, Father of all men; it must believe in men of every tribe, tongue, people, and nation, as God's children; it must believe in the Kingdom of God on earth. The spirit of Christianity is not narrowly nationalistic, but universally inclusive. When the world, therefore, organizes itself on the basis of belligerent nationalism the very genius of the Christian Gospel is at stake. Once more we can have our old war systems with their appalling modern developments, or we can have Christianity, but we cannot permanently have both. They worship irreconcilable gods.

I need not, and I must not, press the analysis further. Two generations ago one of our great statesmen, Charles Sumner, said, "Not that I love country less, but Humanity more, do I now and here plead the cause of a higher and truer patriotism. I cannot forget that we are men by a more sacred bond than we are citizens—that we are children of a common Father more than we are Americans." Shall not each one of us here pray for his own country, as I pray earnestly for mine, that that spirit may come into the ascendancy? Christianity essentially involves it.

The first Christians saw this. "The early Christian Church," says a recent writer, "was the first peace society." Then came Christianity's growing power—the days when Christians, no longer outcast, were stronger than their adversaries, until at last the imperial household of Constantine himself accepted Christianity. Then Christianity, joined with the state, forgot its earlier attitudes, bowed to the necessities of imperial action, became sponsor for war, blesser of war, cause of war, fighter of war. Since then the Church has come down through history too often trying to carry the cross of Jesus in one hand and a dripping sword in the other, until now when Christians look out upon the consequence of it all, this abysmal disgrace of Christendom making mockery of the Gospel, the conviction rises that we would better go back to our first traditions, our early purity, and see whether those first disciples of the Lord were not nearer right than we have been.

We cannot reconcile Jesus Christ and war—that is the essence of the matter. That is the challenge which today should stir the conscience of Christendom. War is the most colossal and ruinous social sin that afflicts mankind; it is utterly and irremediably unchristian; in its total method and effect it means everything that Jesus did not mean and it means nothing that He did mean; it is a more blatant denial of every Christian doctrine about God and man than all the theoretical atheists on earth ever could devise. It would be worth while, would it not, to see the Christian Church claim as her own this greatest moral issue of our time, to see her lift once more, as in our fathers' days, a clear standard against the paganism of this present world and, refusing to hold her conscience at the beck and call of belligerent states, put the Kingdom of God above nationalism and call the world to peace? That would not be the denial of patriotism but its apotheosis.

Here today, as an American, under this high and hospitable roof, I cannot speak for my government, but both as an American and as a Christian I do speak for millions of my fellow citizens in wishing your great work, in which we believe, for which we pray, our absence from which we painfully regret, the eminent success which it deserves. We work in many ways for the same end—a world organized for peace. Never was an end better worth working for. The alternative is the most appalling catastrophe mankind has ever faced. Like gravitation in the physical realm, the law of the Lord in the moral realm bends for no man and no nation: "All they that take the sword shall perish with the sword."

A DICTATORSHIP OF THE PROLETARIAT

Nikolai Lenin

(1870-1924)

Nikolai Lenin, the Russian socialist, began his revolutionary activity when a youth and by 1890 had become identified as a leader among the radical socialists. Much of his life he spent in exile from Russia to avoid imprisonment for his socialist views. These exiles he utilized to do his political and economic writings. It was the Bolsheviki, led by Lenin and Trotsky, who overthrew the Kerensky regime in 1917, executed the Czar, and established the dictatorship of the proletariat. Thereafter Lenin established in each district of Russia a soviet which he united into the Union of Soviet Socialist Republics of modern Russia.

An idealist, yet a man of vigorous and almost ruthless action, Lenin was a political genius whose extraordinarily strong personality made him virtually the dictator of Russia. Today his tomb in the Red Square at Moscow is the scene of daily pilgrimages by communists.

Included here is an excerpt from a speech delivered by Lenin on March 8, 1919, before the International Communist Congress.

The growth of the revolutionary movement of the proletariat in all countries has called forth convulsive efforts of the bourgeoisie and its agents in workmen's organizations, to find ideal political arguments in defense of the rule of the exploiters. Among these arguments stands out particularly condemnation of dictatorship and defense of democracy. The falseness and hypocrisy of such an argument, which has been repeated in thousands of forms in the capitalist press and at the conference of the yellow International in February, 1919, Berne, are evident to all who have not wished to betray the fundamental principle of socialism.

First of all, this argument is used with certain interpretations of "democracy in general" and "dictatorship in general" without raising the point as to which class one has in mind. Such a statement of the question, leaving out of consideration the question of class as though it were a general national matter, is direct mockery of the fundamental doctrine of socialism, namely, the doctrine of class struggle, which the socialists who have gone over to the side of the bourgeoisie recognize when they talk, but forget when they act. For in no civilized capitalist country does there exist "democracy in general," but there exists only bourgeois democracy, and one is speaking not of "dictatorship in general" but of dictatorship of the oppressed classes, that is, of the proletariat with respect to the oppressors and exploiters, that is, the bourgeoisie, in order to overcome the resistance which the exploiters make in their struggle to preserve their rule.

History teaches that no oppressed class has ever come into power and cannot come into power, without passing through a period of dictatorship, that is, the conquest of power and the forcible suppression of the most desperate and mad resistance which does not hesitate to resort to any crimes, such has always been shown by the exploiters. The bourgeoisie, whose rule is now defended by the Socialists who speak against "dictatorship in general," has won power in the progressive countries at the price of a series of uprisings, civil wars, forcible suppression of kings, feudal lords, and slave owners, and of their attempts at restoration. The Socialists of all countries in their books and pamphlets, in the resolutions of their congresses, in their propaganda speeches, have explained to the people thousands and millions of times the class character of these bourgeois revolutions, and of this bourgeois dictatorship. Therefore the present defense of bourgeois democracy in the form of speeches about "democracy in general," and the present wails and shouts against the dictatorship of the proletariat in the form of wails about "dictatorship in general," are a direct mockery of socialism, and represent in fact going over to the bourgeoisie and denying the right of the proletariat to its own proletarian revolution, and a defense of bourgeois reformism, precisely at the historic moment when bourgeois reformism is collapsing the world over, and when the war has created a revolutionary situation.

All socialists who explain the class character of bourgeois civilization, of bourgeois democracy, of bourgeois parliamentarism, express the thought which Marx and Engels expressed with the most scientific exactness when they said that the most democratic bourgeois republic is nothing more than a machine for the suppression of the working class by the bourgeoisie, for the suppression of the mass of the toilers by a handful of capitalists. There is not a single revolutionist, not a single Marxist of all those who are now shouting against dictatorship and for democracy, who would not have sworn before the workmen that he recognizes this fundamental truth of socialism. And now, when the revolutionary proletariat begins to act and move for the destruction of this machinery of oppression, and to win the proletarian dictatorship, these traitors to socialism report the situation as though the bourgeoisie were giving the laborers pure democracy, as though the bourgeoisie were abandoning resistance and were ready to submit to the majority of the toilers, as though there were no state machinery for the suppression of labor by capital in a democratic republic. . . .

Dictatorship of the proletariat resembles dictatorship of other classes in that it was called forth by the need to suppress the forcible resistance of a class that was losing its political rulership. But that which definitely distinguishes a dictatorship of the proletariat from a dictatorship of other classes, from a dictatorship of the bourgeoisie in all the civilized capitalist countries, is that the dictatorship of the landlords and of the bourgeoisie was the forcible suppression of the resistance of the overwhelming majority of the population, namely, the toilers. On the other hand, the dictatorship of the proletariat is the forcible suppression of the resistance of the exploiters, that is, of an insignificant minority of the population—of landlords and capitalists.

It therefore follows that a dictatorship of the proletariat must necessarily carry with it not only changes in the form and institutions of democracy, speaking in general terms, but specifically such a change as would secure an extension such as has never been seen in the history of the world of the actual use of democratism by the toiling classes.

The essence of the Soviet authority consists in this, that the permanent and sole basis of all State authority, of the entire apparatus of government, is the mass organization precisely of those classes which were oppressed by capitalism, that is, of the workmen and of the half-proletarians (peasants who did not exploit the labor of others and constantly had to sell at least a portion of their labor strength). Precisely those masses which even in the most democratic bourgeois republics had equal rights before the law but in fact were deprived of participation in the political life of the country, and by thousands of tricks and traps of the use of democratic rights and liberties, are now brought into constant and actual, and, in addition, decisive participation in the democratic administration of the State.

SPEECH BEFORE THE REPUBLICAN PARTY [4]

Mustapha Kemâl Atatürk

(1881-1938)

Kemâl Atatürk, first President of the Turkey, entered on military training at the age of 12 and finished at the Imperial Military School at Constantinople. He early joined a revolutionary organization, known as the Society of Union and Progress. During the World War he distinguished himself in the Gallipoli campaign against Great Britain. After the armistice Kemâl Atatürk returned to Constantinople and set out on a program of internal reform, but shortly thereafter left for Asia Minor where he organized a Nationalist Party. In 1919 he called a National Assembly and set up a government at Angora of which he became the head. With his National Army he defeated Greece in 1922 and expelled all Greeks from Asia Minor, Anatolia, and Thrace. For his numerous military services he was named by his people "Conqueror" or *Ghazi*. That same year the National Assembly overthrew the Sultanate, took control of Constantinople and elected Kemâl Atatürk president of the National Assembly; in 1923 Angora was made the Turkish Capital, and in October 29, 1923, Turkey was proclaimed a Republic with Kemâl as its president. In 1924 the Caliphate was abolished.

Among the numerous reforms inaugurated by Kemâl are the abolishment of the use of the Arabic alphabet; the adoption of the Gregorian calendar and the Swiss Civil Code; the emancipation of women; monogamy has supplanted polygamy; western ideas and dress have been adopted; and European languages are taught in the schools, rather than Arabic and Persian.

Kemâl was an emphatic and powerful speaker, advocating international cooperation and self defense as an assurance of

[4] Abridged.

peace. His most influential as well as most unusual speech was delivered at Angora over a five-day period, October 15-20, 1927, before the deputies and representatives of the "Republican Party" which he had founded, reviewing the activities of Turkey under his leadership.

Included here are the introduction and peroration of the speech.

The main point was that the Turkish nation should be free to lead a worthy and glorious existence. Such a condition could only be attained by complete independence. Vital as considerations of wealth and prosperity might be to a nation, if it is deprived of its independence it no longer deserves to be regarded otherwise than as a slave in the eyes of civilized humanity.

To accept the protectorate of a foreign power would signify that we acknowledge that we lack all human qualities; it would mean that we admit our own weakness and incapacity. Indeed, how could we make people understand that we cannot accept a foreign master if we have not descended to this degree of abject servitude?

But the Turk is both dignified and proud; he is also capable and talented. Such a nation would prefer to perish rather than subject itself to the life of a slave. Therefore, Independence or Death!

This was the rallying cry of all those who honestly desired to save their country.

Let us suppose for a moment that in trying to accomplish this we had failed. What would have been the result?—why, slavery!

In that case, would not the consequence have been the same if we had submitted to the other proposal? Undoubtedly, it would; but with this difference, that a nation that defies death in its struggle for independence derives comfort from the thought that it had resolved to make every sacrifice compatible with human dignity. There is no doubt whatever that in the eyes of both friend and foe throughout the world its position is more respected than would be that of a craven and degraded nation capable of surrendering itself to the yoke of slavery.

. . .

Moreover, the labour for the maintenance of the Ottoman dynasty and its sovereign would have been to inflict the greatest injustice upon the Turkish nation; for, if its independence could have been secured at the price of every possible sacrifice, it could not have been regarded as secure so long as the Sultanate existed. How could it be admitted that a crowd of madmen, united by neither a moral nor a spiritual bond to the country or the nation as a whole, could still be trusted to protect the independence and the dignity of the nation and the state?

As for the Caliphate, it could only have been a laughing-stock in the eyes of the really civilised and cultured people of the world.

As you see, in order to carry out our resolution, questions had to be dealt with about which the nation had hitherto known practically nothing. It was imperative that questions should be brought forward that could not be discussed in public without giving rise to serious dissentions.

We were compelled to rebel against the Ottoman Government, against the Padishah, against the Caliph of all the Mohammedans, and we had to bring the whole nation and the army into a state of rebellion.

It was important that the entire nation should take up arms against those who would venture to attack the principal part of Turkey and its independence, whosoever they might be. It would undoubtedly have been of little advantage if we had put forward our demands at the very beginning in a resolution of such far reaching importance. On the contrary, it was necessary to proceed by stages, to prepare the feeling and the spirit of the nation and to try to reach our aim by degrees, profiting meanwhile by our experience. This is actually what happened.

If our attitude and our actions during nine years are examined in their logical sequence, it is evident from the very first day that our general behaviour has never deviated from the lines laid down in our original resolution, nor from the purpose we had set out to achieve.

In order to dispel any doubts which might still be entertained, one fact is urged upon us for mutual examination. As the national struggle, carried on for the sole purpose of delivering the country from foreign invasion, developed and was crowned with success, it was natural and inevitable that it would gradually, step by step to the present day, have established all the principles and forms of government founded on national sovereignty. The sovereign of the dynasty who, thanks to his traditional instincts, foresaw this fatal course of historical events, declared himself from the very beginning the most embittered enemy of the national struggle. I, also, from the first could see what would be the result. But we never disclosed the views we held. If we had done so we would have been looked upon as dreamers and illusionists. If we had offered explanations we might from the outset have alienated those who, discouraged by the possibilities arising from dangers that threatened from abroad, were fearful of eventual revolutionary changes which would be contrary to their tradition, their way of thinking and their psychology. The only practical and safe road to success lay in making each step perfectly understood at the right time. This was the way to ensure the development and restoration of the nation.

This was how I acted. This practical and safe way, however, as may easily be understood, provoked certain differences of opinion of more or less importance, and even the discouragement and dissension which was observable from time to time between us and our most intimate co-workers: differences of opinion, sometimes in regard to principles, at others as to the method of the execution of our programme. Some of my companions who had entered into the national fight with me went over to the opposition, according as the limitation of their own mental appreciation led them and their moral courage succumbed in the effort to develop national life, to proclaim the Republic and enact its laws. I shall refer to these cases individually as I proceed with my statement.

To summarize what I have been saying, I may add that it was incumbent upon me to develop our entire social organization, step by step, until it corresponded to the great capability of progress which I perceived in the soul and in the future of the nation and which I kept to myself in my own consciousness as a national secret. . . .

These detailed descriptions, which have occupied you for so many days, are, after all, merely a report of a period of time, which will henceforth belong to the past.

I shall consider myself very happy if I have succeeded in the course of this report in expressing some truths which are calculated to rivet the interest and attention of my nation and of future generations. Gentlemen, I have taken the trouble to show, in these accounts, how a great people, whose national course was considered as ended, reconquered its independence; how it created a national and modern state founded on the latest results of science.

The result we have attained today is the fruit of teachings which arose from centuries of suffering, and the price of streams of blood which have drenched every foot of the ground of our beloved Fatherland.

The holy treasure I lay in the hands of the youth of Turkey.

Turkish Youth! your primary duty is ever to preserve and defend the national independence, the Turkish Republic.

That is the only basis of your existence and your future. This basis contains your most precious treasure. In the future, too, there will be ill will, both in the country itself and abroad, which will try to tear this treasure from you. If one day you are compelled to defend your independence and the Republic, then, in order to fulfill your duty, you will have to look beyond the possibilities and conditions in which you might find yourself. It may be that these conditions and possibilities are altogether unfavourable. It is possible that the enemies who desire to destroy your independence and your Republic represent the strongest force that the earth has ever seen; that they have, through craft and force, taken possession of all the fortresses and arsenals of the Fatherland; that all its armies are scattered and the country actually and completely occupied.

Assuming, in order to look still darker possibilities in the face, that those who hold the power of government within the country have fallen into error, that they are fools or traitors, yes, even that these leading persons identify their personal interests with the enemy's political goals, it might happen that the nation came into complete privation, into the most extreme distress; that it found itself in a condition of ruin and complete exhaustion.

Even under those circumstances, O Turkish child of future generations! it is your duty to save the independence, the Turkish Republic.

The strength that you will need for this is mighty in the noble blood which flows in your veins.

Printed by courtesy of His Excellency, Mehmet Münir Ertégün,
Turkish Ambassador to the United States, Washington, D.C.

THE NEW SOCIAL ORDER

Toyohiko Kagawa

(1888-   )

Toyohiko Kagawa, the regenerator of Japan, was born in Kobe, Japan. His mother was a dancing girl whom his father, a politician of some repute in the village of Awa, had met on a trip to Kobe. Left an orphan at four years of age by the death of both of his parents, Kagawa was reared in Awa, and from the loneliness of his life found a solace in communing with nature. His education, which was started in a Buddhist temple, was continued in Kobe, where he came under the influence of an American missionary, Dr. Henry Myers, who led him out of his loneliness into a realization of the abundance of life in Christ Jesus. In 1905 Kagawa, with the assistance of Dr. Myers, entered the Presbyterian College at Kobe to study for the ministry, but he found his interest in helping the destitute people of the slums of the city rather than in a study of the creeds of religion, and set up at Shinkawa a home for these miserable people. In 1914 he came to America, where he studied at Princeton Theological Seminary and investigated social service institutions in America. On his return to Japan he resumed his work in the slums, assisting the farming classes of his country, and teaching scientific methods of hospitalization, cooperative banking, and similar reforms.

Although proclaiming himself a Socialist, Kagawa has opposed violence and hatred between social classes and has voiced opposition to the imperialistic policies of the government since 1931. While engaged in his manifold activities of directing numerous social service organizations, Kagawa has also been a prolific writer, but has turned the $1,000,000 received in royalties from his books to social settlement work for the laborers and peasants.

From his home in a small village outside Tokyo, Kagawa meets the demands of his numerous enterprises all over the kingdom, but the urgent calls for his counsel and message in all parts of the world force him to spend a great deal of his time in travel, lecturing, and preaching. He is not a powerful speaker, for he is a man of frail physique, but the results of his message testify to its efficacy.

It is strange how the cities of today are all fed by the villages. The cities have neither lumber nor sheep; villages supply the rice and the cotton. There are neither hospitals nor good schools nor universities in the villages. The cities are developed culturally and mentally. The machine-shops are places for the convenience and the development of the ability of man—so in the same way are the cities. The villages feed and therefore maintain the cities. Suppose the villages refused to feed them; if the urban people were not fed they would say, "Ah, revolution—to arms!" But the people in the villages might say, "When we take food to the cities, we have no returns, so let's not give them any more!" and then produce it secretly for themselves. In four days' time the food in the cities would entirely disappear.

As the result of revolution there is always famine. At the time of the French Revolution about fifty thousand were killed, but three million five hundred thousand died of famine. In 1917, about seven thousand were killed during the revolution in Russia, but about eighteen million were in a state of famine. The number of people who die as the result of famine is always greater than those who are killed in revolution. Therefore, if revolution broke out in Japan and was followed by famine it would be terrible. Furthermore, when there is revolution by violence, only great disorder follows. A good social order must be built according to the needs of mankind, according to their conceptions of labour and of personality; otherwise a genuine society cannot be developed.

In speaking of the controlling of the desires: though we tell people to stop drinking sake and smoking tobacco, they will not stop; nor will they overcome the greed that is in their hearts; this must be done through the power of religion. In India some two hundred million people are vegetarians, because their religion teaches it. But because they are made to work at the point of the bayonet there is no efficiency; in fact, efficiency is less than one-third the normal. On the other hand if they were given freedom they would perhaps become efficient. A real change cannot be brought about by revolution based on arms. The change must be based on the reconstruction of the desires of labour and of personality; on the regeneration of the conscience, so that all will have the spirit of cooperation. In England there are cooperative societies, which are trying to bring about a spirit of cooperation. Recently Germany unified her factories under this plan. The German people are most systematic; for example, if there are forty-two different trades, these forty-two are well organized and everything goes steadily ahead, like Japanese chessmen. But in Japan things are in confusion. In some respects we do things in the Russian way. We cannot bring about a change for the better unless we have our eyes opened.

Without a spiritual foundation we cannot hope to lead in this social order nor help to make a good country. When bolshevism is repressed it tends to become worse. We must conquer thought with thoughts. If the other party puts forth Marxian ideas, we on our side must put forth the ideas of love and sacrifice. England, having a religion of love and helpfulness, may laugh and say, "Marxism? It is only a name here." Marxism has not greatly invaded England, but Japan, where there is not that love and mutual helpfulness, is just the soil for this thought to flourish. Although it may take a long time to accomplish, we must persist in founding a deeply spiritual movement.

In Denmark mutual helpfulness is growing. The cooperative system is being taught, and because the social order there is founded on religion, there is a spirit of confidence. For this reason it is possible to travel on credit-slips, without any money. If we wish to build such a society we must found it on the idea of mutual aid. Hard times have only hit half of England. She has not been deeply affected, because so many of her people belong to the cooperative societies. During the War, England's losses were ten times as great as the earthquake losses in Japan, but she is not so deeply affected. The reason Japan was so greatly troubled is because she is so unstable. If even half of the population belonged to cooperative societies, as in England, we should not be so troubled when calamities overtake us.

With high ideals, a great yearning for God, and the spirit of prayer, we must take responsibility for the proletariat. If we do not have the spirit of love for each other, the spirit of the Christ who joyfully suffered, even hung on the Cross for man, Japan will not become better. This is what we mean by "the spirit of the Cross." If we are selfish, this country will not improve. We must work with all our might and main. That does not mean to work without any food, though.

We must work during these next few years with untiring spirit at great sacrifice, in a prayerful attitude, until economic and social conditions become better here. Where is there a movement in all of Japan like the earnest spiritual movement in Germany, where a hundred thousand of the young men have joined together in prayer for their country, while eating only common potatoes and wearing simple clothes? How can the morale of a people be raised up if all the young men visit places like cafés? Like Germany, we must face heaven and throw out all sins of the past, and even though it should mean that we must go to Siberia or Manchuria empty-handed, wherever we go we must go on praying for God's help. In order to do this, we must have a manly spirit and a strong faith. We cannot work as small units, but must work all together in the Kingdom of God movement, for the purpose of establishing the New Social Order. Prayer:

O marvellous God, Who teachest us that we should use love and the blood of sacrifice instead of violence, military power or authority, save Japan by Thy wonderful power, affecting both her inner and outer life. May we not divide into upper and lower classes; draw the villages and cities together. Many people have become weakened through anguish and suffering; the Middle School students are studying under great difficulties, and even the university graduates cannot get positions. Help us at this time to be of good cheer and help the people, loving them and making mutual concessions. May those who labour, serve by labour; may those who have wisdom, offer wisdom for the cause. O God, give us power that Japan may become a country desirable to live in. In Japan, the land of the fair name where there is civilization and history, initiate, we pray, the Spirit of the Kingdom of God movement. In a special sense raise up the soul of the youth, and in this way the nation of Japan. In the Name of Christ Jesus we pray. Amen.

MESSAGE FOLLOWING THE SIAN COUP

Chiang Kai-Shek
(1886-   )

Chiang Kai-Shek, Chinese general and leader of modern China, was born in Ningpo, Province of Chekiang, China, the son of a wine merchant. He was educated at the Paotingfu Military Academy and also in the Military Staff College of Japan. During the Revolution of 1911 Chiang Kai-Shek was an ordinary sailor but afterwards became connected with the leader of the Revolution, Sun Yat-Sen, who had accomplished the overthrow of the Manchu Dynasty and founded the Chinese Republic. It was Sun Yat-Sen who in 1923 made Chiang Kai-Shek the commander of the Whampoa Military Academy, the cadets of which were the mainstay of Sun Yat-Sen's army. After the death of Sun Yat-Sen in 1925, Chiang Kai-Shek became commander-in-chief of the army, was instrumental in forming the Nationalist Government of China, and on October 10, 1928, was inaugurated President of the Nationalist Government.

Among Chiang's foremost speeches was one delivered on New Year's Day in 1930, entitled *A Sense of Honour as the Foundation of Party and Government.* On December 15, 1932, he delivered a momentous speech on *Domestic Reform* in which he denounced corruption and inefficiency in the government and said: "We must set our own house in order before we can successfully resist outside aggression." On February 19, 1934, Chiang addressed a mass meeting of 50,000 people and inaugurated the New Life movement of China. This movement has been likened to the Renaissance in Europe as a rebirth of the Chinese nation. In this inaugural speech Chiang laid emphasis upon knowledge and virtue as the foundations of national greatness. The unification of China has been his chief endeavor, a difficult task because of the diversities of race and language and the volume of population and vast land area of China.

It was in December of 1936, after nearly thirty years of revolution and civil war in China, that the entire world was shocked by the sensational kidnapping of the great Chinese leader, Chiang Kai-Shek, at Sian. The peaceful outcome of this mutiny, upon which hinged the future of China, was a triumph of sanity and reason over force of arms, and therefore the speech delivered by Chiang Kai-Shek following the Sian coup is of great significance. A new chapter in Chinese history dates from the united front attained by the factions on this occasion.

Madame Chiang Kai-Shek has been a tremendous influence in the life and work of her husband. She is of the famous Soong family, a Christian Chinese family of great wealth and prominence in the Constitutionalist party. In 1917 she was graduated from Wellesley College in the United States with high honors. Her marriage in 1927 to Chiang Kai-Shek was followed by his conversion to the Christian faith. One of his most important radio speeches was delivered on the subject, *Why We Believe in Jesus,* and is indicative of the spirit in which these two people have dedicated their lives to China. Madame Chiang has been active in public and political life largely in behalf of the women and children, and her writings and speeches have helped to mold modern China. During the Japanese crises in China these two leaders have been indefatigable in their work for their country. They are symbols of Chinese unity and the personification of Chinese resistance against Japan, ever working for the expression of Chinese nationalism.

The coup d'état is an act which gravely affects both the continuity of Chinese history of five thousand years and the life and death of the Chinese nation, and it is a criterion whereby the character of the Chinese race may be judged. Since today you have shown due regard for the welfare of the nation and have decided to send me back to Nanking and no longer try to make any special demands or force me to make any promise or give any orders, it marks a turning point in the life of the nation and is also an indication of the high moral and cultural standard of the Chinese people.

It is an ancient Chinese saying that a gentleman should correct his mistakes as soon as he realizes them. The present outcome of the coup d'état shows that you are both ready to correct your own mistakes, and that is creditable to you as well as auguring a bright future for the Chinese race. Since you are now so convinced of my sincerity towards you that you have the courage to acknowledge your wrongdoing you are entitled to remain as my subordinates. Furthermore, since you can be so readily converted it will be easier for your subordinates to follow suit.

Formerly you were deceived by reactionaries and did not believe that I treated the people fairly and squarely and that I was loyal to our revolutionary ideals. But now you have read my private diary for this whole year, the public and private telegrams and documents numbering some fifty thousand words that have passed through my hands during the past two months, as well as my plans for the salvation of the nation and those relating to internal administration, foreign affairs, military finance, and education, numbering some one hundred thousand words, you must now know that there is not a single word which would condemn me of any self-interest or insincerity on my part.

I have always told my subordinates that when they make mistakes their superiors must also be blamed for not having given them adequate training. As I am in supreme command of the army, your fault is also my fault, and I must ask for punishment by the Central Authorities. At the same time I will explain to them that you sincerely regret what you have done. As you have rectified your mistake at an early stage, the crisis has not been prolonged, and I believe the Central Authorities should be able to be lenient with you.

Meanwhile you should tell your subordinates how you have been deceived by reactionaries and how I have always held the welfare of the nation at heart, so that they will not be unduly disturbed over whatever decisions the Central Government may make.

I have always impressed upon my people the importance of ethical principles and integrity to cultivate a sense of probity and shame, to bear responsibility, and to obey discipline.

We must always remember that the life of the nation is more important than anything else. We should not care for ourselves although our personal integrity must be preserved in order that the nation may exist on a firm foundation. Our lives may be sacrificed, but the laws and discipline of the nation must be upheld. Our bodies may be confined, but our spirit must be free. No matter whether it be an individual or a nation, the loss of integrity is tantamount to death itself. For the upholding of those moral principles which I have repeatedly emphasized to the people, I am ready to undergo any sacrifice. If I do not carry out my own teachings, my subordinates as well as the people of the country will not know what to follow, and the nation will be as good as destroyed.

From this coup you should learn a definite lesson; that integrity is more important than anything else and that national interests should precede personal ones. If you commit mistakes do not hesitate to admit them and make corrections. You should bear responsibility for what you have done and should make these things plain to your subordinates.

Dr. Sun Yat-Sen used to instruct us that we must rebuild the moral fibre of the nation before we could effect a national revival. Honesty, righteousness, and love of peace are important characteristics of our country. For more than ten years I have devoted myself to uniting the nation, politically and spiritually, for national salvation and honesty and righteousness are of particular importance. I have always tried to carry out my own words. Anything that is beneficial to the country and the people I will do with total disregard of my personal interests. Recommendations of this nature have always been accepted and put into practice.

The policy of the Central Government for the last few years has been to achieve peace in and unification of the country and to increase the strength of the nation. Nothing should be done to impair this strength. During the present crisis, as you engineered the coup, you are responsible for bringing about warfare in the country. But as you have expressed remorse; I shall recommend the Central Government to settle the matter in a way that will not be prejudicial to the interests of the nation.

In short you now know the situation of our country as well as my determination to save it. I always give first thought to the life and death of the nation as well as the success or failure of the Revolution and do not pay any attention to personal favours or grudges. Questions of personal danger or loss are of no interest to me. I have had the benefit of receiving personal instruction from Dr. Sun concerning broadmindedness, benevolence, and sincerity, and am not vindictive with regard to things that have passed. As you felt remorse very early, it shows that you know that the welfare of the nation is above everything else. That being the case, you ought to obey unreservedly the orders of the Central Government and carry out whatever decisions it may make. This is the way to save the nation from the dangers it is facing, and this is the way to turn a national calamity into a national blessing.

SPEECH IN LONDON, 1931

Mohandas Karamchand Gandhi
(1869-   )

Mahatma Gandhi, the saint of India, has become the saviour of his people, and his numerous messages delivered in their behalf have made him an international force. Born in a caste-burdened country, it has been Gandhi's life work to bind together the people of India, to win for them national independence, and to establish among them their own economic democracy. He is a pacifist and an idealist and believes that love can conquer the world. His fight for Indian independence is based on the non-violent theory of "moral resistance," which he claims is through its boycott stronger than any army or navy India could produce. Gandhi is a psychologist and understands men both black and white, and has also the adaptable power of an opportunist so necessary in a statesman. Far from commanding in appearance, this little, brown, wizened philosopher of India in a voice clear and vibrant and with eyes gleaming delivers his speeches quietly and without a trace of passion or malice; yet their power is almost hypnotic.

Born the son of a government official, Gandhi was educated in law in London and admitted to the Inner Temple. In 1891 he went to South Africa and suffered persecution because of racial prejudice, but through it all maintained loyalty to Britain. It was in about 1916 that Gandhi was converted to the Tolstoian philosophy which became a dominant force in his life. After the passage of the Rowlatt Act in 1918 Gandhi initiated the non-cooperative movement against the government and in 1919 issued his famous pledge of "Passive Resistance." As leader of the Home Rule Party Gandhi was made sole executive of the non-cooperative forces; following a series of riots he was arrested and imprisoned by the British Government in 1922; was released in 1924 and in 1927 was the leader of the Indian National Congress. Again in 1930 Gandhi was jailed for violating the salt laws, but again was released and in 1931 headed the delegation to London. On his return to India Gandhi launched his "Untouchability Campaign." This was followed by another arrest.

After a long period of self-imposed silence and inactivity this Hindu mystic who had led India's millions toward nationalism, on May 14, 1938 culminated a virtual agreement between the Hindu and Mohammedan communities of India on most of their outstanding differences. Thus one of the last barriers to the political unity of India's 360,000,000 people was removed.

Gandhi, the apostle of peace and passive resistance, now exercises almost dictatorial power in British India. Through his efforts Britain's conciliatory measures have introduced a new spirit of mutual confidence and hope throughout India.

Gandhi's purpose is to live to see India become a dominion and achieve thereby her independence.

Included here is an abridgment of a speech delivered before the Gandhi Society and the Indian Congress League in London in 1931 which expresses his principles in the fight for Indian independence.

It is terribly difficult, almost impossible, for Englishmen to realize that Indians believe that the sum total of the activities of British administration in India has been harmful rather than beneficial to the nation. India might have received many benefits from the British connection. But it is of vital importance to sum up the good and evil and find out how India has fared.

I have two infallible tests: Is it or is it not a fact that India today is the poorest country in the world, having millions of people remaining idle for six months of the year?

Is it or is it not a fact that India has been rendered emasculated not merely through compulsory disarmament but also through being denied so many opportunities that members of a free nation are always entitled to?

If you find upon investigation that in these two cases England has failed, I do not say hopelessly, but to a very large extent, is it not time that England revised her policy?

As a friend said, as the late Lokamanya Tilak said repeatedly from thousands of platforms: "Freedom and independence were India's birthright." It is not necessary for me to prove that British rule has been in the end British mis-rule. It is enough for me to state that, mis-rule or good rule, India is entitled to her independence immediately. There is a demand made for it on behalf of her voiceless millions.

It is no answer to be told that there are some in India who are afraid of the words "freedom" and "independence". There are some of us, I admit, who are afraid of talking about the freedom of India if the British protection—so-called—is withdrawn from India. But I assure you that the starving millions and those who have become politically conscious entertain no such fear and they are ready to pay the price for the sake of freedom. There are, however, well-marked limitations so long as the Congress retains her present workers and her faith in her present policy. We do not want the freedom of India to be bought at the sacrifice of the lives of others, to be achieved by spilling the blood of the rulers. But, if any sacrifice can be made by the nation, by ourselves, to win that freedom, then you will find that we will not hesitate to give a Ganges full of blood to flow in India in order to obtain the freedom that has been so long delayed. I know, as you, sir, reminded me, that I was not a stranger in your midst but that I was a comrade. I know that I have this absolute assurance that so far as you are concerned and those whom you represent are concerned, you would always stand by us and prove once more to India that you are friends in need and, therefore, friends indeed.

I thank you once more for the great reception you have given to me. I know that it is not an honor done to me. You have done that honor to the principles which, I hope, are as dear to me as to you—if possible dearer—and I hope with your prayers and your assistance I shall never deny the principles that I today proclaim.

PROTECT THE DEMOCRACIES

Stanley Baldwin

(1867-   )

Stanley Baldwin, British statesman and conservative, whose proceedings in connection with the abdication of King Edward VIII of England in 1936 caused such violent criticism in liberal circles, has had a remarkable career in English politics. His father was a wealthy ironmaster from whom Baldwin inherited his great wealth, one-fourth of which he gave to the government at the outbreak of the World War; his mother was one of the four famous daughters of the Reverend George Macdonald, a Methodist minister. Both parents were of staunch Puritan stock.

Baldwin received his education at Harrow and in 1888 took his A.B. at Trinity College, Cambridge. After his graduation, when his father entered Parliament, Stanley took over his father's business which became his central interest for twenty years. It was not until 1908 that Baldwin himself entered the House of Commons. His maiden speech was modest and sane, on the subject of the coal mines. The following year he spoke as an ardent protectionist on the matter of British capital abroad. For nine years he was thus in a modest yet effective manner a "backbencher" until Lord Talbot singled out his ability and Baldwin sprang into the lime-light, first as Financial Secretary from 1917-1921; then as a member of the Privy Council and of the Cabinet in 1920, and in 1921 as President of the Board of Trade.

In 1922 came Baldwin's great opportunity when in a characteristically brief and direct speech he courageously spoke in behalf of what he considered right in the principles of the old conservative party. The occasion marked not only a turning point in Baldwin's career but in the history of modern conservatism. The result was the overthrow of the Coalition led by Lloyd George and the re-establishment of a strictly Conservative gov-

ernment. In 1923 Baldwin became Premier under the Conservative government and again in 1935. It was during the last term
in 1936 that the abdication of King Edward VIII to wed Wallis
Simpson, twice a divorcee, was accomplished by the combined
conservative forces of the Church and the State and was followed
by the accession to the throne of England of George VI, younger
brother of Edward, and second son of Queen Mary and the deceased King George V. On May 28, 1937, Baldwin resigned the
Premiership.

Baldwin, who always has stood for peace and conciliation in
industry, made a number of notable addresses in 1925 in an appeal for mutual understanding and toleration between the opposing interests in industrial disputes. He is slow of speech but
simple, sincere, and disinterested as well as shrewd. His thoughts
are labored and this he reveals through a peculiar puckering of
his brows. He has a dry and at times caustic humor, and is
forceful and direct in expressing his judgments. A true patriot,
a puritan, who adheres vigorously to what he thinks is right,
Baldwin's keen intellect and broad interests have made him an
outstanding figure in English political history.

We include here his last speech made before a great audience
as Prime Minister of England. The occasion was the Youth of
the Empire Conference held in Albert Hall, London, May 18,
1937.

I have often stood upon this platform facing a great audience as I
face you tonight. But you are different from every other audience that
I have ever faced. I have presided over conferences of elder statesmen;
you are a conference of youth, and of the youth of the empire. I probably see before me in this hall potential statesmen, potential poets, potential businessmen; in fact, the great men and women of the rising
generation.

I have had my hour. I pass soon into the shade; but for you life
lies before you like a boundless ocean, and the imagination of youth is
busy launching flotillas of dream ships upon its waters.

It's not only young men who dream dreams, nor old men who see
visions. I have dreams and I am sure you have visions, and let us
tonight combine our dreams and our visions, your eagerness, your courage, your strength, and my experience.

In the next quarter of a century, as you come to play your part in the great world, the big problems will be the problems of government. The peoples of the world, disillusioned by the horrors of the war, are all seeking eagerly, earnestly for what they conceive to be the best form of government in which their peoples may find happiness, security, and develop their talents to their best. So I say to you, take an interest in government.

You may not wish to enter politics. You may have no taste. But governments of whatever kind tend more and more to influence the life of the individual, and, if liberty of the individual is to be preserved, it is vital that the individual should know what is going on, should form his opinion, should give his judgment, for that is the foundation of orderly democratic government.

And first let me say this to you, from tonight onwards—and all your lives—put your duty first and think about your rights afterward.

There was a very wise man called Edmund Burke who lived about five generations ago and he said these words and I want to give you just these sentences and it is a text:

"In order to perform the part of a citizen wisely and well, it is needful carefully to cultivate our minds; to rear to the most perfect vigor and maturity every sort of generous and honest feeling that belongs to our nature; to bring the dispositions that are lovely in private life into the service and conduct of the commonwealth. So to be patriots and not to forget we are gentlemen, public life is a situation of power and energy."

He trespasses against his duty who sleeps upon his watch, as well as he who goes over to the enemy. In war, the sentry who sleeps upon his watch is shot. And so, you see, a responsibility rests upon every one of you, whether you like it or not. Upon some of you the responsibility is for England; upon some for Scotland, for Wales, for Ireland; upon some for Canada, some for Australia, for New Zealand, for South Africa, and every colony; in fact, your country. And beyond your country, the empire of which we are all constituent parts.

And when I talk of your country, I mean all its activities, all that it comprehends, the well-being of the people, their content, their education, their religion, their professions, their business, their public affairs, the capital of the village, of the country, of the province, of the country.

All that is inevitably committed to you, inevitably so, whether you realize it or desire it or not, for as the whole is the sum of its parts, you are a part and you're bound to have influence—good and bad where you live. You're bound to be of some effect for good or for evil in your neighborhood and in your country. Do your best by it, for your own sakes and for the sake of your children.

We are passing. You are the governors of the future. We vest in you the duty of guarding and safeguarding what is worthy and worthwhile in our past, our heritage, and our traditions. You are in charge of our honor and of all our votes.

The beauty of the countryside is yours, the green fields, the trees, the wildflowers, the rivers, the moors, the prairies, and the hills, and the treasures from the ages of literature and art, all these are yours. The accumulated wealth, material and moral, is being and will be transferred to your account that you may enjoy it.

Certainly enjoy it, but also hold it and, I hope, enhance it, because you are trustees in every sense of that noble word, and what is coming to you is a trust and not merely a benefit which develops upon you. It's a trust that you'll hold and will try to hold for future generations, and unless you rise to the trust there'll be little benefit for you or for your children to enjoy.

And it will be for you to protect the democracies in whatever part of the empire you may live. They must be defended from without; and equally they have to be defended from within. And it may well be that you will have to save democracy from itself.

You have to show the world, and in many parts of it an exceeding critical world, but there is nothing in democracy and its principles, its purposes or its methods which naturally breeds timidity of outlook or mediocrity of achievement. Courage, discipline, and efficiency are as necessary to democracy as they are to any dictatorship, and democracy implies and demands leadership as essentially as any dictatorship, for it is a leadership which has not force behind it; it is the leadership of faith and character, and democracy is crying to you today for the leadership of the next generation.

I am not going to try to describe to you the shape of things to come. I know far more of the world that was and that is than of the world that is to be. Probably all of you were born on this side of the great divide which apportions the lives of all grownups into "before and after."

I was born on its far side in the year which saw two symbolic things happen, the publication of Marx's "Capital" with its gospel of economic fatalism, and the extension of the franchise to working men with its faith in expanding freedom. I mention those two events, partly because they're the keys to much of what has happened in the subsequent seventy years and partly for another reason.

I'm not going to dogmatize tonight; dogmatism is a prerogative of youth. I don't know that many people, old or young, can tell you what is happening around you, or what will happen. But I mentioned that fact a few minutes ago because I want to ask you: Who realized in 1867 what the implications of those two events were? Very few, if any. It is given to few to understand the times in which they live.

Our friend, General Smuts, used this fine phrase, "Humanity has struck its tents and is once more on the march," but it is not yet certain whether it is marching forward to the promised land or backward to a

808 ANTHOLOGY OF PUBLIC SPEECHES

wilderness of suffering and of sorrow such as we went through twenty
years ago.

You were born in the backwash of that overwhelming wave which
spread desolation over Europe. Your fathers and brothers, who fell
fighting in the Great War, thought that they were making the world
a fairer, sweeter place for you to live in. But mankind cannot commit
a great sin without paying for it. The twenty post-war years have shown
that war does not settle the accounts; there is a balance brought forward.
When an emancipation is achieved a new slavery may begin. The
moment of victory may be the beginning of defeat.

The days which saw the framing of the League of Nations saw the
signing of the Treaty of Versailles. Should both be entered on the
credit side? Twenty years ago we would all have said "Yes"; today
the reply would be doubtful, for both have belied the hopes of mankind
and they have given place to disillusion.

Freedom for the common men, which was to have been the fruit
of victory, is once more in jeopardy, because it has been taken away
from the common men in other lands. You may attempt to explain
these twenty years in terms of economics or in terms of politics; some
see only the one and some only the other. Some blame the treaty, some
the banker, some the statesmen, some the diplomats. Some simplify
the causes of the tragedy and make scapegoats of some half dozen prominent figures on the European stage.

But what is clear is that today Europe is neither at war nor at peace,
but stands at armed attention. For every soldier who died at the front
another is taking his place; for every ship sent to the bottom of the sea
another rides the waves, and for every airplane brought down to earth
twenty new ones sail the skies. And that in itself is a sufficiently
melancholy, devastating reply to all the efforts of the lovers of peace.

But what is worse than this, peace in some quarters is proclaimed
as a bad dream and war is glorified as an ideal for rational men. As
long as the British Empire lasts we will raise our voice against these
false gods.

Let me end in this, the last speech I shall make before a great audience as Prime Minister of this country, let me proclaim my faith, which
is the faith of millions of all races from end to end of the British empire:

Here we have ceased to be an island, but we are still an empire.
And what is her secret? Freedom, ordered freedom within the law,
with force in the background and not in the foreground; a society in
which authority and freedom are blended in due proportions, in which
State and Citizen are both ends and means. An Empire, organized for
peace and for the free development of the individual in and through
an infinite variety of voluntary associations that neither defy the State
nor its rulers.

The old doctrine of the Divine Right of Kings has gone, but we
have no intention of erecting in its place a new doctrine of the Divine

Right of States, for no State that ever was is worthy of a free man's worship.

The young king and queen, whom we have delighted to honor in these memorable days, are the servants of the sovereign people. To them, as your chairman told you, they have dedicated themselves. That is the magic of monarchy which is everlasting.

The king is the symbol of the union, not only of an empire, but of a society which is held together by a common view of the fundamental nature of men. It is neither the worship of a tribe nor of a class. It is a faith, a value placed upon the individual, derived from the Christian religion. The Christian State proclaims human personality to be supreme; the servile State denies it.

Every compromise with the infinite value of the human soul leads straight back to savagery and to the jungle. Dispel truths of our religion, and what follows? The insolence of dominion and the cruelty of despotism. Denounce religion as the opium of the people, and civil liberty as opium. Freedom of speech goes, intolerance follows and justice is no more.

The fruits of the free spirit of men do not grow in the garden of tyranny. It's been well said that slavery is a weed that grows in every soil. As long as we have the wisdom to keep the sovereign authority of this country as the sanctuary of liberty, the sacred temple consecrated to our common faith, men will turn their faces toward us and draw their breaths more freely.

Association of the peoples of the empire is rooted, and their fellowship is rooted in this doctrine of essential dignity of the individual human soul. That is the English secret, however feebly and faintly we have at times and places embraced and obeyed it.

The torch I would hand to you and would ask you to pass from hand to hand along the pathways of the empire is a great Christian truth rekindled anew in each ardent generation. Use men as ends and never merely as means and live for the brotherhood of man, which implies the fatherhood of God.

The brotherhood of man today is often denied and derided and called foolishness, but it is in fact one of the foolish things in the world which God has chosen to confound the wise, and the world is confounded by, daily. We may evade it; we may deny it, but we shall find no rest for ourselves nor the world until we acknowledge it as the ultimate wisdom.

That is the message I've tried to deliver as Prime Minister of England in a hundred speeches. I can think of no better message to give you to take away tonight than that.

INAUGURAL ADDRESS

Franklin Delano Roosevelt
(1882-   )

Franklin D. Roosevelt, 32nd President of the United States, enjoyed in his youth the advantages of wealth and culture. The Roosevelt family travelled frequently abroad, so that Franklin became acquainted with the peoples, languages, and customs of Europe at an early age. His school years were happy years, for his personality, exuberance, and talent for fluent conversation won him many friends. At Harvard University he was a leader, and it was during the years spent there that he became actively interested in the United States Navy. After leaving Harvard, Roosevelt attended the Columbia Law School in New York and was admitted to the bar in 1907. In 1905, he married Eleanor Roosevelt, the daughter of Elliot Roosevelt, who was the only brother of President Theodore Roosevelt—a woman ably fitted by her intelligence, temperament, social interests, and sense of humor to be his partner in his political career. In 1910 Roosevelt was elected a member of the New York State Senate, resigning that post in 1913 to become Assistant Secretary of the Navy, which post he held until 1920. During the World War Roosevelt had charge of the inspection of naval forces in European waters, and following the war he supervised naval demobilization. Here again his talent for organization and his ability to gain loyalty and friendship were conspicuous. He was, with Wilson, an ardent advocate of the League of Nations and made many speeches in its behalf.

In 1921 an attack of infantile paralysis tested Roosevelt's mettle. He fearlessly and cheerfully worked for his recovery and later established the foundation for the treatment of infantile paralysis at Warm Springs, Georgia. In 1924 Roosevelt's appearance on crutches at the Democratic Convention in the Madison Square Garden electrified the audience. His speech on this occasion in which he nominated Smith for the presidency was a masterpiece.

In 1928 Roosevelt became Governor of New York State and his record for reform in this office combined with his personality, his popularity, and his ability as a public speaker on the numerous occasions upon which he was called to speak made him an inevitable candidate for the Presidency of the United States in 1932. Roosevelt received the news of his selection over the radio and with Mrs. Roosevelt flew to the Convention at Chicago to accept the nomination. On this occasion he delivered a speech which promised the United States a liberal government and a "new deal." In a landslide majority Roosevelt defeated Herbert Hoover for the Presidency and on March 4, 1933, was inaugurated as President of the United States. President Roosevelt has for two terms served his country in one of the greatest crises of her history. Not only has he fought for legislation to bring about recovery in his own country, but he has tried to establish a policy of good neighborliness with other countries. Particularly conspicuous among these efforts was his visit to South America in 1937 in the interests of establishing Pan American goodwill.

Roosevelt is an effective and forceful speaker with a pleasing and convincing voice, an informal manner and a leaven of humor. These virtues combined with his skillful understanding of human nature have made him conspicuous as one of the world's foremost orators. He has made excellent use of the radio and has achieved many of his successes by this direct contact with the people.

Included here is Roosevelt's *First Inaugural Address* delivered March 4, 1933, which historians have stated marked the turning point of the great world depression.

This is a day of national consecration, and I am certain that my fellow Americans expect that on my introduction into the Presidency I will address them with a candor and a decision which the present situation of our nation impels.

This is preeminently the time to speak the truth, the whole truth, frankly and boldly. Nor need we shrink from honestly facing conditions in our country today. This great nation will endure as it has endured, will revive and will prosper.

So first of all let me assert my firm belief that the only thing we have to fear is fear itself—nameless, unreasoning, unjustified terror which paralyzes needed efforts to convert retreat into advance.

In every dark hour of our national life a leadership of frankness and vigor has met with that understanding and support of the people themselves which is essential to victory. I am convinced that you will again give that support to leadership in these critical days.

In such a spirit on my part and on yours we face our common difficulties. They concern, thank God, only material things. Values have shrunken to fantastic levels; taxes have risen; our ability to pay has fallen; government of all kinds is faced by serious curtailment of income; the means of exchange are frozen in the currents of trade; the withered leaves of industrial enterprise lie on every side; farmers find no markets for their produce; the savings of many years in thousands of families are gone.

More important, a host of unemployed citizens face the grim problem of existence, and an equally great number toil with little return. Only a foolish optimist can deny the dark realities of the moment.

Yet our distress comes from no failure of substance. We are stricken by no plague of locusts. Compared with the perils which our forefathers conquered because they believed and were not afraid, we have still much to be thankful for. Nature still offers her bounty and human efforts have multiplied it. Plenty is at our doorstep, but a generous use of it languishes in the very sight of the supply.

Primarily, this is because the rulers of the exchange of mankind's goods have failed through their own stubbornness and their own incompetence, have admitted their failure and abdicated. Practices of the unscrupulous money changers stand indicted in the court of public opinion, rejected by the hearts and minds of men.

True, they have tried, but their efforts have been cast in the pattern of an outworn tradition. Faced by failure of credit, they have proposed only the lending of more money.

Stripped of the lure of profit by which to induce our people to follow their false leadership, they have resorted to exhortations, pleading tearfully for restored confidence. They know only the rules of a generation of self-seekers.

They have no vision, and when there is no vision the people perish.

The money changers have fled from their high seats in the temple of our civilization. We may now restore that temple to the ancient truths.

The measure of the restoration lies in the extent to which we apply social values more noble than mere monetary profit.

Happiness lies not in the mere possession of money; it lies in the joy of achievement, in the thrill of creative effort.

The joy and moral stimulation of work no longer must be forgotten in the mad chase of evanescent profits. These dark days will be worth all they cost us if they teach us that our true destiny is not to be ministered unto but to minister to ourselves and to our fellow men.

Recognition of the falsity of material wealth as the standard of success goes hand in hand with the abandonment of the false belief that public office and high political position are to be valued only by the standards of pride of place and personal profit; and there must be an end to a conduct in banking and in business which too often has given to a sacred trust the likeness of callous and selfish wrongdoing.

Small wonder that confidence languishes, for it thrives only on honesty, on honor, on the sacredness of obligations, on faithful protection, on unselfish performance. Without them it cannot live.

Restoration calls, however, not for changes in ethics alone. This nation asks for action, and action now.

Our greatest primary task is to put people to work. This is no unsolvable problem if we face it wisely and courageously.

It can be accomplished in part by direct recruiting by the government itself, treating the task as we would treat the emergency of a war, but at the same time, through this employment, accomplishing greatly needed projects to stimulate and reorganize the use of our natural resources.

Hand in hand with this, we must frankly recognize the overbalance of population in our industrial centers and, by engaging on a national scale in a redistribution, endeavor to provide a better use of the land for those best fitted for the land.

The task can be helped by definite efforts to raise the values of agricultural products and with this the power to purchase the output of our cities.

It can be helped by preventing realistically the tragedy of the growing loss, through foreclosure, of our small homes and our farms.

It can be helped by insistence that the federal, state and local governments act forthwith on the demand that their cost be drastically reduced.

It can be helped by the unifying of relief activities which today are often scattered, uneconomical, and unequal. It can be helped by national planning for and supervision of all forms of transportation and of communications and other utilities which have a definitely public character.

There are many ways in which it can be helped, but it can never be helped merely by talking about it. We must act, and act quickly.

Finally, in our progress toward a resumption of work we require two safeguards against a return of the evils of the old order; there must be a strict supervision of all banking and credits and investments;

there must be an end to speculation with other people's money, and there must be provision for an adequate but sound currency.

These are the lines of attack. I shall presently urge upon a new congress in special session detailed measures for their fulfillment, and I shall seek the immediate assistance of the several states.

Through this program of action we address ourselves to putting our own national house in order and making income balance outgo.

Our international trade relations, though vastly important, are, in point of time and necessity, secondary to the establishment of a sound national economy.

I favor as a practical policy the putting of first things first. I shall spare no effort to restore world trade by international economic readjustment, but the emergency at home cannot wait on that accomplishment.

The basic thought that guides these specific means of national recovery is not narrowly nationalistic.

It is the insistence, as a first consideration, upon the interdependence of the various elements in and parts of the United States—a recognition of the old and permanently important manifestation of the American spirit of the pioneer.

It is the way to recovery. It is the immediate way. It is the strongest assurance that the recovery will endure.

In the field of world policy I would dedicate this nation to the policy of the good neighbor—the neighbor who resolutely respects himself and, because he does so, respects the rights of others—the neighbor who respects his obligations and respects the sanctity of his agreements in and with a world of neighbors.

If I read the temper of our people correctly, we now realize, as we have never realized before, our interdependence on each other; that we cannot merely take, but we must give as well; that if we are to go forward we must move as a trained and loyal army willing to sacrifice for the good of a common discipline, because, without such discipline, no progress is made, no leadership becomes effective.

We are, I know, ready and willing to submit our lives and property to such discipline because it makes possible a leadership which aims at a larger good.

This I propose to offer, pledging that the larger purposes will bind upon us all as a sacred obligation with a unity of duty hitherto evoked only in time of armed strife.

With this pledge taken, I assume unhesitatingly the leadership of this great army of our people, dedicated to a disciplined attack upon our common problems.

Action in this image and to this end is feasible under the form of government which we have inherited from our ancestors.

Our Constitution is so simple and practical that it is possible always to meet extraordinary needs by changes in emphasis and arrangement without loss of essential form.

That is why our constitutional system has proved itself the most superbly enduring political mechanism the modern world has produced. It has met every stress of vast expansion of territory, of foreign wars, of bitter internal strife, of world relations.

It is to be hoped that the normal balance of executive and legislative authority may be wholly adequate to meet the unprecedented task before us. But it may be that an unprecedented demand and need for undelayed action may call for temporary departure from that normal balance of public procedure.

I am prepared under my constitutional duty to recommend the measures that a stricken nation in the midst of a stricken world may require.

These measures, or such other measures as the Congress may build out of its experience and wisdom, I shall seek, within my constitutional authority, to bring to speedy adoption.

But in the event that the Congress shall fail to take one of these two courses, and in the event that the national emergency is still critical, I shall not evade the clear course of duty that will then confront me.

I shall ask the Congress for the one remaining instrument to meet the crisis—broad executive power to wage a war against the emergency as great as the power that would be given to me if we were in fact invaded by a foreign foe.

For the trust reposed in me I will return the courage and the devotion that befit the time. I can do no less.

We face the arduous days that lie before us in the warm courage of national unity; with the clear consciousness of seeking old and precious moral values; with the clean satisfaction that comes from the stern performance of duty by old and young alike.

We aim at the assurance of a rounded and permanent national life.

We do not distrust the future of essential democracy. The people of the United States have not failed. In their need they have registered a mandate that they want direct, vigorous action.

They have asked for discipline and direction under leadership. They have made me the present instrument of their wishes. In the spirit of the gift I take it.

In this dedication of a nation we humbly ask the blessing of God. May He protect each and every one of us! May He guide me in the days to come.

THE ABSURDITY OF ETERNAL PEACE

Benito Mussolini

(1883-   )

Mussolini, Italian Premier and Dictator, was born in northern Italy at Verano de Costa. His father, a blacksmith, was a staunch socialist and his mother was a schoolteacher, so Mussolini was early exposed to independent thinking. After training at the Normal School at Forlimpopoli, Mussolini himself became a school-teacher, but when 19 years of age he fled to Switzerland to escape military training against which his ardent socialistic tendencies rebelled. After a period of poverty and hardship Mussolini received his degree from the University of Lauzanne in Switzerland. From Switzerland he went to Trent and Austria but was expelled because of his socialistic tendencies and returned to Italy where he served his army term and became editor of the *Avanti,* a violent proletarian journal. During the World War Mussolini fought in the trenches and was wounded. Following the armistice, when Italy was deluged with communism, Mussolini founded the first fascist movement to suppress bolshevism; by 1922 he had 4,000,000 followers. At the fascist conference at Naples that year the party demanded that Mussolini head the government, whereupon the cabinet resigned and the King appointed Mussolini as premier. From this date Mussolini assumed the dictatorship. He became Minister of Foreign Affairs and of the Interior; established a rigorous censorship of the press and prosecuted or drove into exile his chief opponents; executed laws which affected the political, social, and economic life of Italy; and in 1929 terminated the sixty-year dispute between Church and State. Through all these movements Mussolini's dominant policy was to expand the power of Italy and place her on an equality with the great powers of Europe. In 1935 Mussolini began his campaign against Abyssinia—a cold blooded violation of the covenants he had pledged to support. On April 16, 1938, Mussolini's victory in Ethiopia was recognized by the Anglo-Italian Pact.

Mussolini is an emphatic and dynamic speaker. He is the self-asserted "Man of Destiny" whose mission it is to bring Italy into world supremacy.

Officers, non-commissioned officers, soldiers, Black Shirts, and people of Hirpinia:

Listen to me while I speak to you and to the Italian people.

The grand manoeuvres of the fourteenth year of fascism have ended. They have developed, from the first to the last day, in an atmosphere vibrant with enthusiasm.

The generous hospitality of the Hirpinian people has enveloped the participating units in its atmosphere.

Your fervent patriotism and your dedication to the regime make you worthy, O comrades of Hirpinia, of having had take place in your magnificent territory the grand manoeuvres of the first year of the Fascist empire.

Tomorrow on the plains of Volturara, before His Majesty Victor Emmanuel, King of Italy and Emperor of Ethiopia, will pass more than 60,000 men, 200 tanks, 400 pieces of heavy artillery, 400 mortars, 3,000 machine guns, and 2,800 armored cars.

This aggregation of men and means is imposing, but it represents at most a modest and almost insignificant total in comparison to the total of men and means on which Italy can surely count.

I invite Italians to take absolutely to heart this declaration of mine.

Not despite the African war, but as a consequence of the African war all the armed forces of Italy today are more efficient than ever.

We always, in the course of a few hours and after a simple order, can mobilize 8,000,000 men.

It is a formidable bloc that fourteen years of Fascist regime have prepared at white heat with great sacrifice.

The Italian people should know that their internal peace and that abroad will be protected and, with it, the peace of the world.

With the most crushing of victories in one of the most just wars, Italy, with war in Africa, has acquired an immense, rich, imperial territory where for many decades she will be able to carry out the achievements of her labors and of her creative ability.

For this reason, but only for this reason, will we reject the absurdity of eternal peace, which is foreign to our creed and to our temperament.

We desire to live a long time at peace with all; we are determined to offer our lasting, concrete contribution to the project of collaboration among peoples. But after the catastrophic failure of the disarmament conference, in the face of an armaments race already under way and irresistible from this time on, and in the face of certain political situations which now are in the course of uncertain development, the order of the day for Italians, for Fascist Italians, can be only this:

We must be strong. We must be always stronger. We must be so strong that we can face any eventualities and look directly in the eye whatever may befall.

To this supreme principle must be subordinated and will be subordinated all the life of the nation.

The conquest of the empire was not obtained by compromises on that table of diplomacy. It was obtained by fine, glorious, and victorious battle, fought with the spirit which has overcome enormous material difficulties and an almost world-wide coalition of nations.

It is the spirit of the Black Shirt revolution, the spirit of this Italy, the spirit of this populous Italy, warlike and vigilant on sea, on land, and in the heavens.

It is the spirit I have seen shining in the eyes of the soldiers who have manoeuvred in these past days, the spirit we shall see shine when King and country call them.

Since the manoeuvres last year, twelve months have passed: twelve months only, but how many events, how much history, has passed in these twelve months! They have been rich in events the influence of which is felt today but will be felt still more in the course of time.

Before concluding this meeting I ask you:

Were old accounts settled?   (The crowd shouted "Yes!")

And have we marched straight ahead up to now?   (The crowd: "Yes!")

I tell you, I promise you, we will do likewise tomorrow and always.

GERMANY COULD NO LONGER REMAIN IDLE

Adolph Hitler
(1889-   )

Adolph Hitler, the Chancellor and leader of New Germany, was born at Brunau, Austria; his father was an Austrian customs official. Rebelling against his studies in the Realschule, Hitler as a youth went to Vienna and apprenticed himself as a carpenter. From there he went to Munich where he enlisted in the World War in which he was gassed and temporarily blinded. After the armistice, in spite of his four years of service and the attainment of the Iron Cross gained for valor in the war, Hitler was refused citizenship in the German army because he was of Austrian birth. He returned to Munich and became a leader of the National Socialist German Labor Party.

It was the Treaty of Versailles with its lack of consideration for the recovery of Germany which gave Hitler subject matter for his speeches, and he incited the German people through his oratorical presentation of the injustice done to them. His action gave power to his words. In 1923 his "storm-troopers," a military organization, were instigated by Hitler's dramatic oratory to try to overthrow the government. Hitler, as the prime agent, was imprisoned, and during his imprisonment wrote his autobiography, *Mein Kampf*, which became the Bible of his followers. After his release, both through his convincing oratory and his personality, Hitler built up the Nazi Party until it dominated all of Germany. Through the doctrines of nationalism, anti-semitism, and socialism as well as his efficient military organization the fiery Hitler swayed the German people. On January 30, 1933, Hitler became Chancellor of the Reich; in 1934 he quelled a revolt within the Nazi ranks through force and conducted an antisemitic purge through blood-shedding, execution, and exile. On the death of von Hindenburg on August 2, 1934, Hitler became both Chancellor and Reichsfuehrer of all Germany; he censored the press, and abolished the Wiemar Constitution which had existed since the World War. In 1935 Hitler re-established conscription in Germany and enlarged his air fleet, negotiating a naval agreement with Great Britain for expansion of the German navy.

Hitler's mission has been frequently defined as an effort to create a Germanic state by regaining the territory lost by the Treaty of Versailles. Time and again this theme has been evident in his speeches to the German people. On March 11, 1938, Hitler realized one of the greatest triumphs of his career, when his army marched into Vienna and in a bloodless conquest forced the resignation of the Austrian Chancellor and reclaimed for Germany the land of his birth, Austria. While his troops were pouring into Vienna from the German border, Hitler before a cheering crowd delivered a speech which was broadcast over the entire world.

Following the conquest of Austria came another victory for Hitler when his troops entered Czechoslovakia. Pressing his claims still further to the free city of Danzig and the Polish Corridor Hitler won the opposition of England and France, aligned to protect Poland through treaty alliances, and thereby plunged Europe into another major war. The conquest of Poland quickly expedited with the assistance of Russia, Hitler turned his attention to the armies of England and France who had on September 3, 1939, declared war upon Germany. Included here is the speech made by Hitler before the German Reichstag on September 1, 1939, entitled *Germany Could No Longer Remain Idle,* in an attempt to vindicate himself to the German people.

Delegates and men of the German Reichstag: For months long we have been suffering under the torturing problem which the Versailles treaty, that is the dictate of Versailles, once left us, a problem which in development and distortion has become unbearable for us.

Danzig was and is a German city. The Corridor was and is German. All these territories owe their cultural development only to the

German people.   Without the German people, the lowest barbarism would reign in all these eastern districts.

Danzig was separated from us.   The Corridor with her German districts in the East was annexed by Poland, and above all the German minority living there was mistreated in the most fearful fashion.

About 1,000,000 people of German blood were forced to leave their homeland in 1919 and 1920.   As always, I attempted here also to achieve alteration of this unbearable situation by peaceful proposals and revision.   It is a lie when it is maintained abroad that we realized our revisions only through pressure.

Fifteen years before National Socialism came to power there was opportunity to carry out revision by the most peaceful agreements, by peaceful understanding.   This was not done.   In every single case, I then and later, not once but many times, made proposals for revision of the unbearable conditions.

All these proposals were, as you know, refused.   I need not singly enumerate proposals for arms limitation—yes, even if necessary the abolition of arms—proposals for restrictions of waging war, for elimination of what in my eyes were methods of waging war incompatible with international law.

You know the German proposals were for re-establishment of German soveriegnty over German Reich territory, you know the endless attempts which I made in order to come to a peaceful settlement of the Austrian and later the Sudeten, Bohemian, Moravian problems—they were all in vain.

One thing is impossible: that an impossible situation be settled by way of peaceful revision and then absolutely decline this revision.

It is also impossible to say that he who, in such a situation, takes revision into his own hands, is violating law, for Versailles is no law for German people.

It is impossible to force some one at pistol's point and threat, let millions starve to death and then proclaim a solemn law document with a thusly enforced signature.   Therefore, I also tried, apropos of the Danzig Corridor, to solve problems by proposing peaceful discussion. That these problems must be solved was clear.   It is understandable to us that for western powers the date of such settlement might perhaps be uninteresting.   But to us Germans the date is not immaterial—could not be immaterial—could not be immaterial to victims who suffered the most.

In discussions with Polish statesmen I have ventilated and talked over such ideas as you heard here from my latest, previous Reichstag speech.   I formulated the German proposals, and I must repeat once more there could be nothing fairer or more modest than these proposals.

I wish to say here before the world that I alone was in a position to make such proposals because I know that thereby I opposed the ideas of millions of Germans. These proposals were rejected. Not only that, they were answered firstly with mobilization, with increased terrorism and pressure against Germans in this territory, and with a steady campaign of strangulation against the city of Danzig, first economic and political, and, in recent weeks, military.

Poland has engaged in a struggle against the free state of Danzig. Poland was not ready to settle the corridor problem in a way satisfactory to both parties nor did she intend to carry out her obligation to the minorities. I must here make clear that Germany has honored her obligations toward minorities in Germany.

For four months I watched these developments calmly, although not without repeated warnings. I strengthened these warnings recently. I caused the Polish ambassador to be informed over three weeks ago that if Poland continued to deliver ultimate notes to Danzig and used further measures of pressure against Germans there, or if she sought to destroy Danzig economically through a customs war, then Germany could no longer remain idle.

And I left no one in doubt that in this connection Germany of today could not be confused with the Germany that preceded. An attempt was made to excuse actions against Germans by claiming these Germans had engaged in provocations. I did not know what provocations these women and children committed who were mistreated or dragged off or what those provocations were on the part of those who were mistreated and killed in terrorizing, sadistic fashion.

I do not know that, but I do know that there is no great power with honor that would watch such a situation indefinitely.

I even attempted for the last time, although I admit I was innerly convinced that the Polish government, perhaps of its dependence on now wildly unleashed Soldateska (a scornful term for Slavic soldiery which was also used in reference to Czech soldiers) was not seriously inclined to achieve real understanding. I attempted for the last time to accept an offer of mediation on the part of the British government. The British government proposed that itself should not conduct negotiations but proposed to establish direct contact between Germany and Poland in order in this way to initiate conversation.

I must now state the following: I accepted this proposal. I worked out the basic points for the conversations which are known to you, and I and my government now sat there for two full days and waited until it should suit the Polish government to at last send us a man with full powers.

By last night they had not sent a plenipotentiary, but they let us know through their Ambassador they were now contemplating whether and how far they were able to consider British proposals. They would let England have their decision.

My deputies: If it was possible to make the German Reich and its head of state take this, and if the German Reich and its head of

state would suffer it, then the German nation would not deserve anything better than to disappear from the political stage. And there's
where they have been essentially wrong. My love of peace and endless
patience would not be confounded with weakness or even cowardice.
Hence, I decided last night to communicate also to the British government that I could not find any inclination on the part of the Polish
government to enter with us into any really serious conversation.

Therewith, an attempt at mediation had failed. Meanwhile general
mobilization was given as Poland's first answer to this proposal for
mediation and, as further answer, there were new atrocities. These
events have been repeated today. After recently in a single night
twenty-one frontier incidents occurred, last night fourteen were perpetrated, including three extremely serious ones. I, therefore, decided
to answer Poland in the same language it already was employing against
us for several months. If now western statesmen declare that this is
touching on their interests, then I can only regret such a statement.
It can, however, not shake me for a second from fulfilling my duty.

What more does one want? I have solemnly declared and I repeat:
we do not want anything of the western states and we never shall. I even
assured them that the frontier between France and Germany is a
definite one. Time and again I offered England friendship and, if
necessary, closest cooperation. Yet love cannot be offered from one
side only, it must be reciprocated by the other. Germany has no
interests in the West. Our western wall is simultaneously and for all
times the Reich frontier in the West. We have also no aspiration for
the future. This attitude of the Reich will not be changed. Other
European states partly understand our attitude. I wish to thank here
especially Italy which supported us during the entire period. But you
will also understand that in carrying through my struggle I do not
want to appeal to foreign assistance.

We will ourselves solve our task. Neutral states of their own
volition have reaffirmed their neutrality exactly as we had guaranteed
it to them. This assurance is our sacred earnest [trust,] and as long
as no other violates their neutrality we ourselves will scrupulously
respect it. What should we wish or want of them? I am happy,
however, to report to you a far-reaching event. You know that Russia
and Germany are ruled by two different doctrines. There was only
one question that remained to be cleared. Germany does not intend
to export its doctrine to Russia. I see no reason that we ever again
will take stand against one another.

We both realize this, that every fight of our peoples against one
another would be advantageous only for others. We, therefore, agreed
to conclude a pact which excludes for all the future any application
of force between us, which obligates us to consultation in certain
European questions and makes possible economic collaboration and,
above all, assured each other that the forces of these two great states

are not spent with each other or against each other. Any attempt of the West to alter this will fail. I would like to assure here that this political decision means a tremendous change for the future and that it will be conclusive.

I believe the entire German people will welcome my political attitude, because both Russia and Germany fought against each other in the World War and in the end both were left holding the bag. This shall not happen again. The non-agression consultation pact which was in force the day it was signed, yesterday received ultimate ratification in Berlin and also at Moscow, where the pact was welcomed the same as you welcome it here.

I can indorse word for word a speech by the People's Commissar Molotov, the Russian Foreign Minister. As to our aims: I am firstly determined to solve the Danzig problem; secondly, to settle the problem of the Corridor, and thirdly, take care that German-Polish relations will be changed in a way permitting peaceful living side by side. I, therefore, am determined to fight until either the Polish government is ready to bring about such connections or until another Polish government is inclined to do so.

I want to banish from the German boundaries the element of insecurity, the atmosphere of permanent conditions that approximate civil war. I want to achieve that peace on our eastern border which will be no different than peace as we know it on our other borders. I want to undertake the necessary action in fashions that will not contradict what I announced here as proposals. I will not wage a fight against women and children. I similarly have given my air force orders to restrict its actions to military objectives. But if the enemy attempts to construe from this a permission for him to fight with opposite methods, then he will receive an answer that will strike him dumb and blind.

Poland last night for the first time shot at our territory with regular soldiers. Since 5:45 a.m. we have been returning fire and from now on we will answer bomb with bomb, and he who fights with poison will be fought with poison gas. He who does not follow the rules of humane war can expect nothing from us but that we take the same step. I will wage this fight—no matter against whom—until the security of the Reich and its rights is achieved.

I have now labored over six years on construction of the German armed forces. During this time over 90,000,000,000 marks (nominally $36,000,000,000) have been spent for construction of armed forces. It today is the best equipped and far above comparison with the forces of 1914. My trust in it is unshakable. I am justified if I call up this armed force, and when I now demand sacrifice and, if necessary, all sacrifices from the German people.

I myself am today as ready as I once was to make every personal sacrifice. I expect no more of any German than what I for four years was voluntarily prepared to do. There shall be no privations in Germany which I myself will not immediately endure. My whole life from now on belongs to my people. I now do not want to be anything but the first soldier of the German Reich.

I, therefore, again put on the uniform which once had been most sacred and dearest to me. I will take it off only after victory.

Should something happen to me during battle my successor will be party chief Goering. (Air Marshal Hermann Wilhelm Goering.) Should something happen to Goering his successor will be Hess. (Rudolf Hess, deputy chief of the Nazi party.) You then would be pledged to this fuehrer in the same blind loyalty and obedience as to me.

Should something happen to him, I will, through law, have the senate called, which will choose the worthiest, that is the bravest from its midst. I enter this fight with a strong heart as a National Socialist and a German soldier. My whole life was nothing more than a single struggle for my people. I never learned one word—capitulation—and if any one believes we perhaps are approaching a difficult time, then I ask him to consider that once a Prussian king with a ridiculously small state rose against one of the greatest coalitions and was successful after three battles because he had a heart strong in its faith such as we need in these times.

I, therefore, want to assure the entire world that November, 1918, will never again be repeated in German history.

I am ready at any time to stake my life. Any one may take it for my people and Germany. I demand that of every other. Whoever believes himself able directly or indirectly to withstand this national command will fall. Traitors can expect nothing but death. We all recognize an old fundamental principle. It is totally unimportant whether we live, but it is essential that Germany lives. I expect of you, as deputies of the Reich, that each of you at his post performs his full duty. You must be flagbearers of the cause, cost what it may. You are vehicles of that sentiment in your districts, and I am responsible for the sentiment of the entire German people. We are not to concern ourselves with this or that sentiment but exclusively with our duty, which is clear. Sacrifice which is asked of us is no greater than that which has been asked of others. Other men who entered the cause for Germany trod the hard and bitter road of sacrifice which we must tread. Their sacrifice was not easier, less painful, than the sacrifice required of us.

I also expect from German women that they enter this common struggle in a spirit of iron discipline. German youth will fulfill with glowing hearts that which the National Socialist state expects and demands. If we construct this community resolved to never capitulate on our demands, then our wills can master every situation. And I want to close with a confession I once made when I commenced my struggle for power. I said then that when our will power is so strong that no calamity could force it down, then our will power and our steel would also be able to conquer any emergency.

Deutschland sieg heil!

BRITAIN MUST GO TO WAR

Neville Chamberlain
(1869-   )

The Right Honorable Arthur Neville Chamberlain was born on March 18, 1869; was educated at Rugby and Mason College, in Birmingham, England, his home town, where he resided until he was nearly forty-five years of age, with the exception of the years 1890-97 when he lived in the Bahamas.

Until the end of the World War, Chamberlain had a purely Birmingham reputation. He had been Lord Mayor of Birmingham; Director of the National Service under Lloyd George; postmaster general under Stanley Baldwin in 1922; thereafter serving twice as Minister of Health and twice as Chancellor of the Exchequer. It was his strong political friendship with Baldwin which carried him into the position of Prime Minister.

Chamberlain is in no sense of the word an orator; incapable by nature of the memorable sentence or the inspired phrase, he speaks clearly and is a useful debater in the sense that he is quick to see the weak points in an opponent's case. He is a splendid administrator and an excellent committeeman.

He is honest, precise, energetic, but at a time which called for imagination, vision, and experimentalism with all the new hopes that are striving for expression today, Chamberlain was thrust into a position in which he was a misfit. This was the man who came to the leadership of Great Britain at an extraordinarily critical period and incongruously it was this man who in spite of, or perhaps because of, the Munich Conference was called upon to make the declaration of war upon Germany on September 3, 1939. There follows the speech made by Chamberlain as Prime Minister of Great Britain before the House of Commons, on September 1st, presenting the facts leading up to the formal declaration of war on the 3rd.

I do not propose to say many words tonight. The time has come when action rather than speech is required. Eighteen months ago I prayed that the responsibility would not fall upon me to ask this country to accept the awful arbitrament of war. I fear that I may not be able to avoid that responsibility, but, at any rate, I could not wish that conditions in which such a burden should fall upon me were clearer than they are today.

No man could say that the government could have done more to try and keep open the way for an honorable and equitable settlement for the dispute between Germany and Poland, nor have we neglected any means of making crystal clear to the German Government that if they insisted on using force in the manner in which they have used it in the past, we were resolved to oppose them by force.

Now that all the relevant documents are being made public, we shall stand at the bar of history knowing that the responsibility for this terrible catastrophe lies on the shoulders of one man. The German Chancellor has not hesitated to plunge the world into misery in order to serve his own senseless ambitions.

I would like to thank the House for the forbearance they have shown me on two recent occasions in not demanding from me information which they recognize I could not give while these negotiations were still in progress.

All correspondence with the German Government is being published in the form of a White Paper which will be available to Members, coming in relays, while the House is sitting.

I do not think it necessary for me to refer in detail now to these documents, which are already past history. They make it perfectly clear that our object has been to try to bring about discussions about the Polish-German dispute between the two countries themselves, on terms of equality, the settlement to be one which safeguarded the independence of Poland and which secured its due observance by international guarantees. There is just one passage from a recent communication of ours, dated Aug. 30, which I should like to quote, for it shows how easily the final clash might have been avoided if there had been the least desire on the part of the German Government to arrive at a peaceful settlement.

In this document we state this:

"This government fully recognizes the need for speed in the initiation of discussions. They share the apprehensions of the Chancellor arising from the proximity of two mobilized armies standing face to face. They accordingly most strongly urge that both governments should undertake that during the negotiations no aggressive military movements will take place. His Majesty's government feels confident that they can obtain such an undertaking from the Polish Government if the German Government will give similiar assurances."

That telegram, which was repeated to Poland, brought an instantaneous reply from the Polish Government, dated Aug. 31, in which they say that the Polish Government are also prepared, on a reciprocal basis, to give a formal guarantee, in the event of negotiations taking place, that Polish troops will not violate the frontier of the German Reich, provided that a corresponding guarantee is given that there would be no violation of Poland by troops of the German Reich.

We never had any reply from the German Government to that suggestion. It was one which, if it had been followed, must have saved the catastrophe which took place this morning. In the German broadcast last night, which recited the sixteen points of the proposals which they had put forward, there occurred this sentence: "In these circumstances, the Reich Government considered its proposals rejected."

I must examine that statement. I must tell the House what are the circumstances.

To begin with, let me say that these proposals have never been communicated by Germany to Poland at all. On Tuesday, Aug. 29, in replying to a note which we had sent to them the German Government said that they would immediately draw up proposals for a solution, acceptable to themselves, and would, if possible, place them at the disposal of the British Government before the arrival of the Polish negotiators.

It will be seen by an examination of the White Papers that the German Government has stated that they counted on the arrival of a plenipotentiary from Poland in Berlin on the 30th, the following day. In the meantime, of course, we were awaiting these proposals, but the next thing was that when our Ambassador saw Herr von Ribbentrop, the German Foreign Secretary, he urged upon him that when these proposals were ready—for we had heard no more about them—he should invite the Polish Ambassador to call and should hand him the proposals for transmission to his government.

Thereupon, reports our Ambassador, in the most violent terms Herr von Ribbentrop said he would never ask the Ambassador to visit him. If, he added, the Polish Ambassador asked him for an interview it might be different.

The House will see this was on Wednesday night, which, according to the German statement of last night, is now claimed to be the final date after which no negotiation with Poland would be possible.

It is plain, therefore, that Germany claims that Poland was in the wrong because she had not on Wednesday entered into negotiation with Germany on proposals which she (Poland) had never heard. Now, what of ourselves? On that Wednesday night, at the interview to which I have just referred, Herr von Ribbentrop produced a lengthy document which he read aloud in German at rapid speed. Naturally, on this meeting our Ambassador asked him for a copy of the document. He replied that it was now too late, as the Polish representative had not arrived at Berlin at midnight and so we never got a copy of those proposals. The first time we heard them was on the broadcast last night. These were the circumstances in which the German Government said they considered their proposals were rejected. It is now clear that their conception of negotiation was that on an almost instantaneous demand the Polish plenipotentiary should go to Berlin, where others have been before him, and should then be confronted with a statement of the demands to be accepted in their entirety or refused.

I am not pronouncing an opinion of the terms themselves, for I do not feel called upon to do so. The proper course, in my view, was that these proposals should have been put before the Poles, who would have been given time to consider them and to say whether in their opinion they did or did not infringe those vital interests of Poland which Germany had assured us on a previous occasion she intended to respect.

Only last night the Polish Ambassador did see the German Foreign Secretary, Herr von Ribbentrop. Once again he expressed to him what indeed the Polish Government had already said publicly—that they were willing to negotiate with Germany about their disputes on an equal basis.

What was the reply of the German Government?

The reply was that without another word German troops crossed the Polish frontier this morning at dawn and are since reported to be bombing open towns. In these circumstances there is only one course open to us.

His Majesty's Ambassador in Berlin and the French Ambassador have been instructed to hand the German Government the following document:

"Early this morning the German Chancellor issued a proclamation to the German Army which indicated clearly that he was about to attack Poland. Information which has reached His Majesty's Government in the United Kingdom and the French Government indicates that German troops have crossed the Polish frontier and attacks on Polish towns are proceeding.

"In these circumstances it appears to the governments of the United Kingdom and France that by their action the German Government have created conditions—namely, an aggressive act of force against Poland threatening the independence of Poland—which call for the immediate implementation by the governments of the United Kingdom and France of the undertaking to Poland to come to her assistance.

"I am accordingly to inform Your Excellency that unless the German Government are prepared to give His Majesty's Government an assurance that the German Government have suspended all aggressive action against Poland and are prepared to withdraw their forces from Polish territory His Majesty's Government in the United Kingdom will, without hesitation, fulfill their obligations to Poland."

If the reply to this last warning is unfavorable, and I do not suggest it is likely to be otherwise, His Majesty's Ambassador is instructed to ask for his passport. In that case we are ready.

Yesterday we took further steps toward the completion of our defence preparations.

This morning we ordered complete mobilization of the whole of the navy, army and air force. We have also taken a number of measures both at home and abroad which the House perhaps would not expect me to specify in detail.

Briefly, they represent the final steps in accordance with a pre-arranged plan. These last will be put into force rapidly and are of such a nature that they are deferred until war seems inevitable.

Steps have also been taken under powers conferred by the House last week to safeguard the position in regard to stocks and commodities of various kinds.

The thoughts of many of us must inevitably at this moment be turning back to 1914. In comparison with our position then how do we stand at this time? The answer is that all three services are ready and that the situation in all directions is far more favorable and reassuring than in 1914.

For beside the fighting services we have built up a vast organization of civil defence under the scheme of air-raid precautions.

As regards immediate man power requirements, the navy, the army, and the Royal Air Force are not in the fortunate position of having almost as many men as they can conveniently handle at this moment.

There are, however, certain categories of service in which men are required immediately both for military and civil defenses. These will be announced in detail through the press and the British Broadcasting Corporation. It is most satisfactory to observe that there is today no need to appeal in a general way for recruits, such as there was issued by Lord Kitchener twenty-five years ago. That appeal has been anticipated by many months, and men are already available.

So much for the immediate present.

Now we must look for the future. It is essential in fact of the tremendous task which confronts us, more especially in view of our past experience in this matter, to organize our man power this time upon as methodical, equitable and economical a basis as possible. We therefore propose immediately to introduce legislation directed to that end, and a bill will be laid before you which, for all practical purposes, will amount to an expansion of the military training act.

Under its operation all fit men between 18 and 41 will be rendered liable to military service if and when called upon. It is not intended at the outset that any considerable number of men, other than those already liable, will be called up, and steps will be taken to insure that men essentially required by industry will not be taken away.

One other allusion before the close of my speech, and that is to record my satisfaction and the satisfaction of His Majesty's Government throughout these days of crisis to Signor Mussolini, who has been doing his best to reach a peaceful solution.

It only remains to set our teeth and enter upon this struggle, which we so earnestly endeavored to avoid, with a determination to see it through to the end.

We shall enter it with a clear conscience and with the support of the Dominions and the British Empire and the moral approval of the greater part of the world. We have no quarrel with the German people except that they allowed themselves to be governed by a Nazi government. As long as that government pursues the method which it has so persistently followed during the last two years there will be no peace in Europe.

We should merely pass from one crisis to another and see one country attacked by another by methods which have now become familiar to us with their sickening technique. We are resolved that these methods must come to an end, and if, after the struggle, we can reestablish in the world the rules of good faith and the renunciation of force, then even the sacrifices entailed upon us will find their fullest justification.

FRANCE CANNOT STAND BY

Édouard Daladier

(1883-   )

Édouard Daladier, Prime Minister of France at the time that war was declared on Germany in 1939 by England and France, was born on June 18, 1883, the son of an obscure baker at Carpentras in the Rhône Valley. The lad acted as his father's delivery boy and, while working hard in this capacity, was awarded a fellowship at the Carpentras High School; then followed college and university fellowships which enabled him to get a professorship in history and later to be appointed to the Lycée Condorcet in Paris.

Daladier's interest in politics began early, for while still a he fought as an infantryman for four years. Starting as a corpentras political club of young men. His political career, however, did not actually begin until after the World War in which he fought as an infantryman for four years. Starting as a corporal he rose to a captaincy, and was awarded the Legion of Honor, the Croix de Guerre, and three citations for bravery; he was wounded three times.

Daladier was elected a Deputy in the department of Vaucluse (his home town department) in 1919 and was reelected regularly in 1926, 1928, 1932, 1936, always on the same Radical Socialist ticket. Premier Herriot, who is often regarded as having influenced Daladier's early political career, assigned him to his first cabinet post in 1924. Since then Daladier has been a minister seventeen times and Prime Minister of France three times. In the meantime, he was elected President of the Executive Committee of the Radical Socialist Party in 1927 and President of the Radical Socialist Party, in January, 1934, succeeding Édouard Herriot.

Daladier's greatest activity has been in the capacity of War Minister, or Minister of National Defense, as the post is now termed. That he is not a newcomer in this field is shown by the fact that, back in 1924, when the Radical Socialist Party edited a book on "The Republican Policy" to serve as a platform for the coming elections Daladier was assigned the chapter about the military organization of France.

According to an article published in the "Revue de Paris," September 15, 1938, some of Daladier's main political ideas are as follows:

"The State must be strong and independent. The defense of the Republican ideal is part of the program of national defense. France must herself assure her own security and it is French force which constitutes the best guarantee of peace. But French force is a composite whose principal elements are the effort of all, the development of economic activity and financial equilibrium. Thanks to this force, it will be possible to render useful service to international relations and the cause of peace."

Daladier is known to be a man of few words. He has always worked hard and spoken little, but when he does speak he means what he says. The speech which follows was made before the Chamber of Deputies, September 2, 1939.

Today the government has ordered general mobilization. The whole nation has answered the call with grave and resolute calm. Our young men have joined their regiments. They are now on guard along our frontiers.

The example of dignity and courage which they have set before the world must give the key for our discussions. In their spirit of national brotherhood they have forgotten every other thing which even yesterday held them apart. They know no other service but the service of France

And in addressing to them the grateful salutation of the nation, let us take an oath to show ourselves worthy of them.

The government has put France in a position to act in accordance with her vital interests and her honor.

Its duty now is to set before you the facts to their fullest extent and with frankness and clarity.

It is now several days since peace became once more endangered German exactions from Poland threatened to create a conflict. In a moment I will show you how all the peaceful influences in the world were concerted during these last few days in order to save peace. But at the moment when it could be hoped that all these constantly renewed efforts were going to be crowned with success, Germany brutally reduced them to nothing.

During the day of August 31, the crisis reached its culminating point. As soon as Germany informed Britain she would accept direct negotiation with Poland, Poland, despite the menace caused by the sudden military invasion of Slovakia by the German armies, immediately tried to have recourse to this peaceful method.

At 1 o'clock that afternoon Ambassador Lipski asked for an audience with Foreign Minister von Ribbentrop. Peace seemed to have been saved. But the Reich's Foreign Minister would not receive M. Lipski until 7:45. Although the latter announced the agreement of his government to direct conversations, the German Minister refused to communicate Germany's demands to the Polish Ambassador, on the pretext that he did not possess the full power to accept or reject them on the spot.

At 9 o'clock the German radio made known the nature and extent of these demands and added that Poland had rejected them. It was a falsehood, since Poland had not even been informed of them.

On September 1 at dawn the Fuehrer gave his troops an order to attack. Never was aggression more evident or more unjust. Never was such a work of falsehood and cynicism invented to justify aggression.

Thus war was launched at a moment when great forces had been set in motion for peace and when the most respected authorities of the entire world were exerting their influence on the two parties to induce them to open negotiations for a direct settlement of the conflict which was confronting them.

The head of Christianity had made his voice heard in favor of reason and fraternity: President Roosevelt had sent moving appeals for a general conference; neutral countries actively proffered their good offices for impartial mediation.

Is there any need for me to say that each of these pleas received an immediate warm reception from the French Government?

I myself, gentlemen, felt it was my duty to intervene directly with M. Hitler. The head of the German Government on August 25 had made known to me through Ambassador Coulondre that he deplored that a conflict between Germany and Poland could cause French and German blood to be spilled.

I immediately had transmitted to the Fuehrer a positive proposal, framed with a sole view to saving peace without delay.

You have been able to read those texts. You know the answer that was given. I shall not dwell upon it.

But we were not discouraged by the failure of this step, and a second attempt was made by M. Chamberlain with his magnificent perseverance.

The documents exchanged between London and Berlin have been published. On the one hand, they showed impartial and steadfast loyalty; on the other, embarrassment, false answers and evasions.

I am also happy to pay homage to the noble efforts made by the Italian Government. Even yesterday we were still trying to unite all the forces of good-will in order to avoid hostilities and obtain the methods of conciliation and arbitration instead of the use of violence.

These efforts for peace, if they have been ineffectual thus far, have at least placed the responsibility upon Germany. They have assured for Poland as the victim, the effective aid and moral support of free nations and free men.

All that we did before the outbreak of hostilities we are still ready to do. If a move for conciliation is renewed we still are ready to join in it. If the fighting should cease and if the aggressors should return within their borders, and if free negotiations could then begin, you may believe me, gentlemen, that the French Government would spare no effort to attain success, even now, in the interests of world peace.

But time is pressing. France and Britain cannot stand by and witness the destruction of a friendly people which foreshadows other violent attacks to be directed against themselves.

Is this the simple question of the German-Polish conflict? No, gentlemen, it is a new phase in the march of Hitler dictatorship toward its goal—domination of Europe and of the world. How, indeed, can it be forgotten that German claims to Polish territory have long been written on the map of Greater Germany and were only camouflaged for a few years in order more easily to accomplish other conquests!

As long as the German-Polish pact was profitable to Germany it was respected by her. The day when it became an obstacle in the march toward hegemony she did not hesitate to abrogate it.

We are told today that once the German claims on Poland have been satisfied Germany will bind herself to everlasting peace with the world. You may recognize these words!

On May 25, 1935, Hitler agreed not to intervene in the internal affairs of Austria and not to add Austria to the Reich. And on the eleventh of May, 1938, the army entered Vienna, and Dr. Schuschnigg, for having dared to defend the independence of his country, was thrown into prison, and no one can say today what has been his true fate after untold sufferings.

But it seems that it was Chancellor Schuschnigg's provocations which caused the invasion and servitude of his country!

On September 12, 1938, Hitler said that the Sudeten problem was an internal question which concerned only the German minority in Bohemia and the Czechoslovak Government. A few days later he unmasked his ambitions, pretending they had been legitimatized by violence of Czech persecutions.

On September 26, 1938, Hitler declared that the Sudeten territory represented the last territorial claims he had to make in Europe. On March 14, 1939, President Hacha was called to Berlin and ordered in the harshest terms to accept an ultimatum. A few hours later Prague was occupied without regard for the given signatures.

There again Hitler attempted to throw upon the victim blame which hung solely on the aggressor.

Finally, on January 30, 1939, Hitler lauded the pact of nonaggression which he signed five years previously with Poland. He hailed this accord as a contribution to freedom and solemnly proclaimed his intention to respect its clauses.

But it is Hitler's acts which count and not his words.

What, then, is our duty now? Poland is our ally. We contracted agreements with her in 1921 and 1925. These agreements have been confirmed. From the tribune of this chamber last May 11, I said:

"Following Foreign Minister Beck's visit to London and in accord with the giving of reciprocal guarantees between Britain and Poland, we made a common accord with that noble and courageous nation for measures of direct immediate application of our treaty of alliance."

"Parliament unanimously approved this policy."

"Since then we never ceased in diplomatic negotiations and public statements to show ourselves faithful to this pact. Our Ambassador to Berlin several times recalled to Hitler and his collaborators that if German aggression against Poland should take place we would fulfill our engagements. And on July 1 in Paris our Minister of Foreign Affairs told the German Ambassador:

"France has definite agreements with Poland and these have been strengthened since the recent events, and consequently France will be on Poland's side immediately as soon as she takes up arms to defend herself."

Poland has been the object of the most unjust and brutal aggression. Nations that guaranteed her independence are bound to intervene and come to her defense. Britain and France are not countries which disregard their signatures.

Yesterday evening, September 1, the Ambassadors of France and Britain made a common demarche with the German Government. They placed in Herr von Ribbentrop's hands the following communication which I will read to you:

"Early today the German Chancellor published a proclamation to the German Army which clearly indicated that he was about to attack Poland.

"The information which reached the French Government and the United Kingdom that by its actions the German Government has created conditions (that is to say, German acts of force of an aggressive character threatening that country's independence) which demand execution by the Governments of France and Great Britain of their obligation to come to Poland's aid.

"Consequently, I must inform Your Excellency that unless the German Government is disposed to give the French Government satisfactory assurance that the German Government has suspended all aggressive action against Poland and is ready promptly to withdraw its forces from Polish territory, the French Government will without hesitation fulfill its obligations with regard to Poland."

Moreover, gentlemen, it is not alone a question of our country's honor. It also concerns the protection of her vital interests. For a France which has failed to keep its signature would soon become a France despised and isolated, without allies and without support, and would soon be subjected to a dreadful onslaught.

What worth can be attached to a guarantee given for our eastern frontier for Alsace-Lorraine after disavowal of guarantees given to Austria, Czechoslovakia, and Poland? Rendered more powerful by their conquests, gorged with the plunder of Europe and masters of an inexhaustible natural wealth, the aggressors would soon turn on France with all their force.

Our honor, therefore, is today the gage of our security. It is not the abstract, archaic honor which conquerors talk about to justify their violences. It is the dignity of a pacific people which entertains no hatred for any other people in the world and which engages in no undertaking except for the safety of its liberty and life.

At the price of our honor we could only purchase a precarious peace which would be revocable, and when later we should have to accept the struggle, having lost the respect of other nations, we would no longer be anything but a miserable people doomed to defeat and servitude.

I am sure there is not a Frenchman who would embrace such thoughts. But I know nevertheless, gentlemen, that it is hard for those who have devoted their whole life to defending peace and who have always been inspired with that ideal to meet acts of violence with force. It will not be I, as head of the government, who will present any excuses for war.

I fought, like the greater number of you. I remember. I will not speak one single word which veterans would think a sacrilege. I shall simply do my duty as an honest man.

While we are deliberating Frenchmen are joining their regiments. Not one of them permits himself to be mastered by a spirit of violence and brutality. But every one is ready to do his duty with calm courage, which is inspired by a clear conscience.

You who know, gentlemen, what Frenchmen think, you who even yesterday were among them in our provincial towns, our countryside, you who saw them leave, you will not contradict me if I evoke their thoughts. They are pacific men but determined to make all sacrifices to defend the dignity and freedom of France.

If they answer our appeal as they have done, without hesitation, without murmur, it is because they all feel France's existence is in danger.

You know better than any one that nothing could mobilize France for a mere adventure. It will not be Frenchmen who will rise to invade the territory of a foreign State. Their heroism is that of defense, not that of conquest. When France rises it is because she feels threatened.

It is not only France who has risen, but all the immense empire that lives under the protection of our tricolored flag. From all corners of the world moving testimonials of loyalty arrive these days in the mother country. To the union all Frenchmen reply. Also beyond the seas all the peoples living under our protection in this hour of peril offer us their arms and hearts.

I want also to salute those foreigners living on our soil who today by the thousands—as volunteers of peace in danger—place their courage and lives in France's service.

Our duty is to finish with enterprises of aggression and violence. By peaceful settlements, if we still can. By the use of our force, if all moral feeling and all light of reason have disappeared from our aggressors.

If we did not keep our pledges, if we let Germany crush Poland, within a few months, weeks, perhaps, what could we tell France if she should again rise to meet the aggressor?

Then these so determined soldiers would ask what we had done about our friends. They would feel alone before the most terrible menace and would lack, perhaps, the confidence that animates them today.

In these hours when the destiny of Europe is being decided, France speaks to the United States through the voice of her sons and all those who have accepted the supreme sacrifice if necessary. Let us find, like them, the spirit which animated all the heroes of our history. France does not rise with such spirit except when she believes she is fighting for her life and independence. It is France today who gives us her commands.

THIS NATION WILL REMAIN NEUTRAL
(Radio address, September 4, 1939)

Franklin Delano Roosevelt [6]
(1882-   )

Tonight my single duty is to speak to the whole of America. Until 4:30 o'clock this morning I had hoped against hope that some miracle would prevent a devastating war in Europe and bring to an end the invasion of Poland by Germany.

For four long years a succession of actual wars and constant crises have shaken the entire world and have threatened in each case to bring on the gigantic conflict which is today unhappily a fact.

It is right that I should recall to your minds the consistent and at times successful efforts of your government in these crises to throw the full weight of the United States into the cause of peace. In spite of spreading wars I think that we have every right and every reason to maintain as a national policy the fundamental moralities, the teachings of religion and the continuation of efforts to restore peace—for some day, though the time may be distant, we can be of even greater help to a crippled humanity.

It is right, too, to point out that the unfortunate events of these recent years have been based on the use of force or the threat of force. And it seems to me clear, even at the outbreak of this great war, that the influence of America should be consistent in seeking for humanity a final peace which will eliminate, as far as it is possible to do so, the continued use of force between nations.

It is, of course, impossible to predict the future. I have my constant stream of information from American representatives and other sources throughout the world. You, the people of this country, are receiving news through your radios and your newspapers at every hour of the day.

You are, I believe, the most enlightened and the best-informed people in all the world at this moment. You are subjected to no censorship of news, and I want to add that your government has no information which it has any thought of withholding from you.

At the same time, as I told my press conference on Friday, it is of the highest importance that the press and the radio use the utmost cau-

[6] A sketch of the life of Roosevelt appears on page 810.

ANTHOLOGY OF PUBLIC SPEECHES

tion to discriminate between actual verified fact on the one hand and mere rumor on the other.

I can add to that by saying that I hope the people of this country will also discriminate most carefully between news and rumor. Do not believe of necessity everything you hear or read. Check up on it first.

You must master at the outset a simple but unalterable fact in modern foreign relations. When peace has been broken anywhere, peace of all countries everywhere is in danger.

It is easy for you and me to shrug our shoulders and say that conflicts taking place thousands of miles from the continental United States, and, indeed, the whole American hemisphere, do not seriously affect the Americas, and that all the United States has to do is to ignore them and go about our own business.

Passionately though we may desire detachment, we are forced to realize that every word that comes through the air, every ship that sails the sea, every battle that is fought does affect the American future.

Let no man or woman thoughtlessly or falsely talk of America sending its armies to European fields. At this moment there is being prepared a proclamation of American neutrality. This would have been done even if there had been no neutrality statute on the books, for this proclamation is in accordance with international law and with American policy.

This will be followed by a proclamation required by the existing Neutrality Act. I trust that in the days to come our neutrality can be made a true neutrality.

It is of the utmost importance that the people of this country, with the best information in the world, think things through. The most dangerous enemies of American peace are those who, without well-rounded information on the whole broad subject of the past, the present and the future, undertake to speak with authority, to talk in terms of glittering generalities, to give to the nation assurances or prophecies which are of little present or future value.

I, myself, cannot and do not prophesy the course of events abroad—and the reason is that because I have of necessity such a complete picture of what is going on in every part of the world, I do not dare to do so. And the other reason is that I think it is honest for me to be honest with the people of the United States.

I cannot prophesy the immediate economic effect of this new war on our nation, but I do say that no American has the moral right to profiteer at the expense either of his fellow citizens or of the men, women and children who are living and dying in the midst of war in Europe.

Some things we do know. Most of us in the United States believe in spiritual values. Most of us, regardless of what church we belong to, believe in the spirit of the New Testament—a great teaching which opposes itself to the use of force, of armed force, of marching armies and falling bombs. The overwhelming masses of our people seek peace.